Sociology and Post-Socialist Transformations in Eastern Europe

Borut Roncevic • Tamara Besednjak Valič
Editors

Sociology and Post-Socialist Transformations in Eastern Europe

A Cultural Political Economy Approach

Editors
Borut Roncevic
School of Advanced Social Studies
Nova Gorica, Slovenia

Tamara Besednjak Valič
School of Advanced Social Studies
Nova Gorica, Slovenia

ISBN 978-3-031-65555-5   ISBN 978-3-031-65556-2 (eBook)
https://doi.org/10.1007/978-3-031-65556-2

© The Editor(s) (if applicable) and The Author(s), under exclusive license to Springer Nature Switzerland AG 2024

This work is subject to copyright. All rights are solely and exclusively licensed by the Publisher, whether the whole or part of the material is concerned, specifically the rights of translation, reprinting, reuse of illustrations, recitation, broadcasting, reproduction on microfilms or in any other physical way, and transmission or information storage and retrieval, electronic adaptation, computer software, or by similar or dissimilar methodology now known or hereafter developed.

The use of general descriptive names, registered names, trademarks, service marks, etc. in this publication does not imply, even in the absence of a specific statement, that such names are exempt from the relevant protective laws and regulations and therefore free for general use.

The publisher, the authors and the editors are safe to assume that the advice and information in this book are believed to be true and accurate at the date of publication. Neither the publisher nor the authors or the editors give a warranty, expressed or implied, with respect to the material contained herein or for any errors or omissions that may have been made. The publisher remains neutral with regard to jurisdictional claims in published maps and institutional affiliations.

This Springer imprint is published by the registered company Springer Nature Switzerland AG
The registered company address is: Gewerbestrasse 11, 6330 Cham, Switzerland

If disposing of this product, please recycle the paper.

Acknowledgements

This book was in preparation for a long time. The first interview for a preliminary study that was used to develop our conceptual and analytical framework was conducted on the very distant 16th of September 2016. What is our excuse for taking it so long? Well, as the editors learned, regardless of the importance of the topic, not many funding authorities are prepared to finance research on the role of sociologies in societal transformations. Thus, our endeavour was more of an afternoon activity, carved out of our private lives, after finishing teaching, funded research, and academic administrative duties.

However, we realised quite early that it is an interesting topic and one that can attract the attention of our peers. The first indication was that it was quite easy to reach the respondents for interviews for our preliminary study, although all of them are quite well-established and very busy. The second was the reaction we received during the Third International Conference on Cultural Political Economy, which took place on 6–8 September 2017 in Lancaster, United Kingdom, where we first presented the results of the preliminary study. The third such indication was a presentation during the 5th Council of National Associations Conference of the International Sociological Association, which we hosted at the School of Advanced Social Studies in Nova Gorica, Slovenia, 21–24 November 2022.

Many people have contributed to the production of this book with their ideas and work. For early insights and discussions, we are thankful to Andrzej Rychard, Nikolai Genov, Ivan Bernik, Pal Tamas, Marju Lauristin, Elena Danilova, Siniša Zrinščak, Natalia Vladicescu, Dumitru Sandu, and Marija Babović.

We are also thankful to the International Sociological Association, who supported the production of this book with its grant to the Slovenian Social Science Association, to organise a seminar on 21–23 September 2017 in Ljubljana, during which this topic was discussed. The Executive Secretary of the ISA, Isabela Barlinska, was a great help with the administrative aspects of handling this grant. Additional financial support for this event was provided by the national UNESCO Management of Social Transformations programme. The event was a great opportunity for a reflection on our conceptual framework, which was provided by Bob Jessop and Ngai-Ling Sum. Other colleagues contributed valuable additional insights: Zenonas Morkus, Vaidas Morkevicius, Olga Kutsenko, Svitlana Babenko, Dejan Jelovac, Agnieszka Kolasa-Nowak, Larissa Titarenko, Mikko Lagerspetz, and Urban Vehovar.

We would also like to acknowledge the support of Victor Cepoi in conducting some of the interviews and Nadia Capraga for providing transcripts. Rossine Fallorina, Terry Jackson, and Ksenia Gromova contributed immensely to the technical preparation of this book.

One of the editors of this book (Borut Rončević) was a Fulbright Scholar-in-Residence at Troy University, USA, during the final stages of preparing this volume. Thanks to colleagues, especially Michael Slobodchikoff and Doug G. Davis, for providing a supportive academic environment.

Contents

1 **Sociologies in Post-Socialist Transformations in Central and Eastern Europe: Towards Conceptual and Analytical Framework** 1
Borut Rončević

2 **The Sociology of Sociological Interventions: Do Sociologists Make a Social Difference?** 25
Patricia Ahmed, Rebecca Jean Emigh, Dylan Riley, and Nancy Wang Yuen

3 **Sociologists as Intellectuals and Their Role in Post-Communist Transformation** 51
Matevž Tomšič

4 **Sociology and Post-Communist Transformations: The Uniqueness of the Albanian Case in the East-European Context** 67
Leke Sokoli

5 **Sociology in Belarus: Where To Go?** 87
Larissa Titarenko

6 *Mission Impossible*: **The Role of Sociology When There Is No Society** 111
Vedad Muharemovic

7 **Sociology as Factor of Change: Reflections on the Bulgarian Experience** 133
Nikolai Genov

8 **Sociology in Post-transition Transformations of Croatian Society** 151
Jasminka Lažnjak

9	**Czech Sociology and Transformation** Ladislav Cabada	169
10	**Sociology and Sociologists During the 30 Years of Estonia's Post-socialist Transformation** Mikko Lagerspetz	189
11	**Hurried Professionals: Sociology in Latvia** Emils Kilis	207
12	**The Contribution of Sociology to Post-communist Restoration in Lithuania** Zenonas Norkus and Vaidas Morkevičius	227
13	**Sociology in Macedonian Society in Transition** Konstantin Minoski and Antoanela Petkovska	249
14	**Moldovan Post-socialist Transformation: The (Un)successfulness of Sociology** Victor Cepoi	273
15	**Sociology as a Witness to the Value Dormancy of Post-socialist Society or Ideological Subjugation** Vladimir Bakrač and Predrag Živković	289
16	**Polish Sociology and the Post-socialist Transformation** Agnieszka Kolasa-Nowak	307
17	**From Past to Present: An Overview of the History of Sociology in Romania** Sorana Constantinescu and Gabriel Bădescu	325
18	**Sociology in Subaltern Conditions: A Story About Russian Sociology** Elena Zdravomyslova	345
19	**The Role of Sociology in Post-Socialist Transformation in Serbia** Marija Babović, Jelena Pešić, and Ivana Spasić	371
20	**Slovak Sociology and Postcommunist Transformation** Robert Klobucký and Silvia Miháliková	401
21	**The Role of Slovenian Sociologists in Shaping National Imaginary Through Discursive Practices** Tea Golob and Tamara Besednjak Valič	421
22	**The Power of Ukrainian Sociology in Post-USSR Transformations and Russia's War in Ukraine** Olga Kutsenko and Svitlana Babenko	437

Index 463

Chapter 1
Sociologies in Post-Socialist Transformations in Central and Eastern Europe: Towards Conceptual and Analytical Framework

Borut Rončević

1.1 Filling the Void: Sociologies' Unexplored Role in Central and Eastern Europe's Post-Socialist Transformations

What was the role of sociologies in societal transformations since the beginning of East European post-socialist transitions towards the end of the 1980s? This question requires professional self-reflection and, at the same time, touches upon complex, ambiguous, and often controversial issues of developmental trajectories of the former post-socialist societies. Processes of post-socialist transitions, their assumed successes (Shleifer & Treisman, 2014; Adam et al., 2005), and apparent failures (Berend & Bugarič, 2015) are relatively well documented, sometimes in quite innovative ways (Rončević et al., 2018). This is also true for the evaluation of their results in view of more recent challenges, such as the global financial crisis (Kattel, 2010) or the COVID-19 pandemic with its health, social, political, and economic implications (Chepurenko & Szanyi, 2023; Győrffy, 2022). This has resulted in a large body of literature, reports, and other documents collected for both reflective and instrumental purposes. Nielsen and colleagues stated in the mid-1990s that in the light of so many emerging publications about post-socialist transformation, every author should have a very good reason for additional enlargement of the already expansive corpus of literature (Nielsen et al., 1995, p. 3). They substantiated their contribution by researching dialectics, structure, and strategic action in the processes of post-socialist transformation, linking their research of unique

---

B. Rončević (✉)
School of Advanced Social Studies, Nova Gorica, Slovenia

Faculty of Information Studies, Novo Mesto, Slovenia

Rudolfovo–Science and Technology Centre, Novo Mesto, Slovenia
e-mail: borut.roncevic@fuds.si

© The Author(s), under exclusive license to Springer Nature Switzerland AG 2024
B. Roncevic, T. Besednjak Valič (eds.), *Sociology and Post-Socialist Transformations in Eastern Europe*,
https://doi.org/10.1007/978-3-031-65556-2_1

processes in Eastern European countries with general problems of political economy and social theory. So, what is our excuse for producing this book, published a full three decades and a half since the beginning of post-socialist transformations in Central and Eastern Europe?

Setting aside the obvious argument that there still is no consensus regarding the outcome of these processes, we argue, first, that this book does not belong to the classical East European 'proto-sciences' (Schmitter, 1994) of transitology or consolidology (Schmitter & Karl, 1994) nor is it an attempt at their revival (Ould & Sisk, 2017). While the book focuses on transformations that started with a change from one political and economic regime to another, its scope is closer to the East European area studies and post-socialist transitions are just the first part of our research interest. Our temporal perspective does not end with the official transformation to the new political and economic regime, or the consolidation period of the 1990s when the consequences of transitions unfolded, or even later, when many of these countries entered the European Union or at least became increasingly integrated with it. Thus, we are not focusing on a temporally delimited phase of post-socialist development, and we are not restricting our interest to research on specific narrow aspects of developmental trajectories of post-socialist societies. On the contrary, we are tackling the issues of universal and continually emerging problems of strategic steering of social, political and economic development in societies with deeply rooted socialist legacies. The current resurgence of populist politics with emergence of a coherent economic system in some Central and East European countries (Feldmann & Popa, 2022) and the reestablishment of neo-totalitarian or electoral authoritarian regimes in Belarus (Usov, 2023) and Russia (Chaisty & Whitefield, 2023) in which the freedom of academic expression is severely limited (Academic Freedom Index, 2023) is as relevant as exploration of the early years of post-socialist transformations.

Second, the topic of this paper—the role of sociologies in post-socialist transformations in Central and Eastern Europe—is far from being exhaustively researched. On the contrary, a detailed literature review unveils numerous unresolved questions and dilemmas. The position of sociologies in the communist countries of Eastern Europe, their institutional development, specifics of national sociological traditions (Genov, 1989), its often controversial and ambiguous relationship with the political system, and (limited) debates with the international sociological community were (Denitch, 1971; Kaase et al., 2002) and continue to be (Zysiak, 2023) the subject of sociological research. We also have a relatively good overview of the state of development of sociologies and its institutional conditions in post-socialist Eastern Europe (see Kaase et al., 2002; Keen & Mucha, 2003).[1] However, the role of sociologies—their agency—in the processes of East European post-socialist transformations remains under-researched, if not completely overlooked. Consequently, we

---

[1] We should specifically emphasise the project, 'The State of the Three Social Science Disciplines in East Europe', focusing on economics, political sciences, and sociology in ten Central and Eastern European Countries seeking to enter the European Union (EU). More than 60 scholars participated in a detailed overview, with the support of the EU Fifth Framework Programme.

have relatively little structured and reliable information about the role of sociologies as the agent of profound societal transformations in post-socialist countries of Central and Eastern Europe. This should not be too surprising, although processes of East European transformations were and continue to be the subject of immense research interest. 'Sociology of sociology' generally seems to be primarily interested in the role of social, political and economic contexts in the production of sociological knowledge (e.g., Halsey, 2004) and not so much with reflection on the societal impact of sociology.

This is somewhat surprising, since agency-structure divide and integration in its many theoretical conceptualisations is a key part of foundational paradigmatic debates in sociological theory. Also, sociology does have a propensity to deal with itself. The International Sociological Association (ISA) has had a Research Committee 08 on the History of Sociology since 1971. And we could, in fact, go earlier in history. A plenary session of the fourth World Congress of Sociology in Amsterdam in 1959 focused on systematic and critical analysis of the development of modern sociology, examining the social and intellectual influences that affected its form and content in diverse contexts (countries). One of the founding fathers of modern sociology, Robert Merton, was among the contributors. However, while we can say that this debate was still focused more on sociology as an *object* of social influences and changes and not as an *agent with* influences, more emphasis on the agency of sociology has developed in recent decades.

One of the more important contributions is Michael Burawoy's (2005) call for a public sociology, in which he made two important points. The first is that the division of labour among sociologists requires that sociology addresses not only academic but also extra-academic audiences (e.g., professionals, policy-makers, politicians, and the general public). The second is that it should not only engage in the production of reflexive knowledge (involving self-awareness and introspection, contributing to a more nuanced and self-aware approach to understanding the world and oneself) but also instrumental knowledge (practical or utilitarian knowledge that is acquired and applied to achieve specific goals or tasks.). In fact, Burawoy makes a point that this division of labour per se is not a professional degradation of sociology but is indeed a legitimate endeavour that can help invigorate the discipline as a whole.

Of course, not everybody would agree with this. Turner (2019), for example, outlines a number of issues with policy, practice, applied and clinical sociology and claims that in an ideal scenario, the fundamental focus of sociologists' endeavours to address real-world issues should revolve around theoretical explanations derived from the data collected by sociologists and other social scientists. Turner (2019) concludes that increased efforts of sociology to make it relevant in solving societal issues just make it less and less relevant.

However, much focus was put on the public role of sociology. While Burawoy's initial call for a public sociology was his American Sociological Association (ASA) presidential address, he later became the president of the ISA (2010–2014), which undoubtedly brought additional attention to his ideas. His ISA presidential address strongly reiterated his message by stating: 'To face an unequal world requires us to interpret and explain it, to be sure, but also to engage it, that is, to recognize that we are part of it and that we are partly responsible for it' (Burawoy, 2015, p. 5) In his more recent reflection on public sociology, he clearly reiterated that sociology as a profession needs to play a role in societal development (Burawoy, 2021, p. 214). He asserted that the present moment calls for sociology to reawaken and assert itself, rediscovering its initial purpose of safeguarding society from an overpowering state and unregulated market alike and actively confronting the threats of extinction by crafting visions that emerge within the gaps of capitalism.

The idea of sociology assuming an active role and responsibility for the world was also resonating among successive ISA presidents. Margaret Abraham (ISA president 2014–2018) emphasised her belief that we are at a critical juncture in our human history in her presidential address and exclaimed: 'We sociologists need to step up now, with purpose, and draw upon our theories, research, and practice in the best interests of humanity' (Abraham, 2019). Sari Hanafi (ISA president 2018–2023), in his presidential address, outlined the entangled pathologies of late modernity, namely the emergence of authoritarianism in the South and right-wing populism in the North, rising trends in inequality, precarity exclusion, and hierarchical social polarisations and claimed that 'to address the inherent problems with Symbolic Liberalism and as an alternative to it, I propose Dialogical Sociology as a form of balance between collective and individual political liberal project' (Hanafi, 2024, p. 3). Jeffrey Pleyers, ISA president since 2023, has yet to deliver his presidential address at the XXI World Congress of Sociology in Gwangju (South Korea), but in his work, he emphasises the necessity to engage in dialogue between sociologists and actors in social movements, a process in which 'sociology becomes a collective project that combines researchers' and actors' reflexivities in a common quest to a better understanding of social movements, our world and how to transform it' (Pleyers, 2023). Many other authors have argued in this direction, for example for clinical sociology (Fritz, 2021) as a specialised field characterised by creativity, a humanistic approach, and an interdisciplinary focus, with the primary aim of enhancing the well-being and quality of life for individuals, or for publicly engaged sociology encompassing reframing/debunking sociology, institutionally engaged sociology, and community-engaged sociology (Smith, 2022), and so on.

However, despite growing awareness and even requests that sociologies can be agents of social transformation, we know very little about their role in Central and Eastern European post-socialist transformations. This book will fill part of the void in knowledge on the topic in a systematic way and with a broad geographical coverage. In this introductory chapter, we will first provide the analytical framework required to analyse the possible transformative role of sociologies. It will be based on Cultural Political Economy, a post-disciplinary approach that provides an approach that seeks to understand the dynamic interplay between culture, politics, and the economy (Sum & Jessop, 2015) and shows how imaginaries can have a real constitutive role in the real world. We will then present the results of a pilot study on the role of sociologies in societal post-socialist transformations, used to determine the main mechanisms for a transformative role of sociologies and how this role was changing over time. Due to a lack of research on this topic, primary research was the only approach that could provide us with reliable and structured information. We will conclude this chapter by introducing the rest of the volume.

In this chapter, we use both *sociology* (singular) and *sociologies* (plural). *Sociologies* are often used to recognise and appreciate the various approaches, perspectives, and specialisations that exist within our discipline and reflect the diversity and richness of the discipline, acknowledging that sociologists can approach our work from different angles and explore a wide range of social phenomena. In addition to this, when referring to sociologies in this chapter, we emphasise the plurality of both (national) sociological communities that can exert very different levels of agency within their national context, as well as the plurality of the ways in which the discipline, its community and individual members can play a transformative role. We take into account both its emergent level, understanding either sociology as a science and specific expertise communicating with other disciplines and systems, or a national disciplinary community, and individual level, implying the impact of individual sociologists through their diverse roles as academics, educators, public intellectuals, experts, politicians, civil society activists, as well as their hybrid roles or shifting between different roles.

1.2 Towards Conceptual Framework: Discourses, Evolutionary Mechanisms and Selectivities

To explore the role of sociologies in post-socialist transformations in Eastern Europe, we adopted the Cultural Political Economy approach (CPE) (see Sum & Jessop, 2015; Jessop & Oosterlynck, 2008; Fairclough et al., 2004). CPE provides a conceptual framework for the analysis of the semiotic structuration of social imaginaries. While the modern conception of the imaginary was outlined by Sartre (2004) in 1940, he limited his interest in the imaginary to the context of existence. It was introduced to social analysis by Castoriadis (1975), who emphasised social imaginary as a key concept, as a realm of collective and individual meaning-making, where societies and individuals create and project their values, institutions, and interpretations of the world. He emphasised the importance of imaginaries for shaping the real existing societies: 'What we call "reality" and "rationality" are its works' (Castoriadis, 1975, p. 3) and as such, although it is assumed that social imaginaries are separate from the real, 'on the social plane, which is our main interest here, the emergence of new institutions and of new ways of living is not a "discovery" either but an active constitution' (Castoriadis, 1975, p. 133). The impact of imaginaries on real existing societies was further explored and conceptualised in CPE, where the term 'imaginary' belongs to a group of terms referring to semiotic systems that influence lived experiences within a complex world. In essence, discourse and imaginaries can be analysed as sets of mechanisms playing a vital role in the continual and unstable process of societal reproduction and transformation (Sum & Jessop, 2015, p. 26).

Engaging CPE for our analysis, therefore, enables us to focus on how sociology and sociologies shape social, political and economic imaginaries in their (re-)articulation of various genres, discourses, and styles around a particular conception of society, economy and politics and its 'extra-economic conditions of existence' (Jessop & Oosterlynck, 2008, p. 1158). This framework thereby enables the analysis of how the intellectual forces can redefine the imaginaries and influence societal transformations, which touches the very core of our research interest. By employing CPE to analyse the role of sociologies in East European transformations, we are responding to an early call for a critical CPE (Sayer, 2001) and extending it to include critical reflection of sociology itself.

Imaginaries are not fixed. They are continuously (re)shaped through discourses and are themselves contributing to the shaping of discourses. Imaginaries and discourses are mutually constitutive.

1.2.1 Sociologies, Discourses, and Evolutionary Mechanisms

For this exploration, we will be analysing the data on sociologies exercising their influence through, first, a series of semiotic evolutionary mechanisms (Fairclough et al., 2004; Jessop & Oosterlynck, 2008) and, second, a combination of four selectivities (Sum & Jessop, 2015).

First, we explore the contribution of sociologies to processes of *variation of discourses and practices*, which may lead to a variety of alternative paths. The post-socialist transformation involved a quite radical redefinition of social, political, and economic imaginaries, that is, the semiotic systems providing the foundations for the living existence with a constitutive role in real existing East European societies; the question is: what role did sociologies play in developing the variation of these discourses? Imaginary that is not created or imported cannot be selected. At the beginning of the post-socialist transformation, we had a significant variation of discourses on economic and social policies, privatisation, and other issues on national and transnational levels, resulting in relevant debates, for example, big bang vs. gradualism, and different nuances of these debates (Šušteršič, 2009). How were these variations introduced on the national levels in different countries? Did sociologists influence the variability of discourses, and if so, how did they do it? Did sociologies contribute to any significant theoretically and practically relevant indigenous discourses? How did the indigenisation of imported discourses proceed, and what role did sociologies play in these processes?

Second, we scrutinise the *selection of particular discourses*, a process in which sociologies could play a role by privileging and interpreting some of these discourses by providing legitimisation through the interpretation of specific phenomena. The question is: What were the processes determining the selection of dominant discourse? Was this selection indigenous, and was it really a choice? What determined the outcome? More specifically, what was the role of sociologies leading to dominant social imaginary? How did sociologies get involved in the process of selection? Did sociologies contribute to the legitimation of particular discourses over others? If so, what mechanisms did sociologies use for that, for example, specific interpretations of social phenomena? What motivated sociologies for this?

Third, sociologies can contribute to the *retention of specific resonant discourses*, a process in which discourses and practices are included in individual and collective routines and identities, in widely accepted strategies and state projects and are even materialised in the physical environment. In the mid-1990s, dominant discourses crystallised. This does not imply that strategic reorientation is not a possibility, as evidenced by the strategic changes in Croatia or Russia after the year 2000 or more recent developments in Hungary, Poland, and others (Berend & Bugarič, 2015). How did sociologies contribute to this process? What mechanisms did sociologies use for the retention of dominant discourses: for example, how did this show in its research, education (curricula), consulting or political activities?

Fourth is the *reinforcement of dominant discourses*. Sociology can be a device that privileges some discourses over others. Did sociologies provide any mechanisms for discursive selectivity for privileging and reinforcing dominant discourses and filtering out the competing ones (that is, by privileging particular styles and genres) or for material selectivity (that is, privileging certain sites or institutions through specific organisational and institutional orders, financial mechanisms, etc.)?

Finally, we explore the processes of selective recruitment, inculcation, and retention by national sociological communities, associations and academic institutions by privileging those individuals that correspond with dominant discourses. Did sociologies contribute to any processes of selective recruitment, inculcation and retention? Did this also happen within national sociological communities, associations and academic institutions? What were the mechanisms and consequences? What was the extent of these consequences?

1.2.2 Sociologies, Selectivities and Discourses

Exploration of the role of sociologies in societal transformation also needs to analyse four selectivities, as defined by Sum and Jessop (2015). First is *structural selectivity*. States and other actors strategically choose specific policies, interventions, or areas of focus rather than pursuing comprehensive and all-encompassing strategies. This selectivity is driven by various factors, including political considerations, economic interests, and the specific challenges or crises facing the state. We can explore the question: How did sociologies contribute to (un)equal arrangement of limitations and possibilities that affect social forces in their pursuit of specific goals? This arrangement is only present to the extent that it is repeatedly seen in social practices and can evolve over time through gradual changes or intentional efforts to alter the constraints and opportunities in societal transformation. The outcomes of these efforts, successful or not, tend to leave lasting influences on social reality.

The second is *discursive selectivity*. This describes the uneven constraints and opportunities embedded in specific genres, styles, and discourses. This involves what can be expressed, who has the authority to express it, and how these expressions enter interconnected textual, discursive, and contextual domains. Did sociologies in East and Central European post-socialist societies place limitations on what can be envisioned, themes that can be articulated, or the adoption of certain subject positions? Did sociologies permit and forbid certain expressions within the confines of specific languages and the forms of discourse existing within them? Did it shape the ease with which specific appeals, arguments, or legitimisations can be developed?

Third is *technological selectivity*. This encompasses the entire spectrum of the technical and social relations involved in the social division of labour, not only from a technological perspective. How did sociologies shape objects, create subject positions, recruit subjects, and, particularly in this context, establish power/knowledge relations and possibilities? Did it shape the asymmetries embedded in the use of technologies in shaping object and subject positions that contribute to the formation of dispositives and truth regimes in post-socialist transformations in Central and Eastern Europe?

Finally, *agential selectivity*. It refers to the varying ability of agents to engage in strategically calculated actions aligned with other selectivities, not only in abstract terms but also to specific circumstances, in this case, in the processes of dramatic and rapid transformations in Central and Eastern Europe. Sociologists can have, at least in principle, an impact due to their diverse abilities to persuade, interpret specific circumstances, engage ideological opponents, and effectively reshape discourses and imaginaries. Agential selectivity hinges on the unique contributions that specific actors (or social forces) make in particular circumstances.

While answering these questions, we also need to touch upon the professional status of sociologies and their possible changes throughout time has to be touched upon. Is sociology in a nation a strong and autonomous professional community, or is it a weak and dependent profession? While answering this question, one should deal with the issue of the availability of appropriate institutional infrastructure and funding, the availability of funding for social research, the availability of relevant empirical data for social research, as well as professional ethics and (in)dependence from political influence. Appropriate funding, both in terms of its sufficiency as well as strings attached to it, is crucial as it empowers researchers to independently investigate societal issues, contribute to evidence-based policy-making, and promote relevant social issues. This support ensures that sociologists can pursue critical research, enrich education, and engage with the public, exercising their role in societal transformations. Funding regimes significantly contributing to 'national histories of sociology' (Collyer & Manning, 2022) are a source of friction and are supporting knowledge hierarchies and disparities both within sociology (Larregue & Nielsen, 2024), among social sciences and between disciplines (Solovey, 2020).

1.3 Transformative Power (or Lack Thereof) of Sociologies: First Empirical Results

Using this analytical framework, we started our exploration already in the period between September 2016 and April 2017 with a series of ten semi-structured expert interviews with academic sociologists from ten East European countries (Bulgaria, Croatia, Estonia, Hungary, Moldova, Poland, Romania, Russia, Serbia, Slovenia) in the period. The experts were selected to provide an in-depth view of the situation in their countries. All interviewees are well-established academic sociologists who were already in academic careers at the end of the 1980s and have been able to observe societal transformations in their profession since then (Fig. 1.1).

Our interviews revealed two interesting and general oversights by East European sociologists.

East European sociologists seem *oblivious to the transformative power of sociologies*, understood either as a profession or through the participation of sociologists in politics. True, the literature review reveals that this is shared with other sociologists researching Central and Eastern Europe and is evidence of the overall failure of sociologies to reflect upon their transformative power, leading to an identified lack of knowledge on the topic. Interviewees were generally relatively knowledgeable about the literature on how transition influenced the sociological profession, even in cases in which they were not specialising in transitological research, or at least had a relatively good overview of the state of the social sciences generally and sociology, more specifically. However, almost without exception,

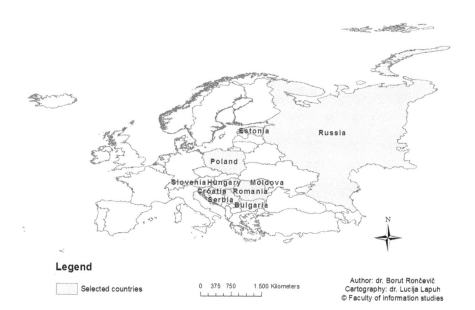

Fig. 1.1 East and Central European post-socialist countries included in the preliminary study

they were quite surprised by the question on the role of sociologies in post-socialist transformation and did not have the answer to the question of what should be the key points of this line of research in this sociology of sociology or what this research should focus on in the future. In cases in which interviewees would reflect on the role of sociologies, they claimed a minuscule role, a consequence of either the impact of politics (which perceived sociologists as ideologically inappropriate) or the successful competition of other, more 'practical' sciences like economics, political sciences, or legal sciences, or in the case of Poland, interestingly, history, which became more influential.

They exhibit almost a general *failure to recognise the variability of imaginaries* in the early stages of post-socialist transitions. Transitions were a complex multidimensional process from planned to market economy, from undemocratic totalitarian to democratic regime, from autarchy or limited integration to international integration (Adam et al., 2005) and in some cases even included the process of nation-building. At some point, strategic decisions were made, resulting in very different social and economic policies (Šušteršič, 2009). However, there seems to be a relatively general defeatist consensus among interviewees that in these initial times, there was no space for strategic choices and that the dramatic economic situation allowed no other policies, namely, the policies undertaken were the only options available.

1.3.1 How Sociologies Can Play Their Role

Our interviews revealed two dimensions determining the way sociologies impact post-socialist transformations in Central and Eastern Europe. The first is the *status of the profession*, best described by the continuum between sociology with professional autonomy on one side and professional dependence on the other. The second is the *transformative power of sociology*, simply described by the continuum between strong and impactful on one side and weak and irrelevant roles in post-socialist transformations on the other.

1.3.1.1 The Status of Profession

Professional autonomy can be defined differently in different social settings. In the context of Eastern Europe, the following aspects appeared most relevant.

Availability of institutional infrastructure and funding. The situation varies across East European countries, and the legacy of socialism plays an important role in determining the current status. The situation is well known from extensive previous research (see Kaase et al., 2002; Keen & Mucha, 2003) and this volume reaffirms this conclusion, as well as provides information on more recent developments. In some countries, the institutional infrastructure was well developed, and sociology as a profession was well embedded in national academic communities, even allowing a certain degree of intellectual freedom and different schools of thought to develop. In others, the situation was much less positive.[2]

Availability of funding for social research is a key determinant for the functioning of institutions, enabling them to conduct social research and have a good overview of rapid societal transformations, replace retired professors, or even strengthen their ranks (e.g., in Slovenia). In other countries, the situation was less positive, for example, in Bulgaria, where the ranks of academic sociology were thinned, or even worse, in Croatia or Bosnia, where research was not only made difficult due to the war situation but initially made it virtually impossible by the lack of funding for empirical research. In some countries, external funders were able to support small-scale research, mostly on the level of individual researchers, but they were not able to replace national funding systems, and in most cases, they did not support primary research. Furthermore, relying on external funders submits researchers to the bias and interests of these funders and, at the same time, ignores the topics perceived as relevant by indigenous researchers, for example, the topic of the 'destruction of society' in Serbia.

Insufficient funding translates directly to poor availability of empirical data. Although some institutions are well-staffed, they lack the ability to do empirical research. The lack of concrete high-quality data renders any kind of relevance of sociologies in policy-making unfeasible. The worst was, for example, the situation in Bosnia, a devastated country and deeply divided along ethnic and religious lines with virtually no empirical data except the most basic types and, in some cases, not even that but only estimates. The situation has changed more recently, either due to the improvement of the economic situation or due to access to external sources of funding, especially the variety of European Union mechanisms. Furthermore, nowadays, it is possible to do substantial secondary research by relying on a number of information from international reports (Global Competitiveness Report, World Competitiveness Yearbook, Transparency International, World Bank Governance Indicator, Human Development Report and many more). In the 1990s, relatively few, except the most advanced and well-off post-socialist countries, were included in these reports, making any kind of comparative research very difficult.

Another key dimension is the level of professional ethos of sociologists and their independence from politics. Here, we are referring to respect for academic autonomy, professional ethics and responsibility. The legacy played a very important role. For example, Polish, Hungarian, and Slovenian sociological communities were relatively independent during the socialist period. This does not imply that they were not ideologised and used as a means for the reproduction of socialist imaginaries. However, the differences in the degree to which sociologists claimed and exercised their professional autonomy and to which political systems allowed for intellectual independence from official ideology were substantial, as were the differences in the degree to which sociologists were able to find ways around the

---

[2] The situation was particularly interesting in former Yugoslavia, a federal state, where the state apparatus within individual republics adopted different approaches towards intellectual freedom and dissent.

official rules.[3] These differences translated to differences in the ability of national sociological communities to contribute to the variability of discourses.

The last was the theoretical competence of national sociological communities, giving them the ability to connect observations and information, similar to sociological theories and global trends. Here, the political openness of the national regimes played a very important role. For example, in Slovenia, a number of young sociologists were allowed to spend time in Germany or even to pursue their doctoral degrees in the US, some of them actually playing important roles in political processes leading to independence and systems transformation.[4] In Hungary, ironically, the political system contributed to profession building by exiling sociologist Ivan Szeleny after the publication of work critical of communism.[5]

1.3.1.2 Transformative Power of Sociologies

The second dimension is the transformative power of sociologies. Let us first note that sociologists can perform their transformative role in a number of ways.

Academic sociologists performing their role as researchers and educators. In this role, sociologists are performing several important functions. While being done professionally and keeping up with the best practices in scientific research, the research process can still be influenced by the personal beliefs or agenda of individual researchers (e.g., libertarian or social-democratic worldviews). Academic sociologists, as educators, influence generations of new intellectuals, politicians, civil servants, journalists, and other professionals.

As experts and consultants, sociologists can play the role of interpreting possible scenarios, alternative paths and discourses for politicians and policy-makers. While this role is not related to power, it can be linked with significant influence over the final policy outcome. Furthermore, sociologists can give credibility and legitimacy to specific discourses.

In some cases, sociologists shift between political and academic careers. Interviews revealed that this is a rather common occurrence in most countries, although their political influence can vary substantially, from being very strong (e.g., in Slovenia, sociologists not only contributed to initial democratic reforms, but reshaped educational system, adjusted system of social policy, and contributed to building of foreign policy) to relatively weak or ineffectual. In a number of cases in many countries, they later returned to academic careers, and although interviews

---

[3] For example, to introduce knowledge about non-Marxist theories, the so-called bourgeois sociology, by publishing carefully worded critiques of these theories or by evading the censorship process by declaring a lower number of printed copies of books below that of censorship threshold.

[4] Some of the political actors who contributed significantly and historically to processes leading to the breakup of the socialist regime were sociologists who received doctorates from universities in the USA or spent extended periods of time in Western countries.

[5] Ivan Szeleny is one of the most prominent sociologists of Hungarian origin and proved very instrumental to opening doors to generations of young Hungarian sociologists.

revealed that this is frowned upon by some of their academic peers, it can be interpreted as evidence of the transformative power of sociologies.

Sociologists are relatively active in civil society, voicing their opinions and contributing alternative discourses or legitimating existing ones. Even in cases in which sociologists did not play a hugely important role and were rather marginalised, they may play a significant role in specific topics, for example, gender issues, family violence, and family policy in Croatia.

Sociologists as public intellectuals step beyond strict disciplinary and scientific boundaries and engage with wider audiences in a 'dialogic relation between sociologist and public in which the agenda of each is brought to the table' (Burawoy, 2005, p. 9) to address relevant public issues (Agger, 2000). In this role, sociologists can potentially play a major role in various social movements by creating and disseminating discourses in the public sphere.

1.3.1.3 Four Ideal Types of the Role of Sociologies in Society

If we take these two dimensions into account, we can see that sociologists can play very different roles in societal transformations at any particular time. Combining two dimensions can provide us with four ideal types, as presented in Fig. 1.2.

Our exploration of the role of sociologies in Central and East European post-socialist transformations provided the opportunity to delve into a topic that is little known or explored; hence, we can follow Max Weber's approach to the application of ideal types in social science research, that is, to develop ideal types by selecting and accentuating key elements which are deemed crucial for sociologies playing role in societal transformations, to help us grapple with an 'empirical reality [...] that is primarily [achieved] through a comparison of reality with the ideal type' (Swedberg, 2018, p. 184). Since 'ideal types are defined by specifying multivariate profiles that represent the ideal types of organisations identified in the theory' (Doty

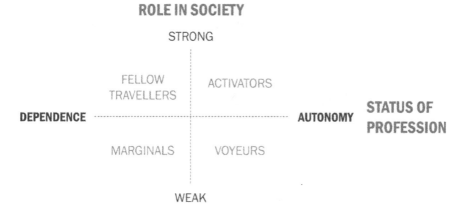

Fig. 1.2 Four ideal types of the role of sociologies in society

& Glick, 1994, p. 237), they can be used in empirical exploration to determine the extent to which each specific case conforms to or diverges from a specific ideal type. This does not negate the fact that 'there must be a closer fit, than Weber standardly admits or allows between ideal-types and the usual or average manifestations and tendencies as empirically observable' (Aronovitch, 2012, p. 361). Developing ideal types 'involves selectivity at the theoretical level, just as the interpretation of experience by agents involves selectivity at the existential level' (Aronovitch, 2012, p. 361).

The formation of ideal types should not be perceived as a mere undertaking in taxonomy or classification (Fric et al., 2023). Classifications and taxonomies aid in constructing concepts and organising empirical instances of specific phenomena, drawing from the empirical realm to conceptualisation. In contrast, ideal types originate as conceptual frameworks and possess significant potential for theory construction, representing, when appropriately developed, relatively intricate theoretical assertions that warrant thorough empirical scrutiny. While we will not go as far in this volume, we can see it as a first step in this direction.

Sociologies as Activators This type implies a competent sociological community with good institutional infrastructure, well-funded and able to conduct empirical research yielding vital information on social trends, and at the same time motivated and successful in its attempts to play an important role in societal transformations. It creates and contributes to alternative discourses and participates in the selection and retention of these discourses. This does not imply that sociologists are the key actors or drivers of social transformations, but they play a relatively prominent role in interaction and in synergy with other professional communities (economists, political scientists, historians, legal scientists, etc.) and other collective actors. In this interconnected network of expertise and implementation, sociologies contribute unique insights, (re)shape imaginaries and contribute to their application.

Sociologies as Voyeurs These sociologies would be closest to Burawoy's critical sociology and possibly public sociology in the division of sociological labour. This type describes competent, academically autonomous, and well-funded sociological communities that are not motivated or fail to be an agent in societal transformations. Sociologists may contribute to the variation of discourses out of scientific curiosity but do not contribute to their selection, retention, and reinforcement of dominant discourses. These strong sociological communities are observing, reflecting and criticising societies.It must be acknowledged that new discourses can indeed emerge as a result of these critiques, adding diversity to the intellectual landscape, even if the communities themselves are not actively involved in steering societal transformations.

Sociologies as Fellow Travellers This mode describes institutionally or ethically weak, professionally dependent sociological communities, without the ability to collect relevant primary data or to use them for socially relevant scientific observations. These sociological communities do play a societal role, though, by contributing to the selection, retention, and reinforcement of particular discourses as the clients of dominant political elites or sometimes even by contributing to the variation of discourses, either in connection to political opposition or as agents of external funders, for example, intentional organisations (e.g., World Bank) or ideologically relevant foundations (e.g., various German political party foundations, Open Society Foundations etc.). Is this close to Burawoy's policy sociology, which is 'sociology in service of a goal defined by a client' (Burawoy, 2005, p. 9)? Not necessarily. As per Burawoy (2005, p. 9), 'policy sociology's raison d'etre is to provide solutions to problems that are presented to us, or to legitimate solutions that have already been reached'. Despite the patron-client relationship, this can still be done by a competent and relatively autonomous sociology, serving in the role of an expert. In contrast, fellow travellers are not autonomous at all. Interestingly, in the Soviet Union, Leon Trotsky popularised the term *poputchik* to describe intellectual supporters of the government.

Sociologies as Marginals This type delineates sociological communities that are notably underdeveloped in a professional capacity, lacking a substantial role in influencing societal transformations and not engaging in semiotic practices that contribute to political changes. These communities find themselves at a point where their sociological influence is limited, and they are not actively participating in the intricate processes that lead to significant shifts in society and the impactful use of signs and symbols in political transformations. In essence, they exist on the periphery of societal dynamics, displaying a marked absence of substantial involvement in shaping the sociopolitical landscape through their sociological contributions and semiotic engagements.

We should add that since these are ideal types in the making, we cannot expect that we will find these types as such in any of the countries. It is not a descriptor; it is a tool utilised in practical investigation to assess the degree to which individual cases adhere to or deviate from a particular ideal type. Furthermore, as national case studies in this book show, in most countries, it is possible to observe a certain level of internal differentiation of sociological communities, or alternatively, these communities exhibit qualities of more than one type or are somewhere in between on continuums described above. In some, if not most, cases presented in this edited volume, we can observe the existence of several communities in a single country.

1.3.2 Temporal Perspective

The above-presented classification of transformative roles of sociologies in a society does not exist in a vacuum. Specific constantly changing external circumstances (political, economic, etc.) and internal disciplinary conditions (positive or negative trends in disciplinary development, that is, increasing or decreasing autonomy) play an important role. This emphasises the importance of temporal perspective. Our

Fig. 1.3 Time perspective: Sociology and topics over time

empirical analysis, as well as exploration of the body of literature on East European transformation (e.g., Berend & Bugarič, 2015), shows that we can distinguish four relevant phases. Here, we omit the extended pre-phase of the socialist period, which played an important role in setting the stage but has already been reflected upon in great detail (e.g., Denitch, 1971; Kaase et al., 2002; Zysiak, 2023; Keen & Mucha, 2003) (Fig. 1.3).

The Nascent Phase The first relevant phase is the period of setting the stage of societal transformation and its early phase, specifically, the end of the 1980s and the beginning of the 1990s. In addition to the post-socialist transition, this was also the period of disciplinary transition from ideologised to professional sociology. In the nascent phase, Eastern European sociologies were dealing with two quite separate yet important topics. In countries where sociology was relatively developed and enjoyed a relatively high level of professional autonomy, sociologists were able to reflect upon—regardless of whether they played the role of activists or voyeurs—the key issues of the time, that is, transitions to democracy, transition to market economy and, where necessitated by the situation—on the issues of nation building, not necessarily in the same order of precedence. Professionally dependent sociological communities, in contrast, were dealing with prolonged yet ambitious processes of profession building. This not only implied emancipation from direct political control but also upgraded institutional infrastructure, collection, and archiving of data from social science research.[6] It also implied the need for staffing, which was a precarious process in times of financial scarcity in a period of systemic

---

[6]For example, initiatives by GESIS to support the social science data archives in East Central Europe, or the current project encouraging social science data archives supported by the Swiss SCOPES programme.

transformation, drastic decreases in economic activity (reduction in gross domestic product/GDP) and consequent reductions in funding for scientific research, especially for non-applied research. Furthermore, there was a realistic need for internal disciplinary differentiation, shifting sociology from a situation in which entire national professional communities were dominated by a single theoretical paradigm to communities providing the ability to accommodate differentiated sociological perspectives. Although unreflected by the community, in this period, sociology became embedded in dominant discourse, supplying data and thereby contributing to the legitimation of predominant discourses.

The Reflective Phase Regardless of the outcome of the nascent phase, in the mid-1990s, the sociological communities reoriented themselves towards rethinking the outcomes of the first phase of post-socialist transitions, to some extent caused by the 'disappointments' of the first phase of transitions, in which results did not meet the expectations. This was evident in various fields. In the economy, the transformation from planned to market economy did not yield appropriate results, as evidenced by a dramatic decrease in GDP (it took years to return to pre-transition levels) and the dramatic breakdown of entire industrial sectors or regions. This was accompanied by a huge increase in employment or, to be more accurate, the transformation from hidden employment (underemployment) in state-owned companies to open unemployment. These trends were offset by failing social policies, which could not be afforded by impoverished states, leading to immense social costs of transition, increases in inequality and especially poverty. Therefore, it is not surprising that in the political fields, unstable democratic systems were present, in which power was in many cases returned to the reformed communists or their descendants after the second elections. In contrast, this reflection was to some extent caused by the external actors, that is, international organisations (the European Union, the World Bank, etc.) or foundations (e.g., the German foundations like Friedrich Ebert Stiftung, Konrad Adenauer Stiftung) who financed local researchers to conduct case studies on East European 'laboratory' of social transformations.

The Reorientation Phase After the year 2000, the attention of sociological communities seems to have shifted somewhat towards new topics. This was the period of important strategic reorientations. Some East European societies, especially those from East Central Europe, started making determined steps towards EU membership, which opened a whole set of new topics. This was also the period in which the EU started to actively encourage the integration of researchers into various EU programs and initiatives, including the FP programmes, Erasmus exchange, Tempus, and various pre-accession funds. This not only provided the possibility of obtaining additional funding for sociological research but also enabled the continued integration of sociological communities to the international sociological community. In effect, East European sociologists had the opportunity to actively engage, which further contributed to profession building. For some other countries, this implied a completely different set of strategic reorientations. In Russia, the change from the Yeltsin to Putin era was a major transformation. In Croatia, the death of President

Tudjman and the electoral defeat of his conservative Croatian Democratic Union led to a strategic change from isolationist policy towards European integration. Likewise, in Serbia, the defeat of the Milosevic regime led to the opening of the country towards European integration, although this process has yet to conclude with EU membership.

The New Crises and Challenges Accession to the European Union of the majority of East European countries did not lead towards some new 'end of history'. In addition to being subjected to dynamic global trends (Genov, 2016), they have entered a period of major new challenges, such as social, economic and cultural consequences of mass illegal migration to Europe from Africa, Asia and the Middle East, as well as related political conflicts (Ben-Arieh & Heins, 2021), Brexit and the resulting crisis of the European Union (Markakis, 2020), the COVID-19 pandemic with its varied enduring impacts (Charron et al., 2023) and the reassertion of Russian imperial ambitions, of which war in Ukraine is one demonstration (Oksamytna, 2023). They have all opened the new crisis phase, and like every crisis, it opens the space for new alternative discourses. Currently, we are in the phase of variation of discourses, and its outcome, as well as the role of sociologies in this process, is the question for future research.

1.3.2.1 Two Modes of Sociology

Temporal analysis of the role of sociologies in East European transitions revealed two modes of sociology, namely sociology as a crisis science and sociology as a service science.

Sociology as a Crisis Science Initially, sociologies played a relatively important role in some of the Central and East European countries undergoing post-socialist societal transformations. The initial period of transition provided an opportunity for a critique of the outgoing regime. This period was followed by major societal transformations, disruptions of social order, and related challenges. These are the conditions of crisis in which sociology as a discipline thrives, performing its role as a critical science as a crisis science. This is not something new or unprecedented; in fact, sociology was formed more than a century earlier as an academic response to the demand for analysis of immense social changes stemming from the Industrial Revolution—a complex of social and technological innovations that permeated all areas of social life—that fundamentally transformed most societies in the second half of the nineteenth century. These changes in the social and material world also fundamentally shaped early sociological imaginaries and resulted in a number of well-known dichotomies like Ferdinand Tönnies' Gemeinschaft and Gesellschaft, Emile Durkheim's *mechanical and organic* solidarity, as well as Herbert Spencer's theory of evolution. The 'crisis' situation even influenced Albion Small to announce the 'era of sociology' in his editorial to the introductory issue of the American Journal of Sociology (Small, 1895). We should add that the new challenges and paths phase seems to continuously provide new opportunities for the reinvigoration of sociology as a crisis science.

Sociology as a Service Science There was a general perception among the interviewed sociologists that this opportunity for sociology was changed relatively dramatically immediately after the transition commenced, and sociology lost its social impact and appeal. This transition is described as a shift from 'real' science to service science; this was meant pejoratively, reflecting the feeling of resentment, feeling that the instrumentalisations of sociology undermine its status as a science, that sociology can exist only as a critical science and that once sociology is not required anymore as a critical science, sociology is in crisis. One could comment with a bit of cynicism that either society is in crisis, or sociology is in crisis. The perception is that if sociology as a real critical science does not give way to sociology as a service science, it risks becoming a marginal science, especially in comparison with more 'applied sciences' (law, economics, political science).

In reality, the line between sociology as a crisis science and as a service science can become blurred. For example, during the reflection in the mid-1990s, both modes overlapped in many countries, as it was the period of both critical reflection as well as the opportunities to conduct applied instrumental research.

Further research is required to determine the reasons for this attitude among sociologists and the consequences it has for the societal role of sociologists. Could this negative perception of the applied nature of sociology be the reflection of experience from the socialist times, in which sociology was misused and abused as a tool for the reproduction of the regime, to contribute to retention, reinforcement, and selective recruitment for the socialist system, leading to the misinformed conclusion that only science removed from the practicalities is the real science? In fact, the current situation provides ample opportunities for sociologies to assume a more substantial role in steering societal transformations, not only in Central and Eastern Europe. We are referring to a general trend towards practical applications of sociology in Europe. This was, to some extent, institutionalised in Horizon 2020 and continued in Horizon Europe, from which relatively little funding is available for focused basic reflective sociological research. Instead, funding is increasingly aimed towards solving societal problems by application of Mode 2 (Gibbons et al., 1994) and Mode 3 production of knowledge (Carayannis & Campbell, 2006) within the Quintuple Helix approach (Carayannis & Campbell, 2021), which is driven by specific (applied) problem, depends on specific context—thereby eschewing generalisations and contributions to purely basic scientific exploration—and which, as a consequence, requires the cooperation of researchers from different disciplines, not only in the framework of social sciences but even cooperation of social and hard sciences. Nowadays, it is not uncommon to find academic sociologists working in interdisciplinary and multisectoral teams with hard scientists, as well as people from the private sector, creative industries, public administrations, nongovernmental organisations, and others (e.g., Interreg projects, which are relatively abundant and well-funded). In fact, a substantial part of research is 'carried out in a context of application, arising from the very work of problem-solving and not governed by the paradigms of traditional disciplines of knowledge' (Limoges, 1996, pp. 14–15). Traditional research is supported by relatively limited funds in national funding, ERC grants and others, limiting the opportunities for traditional academic mode of knowledge production.

Recent developments in Central and Eastern Europe—notably shifts towards nationalism and less democratic forms of governance—imply an increased role that sociology may play in reflecting and moderating these processes, so the knowledge about specific mechanisms of the role of sociology in societal steering is of vital importance.

1.4 Conclusion

The post-socialist transition in Central and Eastern Europe was a major societal transformation and involved (sometimes) radical redefinitions of social, economic, and political imaginaries, specifically the semiotic systems providing the foundation for the living experience in an extraordinary complex world with a constitutive role in real existing societies. We should further note that imaginaries are especially susceptible to changes in periods of crisis, which opens space for variation of discourses, followed by selection of a specific discourse, retention of specific resonant discourse, reinforcement of dominant discourses, and processes of selective recruitment, inculcation, and retention. Sociology, like the other social sciences, had the potential to play a significant role in these processes. However, our empirical analysis based on semi-structured expert interviews showed that this is not the only possible outcome. In fact, the role of sociologists can vary substantially between countries, from having a relatively important activist role to being completely marginal.

This introductory chapter presented a preliminary analysis as the first step to filling the gap in research on sociologies as the actors of post-socialist societal transformations in Central and East European countries. This volume as a whole is expanding and upgrading this exploration both on the theoretical-conceptual level and with more detailed empirical analyses through in-depth case studies of national sociological communities in 19 Central and East European countries. These case studies use a conceptual framework developed in initial exploratory analysis and provide detailed information about the transformative power of sociologies in specific national contexts. Additionally, they provide answers to some specific questions that were previously unanswered. For example, why is the role of sociologies in processes of post-socialist transition so un-reflected? What was the impact of the transition of sociologists between academic and political careers? What were the mechanisms of politics to influence sociologies, and what were the mechanisms of sociologies to influence politics? How important was the communication with the other social sciences and humanities (political science, economics, legal sciences, history, philosophy)? What was the role of sociologies in the operation of four selectivities? More specifically, did sociologies enhance or limit the scope for path-shaping by contributing to social structures favouring specific hegemonic discourses, specifically interests, identities, agents, spatiotemporal horizons, strategies, and projects (structural selectivity)? Did they contribute to the discursively enforced selection of sense and meaning, inscribing cognitive frames and limiting possible imaginaries and discourses (discursive selectivity)? In what way did sociologies contribute to dominant repositories of knowledge, governmental rationalities, sites and mechanisms of rational intervention (technological selectivity)? Did sociologists, in their various roles, have the capacity, and did they act upon this capacity to contribute to the establishment of a specific hegemonic discourse and economic imaginary (agential selectivity)?

While answering these questions, the professional status of sociologies and its possible changes throughout time has to be touched upon. Is sociology in a nation a strong and autonomous or weak and dependent profession? While answering this question, the authors of the case studies also touched upon the issues of the availability of appropriate institutional infrastructure and funding for social research, the availability of relevant empirical data for social research, the issues of professional ethics and (in)dependence from political influence. In some cases, the role of sociologists from the diaspora played an important role.

We aim to answer these and more questions in this book. First is a chapter by Ahmed and colleagues, who ask the question: Can sociologists make a difference with their intervention? They present three theoretical traditions that underlie the sociology of intellectuals and link positions to the type of concrete social intervention. They assert that the effectiveness of interventions is influenced by the strength and unity of intellectuals, emphasising that effectiveness will be restricted in areas or times where intellectuals lack power or are divided. Tomšič narrows the debate specifically on sociologists as intellectuals and their role in East and Central European post-socialist transformations and claims that the intellectual engagement of sociologists is necessary for successful societal transformation in former Communist countries. He outlines the conditions for their successful developmentally beneficial intellectual engagement to take place. Next, follow the case studies from 19 East and Central European countries. They offer good insight into processes that unfolded in the previous three to four decades, in some cases even more. We are especially happy that we were able to include countries that were, for various reasons, rarely studied in earlier periods, such as Albania, Bosnia and Herzegovina, and Moldova.

While this book does not provide definitive and final answers, it provides a good overview and a starting point for further debates on the topic at hand.

If we may use the vocabulary of some of my interviewees, it seems that we have entered a period of 'crisis', in which established patterns and assumptions are challenged. The future of European integration, the challenges of mass migration into the developed world, the looming possibilities of environmentally induced social, political and economic transformations on a global scale, as well as possible reversal of two of the key trends—from the globalisation of market economy to economic nationalism and from democratisation to spreading of populism and rise of authoritarian leaders and many more—imply that there is again the need for new social, political, and economic imaginaries, in which sociology as a crisis science has the opportunity to play an increasingly important role. There will also be ambition to instrumentalise sociology for political purposes or—where sociology will resist such attempts—to suppress freedom of sociological imagination and expression.

Competing Interests The author has no conflicts of interest to declare that are relevant to the content of this chapter.

References

Abraham, M. (2019, July 15). Power, violence, and justice: Reflections, responses and responsibilities: Presidential address—XIX ISA world congress of sociology. *International Sociology, 34*(3), 243–255.
Academic Freedom Index. (2023). *Friedrich-Alexander-Universität*. Erlangen-Nürnberg Germany.
Adam, F., Makarovič, M., Rončević, B., & Tomšič, M. (2005). *Challenges of sustained development: The role of socio-cultural factors in East-central Europe*. Central European University Press.
Agger, B. (2000). *Public sociology: From social facts to literary acts*. Rowman & Littlefield Publishers.
Aronovitch, H. (2012). Interpreting Weber's ideal-types. *Philosophy of Social Sciences, 42*(3), 356–369.
Ben-Arieh, G., & Heins, V. M. (2021). Criminalisation of kindness: Narratives of legality in the European politics of migration containment. *Third World Quarterly, 42*(1), 200–217.
Berend, I., & Bugarič, B. (2015). Unfinished Europe: Transition from communism to democracy in Central and Eastern Europe. *Journal of Contemporary History, 50*(4), 768–785.
Burawoy, M. (2005). 2004 American sociological association presidential address: For public sociology. *American Sociological Review, 70*(1), 4–28.
Burawoy, M. (2015). Facing an unequal world. *Current Sociology, 63*, 5–34.
Burawoy, M. (2021). *Public sociology between utopia and anti-utopia*. Polity Press.
Carayannis, E. G., & Campbell, D. F. J. (2006). Mode 3: Meaning and implications from a knowledge systems perspective. In E. G. Carayannis & D. F. J. Campbell (Eds.), *Knowledge creation, diffusion, and use in innovation networks and knowledge clusters: A comparative systems approach across the United States, Europe and Asia* (pp. 1–25). Praeger.
Carayannis, E. G., & Campbell, D. F. J. (2021). Helix trilogy: The triple, quadruple, and quintuple innovation helices from a theory, policy, and practice set of perspectives. *Journal of the Knowledge Economy, 13*, 2272–2301.
Castoriadis, C. (1975). *The imaginary institution of society*. Polity Press.
Chaisty, P., & Whitefield, S. (2023). Building voting coalitions in electoral authoritarian regimes: A case study of the 2020 constitutional reform in Russia. *Post-Soviet Affairs, 39*(4), 273–290.
Charron, N., Lapuente, V., & Rodriguez-Pose, A. (2023). Uncooperative society, uncooperative politics or both? Trust, polarization, populism and COVID-19 deaths across European regions. *European Journal of Political Research, 62*(3), 781–805.
Collyer, F. M., & Manning, B. (2022). Writing national histories of sociology: Methods, approaches and visions. *Journal of Sociology, 58*(4), 481–498.
Chepurenko, A., & Szanyi, M. (2023). Parallel processes and divergent outcomes: The transformation of the economies of former socialist countries. In B. Dallago & S. Casagrande (Eds.), *The Routledge handbook of comparative economic systems* (pp. 411–431). Routledge.

Denitch, B. (1971). Sociology in Eastern Europe: Trends and prospects. *Slavic Review, 30*(2), 317–339.

Doty, H., & Glick, W. (1994). Typologies as a unique form of theory building: Toward improved understanding and modeling. *The Academy of Management Review, 19*(2), 230–251.

Fairclough, N., Jessop, B., & Sayer, A. (2004). Critical realism and semiosis. In S. Fleetwood & J. M. Roberts (Eds.), *Realism, discourse and deconstruction* (pp. 23–42). Routledge.

Feldmann, M., & Popa, M. (2022). Populism and economic policy: Lessons from Central and Eastern Europe. *Post-Communist Economies, 34*(2), 219–245.

Fric, U., O'Gorman, W., & Rončević, B. (2023). Strategic competence model for understanding smart territorial development. *Societies, 13*(3), 76.

Fritz, J. M. (2021). The basics: From concepts to models. In J. M. Fritz (Ed.), *International clinical sociology* (2nd ed., pp. 17–32). Springer.

Genov, N. (2016). *Global trends in Eastern Europe*. Ashgate.

Genov, N. (Ed.). (1989). *National traditions in sociology*. Sage.

Gibbons, M., Limoges, C., Nowotny, H., Schwartzman, S., Scott, P., & Trow, M. (1994). *The new production of knowledge: The dynamics of science and research in contemporary societies*. Sage.

Győrffy, D. (2022). The middle-income trap in Central and Eastern Europe in the 2010s: Institutions and divergent growth models. *Comparative European Politics, 20*(1), 90–113.

Halsey, A. H. (2004). *A history of sociology in Britain: Science, literature and society*. Oxford University Press.

Hanafi, S. (2024). Toward a dialogical sociology: Presidential address—XX ISA world congress of sociology 2023. *International Sociology, 39*(1), 3–26.

Jessop, B., & Oosterlynck, S. (2008). Cultural political economy: On making the cultural turn without falling into soft economic sociology. *Geoforum, 39*, 1155–1169.

Kaase, M., Sparschuh, V., & Wenninger, A. (Eds.). (2002). *Three social science disciplines in Central and Eastern Europe: Handbook on economics, political science and sociology (1989–2001)*. GESIS.

Kattel, R. (2010). Financial and economic crisis in Eastern Europe. *Journal of Post Keynesian Economics, 33*(1), 41–60.

Keen, M. F., & Mucha, J. (Eds.). (2003). *Sociology in Central and Eastern Europe: Transformation at the dawn of a new millennium*. Praeger.

Larregue, J., & Nielsen, M. W. (2024). Knowledge hierarchies and gender disparities in social science funding. *Sociology, 58*(1), 45–65.

Limoges, C. (1996). *L'université à la croisée des chemins: Une mission à af rmer, Une gestion à réformer, Colloque Le lien formation-recherche à l'université: Les pratiques aujourd'hui*. Association canadienne-français pour l'avancement des sciences et le Conseil de la science et de la technologie et le Conseil supérieur de l'education.

Markakis, M. (2020). Differentiated integration and disintegration in the EU: Brexit, the Eurozone crisis, and other troubles. *Journal of International Economic Law, 23*, 489–507.

Nielsen, K., Jessop, B., & Hausner, J. (1995). Institutional change in post-socialism. In J. Hausner, B. Jesop, & K. Nielsen (Eds.), *Strategic choice and path-dependency in post-socialism: Institutional dynamics in the transformation process* (pp. 3–44). Edward Elgar.

Oksamytna, K. (2023). Imperialism, supremacy, and the Russian invasion of Ukraine. *Contemporary Security Policy, 44*(4), 497–512.

Ould, M., & Sisk, T. D. (2017). Reviving transitology: Democratisation then and now. In O. Mohamedou & T. D. Sisk (Eds.), *Democratisation in the 21st century: Reviving transitology*. Routledge.

Pleyers, G. (2023). For a global sociology of social movements: Beyond methodological globalism and extractivism. *Globalizations, 21*(1), 183–195.

Rončević, B., Makarovič, M., Tomšič, M., & Cepoi, V. (2018). Methodological solutions for comparative research on transformations. In P. Vihalemm, A. Masso, & S. Opermann (Eds.), *The Routledge international handbook of European social transformations* (pp. 57–70). Routledge.

Sartre, J.-P. (2004 [1940]). *The imaginary: A phenomenological psychology of the imagination*. Routledge.
Sayer, A. (2001). For a critical cultural political economy. *Antipode, 33*(4), 687–708.
Schmitter, P. C. (1994). The proto-science of consolidology: Can it improve the outcome of contemporary efforts at democratization? *Politikon, 21*(2), 15–27.
Schmitter, P., & Karl, T. L. (1994). The conceptual travels of transitologists and consolidologists: How far to the east should they attempt to go? *Slavic Review, 53*(1), 173–185.
Shleifer, A., & Treisman, D. (2014). Normal countries: The east 25 years after communism. *Foreign Affairs, 93*(6), 92–103.
Small, A. W. (1895). The era of sociology. *American Journal of Sociology, 1*(1), 1–15.
Smith, R. C. (2022). Advancing publicly engaged sociology. *Sociological Forum, 37*(4), 926–950.
Solovey, M. (2020). *Social science for what? Battles over public funding for the "other sciences" at the national science foundation*. MIT Press.
Sum, N. L., & Jessop, B. (2015). *Towards a cultural political economy: Putting culture in its place in political economy*. Edward Elgar.
Šušteršič, J. (2009). Endogenous gradualism and the Slovenian puzzle. *China Economic Review, 20*(2), 265–274.
Swedberg, R. (2018). How to use max Weber's ideal type in sociological analysis. *Journal of Classical Sociology, 18*(3), 181–196.
Turner, J. H. (2019). The more American sociology seeks to become a politically-relevant discipline, the more irrelevant it becomes to solving societal problems. *The American Sociologist, 50*, 456–487.
Usov, P. (2023). From authoritarianism to neo-totalitarianism in Belarus. In R. Zięba (Ed.), *Politics and security of Central and Eastern Europe: Contemporary challenges* (pp. 33–56). Springer.
Zysiak, A. (2023). How sociology shaped postwar Poland and how stalinization shaped sociology. In D. Fassin & G. Steinmetz (Eds.), *The social sciences in the looking glass: Studies in the production of knowledge* (pp. 175–194). Duke University Press.

Borut Rončević, PhD is a Professor of Sociology at the School of Advanced Social Studies (Nova Gorica, Slovenia), Faculty of Information Studies (Novo mesto, Slovenia) and senior research fellow at Rudolfovo-Science and Technology Centre (Novo mesto). He is a member of the Executive Committee of the International Sociological Association. He held the prestigious Marie Curie Fellowship at Aalborg University (Denmark) and was a Fulbright Scholar-in-Residence at the Troy University (USA) and Jean Monnet Chair. In his work, he focuses on developmental performance in East and Central Europe, and issues of regional development, innovations and circular economy. He was a visiting scholar at institutions in the United States of America, the United Kingdom, Germany, Ireland, Russia, Denmark, Norway, Lebanon, and Croatia.

Chapter 2
The Sociology of Sociological Interventions: Do Sociologists Make a Social Difference?

Patricia Ahmed, Rebecca Jean Emigh, Dylan Riley, and Nancy Wang Yuen

The term 'intellectual' as a group identifier first emerged during the Dreyfus Affair of 1897–1899 (Ringer, 1992, p. 219), when some French writers and academics protested and successfully mobilised against the conviction of a Jewish military officer imprisoned for treason (Jennings & Kemp-Welch, 1997, p. 7; Kurzman & Leahy, 2004, p. 942; Kurzman & Owens, 2002, p. 64). The 'Dreyfusards' were linked to the most academically prestigious institutions. The 'anti-Dreyfusards', in contrast, were more market-dependent writers and professionals (Debray 1979/1981, p. 58; Ringer, 1992, p. 221). Thus, the Dreyfusard mobilisation, in which intellectuals intervened in public debate *qua* 'men of knowledge', was made possible by the rise of a powerful system of higher education in the French Third Republic (Debray, 1979/1981, pp. 42–43; Ringer, 1992, p. 220). Self-identified intellectuals, inspired by their Dreyfusard French colleagues, globally united around the designation of 'intellectuals', sparking a positive, almost messianic collective identity among themselves during the early twentieth century (Kurzman & Leahy, 2004, p. 943; Kurzman & Owens, 2002, p. 64). Initially, strong solidarity and belief in their importance fostered their support of democratisation (Kurzman & Leahy, 2004,

---

P. Ahmed
South Dakota State University, Brookings, SD, USA
e-mail: patricia.ahmed@sdstate.edu

R. J. Emigh (✉)
University of California, Los Angeles, CA, USA
e-mail: emigh@soc.ucla.edu

D. Riley
University of California, Berkeley, CA, USA
e-mail: riley@berkeley.edu

N. W. Yuen
Independent Scholar, Los Angeles, CA, USA

© The Author(s), under exclusive license to Springer Nature Switzerland AG 2024
B. Roncevic, T. Besednjak Valič (eds.), *Sociology and Post-Socialist Transformations in Eastern Europe*,
https://doi.org/10.1007/978-3-031-65556-2_2

p. 944). However, during the interwar period, intellectuals became disillusioned and disorganised and participated more in radical movements of the right and left (Kurzman & Leahy, 2004, p. 944). As a result, intellectuals underwent a period of intense self-criticism, questioning their ability to intervene positively and politically to serve the general public (Michels, 1932, p. 123). The sociology of intellectuals took form during this period (Kurzman & Owens, 2002, p. 63).

The emphasis on sociological interventions followed a roughly similar time frame. In its earliest inception in the nineteenth century, sociology focused on social intervention. In the United States, for example, it took the form of a dialogue between sociologists and various philanthropic and reformist groups (Burawoy, 2005a, p. 19). From the 1920s to the 1940s, sociological work came to be sponsored by government or corporate sources, leading it away from its public (Burawoy, 2005a, p. 19). In the late 1930s, a critical reaction reevaluated sociology's role in transforming society (Burawoy, 2005a, p. 19). More recently, the discipline may have continued to shift back to its roots, increasingly seeking ways to transform knowledge and expertise into interventions in civil society or the public sphere (Eyal & Buchholz, 2010, p. 117).

In addition to this possible historical shift in the interest in social interventions, the development of an explicit theoretical apparatus, and in particular a sociology of intellectuals, shaped how sociologists conceptualise their sociology of interventions. Below, then, we review the sociology of intellectuals and their conceptualisation of social interventions, drawing out three main positions: (1) intellectuals are a group or stratum situated between classes but shaped by class struggles ('intellectuals as a stratum', e.g., Marx, Gramsci); (2) intellectuals are a group, or indeed a class, who pursue their own class interest ('intellectuals as a class', e.g., Bakunin, Djilas, Konrád and Szelényi, Gouldner); and (3) intellectuals are a universal group because their ideas apply to all social groups ('intellectuals as universal', e.g., Benda, Mannheim, Shils, and Bourdieu). These three positions have different implications for intellectuals' social interventions: the first position led to diverse calls for a public sociology, exemplified by Burawoy (2005a, p. 4); the second position is similar to Touraine's (1981, pp. 139–140) 'sociological interventions'; and the third position has led to calls for civic sociology (Lybeck et al., 2018, n.p.) and humane translations of sociological ideas (Abbott, 2007, pp. 202–203).

2.1 Intellectuals as a Stratum

2.1.1 The Sociology of Intellectuals

The first set of theories, the Marxist account of intellectuals, portrays the intelligentsia as a stratum whose political and social character derives from its position in particular modes of production and class structures. Marx (1932/1994, p. 118) hinted at the problem of intellectuals in 'The German Ideology' in which he linked their idealism to the separation of mental from manual labour. The topic became pressing during the Second International. In his famous critique of the Austrian Social Democratic Party programme of 1899, Kautsky (1901–1902, p. 80) rejected the view that socialist consciousness directly stemmed from proletarian class struggle. It was not created by the proletariat but had to be brought from the outside. In fact, 'the bearer of science is not the proletariat, but rather the bourgeois intelligentsia' (Kautsky, 1901–1902, p. 79). Lenin (1902/1975, p. 28), drawing on Kautsky, suggested that the creation of socialist intellectuals was a central task of party formation.

Gramsci attempted to develop a more sophisticated and historically grounded account of intellectuals. He made three decisive contributions. First, he developed a more sophisticated typology of intellectuals than the crude contrast between bourgeois intellectuals and the proletariat current in the Second International of the early twentieth century. Second, he recast the relationship between ideology and science in accordance with his sharply anti-positivist epistemological stance that distinguished him from both Kautsky and Lenin. Third, he recast the connection between political engagement and cognitive validity, making the latter dependent on the former. We trace all three contributions here.

First, Gramsci (1971/1992, p. 1) dismissed the idea of intellectuals forming a separate class. Instead, intellectuals' position in the social structure was shaped by the overall configuration of knowledge and production in different modes of production (Gramsci, 1971/1992, pp. 5–6). For Gramsci (1971/1992, p. 12), intellectuals had a variable relationship to the process of production in different class societies. In pre-capitalist societies, Gramsci claimed that knowledge and production were structurally separated from one another, so intellectuals formed an insulated caste, whom he called 'traditional intellectuals'. They were exemplified by the clergy, who viewed themselves as an autonomous group by virtue of historical continuity (Gramsci 1971/1992, pp. 7–8). Organic intellectuals, in sharp contrast to traditional intellectuals, developed under capitalism, a mode of production characterised by the systematic integration of knowledge into production. Unlike traditional intellectuals, organic intellectuals took on specialised roles within their originally undifferentiated class (Gramsci, 1971/1992, p. 5).

Given the uneven development of capitalism, especially in Italy, organic and traditional intellectuals could exist contemporaneously. Gramsci (1971/1992, pp. 7–8, 10) saw the central task of party formation as the attempt to link the two types of intellectuals together. Thus, he argued that classes, in the fight to achieve hegemony, 'struggle to assimilate and to conquer "ideologically" the traditional intellectuals' (Gramsci, 1971/1992, p. 10). Indeed, this struggle was the main task of organic intellectuals acting either in the interests of the proletariat in their struggle to overthrow capitalism or in the interests of the capitalist class in their struggle to preserve existing property relations (Gramsci, 1971/1992, p. 12). Likewise, the proletariat could produce its own organic intellectuals (Gramsci, 1971/1992, p. 334). This long process, fraught with difficulties, was most likely to occur during crises, with the intervention of discontented traditional intellectuals (Filippini, 2017, pp. 69–70; Gramsci, 1971/1992, pp. 210, 334).

Gramsci's second contribution was to recast the relationship between science and ideology. Intellectuals draw on lay categories or everyday forms of consciousness, which Gramsci (1971/1992, pp. 333, 348–351) also called 'common sense', to elaborate worldviews and ideologies (review in Emigh et al., 2016, p. 25). Common sense has a dual nature: through activity, it unites individuals with each other in the practical transformation of their current reality; through language, it reflects an inherited tradition (Gramsci, 1971/1992, p. 333). By noting this dual foundation of common sense, Gramsci reformulated Marxist theories of ideology and false consciousness with the idea of 'contradictory consciousness'. For Gramsci, contradictory consciousness stemmed from a difference between individuals' understanding of their current situation simultaneously through their own experience and some more general, widespread social and cultural formations (Emigh et al., 2016, p. 25). Intellectuals can then systematise and clarify common sense, thereby transforming it into good sense. They can also point to the contradictions that arise between practice and received knowledge (Gramsci, 1971/1992, pp. 9, 334–335). Thus, where and when lay categories get translated into scientific ones is historically contingent upon the practices of intellectuals within particular social and historical configurations (Gramsci, 1971/1992, pp. 5, 334–335).

At the same time, the political deployment of these translated categories and their influence over social structures are historically contingent (Gramsci, 1971/1992, p. 12). Intellectuals can either sustain or transform these structures because they are attached to different economic and social bases; consequently, they have different interests, powers, and capacities, as well as different relationships with the state and civil society in different historical settings (Gramsci, 1971/1992, pp. 5–7, 12; cf. Crehan, 2002, pp. 136–137). Elite and non-elite social actors struggle politically over categories, as intellectuals' systematisations are, or are not, reincorporated into lay practices through political action (Gramsci, 1971/1992, pp. 9, 334–335). Gramsci's approach, therefore, exemplifies a sophisticated formulation of the connections between intellectuals and social classes.

The notion that intellectuals can serve powerful interests is also common in non-Marxist literature. For example, C. Wright Mills (1945, pp. 235–236) believed that intellectuals succumbed to career pressures that fuelled self-intimidation, 'sometimes politely known as "discretion", "good taste", or "balanced judgment"', thus losing intellectual freedom. Chomsky (1978, p. 11) viewed intellectual intervention more cynically, describing intellectuals as 'experts in legitimation' who ensure that beliefs are properly inculcated; these beliefs serve the interests of power.

Emigh et al. (2016, p. 25) used Gramsci's insights to explore the role of intellectuals in official information gathering in three ways. First, they argued that the basic technology for information gathering (like all practical activity) must be based on common sense. Second, they defined 'information intellectuals' as social actors who develop explicit ways of recording information based on common-sense knowledge (Emigh et al., 2016, p. 25). Like Gramsci, they intentionally specified information intellectuals as social (not state) actors in civil society, thus allowing consideration of how intellectuals and state actors interact to gather information (Emigh et al., 2016, p. 25). Third, they maintained that the ability of information intellectuals to deploy their ideas depends on their social location and their level of power (Emigh et al., 2016, p. 26). They may preserve or transform common sense as well as political and social structures, and they may do so in different roles on behalf of different individuals or groups in the state or society (Emigh et al., 2016, p. 26). They may collect or systematise information to assist the state, or they may demand that the state undertake certain information-gathering activities (Emigh et al., 2016, p. 26).

Intellectuals' translation of lay categories into information categories can be supported or resisted by other social actors (Emigh et al., 2016, p. 26). Nonstate elites (elites are embedded within a distinct organisational apparatus and have the capacity to appropriate resources from non-elites; Lachmann, 2000, p. 9) influence where and when lay categories are translated and deployed as information categories (review in Higgs, 2004, pp. 16, 20–21). Like information intellectuals, elites have different roles. They may prevent state actors from collecting information; they may force state actors to adopt some but not other lay categories; or their interests may simply coincide with those of state actors, adding subtle pressure for the adoption of particular lay categories (Emigh et al., 2016, p. 26). Non-elites' direct influence in this regard is limited; power stems mostly from their role as repositories of common-sense knowledge (Emigh et al., 2016, p. 27). Consequently, one of their common influences is to resist information gathering, thereby undermining the efforts of state actors and intellectuals (e.g., Bulmer, 1986, p. 474; Starr, 1987, pp. 12–13, cf. Loveman, 2007, pp. 8–9).

Emigh et al. (2016, pp. 24–30) also expanded on Gramsci's work. While Gramsci focused on how the class alignment of intellectuals with common sense depended upon social and historical conditions, Emigh et al. (2016, pp. 15–16, 40), by combining Weber with Gramsci, investigated the micro-level social interactional backdrop to common sense as well as the macro-level political effects of intellectuals' alignment on political and social structures. Their work then showed how intellectual interventions have implications at various levels of the social structure (micro, meso, and macro). This theorisation provides an alternative view not only of intellectuals but also of a more general sociology of knowledge that challenges the prevalent science and technology studies approach (Riley et al., 2021, pp. 331–334).

Brym (2015, p. 279; Nakhaie & Brym, 1999, p. 345), drawing upon Gramsci, similarly considered how social conditions affect intellectual intervention by showing how the social origins of intellectuals determine their ideologies and political allegiances and structure their opportunities for education, employment, and political intervention. These opportunity structures are, in turn, shaped by the relative power of major social classes (Brym, 2015, p. 280). Thus, intellectuals' ideologies and political allegiances can only be understood in terms of their paths of social mobility, as they are shaped by the capacity of social groups, such as classes, ethnic groups, and religious orders (Brym, 2015, p. 280). Therefore, in Brym's (2015, p. 280) approach, conceptualising intellectuals in terms of their relationship to class is an oversimplification. Intellectuals are embedded in social networks whose ties to various classes and other collectivities shift over time and help account for their ideologies and political allegiances (Brym, 2015, p. 280; Nakhaie & Brym, 1999, pp. 345, 348).

Gramsci's third contribution was to re-think the relationship between political engagement and scientific knowledge. Political engagement for Gramsci was the pre-condition for valid social knowledge, not an obstacle to it. Gramsci developed this highly politicised epistemology in his theory of 'prediction and perspective'. According to Gramsci, valid knowledge itself resulted from a political stance towards social reality because only the individual 'who wills something strongly can identify the elements which are necessary for the realization of his will' (Gramsci, 1971/1992, p. 171; see also Riley, 2018, p. 122). This position underlies Gramsci's (1971/1992, p. 214) view that the best social analyses are produced either by people seeking to overthrow an existing state of affairs (revolutionaries) or by those actively engaged in sustaining the existing order (counter-revolutionaries). On this basis, Gramsci accorded a methodological significance to mass political parties that fused common sense and expert knowledge, thereby transforming both (Riley, 2018, pp. 122–123).

Like Gramsci, Foucault (1984, pp. 69–70; review in Eyal & Buchholz, 2010, p. 119) differentiated between two different types of intellectuals, which he labelled 'universal' and 'specific'. Foucault (1984, pp. 68, 70; review in Kurzman & Owens, 2002, p. 70) suggested that intellectuals became more aligned with the proletarian masses (i.e., more class-bound) over time. Universal intellectuals, dating back to the nineteenth and early twentieth centuries, were autonomous individuals dedicated to universal justice and equity (Foucault, 1984, p. 69; Foucault & Deleuze, 1977, pp. 207–208). Their preferred mode of intervention was politicised writing (Foucault, 1984, p. 68). An increasing need for scientific credentials gave rise to specific intellectuals grounded within particular areas of expertise (Foucault, 1984, p. 69). Subsequently, intellectuals became embedded within sectors where they were shaped by their conditions of life and work (Foucault, 1984, p. 68). Thus, they were more keenly aware of the struggles faced by the masses because they shared the same adversaries, such as multinational corporations and policing units (Foucault, 1984, p. 68). The intellectual's role is, therefore, to resist power in the spheres of knowledge, truth, consciousness, and discourse (Foucault & Deleuze, 1977, pp. 207–208).

2.1.2 Public Sociology

Public sociology is consistent with the 'intellectuals as a stratum' perspective. Intellectuals can draw on their knowledge to act on behalf of individuals in society, depending on the configuration of civil society and the intellectuals' positions within it. Indeed, public sociology was central to the discipline from its founding, especially among those marginalised by civil society and academia, which had long privileged White males (Morris, 2017, pp. 3, 11–12). W.E.B. Du Bois founded the National Association for the Advancement of Colored People between academic stints that produced two major monographs, *The Philadelphia Negro* (1899/2007a, b) and *Black Reconstruction* (1935/2007) (Burawoy, 2005a, p. 14). The question of whether sociological knowledge should be used to initiate change was not merely theoretical for sociologists of colour like Du Bois, who faced violence, economic exploitation, political disenfranchisement, and daily insults just to live and work as a Black sociologist at the turn of the twentieth century (Morris & Ghaziani, 2005, p. 48). This historical legacy prompted Du Bois and other scholars, such as Ida B. Wells, to advance a sociological epistemology focused on Black people, which aimed to produce and disseminate knowledge for emancipatory purposes (Brooks & Wright, 2021, pp. 321–324; Crenshaw et al., 2019, p. 11; Hunter & Robinson, 2016, pp. 388–390; Morris, 2017, pp. 10–11; Wells, 1892, pp. 22–23; Wells, 1895, pp. 7–15, 96). Double consciousness, for example, stemmed directly from Black persons' social locations and could promote both despair as well as positive social change (Du Bois, 1903/2018, pp. 3–4). Analogously, Jane Addams (1905, pp. 6–12; 1910, pp. 6–16, 133–135) advocated for democracy, women, and girls, contributing to public sociology as well as to the Chicago School of Sociology (Deegan, 1988, pp. 1–3; Knight, 2005, pp. 1–4).

Public sociology, highlighted by Gans at the 1988 American Sociological Association presidential address (1989, pp. 5–9), gained prominence when Burawoy (2005a, p. 4) made it the theme of his own 2004 presidential address to the same organisation (Gans, 2016, p. 3). He argued that sociology had succumbed to normalising pressures that privileged academic credentials (e.g., publications, tenure, and citations) at the expense of its original moral impetus of positive social intervention (Burawoy, 2005a, p. 5). He contended that sociologists are poised to undertake a 'systematic back-translation', giving back knowledge to those from whom it came and restoring sociology's original passion for social justice (Burawoy, 2005a, p. 5).

Public sociology intervenes outside academia to engage diverse publics in dialogue about fundamental values (Kennedy, 2015, p. xiv; Zussman & Misra, 2007, p. 5). For Fischer (2020, p. 26), this intervention operates at two levels: first, by clearly articulating research results to the public, and second, by publicly conveying a general sociological understanding of how structural, institutional, and cultural contexts shape individuals' actions. Thus, public sociology is rooted in engagement, a mutual connection between researcher and community that informs both the means and purpose of sociological research (May et al., 2020, p. 591).

While noting a multiplicity of public sociologies, Burawoy (2005a, pp. 7–8) emphasised two variants: traditional public sociology and organic public sociology (with obvious similarities to Gramsci). The former consists of any sociological product that garners the attention of some publics within the general public (Gans, 2016, p. 4). These publics are usually relatively invisible, thin, and passive (Burawoy, 2005a, p. 7). The latter, making up the bulk of public sociology, has a close relationship to a visible, thick, active, local public that is typically engaged in active organising or protest (Burawoy, 2005a, pp. 7–8). Public sociology starts with the common sense of various communities and interrogates that common sense for generalisable principles; it then develops a design that other communities can access and discuss

(Burawoy, 2005b, p. 325). More recently, Schneider and Simonetto (2017, p. 236) identified a third, hybrid form, *E-public sociology,* which merges elements of traditional (e.g., publishing tweets) and organic (e.g., interactive dialogue with publics on Twitter) forms of public sociology.

As a discipline, sociology is tied to civil society; that is, it studies institutions from the perspective of civil society (Burawoy, 2005a, p. 24). In turn, public sociology is tied to the defence of civil society (Burawoy, 2005a, p. 24). In times of market tyranny and state despotism, public sociology intervenes on behalf of humanity's interests (Burawoy, 2005a, p. 24). Furthermore, sociology depends on civil society. When civil society disappears, as in Stalinist Russia or Pinochet's Chile, sociology disappears (Burawoy, 2005a, p. 24). Conversely, sociology flourishes where civil society flourishes (Burawoy, 2005a, p. 24). The possibility for public sociology itself emerges from sociology's reflexive relation to civil society (Burawoy, 2005b, p. 324).

Historically, however, civil society was White and male (Burawoy, 2005a, p. 25). Though civil society has gradually become somewhat more inclusive, this has occurred concomitantly with co-optation by market and political forces, reflected by sociology's uncritical use of terms such as 'social capital' (Burawoy, 2005a, p. 25). Nonetheless, Burawoy (2005a, p. 25) maintained that civil society remains an effective arena for intervention and engagement greatly bolstered by a critically disposed public sociology. Thus, he called on sociologists to foster public sociologies that bolster civil society rather than radicalising professional sociology (Burawoy, 2005b, p. 319). Public sociology can be crucial in addressing debates based on ideology, not facts. For example, the widespread attack on Critical Race Theory (CRT), a framework for legal analysis (Bell, 1992, pp. 2–14; Crenshaw, 1995, p. 369; Delgado & Stefancic, 2001, pp. 2–4), has led several US states to ban its use in public schools (Ray & Gibbons, 2021, n.p.). These calls to ban CRT have occurred despite its firm establishment in academia and irrespective of whether CRT theory is actually being taught. As this important issue shows, therefore, the need for a critically disposed and widely disseminated public sociology is more important than ever.

True to its roots, much public sociology comes from Black sociologists and feminists who blended public and professional sociology to affect both theoretical debates and broader social changes around race and gender (Collins, 2007, pp. 101–102; Crenshaw, 1995, p. 358; Wilson, 1987, pp. 3–19; 2009, p. 3). These contributions reshaped sociology, as well as academia more generally, despite the privileges given to White men by the discipline and civil society and despite the marginalisation of women and BIPOC scholars that silenced their voices, smothered their ideas, and diminished the value of their research (Collins, 2019, pp. 118–119, 133–135; Crenshaw et al., 2019, p. 12). Repressive tendencies such as these promote a public sociology that fails to articulate the needs of communities of colour (Brooks & Wright, 2021, p. 323; Morris, 2017, p. 12).

The public sociology promoted by scholars of race, ethnicity, and gender addresses these issues. Contemporary Du Boisian scholar-activists continue to view knowledge production as an emancipatory project tied to activist goals (Daniels,

2018, p. 1075). Crenshaw et al. (2019, p. 1) championed critical race projects that challenge existing epistemologies of racial power to enhance emancipatory possibilities both within and outside of academia. Specifically, Crenshaw (1995, p. 358) coined the term 'intersectionality' to address the effect of multiple forms of inequality and identity, such as race, class, gender, and disability, not just analytically but in an applied fashion. In doing so, Crenshaw (1995, p. 377) envisioned a public application of intersectionality to analyse social problems, shape interventions, and promote more inclusive coalitional advocacy. Indeed, this concept has become widely used academically and publicly. For example, Collins (2019, pp. 116–119), drawing on Crenshaw's (1989, p. 140) concept of intersectionality, articulated a theory of 'resistant knowledge', that is, knowledge production that fosters social action to challenge structural inequalities based in race, gender, and colonialism. Intersectionality powerfully illustrates how emancipatory ideas are shaped by scholars' social locations, as the 'intellectuals as a stratum' perspective suggests.

In the United States, instrumental knowledge is often privileged over reflexive knowledge, and this relationship, in turn, privileges professional sociology over public sociology (Burawoy, 2005a, pp. 17–18). Public sociology, however, often attracts graduate students to the discipline. By marginalising public sociology, sociologists are rendered dispassionate about the discipline (Burawoy, 2005a, pp. 13–15). Bonilla-Silva (2017, p. 183) argued that sociologists should abandon the idea that they exist 'above the social fray' and recognise that they do not sacrifice scientific rigour by committing to social change. Pedagogy is crucial to public sociology: the classroom is an inherently political arena where exclusionary practices can be challenged (Ochoa & Ochoa, 2004, p. 60).

While many sociologists remain open to the promise of public sociology (Abbott, 2018, p. 164; Calhoun, 2005, p. 362; Gans, 2016, p. 10), Burawoy's approach has been widely critiqued. The first set of criticisms revolves around the possibility of reforming professional sociology. Burawoy (2005a, p. 20) asserted that professional sociology had matured to the point that it could return to its roots and promote public sociology from a position of strength. Feagin et al. (2009, p. 76) questioned this position, suggesting that power rarely concedes space without insistent demands. They proposed a 'countersystem' perspective that would directly challenge the concepts, methods, and overall framework of mainstream sociology and that would attempt to remould or undo professional sociology to reduce social inequality and injustice (Feagin, 2001, p. 6; Feagin et al., 2009, p. 76). A countersystem would require revisiting the ideas and actions of the early sociologists committed to social-scientific knowledge as well as social justice, equality, and democracy to develop a 'new conceptual paradigm for sociology' (Feagin, 2001, pp. 6–7, 11; Feagin et al., 2009, p. 77). This countersystem could be developed through thorough empirical documentation of major social injustices, both nationally and internationally, and by generating conceptual work that develops and enriches the concepts of social justice and equality (Feagin, 2001, pp. 6, 11; Feagin et al., 2009, p. 77). Similarly, Hays (2007, p. 80) expressed concerns over the tendency to accept existing hierarchies within sociology and simply insert public sociology into them. This compartmentalisation of public sociology reproduces its secondary status, thus protecting the existing intellectual insularity within the discipline (Hays, 2007, p. 80). Brady (2004, pp. 1632–1633) noted that as long as professional sociology remains incentivised, public sociology will remain an isolated island within academia.

Other critiques focused on the status of race and gender within Burawoy's public sociology. Collins (2007, p. 104), though herself highly successful at combining professional and public sociology, suggested that Burawoy's approach may lend itself to a 'kind of sociological ghettoisation' because those attracted to public sociology often have subordinate status within the discipline (Collins, 2007, p. 104; see also Arribas Lozano, 2018, p. 94). Thus, public sociology may channel faculty of colour, women, and community college teachers into the service work of the discipline: teaching, serving on endless committees, and clarifying sociology to multiple publics (Collins, 2007, pp. 104–105). Feagin et al. (2009, p. 82) relatedly asserted that racial and gender domination and exploitation are not fully clarified or stressed in Burawoy's approach, though these should be central concerns. Piven (2007, p. 163) went even further, arguing that the felt needs of the poor, migrants, and minorities, both locally and globally, should become central sociological problems. In short, she called for the development of a critical, dissident public sociology (Piven, 2007, pp. 163–166).

Others questioned the lack of neutrality and the use of the term 'standpoint' in Burawoy's public sociology. Massey (2007, pp. 146–147) expressed concerns about mixing science and politics; in his view, sociologists collectively should avoid taking broad political positions in public debates. Tittle (2004, pp. 1639–1641) concurred, fearing that shifting from knowledge production to advocacy of particular causes would undermine sociology's public legitimacy. Feagin et al. (2009, pp. 81–82) questioned Burawoy's Marxist leanings, not so much for radicalism, but rather for limiting pluralism: Burawoy's public sociology focused on criticisms of the state's promotion of a market economy. Calhoun (2005, p. 361), in contrast, argued that Burawoy's (2005a, p. 17) use of standpoint did not mesh well with his previous conceptualisation of sociology as a disciplinary field. While Calhoun (2005, p. 361) agreed that sociology is socially situated, he noted that perspectives are shared by social locations and that knowledge is contingent upon social conditions, so the notion of a standpoint may convey an epistemological privilege to a particular substantive location or commitment.

2.2 Intellectuals as a Class

2.2.1 The Sociology of Intellectuals

A second set of theories, rooted in Bakunin's critique of Marx, suggests that intellectuals form a class of their own. Bakunin (1873/2005, pp. 134, 137) claimed that Marxism, despite its explicit demand to eliminate the state, was an authoritarian ideology of planning by a dictatorship of 'scholars' and 'metaphysicians'. He thus predicted the rise of a new class of intellectuals, comprised of both real and pseudo scientists and scholars, dividing the world into a minority ruling an immense uneducated majority through knowledge (Bakunin, 1872/1972, p. 319).

This critical stance carried over into the 'new class' scholarship on communism. Expanding upon Djilas's (1957, pp. 38–39) work, intellectuals were positioned at the centre of socialist administration (Gella, 1976, pp. 9–27; Konrád & Szelényi, 1979, p. 9; Szelenyi, 1982, p. S287). In Eastern Europe, intellectuals' technical expertise, crucial for the implementation of rational distribution in planned economies, was the basis of their class power (Konrád & Szelényi, 1979, pp. 9, 60, 97; Szelenyi, 1982, p. S287; Szelenyi & Martin, 1988, p. 657).

The new class approach was adapted by Western theorists. Bell (1973/1976, p. 374) believed that scientific knowledge would drive economic and social progress in post-industrial society, facilitating a new knowledge class. Gouldner (1979, p. 83) agreed that the 'new class' would possess the technical skills needed to sustain modern production; at the same time, this new, albeit flawed, universal class would replace the proletariat as the future vehicle of human emancipation. Aronowitz (1990, pp. 50, 52) suggested that in knowledge economies, a new class was emerging that sought the implementation of new political principles by signalling that effective administration, scientific and technical progress, and cultural propagation should include social justice. King and Szelényi (2004, p. viii) suggested that future social change could depend on an alliance among capital, labour, and a new technostructure. Yet the new class concept seems to be waning in significance; even Szelényi backed away from the concept, urging a reconstruction of study centred on 'symbolic domination' (Kurzman & Owens, 2002, p. 74; Szelenyi & Martin, 1988, pp. 663–664).

Bauman offered a postmodern twist to this approach. For him, the question 'Who are the intellectuals?' was difficult to answer since the category of intellectual does not objectively define a particular area (Bauman, 1987, p. 5; 1992, p. 81). Rather, it is self-referential because it arouses concerns, mobilises loyalties, and prompts self-definitions; thus, in any given time and place, intellectuals as an educated class come into being as a result of mobilisation and self-recruitment (Bauman, 1987, pp. 5–6; 1992, p. 81). Bauman distinguished between two historically contingent roles of intellectuals. First, he characterised intellectuals in the modern era as 'legislators' who make authoritative statements that arbitrate disputes and make binding decisions (Bauman, 1987, p. 8). Goldfarb (1998, p. 1) similarly focused on the structural position of intellectuals, arguing that they are particularly competent at addressing the pressing need of democracies to deliberate over common problems and to cultivate civility in public life (review in Kurzman & Owens, 2002, p. 77). Their authority therein is legitimated by their superior knowledge (Bauman, 1987, p. 8). Second, Bauman (1987, p. 8), in contrast, characterised intellectuals in the postmodern era as 'interpreters' who translate statements based on one area of knowledge into a different knowledge system.

2.2.2 Sociological Interventions

Public sociology, flowing from the idea that intellectuals form a stratum, is well-developed conceptually, well-populated with examples, and well-critiqued. However, there is no similarly well-developed sociology of interventions based on the new class position in US sociology, perhaps for two reasons. First, as King and Szelényi (2004, p. ix) noted, intellectuals never established themselves anywhere as a dominant class; in Eastern Europe, intellectuals may have been prominent even if not dominant, but in the West, they played no such prominent role. Second, new class theory was originally developed for socialist societies, where a critically reformulated Marxist theory implied that intellectuals could form a new class. However, in the capitalist West, the reformulation of a class theory around a knowledge elite is probably relatively uncomfortable for most sociologists, who view themselves either as critics or as observers of consumer capitalism and its cultural forms, not as avid promoters of it. Although Western theorists such as Bell, Gouldner, and Aronowitz proposed that a new class of knowledge producers could promote positive change, their sociology of intellectuals did not propose how sociologists might implement this.

The closest to a new class theory of interventions comes from Touraine's (1981, p. 140) work. Like other representatives of new class theory, Touraine (1981, pp. 6–13) was influenced by both Marxism and postmodernism, so he focused on the labour of knowledge producers in the shift to information-based production (Rose, 1996, p. 33; Scott, 1996, p. 81). Major social conflicts would occur between those who had knowledge and those who did not (Scott, 1996, p. 81; Touraine, 1981, p. 11).

His 'sociological intervention' was a method of social action whereby sociologists transferred knowledge to ordinary social actors to empower them to create social change through collective action (Touraine, 1981, pp. 139–140). For Touraine (1981, p. 139), sociology was the study of social relations, and in particular social domination. Since most domination was hidden, the task of a sociological intervention was to reveal this domination by interacting with small groups of ordinary actors (e.g., students and workers) through the method of participant observation (Dubet & Wieviorka, 1996, pp. 59–60; Gorz, 1997/1999, pp. 137, 145; Touraine, 1981, pp. 139–144). Although sociologists clearly did not form a dominant class, they could transfer their general disciplinary knowledge and methodological expertise to ordinary actors to induce social change. Unlike public sociology, the knowledge transferred to lay actors through sociological interventions was not topically specific to the actors' social characteristics. Instead, it was a general knowledge of how domination configured social relations, which the group members could then apply to their situations. Thus, Touraine's sociological intervention, though not a perfect fit, is congruent with many of the ideas of intellectuals as a knowledge class. Of course, sociologists do not form their own class, but as part of a knowledge class, they can explicitly use their knowledge to rearrange patterns of class-based domination.

Touraine's criticisms of Burawoy also illustrate how Touraine's sociology of interventions contrasts with public sociology. Touraine (2007, p. 77) noted the utility of Burawoy's division of sociology into four types (i.e., public, professional, policy, and critical sociology), but he argued that the key to a more interventionist mode of general sociology lies in merging sociology's internal differentiation with (at the very least) the integration of the mutual influence of these four sociological approaches (Touraine, 2007, pp. 77–78). In Touraine's (2007, p. 71) view, sociology must resist domination; therefore, sociology's key concern is the study of all forms of resistance to powerful transactions and institutions. Thus, Touraine (2007, pp. 68–69) called for sociologists to move from practising a sociology focused on society and social systems to one that elucidates how economic and political factors can be linked with culturally and socially defined individuals and groups to generate collective action, political processes, and personal and collective attitudes. Touraine (2007, p. 72) further advocated for the creation of new institutions that defend actors against internal or external constraints in the form of a new publicly oriented, interventionist, and professional sociology.

This method of sociological intervention also has been widely critiqued. One of the most pointed criticisms suggested that conflict often develops between the sociologist and the group members, especially when the group wants an outcome that the sociologist finds unethical (Brincker & Gundelach, 2005, pp. 372–373). The method is also extremely time-consuming and burdensome to implement, as well as awkward to teach at universities (Cousin & Rui, 2011, p. 132). Even Wieviorka (2014, p. 251), one of its proponents, noted that the method can lead to frustration because it can help group members articulate grievances without formulating solutions. Like public sociology, it is impossible to implement where there is no civil society (Cousin & Rui, 2011, p. 133).

2.3 Intellectuals as Universal

2.3.1 *The Sociology of Intellectuals*

In contrast to the previous approaches, the third set of theories portrays intellectuals as universal. Mannheim (1929/1946, pp. 137–141), for example, viewed intellectuals as a relatively classless and socially unattached group. Free of class interests, intellectuals intervene in social conflicts to promote mutual understanding, thus preserving the interests of the whole (Mannheim, 1929/1946, pp. 140, 142). Parsons (1969, pp. 21, 23; review in Kurzman & Owens, 2002, p. 69) similarly viewed intellectuals as unbound to class because they were relatively unattached to political and economic power. Instead, intellectuals primarily intervened in society as 'cultural specialists' and elaborators of the society's symbolic system (Parsons, 1969, pp. 4, 11, 14, 20). Shils (1969, p. 25) similarly suggested that intellectuals, more than ordinary individuals, desired to work with general symbols instead of everyday, concrete situations. Expanding upon Parsons, Shils (1969, p. 28) credited intellectuals with eliciting, guiding, and moulding expressive dispositions within society by presenting and providing models, standards, and symbols.

However, Shils (1969, pp. 30–31) noted an inevitable tension between the intellectuals' universalist orientation and the value orientation of specific societal institutions, which could lead to alienation or dissent within their ranks. Dahrendorf (1969, p. 50) noted a similar tension with respect to intellectuals' freedom and social hierarchy. Like a court jester, intellectuals can speak from outside as well as inside the social order without committing to it (Dahrendorf, 1969, p. 50). Thus, the jester points out social problems without fear (Dahrendorf, 1969, p. 50). In this role, Dahrendorf (1969, p. 51) enjoined intellectuals to intervene critically in society by doubting everything that is obvious, making relative all authority, and asking all questions no one dared to ask. Schumpeter (1942/2012, pp. 178, 181) linked the intellectuals' position as both onlookers and outsiders to their tendency to foster, organise, and lead resentment in society. Aron (1957, p. 210) similarly called intellectuals' tendency to critique the social order 'the occupational disease of the intellectuals'.

The most influential contemporary exponent of this position is Bourdieu. Using a field approach, he conceptualised intellectuals as occupying a space or field of scientific positions (Bourdieu, 1975, p. 19; 1984/1988, pp. 3, 40). Field participants (i.e., individuals, schools, or academic disciplines) are embedded within a network of relationships. Each exhibits a specific 'weight' or authority; thus, the field distributes power (Bourdieu, 1984/1988, p. 41; Ringer, 1990, p. 270). In a sense, Bourdieu's (1984/1988, p. xvii) sociology of intellectuals is aimed at unmasking the material interests that undergird intellectuals' purported disinterestedness since he aimed to show how the political stances of intellectuals are a lightly euphemised expression of their position in the field of cultural production.

Bourdieu (1976, pp. 97–98) insisted that the insulation of the scientific field is the key to the production of disinterested truth: intellectuals paradoxically possess an interest in disinterestedness. This scientific field operates to guarantee disinterestedness for three reasons: first, the researchers' audience is composed of their professional peers; second, this field strives to monopolise the 'scientifically legitimate representation of the "real"'; and third, it requires participants to master tools for theoretical construction and empirical verification or falsification (Bourdieu, 2001/2004, pp. 69–71; Swartz, 2013, p. 162). With respect to intervention, the second characteristic is key, as it implies a tacit acceptance of the 'arbitration of the real' by intellectuals embedded within the field (Swartz, 2013, p. 162). Bourdieu et al. (1991, p. 656) thus characterised intellectuals as bi-dimensional. On the one hand, they belong to an autonomous intellectual field; on the other hand, they must invest the competence and authority acquired in the intellectual field in outside political intervention. Thus, scholarship adopting the field approach creates a space within which intellectual attributions and related values are created and contested (Bourdieu, 1987/1990, pp. 140–141; review in Eyal & Buchholz, 2010, p. 124). The space occupied varies. It could be a 'space of opinion' that facilitates private commentary (Jacobs & Townsley, 2011, p. 7) or, more generally, a space for public engagement (Sapiro, 2009, p. 9; review in Eyal & Buchholz, 2010, p. 124). Thus, Bourdieusian intellectuals achieve truth insofar as they are autonomous from society; in contrast, as we noted above, for Gramscians, truth requires a political link to society (Riley, 2018, pp. 116–120, 122).

This theorisation of fields is a criticism of the other two theories of intellectuals as a stratum or a class (Eyal & Buchholz, 2010, pp. 123–124; Rahkonen, 1999, pp. 70–71). Camic and Gross (2004, p. 242), for example, asserted that classifying intellectuals as such obscured key distinctions among specialised knowledge producers. They further noted that so-called inherent characteristics, such as intellectual standing and authority, are valuable and rare resources for which all knowledge producers compete, significantly affecting the ideas they promote (Camic & Gross, 2004, p. 242). Ringer (1990, pp. 281–282, 284) similarly asserted that no single definition of the intellectual's qualities applies universally, emphasising rather the historical contingency and malleability of intellectual roles shaped by objective conditions and conceptual schemes.

The Bourdieusian position produced a vast outpouring of work. For example, Ringer (1990, p. 272) showed that historical and cross-cultural comparisons illuminate how meanings of propositions or doctrines are defined by their place in an intellectual field, using the comparative history of positivism in Germany (where it was criticised) and France (where it was largely accepted). Thus, public intervention was characterised, in this instance, as competition over establishing meaning. Drawing on Bourdieu's field concept, Sapiro (2003, pp. 633–634; 2009, p. 9) conceptualised the French intellectual field as a space occupied by various cultural producers vying to impose their legitimate vision of the social world upon the public. She linked different modes of public intervention (e.g., style (ranging from prophecy or expertise), discursive forms (the pamphlet or the diagnosis), or modes of intervention (individual or collective)) practised by different cultural producers to their position in the intellectual field (Sapiro, 2009, pp. 10–15; review in Eyal & Buchholz, 2010, p. 127). Eyal (2000, p. 54; 2003, pp. 11–13, 26–34, 59–92) similarly extended Bourdieu's field approach to elite class formation in late communist Czechoslovakia in terms of four discursive strategies: dissidence, internal exile, reform communism, and co-optation. These strategies were probabilistically related to different social positions in the late communist field of power and served to explain political affinities and alliances among intellectual fractions within it (Eyal, 2000, p. 54; 2003, pp. 11–13, 26–34, 59–92).

This view of intellectuals as pursuing universal values leads to a particular criticism, or negative view, of intellectuals when they are beholden to specific social interests. Thus, a common move among these thinkers, starting with Benda in the 1920s, was to bemoan intellectuals' links to academic institutions, the market, or political ideologies. These works, because they were posed as criticism of intellectuals who did not pursue universalism, had a moral dimension that Bourdieu and his followers lacked. Benda (1928, pp. 71–77, 172–176), writing at a time of increasing rightist nationalism, assaulted irrationalism as a betrayal of intellectuals' universalistic vocation. The modern clerks, according to Benda (1928, pp. 43–47, 126–127,

139; review in Kurzman & Owens, 2002, pp. 64–65), had renounced their vocation of defending the ideas of justice and law to worship state power.

Like Benda, for Coser (1965, p. viii), intellectuals were knowledge producers who possessed a capacity for detachment. Coser (1965, pp. 147–157, 157–167, 183–186) thus critiqued the Jacobins, the Bolsheviks, and the New Dealers for pursuing power rather than maintaining this detachment. The collective status of intellectuals allowed them to mobilise and intervene in political affairs (Benda, 1928, pp. 5, 99–102; Coser, 1965, pp. 144–167). Similarly, Kurzman (2008, p. 54) spoke of intellectuals as potentially constituting a class, but he defined their class nature in terms of pro-democracy values. Thus, like Benda, he provided a moral definition of intellectuals in terms of how they think, not a structural conception that located them in society.

Another strand of this criticism suggests that intellectuals are declining and disappearing, a trend particularly pronounced in the US debate on public intellectuals (review in Eyal & Buchholz, 2010, p. 118). Posner (2001, p. 3) characterised public intellectuals as 'safe specialists', ill-equipped to assume the role of the public intellectual's most distinctive role: a critical commentator addressing non-specialist audiences on matters of general public concern. Their public interventions, thus, are mistaken prophecy and superficial policy advice (Posner, 2001, p. 5).

Jacoby (1987, p. 6), in contrast, believed that public intellectuals have all but disappeared. Younger intellectuals firmly ensconced in academia no longer desire nor require a public (Jacoby, 1987, p. 6; 2009, p. 39). Their message is contained within academic publications and limited to their colleagues (Jacoby, 1987, p. 6). Fleck and Hess (2014, p. 10) likewise noted a decline of public intellectuals in US sociology. They attributed this lack of public intervention partly to fragmentation and division into rival schools and approaches that limit consensus (Fleck et al., 2009, p. 7). Furthermore, sociologists who regularly participate in public debates do so at the expense of their scholarly reputations (Fleck et al., 2009, p. 7). In contrast, Fleck and Hess (2014, p. 10) noted that European public intellectuals enjoy a broad public resonance. Another strand of research, however, questioned the decline of public intellectuals in the United States by pointing to the diversification of intellectual interventions (review in Eyal & Buchholz, 2010, pp. 117–119; Jacobs & Townsley, 2011, p. 236). These various analyses implicitly suggest that the true intellectual is autonomous from power, pursues universal values, and speaks on broad public issues. When knowledge producers do not act in this way, they are not intellectuals. Thus, references to the decline of intellectuals refer more to a changing moral attitude than to a structural fact.

2.3.2 Humane Translation

Although the emphasis on universal values might seem to preclude sociological interventions, at least two attempts outline such a path. The first is Abbott's (2007, pp. 202–203) call for 'humane translation'. For Abbott (2001, p. 5), the goal of social science is to produce sharable universal knowledge of society emerging from accommodation and conflict, thus tentatively bridging local pieces of knowledge and allowing interchange between fundamentally different people. Yet, the structure of academic disciplines limits how and the extent to which intervention occurs outside of academia (Abbott, 2001, p. 141).

Academic activity is composed of two analytically distinct fields: the bodies of potential academic work and bodies of people who do that work, and the tangled clusters of ties between and within them (Abbott, 2001, p. 137). These clusters comprise the academic 'settlement' (Abbott, 2001, p. 137). In this interactional field, no individual tie changes without affecting the ties around it (Abbott, 2001, p. 137). Disciplines cannot gain or lose authority in an area without displacing or enticing other disciplines (Abbott, 2001, p. 137).

Typically, academic settlements interact with two audiences, an immediate and a distant one (Abbott, 2001, p. 141). Students, administrators, and other academics comprise the former; parents, trustees, legislators, and the general public comprise the latter (Abbott, 2001, p. 141). In sociology, the cleavage between these two audiences is so pronounced that departments split into theoretical and applied areas based on their targeted audiences (Abbott, 2001, p. 141). Like any social structure, professions typically accord prestige to those who most closely associate with their organising principles (i.e., those who apply knowledge in its most pristine form) (Abbott, 2001, p. 145). In academia, those who teach as little as possible (or limit their instruction to graduate students) have the highest esteem (Abbott, 2001, p. 146). Therefore, academics, like other professionals, are inclined to regress to professional purity (Abbott, 2001, p. 146). Professional regression thus entails faculty moving out of applied academic work such as teaching (Abbott, 2001, p. 145). Similarly, public sociology involves privileging some values over others, resulting in a politicisation that undermines its 'expert legitimacy' in public forums (Abbott, 2007, p. 202).

Professional regression also produces shifts in settlement power (Abbott, 2001, p. 147). Changes to research practices, genres, and rhetorics can create or close off openings for other disciplines (Abbott, 2001, p. 147). For example, a discipline that produces easily transposable, commodified knowledge (e.g., anthropology or statistics) can lose power (Abbott, 2001, p. 147). Disciplines can also create power by developing novel and crucially important types of knowledge (e.g., Keynesian economics) (Abbott, 2001, p. 147). These forces are constantly disrupting relations between disciplines and their fields of inquiry (Abbott, 2001, p. 147).

Yet despite this, the US disciplinary structure and its modes of engagement with its audiences remain stable. Abbott (2001, p. 126) attributed this incredible resilience to dual institutionalisation: the disciplines comprise the macrostructure of the faculty labour market, while the system comprises the microstructure of individual universities (e.g., most arts and sciences faculties contain the same departments) (Abbott, 2001, p. 126). Therefore, universities cannot challenge the disciplinary system without depriving Ph.D. graduates of their academic future (Abbott, 2001, p. 126). Departments likewise perpetuate the disciplinary system by recruiting faculty in their own disciplines (Abbott, 2001, pp. 126–127). The role of disciplines in undergraduate education likewise perpetuates this stability: the major has the largest impact (Abbott, 2001, p. 127). The spread of majors occurred at the same time as the spread of departments and, once institutionalised, was not questioned (Abbott, 2001, p. 127). Indeed, the number of majors is commonly used to allocate faculty positions to departments (Abbott, 2001, p. 127).

Disciplines also support academics beyond organising labour markets and university structures (Abbott, 2001, p. 130). First, they facilitate reproduction: academia is, for all intents and purposes, the only practical recourse for US intellectuals (Abbott, 2001, p. 130). Departments must train able and committed people in the skills and moral character required by the discipline rather than shift the focus to public sociology (Abbott, 2007, p. 207). If training is weakened, sociology will cease to exist as a discipline (Abbott, 2007, p. 207). Thus, Abbott (2007, pp. 202–207; 2018, p. 164) admired Burawoy's vision of public sociology but was critical of his call to make professional sociology more public. This move, according to Abbott's view, would undermine the discipline by undermining the training of disciplinary scholars with strong claims to producing abstract, universal knowledge.

Rather, given that US sociology is embedded within the US disciplinary structure of academia, Abbott (2007, pp. 202–203) called for sociologists to engage in 'humane translation'. This involves shifting from scientific research to humane research (Abbott, 2007, p. 203). It also emphasises giving a voice to subjects by translating their moral activity into sociological ways of envisioning what happens to them in the social process (Abbott, 2007, p. 203). To move towards a more engaged public sociology, Abbott (2018, p. 178–179) proposed the development of a new normative subdiscipline of sociology organised around canons and moral critiques of examples and works. This framework for public sociology would inform normatively driven, as opposed to simply politicised, sociological engagement.

2.3.3 Civic Sociology

A final emerging scholarship, civic sociology, proposes a model of intellectual intervention also based on universal intellectuals. Wacquant (2009, p. 161) defined civic sociology as an effort to deploy social science tools to engage in important public debates. Patterson (2007, p. 187) stressed the role of politically engaged scholars in this enterprise. In this respect, civic sociology aims to reconstruct the disciplinary knowledge of sociology by redirecting research into three specific areas of intervention: problem-solving and professional practice, local and regional issues, and normative and ethical reflection (Lybeck et al., 2018, n.p.). While these three areas are not exclusive to the enterprise of civic sociology, taken together, they help promote a better understanding of local and regional particularities, which in turn prompts more effective and ethical interventions into systemic social issues (Lybeck et al., 2018, n.p.). Thus, not only would sociological research be more relevant, but it would also spawn novel integrative, synthetic, and reflexive forms of social knowledge, taking scholarship in new directions (Lybeck et al., 2018, n.p.).

Thus, civic sociology aspires to reinvigorate sociology as a profession: one that is not solely academic but rather intervenes in communities to solve problems (Lybeck et al., 2018, n.p.). This perspective also draws inspiration from the work central to public sociology we reviewed above, including Jane Addams and W.E.B. Du Bois. Civic sociology derives models from these earlier works, striving to integrate sociological knowledge into society (Lybeck et al., 2018, n.p.).

Finally, Lybeck (2011, p. 182) critiqued Burawoy's call for sociologists to be 'partisans of civil society' as impractical. In Lybeck's view, civil society as such does not exist due to widespread passivity. Lybeck (2011, p. 181) called instead for a 'critical public pragmatism' to work towards establishing a dynamic public sphere receptive to the creative action of neopragmatist sociologists. Lybeck et al. (2018, n.p.) noted that while civic sociology and public sociology share similarities, they differ in that while public sociology distinguishes itself from 'professional', 'policy', and 'critical' sociology, civic sociology seeks to integrate all four of these forms of research.

2.4 Conclusions

The sociology of intellectuals conceptualises the role of intellectuals in society as groups with different social relations that shape their knowledge (intellectuals as a stratum, intellectuals as a class, intellectuals as universal). The three perspectives suggest somewhat different social conditions that have led to the rise of intellectuals: social inequality prompting participation in class struggle (intellectuals as a stratum), exclusive access to technical expertise used to promote their own interest or that of society (intellectuals as a class), and the differentiation of intellectual social spaces that creates specialised knowledge among intellectuals who nevertheless ideally promote shared values and critically interrogate power structures (intellectuals as universal). These three perspectives, however, also differ in how they conceptualise the configuration of the group and its relationship to the rest of society. Intellectuals who form a stratum float between classes and may act on behalf of a particular group; intellectuals who form a class have similar economic class characteristics and act on behalf of their class; while universal intellectuals need not share any specific characteristics, so they do not necessarily act on behalf of any particular group.

In turn, these conceptualisations shape how sociological interventions are framed. Across these perspectives, the possibility of sociological interventions is shaped by social conditions. These interventions may be unintended as intellectuals produce knowledge that is diffused throughout society. All three perspectives, however, suggest that explicit interventions are possible by motivated academics, whether through public sociology (intellectuals as a stratum), through a new, integrated and interventionist professional sociology (Touraine, the closest example to intellectuals as a class), or through humane translation or civic sociology (intellectuals as universal). Even proponents of explicit interventions suggest that a civil society is key to implementing interventions; without a well-developed civil society, neither sociology nor sociological interventions are possible. The power of intellectuals affects where and when these interventions will be efficacious. Where intellectuals are weak or divided, their interventions will be limited.

Beyond this, the perspectives on interventions diverge and not necessarily in ways that correspond to their sociologies of intellectuals. Proponents of public and civic sociology, though motivated by different sociologies of intellectuals (intellectuals as a stratum versus intellectuals as universals), seem to suggest that explicit interventions are possible by engaged academics, while humane translations (motivated by intellectuals as universals) are desirable as explicit interventions, but seem more limited in scope because of the organisational structure of disciplines. Today, digital media has facilitated civic sociology by enabling sociologists to directly communicate ideas and connect with people around the world (Healy, 2017, p. 771). Explicit public engagement and interventions (via social media) are thus no longer exclusive to a few motivated intellectuals. These new forms of interventions may, therefore, combine with older repertoires of speaking and writing to facilitate sociological interventions (Emigh 2024, p. 716).

Acknowledgments We would like to thank Corey O'Malley and Johanna Hernández Pérez for their research assistance. A grant from the UCLA Faculty Senate supported this work.

Competing Interests The authors have no conflicts of interest to declare that are relevant to the content of this chapter.

References

Abbott, A. (2001). *Chaos of disciplines*. University of Chicago Press.
Abbott, A. (2007). For humanist sociology. In D. Clawson, R. Zussman, J. Misra, N. Gerstel, R. Stokes, D. L. Anderton, & M. Burawoy (Eds.), *Public sociology: Fifteen eminent sociologists debate politics and the profession in the twenty-first century* (pp. 195–209). University of California Press.
Abbott, A. (2018). Varieties of normative inquiry: Moral alternatives to politicization in sociology. *The American Sociologist, 49*(2), 159–180.
Addams, J. (1905). *Democracy and social ethics*. The Macmillan Company.
Addams, J. (1910). *The spirit of youth and the city streets*. The Macmillan Company.
Aron, R. (1957). *The opium of the intellectuals* (trans: Kilmartin, T.). Doubleday.
Aronowitz, S. (1990). On intellectuals. In B. Robbins (Ed.), *Intellectuals: Aesthetics, politics, academics* (pp. 3–56). University of Minnesota Press.
Arribas Lozano, A. (2018). Reframing the public sociology debate: Towards collaborative and decolonial praxis. *Current Sociology, 66*(1), 92–109.
Bakunin, M. (1972). The international and Karl Marx. In S. Dolgoff (Ed.), *Bakunin on anarchy: Selected works by the activist-founder of world anarchism* (pp. 286–320) (trans: Dolgoff, S.). Vintage Press. (Original work published 1872).
Bakunin, M. (2005). *Statism and anarchy* (trans: Shatz, M. S.). Cambridge University Press. (Original work published 1873).

Bauman, Z. (1987). *Legislators and interpreters: On modernity, post-modernity and intellectuals*. Cornell University Press.
Bauman, Z. (1992). Love in adversity: On the state and the intellectuals, and the state of the intellectuals. *Thesis Eleven, 31*(1), 81–104.
Bell, D. (1976). *The coming of post-industrial society: A venture in social forecasting*. Basic Books. (Original work published 1973).
Bell, D. (1992). *Faces at the bottom of the well: The permanence of racism*. BasicBooks.
Benda, J. (1928). *The treason of the intellectuals* (trans: Aldington, R.). William Morrow.
Bonilla-Silva, E. (2017). What we were, what we are, and what we should be: The racial problem of American sociology. *Social Problems, 64*(2), 179–187.
Bourdieu, P. (1975). The specificity of the scientific field and the social conditions of the progress of reason. *Social Science Information, 14*(6), 19–47.
Bourdieu, P. (1976). Le champ scientifique. *Actes de la recherche en sciences sociales, 2*(2–3), 88–104.
Bourdieu, P. (1988). *Homo academicus* (trans: Collier, P.). Polity Press. (Original work published 1984).
Bourdieu, P. (1990). *In other words: Essays towards a reflexive sociology* (trans: Adamson, M.). Polity Press. (Original work published 1987).
Bourdieu, P. (2004). *Science of science and reflexivity* (trans: Nice, R.). University of Chicago Press. (Original work published 2001).
Bourdieu, P., Sapiro, G., & McHale, B. (1991). Fourth lecture. Universal corporatism: The role of intellectuals in the modern world (trans: Sapiro, G.). *Poetics Today, 12*(4), 655–669.
Brady, D. (2004). Why public sociology may fail. *Social Forces, 82*(4), 1629–1638.
Brincker, B., & Gundelach, P. (2005). Sociologists in action: A critical exploration of the intervention method. *Acta Sociologica, 48*(4), 365–375.
Brooks, M. A., & Wright, E., II. (2021). Augustus Granville Dill: A case study in the conceptualization of a Black public sociology. *Sociology of Race and Ethnicity, 7*(3), 318–332.
Brym, R. J. (2015). Sociology of intellectuals. In J. D. Wright (Ed.), *International encyclopedia of the social and behavioral sciences* (Vol. 12, 2nd ed., pp. 277–282). Elsevier.
Bulmer, M. (1986). A controversial census topic: Race and ethnicity in the British census. *Journal of Official Statistics, 2*(4), 471–480.
Burawoy, M. (2005a). For public sociology. *American Sociological Review, 70*(1), 4–28.
Burawoy, M. (2005b). The critical turn to public sociology. *Critical Sociology, 31*(3), 313–326.
Calhoun, C. (2005). The promise of public sociology. *The British Journal of Sociology, 56*(3), 355–363.
Camic, C., & Gross, N. (2004). The new sociology of ideas. In J. R. Blau (Ed.), *The Blackwell companion to sociology* (pp. 236–249). Blackwell Publishing.
Chomsky, N. (1978). *Intellectuals and the state*. Het Wereldvenster.
Collins, P. H. (2007). Going public: Doing the sociology that had no name. In D. Clawson, R. Zussman, J. Misra, N. Gerstel, R. Stokes, D. L. Anderton, & M. Burawoy (Eds.), *Public sociology: Fifteen eminent sociologists debate politics and the profession in the twenty-first century* (pp. 101–113). University of California Press.
Collins, P. H. (2019). *Intersectionality as critical social theory*. Duke University Press.
Coser, L. A. (1965). *Men of ideas: A sociologist's view*. The Free Press.
Cousin, O., & Rui, S. (2011). Sociological intervention: Evolutions and specificities in a methodology (trans: O'Mahony, M.). *Revue française de science politique* (English edition), *61*(3), 123–142.
Crehan, K. (2002). *Gramsci, culture and anthropology*. University of California Press.
Crenshaw, K. (1989). Demarginalizing the intersection of race and sex: A Black feminist critique of antidiscrimination doctrine, feminist theory and antiracist politics. *University of Chicago Legal Forum, 1989*(1), 139–167.

Crenshaw, K. W. (1995). The intersection of race and gender. In K. Crenshaw, N. Gotanda, G. Peller, & K. Thomas (Eds.), *Critical race theory: The key writings that formed the movement* (pp. 357–383). The New Press.

Crenshaw, K. W., Harris, L. C., HoSang, D. M., & Lipsitz, G. (2019). Introduction. In K. W. Crenshaw, L. C. Harris, D. M. HoSang, & G. Lipsitz (Eds.), *Seeing race again: Countering colorblindness across the disciplines* (pp. 1–19). University of California Press.

Dahrendorf, R. (1969). The intellectual and society: The social function of the "fool" in the twentieth century. In P. Rieff (Ed.), *On intellectuals: Theoretical studies, case studies* (pp. 49–52). Doubleday.

Daniels, J. (2018). W. E. B. DuBois for the twenty-first century: On being a scholar-activist in the digital era. *Sociological Forum, 33*(4), 1072–1085.

Debray, R. (1981). *Teachers, writers, celebrities: The intellectuals of modern France* (trans: Macey, D.). New Left Books. (Original work published 1979).

Deegan, M. J. (1988). *Jane Addams and the men of the Chicago school, 1892–1918*. Transaction Books.

Delgado, R., & Stefancic, J. (2001). *Critical race theory: An introduction*. New York University Press.

Djilas, M. (1957). The new class: An analysis of the communist system. Harcourt Brace Jovanovich.

Dubet, F., & Wieviorka, M. (1996). Touraine and the method of sociological interventions. In J. Clark & M. Diani (Eds.), *Alain Touraine* (pp. 55–75). Falmer Press.

Du Bois, W. E. B. (2007a). *The Philadelphia negro: A social study*. Oxford University. (Original work published 1899).

Du Bois, W. E. B. (2007b). *Black reconstruction in America: An essay toward a history of the part which Black folk played in the attempt to reconstruct democracy in America, 1860–1880*. Oxford University Press. (Original work published 1935).

Du Bois, W. E. B. (2018). *The souls of Black folk: Essays and sketches*. University of Massachusetts Press. (Original work published 1903).

Emigh, R. J., Riley, D., & Ahmed, P. (2016). *How societies and states count*. Vol. 1, *Antecedents of censuses from medieval to nation states*. Palgrave Macmillan.

Eyal, G. (2000). Anti-politics and the spirit of capitalism: Dissidents, monetarists, and the Czech transition to capitalism. *Theory and Society, 29*(1), 49–92.

Eyal, G. (2003). *The origins of postcommunist elites: From Prague spring to the breakup of Czechoslovakia*. University of Minnesota Press.

Eyal, G., & Buchholz, L. (2010). From the sociology of intellectuals to the sociology of interventions. *Annual Review of Sociology, 36*, 117–137.

Feagin, J. R. (2001). Social justice and sociology: Agendas for the twenty–first century. *American Sociological Review, 66*(1), 1–20.

Feagin, J., Elias, S., & Mueller, J. (2009). Social justice and critical public sociology. In V. Jeffries (Ed.), *Handbook of public sociology* (pp. 71–88). Rowman & Littlefield.

Filippini, M. (2017). *Using Gramsci: A new approach* (trans: Barr, P.). Pluto Press.

Fischer, C. S. (2020). Of modernity and public sociology: Reflections on a career so far. *Annual Review of Sociology, 46*, 19–35.

Fleck, C., & Hess, A. (2014). Introduction: Public sociology in the making. In C. Fleck & A. Hess (Eds.), *Knowledge for whom? Public sociology in the making* (pp. 1–15). Ashgate.

Fleck, C., Hess, A., & Lyon, E. S. (2009). Intellectuals and their publics: Perspectives from the social sciences. In C. Fleck, E. S. Lyon, & A. Hess (Eds.), *Intellectuals and their publics: Perspectives from the social sciences* (pp. 1–16). Ashgate.

Foucault, M. (1984). Truth and power. In P. Rabinow (Ed.), *The Foucault reader* (pp. 51–75). Pantheon Books.

Foucault, M., & Deleuze, G. (1977). Intellectuals and power. In D. F. Bouchard (Ed.), *Language, counter–memory, practice: Selected essays and interviews* (trans: Bouchard, D.F., & Simon, S.) (pp. 205–217). Cornell University Press.

Gans, H. J. (1989). Sociology in America: The discipline and the public: American Sociological Association, 1988 presidential address. *American Sociological Review, 54*(1), 1–16.
Gans, H. J. (2016). Public sociology and its publics. *The American Sociologist, 47*(1), 3–11.
Gella, A. (1976). An introduction to the sociology of the intelligentsia. In A. Gella (Ed.), *The intelligentsia and the intellectuals: Theory, method and case study* (pp. 9–34). Sage.
Goldfarb, J. C. (1998). *Civility and subversion: The intellectual in democratic society*. Cambridge University Press.
Gorz, A. (1999). *Reclaiming work: Beyond the wage-based society* (trans: Turner, C.). Polity Press. (Original publication date 1997).
Gouldner, A. W. (1979). *The future of intellectuals and the rise of the new class: A frame of reference, theses, conjectures, arguments, and an historical perspective on the role of intellectuals and intelligentsia in the international class contest of the modern era*. Seabury Press.
Gramsci, A. (1992). *Selections from the prison notebooks of Antonio Gramsci* (trans: Hoare, Q., & Smith, G.N.). International Publishers. (Original publication date 1971).
Hays, S. (2007). Stalled at the altar? Conflict, hierarchy, and compartmentalization in Burawoy's public sociology. In D. Clawson, R. Zussman, J. Misra, N. Gerstel, R. Stokes, D. L. Anderton, & M. Burawoy (Eds.), *Public sociology: Fifteen eminent sociologists debate politics and the profession in the twenty-first century* (pp. 79–90). University of California Press.
Healy, K. (2017). Public sociology in the age of social media. *Perspectives on Politics, 15*(3), 771–780.
Higgs, E. (2004). *The information state in England: The central collection of information on citizens since 1500*. Palgrave Macmillan.
Hunter, M. A., & Robinson, Z. F. (2016). The sociology of urban Black America. *Annual Review of Sociology, 42*, 385–405.
Jacobs, R. N., & Townsley, E. (2011). *The space of opinion: Media intellectuals and the public sphere*. Oxford University Press.
Jacoby, R. (1987). *The last intellectuals: American culture in the age of academe*. Basic Books.
Jacoby, R. (2009). Last thoughts on *The last intellectuals*. *Society, 46*(1), 38–44.
Jennings, J., & Kemp-Welch, T. (1997). The century of the intellectual: From the Dreyfus affair to Salman Rushdie. In J. Jennings & A. Kemp-Welch (Eds.), *Intellectuals in politics: From the Dreyfus affair to Salman Rushdie* (pp. 1–21). Routledge.
Kautsky, K. (1901–1902). Die Revision des Programms der Sozialdemokratie in Oesterreich. *Die Neue Zeit: Wochenschrift der deutschen Sozialdemokratie, 20*(1), 68–82.
Kennedy, M. D. (2015). *Globalizing knowledge: Intellectuals, universities, and publics in transformation*. Stanford University Press.
King, L. P., & Szelényi, I. (2004). *Theories of the new class: Intellectuals and power*. University of Minnesota Press.
Knight, L. W. (2005). *Citizen: Jane Addams and the struggle for democracy*. University of Chicago Press.
Konrád, G., & Szelényi, I. (1979). *The intellectuals on the road to class power* (trans. Arato, A., & Allen, R. E.). Harcourt Brace Jovanovich.
Kurzman, C. (2008). *Democracy denied, 1905–1915: Intellectuals and the fate of democracy*. Harvard University Press.
Kurzman, C., & Leahey, E. (2004). Intellectuals and democratization, 1905–1912 and 1989–1996. *American Journal of Sociology, 109*(4), 937–986.
Kurzman, C., & Owens, L. (2002). The sociology of intellectuals. *Annual Review of Sociology, 28*, 63–90.
Lachmann, R. (2000). *Capitalists in spite of themselves: Elite conflict and economic transitions in early modern Europe*. Oxford University Press.
Lenin, V. I. (1975). What is to be done? Burning questions of our movement. In R. C. Tucker (Ed.), *The Lenin anthology* (pp. 12–114). W. W. Norton. (Original publication date 1902).
Loveman, M. (2007). Blinded like a state: The revolt against civil registration in nineteenth-century Brazil. *Comparative Studies in Society and History, 49*(1), 5–39.

Lybeck, E. R. (2011). For pragmatic public sociology: Theory and practice after the pragmatic turn. In H. F. Dahms (Ed.), *The diversity of social theories* (pp. 169–185). Emerald Group.

Lybeck, E., & the Editorial Board. (2018). Aims and scope: The vision for civic sociology. *Civic Sociology*. Accessed Sep 8, 2018, from https://www.civicsociology.com/aims-and-scope

Mannheim, K. (1946). *Ideology and utopia: An introduction to the sociology of knowledge*. Harcourt Brace. (Original publication date 1929).

Marx, K. (1994). The German ideology. In L. H. Simon (Ed.), *Karl Marx: Selected writings* (pp. 102–156). Hackett. (Original publication date 1932).

Massey, D. S. (2007). The strength of weak politics. In D. Clawson, R. Zussman, J. Misra, N. Gerstel, R. Stokes, D. L. Anderton, & M. Burawoy (Eds.), *Public sociology: Fifteen eminent sociologists debate politics and the profession in the twenty-first century* (pp. 145–157). University of California Press.

May, M. L., Treviño, L., & Garcia, E. (2020). Discerning the heart and soul of public sociology. *The Sociological Quarterly, 61*(3), 588–608.

Michels, R. (1932). Intellectuals. In E. R. A. Seligman & A. Johnson (Eds.), *Encyclopaedia of the social sciences*. Vol. 8, *Industrial revolution—labor turnover* (pp. 118–124). Macmillan.

Mills, C. W. (1945). The powerless people: The social role of the intellectual. *Bulletin of the American Association of University Professors (1915–1955), 31*(2), 231–243.

Morris, A. (2017). W. E. B. Du Bois at the center: From science, civil rights movement, to Black lives matter. *The British Journal of Sociology, 68*(1), 3–16.

Morris, A., & Ghaziani, A. (2005). DuBoisian sociology: A watershed of professional and public sociology. *Souls: A Critical Journal of Black Politics, Culture, and Society, 7*(3–4), 47–54.

Nakhaie, M. R., & Brym, R. J. (1999). The political attitudes of Canadian professors. *Canadian Journal of Sociology, 24*(3), 329–353.

Ochoa, G. L., & Ochoa, E. C. (2004). Education for social transformation: Chicana/o and Latin American studies and community struggles. *Latin American Perspectives, 31*(1), 59–80.

Parsons, T. (1969). "The intellectual": A social role category. In P. Rieff (Ed.), *On intellectuals: Theoretical studies, case studies* (pp. 3–24). Doubleday.

Patterson, O. (2007). About public sociology. In D. Clawson, R. Zussman, J. Misra, N. Gerstel, R. Stokes, D. L. Anderton, & M. Burawoy (Eds.), *Public sociology: Fifteen eminent sociologists debate politics and the profession in the twenty-first century* (pp. 176–194). University of California Press.

Piven, F. F. (2007). From public sociology to politicized sociology. In D. Clawson, R. Zussman, J. Misra, N. Gerstel, R. Stokes, D. L. Anderton, & M. Burawoy (Eds.), *Public sociology: Fifteen eminent sociologists debate politics and the profession in the twenty-first century* (pp. 158–166). University of California Press.

Posner, R. A. (2001). *Public intellectuals: A study of decline*. Harvard University Press.

Rahkonen, K. (1999). *Not class but struggle: Critical overtures to Pierre Bourdieu's sociology* (Research report 1/1999). Department of Social Policy, University of Helsinki.

Ray, R., & Gibbons, A. (2021). Why are states banning critical race theory? *Brookings*. Accessed Aug 19, 2021, from https://www.brookings.edu/blog/fixgov/2021/07/02/why-are-states-banning-critical-race-theory/

Riley, D. (2018). Science and politics: A response to Burawoy, Heilbron, and Steinmetz. *Catalyst, 2*(1), 89–132.

Riley, D., Ahmed, P., & Emigh, R. J. (2021). Getting real: Heuristics in sociological knowledge. *Theory and Society, 50*(2), 315–356.

Ringer, F. (1990). The intellectual field, intellectual history, and the sociology of knowledge. *Theory and Society, 19*(3), 269–294.

Ringer, F. (1992). *Fields of knowledge: French academic culture in comparative perspective, 1890–1920*. Cambridge University Press.

Rose, M. (1996). Skill, flexibility and effort in a post-factory world: Evidence from Britain. In J. Clark & M. Diani (Eds.), *Alain Touraine* (pp. 33–54). Falmer Press.

Sapiro, G. (2003). Forms of politicization in the French literary field. *Theory and Society, 32*(5–6), 633–652.

Sapiro, G. (2009). Modèles d'intervention politique des intellectuels: Le cas français. *Actes de la recherche en sciences sociales, 176–177*(1), 8–31.

Schneider, C. J., & Simonetto, D. (2017). Public sociology on twitter: A space for public pedagogy? *The American Sociologist, 48*(2), 233–245.

Schumpeter, J. A. (2012). *Capitalism, socialism, and democracy*. Start Publishing. (Original publication date 1942).

Scott, A. (1996). Movements of modernity: Some questions of theory, method and interpretation. In J. Clark & M. Diani (Eds.), *Alain Touraine* (pp. 77–91). Falmer Press.

Shils, E. (1969). The intellectuals and the powers: Some perspectives for comparative analysis. In P. Rieff (Ed.), *On intellectuals: Theoretical studies, case studies* (pp. 25–48). Doubleday.

Starr, P. (1987). The sociology of official statistics. In W. Alonso & P. Starr (Eds.), *The politics of numbers* (pp. 7–57) Russell Sage Foundation.

Swartz, D. L. (2013). *Symbolic power, politics, and intellectuals: The political sociology of Pierre Bourdieu*. University of Chicago Press.

Szelenyi, I. (1982). The intelligentsia in the class structure of state-socialist societies. *American Journal of Sociology, 88*(Supplement), S287–S326.

Szelenyi, I., & Martin, B. (1988). The three waves of new class theories. *Theory and Society, 17*(5), 645–667.

Tittle, C. R. (2004). The arrogance of public sociology. *Social Forces, 82*(4), 1639–1643.

Touraine, A. (1981). *The voice and the eye: An analysis of social movements* (trans: Duff, A.). Cambridge University Press.

Touraine, A. (2007). Public sociology and the end of society. In D. Clawson, R. Zussman, J. Misra, N. Gerstel, R. Stokes, D. L. Anderton, & M. Burawoy (Eds.), *Public sociology: Fifteen eminent sociologists debate politics and the profession in the twenty-first century* (pp. 67–78). University of California Press.

Wacquant, L. (2009). *Prisons of poverty*. University of Minnesota Press.

Wells, I. B. (1892). *Southern horrors: Lynch law in all its phases*. The New York Age Print.

Wells, I. B. (1895). *A red record: Tabulated statistics and alleged causes of lynchings in the United States, 1892–1893–1894*. Donohue & Henneberry.

Wieviorka, M. (2014). Sociology's interventions: Engaging the media and politics while remaining a social scientist. *Current Sociology Monograph, 62*(2), 243–252.

Wilson, W. J. (1987). *The truly disadvantaged: The inner city, the underclass, and public policy*. University of Chicago Press.

Wilson, W. J. (2009). *More than just race: Being Black and poor in the inner city*. W. W. Norton.

Zussman, R., & Misra, J. (2007). Introduction. In D. Clawson, R. Zussman, J. Misra, N. Gerstel, R. Stokes, D. L. Anderton, & M. Burawoy (Eds.), *Public sociology: Fifteen eminent sociologists debate politics and the profession in the twenty-first century* (pp. 3–22). University of California Press.

Patricia Ahmed is an Assistant Professor of Sociology and Criminology at the South Dakota State University. Her research interests include comparative/historical sociology, cross-cultural sociology, and globalisation. Her recent publications include works on census categorisation in Puerto Rico and the sociology of knowledge (with Rebecca Jean Emigh and Dylan Riley).

Rebecca Jean Emigh is a Professor of Sociology at the University of California, Los Angeles. She is a comparative historical sociologist who specialises in long-term social change. She is the author of multiple prize-winning articles and books on a range of topics, including capitalism, censuses, social theory, and historical demography. She is the past chair of the Comparative-Historical Section of the American Sociological Association and is the chair elect of the Theory Section of the American Sociological Association.

Dylan Riley is a Professor of Sociology at the University of California, Berkeley. He is the author of *The Civic Foundations of Fascism in Europe: Italy, Spain, and* Romania *1870–1945* (Johns Hopkins University Press, 2010, Verso, 2019) and *Microverses: Observations from a Shattered Present* (Verso 2022), as well as co-author with Rebecca Jean Emigh and Patricia Ahmed of *Antecedents of Censuses: From Medieval to Nation States* and *Changes in Censuses: From Imperialism to Welfare States* (Palgrave 2016). In addition to these books, he has published articles in the *American Journal of Sociology, American Sociological Review, Catalyst, Comparative Sociology, Contemporary Sociology, Comparative Studies in Society and History, Social Science History, The Socio-Economic Review, Theory and Society* and the *New Left Review* (of which he is a member of the editorial committee). His work has been translated into German, Portuguese, Russian, and Spanish.

Nancy Wang Yuen is a sociologist and public scholar. She is the author of *Reel Inequality: Hollywood Actors and Racism* and a guest writer at CNN, *Elle, LA Times, NBC, Newsweek, Today, and Vanity Fair are magazines*. She has appeared on PBS, NPR, MSNBC, BBC World, and Dr. Phil. For more details, see: www.nancywyuen.com

Chapter 3
Sociologists as Intellectuals and Their Role in Post-Communist Transformation

Matevž Tomšič

3.1 Introduction

When discussing society's system transformation, one can hardly avoid the question of its main actors, the ones with the capacity to influence the nature of social change. Who are the ones that impact the constitution of institutional relationships that define the principles of society? That is to say, societal transformation is not merely an automatic product of certain cultural, historical, and material circumstances. The process of transformation is introduced, steered, and maintained by concrete 'agents' with their values, ideas, and interests.

The selection of a particular type of institutional setting is not the mere decision of political power-holders. For its successful implementation to take place, it has to be accepted as legitimate by relevant stakeholders. It has embedded in particular value systems and effectively communicated to different publics. This implies the importance of particular 'strategic groups'. As stated by Sum and Jessop (2013, p. 220): 'Some agents, by virtue of their nodal position in social networks, have better capacities to read particular conjunctures, refocus arguments, displace opponents, structure responses, introduce timely imaginaries and worldviews'. This particularly applies to intellectuals as main bearers of cultural capital and providers of interpretations of societal reality as well as inventors of collective identities, both at national and transnational levels (Giesen, 2009).

Sociologists, particularly those who are engaged in academia, that is, scholars, researchers, and professors, undoubtedly belong to the intellectual elite. They deal

---

M. Tomšič (✉)
School of Advanced Social Studies, Nova Gorica, Slovenia

Faculty of Information Studies in Novo Mesto, Study Centre for National Reconciliation, Novo Mesto, Slovenia
e-mail: matevz.tomsic@fuds.si

© The Author(s), under exclusive license to Springer Nature Switzerland AG 2024
B. Roncevic, T. Besednjak Valič (eds.), *Sociology and Post-Socialist Transformations in Eastern Europe*, https://doi.org/10.1007/978-3-031-65556-2_3

with social relationships, the social essence of the human being, and the conditions of human life in society. As a universally oriented discipline, sociology is well-equipped for critical reflection on human and social life. Due to their area of expertise, sociologists (as well as academics from other social science disciplines) are usually more actively involved in public life (compared to academics from natural and life sciences).

Intellectuals from Central and Eastern Europe (including those from the field of sociology) were intensively engaged in developments that finally brought about the collapse of communist regimes. They positioned themselves as a moral elite, 'articulating a promise of morality in an immoral society became its main function' (Oushakine, 2009, p. 245). With the immense assistance of the intellectual elite, the defining twentieth-century struggle, between liberal democracies and authoritarian communist regimes, came to a sudden and unexpected demise (Falk, 2003).

However, circumstances have changed substantially since then. The old political-ideological corpus has fallen apart, and these countries have undertaken a journey on the long and, in many respects, uncertain path of social transformation. We can claim that they are undergoing the 'Europeanisation' process, both regarding formal integration into the European Union's (EU) institutional framework (which countries from East-Central Europe have completed) and content-wise, acquiring and enacting fundamental cognitive and behavioural standards characteristic of developed European societies. Moreover, what is the place the sociologists occupy in these processes? What impact do they exert on the course of systemic transformation? What is their contribution to the processes of variation of different developmental alternatives, to selection, retention and reinforcement of particular social discourses and practices? Furthermore, what is their relationship to other strategic elites in their societies?

In our discussion, we selected sociologists as a group from the ranks of academic intellectuals. Specifically, in countries from Central and Eastern Europe, members of this group of academics are among the most intellectually active in terms of involvement in public life. Furthermore, they were strongly represented in the ranks of opponents of the communist regime. To be sure, one should not neglect the differences between these countries in terms of the engagements of both two groups.

The main claim of this chapter is that the intellectual engagement of sociologists is necessary for successful societal transformation in former communist countries. However, it brings a threat of ideologisation and politicisation of academic space. For developmentally beneficial intellectual engagement to take place, several conditions (at both the personal and systemic levels) must be fulfilled. One can speak about intellectual imagination (avoidance of stereotypes and clichés), autonomy (toward political elite and other power-holders), critical distance (especially toward one's own ideological orientations and political beliefs), dedication (devoting time and energy to public causes) and pluralism (existence of different ideological strains within intellectual circles).

The following section deals with the characteristics of intellectuals and their position in modern society. Then, the specifics of the intellectual situation in Central and Eastern Europe and the role of intellectuals in the deconstruction of communist regimes are discussed. Further, the analysis focuses on the place and role of sociologists as intellectuals in the post-communist period.

3.2 Intellectuals as Part of the Cultural Elite

The term 'intellectual', often found in scientific and everyday vocabulary, is anything but clear. It is often mistaken for some other notions, especially the notion of the intelligentsia since the two are used practically as synonyms in everyday speech. Some sociologists (e.g., Mannheim, Konrad, and Szelenyi) also equate these two terms and use them to describe the holders of higher education. For others, the intelligentsia is a broader notion of the group of educated people, and the intellectuals are a subgroup of the intelligentsia with their own attributes, especially those concerning their relationship to society, such as a critical orientation, a sense of responsibility and personal risk (Tomšič, 2016a).

There are two dimensions individual authors addressing the treatment of intellectuals as knowledge holders focus on (with varying accents, of course). The first concerns the cognitive capabilities of the individual and treats them as the key factor making an individual an intellectual. The second sees the intellectual as a social function and thus as a position in terms of the performance of a social role, one which involves the articulation of ideas communicated to a general public (Eyerman, 2011). However, the position and role of intellectuals certainly depend on the cultural-historical context within which certain intellectual traditions emerge and consequently define the intellectual and his or her actions.

The term 'intellectual' emerged in France at the end of the nineteenth century in reference to the so-called Dreyfus affair (Eyerman, 1994). At first, it had a negative connotation and referred to a group of respectable public figures, writers and thinkers (Émile Zola, Anatole France, Émile Durkheim, etc.) who spoke up against the abuse of authority. In doing so, they decisively shaped the European, mostly French, tradition of a confrontation between people of reason and culture with the ruling elite.

The question of knowledge and its holders is especially relevant in the context of contemporary (post)industrial societies with their characteristic devaluation of classical industrial work and the ever-growing emphasis on various service activities and production based on highly expert work, which was referred to with concepts such as the 'new economy' (see, for example, Hübner, 2005). Thus, the so-called cultural capital, that is, the capability of individuals to master special languages, cultures, techniques and their respective skills, is becoming ever more important. Some sociological theories argue that this process is leading to changes in the social structures of these societies. Two examples of this are Gouldner's theory of the 'new class' (Gouldner, 1985) and Bell's theory of the 'knowledge class' (Bell, 1991), both presupposing that the shaping of the new social group (class) is based on the mentioned cultural capital (education). Gouldner speaks of the so-called 'culture of critical discourse', which is based on a relatively 'situation-independent discourse' within which everything and everybody should be open to criticism and thus rejects the reference to the authority and the social position of the speaker.

However, the notion of the intellectual cannot be used to describe the entire strata of highly educated people; on the contrary, people defined as intellectuals represent a minority of these strata. Eva Etzioni-Halevy (1985, p. 9), for instance, defines intellectuals as those people who deal professionally with the creation, training and spreading of theoretical knowledge, ideas and symbols. People who only transmit or use the knowledge are not included among them. According to these criteria, members of the same profession can be intellectuals or not. For example, a physician inventing new treatments is an intellectual, while his colleague who merely uses these methods for his treatments is not.

We can state that a considerable part of academia can qualify for this category. Everyone who wants to become eligible for a professorship or other types of academic tenure has to publish several scientific works that include original ideas and contributions to the knowledge base of a particular science discipline.

However, sheer expertise in a specific area expressed through the possession of knowledge and its creative use does not make one an intellectual. He is defined as an intellectual by their social role, their relation to social problems and their public engagement. To be considered an intellectual, one must interpret general problems using their scientific cognition and skills. We could claim that the intellectual is in a paradoxical situation, being, on the one hand, a sceptic and a critic of the existing values and the state of mind and, on the other, their creator.

There are three different approaches toward the thematisation of intellectuals as a social group. They can be perceived as class-in-themselves, class-bound or classless (Kurzmann & Owens, 2002). The above-mentioned conceptions of a 'new' class belong to the first category, in which intellectuals as 'knowledge-holders' hold to their own mentality or ideology, meaning they are class on their own. The notion of intellectuals as bound to their class of origin was pursued by Antonio Gramsci (1971) with his concept of 'organic intellectuals' (by which each class produce its own). In contrast, Karl Mannheim (1985) claimed that intellectuals transcend class, at least to some degree, and are thus socially relatively unattached since their education provides them with critical distance from their social origins.

The position of intellectuals is specific in that their 'self-interest', at least potentially, corresponds to the universal interests (Kurzmann & Owens, 2002, p. 79). They are, according to Bourdieu (1989), 'bearers of universal reason' since their field of engagement rewards 'defence of universal causes', and since being in possession of cultural capital, they can apply critical reflexivity to transcend their social position. Some theorists, such as Karl Mannheim (1985, 1993) and Zygmunt Bauman (1984), consider intellectuals as the one social group that can, due to its unrestrainedness with the class (Mannheim uses the term 'free-flowing intelligentsia'), act as a mediator between the various social strata (classes) and also, due to its cultural openness and sensibility, as a mediator of information and ideas between one's own culture and those of others. However, despite shared interests, they do not represent a homogeneous entity, so they rarely act collectively.

When defining the public character of the actions of intellectuals, one necessarily comes to the question of their relationship with politics and politicians. The fields of politics and intellectual life cannot be perceived as fully separated since their boundaries are often blurry (Eyal & Buchholz, 2010). Debates concerning the political engagement of intellectuals are long-standing. In his book *La Trahison Des Clercs* (*The Treason of the Intellectuals*) from 1927, Julien Benda fiercely criticised those intellectuals who had entered the political arena and consequently helped mobilise political hatred. By doing so, they had, according to him, abandoned the traditional role of intellectuals as safeguards of the mind and reason against sensuality and passions; they had become the ideologists and messiahs of various civic religions, and thus the agitators of political passions (Benda, 1997).

The political engagement of intellectuals and artists within Western culture has a rich history, and its consequences have never been univocal. As much as intellectuals have often sensitised the public to key social problems regarding issues of freedom and human rights, they have also frequently contributed to their limitation by cooperating with various extremist ideological endeavours. However, it has to be stated that intellectuals cannot control how their 'products' (concepts, ideas) are applied in political processes (Bourdieu, 2008), meaning that they are not always the ones to be blamed for their (mis)use.

3.3 The Role of Intellectual Elite in Dismantling Communism in Central and Eastern Europe

The so-called 'revolutions of 1989', which led to the final collapse of the communist regimes in the countries of the eastern half of Europe, can certainly not be understood without the knowledge of the role of intellectuals in them (and therefore, some, maybe somewhat exaggerated, call them 'revolutions of intellectuals'). As described by Timothy Garton Ash (1993, p. 136):

> To be sure, the renewed flexing of workers' muscle in two strike waves in 1988 is what finally brought Poland's communists to the first Round Table of 1989. To be sure, it was the masses on the streets in demonstrations in all other Eastern European countries that brought the old rulers down. But the politics of the revolution were not made by workers or peasants. They were made by intellectuals.

This public engagement of intellectuals from the region was part of longer tradition. Their impact on society's development was greater than that of their Western counterparts (Szakolczai, 2005).[1] Over the last two centuries, the intellectuals (mostly including people from the arts and humanities) in Central and Eastern Europe played very important social and political roles. The main characteristic was the feeling of a general social mission in the sense of the development and

---

[1] According to Michael Kennedy (1992, p. 29), intelligentsia represented 'a culturally constituted group whose claim to authority is its historic role as leaders of East European nations'.

modernisation of backward societies, along with the related need for public actions. It was about the 'enlightening' of the masses in the form of education or direct political engagement (Szablowski, 1993). Intellectuals were (and often still are) prone to speak in the name of the people as a whole (Fuller, 2000). The more undeveloped a country was, the bigger the gap between the educated elite and the uneducated masses (Bozoki, 1999, p. 1). In the countries of Central Europe, where there have been greater possibilities for professional development since the beginning of the twentieth century onward, there has also been a fair number of intellectuals who have 'stuck' to their fields of expertise, in addition to those who were socially engaged. Meanwhile, intellectual elites in the Eastern and Southeastern parts of Europe have represented some sort of social and cultural enclaves from which social reformists and protagonists of both leftist and rightist radical movements have evolved.

Another moment that has characterised the role of the intellectual elite in this space needs to be mentioned. Namely, it is characteristic of the Central European space to be populated mostly by countless nations which did not have a special historical constitutional tradition and/or whose destiny was exposed to manipulation by their larger neighbouring nations and whose national existence was constantly unclear; this is something for which they have always had to strive. With the absence or weakness of their own political institutions, it was culture (mostly literature) that represented the basis of maintaining their national, and its elite was the main holder of national ideas and struggled for national self-constitution (whose final goal was almost without exception a state of its own). Milan Kundera (1984, p. 3466) gives a good example of this when he wrote: 'The upheavals in the Middle Europe were not supplied by newspapers, radio and television—the media. They were prepared, designed and carried out by novels, poetry, theatre, film, historiography, literary magazines, human comedies and cabarets, philosophical debates—the culture'.

This role of intellectuals was also maintained during communism. Control over all of society by the ruling party elite and its branches typified communist rule. Specifically, its goal was to create a 'new' society in accordance with the dogmas of the ruling Marxist-Leninist ideology, and thus, it had to control all key social areas. Intellectuals in these circumstances, like other members of the highly educated strata, found themselves in various positions in the opposing ruling elite. Despite the once-influential thesis by Konrad and Szelenyi (1979) about the 'road of intellectuals to power', which was supposed to happen in the phase of 'mature socialism' when the intelligentsia was to become the dominant social class and take over the leading position in all key segments of society, including politics,[2] most intellectuals were nowhere near positions of social power. But it is a fact that only a small share of them were actively opposing the regime and cooperating in undermining the monopoly of the ruling party elite.

---

[2] It is worth mentioning that the two authors define intelligentsia in the broadest sense as a group of people with a university education.

This minority, consisting of active opponents of the regime, could be categorised as non-conformist marginal intellectuals. Their actions are often referred to by the concept of dissidence. However, the notion of a dissident is narrower since it is not only characterised by clear opposition to the regime but also by a repressive attitude toward members of the opposition, whereas all those actions not fitting into the context of the ruling ideal and normative complex or overtly opposing it could be called non-conformist and thus automatically placed at the social margin. The inability to access political power is common to both; also, it is worth noting that the boundary between the two was not as sharp since non-conformism in certain circumstances could quickly become dissident behaviour.

Most non-conformist intellectuals came from cultural, mainly literary circles. The reason for that lies in the nature of this sphere or the nature of cultural (mostly artistic) production, which requires a relatively free flow of information. Specifically, art is based on mechanisms of the imagination, that is, the free play of ideas, and thus, it does not stand external (especially ideologically motivated) interventions. We could even claim that the world of art is some sort of a special reality.[3] However, it is not independent of the external world since it uses elements of everyday reality as 'material' for its 'processing'. In this way, truths unpleasant for the regime concerning the state of social reality could be articulated through artistic discourse. This was a common practice in communist societies where the position of artistic (especially literary) works was, given the absence of political and media pluralism, one of the main sources of independent information, unfiltered by the 'ideological state apparatus'.

Non-conformism, which had its focus in the field of culture, where an important role was played by various cultural magazines, shaped a relatively regime-independent sphere that became the generator of criticism of the existing system. However, to successfully confront the ruling apparatus, it was necessary to exceed the non-conformism, which was limited to smaller groups of intellectuals through mutual connection and organisation. These kinds of engagement initially took the form of social opposition, labelled by György Konrad (1988) as 'anti-politics' since the aspirations of the majority of its protagonists were not focused on the struggle to gain power. According to Eyal (2000, p. 65), 'anti-politics signified the dissidents' renunciation of political power in favour of pastoral power'.

In the context of the ever-growing sterility of the regime that was incapable of fending off social challenges and the related decline of people's trust, the influence of independent intellectuals, their ideas and concepts grew stronger. It was realised over time that the essential social changes required an autonomous political organisation. Thus, political counter-elites were formed that were capable of pursuing its social change programme in an organised and systematic way. Nevertheless, certain anti-political moments were still maintained, a fact expressed in the numerous

---

[3] Thus, the phenomenological theory of Alfred Schutz considers art as one of the independent areas of meaning, with a characteristic cognitive style and the mutual harmony and compatibility of experiences according to this style, which enables it to achieve the 'accent' of truth. For details, see Alfred Schutz (1971).

forms of resistance against the Western patterns of political, mainly party, actions (see Havel, 1990). That is why various mass democratic movements, such as the *Civic Forum* in the Czech Republic, *Public Against Violence* in Slovakia, and the *Slovenian Democratic Union* in Slovenia, in which people from the cultural sphere played an important or even leading role, emerged before any conventional political parties. (This is even the case with the Polish *Solidarity*, which was originally a trade union).

It should be noted that the independent intellectuals were a heterogeneous group. Indeed, they were united by the opposition against the 'iron grip' of the communist regime, their striving for civil rights and respect for the principles of civil society. However, there were substantial differences in their worldviews and the pertaining perceptions of the development of society and their own role in it.

3.4 The Place and Role of Intellectuals in Post-Communism

By successfully dismantling the 'ancient regime', the structural conditions emerged for establishing the Western type of social organisation with a parliamentary democracy and a market economy as its key components. The independent and critical intellectuals who shaped this concept ideally, thus, in the new circumstances, found themselves in a dilemma regarding their (future) attitude to politics. These dilemmas concerned a concrete political engagement question: whether to join a specific political party and perhaps participate in government or to remain politically free, as well as the general social critical stance on whether to follow the social happenings or withdraw to one's own field of expertise. These decisions made by intellectuals varied, but in no case was their position unproblematic.

Many leading opponent intellectuals occupied key positions in politics and the ruling structures after the victory of democratic forces. We may claim that politics intellectualised itself in the new circumstances since most of the leading positions among politicians of the new democratic parties and the renewed parties were taken over by more educated people. Thus, in the newly elected 1990 Hungarian parliament, 90% of the representatives had a bachelor's degree, and half had a doctoral degree. According to Konrad and Szelenyi, the intelligentsia shaped the new political speech, which was founded on the mentioned 'culture of critical discourse' (Kempny, 1999, p. 154).

Nonetheless, the position of intellectuals in politics was in many ways problematic and contradictory. The origin of this lies in the nature of the political sphere, which requires a different way of acting than in the cultural sphere, which the intellectuals had been accustomed to. According to Daniel Bell (1996), culture and politics are two spheres in which adverse 'axis principles' are detectable in contemporary society, that is, different behaviour and various techniques and norms of legitimisation. The axis principle of (democratic) politics represents legitimacy, that is, the authority of the ones ruling approved by the ruled ones. This principle is realised through formal mechanisms that presuppose equality, and the decision-making takes place according to criteria of formal rules and consensus, subsequently enabling the basic tasks of political order to be realised. In contrast, the axis principle of culture is represented by the self-realisation of the individual, that is, his/her existential self-fulfilment or self-confirmation. This is the core of the conflict between the roles of an intellectual and a politician. Some intellectuals were quite successful in politics but had to adapt to the basic principles of political actions (and thus represented the political and not the cultural elite). However, many of them continued to act individualistically despite being representatives of the authorities and relied more on their spiritual and moral capital (acquired by being opponents of the former regime) than on formal rules and authority. Some typical intellectual characteristics, such as a critical attitude and an unconditional commitment to finding the truth, turned out to be somewhat inappropriate predispositions for the tactfulness and compromise-making essential for success in politics. Even political parties deriving from some sort of intellectual associations had no long-term success in politics without first changing their form.

In contrast, the 'depoliticisation' of intellectuals in the sense of their withdrawal from political institutions meant a denunciation of the power to decide on the strategic orientations of society. The 'weight' of their word has fallen drastically since the fall of communism, which had been the main subject of their criticism. Their courageous stand against the regime, the source of their moral authority, has slowly faded into oblivion; for some, the public presence of former dissidents has even become disturbing since they, with their pose, were a living witness to the conformism and the opportunism of the majority. Moreover, the legacy of anti-intellectualism must be mentioned. It derived mainly from the ideology of the former regime and was a consequence of the undeveloped political culture; it has also been often expressed in post-communist times. These are the reasons for the substantial discomfort about the new circumstances felt by the majority of intellectuals, which has led some to withdraw into privacy and others into uncompromising criticism of the new state of affairs and related deformations. Hence, some analysts believe that non-conformist intellectuals somehow belong to the losers of transition or at least to the 'losers among the winners' (Bernik, 1999) because their gains were presumably much smaller than those made by other segments of the educated strata (which deserve significantly less merit for the democratisation processes). Specifically, the political regulation of material resources in the new circumstances was mainly replaced by market regulation in relation to which the former non-conformist intellectuals, mostly coming from the social sciences, the humanities and culture, are in a much weaker position than others (e.g., economists, lawyers, etc.).

Despite the correctness of some of the above assessments, theses on intellectuals being the losing social group in the new circumstances are disputable or at least exaggerated (Tomšič, 2016a). They can be perceived as such only if their ambitions were to occupy the position of the new political elite or to somehow play the role of a 'collective nation leader'. However, such a role is in no way in line with the structure and principles of contemporary society. Namely, these are defined by two basic sets of processes: functional differentiation and culture-value pluralisation. Functional differentiation presupposes the functioning of various social fields in accordance with their own principles, that is, autonomy; this autonomy was limited by communism, similarly to all undemocratic forms of social organisation (Makarovič, 2001). The autonomy that represents the freedom of intellectual actions is now ensured, at least in an institutional sense, and this undoubtedly represents a big (we could even say essential) gain for the intellectual sphere. Furthermore, pluralisation, which is an element of the democratisation process, is leading to a change in relations among the intellectuals themselves. The worldviews of the various groups of intellectuals who gathered around some magazine or society, which were strongly personally or ideally connected during communism, started to differentiate. Thus, various combinations and alliances are emerging on the intellectual scene, characterised by an explosion of differences and 'autopoetics'. The removal of ideological pressure undoubtedly enabled the manifestation of differences in thought and the free flow of ideas, along with the consequential individualisation of intellectual work, with the accompanying pluralism of artistic genres, forms, and theoretical concepts, which is certainly an enrichment of the cultural space.

However, this 'normalisation' of the situation concerning the social placement of intellectuals does not mean their public engagement is unnecessary or even unwanted. Or, if we return to the above dilemma, just as the traditional role of Eastern and Central European intellectuals as the moral and political leaders of the nation is not in accordance with the postulates of a contemporary plural and functionally differentiated society nor with the principles of a liberal democracy (where in principle everyone has equal chances of political leadership), the withdrawal of intellectuals into privacy, behind the walls of carefully delimited professional fields, does not help strengthen democracy in any way. The place of the social engagement of intellectuals is in the sphere of public and civil society: a formal political transformation in the sense of the establishment of democratic institutions is a necessary but not also a sufficient condition for the successful democratisation of post-communist societies. A strong, dynamic and plural civil society is also needed, which can act as a partner of the political elite in setting social goals and shaping policies in various fields. We can say that the relationship between the state and civil society is reciprocal. The existence of legitimate power and a legal state is a condition for the development of civil society. In contrast, the civil-norms-compliant state organisation requires control, including by civil society and an independent public.

3.5 Academic Sociologists and Post-Communist Transformation

With the transition to democracy, academia found itself with a new independence free of the ideological and intellectual restrictions that had been imposed by the previously ruling communist authorities. State/bureaucratic regulation in normative terms is replaced with principles of institutional and professional autonomy. The status, prestige and reputation of scientists and their work have been made increasingly dependent on market principles and on the evaluation of their peers (Peteri, 1995, p. 306).

On the situation academic intellectuals are facing, post-communist countries differ on (1) the influence of academic intellectuals, (2) the level of pluralism, and (3) the ability to maintain intellectual autonomy and moral integrity. These differences are related to the dynamics of change in different fields of society. What is of special importance is the composition of national elites after the democratic transition. We can speak about two types of dynamics of change in elite positions: elite reproduction and elite circulation (see, for example, Szelenyi & Szelenyi, 1995; Tomšič, 2016b). Elite reproduction meant that changes in Eastern and Central Europe did not have an impact on the composition of elites since the nomenclature was able to remain at the top of the social structure. In contrast, elite circulation brought about structural changes at the top of the social hierarchy, that is, key positions occupied by new people on the basis of new principles.

In the countries of East-Central Europe, the principle of circulation prevails, while in the countries of Eastern and South-Eastern Europe, the principle of reproduction is dominant.[4] The latter also applies dynamics in the field of academia. A high level of academic elite reproduction causes the retention of old principles, that is, the ones that were in place during the communist period. In contrast, circulation leads to increased pluralism within the intellectual community and the prevalence of new ideas and values that are in line with the principles of established Western democracies.

Newly established academic freedom and autonomy were of particular relevance for the social sciences, which enjoyed special attention of the regime and were exposed to particularly tight control and strong ideological penetration. In this context, sociology plays a central role among social science disciplines in many aspects since its mission is a reflection of societal change in different fields. Furthermore, its role is inherently political. For Bourdieu (2008, p. 14), politics and sociology are 'two sides of a single work, one of analysis, deciphering and critique of social reality, with a view to assisting its transformation'.

Sociologic communities awaited the end of communist rule in different conditions. The first factor of variance was the strength of national traditions. For example, Poland, Romania, the Czech Republic, and Hungary had long and strong traditions; Estonia, Latvia, and Lithuania have had relatively small sociological communities, which were only recently established, initially under the umbrella of the Soviet Union (Keen & Mucha, 2004, p. 125). A very important factor was also the nature of the communist regime. In countries like Hungary, the former Yugoslavia and Poland, where political control and ideological pressure on academia were not

---

[4] A lengthy international comparative study of national elites (which formed part of the research project 'Social Stratification in Eastern Europe') was conducted in several countries of the post-socialist transition in 1990–1994. It was carried out by Ivan Szelenyi and his colleagues and initiated in 1990. By mid-1994, surveys had been completed in six countries: Bulgaria, Czech Republic, Slovakia, Hungary, Poland and Russia. The new findings (2000–2004) are presented and elaborated in Lengyel et al. (2007).

so persistent, with some longer periods of liberalisation, sociology had some relevant experience with autonomous academic research and intellectual involvement. In other cases, when the regime retained its orthodox character until its end, sociologists suffered from the lack of academic freedom, and their independent critical research works were only possible to be published in samizdat form.

Countries with the strongest and longest traditions and the largest intellectual and sociological communities were typically at the forefront in terms of institutionalisation of sociology (Keen & Mucha, 2004, p. 128). One should not also neglect the general socio-economic situation in these countries. The more successful the institutional transformation was and the better the economic conditions were, the easier the consolidation of academic sociology was (this is also true of other scientific disciplines).

The abolishment of ideological control brought freedom of choice of research topics, and theoretical concepts and research methods were re-established (see Kaase et al., 2002). The consequence of this is scientific pluralism, where different conceptual and methodological approaches are confronting and competing. The second major change can be found in the internationalisation of disciplines in terms of the availability of Western concepts and methods as well as actual international cooperation in terms of intensified participation of sociologists from Central and Eastern Europe at international scientific events and their involvement in transnational research projects. Sociology in Central and Eastern Europe has increasingly become similar to Western sociology (Keen & Mucha, 2010).

Sociological research in the region includes a number of highly relevant topics related to the process of social, economic, political and cultural transformation, such as privatisation, industrial relations, social stratification, democratisation, changes in values and ideological orientations, among others, as well as topics related to processes at transnational levels, such as Europeanisation and globalisation. There is a large potential for sociology to make significant contributions to the extended and more profound understanding of social reality. However, these potentials are insufficiently realised for several reasons. Mention should be made of excessive specialisation in terms of the large number of sub-disciplines with (overly) narrow research foci and weak integrations of theoretical and empirical work, which result in either abstract theorisation (detached from reality) or substance-less empiricism. This does not lead to a more in-dept and comprehensive reflection of social phenomena to provide solutions for the most urgent problems of societies. The contributions of sociologists at both the academic and political levels play a considerably less important role than those of some other experts, especially economists; the situation is also characteristic of Western societies (Woolcock & Kim, 2000; Colic-Peisker, 2016). Participation in international research projects funded by international entities (e.g., the European Union), although beneficial in terms of research experience and know-how, could be detrimental since it dictates the topics, objectives, and purposes of the empirical studies so we can speak about outside-induced 'agenda setting' that hinders research freedom. Furthermore, sociologists from Central and Eastern Europe are still often reduced to the role of data suppliers for their Western counterparts, which impedes their creative potential. Another problem is increasing commercialisation, which further limits the range of options for independent sociological research.

The role of public intellectuals is far from being unknown to sociologists from this region. Some of them often appear in mass media as commentators on current developments in politics or other realms of society. However, to a considerable extent, their participation in the public sphere consists of little more than 'sound bite sociology', often with little or no foundation in their scientific research (Keen & Mucha, 2004, p. 142). They are perceived as political commentators or even ideologues more often than as social scientists. In general, the cooperation of sociologist with broader society is insufficient, which harms their identity and social recognition.

On the public role of sociologists in former communist countries, one can state different, even contradictory, problematic points. On the one hand, we can witness their self-marginalisation, that is, retreat to their rather narrow social and professional spaces. In this way, many of them become more or less detached from wider developments in society and thus form problems with which it is faced. On the other hand, there are examples of their political instrumentalisation when sociologists place themselves into the service of power-holders. This is often connected to ideologisation, which is not typical only for post-communist societies. Namely, nowadays, we can witness the appearance of new and the revival of old ideologies (and fusions of both). Peter Berger (2002) sees this ideologisation as one of the main causes of the decline of the relevance of sociology. According to him, it is being transformed from science into an instrument of 'ideological advocacy'. When its protagonist began to engage in activism in terms of representing various (class, gender, racial) particularisms and participating in 'cultural conflicts' (mostly on the one hand, i.e., left-wing), instead of exploring fundamental societal issues, the discipline lost the status of (at least relatively) objective researcher of social life. Although its implementation may be an oversimplification, it nevertheless indicates some (at least in some places) strongly present tendencies (Adam & Tomšič, 2004). Of course, the solution is not to discourage sociologists from speaking publicly through mass media or political forums but to ensure that different opinions are treated equally, as well as in their ability to separate their roles of scientists and active citizens.

3.6 Conclusion

The so-called post-communist transformation in Central and Eastern Europe is not complete. It is still ongoing after more than a quarter of a century. This holds even for the countries that are considered the most successful in this process and are now members of the European Union. We are still waiting for a thorough, comprehensive, and systemic societal change to take place in this part of Europe, resulting in the implementation of an institutional setting comparable to the one in developed Western countries. Instead, we are witnessing a poor institutional performance, clientelism and corruption, and the rise of populism, which lead to political destabilisation and deterioration of democratic standards.

A situation characterised by such negative phenomena calls for active intellectual engagement. The marginalisation of intellectuals, which is not exclusively characteristic of so-called 'new democracies' in Central and Eastern Europe, is very problematic in this regard. For a healthy democracy, critical and autonomous public intellectuals as 'conscience of society' are necessary. In this context, the intellectual contribution of sociologists in terms of reflection on societal change in different fields and a better understanding of the structure and dynamic of society as a whole is highly significant. Although sociologists and other academic intellectuals do not possess a monopoly over truth and justice, they are, due to their cognitive and moral capabilities, qualified to become leading protagonists of the independent public sphere.

Competing Interests The author has no conflicts of interest to declare that are relevant to the content of this chapter.

References

Adam, F., & Tomšič, M. (2004). Sociologija v dobi globalizacije [Sociology in the age of globalisation]. In F. Adam & M. Tomšič (Eds.), *Kompendij socioloških teorij [Compendium of sociological theories]* (pp. 9–23). Študentska založba.
Ash, T. G. (1993). *We the people: The revolutions of 89 witnessed in Warsaw, Budapest.* Granta Books.
Bauman, Z. (1984). *Kultura i društvo [Culture and society].* Prosveta.
Bell, D. (1991). *The winding passage: Sociological essays and journeys.* Transaction Publications.
Benda, J. (1997). *Izdaja intelektualaca* [Treason of intellectuals].. Politička kultura.
Berger, P. (2002). Whatever happened to Sociology? *First Things* 126. Accessed Sep 10, 2023, from https://www.firstthings.com/article/2002/10/whatever-happened-to-sociology
Bernik, I. (1999). From imagined to actually existing democracy: Intellectuals in Slovenia. In A. Bozoki (Ed.), *Intellectuals and politics in Central Europe* (pp. 101–117). Central European University Press.
Bourdieu, P. (2008). *Political interventions.* Verso.
Bourdieu, P. (1989). The corporatism of the uni-versal: The role of intellectuals in the modem world. *Telos, 81*, 99–110.
Bozoki, A. (1999). Introduction. In A. Bozoki (Ed.), *Intellectuals and politics in Central Europe* (pp. 1–15). Central European University Press.
Colic-Peisker, V. (2016). Ideology and utopia: Historic crisis of economic rationality and the role of public sociology. *Journal of Sociology, 53*(1), 1–17.
Etzioni-Halevy, E. (1985). *The knowledge elite and the failure of prophecy.* George Allen and Unwin.
Eyal, G. (2000). Anti-politics and the spirit of capitalism: Dissidents, monetarists, and the Czech transition to capitalism. *Theory and Society, 29*(1), 49–92.
Eyal, G., & Buchholz, L. (2010). From the sociology of intellectuals to the sociology of interventions. *Annual Review of Sociology, 36*(1), 117–137.
Eyerman, R. (2011). Intellectuals and cultural trauma. *European Journal of Social Theory, 14*(4), 453–467.
Eyerman, R. (1994). *Between culture and politics: Intellectuals in modern societies.* Polity Press.

Falk, B. (2003). *The dilemmas of dissidence in east-Central Europe*. CEU Press.
Fuller, L. (2000). Socialism and the transition in the east and Central Europe: The homogeneity paradigm, class, and economic inefficiency. *The Annual Review of Sociology, 26*(5), 585–609.
Giesen, B. (2009). Intellectuals and politics. *Nations and Nationalism, 17*(2), 291–301.
Gouldner, A. (1985). *Against fragmentation: The origins of Marxism and the sociology of intellectuals*. Oxford University Press.
Gramsci, A. (1971). *Selections from the prison notebooks of Antonio Gramsci*. Int. Publishing.
Havel, V. (1990). *Living in truth*. Faber and Faber.
Hübner, K. (Ed.). (2005). *The new economy in a transatlantic perspective: Spaces of innovation*. Routledge.
Kaase, M., Sparschuh, V., & Wenninger, A. (Eds.). (2002). *Three social science disciplines in central and Eastern Europe*. Social Science Information Centre.
Keen, M. F., & Mucha, J. (2010). Post-communist democratization and the practice of sociology in central and Eastern Europe. In S. Patel (Ed.), *The ISA handbook of diverse sociological traditions* (pp. 129–139). SAGE.
Keen, M. F., & Mucha, J. (2004). Sociology in central and Eastern Europe in the 1990s: A decade of reconstruction. *European Societies, 6*(2), 123–147.
Kempny, M. (1999). Between tradition and politics: Intellectuals after communism. In A. Bozoki (Ed.), *Intellectuals and politics in Central Europe* (pp. 151–165). Central European University Press.
Kennedy, M. (1992). The intelligentsia in the constitution of civil societies and post-communist regimes in Hungary and Poland. *Theory and Society, 21*(1), 29–76.
Konrad, G. (1988). *Antipolitika. Srednjevropske meditacije [Anti-politics. Central-European mediatations]*. KRT.
Konrad, G., & Szelenyi, I. (1979). *The intellectuals on the road to class power: A sociological study of the role of the intelligentsia in socialism*. Harcourt Brace Jovanovich.
Kundera, M. (1984). Tragedija srednje Evrope [tragedy of Central Europe]. *Nova Revija, 3*(30), 3456–3468.
Kurzmann, C., & Owens, L. (2002). The sociology of intellectuals. *Annual Review of Sociology, 28*, 63–90.
Lengyel, G., et al. (2007). *Political elites in Central-Eastern Europe*. Friedrich Ebert Stiftung.
Makarovič, M. (2001). *Usmerjanje modernih družb [Steering of modern societies]*. ZPS.
Mannheim, K. (1993). *The sociology of intellectuals* (Vol. 10, p. 69). Sage.
Mannheim, K. (1985). *Ideology and utopia*. Harcourt Brace Jovanovich.
Oushakine, S. A. (2009). Introduction: Wither the intelligentsia: The end of the moral elite in Eastern Europe. *Studies in East European Thought, 61*(4), 243–248.
Peteri, G. (1995). On the legacy of state socialism in academia. *Minerva, 33*, 305–324.
Schutz, A. (1971). *Collected papres I*. Martin Nijhoff.
Sum, N.-L., & Jessop, B. (2013). *Toward a cultural political economy*. Edward Elgar.
Szablowski, G. J. (1993). Governing and competing elites in Poland. *Governance, 6*(3), 341–357.
Szakolczai, A. (2005). Moving beyond the sophists intellectuals in east Central Europe and the return of transcendence. *European Journal of Social Theory, 8*(4), 417–433.
Szelenyi, I., & Szelenyi, S. (1995). Circulation or reproduction of elites during the post-communist transformation of Eastern Europe. *Theory and Society, 24*(5), 615–638.
Tomšič, M. (2016a). Between culture and politics: Dilemmas of the central and eastern European intellectuals. *Research in Social Change, 8*(1), 4–19.
Tomšič, M. (2016b). *Elites in the new democracies*. Peter Lang Verlag.
Woolcock, M., & Kim, J. (2000). Can what is right with sociology fix what is wrong with sociology? A view from the 'Come-Back' generation. *The American Sociologist, 31*(1), 15–31.

Matevž Tomšič is a political sociologist and Professor at the School of Advanced Social Studies in Nova Gorica, Slovenia. He also works at the Faculty of Information Studies in Novo mesto, and the Study Centre for National Reconciliation. His research interests include political elites and political leadership, quality of governance, political culture, Europeanisation, media pluralism, democratisation, and the development of societies from Central and Eastern Europe. Among titles, he published the book Elites in the New Democracies (Peter Lang 2016). He is also co-author of the book The Challenges of Sustained Development (Central European University Press 2005).

Chapter 4
Sociology and Post-Communist Transformations: The Uniqueness of the Albanian Case in the East-European Context

Leke Sokoli

4.1 Introduction

It is not my intention to give a detailed picture of the developments and changes in Albania, in the previous three decades, including the development of sociology and its role in post-communist transformations. What I would like to present is the hypothesis: Is Albania a kind of laboratory for studying the post-communist transition, the features of its transformations, the (old and new) social problems connected with these transformations, and even the correlation between sociology and social transformations? Answering the above questions means analysing the uniqueness of the Albanian case in an East-European context.

Let us begin with an example. By a considered number of authors, Albania is considered an excellent laboratory for studying, for example, the new migratory process, especially for the study of the dynamic and mutually interdependent relationship between migration and development (King et al., 2003; De Zwager et al., 2005; Gëdeshi, 2010; King, 2011). As a matter of fact, regarding migration, Albania can be considered a sui generis case in Central and East Europe and beyond. The massive international migration of the Albanians is perhaps the most significant indicator of the difficult transformations in Albania.

The fall of the Berlin Wall, which symbolised the collapse of the socialist system in Central and Eastern Europe, was viewed with concern by many policymakers in Western Europe who expected their affluent countries to be flooded by immigrants. However, this did not materialise, and post-communist East-West migration was rather moderate. The one exception is Albania, whose emigration displayed features

---

L. Sokoli (✉)
Albanian Institute of Sociology (AIS), University Aleksander Moisiu of Durres, Durrës, Albania
e-mail: lsokoli@sociology.al

© The Author(s), under exclusive license to Springer Nature Switzerland AG 2024
B. Roncevic, T. Besednjak Valič (eds.), *Sociology and Post-Socialist Transformations in Eastern Europe*,
https://doi.org/10.1007/978-3-031-65556-2_4

Table 4.1 Albanian population and emigrants

Total population of Albania	4,229,753
The population in Albania (1 January 2023)[a]	2,761,785
Number of voters (Central Commission of Election, 14 May 2013)[b]	3,650,550
Number of non-voters (0–17 years old)[c]	579,203
Albanian emigrants, in numbers (1–2)	1,467,968
Albanian emigrants, in percentage (5/1)	34.7%
Emigrants in the world, in percentage (Solimano, 2010)	2.7–3.0%

[a]Instat, Albania; https://www.instat.gov.al/al/temat/treguesit-demografik%C3%AB-dhe-social%C3%AB/popullsia/publikimet/2023/popullsia-e-shqip%C3%ABris%C3%AB-1-janar-2023/
[b]Albanian Central Commission of Election, 2023 (20 March); https://mb.gov.al/verifiko-emrin-ne-listen-zgjedhore/
[c]Instat, Albania 2021; https://www.instat.gov.al/al/statistika-zyrtare-femije-dhe-te-rinj/popullsia/numri-i-f%C3%ABmij%C3%ABve-0-17-vje%C3%A7-n%C3%AB-fillim-t%C3%AB-vitit-num%C3%ABr/

of an exodus in terms of its ratio to the country's population, its significant concentration over a short period, and the typology of these moves (Vullnetari, 2011; Sokoli, 2022). No other Central or Eastern European country has been so affected by migration in such a short period as Albania has. The Albanian migration is one of the most spectacular mass migrations ever (Table 4.1).

It is confirmed that 34.7% of Albanians have immigrated to Italy, Greece, the US, the UK, Germany, and more than 30 other countries, while the world migrant average is about 2.7–3.0% (Solimano, 2010). Including the migrants that have spent considerable lengths of time abroad and have made their return to the country, Albania is a country in which more than half the population has experienced migration after the 1990s. In this sense, Albania has broken every record.

Sociology can attempt to explain 'Why?': Why did so many Albanians migrate in such a short time, and why is this so different from the other countries?

It is well-known that multiethnic states can be fragile, especially in the face of internal upheaval or external threats. The Balkans of the 1990s is the most recent example (Giddens, 2004; Rupnik, 2004). However, this is not the case for Albania, the most homogenous Balkan country regarding ethnicity. In Albania, there were no armed conflicts or genocide, persecution, ethnic problems, religious conflicts, political repression, and human rights violations.

However, it is widely accepted that after World War II, the totalitarianism installed in Albania was one of the most savage ever experienced (Rupnik, 2002). However, the Albanian migration wave broke just at the time of the collapse of that regime and not before. To some degree, it can be defined as a 'peaceful' migration or, using Fromm's words, a kind of 'escape from freedom'. In his famous book *Escape from Freedom* Fromm (1941, cit. Funk, 2000), he distinguishes between 'freedom from' (negative freedom) and 'freedom to' (positive freedom). Albanians' massive 'escape from freedom' was just escaping from a negative freedom, as they perceived it. To some extent, this is the kind of freedom typified by the Existentialism of Sartre; according to Fromm, on its own, it can be a destructive force unless accompanied by a creative element: 'freedom to'. In the process of liberation from an authority or a set of values concerned with—as Fromm argues—people are often left with feelings of emptiness and anxiety.

However, migration is one indicator of the extreme and multidimensional changes occurring in Albania. It is also only one of the social problems of present Albania that require a wider analysis.

4.2 Beyond the *En Bloc* Perspective

In my opinion, the keyword of the analysis to explain and understand the transformations of East Europe in the previous three decades is 'uniqueness'.

Why just 'uniqueness'? I will try to explain, based on the 'particular features approach'. Undoubtedly, the post-Communist transition in Central and Eastern European Countries (CEECs)[1] represents a highly complex process not only for its practical management but also for its theoretical interpretations and explanations. It is confirmed that the post-Communist transition was an unprecedented process, and it began having not a theoretical perspective, a theoretical framework on which the Great Transformation, using Brzezinski's concept (1993), would be based. This is confirmed by the absence of scientific literature published up to 1989, the year of the fall of the Berlin Wall, which symbolised the fall of communism and the end of the Cold War. Now, three decades later, there is a clearer picture of the post-Communist transition in CEECs. However, the essential questions are always the same: Is the post-Communist transition over? When can it be considered to be over? What drives the transition and ensures success? When can it be regarded as having been completed?

As we consider these questions, we have to remember that there was no model of the kind of post-Communist transition and transformation on which the region embarked. Rather, despite the similarities of some of their features, there were as many models as there are societies concerned (Gross & Jakubowicz, 2013).

Now, more than three decades later, it has become very clear that the initial view of the post-Communist transformation was too euphoric, and the estimates made by most American and Western European politicians and economists, as well as by numerous scholars, were too rosy. The prevailing predictions were generally based on the assumption that as in the words of the U.S. General Accounting Office Report, 'Poland and Hungary–Economic Transition and US Assistance', 'the democratic and free market institutions would be easily exportable as a "model" and quickly transplanted into the formerly communist-ruled states, and that the transition process would last for about five years' (Tarifa, 1998a, p. 74).

Undoubtedly, positive changes did indeed occur, and most CEECs are now far more open, offering freedoms and liberties, rights, and opportunities. However, the

---

[1] The reference is for 29 ex-communist countries, including the former Soviet Union Republics.

main conclusion is concerned with the fact that the very optimistic and idealistic expectations for a quick democratisation of both political and social systems and Fukuyama's 'end of history'[2] are not confirmed. The transformations in all societal institutions have turned out to be slower than expected, uncertain, and unsatisfying in many aspects of the transformations.

Reflecting on a wide literature of post-Communist transition, we can find, more or less, some stages:

1. The absence of a theoretical perspective or a theoretical framework regarding the (coming) radical transformations (up to or around 1989–1990)
2. The euphoria of the beginning (1989–1995; Fukuyama, 1992, and many others, including official reports of the US and other Western countries)
3. The objections of the initial euphoria (1995–2000 and after) and a more realistic approach (beginning with Brzezinski, 1993, etc.)
4. A kind of return to the classical ideas of Alexis de Tocqueville (2002) on the argument that different peoples would follow very different paths to reach democracy
5. The prediction that the future of post-Communist societies is open for more than one direction (around 1998, and later)
6. Distancing from, or leaving behind, the *en bloc* approach, now based on the assumption that what is relevant for Poland or Hungary is not relevant to all other ex-communist countries and considering the approaches of the particular features of different countries

For the scholars, it was necessary to study this particular 'unknown' process. Diverse literature has been produced on the subject, especially in the second half of post-Communist time, and we can say that a 'transitology' as a separate (sub)discipline of social sciences has emerged.[3]

In conclusion, the post-Communist Transition was considered a 'linear process' of political and economic transformation towards democracy and market economy. Additionally, the transformation was designed *en bloc*, applying the same strategy to all countries of the region, regardless of their local appropriateness. The *en bloc* perspective (*en bloc* = all together, and all simultaneously) characterised almost the literature of the first half of the post-communist epoch. During the Cold War, generally, it was assumed that all communist systems were the same (Crampton, 2013). That was because most Western observers viewed Eastern Europe from the outside

---

[2] In *The End of History*, Francis Fukuyama (1992, p. 18), declared: 'What we may be witnessing is not just the end of the Cold War, or the passing of a particular period of post-war history, but the end of history as such: that is, the end point of mankind's ideological evolution and the universalization of Western liberal democracy as the final form of human government'. A direct response to *The End of History* was *The Clash of Civilizations* by Samuel Huntington (1996).

[3] We can mention some series of publishing, as *Routledge Studies of Societies in Transition+*, *Springer Series of Transitional Justice*, etc., and many works such as Pëllumbi (2015a, 2015b), Gjuraj (2015), Petrovic (2013), Gross and Jakubowicz (2013), Crampton (2013), Simic and Volcic (2013), Edmunds et al. (2006), Polyyzoi et al. (2003); Winiecki (2002), Brabant (1998), Simic and Volcic (2013), and Sokoli (2015).

rather than the inside; their perspectives were distant, and their perceptions were generalised (Petrovic, 2013). From this perspective, even the transformations (of 1989–91) were defined metaphorically as a 'domino effect' (or chain reaction): one after the next, as a mechanical effect (the analogy to a falling row of dominoes), in which the time between successive (similar) events is relatively small.

However, the post-Communist transition produced very different outcomes. This can be confirmed clearly by referring to the gross domestic product (GDP) index by countries (see Table 4.2) and the Democracy Index (2014; see Table 4.3).

As we know, 11 of the post-Communist countries are European Union (EU) Member States: Slovenia, Estonia, Czech Republic, Slovakia, Lithuania, Latvia, Poland, Hungary, Croatia, Romania, and Bulgaria. The average GDP per capita of 29 ex-communist countries (USD 8113) is one-fourth that of the EU average (USD

Table 4.2 GDP per capita of 29 ex-communist countries

Rank	Country	US $
=	*European Union*	*32,006*
35	Slovenia	20,712
40	Estonia	17,425
41	Czech Republic	17,330
44	Slovakia	15,893
50	Lithuania	14,318
51	Latvia	13,729
54	Poland	12,662
56	Hungary	12,021
59	Croatia	11,551
60	Kazakhstan	11,028
=	World	10,023
68	Romania	8807
72	Russia	8447
76	Turkmenistan	7534
78	Azerbaijan	6794
80	Belarus	6583
81	Bulgaria	6582
82	Montenegro	6373
91	Serbia	5102
95	Macedonia	4867
103	Albania	4200
107	Bosnia & Herzegovina	4030
111	Kosova	3898
115	Georgia	3720
116	Armenia	3547
132	Uzbekistan	2130
133	Ukraine	2109
139	Moldova	1740
152	Kyrgyzstan	1198
159	Tajikistan	949

Table 4.3 The number of ex-communist countries and the percentage of the population for each regime type in 2014

Types of the regime	Score (Democracy Index)	Number of countries	Population (million)	% of population
Full democracy	8.0 to 10	=	=	=
Flawed democracy	6.0 to 7.9	14	119	30
Hybrid regimes	4.0 to 5.9	8	66	16
Authoritarian regime	0.0 to 3.9	7	217	53
Total (including Kosovo)	=	29	402	100.0

Source: Countries by population 2015 (http://www.populationmatters.org; available 12.11.2015); our accountings (L.S.)

32,006). Albania and Kosovo are among the countries of the third group, and their average GDP per capita is half that of the average of 29 ex-communist countries, which means one-eighth that of the average GDP of the EU.

Moreover, the average GDP of the three first-ranked countries is 15 times higher than that of the three last-ranked countries. So, economically, the transition has produced very different outcomes.

However, clear differences are also seen in the Democracy Index.[4] None of the CEEC countries is between the 24 countries of 'full democracy'.[5] Comparing the population of each type of regime, the results show that (three decades after the beginning of the transition) the greatest part of the population of the CEECs is under authoritarian regimes.

Showing serious concern about the possible outcomes of the transition in different countries, many scholars have predicted that even the concept of 'post-Communism' has lost its meaning, as Rupnik (2002, p. 129) writes:

> What can the common denominator of Hungary, Albania, Czech Republic, Belarus or Kazakhstan show? Almost nothing! Their communist past cannot help in understanding the different ways that followed these countries after 1989.

It is clear that the approach 'all together, all at the same time' is no longer valid. Even though almost all the works of the previous 5 to 10 years refer to 'communism' and its 'post' (as a whole), the analysis is focused on particular aspects of specific countries, such as socioeconomic and political facts on post-Communist

---

[4] Twenty-nine ex-communist countries and their rank, by the Democracy Index 2014: 'Full democracy' (half country, East Germany): Germany (13); 'Flawed democracy' (14 countries): Czech Republic (25), Estonia (34), Slovenia (37), Lithuania (38), Latvia (39), Poland (40), Slovakia (45), Croatia (50), Hungary (51), Bulgaria (55), Serbia (56), Romania (57), Moldova (69), Macedonia (72); 'Hybrid regimes' (7 countries): Montenegro (77), Georgia (81), Albania (88), Ukraine (92), Kyrgyzstan (95), Bosnia & Herzegovina (103), Armenia (113); 'Authoritarian regime' (7 countries): Belarus (125), Russia (132), Kazakhstan (137), Azerbaijan (148), Uzbekistan (154), Tajikistan (156), and Turkmenistan (160). Kosovo is not evaluated. (http://www.eiu.com/public/topical_report.aspx?campaignid=Democracy0115; retrieved 11 December 2015).

[5] East Germany, with 16 million inhabitants in 1990, is not included because of the German Reunification, immediately following the fall of the Berlin Wall.

transition; the impacts of the pre-communist legacies and geographic position; explanations based on different institutional and behavioural legacies of communism; the pre-communist past and the establishment of communist rule; differing aspects of communism: weak and strong communism; the socio-economic effects of communist institutionalisation and urbanisation; the different roles of the external factors despite the same EU approach and so on.

4.3 Understanding the Albanian Transformations Comparatively

> The past is never dead, it's not even past.
> —William Faulkner

Let us refer to the case of Albania. Change—as the common cliché goes—is a constant of contemporary society. The entire world has changed. However, change in the 'Albanian laboratory' includes extreme and multidimensional transformations. So, the Albanian transition is somewhat unique in its complexity: it is a political, economic, democratic, social, demographic, religious transition, media and public sphere transition, and civil society transition, among others.

The first dimension of change is economic and represents the passing from a totally centralised economy to a 'liberalised and chaotic market economy'. While the economy before the 1990s was based on production and, first and foremost, on the production of the means of production, the new economy was based on consumption and services. This is an 'extroversion' economy, meaning that internal consumption greatly exceeds national production (Sokoli & Hroni, 2009, p. 119). For this reason, the integration of the Albanian economy into global markets remains moderate. Economic change in Albania includes extreme transformations due to the simple (and strange) fact that in Albania, quite different from the other ex-communist countries, the state was and remained (to the very end) the only owner and the only employer.

The *political dimension of change* represents the transition from a Stalinist authoritarian regime to a 'stable' hybrid regime (Democracy Index 2014) after a severe post-communist transition.

The *third dimension of change is social* and represents the passing from 'the equal distribution of poverty' (using Churchill's words) to the most extreme social disparities in Europe.[6]

---

[6] So, even the social change in Albania is characterised by moving between extremes, from the most extreme equality to the most extreme social disparities in Central and East European Countries. It is accounted, for example, that 20 years after the face of the Berlin Wall, the average wealth of 10% of the richest households, compared to 20% of the poorest ones in Albania is 2.5 times higher than the same report referred to Eastern European countries (Sokoli, 2010, p. 8). The growth of the living standard has been accompanied by extreme economic and social differentiation.

As we know, communism atomised the society by destroying virtually all the institutions of autonomous collective actions, which we usually refer to as 'civil society'. Therefore, the post-communist change that took place in Albania was a return to our 'normal identity', first and foremost, a return to freedom, including religious freedom. Also, a moderately liberal public sphere has been created in Albania since the fall of communism. In the early 1990s, an Albanian civil society emerged, overcoming a very difficult period (Tarifa & Sokoli, 2006; Sokoli, 2006; Sokoli, 2009).

Understanding the Albanian transition comparatively, we can say that the post-communist transformations represent a very interesting example for comparative studies: a considerable number of countries began this transformation at the same time (1989), following more or less the same common goal of moving towards a consolidated democracy and a liberal market economy, and get as close to the EU as possible (at least for the European part of ex-communist world). Nevertheless, their communist past can still aid in analysing the different dynamics of development during the transition. As William Faulkner said: 'the past is never dead, it's not even past'. Based on the 'tradition-based methodology', Brzezinski (1993) predicted the historical calendar of those countries, according to the expected rhythm of development of democracy, by listing them in four groups. Albania was set in the last group, predicting a bumpy road to democracy.

The Albanian transition was, in fact, 'a transition on transition', a post-communist transition after a 'communist transition',[7] based on the Marxist theory of transformation from capitalism to communism. Marx (1980, p. 24) writes that 'between capitalist and communist society lies the period of revolutionary transformation of the one into the other. Corresponding to this, there is also a political transition period in which the state can be nothing but the revolutionary dictatorship of the proletariat' (Fig. 4.1).

Marx (1976, p. 226) says that 'the dictatorship of the proletariat is a necessary phase to move to the disappearance of class distinctions generally, to the disappearance of all the relationships in production (which means, first of all, relations of ownership over the means of production) upon which are based these class

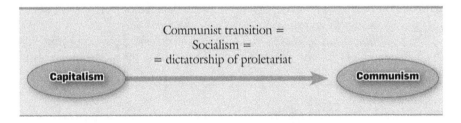

Fig. 4.1 Communist transition, according to Marx (1980, p. 24), own interpretation

---

[7] Even in the official goals of the communist time, the building of communism figured only as a very distant goal.

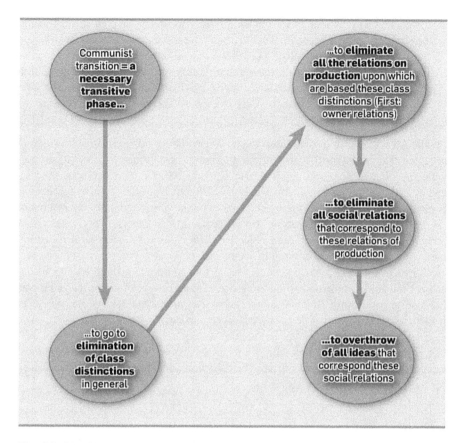

Fig. 4.2 The features of communist transition according to Marx (1976, p. 226), own interpretation

distinctions, the disappearance of all social relations that correspond to these relations in production, the overthrow of all ideas emanating from these social relations'.

Therefore, we have (Fig. 4.2):

Referring to Marx's scheme and judging the depth of the transformations applied in Albania, compared with other countries of Eastern Europe, we can say that:

First, of all types of transitions, *the post-communist transition is perhaps the most difficult one*. This is regarded as the quantity and depth of the transformations performed.

Second, the starting point of post-communist transitions was different in different countries. This depends on three factors: (1) the different levels of development, (2) the degree of application of Marx's formula, cited above, and (3) different levels of previous reforms.

Third, it is confirmed that of all former communist countries, Albania represents *a special case* because in no other country has Marx's formula (quoted above) been implemented so faithfully (or blindly) than in Albania. All other countries corrected the system, at least from the 1960s onward. On the contrary, following the strategy 'neither East nor West', Albania went paradoxically on the opposite side of the reformation: Albania in 1989 was a more communist country than in 1945 or 1960. First, Albania remained the country with the highest concentration of means of production in the state's hands. In Albania, as nowhere else, the state became the *only owner* and the *only employer*. The Albanian people were, as nowhere else, alienated by the state.

The Albanian form of communism was a very 'heavy communism'. It is widely accepted that after World War II, the longest and most savage totalitarianism prevailed in Albania, Romania, and Bulgaria (Rupnik, 2002). It remained up to the very end a 'heavy communism', which is quite different from the 'light communism' experienced in other countries, such as the so-called 'goulash communism' (Hungarian), 'self-administration' (ex-Yugoslavia), or others. This means that Albania has had some additional objective difficulties for a successful transition compared to other former communist countries.

Conversely, Albania has had some 'subjective additional difficulties' for a successful transition compared to the majority of East European countries. That was because, paraphrasing Brzezinski, the behaviour or engagement of the Albanian leaders towards a pluralist democracy has been and still is problematic.

The above arguments lead us to the generalisation: if the post-communist transition is the most representative, the Albanian post-communist transition is the most representative. Therefore, this is why the Albanian transition is a kind of laboratory for the study of transitional processes.

4.4 Transition and Social Problems: An Empirical Approach

In the case of Albania, a strong correlation between post-communist transformations (or transition) and social problems is confirmed. However, first, it is necessary to define the concept of 'social problem'. What is a social problem?

> A social problem is a condition affecting a significant number of people in way considered undesirable, about which it is felt something can be done through collective social action (Horto et al., 1997, p. 2).

This definition has four distinctive ideas: (1) a condition affecting a significant number of people; (2) in a way considered undesirable; (3) about which it is felt something can be done; (4) through collective social action.

Everything in Albania changed after the collapse of the 'Albanian Berlin Wall', but not everything was for the better. In the article 'First impressions of life in Albania', written after his first visit to Albania in 1986, Peter Lucas, from Boston Globe, wrote:

> There is no drug problem in Albania, no pornography, and there is hardly any crime. There were no homeless people sleeping in the streets and in the parks. There was plenty of water and electricity, and there were no prostitutes, no children begging and sleeping on the street,

and no guns [...] There was law and order, but there was no freedom. There was stability and plenty of food, but there was no public discourse [...]. (Lukas, 1998, p. 157).

Three decades after the beginning of the Albanian transition, we can compare two different realities (before and after the transition): the first one was characterised by a simple social reality, mainly rural, homogeneous, and based on a social consensus; the second is a new reality, complex, mainly urban, heterogeneous, a reality that will be faced (as everywhere, but perhaps more than anywhere) with major social problems.

From this analysis, we conclude that the post-communist transition was, at the same time, a period of a flood of social problems in Albania. Previously, they were limited by three factors:

1. The dictate of an 'iron' communist regime[8]
2. Propaganda, which in conditions of total isolation cannot be ineffective[9]
3. Social policies of the state of that time, such as those on employment, education, public health, housing, etc.

However, social problems are 'defeated' only temporarily. They began to boil under the communist regime until they exploded to a size difficult to be managed by the society. Later, changes were rapid and unexpected. The flow of social problems in post-communist Albania was caused, first, by the shock of rapid (but chaotic) change (Sokoli, 2014; Sokoli, 2022). Social problems flowed in proportion to the speed of change. Albanian society was not immune; it did not have the proper instruments (political, social, legal, organisational, etc.) to confront their 'storm'. Let us take, for example, human trafficking. The communist regime avoided it 'in its own way', even without any anti-trafficking law. Before the 1990s, traffickers and the concept of trafficking in human beings were unknown (Luan Omari, in Sokoli & Gedeshi, 2006).[10]

What about the present social problems of Albania? Based on a national survey ($n = 1365$), about 20 problems meet the criteria of being social problems, based on the above-mentioned definition (Horto et al., 1997). Hence, a methodological

---

[8] It is known that the dictatorial regimes realized to repress (even in the embryonic phase) some social phenomena, not to allow them to take dimensions of social problems. This happened not only in communist regimes but generally in totalitarian regimes.

[9] Social problems in communist Albania are considered 'wounds of capitalism and expression of its decay'. Thus, the fight against them was considered part of the so-called 'class struggle'. Here is, for illustration, a paragraph from the most important document of the communist time (the Report of PLA Congress) in which the head of the Albanian State R. Alia (only a few years before the start of transition) stated: 'A new social stratum is created with the so-called excluded from the society, including the world of crime, drug addictions, prostitution, etc. This is a figment of the capitalist system, the very reason for the degeneration of society. Present capitalism has proved that it isn't able to heal any of its wounds' (Alia, 1987, p. 153).

[10] The first law against human trafficking was adopted only in 1995. It was amended in 2001 and 2004. So, only 15 years after the start of trafficking, the legal framework to combat trafficking in human beings was established.

principle is derived: testing of social problems and measurement of the degree of their intensity represents the assessment of public concern for them.

The main social problems and their hierarchy based on the rate of 'perceived public concern' for them are listed in Table 4.4. The concern coefficient of each social problem is calculated based on a standard formula (Sokoli, 2022):

$$Cc = No.vc + \tfrac{1}{2} No.lc - No.Nc \qquad (4.1)$$

where Cc is the coefficient of public perception concern; $N.vc$ is the number of respondents that perceive the given problem as a 'big concern'; $No.lc$ is the number of respondents that perceive the given problem as a 'medium concern'; $No.\,nc$ is the number of respondents that perceive the given problem as having 'no concern' at all, and No is the general number of respondents.

Therefore, we can consider that the volume and intensity of social problems are more than the capacities of society to treat and resolve them. The main conclusion has to do with the political priorities. Surprisingly, we can determine that the coefficient of public concern for education (+0.725) is higher than the coefficient of public concern for other major current social problems, such as unemployment, poverty, level of health service, corruption, degree of law enforcement, the degradation of nature and so on.

We observed that several other social problems are directly or indirectly linked with the school and educational system, such as idle life of the youth (R3), problematic teacher-student relationships (R5), low level of civic education (R11), poor rule of law (R7); discrimination of the poor children from rich families' children (R10);

Table 4.4 The hierarchy of social problems

More concern problems	The concern coefficient	Ranking (R)
Drug abuse	−0.136	18
Alcohol abuse	+0.090	14
Poverty	+0.552	9
Unemployment	+0.707	2
Human trafficking	−0.025	16
Poor rule of law	+0.567	7
Corruption	+0.545	8
Conflicts between neighbours	+0.133	13
Violence in society	−0.029	17
Conflicts between generations	+0.179	12
Low level of citizenship education	+0.480	11
Degradation of nature	+0.578	6
Low level of education	+0.725	1
Problematic relations: teachers-students	+0.580	5
Husband-wife conflicts	+0.026	15
Vanity life of the young people	+0.684	3
Low level of health services	+0.660	4
Discrimination to poor children from rich ones	+0.512	10

conflicts between generations (R13); violence in the society (17); trafficking of human beings (R17); alcohol abuse (R14); and drug abuse (R18). To conclude, based on the 'hierarchy of social problems—a government priority', we can say firstly that education must become a political and social priority.

4.5 The Simultaneous Birth of (Both) Sociology and Social Problems in Post-Communist Albania (The Rise of Albanian Sociology)

About a century ago, the 'father' of Albanian Sociology, Branko Merxhani (2003, pp. 83–84), referring to the 'transitive' Albanian society of that time, wrote:

> Sociology is the most necessary science for every social reform. The reform for the realisation of which should work for the Albanian generation of our time has a wider mission and a more general character than that of those who want to give our legislators. We are at the end of a period and the beginning of a new one, and it is a great danger if this transitional period—that is the period of suspicion, of mental weakness and spiritual crisis—be extended indefinitely. So we need a scientific consciousness, a scientific understanding of our social problems…. The beginning and the basis of our reformative activity, depends from a sociological study of the social problems of the Nation.

It was not easy to engage in sociology in Albania, because, quite unlike other Eastern European countries, in Albania, there was no tradition in sociology prior to the collapse of the Berlin Wall. Under Communist rule, sociology was outlawed because it represented an 'unnecessary' and even 'dangerous bourgeois' intrusion into a system that had already 'perfected' social relations (!). No one referred to sociology as a science; no scientific institute was engaged in sociological research; nowhere was sociology studied as a separate academic discipline; no one ever received training in sociology. To speak of sociology as an independent discipline alongside Marxist historical materialism was regarded as a great sacrilege, and any effort to investigate the social reality from a sociological perspective, using sociological methods, was regarded as politically suspicious (Tarifa, 1998b, p. 28).

Albania was perhaps the only European country where sociology was totally excluded from the university curricula and the foci of scientific research. There had never been a department of sociology at the University of Tirana or any institute of sociology among about 40 institutes of the Albanian Academy of Science. Cultural and scientific exchange between Albania and other countries were minimal, while in the field of sociology, there were absolutely no exchanges for the preparation of sociologists, participation in associations, international scientific activities, exchanges of sociological literature, and similar. More than anywhere else in Eastern Europe, Marxism-Leninism was regarded as the ultimate truth, while the Labour [Communist] Party granted itself a monopoly on truth and was immune to any criticism or empirical evidence on domestic social problems. The traditional schools of thought, including existentialism, Freudian psychology, structuralism, phenomenology, and similar, were forbidden altogether, as were the works of Plato,

Aristotle, Hegel, Dostoevsky, Sartre, and others; the names of many major social theorists, such as Weber, Durkheim, Simmel, Pareto, Popper, Mill, Parsons, Merton, among others meant nothing to us. The fight against sociology was also considered part of the so-called class struggle (Sokoli, 2011a, 2014).

After many ups and downs, the Albanian Sociological Association (ALBSA) was founded in November 2006. Since 16 April 2007, it has been a regular and collective member of ISA, and since 10 October 2008, it has been a member of ESA. The foundation of ALBSA was the real beginning of an institutionalised sociology in Albania. It is quite simple to measure an organisation's progress, such as the ALBSA: count the number of members, participants, registrants, and activities. The figures clearly show how few things have gone wrong and how many have gone right.

The main feature of the sociological development is sustainability. Every year of the previous decade, ALBSA has organised wide-ranging dialogues under the name 'Spring Forums', putting the very concerning problems on the agenda of public debate and leading it. Every November, the annual international conference is held; almost every aspect of Albanian society is studied, and the findings are given to the public and policymakers; a (new) tradition of lobbying is created for the implementation of sociological findings, and so on.

We, a group of pioneers of Albanian sociology, have been actors and factors in the rise of Albanian sociology (of course, through many difficulties); the institutionalisation of sociology in Albania is over. As a delegate of the Albanian Sociological Association in the third International Sociological Association Conference of the Council of National Associations (Ankara, May 2012) 4 years ago, I declared:

> What comes after is concerned with the Albanian 'proactive sociology', with the increasing of the impact of sociology and sociologists in the development of the society.

This is an important phase of conducting sociology as a public need. Sociology is (1) the study of the development, structure, and functioning of human society and (2) the study of social problems (2). The post-Communist transition was, at the same time, the period of the intensive emergence of social problems unknown before (Sokoli & Hroni, 2009; Sokoli, 2009; Sokoli & Malaj, 2013). Albanian society did not have the experience, even the instruments or institutions (political, institutional, social, and legal) to confront the intensive flux of social problems (Sokoli, 2006, 2010, 2011a, 2011b).

Sociologists are called to study these social problems—new or with new nuances—actively and proactively. They are called to be in the first line of treating and resolving social problems without thinking about the 'traditional borders' of sociology. Committed sociology, under these conditions, was a mission, except committed AS a 'cold science'.

In a certain way, we have considered sociology even as a social movement, being conditioned by practical needs. Let me mention the study 'Representation and the Quality of Democracy in Albania; a gender perspective' (Ekonomi et al., 2006). We found that in a district of Elbasan, for example, just in the centre of the country, the Regional Council was composed of 92 members, but all were men, and no one was a woman. It was easy to publish and send the study to the bookshops, thus 'washing the sociological hands'. However, this was not enough, even correct. The ALBSA members moved to resolve the problem practically. They composed a document and named it 'Gender Code', with some specific requests for the political parties, and as an 'alarm bell' for international partners, NGOs and the general public.[11] They travelled throughout the country, arguing their sociological findings and resolving ideas. They engaged auditors, offices, media, and social media and were very active in the legislation process. Thanks to the will of some politicians (in the end, politics decides), the situation is changing. Now, at least 50% of the local councils are women. The Albanian government presently has 19 members (ministers), and ten of them are women. For the first time in the history of Albania, women are the majority in the government. Sociology works as a theory and study of social life. However, it works better when accompanied by the engagement to move things ahead.

It is well known that many sociologists, like Max Weber, are public intellectuals and are not cut out to be politicians. I personally have refused to be a member of any political party. However, experience shows that the political engagement (at least for a certain time) of social scholars does not compromise the values they defended as independent scholars. Actually, many social scholars are engaged successfully in politics. Three ALBSA members, all women and very active in the 'sociological movement' for the Representation of Women in Politics and the Public Sphere, are members of the Albanian government: others are vice-ministers, the present Academic Director of the Albanian Institute of Sociology was the Chair of the Albanian Parliament and others. It is possible to be engaged in politics and not compromise sociology as a science. In our time, politics is not a lifelong profession. Weber's idea of politics as a vocation has to be reevaluated.[12]

---

[11] See, for example 'Ideas and their materialization: Gender Code of the Albanian sociologists' where it is declared that: 'AIS/ALBSA is and remains an institution of scholars and graduates of sociology and social sciences. The study of the phenomena of social life remains its priority. But it is an institution of the engaged intellectuals and citizens, with the objective to provide society with democratic forms and tools, some standards of development'. AIS/ALBSA aims to make gender issues part of the media agenda, political programs, lobbying object etc., according to the principle 'from the conclusions of studies on drafts of laws, decrees, decisions'.

In 2008–2009, AIS organised the so-called 'Gender Convention' as a working and circulating forum throughout the country, proclaiming its 'Gender Code'—a set of principles and requests for equal opportunities and the same status for women and girls in society, including political representation. One of the ultimate requests was: 'Not voting the political parties or coalitions without publishing in advance the list of alternate candidates, male and female, in order to achieve representation of women in Parliament, Local and Regional Councils of above 30%' (Malaj & Hoxha, 2009, pp. 30–32).

[12] 'I never thought of politics as a profession', said the Greek politician, Georgios A. Papandreou. Greece may be suffering the consequences of this perception. Unfortunately, in many countries what Manoj, Sridharan and Kulandaivel concluded in a paper of 2016 is happening, that 'politics acts as a business where politicians invest their money to win a seat in assembly and make money by abusing their power. In order to change this—they proposed—politics should be standardized. Educated and socially aware people should be keen on participating in politics, treating politics as a profession rather than a business', because 'the success or failure of democracy in a country solely depends on the quality of politicians who operate in it' (Manoj et al., 2016, p. 188).

The last initiative of Albanian sociologists is the Move(ment) for a Good Society (MGS). *Good Society* is a comprehensive concept and covers many aspects of society, including democracy, capitalism, social problems, and social politics, among others. And not all these 'belong' to sociologists. Furthermore, the 'Move(ment) for a Good Society' is only one project and engagement of Albanian sociologists and their organisations.

The main objective of this movement is to (1) increase the impact of sociology and sociologists for a better/good society and (2) increase the presence of Albanian sociologists in Albanian society, keeping the charge of sociological organisations through action. All issues related to the concept of 'good society' are controversial because, as human beings, we think of good as what is best for us, not what is best for everyone as a whole (Perrucci & Perrucci, 2014) or even what 'the good society' means, how we would define it, a good society in whose opinion, and similar. There is no pattern of a good society that we or anyone else can decide on and then expect people to conform to. These are the very arguments that the good society is an appropriate theme for the dialogues.

The 'Move(ment) for a Good Society' was founded in January 2016, and the idea of this movement emerged in the dialogue with the students of two main universities in two main Albanian cities, Tirana and Durres, on 'the Year of Aristotle'[13] (2016), The Year of the Great Albanian Mother Teresa (2016),[14] and 'the Year of the Inquiry' (2017).

For Aristotle the final end of human life is to have a good life, living in a good society. All acts should aim at this end. The practical message is: The Good (Society) through Good Acts, and Good Actions.

From Mother Teresa, we have the (sociological) idea of Acting Now: 'Yesterday is gone. Tomorrow has not yet come. We have only today. Let us begin. Act Now!'

The idea of a Good Society comes even from the relationship between science and politics, and *the Inquiry*, founded a century ago, is a good example.[15]

The principles and the main goals of the MGS are declared in its Code, which symbolises the MGS's identity. Its requests must be considered as moral preconditions for its members to engage to:

- Comply with the principle that all men are created equal, that they are endowed by their Creator with certain unalienable Rights, that among these are Life,

---

[13] The year 2016 was 2400th anniversary of the birth of the great Greek thinker Aristotle. The 38th session of the UNESCO General Conference held in Paris was declared Jubilee Year 2016 of Aristotle. Mankind has commemorated the anniversary of the famous philosopher activities worldwide. Aristotle intended authentic friendships Authentic people tend to attract authentic friends: the larger the network of friendship, the greater the measure of a man's virtue.

[14] Mother Teresa (born Anjezë Gonxhe Bojaxhiu; Albanian), known in the Catholic Church as Saint Teresa of Calcutta, was canonized at a ceremony on 4 September 2016 in St. Peter's Square in Vatican City.

[15] 'The Inquiry' was a study group of composed by 150 academics, established in September 1917 by Woodrow Wilson to prepare materials for the peace negotiations following World War I. The head of research was Walter Lippmann, the author of the first book entitled *Good Society* (1937).

Liberty and the pursuit of Happiness (as 'Learning by Heart', and point of reflection and reference in any personal and collective action)
- Increase the role of science, scholars, intellectuals, students, etc., in reforming the society through studies that precede reforms and by engaging in intellectual and social movements, public debates, rallies, petitions, etc.
- Influence that Education would be the National Priority, considering it as a universal key for a Good Society, encouraging the movements 'Good School—Good Society' 'University for the Good Society' etc.
- Develop the 'Kantian' capitalism, where the Man is always the goal and never an instrument
- Assist in the modelling of society according to ethical standards in all its levels, family, neighbourhood and community, work, school, and the whole society; and
- Consider active citizenship as a key for the consolidation of democracy, based on the principle: 'Do not wait, but move for a good life, for a Good Society'

The organisation aspects of the MGS include the Great Network of the Good Society and different small networks (professionals, students, etc.), the Coalition for a Good Society, and the MGS International Steering Board, with Albanian activists in more than 30 countries.

From the ways of achieving the goals, we can mention the studies for sustainable solutions, incitement to commit good stable, lobbying through debates, petitions, and other forms of solving concrete problems, among others.

One of the goals of MGS is to inject the idea of sustainability into Albanian society, instead of the dominant idea of impatience, rapid change, and almost instantaneous economic enrichment. It is a fact that the shock of rapid change created many problems in present Albania. The so-called Shock Therapy proclaimed as a 'pure science' after the fall of communism, resulted in the most dangerous and catastrophic theory in the recent history of Albania; many decisions were realised in radical situations, under mass and political pressure, in the conditions of hunger strikes, and similar. However strange, the symbol of MGS is the tortoise, giving the message of gradual change and offering sustainable solutions.[16]

There is no pattern of a good society. However, the members of MGS are Albanians living in more than 30 countries, and one of the goals of this organisation is to share different experiences and best practices about a good society.

The Good Society emerges not only as an idealistic project but as the long-term practical necessity of a new area in the new conditions, especially in Albania and the Balkan region, traditionally considered a 'powder keg'. The results, however modest, show that moving is the best strategy for increasing the role of sociology and the image of sociologists in society.

As Martin Luther King Jr. said in his famous speech 'Keep Moving':

> If you can't fly, then run, if you can't run then walk, if you can't walk then crawl, but whatever you do you have to keep moving forward...

---

[16] The tortoise has been the symbol of the Fabian Society, founded on 1884 in London. The Fabian Society was named in honour of the Roman general Fabius. His Fabian strategy sought gradual victory against the superior Carthaginian army under the renowned general Hannibal.

Competing Interests The author has no conflicts of interest to declare that are relevant to the content of this chapter.

References

Alia, R. (1987). *Raport në Kongresin e 9-të të PPSH* [Report to the 9th Congress of PLA]. 8 nëntori.
Brabant, J. (1998). *The political economy of transition opportunities and limits of transformation*. Routledge.
Brzezinski, Z. (1993). *The great transformation*. National Interest, (Fall, 93), 3–13.
Crampton, J. R. (2013). Foreword. In P. Milenko (Ed.), *The democratic transition of post-communist Europe*. Palgrave Macmillan.
De Zwager, N., Ilir Gëdeshi, E. G., & Christos, N. (2005). *Competing for remittances*. IOM.
Edmunds, T., Gottey, A., & Forster, A. (Eds.). (2006). *Civil-military relations in post-communist Europe; Reviewing the transition*. Routledge.
Ekonomi, M., Sokoli, L., Danaj, S., & Picari, B. (2006). *Representative and the quality of democracy in Albania—a gender perspective*. Gender Alliance for Development.
Fukuyama, F. (1992). *The end of history and the last Man*. Penguin.
Funk, R. (2000). *Erich Fromm: His life and ideas*. Continuum.
Gëdeshi, I. (2010). *Global crisis and migration: Monitoring a key transmission channel to the Albanian economy*. IOM and UNDP.
Giddens, A. (2004). *Sociology* (4th ed.). Polity Press.
Gjuraj, T. (2015). *Nova demokratia*. UET Press.
Gross, P., & Jakubowicz, K. (eds.). (2013). Media transformations in the post-communist world (Eastern Europe's Tortured Path to change).
Horto, P., Leslie, G., & Larson, R. (1997). *The sociology of social problems*. Prentice Hall.
King, R., Mai, N., & Dalipaj, M. (2003). *Exploding the immigration myth. Analysis and recommendations for the European Union, the UK and Albania*. The Fabian Society and Oxfam.
King, R. (2011). Albania as a laboratory for the study of migration and development. *Perpjekja, 26–27*, 56–72.
Lukas, P. (1998). Albania: No instant democracy. *Sociological Analysis, 1*(2), 151–158.
Malaj, N., & Hoxha, K. (2009). Gruaja në perspektivë komunitariste [woman in a Communitarian perspective]. *Studime Sociale [Social Studies], 2*(2), 27–33.
Manoj, A. K., Sridharan, D., & Kulandaivel, M. (2016). Politics as a profession. *Open Journal of Political Science, 6*, 186–190. https://doi.org/10.4236/ojps.2016.62018
Marx, Karl. ([1875] 1980). *Kritika e programit të Gotës* [Critique of the Gotha Program]. In K. Marx & F. Engels, Vepra të zgjedhura, Vëll. II. 8 nëntori.
Marx, Karl. ([1844], 1976). *Economic and philosophic manuscripts of 1844*. In K. Marx & F. Engels, Collected Works, Vol. 3, 1843-1844 (pp. 229–249). International Publishers.
Merxhani, B. (2003). *Vepra [Works]*. Plejad.
Pëllumbi, S. (2015a). *Përmbysja e komunizmit [The collapse of Communism]*. UET Press.
Pëllumbi, S. (2015b). *Pluralzmi i dytë [The second pluralism]*. Morava.
Perrucci, R., & Perrucci, C. (2014). The good society: Core social values, social norms, and public policy. *Sociological Forum, 29*(1), 245–258.
Petrovic, M. (2013). *The democratic transition of post-Communist Europe*. Palgrave Macmillan.
Polyyzoi, E., Fullan, M., & Anchan, J. (Eds.). (2003). *Change forces in post-communist Eastern Europe*. Routledge.
Rupnik, J. (2002). Tranzicioni në Ballkan [Transition in Balkans]. *Politika & Shoqëria, 1*(10), 129–137.
Rupnik, J. (2004). *Balkans diary*. Kosovo Action for Civil Initiative.
Simic, O., & Volcic, Z. (Eds.). (2013). *Transitional justice and civil society in Balkans*. Springer.

Sokoli, L., & Gedeshi, I. (2006). Trafikimi—rasti i Shqipërisë [Trafficking—the Case of Albania]. *Instituti i. Sociologjisë.*
Sokoli, L., & Malaj, N. (2013). *Probleme sociale bashkëkohore [contemporary social problems].* Albanian Institute of Sociology & Morava.
Sokoli, L., & Hroni, S. (2009). Irregular immigration: The case of Albania. In L. Sokoli (Ed.), *Some present social problems of Albania* (pp. 115–132). AIS.
Sokoli, L. (2006). *Sociologjia dhe jeta e përditshme; Sociologji publike I [Sociology and everyday life; Public Sociology, I].* Albanian Institute of Sociology.
Sokoli, L. (2009). *Some present social problems of Albania.* Albanian Institute of Sociology.
Sokoli, L. (2010). Diferencimi social dhe varfëria: Shqipëria në kontekst eurolindor [social differentiation and poverty: Albania in the East European context]. *Studime Sociale, 4*(1), 5–15.
Sokoli, L. (2011a). "Sociologjia në Shqipëri–rruga e vështirë e lindjes, zhvillimit dhe institucionalizimit të saj" [Sociology in Albania–The difficult road of its birth, development and institutionalization]. *Studime sociale, 5*(1), 87–91.
Sokoli, L. (2011b). Some critical themes regarding the international migration of Albanians. *The Social Studies, 5*(2), 63–75.
Sokoli, L. (2014). The strange trajectory of changes in Albania: A comparative approach. *The Social Studies, 8*(1), 19–31.
Sokoli, L. (2015). Tranzicioni dhe pas tij: Problemet sociale vs. modelet sociale [transition and after: Social problems vs. social models]. *The Social Studies, 9*(1), 85–94.
Sokoli, L. (2022). *Problemet sociale bashkëkohore [Contemporary social problems].* Instituti i Sociologjisë.
Solimano, A. (2010). *International migration in the age of crisis and globalization: Historical and recent experiences.* Cambridge University Press.
Tarifa, F., & Sokoli, L. (2006). Applying Sociology to the construction of a democratic public sphere in Albania. *Sociological Practice, 8*(1), 83–90.
Tarifa, F. (1998a). East European puzzles: Old and new. *Sociological Analysis, 1*(2), 61–76.
Tarifa, F. (1998b). Neither 'Bourgeois' nor 'Communist' science: Sociology in communist and post-communist Albania. *Sociological Analysis, 1*(1), 27–39.
Tocqueville, A. (2002). *Demokracia në Amerikë [Democracy in America].* Fondacioni Soros & Kristalina KH.
Vullnetari, J. (2011). From communist 'gulag' to Balkan 'ghetto': Albania and its migratory policies. *Perpjekja, 26–27,* 34–46.
Winiecki, J. (2002). *Transition economies and foreign trade.* Routledge.

Prof. Dr. Lekë Sokoli is a Full Professor of Sociology at the University Aleksander Moisiu of Durres-Albania. He is also the President of the Albanian Institute of Sociology, founding President and current General Secretary of Balkan Sociological Forum (BSF), and Editor-in-Chief of the journal Social Studies. Since 1986 he has been engaged in research, studies, publishing, teaching and practice in sociology. He is the first doctor of sociology in the history of Albania. He is the author of 25 books, almost all seminal works in Albania, in theoretical sociology, sociology of social problems, and methods of research.

Chapter 5
Sociology in Belarus: Where To Go?

Larissa Titarenko

Each post-Soviet republic, currently an independent state, has some peculiar features in development of sociology (in the Soviet and contemporary periods as well). There are no similar ways of sociology in neighbouring states (such as Estonia and Latvia, Moldova and Ukraine, or Russia and Kazakhstan). Belarus is not excluded from this rule: its sociology has a challenging and difficult way of development. The main trajectories of its post-Soviet changes were not expected during the period of Perestroika and even during the first years of independence (1991–1994), when sociologists were in public demand for electoral surveys, several political campaigns, and the like. In this paper, we follow the so-called cultural, political economy approach in the analysis of sociological development, trying to explain how the Soviet and post-Soviet social processes (economic, political, cultural, etc.) have always structured sociology and influenced the meaning production in this field of study (Sum & Jessop, 2013). The reasons for the developmental peculiarities may differ in every post-Soviet republic. In the case of Belarus, they mainly relate to the nature of the political regime: Soviet and then post-Soviet. It seems paradoxical that one of the major trends of sociological development in the Soviet Union that was hardly tolerated by many democratically oriented scholars, that is, the sociological dependence on the power structures, remained the same in the newly independent Belarus. It was a common mistake of many intellectuals in the late *Perestroika* period to dream about a fast and rapid shift to democracy, together with the end of the Soviet regime. Only very few scholars could imagine that the road to freedom and prosperity might be long, not at all direct and easy. Even fewer experts could predict the possibility of the establishment of a new non-free power regime that would not be 'friendly' to social sciences and civil society but subordinate academia to its own rule. However, this happened in Belarus. Therefore, this paper aims to

---

L. Titarenko (✉)
Belarusian State University, Minsk, Belarus

© The Author(s), under exclusive license to Springer Nature Switzerland AG 2024
B. Roncevic, T. Besednjak Valič (eds.), *Sociology and Post-Socialist Transformations in Eastern Europe*,
https://doi.org/10.1007/978-3-031-65556-2_5

explore the sociological development in the Republic of Belarus, taking into account its Soviet economic and political background, current political regime, and several cultural internal and external factors influencing the major sociological discourses and the role of sociology in contemporary Belarusian society. In accordance with the cultural political economy approach (Sum & Jessop, 2013), we assume that the nature of sociology in Belarus is contingent and tendential. In particular, following this approach, we state that sociology in Belarus is (and has always been) meaningful and structured.

The first part of this paper will describe the Soviet structural and cultural background of the contemporary sociological development in Belarus. The second part is devoted to the emergence and becoming of the post-Soviet social-political situation that made it impossible to develop a free, independent social science with a significant status. Additionally, the factors that influenced this process will be disclosed. A third part of the paper will shed light on different discourses in which sociologists participated in the 1990s, 2000s, 2010s, and 2020s. In the conclusion section, the analytical outcome of this situation is presented.

5.1 Soviet Background of Contemporary Sociology in the Republic of Belarus

The key difference in the official status of sociology in the Soviet and post-Soviet periods relates to the fact that, first, Soviet sociology was a sub-discipline, subordinated to Marxist-Leninist philosophy as a part of its structure (1960s–1980s) and only empirical sociological surveys were allowed on the methodological basis of historical materialism. Therefore, the meaning production in Soviet sociology was subordinated to the principles and statements of Marxist-Leninist philosophy.

In the 1970s, a consensus about the structure of sociological knowledge production was achieved between the sociologists and the party officials who supervised social sciences. According to this model, the highest (methodological) level still belonged to historical materialism, while the second and third levels, special sociological theories and empirical research, represented sociology. This so-called 'three-part structure of sociology' was described and legitimised in the 'Working Book of Sociologists' (Osipov, 1976), the first handbook that provided basic theory and empirical information for sociological research. Sociologists consider this model to be a political tool that may help to institutionalise sociological autonomy in the future. However, on the surface of the situation, it appeared that sociology was still a part of Marxist philosophy, not even a 'small sister' but a servant that had to provide empirical data for philosophy. The leading Belarusian sociologists of this period published both in the philosophy and sociology spheres (Babosov, 1970, 1973; Buslov, 1965; Davidjuk, 1966, 1970). In sociological publications, the Marxist language of description of social phenomena coexisted with the structural-functionalist lexicon and methods incorporated from Western resources (Babosov,

1976). This coexistence was not officially declared, nor were the sources of functionalism: officially, sociologists usually referred to Marxism. Social stratification, social mobility, values, dispositions, roles, expectations: all Western sociological terms became common for Soviet sociology from the mid-1960s to the 1970s, including sociology in Belarus.

Nevertheless, there were no university departments to educate the young generation of sociologists. Professional education did not exist in Belarus as in the USSR in general, except for a semi-legal specialisation of a relatively small group of philosophy students at the Belarusian State University that was opened in the early 1970s and existed for only a few years. When this fact was discovered by Moscow bureaucrats from the Ministry of Education, the specialisation was closed, and the students' education returned to pure philosophy until 1989.

This early period of sociology in Belarus was researched and reassessed only later, in the 2000s, and the importance of this period for sociological development was recognised (Danilov, 2017; Institute of Sociology of National Academy of Sciences of the Republic of Belarus, 2017). In the Soviet and the early post-Soviet period, almost no research was conducted on the self-reflection of Belarusian sociology on its roots and Soviet background; however, many descriptive empirical sociological materials were published in the 1980–1990s (Babosov 1988; Davidjuk, 1988; Nesvetaylov, 1979; Shavel' et al.', 1983; Sokolova, 1989). The main sources of information on this period are the memoirs of the first sociologists who started their careers in the 1970s–1980s and continue to work in the field. Similar to the interviews with Russian sociologists of the 1960s collected by Boris Doktorov and published in the post-Soviet period as electronic books (Doktorov, 2013), Belarusian memoirs allow the current researchers to assess and reassess this period from the contemporary (retrospective and reflective) point of view and compare it with the current period of sociological development.

The lack of academic recognition of sociology in the Soviet era meant that no professional sociological journals in Belarus existed until the 1990s. The first sociological journal, *Sociological Studies*, was founded in Moscow in 1974, and all Soviet sociologists attempted to publish their empirical research results in it, as well as in other social-humanitarian journals (on scientific communism, philosophy, history, and demography). There were no academic degrees in sociology as well until the 1990s. Those who prepared dissertations based on empirical research had to defend them either as economists or philosophers.

Scholars involved in sociological surveys were extremely enthusiastic to develop a new discipline with its own mechanisms of meaning production. Probably, their enthusiasm was backed by the demand for empirical data from the party management and contributed significantly to the successful construction of the first scientific organisations in Belarus in the late 1960s.

In 1967, the scientific research laboratory of problem-oriented sociological studies (PNILSI) was opened at the Belarusian State University in Minsk. Its employees were graduates from the Departments of Philosophy and Economics, as well as some enthusiasts from other fields. Like everywhere in the Soviet sociology of this period, these people had to learn mostly from any sources that they could find (mainly in English) or adopt some methods or approaches from other social sciences (history and demography) or economics. They provided sociological recommendations to the local party managers, especially in the fields of social planning, competition, and city planning (Davidjuk & Pisarenko, 1976). They often had to organise methodological seminars for the staff to provide some sociological knowledge for all, and this type of education and self-education helped them to become more or less knowledgeable and skilful empirical researchers.

In 1967, the Institute of Philosophy and Law, a structural part of the Academy of Science (its Belarusian branch), opened a new sector of concrete sociological research (since 1968, a department). A few academic scholars became the first sociologists there. Such innovations became possible in both cases due to some social changes in a society that allowed the enthusiastic and energetic leaders of the new sociological branches to start this initiative. By doing so, like in the Moscow case, Belarusian leaders always used their personal, friendly relationship with the party and administrative officials (Communist Party Committee, leaders of the university and the Institute of Philosophy): they motivated the officials to take a risk and open new sectors or labs. These organisers of sociology in Belarus are currently considered as its 'fathers' who 'wrote its history': Professors Georgy Davidjuk and Evgeny Babosov. Regardless of their advanced age, they were active in the 1990s and had high respect among the professional community of sociologists in Belarus. Due to the formal status of Soviet sociology under the roof of philosophy and due to the Soviet approach to sociology as an 'additional structural branch' of philosophy (Professional'niy, 1987), the first generation of sociologists educated in Belarus had a mainly philosophical background (however, many other individuals with different background also joint the field because sociology attracted many scholars in this period).

Soon, in the early 1970s, new sociological groups and sectors were established that became the first sociological departments for research, practical education of newcomers, and learning from foreign experience. All these sectors, laboratories, and departments published their results as books and collected volumes in parallel to the analytical research reports regularly presented to the party committees. This was a common Soviet practice: almost all Soviet sociologists followed it (Firsov, 2001).

There was no deep theoretical research in the Soviet period of sociology separated from the empirical surveys. All sociological organisations regularly published monographs on the empirical basis of their surveys. The most popular fields included the sociology of youth, sociology of the family, social stratification, rural sociology (being a half-peasant country until the 1970s, Belarus contributed much to this field), industrial sociology, and the like (Davidjuk et al., 1971; Sokolova, 1980, 1984; Yurkevich, 1970). All these books used the so-called Marxist methodology and explained the data within the framework of historical materialism. The titles of the books in this period reflected this connection and also indicated the main topics of research. The authors of these books (e.g., Evgeny Babosov, Georgy Davidjuk, Galina Sokolova, Sergey Shavel', Nikolai Yurkevich, and many others) can be considered the forerunners of contemporary theoretical discourses.

The first textbooks on sociology were published in the 1970s by Georgy Davidjuk, *Introduction to Applied Sociology* (Davidjuk, 1975) and *Applied Sociology* (Davidjuk, 1979). The term 'applied sociology' was introduced in Soviet sociology for the first time in one of these books. The first Soviet dictionary of applied sociology was initiated by Davidjuk and published in Minsk in 1975 (Davidjuk et al., 1975). This dictionary became popular and was in use among the Soviet sociologists.

5.2 *Perestroika* (The End of the 1980s): Institutionalisation of Sociology

Like in the other Soviet republics, sociology in Belarus was finally institutionalised in 1989 when the Department of Sociology and a sociological speciality for students were opened at the new Faculty of Philosophy and Economics (currently the Faculty of Philosophy and Social Sciences) at the Belarusian State University. Also, in 1989, the Republican Centre of Sociological Studies at the Academy of Sciences (since 1990, the Institute of Sociology, National Academy of Sciences of Belarus) was established. Within the framework of this institute, some Belarusian sociological schools of thought were established (and continue to function). They are classified and named by the field of their research focus and include a school of social stratification and conflict (its leader, Babosov), a school of sociology of labour and economic sociology (Sokolova), a school of methodology and methods (Shavel'), and school of sociology of science (Nesvetaylov) (Institute of Sociology of National Academy of Sciences of the Republic of Belarus, 2017). Overall, Soviet sociology continued its development, and in Belarus, there were no indicators of the coming social crisis. Belarus had a reputation as the most 'calm' and fully 'Sovietised' Soviet republic where the people were tolerant and well-integrated into Soviet society. Therefore, the radical changes of the early 1990s were very painful and produced a kind of social shock or trauma of great social changes, in terms of Sztompka (2000). These changes can be viewed as a demarcation line between the past and present periods in Belarusian sociology that differ significantly.

The Soviet period is important because sociology in Belarus was established first as a structural part of Marxist-Leninist philosophy and, at the very end, as an independent social science. Sociology mainly functioned in accordance with Marxist principles and used the same mechanisms of meaning-making; however, many empirical studies were conducted based on structural functionalism. The first generation of Belarusian sociologists attempted to produce social data that might be useful for the improvement of social management in different spheres of life. It was a common hope among them that the results of their surveys would be implemented for the improvement of social life and the level of management. The public activity of Belarusian sociologists of this period was rather visible, as well as their academic activities in the 1970s and '80s, although this activity was controlled by the Communist party and subordinated to the power institutions.

5.3 Sociological Development in Post-Soviet Belarus

The social sciences in ex-Soviet countries faced tremendous obstacles after the fall of the communist system, both institutional and financial. The scientific and educational institutions remained weak after the fall of the Soviet regime. Overall, the processes of reconstruction of old institutions or, more often, the foundation of the new ones had to be carried out largely by Belarusian scholars who were educated under the Soviet system. As for the younger generation of scholars, its role in these processes was rather limited in post-Soviet social and economic conditions of the 1990s. In the face of low salaries and scarce funding, many talented younger social scientists left Belarus to pursue funding opportunities abroad. Social science in Belarus faced an internal 'brain drain' as did other ex-Soviet countries. Even those promising new young people with university educations who stayed in Belarus were more likely to opt for higher-paying jobs in the private sector beyond the academia or for PR activities in political campaigns rather than in the academy. Some of them quickly moved to Russia and later to other countries (mainly in neighbouring Lithuania and Poland).

Like in other neighbouring countries, social scientists in Belarus were confused about defining and especially critically assessing their new decreasing role in the changing society, as the processes of social transformation mostly required economists and political scholars but not sociologists to be involved. Therefore, in the 1990s, mostly economists, political scholars, lawyers, and journalists were incorporated into the spheres of political and public activities as advisers, analysts, or speech writers. However, none of these social scholars took leading positions in society, unlike some physicists who often shifted to the political sphere in the early 1990s and even later. It is also a paradox that scholars from the natural sciences played an important role in post-Soviet political life while sociologists 'lost themselves' in the instrumentally oriented market surveys that did not have significance for civil society. The physicists Shushkevich and Melenkevich and mathematician Kazulin became significant (although not successful) political figures in Belarus in the 1990s and early 2000s. As for the social scholars, unfortunately, even the economists could not become visible in Belarusian society. There were no economists in Belarus similar to Leszek Balcerowicz in Poland or Yegor Gaidar in Russia. Nevertheless, some historians and philosophers became well-known in the nationalistic intellectual circles when developing new discourses in the 1990s (on national history, national identity, Soviet post-colonial legacy, etc.). Some of these scholars (for example, the philosopher Akudovich) wrote a deep self-reflection on the role of liberal social science and liberal discourses in post-Soviet Belarus. Akudovich (1998) bitterly stated that these discourses are not visible, and the whole virtual intellectual community of liberal-democratic thinkers disappeared (in the case of Belarus, this means that many liberal thinkers either moved out of Belarus or remained unknown even to the academic public).

It is worth mentioning that sociology in Belarus did not pay serious attention to its role in the transitional processes, neither in the 1990s nor in the 2000s. There were no books or articles in which the authors attempted to assess this role and reflect on the sociological trajectories in Belarus. In the summer of 2017, when conducting interviews with some sociologists who came to this field in the Soviet period and had some professional achievements by 1991, it was found that they did not think much about the reasons for the practical decline of their discipline in the post-Soviet era. Ten interviews were conducted with the scholars who were in this field in 2017. All the materials are kept unpublished in the author's personal archive.

One of the interviewees mentioned that the academy stopped providing enough even for the standard of living in the 1990s, and he moved to the commercial market surveys (established a private firm) and was successful until the 2000s when the economic conditions for such business became hard, and he had to quit this field and returned to the educational institute.

A second scholar managed to combine successful business (not related to sociology) and academic surveys sponsored by foreign foundations; he did so successfully in the 1990s and the early 2000s. This scholar made an assessment (not published) of the reasons for general sociological failure in the post-Soviet time, saying that the main reason was a lack of charismatic leaders among sociologists in order for the field to become visible to the public and gain public support.

The third interviewee, a successful university administrator in the late 1990s to early 2000s, left science as soon as he understood that the new power structures controlled any scientific research similar to the Soviet time; he preferred to take an administrative position because of its higher financial level. A similar statement was made by another sociologist, a woman, who preferred to chair a non-sociological department for decades because it was more prestigious. One economist whom I additionally interviewed for comparison also confirmed that economic and political fields were in high demand in the 1990s while sociology was not.

None of the interviewees admitted that their own activities were too small to make any positive changes: they blamed the 'objective market conditions' in a post-Soviet society that depreciated the role of science and deprived sociologists of any social prestige. According to their assessments, social and political conditions decisively influenced the fate of sociology in the period of post-Soviet transformation, and the new cultural composition of social processes produced and promoted the social meanings and values that made sociology even less important than earlier. Thus, the post-Soviet sociological field was structured in a way that sociological analysis became meaningless for the new Belarusian power structures that strongly kept their ideological domination. Paradoxically, the interviewees positively referred to the Soviet period of sociological development as, in comparison with their current social status, the Soviet past provided many more opportunities for the scholars, in their opinions. Their social expectations born in the *perestroika* period disappeared by the early 2000s.

None of the interviewed sociologists shared the opinion that the new social and power systems needed any independent research. Also, they did not understand (or at least did not admit) that 'a democratic window of the opportunities' that was opened in the early 1990s (Titarenko et al., 2001; McCarthy et al., 2008) was closed rather soon in social science, public activities, and society at large. By the end of the

1990s, most sociologists lost their private orders, foreign clients, and personal interest in being active in the sociological field. They worried that the societal feedback was close to zero while their personal efforts to achieve some significant results were high. They gained good social and cultural capital, but there was no public demand to realise their knowledge, skills, and expertise. They often stayed in the field but stopped their academic and/or public activity.

In contrast to these opinions, the director of the Institute of Sociology, who started his sociological career in 1991 after finishing his career in the Communist party, asserts that sociology in Belarus is currently actively working on the orders from the administration that are activated during the period of election campaigns. He stated that the results of sociological research are demanded by the administration for decision-making, especially in the political sphere. He also admitted that sociology in Belarus was treated disrespectfully for a long time and that 'Belarusian sociology has lagged significantly behind both Russian and Western sociology' (Kotljarov, 2015). Such statements prove that post-Soviet sociology stayed subordinated to the power structures and provided career opportunities in Belarusian sociology, mostly for ex-party officials.

5.4 The Main Features of Post-Soviet Sociological Development in Belarus

When attempting to assess post-Soviet sociological development in Belarus, we can select the following features that characterise the political, organisational, international, and professional levels of this process:

Strong influence of the authoritarian political regime (domination of state control on research through the establishment of a special committee to approve or prohibit any national surveys; state selection of research topics to be funded, prohibition for the staff of the state organisations to participate in any civil activities, lack of academic freedoms, and very limited financial resources);

Lack of regular communication and network of sociologists on the national level due to the weak sociological association in Belarus, weak 'virtual professional community', lack of regular contacts with sociological associations in other post-Soviet states, and fragmentation of the existing communities of sociologists;

Weak communication with sociologists abroad on a global level (limited financial resources from abroad in the form of grants and fellowships for young and well-established Belarusian scholars), low level of translation and publication of foreign authors in Belarus (Belarusian sociologists usually rely on Russian translations), very limited participation in the activities of the International Sociological Association, European Sociological Association, and other international meetings as well as in the international surveys (European Social Survey, International Social Survey Program) due to financial reasons; rare invitations from the foreign organisations to visit them or participate in joint research (they exist on personal connections); and.

Poor knowledge of foreign languages, even among the young Belarusian scholars, and lack of institutional access to international sociological journals and other professional resources and databases.

Like Russian sociology of the same period, sociology in Belarus experienced a process of fragmentation of its sociological community. The basis of this differentiation can be interpreted on several criteria:

Structural inequality in the distribution of state resources among the sociological institutions and in their access to state-financed surveys. The government usually orders research only to selected state-owned institutions that are subordinated to it, while NGOs have no chance to obtain financial support for their research.

Limited chances to receive orders for research and finance from foreign organisations. All foreign orders (as well as Belarusian orders from NGOs) have to be officially checked by a special Committee on Public Opinion Research established in 2002 (similar to Soviet censorship) prior to research (Kotljarov, 2015). There is no law on 'foreign agents' as in Russia; however, only those studies ordered by foreign organisations that are backed by the officials appointed to this committee can be approved. In September 2023, all the projects with foreign financial involvement (including those in sociology) were closed according to Decree # 282 issued by the President of Belarus (About closing the projects, 2023).

Separation of the empirical surveys and theoretical research. Scholars involved in conducting empirical research are more financially secure than academic scholars who conduct theoretical studies. Only empirical surveys are needed by the state or commercial firms. Some empirical results have importance on the local level; however, such results are almost not known abroad because there is no professional need and/or financial stimulus for sociologists to publish their articles abroad.

The gap between the academy and universities. These two main centres of sociology in Belarus have poor professional ties due to the constant personal competition of their leaders, unequal funding, etc. A similar situation exists in several other fields of research and even in the opposition (non-state nationalist and liberal) camp: they cannot be integrated even within their own small professional community.

Division of professional functions between the institutions. For those who are employed by the state (almost all universities and the academy), the major function of sociology was reduced to the service to the authorities: they have to be ready to do any surveys on the topic that the government wants. They can apply only for financed research already approved by the state. The public function of sociology is weak. Professional theoretical study is not financed. Therefore, contemporary sociology is functioning mainly as an empirical service tool for the bureaucratic structures in Belarus, and its knowledge production is limited.

5.5 Periods of Post-Soviet Development as Steps in Sociological Evolution

The selection of different periods of the social-political development of Belarus in the 1990–2020s is important to demonstrate the level of dependency of sociology on the power structures and the subordinated nature of its development. Unlike the countries of Central Europe, after the gaining of the official status of the independent state in 1991, Belarus did not rid itself of the political and cultural remnants of its previous historical era. Therefore, the problem of the construction of the nation-state was addressed in parallel with the problem of the formation of national identity and the reassessment of its cultural heritage. Both foreign and Belarusian scholars have contributed to the study of these problems (Babosov, 1999; Marples, 1999; Tereshkovich, 2004; Titarenko, 2006; Mackevich, 2010). This field of study has become very popular among scholars.

The first period (1991–1994) is politically characterised by the existence of the Belarusian parliamentary republic oriented to democracy and market, international ties, and independence. In sociology, the empirical surveys on new current topics prevailed, and many small private firms were established, as well as the major think tanks of this period, such as NOVAK (NOVAK, 2012) and the Independent Institute of Social-Economic and Political Studies (IISEPS) (NISEPI, 2016). During this period, pro-Western discourses appeared and dominated, although not many sociologists participated in them.

The second period (1994–1996) started after the change of the status of Belarus: from a parliamentary republic, it turned into a presidential republic when the first (and still the only) president, Alexander Lukashenko, was elected. This period can be described by the existence of the mild presidential structure that immediately started to struggle with the nationalistic political opposition in the parliament and media). In sociology, different discourses on important topics for Belarus emerged, and sociologists participated more actively in them, including joint projects with foreign scholars (Titarenko et al., 2001).

The third period (1996–2001) was marked by the reinforcement of authoritarian power. It is politically known for expelling the members of political opposition from the parliament, closing the 'windows of democracy' in society, and discriminating against any oppositional thoughts and actions. The political isolation of Belarus on the international level started (Korosteleva et al., 2003). In sociology, it was a period of the legitimisation of the dominant (officially imposed) discourse on the national identity, national development, international relations, and the status of the Republic of Belarus (Danilov, 1997; Babosov, 1999). Other discourses continue their existence in the public discussions, intellectual gatherings of Belarusian scholars abroad, and in the private publication of books (Akudovich, 1998).

The fourth period covers 2001–2014. During this period, the authoritarian political regime strongly controlled society and public thoughts; political opponents were often arrested, and many nongovernmental organisations (NGOs) closed (Balmaceda, 2007; Manayev, 2004, 2006; Leshchenko, 2008). As a result, the international sanctions and political isolation of Belarus increased. These political events negatively influenced social sciences and sociology in particular. Foreign ties became even worse; free thought was prohibited and punished; academic freedoms were very limited. As independent electoral surveys were prohibited, some liberal and foreign-sponsored sociologists had to emigrate. During this period, sociology lost some important liberal-democratic institutions partly or totally sponsored by foreign organisations; the private sociological firm IISEPS moved to Vilnius, and the private research firm NOVAK significantly limited its activity and changed the topics of research before it moved to Warsaw; after losing state accreditation, the European Humanities University moved to Vilnius. Foreign influence was limited, and financial sponsorship was almost halted for scholars living in Belarus. Only those NGOs that conducted socially oriented programmes (like anti-trafficking and anti-AIDS) were easily registered and functioned. The liberal discourses in Belarus were pushed to a semi-legal status (scholars could discuss them in small private bookshops or arrange lectures in private universities without accreditation). Several social-political journals were founded and published in Lithuania in which sociologists could present their critical articles. At the same time, research legitimated by the power structures actively continued (Sharyi, 2001; Kotljarov, 2011; Rotman, 2011; Shavel", 2015), and some scholars published their views on the process of sociological development in the genre of semi-imaginary autobiography (Grishchenko, 2007).

The next period (2014–2019) can be described as an imitation of a 'democratic turn' in Belarus. Politically, these actions contributed to the removal of sanctions and made international relations between Belarus and the EU/US better. However, in sociology, nothing radically changed during this period: the professional structural dependency of sociology and the lack of autonomy remained unchanged, while state funding decreased. All research activities related to IISEPS were prohibited; its founder, Oleg Manayev, emigrated to the US, and the NOVAK founder, Andrey Vardomatskiy, moved to Poland. Under such political conditions, according to the surveys, the top values of the Belarusian population include family, social stability, and health, and exclude democracy and freedoms (Rotman et al., 2016). As Manayev (2017) stated, social stability and the paternalistic expectations of the population remained on top of Belarusian value orientations. Therefore, 'Belarusian society and the authorities are hardly threatened with serious changes in the foreseeable future' (Romanchuk, 2014).

The last (current) period has started in 2020. It is associated, first, with COVID-19 (temporary closure of some enterprises and offices, establishing distance methods for work and study from home, medical problems related to the pandemic that stimulated dissatisfaction of the population with life conditions), and, second, with the presidential election in August 2020, when many people went to the streets protesting the official result of the election. In fact, the last event initiated many articles by Belarusian scholars, published abroad for political reasons (Kascian & Denisenko, 2021; Mudrov, 2021; Titarenko, 2022; Vozyanov, 2021). The problem with the election was a huge gap between the official results and those that were calculated illegally and distributed non-officially by the opposition social networks (NEXTA and other Telegram channels actively functioning from Poland and Lithuania). After a few days, the protests were restrained and then stopped; many people were arrested and sentenced to different terms of punishment for their participation in the protests, among them a few opposition sociologists (e.g., Shelest and Mackevich). Overall, many intellectuals left the country and either continued their activities from abroad (like the former director of the Institute of Sociology Korshunov) or decided to leave the field of sociology. Those who stayed at work had to keep silent because when they expressed negative attitudes to the power structure in public or on the internet, they could be punished at any time. Thus, the chair of the Department of Social Sciences, sociologist Yury Bubnov, was arrested and sentenced in January 2023 after his critical statements were found on an illegal Telegram channel.

However, other sociologists preferred to adjust to the new situation. Since 2021, the Institute of Sociology has conducted several politically oriented surveys ordered by the government; their results were regularly published in the official media. It is difficult to evaluate the accuracy and reliability of data because there are no other organisations to carry out similar national surveys. However, due to the new anti-Belarusian sanctions related to the presidential election (2020) and then to the Belarusian political support for the Russian 'special military operation' (since 2022), almost all institutional contacts with the scholars from the EU were cancelled, and even individual Schengen visas for scholars became problematic due to the Western restrictions (if this scholar is not a victim of the political regime). All internet activities of the people, including sociologists, are under invisible control by the internal power structures, and many internet resources are prohibited. This situation is unfavourable for Belarusian sociology as its Western ties became extremely weak, professional exchange decreased, and joint projects and other activities almost disappeared. Partly for this reason, many non-government liberally oriented sociological firms lost their finance from abroad and were closed, while several NGOs were closed officially after losing accreditation in Belarus. Nevertheless, some non-governmental firms (earlier known as sociological ones) continue their market surveys because they have orders from Belarusian businesses (MASMI, SATIO, Mia research). Some expert centres continue their activities abroad (Political Sphere, Center of New Ideas, Our Opinion); however, their influence is very limited on the public in Belarus.

Currently, several factors continue to influence the trajectories of sociological development. On the political level, it is the authoritarian regime that keeps civil society and social sciences under structural and ideological control. This control is overwhelming in regard to media and institutions within Belarus. In higher education and social research, this control is getting even stronger than earlier. The absence of the national liberal-democratic traditions in societal life aggravates this situation. On the public and professional levels, sociologists cannot enjoy academic freedom, openly express their opinions, or publish research results. The authorities have strong economic and administrative instruments to keep sociologists prudent and refrain from the public expressing their civic positions. Therefore, public sociologists are rare in Belarus: the public function of sociology, as described by Burawoy (2005), is known mainly in theory. The fact that the main sociological organisations (institutions, centres, departments) are still guided by the old-style (educated in the Soviet traditions) cadres appointed by the contemporary state authorities did not contribute to the development of new discourses and the support of free thought.

5.6 Sociological Input in Societal Development and Public Policy

Having a weak status inherited from the Soviet past, post-Soviet sociology had almost no potential and no resources to influence the policymakers in Belarus during the early period of the post-Soviet transition. Sociologists survived after they started commercial surveys for private clients. When the country turned to authoritarianism in the mid-1990s, the state control of cultural, social-economic, intellectual, and political spheres of life increased. There was no public demand for sociology as a social or cultural reservoir of knowledge, and alternative discourses about the future of Belarus were not in demand by society. By the end of the 1990s, sociology returned to the previous Soviet position of a dependent social discipline mainly serving the state's needs. This role of sociology in Belarus can be traced by the following indicators:

Sociology mainly provides empirical (commercial or electoral) data ordered by the state institutions or foreign sponsors (as long as possible: until the early 2000s and then during the 'democratic turn' in 2014–2019);

Serious theoretical results (if any) are known for a limited circle of professionals; they are published in Belarus by private publishers or abroad; however, these results might not be known in the sociological community due to the limited (and state-controlled) access to internet resources and restricted access of the state institutions to the foreign literature;

Overall, the contribution of sociology in policy making, not saying about influencing politicians and their decisions (with some exceptions described above), is not significant.

Public activity of scholars is officially interpreted as their 'service for the state'; therefore, sociologists are not active and not visible (with a small exception of the heads of the sociological organisations) to the public. Sociologists rarely participate in civil society activities and do not initiate new public discourses.

As for the role of international organisations in promoting democratic discourses in Belarus, it is not sufficient. Thus, the European Humanities University (EHU), which was established in Minsk in 1992 with significant financial support from the EU and other foreign sponsors, was the only institution of higher education that promoted liberal values. This university was a 'home' for many research and public projects; its members developed democratic and liberal discourses on the national identity and civil society in Belarus. The EHU translated into Belarusian and published several foreign textbooks on the social sciences. The first sociological courses on gender and research on cultural studies were launched there. In 2004, for formal reasons, EHU lost the state accreditation and moved to Vilnius, Lithuania, where practically all the staff and students found a 'new home' and continued to receive funding. Several foreign-sponsored public journals of democratic and liberal orientation where Belarusian and foreign scholars could publish their findings in the fields of national history, philosophy, sociology, and culture and contribute to public discourses that contradicted state ideology were also published in Belarus and Lithuania (e.g., Arche, Political Spheres, Topos, and Fragmenty). In the early 1990s, some foreign-sponsored think tanks started their activities (IISEPS, NOVAK), as well as many small private sociological firms oriented to foreign clients. The Soros Foundation actively functioned in Belarus in the 1990s, which made it possible for Belarusian scholars to participate in international conferences and training abroad. Most of these activities stopped in the 2000s (a bit earlier than in Russia), so not only NGOs but social sciences lost visible foreign financial support. As the state has never sponsored Belarusian participation in international surveys (like ESS and ISSP), Belarusian sociologists could participate in such research only when they had other sponsors. The Belarusian government did not issue a law on foreign agents, as Russia did: it was enough to use structural factors to stop liberal activities at the institutional and individual levels.

5.7 The Main Intellectual Discourses

In general, the popular discourses that were developed in Belarus with some participation from sociologists are not 'special topics' only for this discipline. First, they were developed for the country: intellectuals and scholars from all social and humanitarian fields participated in them (with different results). These practices have been researched and assessed in Belarus in relation to national culture in general (Abushenko, 2003b). There was no serious assessment of the role of sociology in the development of the civil society. Also, there is no methodological analysis of Belarusian social discourses, and even their classification on some theoretical criteria does not exist. In 2016, the first steps in the analysis of the role of Belarusian civil organisations in the decision-making process (and especially in the changes in policy making) were made. As has been discovered, the input of sociological organisations in social practices and public policy is possible on the stage of discussion but not the decision-making (Chulitskaya, 2016).

As for the theoretical and methodological basis for public discourses in which sociologists participated, in the early 1990s, Western theories of post-Soviet transition, with all their strong and weak features and naive illusions, were in use in Belarusian social sciences. In the 1990s, mostly economists who spoke about the necessity of a fast turn to the market and the future fantastic benefits of the market transition for Belarus and partly political scientists were involved in such discussions. The main interest of these scholars related to the processes of democratisation and building a civil society in Belarus.

The major public and academic discourses of the 1990s were universalistic. They were brought into Belarus and other ex-socialist states from the West. Thus, a popular economic discourse was on 'gradualism vs big-bang economy'. In Belarus, sociologists were not in the public need, even when they wished to take part in this discussion. Another general discourse can be indicated as 'populist nation-building vs. liberal nation-building'. The state-sponsored sociologists contributed to the first one (Babosov, 1999), while the liberally oriented scholars developed the second discourse (Abushenko, 1999). This discourse became popular in Belarus in the 1990s; however, later, near the end of the 2010s, it functioned in the public consciousness as one of the most important for both camps, that is, state-sponsored and liberal sociologists. The discourses of the 1990s reflected possible ways of the state functioning and its future development either as a populist welfare state in which almost nobody would be rich, even if he/she would work hard, because of the redistribution of resources, or as an independent nationalistic state where every citizen can earn according to his/her efforts and capital, and only the old, poorest, and disabled people would have the state subsidy. To make the populist discourse stronger, the state camp referred to the Swedish welfare state model as a 'pattern for Belarus', ignoring the low economic level of Belarusian society. Since the 1990s, the mechanisms of promoting the state discourses included the active propaganda of these ideas in the state-financed journals and media, appointing to the leading positions in the state-financed institutions and universities only those who actively supported the dominant discourses and dismissing their opponents, strong criticism in the media ('getting labels') of those scholars who did not support the dominant discourses, and, finally, closing the non-state organisations promoting the opposite discourses (as it happened in the 2000s with the European Humanities University and later with the Independent Institution of Social-Economic and Political Surveys).

Those scholars (including some sociologists) who supported the opposite discourse stressed that private business would be a driving force for the prosperity of Belarusian society. In general, this camp used some mechanisms of promoting liberal discourses: funding the non-government (non-accredited) educational courses for young people interested in liberal education (the so-called 'Flying University' in Minsk); the presentation of new liberal books in the private bookstores; public lectures of foreign scholars in the private organisations in Belarus; annual congresses of Belarusian studies in Lithuania where liberal scholars from several countries presented their papers and communicated with young Belarusians whose participation was sponsored by the organisers; and critical assessments of Belarusian economic, social, and political actions made by scholars from the non-government think tanks (in the field of sociology, it was IISEPS and later BISS). Internet websites published much information for all kinds of users; however, in the 2010s, Belarusian authorities established strong control on the web resources. By now, all such activities have disappeared.

One more popular public discourse was on democratic freedoms and human rights vs. lack of freedoms and old-style (socialist) democracy. In the early 1990s, when liberal economists promoted the abstract model of democratic freedoms and human rights, it was shown by empirical sociologists that the majority of the common people in Belarus viewed human rights mainly as the rights to have stable jobs to earn, house to live and food to eat. In contrast, liberal economists talked about rights on private property, free elections, and similar. From the early 1990s, democratic freedoms and human rights have become popular in discussions (Danilov, 1998; Manayev, 2004). This discourse has not been popular in society since the 2000s, when it became clear to all scholars that democratic development in Belarus had been halted, and the well-established authoritarian regime would only use democratic rhetoric for ideological needs. While the official ideology assured the people that the Republic of Belarus is a democratic welfare state where its president takes care of all the needs of the common people, there was no room to continue the scholarly discourse on democracy, freedoms, and human rights for other sociologists (Korosteleva & Hutcheson, 2006). Since 2020, the situation has worsened, and the political events in 2022 only continued in the direction that had been selected by the Belarusian authorities.

Since the second part of the 1990s, one of the most important indigenous discourses was related to the alternative ways of the future Belarusian development. It was called 'Union with Russia+ vs the project 'From Baltic to Black Sea'. State ideologists and some well-established sociologists (Babosov, 1999; Lazarevich & Levjash, 2014) supported the state discourse, and some Belarusian liberal historians, philosophers, sociologists, along with the intellectuals from Poland, Lithuania, and Ukraine, supported and discussed in their own intellectual circles the ideas of a union that might compete with the first one. Since the second part of the 1990s, this political issue has become one of the state priorities, and the state ideologists developed it further. Sociologists received many orders to conduct empirical surveys to prove that the Belarusian population supported it and shared similar opinions with the state representatives (Rotman et al., 2005). On the other side, liberal intellectuals developed the opposite discourse of nationalist interests being better protected within the speculative Baltic-Black Sea Union. As in the other cases, sociologists were not active beyond the empirical surveys they conducted: they served as a 'small brother' for political scholars or 'a servant' for state officials.

Later in the twenty-first century, this discourse was transformed into an opposition of two political orientations that were discussed in the public: the possibility of joining the European Union or the Russian Federation as its part. Think tanks (especially IISEPS) conducted regular surveys asking this question, and the results of the surveys were constantly published on its website so that everyone could see them. There was no dominance of any of these orientations: sometimes, more people supported the European Union, and sometimes, they preferred Russia. Analytical reviews on this issue were regularly published on the Internet and the opposition media. Regular surveys organised by IISEPS sometimes indicated a higher level of pro-EU political and value orientations of the people that usually was assessed by the conservative scholars and politicians as manipulation of public opinion of the people in Belarus. Probably, such surveys contributed to the decision of Belarusian authorities in the mid-2010s to ban the IISEPS activities, and this think tank stopped the surveys (Nikoljuk, 2016).

A separate aspect of this discourse related to the discussion of Belarus as a part of the Western-Eastern Borderland that can partly share the culture of both neighbouring cultures but keep its own interests. This discourse was actively developed in the early 2000s (Rusetskaya, 2000; Abushenko, 2003a, 2004; Usmanova, 2004; Muradjan et al., 2014). First, a so-called 'creole' (borderland or post-colonial) national identity of Belarusians was performed by liberal sociologists to oppose the idea of 'citizenship' regardless of any cultural ethnic-national background. It was an opposition between the ethnic-national kind of identity and a civil idea that put forward a concept of the so-called 'people of Belarus'. This discourse was transformed later and merged with anti-Russian discourse. The 'creol identity' was interpreted as a dual one and consisted of two contradictory components: local (internal) and external (colonial). These parts co-existed for a long time and created a symbiosis that is difficult to overcome (Abushenko, 1999, 2003a). It was also recognised as typical and traditional for any borderland region, so some people living in the borderland regions in Poland, Lithuania, and Ukraine also share this identity (Hroch, 1996). The context of this discourse slowly became anti-communist and anti-Russian in the 2020s and shifted from sociology and history in the political and economic spheres, especially when the relatively high cost of Russian gas and oil caused the economic crises in Belarus.

Finally, in 2006, an important public discourse that had been functioning for more than 15 years since the late 1980s re-started: the construction of a nuclear station in Belarus. After the Chornobyl tragedy (1986), Belarusians were against any nuclear energy and were afraid of new radiation accidents (Babosov, 1996). However, massive propaganda in the media helped to slowly change the popular attitudes in Belarus: according to the monitoring data, from 2006 until 2015, the number of those who supported a new nuclear station increased from 25 to 50% (Shavel", 2015). It was enough for the government to conclude that Belarusians approved this station and the state policy. Sociological results contributed to the construction of a new nuclear power plant in Belarus, and authorities referred to the massive support of their decision as a 'popular approval' of their policy.

It is interesting to mention that, in 2023, when tactical nuclear weapons were returned to Belarus under the condition of the war in Ukraine and the potential military threat for Belarus from Poland, a NATO member, no new public discourse was started. Political conditions of contemporary Belarus do not produce a possibility of such discourses, as all the decisions have been made and implemented in practice by the authorities.

5.8 The Roles of Sociologists in Belarus

Out of all possible roles usually prescribed to sociologists—academic, educator, expert, public intellectual, politician, or civil society activist (Burawoy, 2005)—the largest group of sociologists in Belarus consists of educators who teach the new generation of students. In the 1990s, on the wave of existing sociological enthusiasm, young, talented students entered this field. Educators tried to teach them in accordance with the new reality and their own professional experience. During the 1990s, several foreign professors visited Belarus, and many grants and fellowship opportunities were available for the students. Unfortunately, almost all the best sociological students of the 1990s left Belarus, using the chance to study abroad and stay there forever. Currently, one of the best experts on Belarusian studies in the EU and Belarusian graduate, Elena Korosteleva, lives in the UK, and some other graduates moved to France (Belova), Canada (Pendrakovskaya), Spain (Parhomenko) or studied in the Central European University and shifted from sociology to the political science and public activities (Silitsky). Many graduates moved to Russia. Still, some young graduates stayed at home and joined departments of sociology that were opened in many universities. Later, in the mid-2000s, when some exchange programmes functioned actively for Belarusian students, another group of prominent students emigrated. In general, foreign programmes for the students officially aimed to help Belarus improve higher education worked as a legal channel of 'brain drain'. They were closed by the EU partners as a consequence of sanctions after the 2020 presidential election.

A second group of sociologists consists of the academics that are involved in research (mainly empirical, conducted by orders of the state or private clients). They are regularly occupied with data collection, but they do not deeply analyse data and make theoretical generalisations beyond the limits of the official theoretical and social framework and the official ideology aimed at consolidating Belarusian society and achieving social consensus. Therefore, they prefer to support the official discourses in their professional work. Consequently, many potential research topics became marginal (such as gender equality, social conflicts in contemporary society, public passivity, and low economic effects of state reforms). The scholars employed at the state organisations officially have no right to be critical of the current political and economic authorities, and the highest criteria to indicate the border between acceptable and non-acceptable criticism is the state itself (ministry of education, ministry of science, and the like). Before 2020, some private research organisations, such as the Belarusian Institute of Strategic Studies (BISS), or Belarusian scholars living abroad developed these 'marginal' topics: scholars in EHU worked on gender studies and borderland identity of Belarusians, and Korosteleva worked on democracy and political regime. As for Belarusian sociologists, in case of losing state employment, they are at risk of not being hired by any organisation (state or private). Therefore, even earning small salaries, they do not want to take a risk and think about alternatives to state employment. They mainly play a service role for the state collecting the requested data.

The third group consists of experts usually employed by market organisations. Nobody knows their job outside the organisation, and nobody knows which criteria they follow in their sociological expertise. They also play a service role.

A small group of public intellectuals has continued activities in the 2020s; it mainly consists of political scholars and journalists. Currently, there is no room for their activities as the new laws on media (2023–2024) allow the authorities to stop such activities and punish the people involved in them. However, these public intellectuals did sociological analysis, being oriented to the political rather than scientific goals (Mackevich). The emigrated sociologists lost their influence on the public discourses in Belarus, while for those who stayed in Belarus, any critical activity was a major risk. Therefore, sociology in Belarus exists mainly as a service (not a crisis) science (in the terms Rončević used in this volume).

5.9 Conclusions

Currently, sociology in ex-Soviet Belarus is weak and strongly dependent on power structures. Due to the EU sanctions against Belarus, Belarusian sociologists have lost previous contacts with Western colleagues, including finance of the surveys, exchange visits, fellowships, and personal participation in the conferences in the EU states.

The major role of Belarusian sociology differs little from that of the Soviet era: sociology is serving the authorities, doing research for power structures, and developing the topics adopted by the authorities. The state of sociology in Belarus resembles its state in the Soviet Union when sociology was officially totally subordinated to ideology and mainly served the communist party authorities.

The different feature of the current sociology is a lack of the previous enthusiasm of the 1960s–1970s. The cultural role in knowledge production is limited, as well as the role of other social sciences and humanities in Belarus.

In terms of Rončević (elaborated in this volume), the proportions of the four roles differ greatly. Most sociologists in Belarus are employed either at research institutions (or centres) or universities. Therefore, the biggest group of sociologists performs the academic role, that is, research and teaching. Both jobs are not well-financed: the median salary of academic staff is less than the average median salary in Belarus (Komsomolskaya Pravda, 2023).

Sociologists as experts and consultants are rare; usually, they are recruited from the research centres belonging to the state, as the research NGOs were closed after the presidential election in 2020.

Those rare sociologists who shifted to politics belonged to the liberal individuals who worked in the private centres. Currently, they are abroad.

Sociologists as public intellectuals also disappeared after 2020.

Finally, only the group of researchers and educators is relatively large; however, they have to serve the government and perform the roles prescribed by the Ministry of Education or the Academy of Sciences of Belarus.

Competing Interests The author has no conflicts of interest to declare that are relevant to the content of this chapter.

References

About closing the projects (O zakrytii proectov). (2023) *Decree # 282 adopted 08.09.2023 by the President of Belarus.* Accessed Sep 11, 2023, from https://president.gov.by/ru/documents/ukaz-no-282-ot-8-sentyabrya-2023-g

Abushenko, V. L. (1999). Filosofija Latinoamerikanskoy suchnosti (philosophy of Latin-American essence). *Fragmenty filosofii, kulturologii, literatury*, 3–4.

Abushenko, V. L. (2003a). Kreol'stvo I problema natcional'no-kul'turnoy samoidentificacii (creole and the problem of national-cultural self-identity). In *Antologiya suchasnogo Bel-aruskogo myshlenija.* Nevskiy proctor.

Abushenko, V. L. (2003b). Intellectual'nae pole Belaruskay kul'tury. Rolja intelektualau kul'turnaj samaidentyfikacii (intellectual field of Belarusian culture. Role of intellectuals of the cultural self-identity). *Pamiz, 3.*

Abushenko, V. L. (2004). Kreol'stvo kak ino-modernost' Vostochnoy Evropy: Vozmoznye strategii issledovanija (creole as other modernity of Eastern Europe: Possible strategies of research). *Perekrestki, 1–2,* 124–156.

Akudovich, V. (1998). *Mjane njama: Rozdumy na ruinah chalaveka (I do not exist: Reflections on the ruins of man).* Center of European Cooperation EuroForum.

Babosov, E. M. (1970). *Teyardizm: Popytka sinteza nauki i hristianstva (Teilhardism: An attempt of synthesis of science and Christianity).* Vysheyshaya Shkola.

Babosov, E. M. (1973). *Nauchno-technicheskaya revolutsija, communism, chelovek (scientific technological revolution, communism, personality).* Obshestvo Znanie.

Babosov, E. M. (1976). *Sotsial'nie aspekty nauchno-technicheskoy revolutsii (social aspects of scientific-technological revolution).* Belarusian State University.

Babosov, E. M. (1996). Chernobyl'skaya tragedija v ee sotcial'nih izmerenijah (Chernobyl tragedy in its social measurement).. *Pravo I ekonomika.*

Babosov, E. M. (Ed.). (1999). *Dynamika sotsial'nyh processov v uslovijay gosudarstvennoy nezavisimosti Belarusi: Sotsiologicheskiy analyz (dynamics of the social processes in the conditions of the state independence of Belarus: Sociological analysis).* Pravo I Ekonomika.

Balmaceda, M. (2007). Understanding repression in Belarus. In R. Rotberg (Ed.), *The worst of the worst: Rogue and repressive states in the world order* (pp. 193–222). Brookings Institution Press.

Burawoy, M. (2005). For public sociology. *American Sociological Review, 70*(1), 4–28.

Buslov, K. P. (1965). *Sotcial'nye izmenenija rabochego klassa Belorussii (social changes of the working class in Belarus).* Nauka I technika.

Chulitskaya T. (2016). Advocatirovanie v Respublike Belarus': Opyt organizatsiy Graz-danskogo obshestva (advocacy in Belarus: The experience of civil society organizations).. Office of European Expertise and Communication.

Danilov, A. N. (1997). *Perehodnoe obshestvo: Problemy sistemnoy transformatcii (transition society: Problems of the systemic transformation).* Harvest.

Danilov, A. N. (1998). *Vlast' I obshestvo: Poiski novoy garmonii (power and society: Search of a new harmony).* Universitetskoe.

Danilov, A. N. (Ed.). (2017). *PNILSI Belaruskogo gosudarstvennogo universiteta: K 50-letiju sozdanija (problem scientific research Laboratory of Sociological Studies: Towards the fiftieth anniversary).* Belarusian State University.

Davidjuk, G. P. (1966). *Sotcial'nye izmenenija krestjanstva Belorussii (social changes of peasants in Belarus).* Nauka I technika.

Davidjuk, G. P. (1970). *Struktura Sovetskoy Intelligentsii (structure of the soviet Intelli-gentsija).* Nauka I technika.

Davidjuk, G. P. (1975). *Vvedenie v Prikladnuju Sotciologiju (introduction to the applied sociology).* Vyshejshaja schola.

Davidjuk, G. P. (1979). *Prikladnaja Sotciologija (Applied Sociology).* Vyshejshaja schola.

Davidjuk, G. P. (Ed.). (1988). *Effektivnost' sredstv massovoy informacii (the effectiveness of mass media)*. Belarusian State University.
Davidjuk, G. P., & Pisarenko, I. J. (Eds.). (1976). *Sotsialnyi effect sorevnovanija (social effect of competition)*. Belarusian State University.
Davidjuk, G. P., et al. (1971). *Sotsial'nie problemy sela (social problems of village)*. Nauka i technika.
Davidjuk, G. P., Pisarenko, I. J., & Shulga, K. V. (1975). *Slovar' prikladnoy sotciologii (dictionary of the applied sociology)* (1st ed.) Vysheyshaja schkola.
Doktorov, B. Z. (2013). *Sovremennaja Rossiyskaja sotciologija. Istorija v biographijah i biographija v istorii (Modern Russian Sociology. History in biographies and biography in history)*. European University.
Firsov, B. M. (2001). *Istorija Rossiyskoy sotciologii: 1950-1980. Ocherki (History of Russian sociology: 1950–1980. Sketches)*. European University.
Grishchenko, Z. M. (2007). *Sotciologia zhizni, ili zhizn' v sotciologii (sociology of life, or life in sociology)*. Chetyre chetverti.
Hroch, M. (1996). From the national movement to the fully formed nation: The nation building process in Europe. In G. Balakrishnan (Ed.), *Mapping the nation* (pp. 78–97). Verso.
Institute of Sociology of National Academy of Sciences of the Republic of Belarus. (2017). Accessed July 15, 2017, from http://www.socio.bas-net.by
Kascian, K., & Denisenko, V. (2021). Society in the authoritarian discourse: The case of the 2020 presidential election in Belarus. *Intersections. East European Journal of Society and Politics, 7*(4), 124–138.
Komsomolskaya Pravda. (2023). *Stalo izvestno, skolko zarabatyvajut belorusy (It became known how much Belarusians earn)*. Accessed Sep 10, 2023, from https://news.mail.ru/economics/57080662/?frommail=1&utm_partner_id=441
Korosteleva, E. A., et al. (2003). *Contemporary Belarus: Between democracy and dictatorship*. Routledge Curzon.
Korosteleva, E. A., & Hutcheson, D. (2006). *The quality of democracy in post-communist Europe*. Routledge.
Kotljarov, I. V. (2011). *Sotciologija politicheskih partiy (sociology of the political parties)*. Belaruskaja navuka.
Kotljarov, I. V. (2015). *'U parushenne usih satcijalagichnyh kanonau my shukaem adkaz na pytanne jak bylechyt' hvarobu' (In violation of all sociological canons, we are looking for an answer to the question of how to cure a disease)*. Accessed July 15, 2017, from http://zviazda.by/2015/06/87616.html
Lazarevich, A. A., & Levjash, I. J. (2014). *Belarus': kul'turno-civilizatcionnyi vybor (Belarus: cultural-civilization choice)*. Belaruskaya Navuka.
Leshchenko, N. (2008). The national ideology and the basis of the Lukashenka regime in Belarus. *Europe–Asia Studies, 60*(8), 1419–1433.
Mackevich, V. (2010). *Pereocenka tsennostey v kul'ture I istorii Belarusi (revaluation of val-ues in the culture and history of Belarus)*. Logvinov.
McCarthy, J., et al. (2008). Assessing stability in the patterns of selection bias in newspaper coverage of protest during the transition from communism in Belarus. *Mobilization: An International Quarterly, 13*(2), 127–146.
Manayev, O. T. (Ed.). (2004). *Nezavisimye issledovanija v nezavisimoy Belarusi: V bor'be za real'nost' (independent research in independent Belarus: In struggle for reality)*. Vodoley.
Manayev, O. T. (2006). *Presidentskie vybory v Belarusi: Ot ogranichennoy demokratii k neogranichennomu avtoritarizmu (1994–2006) (presidential elections in Belarus: From lim-ited democracy to unlimited authoritarianism)*. Vodoley.
Manayev, O.T. (2017). *Belorusskoe obshestvo samo legitimiziruet vlast' Lukashenko (Bela-rusian society legitimizes Lukashenko's power)*. Accessed July 11, 2017, from http://www.dw.com/ru
Marples, D. (1999). *Belarus: A denationalized nation*. Harwood Academic Publishers.

Mudrov, S. (2021). Doomed to fail? Why success was almost not an option in the 2020 pro-tests in Belarus. *Journal of Contemporary Central and Eastern Europe, 29*(1), 109–120.

Muradjan, E., Salnikova, S., Titarenko, L., & Shirokanova, A. (2014). *Dinamika tsennostno-normativnoy sistemy I zhiznennye shansy: Opyt post-sovetskoy transformacii v pogranich'e (dynamics of the value–normative system and life chances: The experience of post–soviet transformation in the borderland).* European Humanitarian University.

Nesvetaylov, G. A. (1979). *Nauka I ee effektivnost' (science and its effectiveness).* Nauka i technika.

Nikoljuk, S. (2016). *Polagaju, NISEPI bol'she net' (I believe that IISEPS is no more).* Accessed Aug 25, 2017, from https://thinktanks.by/publication/2016/08/10/sergey-nikolyuk-polagayu-nisepi-bolshe-net.html

NISEPI. (2016). *Wikipedia.* Accessed Aug 25, 2017, from https://ru.wikipedia.org/wiki/НИСЭПИ

NOVAK. (2012). Accessed Aug 10, 2017, from http://www.novak.by/about

Osipov, G. V. (Ed.). (1976). *Working book of sociologist.* Nauka.

Professional'niy. (1987). *Kodeks Sovetskoy Sotciologicheskoy Assotciacii (professional statutes of the soviet sociological association).* Sovetskaya Sotciologicheskaya As-sotciacija.

Romanchuk, Ya. (2014). *Systema.* Tsennosti belorusov (System. Values of Belarusians). Accessed Sep 12, 2017, from http://naviny.by/rubrics/opinion/2014/09/10/ic_articles-410-186671

Rotman, D. G., et al. (2005). *Artual'nie problemy sovremennogo belorusskogo obshestva: Sotciologicheskiy aspect (actual problems of the modern Belarusian society: Sociological aspect).* Belarusian State University.

Rotman, D. G. (Ed.). (2011). *Aktual'nie problemy sovremennogo belorusskogo obshestva: 2005–2010 (actual problems of modern Belarusian society).* Belarusian State University.

Rotman, D. G., et al. (2016). *Tsennostnyi mir sovremennogo cheloveka: Belarus v proekte 'issledovanie evropeyskih tsennostey (world of values of modern personality: Belarus in the European values survey).* Belarusian State University.

Rusetskaya, V. I. (2000). *O sotciologii Pogranichja (on the sociology of the borderland).* Belaruskaya navuka.

Sharyi, I. N. (2001). *Nauchnaya politika v perehodnyi period (scientific policy in the period of transformation).* Belaruskaya navuka.

Shavel', S. A. (2015). *Perspektivy razvitija sotciuma (perspectives of societal development).* Belarusskaja navuka.

Shavel', S. A., et al. (1983). *Sovetskiy rabochiy: sotcial'nyi I duhovnyi oblik (soviet worker: Social and spiritual image).* Nauka I technika.

Sokolova, G. N. (1980). *Trud I professional'naja kultura (labor and the professional culture).* Belarusian State University.

Sokolova, G. N. (1984). *Kul'tura truda v sotcial'nom razvitii rabochego klassa (culture of labor in the social development of the working class).* Nauka I technika.

Sokolova, G. N. (1989). *Kul'tura truda v sotcial'nom razvitii technicheskoy intelligentsia (Cul-ture of labor in the social development of technological intelligentsia).* Nauka I technika.

Sum, N.-L., & Jessop, B. (2013). *Towards a cultural political economy: Putting culture in its place in political economy.* Edward Elgar.

Sztompka, P. (2000). *Trauma wielkiej zmiany. Społeczne koszty transformacji (trauma of a great change. Social costs of transformation).* ISP PAN.

Tereshkovich, P. (2004). Ukraintcy I belorusy: sravnitel'nyi analiz formirovanija natciy na fone istorii Central'no-Vostochnoy Evropy XIX—Nachala XX v. (Ukrainians and Bela-rusians: A comparative analysis of the formation of nations against the backdrop of the his-tory of Central Eastern Europe XIX - early XX century). *Perekrestki, 1–2,* 10–32.

Titarenko, L. (2006). *Natcional'naya identichnost' I sotcikul'turnye tcennosti naselenija v sovremennom belorusskom obshestve (national identity and social-cultural values of the population in modern Belarusian society).* Respublicanskiy Institut Vysshey Scholy.

Titarenko, L., John McCarthy, J., McPhail, C., & Boguslaw, A. (2001). The interaction of state repression, protest form and protest sponsor strength during the transition from communism in Minsk, Belarus, 1990–1995. *Mobilization: An International Quarterly, 6*(2), 129–150.

Titarenko, L. (2022). Digitalized protests in Belarus and symbolic walls: Some lessons relat-ed to youth. *Demokratizatsiya: The Journal of Post-Soviet Democratization, 30*(4), 473–483.

Usmanova, A. (2004). 'Konceptualisiruja pogranich'e: Ot kulturnoy antropologii k semiotike kul'tury (conceptualizing the borderland: From cultural anthropology to semiotics of cul-ture). *Perekrestki, 1–2*, 209–234.

Vozyanov, A. (2021). Grassroots sociology and possibilities to pose relevant questions about Belarus during the repression. *Topos, 2*, 175–196.

Yurkevich, N. G. (1970). *Sovetskaya sem'ja: Funktsii I uslovija stabil'nosti (the soviet family: Its functions and conditions of stability)*. Belarusian State University.

Larissa Titarenko is a Full Professor of Sociology at the Belarusian State University, Minsk, Belarus. She contributed in several books on social theory and history of sociology, including After the Soviet Empire. Legacies and Pathways (Brill 2015), The EU's Eastern Neighborhood. Migration, Borders, and Regional Stability (Routledge 2016), Sociology in Russia. Brief History (Palgrave Macmillan 2017), 25 Years of Transformation of Higher Education Systems in Post-Soviet Countries (Palgrave MacMillan 2018). She has published more than ten books and 500 articles in eight languages.

Chapter 6
Mission Impossible: The Role of Sociology When There Is No Society

Vedad Muharemovic

It is true that social organisations are not superhuman and omnipotent entities that entirely determine human behaviour but are processual and dynamic entities created by and reliant on continuous human action. Nevertheless, it is precisely these dynamic, historical contingencies that have ultimately created the situation wherein human beings require, and in some ways feel comfortable with, the prevalence of social organisations around them. The cumulative bureaucratisation of coercion is a historical process that, for the most part, does not go against the grain of the popular doxa: although it is essentially a coercive mechanism, it is not something superimposed on individuals against their will. Instead, it is a process that entails tacit and sustained support at all levels of society. It is a product of long-term human action and, as such, is much more overbearing precisely because it necessitates and grows on continuous ideological legitimation. To summarise, the bureaucratisation of coercion is cumulative because it is an ongoing historical process that involves the constant increase of an organisational capability for destruction; it is bureaucratic since it entails ever-expanding bureaucratic rationalisation in the Weberian sense, which originated in the military sphere; and it is coercive since it involves not only the control and employment of violence and the waging of wars but it is also able to internally pacify social order by establishing the monopolistic threat on the use of violence (Malešević, 2010, pp. 7–8).

Sociology is socially weak, and all the weaker, no doubt, the more scientific it is. […] Sociology cannot hope for the unanimous recognition enjoyed by the natural sciences (whose objects are no longer at all—or not very little—at stake in social

---

V. Muharemovic (✉)
Department of Sociology, Faculty of Philosophy, University of Sarajevo, Sarajevo, Bosnia and Herzegovina
e-mail: vedad.muharemovic@ff.unsa.ba

struggles outside the field), and it is condemned to be contested, 'controversial' (Bourdieu, 2004, p. 88).

6.1 Introduction

The contemporary social world is filled with a multitude of unpredictable social phenomena, relationships and their consequences that are difficult to control. We witnessed a change in social arrangements, a change in the very concept of sociality, a change in social behaviourism and the mode of 'control and power' in the period of the COVID-19 pandemic. We are witnessing the war in Ukraine, which in itself can have different implications, outcomes, and consequences. We witness wars in other parts of the world, and we skim the news and horrible events about them on social networks and the news because they are happening 'somewhere else'. The same situation existed when European Jews were liquidated systematically with the ultimate rational calculations and strategies throughout Europe, while the rest of the world, including those who until yesterday were compatriots and neighbours, looked at these events ignorantly as something that was happening 'somewhere out there', to someone beyond us, or the events were viewed with perverted delight and eclipse of basic concepts of humanity. We normatively said that Auschwitz must never happen again, but the empirical verifications were something else entirely.

> As Europe expands, diversifies, and intervenes more in the lives of its member states, it seems to be closing in on itself on its internal problems while not always playing a significant role in world affairs. What European can mention Europe's inability to prevent the massacres in Bosnia and impose a peace on the belligerents without a strong sense of shame? What European can be content with Europe when the names of Sarajevo, Vukovar and Srebrenica are pronounced? (Touraine, 2007, p. 37).

We witnessed an aggressive war and an attempt to eliminate Bosnia and Herzegovina as a historical European objectivity. Today, in Bosnia and Herzegovina, almost three decades after the war, the situation remains more or less the same, if not worse. What is the role of sociology in all this? Does it itself, as a kind of epistemic construction, construct some material and symbolic facts, or does it reveal their contradictions, or does it speak of some kind of *demagogic construction of reality*, the kind that the great writer Miroslav Krleža (1935) warned us about in his essay *Europe Today*?[1]

---

[1] These are some of Krleža's reflections on Europe: 'Standing up to knees in blood from its own slaughterhouse, Europe gives much attention to proper ways of tying a necktie, setting a tablecloth, to issues of napkins, oysters, fish, proper blanching of muskmelons and peaches, edible plants in general, or to painting, and having looked under the microscope all of its brain tissue cells, having counted several tens of thousands animal and human diseases, having observed life of plant lice, moving of stars and the invisible, having disembowelled all known animals: from a dog's head to Radiolaria, in the end, Europe today still does not know if its thinking with its own head or not, it is still inclined to believe that its way of thinking has divine, ethereal origin. [...] Typical European occurrence is that European biggest truths have been told on the gallows, at execution sites, in

6 *Mission Impossible*: The Role of Sociology When There Is No Society

In *Constitution of Society*, Anthony Giddens (1984, p. xvii) says that 'the main concern of social theory is the same as that of the social sciences in general: the illumination of concrete processes of social life'. Bosnia and Herzegovina is maybe the most complicated historical puzzle in the current social constellations and, at the same time, it is quite a challenging one for sociologists who tend to (in the Weberian sense) rationally understand (*Verstehen*) and not only to get an explanation (*Erklärung*) of the social processes and transformations. Bosnia and Herzegovina is a specific social, political, historical, cultural, and sociological reality. As a specific case study, for over 30 years, Bosnia and Herzegovina has functioned as a complicated and controversial social and political phenomenon and *sociological contradiction*. However, what is important to emphasise here is that this *contradiction* is a socially intentional construction that is imposed as a type of naturalisation, both on the citizens of Bosnia and Herzegovina and the international public. Furthermore, that is its greatest and the most dangerous ideological trap. In other words, talking about sociology means talking about conceptual and descriptive constructions that deal with contingencies, constructions of something we call 'society'. In the case of Bosnia and Herzegovina, we are talking about a complex social construction (state and social structure) that was created as a product of political actors who participated in the construction of what we call 'Bosnian society' beyond any rational, logical, ethical, geographical, historical, and symbolic logic. Such a construction is opposed to the constructions of other European societies (even wider), and if we can talk about some kind of rationality, then it is a *rational intention to naturalise the irrational* and impose it as a rationally acceptable social fact.

Since 1995, Bosnia and Herzegovina has existed as a paradigm of disharmony and contradictions, a paradoxical social state that, following the collapse of the socialist system and (soon after) aggressive war, transformed historical, geographic, cultural, economic, educational, political and mental structures and their logic in a revolutionary manner, by imposing a new social and state order as a product of subjectivistic and psychotic actions, opposing logic and history, carried out by certain political entities that were decisive and dominating participants who, as absolute sovereigns, managed to instrumentally transform their mental, psychotic and subjective intentions, wishes, aspirations, moments of current and impulsive decisions and personal frustrations, ideological preparations and simple hunger for power into a category of binding and forced social facts. Any type of social action has been and remains contingent upon such facts. In other words, the Bosnian experience is a paradigmatic example of the state in which individual, psychological, subjective intentions, behaviour, and actions have become objectified and imposed as a form of objective historical laws of this country

---

dungeons and during great ordeals, and those crucified and disgraced truths became European flags that have flown for centuries. Names that were humiliated and disgraced, marked by contempt and positive laws, names that were trampled as embarrassing by cynicism of public opinion became European lighthouses illuminated for grateful generations as only hope in the universe"' (see Krleža, 1935).

(Komšić, 2012). Bosnia and Herzegovina, as a state that institutionally, as well as outside institutions, represents individual and collective identities through groups of common values and obligations of all their members, exists in the form of an artificial framework since political ontology is focused towards eliminating all attributes on the basis of which it is possible to determine the distinctive characteristics of a society. First, political instrumentalisation and violent nationalism resulted in the legitimation of a state that incorporates values based on violence and genocide and pure ethnic and religious territories and viewpoints that dispute fundamental elements of a nation (in this case, of the nation and national identity of Bosnia and Herzegovina): historical territory and common historical memories, since the historical continuity of Bosnia and Herzegovina is disputed, along with any type of relationship with its heritage (war is an appropriate type of social conflict that is able to remove, among other things, all historical marks and cultural, material and spiritual heritage affirming that history), or, in its most benign form, they are treated as a form of 'false consciousness' or pre-history, while a type of 'only and true history' takes place after the end of the war and the constitution derived from Dayton Peace Agreement.

Thus, we may ask ourselves: Can contemporary sociology deal with these controversial aspects of social ontology and social phenomenology and is contemporary sociology capable of 'illuminating' all structural and functional key components to understand and have an active role in societal transformations since the end of the 1980s to the present day? Is sociology a social science that has a privileged field of competence? Whether the role of sociology in the post-socialist transformations is affirmative and critical or is it just a mere descriptive reception of the social and polity structure of the country that has experienced radical and revolutionary transformations of all its political, economic, cultural, even geographic, and mental components in a direction that does not correspond to its historical logic? To argue about the potentially significant role of sociology in the societal transformations of the Bosnian society in the post-socialist sense is inseparable from the transformations caused by the war in 1992–1995 and the Dayton Agreement that has stopped the war and has imposed itself as the Constitution of Bosnia and Herzegovina (*Dayton Agreement as a Bosnian Politeia*) and it is also inseparable from all those consequences of the social and polity organisation of this country that is determined by this agreement and post-war processes. Therefore, the role of sociology in the post-socialist transformations of Bosnia and Herzegovina is closely related to the ways these transformations have occurred. We are not dealing with the 'transferable causality' (Komsic, 2017), where we can explain the transition from socialism in some quite indefinite post-socialist sociopolitical and cultural order since this transition did not occur spontaneously and gradually. Quite the contrary, it occurred through military, ideological and violent means, through a war that tended to finally shape national states at the expense of Bosnia and Herzegovina as a state, by the total elimination of its *Objective spirit* in a Hegelian sense and by the destruction of its multi-religiousness, plurality, and its distinctive history.

6.2 Sociology of a Depressed and Fragmented Society

To discuss the meaning and the significant role of sociology implicates the discussion of the ability and potentiality of sociology to display some answers related to:

- Key issues of the contemporary post-socialist constellations
- Issues about the meaning of the social and political actors that caused these rapid transformations
- Issues about the meaning of modes through which Bosnian society is getting into the present
- Issues on its deliberate cleavage into ethnoreligious components

It also raises the question of the rationally constructed social reality of Bosnia and Herzegovina as a highly complex societal and national community and the *intentional absence* of elements that every other country has (single national language, national culture, national educational system, national associations, national territory, and its symbolic and material signifiers, etc. along with the recognition and acceptance of other cultures, values, lifestyles, languages, religions, etc.). Hence, it raised the question about ideology focused towards the idea of 'autonomy', 'unity', and 'identity' of one nation and the absence of this ideology in the case of Bosnia and Herzegovina (Smith, 1991). Within this, it also highlights the questing concerting its economic system, privatisation, the transformation of social and state property into private property,[2] problems of emigration and demographic changes caused by war and post-war processes, among other issues. The transition from Socialism to something quite uncertain must (even more so) serves as a challenge for Bosnian sociologists and sociologists in general since they are directly affected and immersed in these sociopolitical puzzles. Can sociology be able to participate in these transitions, and what is the course of these transitions?

---

[2] Martina Fischer, for example, wrote that 'the privatisation of social property took place in the political vacuum caused by war. The process of privatizing the former state-owned firms and social property was marked by large-scale corruption. [...] Timothy Donais, an analyst from York University, states: 'What international advisors originally envisaged as an apolitical, rapid and orderly transfer of assets from public to private hands has become a corrupt, ethnicised, and protracted struggle for power, which has done little to stimulate economic growth or promote interethnic reconciliation'. On the contrary, economic transition 'has exposed rifts not only between the goals of the international community and local political actors but also among international agencies. It has ultimately produced little in the way of concrete benefits for ordinary Bosnians' (Fischer, 2007, pp. 448–449).

Despite the fact that the term 'international community' (something like the term 'humanity') itself is not clear from my point of view, and is rather general and elusive, it is questionable to what extent it is possible to talk about an exclusively *innocent* and *utopian-optimistic* attitude of the 'international community', 'international advisers' and international agencies on the issue of the transformation of state and social property into private property in Bosnia and Herzegovina, in the sense that the outcome and consequences of such systemic privatisation with the economic desubstantialisation of the state could not be anticipated. The final implication is a permanent dependence on transnational institutions and 'credit slavery' that will reflect on the lives of the future generations of Bosnians and Herzegovinans.

To argue about these issues and the role of sociology in this 'societal puzzle', something that is totally basic and brutally certain, needs to be taken into account.

> The degree of wartime devastation may be illustrated using the following indicators:—The total number of recorded deaths, i.e. persons killed for whom reliable evidence exists with names and surnames, from 1992 to 1995 was 113,000; [...] The number of missing persons still being sought is around 40,000; [...] The number of persons who fled abroad because of the war and have not returned to BiH is around 450,000; [...] The Foreign Trade Chamber of BiH estimates the extent of wartime damage to personal and business assets to be in the range of 30 to 50 billion USD; and [...] The lost GDP in the four-year period is about 40 billion USD (pre-war GDP of BiH was some 10.3 billion USD in 1991 USD terms) (Zupcevic & Causevic, 2009, p. 13).

So, to stress the impact and the role of sociology in the societal transformations of Bosnia and Herzegovina, there are some basic facts that cannot be neglected for scientific, methodological and, finally, historical and humanistic reasons.

The role of sociology in the societal transformations of Bosnia and Herzegovina from *one time/social unit* (socialism) to *another time/social unit* (post-socialism) necessarily implicates a discussion on the ability of sociology to adequately understand (if not even participate) the phenomenon based on the conflict and violence that functions as a totally normal and rationally accepted social fact and as a rationally accepted set of social actions. These social facts that originate in conflict and violence have a *compelling* character on all citizens and social actors of Bosnia and Herzegovina in the Durkheimian sense.

> The danger primarily arises from the fact that in the case of Bosnia and Herzegovina, the international community accepted and legalized violence as a method of solving political, ethnic and historical issues, thus practically giving *carte blanche* to any similar future effort and method of solving such issues (Filipović, 2003, p. 177).

The end of the 1980s and the beginning of the 1990s was a period of social and political crisis. The collapse of socialism coexisted with the disappearance of Marxism as a privileged and most relevant discipline that describes, understands, supports, and anticipates the future of social reality and has its corrective meaning. It served as an ideological and educational perpetuation of a dominant political and social discourse that, in the political ideology of socialism and communism, sees an eschatological path toward the final effectuation of the *Weltgeist*: equality, freedom and righteousness in the era of the Socialist Millennium. Sociology no longer existed as a mere service within the dominant vocabulary of classless society, self-governing socialism, and the relations between civil versus Marxist sociology but transformed itself toward the social science that saws its meaning and autonomy in a critical reflection of new social relations shaped by a market economy, democracy, and changes in worldviews in general. The fall of the Berlin Wall, on the symbolic level, represents this transition from one temporal and historical unit to another. On the social and political level of Bosnia and Herzegovina, this collapse implied a democratic process within which the national political parties (which acted on behalf of national self-determination) had one single enemy: Communism as a brute that needed to be eradicated from the historical map of Bosnia and Herzegovina.

However, the absence of this brute did not eliminate a series of events, facts and phenomena which appeared shortly afterwards.

So, where does sociology stand within this context? Is it possible to speak about sociology as an emancipatory science that acts autonomously, and can sociology offer some alternative solutions and explanations of social and political challenges contrary to those actions originating in dominant political discourses (discourses of ethnoreligious separation and exclusiveness), or is it just has a mere descriptive character in a sense that sociology closes itself within the framework of the academic community and faculty lectures with no influence on the processes of deliberative democracy and others?

6.3 Sociology as a Science of Fragmented Society and Isolated Personal/Group Activity

The central problem with the role of sociology in the societal transformations of Bosnia and Herzegovina lies not only in the state in which political ontology tends to subject all spheres of social ontology to its own interests, intentions, projects, and constructions. We are not dealing only with the state structure in which social science is treated as a mere instrumental activity of political elites; states in which some of the elements of social science are highly constructed and determined by the political ontology and dominant political ideologies and discourses. In these states, social theories (including those of sociology) perpetuate a description of social reality from the matrix of dominant political practices and values within which every kind of critical distance has only ephemeral and sporadic, almost incidental meaning. The specific position of sociology within Bosnian political and social ontology lies in its academic, professional, and institutional fragmentation that generates academic, professional and institutional activities and practices that are often mutually excluded, isolated and opposite. Their interactivity is effective on the level of discourses of the impact and the role of classical or/and contemporary sociology on societies in some universally accepted manner (on the level of Wallerstein's 'Culture of Sociology'). However, when we deal with the discourses on social ontology and phenomenology, social structure and social actions on the level of one single social fact that as an 'institutional fact' is appointed as 'Bosnia and Herzegovina' then we deal with the situation in which there is no kind of *sociological collective intentionality* that can be objectified into a sociologically institutional form that would have the power to illuminate Bosnian social organisation and its social reality in general. There is no single national strategy that could be sufficiently potent to efficiently deal with certain and concrete economic, political, cultural, and societal issues in the level of academic activity, as well as organised critical argumentative and communicative practice, which is an issue that could be solved and through which Bosnia and Herzegovina can finally become a part of a rationally constructed and politically stable social and political subject analogous to those states and societies that are part of the European Union (EU), for example. Instead of strategic and interdependent action of political actors, intellectuals (sociologists in this sense) and citizens on institutional and non-institutional levels, there are only isolated efforts of sociologists as insiders who attempt to accentuate all contradictions that this country faces every day:

> [...] the political ontology of Bosnia and Herzegovina and its social ontology are in collision with what is rationally acceptable and with the historically achieved model of a developed society and politics in Europe. Prior to that, they are in an internal collision with the logical structure of a normal society, with the functioning principles of any practice as part of which man purposefully uses certain means for achieving certain objectives. In the background of the creation of these collisions (external and internal) lies dogmatism, and it is always connected to the absolute concept. This means that the political ontology of Bosnia and Herzegovina is formulated on tautologies and contradictions, on the opposition of 'absolutely true' (tautological, hyper-national) and 'absolutely untrue' (contradictory, anti-national) ideological concepts, rather than on possible forms of existence of a normal society compatible and convergent to the communities of nations united within the European frameworks of partnership and cooperation (Ibrulj, 2008, p. 205)

.Why do we go backwards to a level of social facts produced by war and violence? Because sociology cannot (even if it wants to) escape the issues of its own subject matter, and in this case, these are the social facts and social actions that determine the individual and collective identities of Bosnia and Herzegovina, the practices and habits of these identities, their sequences in everyday life, their routines and behaviours that are shaped by the existing social and polity structure of this country. To display Bosnia and Herzegovina as a complex and *intentionally contradictory social fact* (in a Durkheimian sense of *social facts*) implies pointing to a structural fragmentation and artificial sociopolitical construction that affects the fragmentation of the educational system, cultural system, economic system, health care system, administrative system (it implies the fragmentation of territory, language, culture, norms, values and finally the fragmentation of symbolic interactions and practices). The final goal of some political and intellectual elites is to *plant these social facts as natural facts* with unquestionable and almost axiomatic characterisations. Since there is an absence of a single national territory, single collective representations, single language, or single educational system, there is *eo ipso* an absence of academic community or academic institutes, associations and organisations that would represent a single platform oriented toward the representation of Bosnia and Herzegovina as a functionally organised state composed with attributes similar to those of the states in the region, EU and worldwide.[3] So, to argue about a specific

---

[3] Sociology as an academic discipline is not excluded from these tendencies and projects. Such political and ideological programmes resulted in the creation of 'institutional facts' disputing or imposing as 'institutional facts' of the same value as 'institutional facts' and other types of distinctions that represent Bosnia and Herzegovina. Such facts are particularly strong as a form of cultural indicators (ethnic and symbolic interpretation of nations and nationalism is very significant here) which socialises, internalises and cultivates (in the sense of internalization-externalization-objectification as Berger and Luckmann have pointed out) the notion of separate state within Bosnia and Herzegovina in a most efficient manner. That is why it is no accident that (to name but a few examples) along with the Academy of Sciences and Arts of Bosnia and Herzegovina,

role of sociology in the societal transformations of Bosnia and Herzegovina, sociology itself cannot be viewed only as a scientific platform of rationally composed social facts and interpersonal relations that needs to be transparent in a methodologically right manner, in a manner of this or that sociological theory or sociological discourse. This means that sociology cannot rely solely on consensual practices and distinctively personal and group behaviours through which sociology explains objective social facts and consequences. In stable states and societies, this can be the case, but in all other social relations (in which we testify contradictions, obstructions, the absence of citizenship and the direct relation of citizenship to his/her motherland/fatherland and political objectivity in the form of the state, similar to those states in Europe) the position of sociology is quite different. So, the first dimension of reality that sociology deals with is the one in Schutz's manner: 'Living in the world, we live with others and for others, orienting our lives to them. In experiencing them as *others*, as contemporaries and fellow creatures, as predecessors and successors, by joining with them in common activity and work, influencing them and being influenced by them in turn—in doing all these things, we *understand* the behaviour of others and assume that they understand ours' (Schutz, 1967, p. 9).

The second dimension of reality that sociology deals with is the sociopolitical reality of Bosnia and Herzegovina. This constructed reality (post-Dayton reality) is, in fact, dispersed in fragmented realities, and in many cases, these fragmented realities are monadic and mutually excluded.

Thus, the specific role of sociology in this concrete case study cannot be reducible to a mere realm of understanding the *behaviours of others* and vice versa, at least for three main reasons:

the *Other* (to live with others and for others) is never an abstract personality or a group; the Other is different, and over the *other identity*, I can know *my own identity*.

National Museum of Bosnia and Herzegovina, the anthem of Bosnia and Herzegovina, the flag of Bosnia and Herzegovina, National Theatre etc., there are also Academy of Sciences and Arts of the Republic of Srpska, Museum of the Republic of Srpska, anthem of the Republic of Srpska, flag of the Republic of Srpska, Museum of Contemporary Art of the Republic of Srpska, National Theatre of the Republic of Srpska. In addition, National Library of Banja Luka from 1935 was transformed into National and University Library of the Republic of Srpska. Other areas, for example, the educational system, is completely fragmented in the territory of Bosnia and Herzegovina, and the concept of national educational system of Bosnia and Herzegovina is definitely non-existent. While there is no educational system of the Federation of Bosnia and Herzegovina, but only a series of systems on level of Cantons, the Republic of Srpska has unitarily created educational system in its entire territory (which itself is one of the characteristics of a national state) with strong religious indicators that also have an important role in a form of religious protectors of an entire entity. Patron saint of the Republic of Srpska is Saint Archdeacon Stephen, and institutions of high education, faculties and academies have their own 'Slava' ('celebration'). For example, *Slava of the University of Eastern Sarajevo* is on 24 May, Saints Cyril and Methodius' Day. Not only does this show the lack of university's independence with regard to political and religious system, but it also shows strong sacralisation and ethnic and religious homogenisation of all elements of society and state in general. (For more on *Slava* of the University of East Sarajevo, see University of East Sarajevo n.d.-a., n.d.-b, n.d.-c).

This common notion is an *intentionally constructed social fact* on which social actions depend; that is to say, the notion about other is always the notion of other as someone who is shaped by this or that political, ideological, and religious identities and interests. In the Bosnian context, certain ideologies want to represent the other as something that is not near me, for me and with me (as a part of my identity) but as something that needs to be excluded, eliminated, ignored, or even be substituted with the other in the sense of someone who is ideologically, politically, religiously and in the sense of the same interests identical to me. So, to speak about the *Other* as someone who needs to be *understood* means to speak about the *Other* who is either an *enemy* (or a *stranger*) or the *Other* as someone who is *identical to me* and my own group identity. The other is not my neighbour but someone who can be miles away but shares the same ideological or some other values and worldviews.

The process of *understanding* that sociology needs to be aware of is not one-dimensional in the sense that it is always cognitively and socially correct. As Bourdieu accents, 'the established order' and its 'symbolic effect that they exert' can be 'misrecognised and recognized' (Bourdieu, 1990, p. 135). So, to speak about social facts, we need to take into account 'that these realities owe to the fact that they are objects of cognition (albeit a misrecognition) within the very objectivity of social existence' (Bourdieu, 1990, p. 135). What is more significant (and in addition to this) is that to *understand* social facts and social actions, we need to take into account the *intentional or deliberate misunderstandings of the Other* (personal and group identity). Sociology must take this reality into account in order to be functional in understanding and analysing societies that are intentionally or violently ruptured or transformed into something quite indefinite, which is often termed a *transition society*.

Sociologists can be active reflexive subjects capable of properly *understanding* how society works and what is crucial for society to be not only a new one but a better one (in the sense of plurality, inclusivity, and the acceptance of universal moral norms) especially those involved in societal transformations from one political ideology and a type of social and political order to another. However, we must not neglect the fact that without some form of deliberative democracy through social movements and organisations, sociology (and other social sciences and humanities) is condemned to a mere theoretic reflection. In this sense, the *capacity to understand* needs to be combined with the capacity to make social behaviour and social action correspond to these understandings and objective meanings. In other words, a social fact X *can be properly understood and/or explained*, but this is not the only condition for transformation processes since the political epistemology operates as a self-sufficient criterion of social reality.

Therefore, social fragmentation follows the fragmentation of all its components. There are no sociological associations on the level of national organisations, and there is no research found that could act outside of the current dominant political order of this country. The fragmented image of Bosnian society implies a fragmented image of science, scientific research, and sociology in particular (as a science of these facts and actions) is not immune to these issues and trends. As Ivan Cvitković, a prominent sociologist, has pointed out: 'We have no sociological journal (unlike colleagues in Serbia, Croatia, Slovenia). At one time, we had an Association of Sociologists with the highest number of members compared to nine republic associations in Yugoslavia. Today, only the Association of Sociologists of the Republic of Srpska operates. In the Federation of Bosnia and Herzegovina, there are no associations' (Cvitković, 2010). This fragmentation, on the one side, the absence of national associations and the absence of a single and organised academic and professional space and engagement is not a matter of coincidence, arbitrariness, and spontaneity. Quite the contrary, we are dealing with organised actions oriented to eliminate every kind of national unification in the sense of the *distinctively nationally recognised Bosnian society*. Thus, it is not accidental that, on the one side, there is a Section of social sciences of the Academy of Science and Art of Bosnia and Herzegovina (within which some sociologists act and attempt to argue on the level of national unity analogous to those unities in other countries) that are financed on the level of the Kanton Sarajevo (the Kanton is an administrative, socio-political and economic unit of the Federation of Bosnia and Herzegovina) and exists on a mere normative level as a matter of the state of Bosnia and Herzegovina. This academy attempts to affirm the idea of Bosnian history as an idea of continuity and to represent the idea of historical and social distinctiveness of this state; within this, social scientists and sociologists are attempting to deal with the social issues that shape social reality today. On the other side, there is a Sociological Society of the Republic of Srpska[4] as a part of the system that tends to the organisation and the construction of all material and symbolic elements that could be able to represent national distinctively and its political objectivation in the form of a national state. It is interesting that the Sociological Yearbook is published by the Sociological Society of the Republic of Srpska and the Serbian Sociological Society (Republic of Serbia).

Contrary to an absence of institutionally organised action at the level of a single academic space, a single educational system, or a social organisation such as the Association of Sociologists of Bosnia and Herzegovina, or something similar to that, there is an engagement of secluded individuals who are attempting to influence societal transformations and to be their integral and active part. These are the individual researchers/sociologists who are attempting to shape the public sphere and to be engaged within the sphere of civil society as a platform for redefining and reconstructing social reality or to indicate the factors that are necessary for these reconstructions. They act within the faculties as university professors and researchers with the intention of creating an environment of scientific action independent of political impacts and dominant political and ideological discourses. One positive example is the Scientific-Research Incubator (ZINK), the first Bosnian incubator

---

[4] On the home page of *Society* it is stated, among other things: 'Today, the membership of the society consists of sociologists from Republika Srpska, Serbia and Montenegro, and colleagues from the Federation of Bosnia and Herzegovina, Slovenia, Macedonia, Croatia, Sweden, USA, Mexico, and other countries participate in our activities'. Coincidentally or not, the entity of the Federation of BiH is classified as a *state* analogous to other mentioned states, which, reversibly, can be interpreted as a way of treating another entity (Republika Srpska) as a *potential or actual state* (see Sociological Society of the Republic of Srpska, n.d.).

that was organised at the Department of Philosophy and Sociology with Nijaz Ibrulj as its founder. This incubator aims to coordinate with all organisations and institutions in Bosnia and Herzegovina that have the capability and means to employ experts in their projects that could lead to significant social progress and transformations. Its main goal is to affirm young researchers as critically organised actors and scientists (among which students of sociology, assistants and assistant professors have a significant place) to have an active role in societal and cultural transformations and decision-making processes on the level of education, politics, culture, economy and issues that concerns the integration of Bosnia and Herzegovina in the EU, diaspora issues, migrations and all other challenges which stand in front of the Bosnia and Herzegovina today, including the uncertainties that faced us all.

6.4 One Example of Engagement in Societal Transformations Affecting the Return of Dignity of Sociology and Its Application in the Public Sphere

There are some persons who, as social actors and as intellectuals, need to be mentioned here. Muhamed Filipovic, although not a sociologist in the sense of formal education, had an enormous influence on the formatting of the study of Sociology at the Faculty of Philosophy in Sarajevo and afterwards at the Faculty of Political Sciences in Sarajevo. He also contributed to an affirmation of the journal for social issues. *Pregled*, he organised teaching processes in sociology (especially in the fields of methodology, industrial sociology, and sociology of culture) and served as a mentor for several master's and doctoral dissertations in sociology. Filipović is also known for his public and political analysis and appearances, and he served as ambassador of Bosnia and Herzegovina in the United Kingdom and Switzerland. His philosophical and sociological knowledge enabled him to perform and witness a series of events that were crucial for the existence of Bosnia and Herzegovina during the war and postwar period. His activity (teaching, scientific interest, political and diplomatic actions) has influenced the popularisation of sociology, philosophy, and social theory as scientific disciplines, which have a crucial role in constructing and understanding societal processes. In his essay 'The status of sociology as a science in the present Bosnia and Herzegovina and some examples related to this issue', this author highlights that social science and sociology, in particular, did not anticipate all the horror and all the levels of collapse at the beginning of the societal transformations from communism to democracy, or more concretely, when this political ideology was radically collapsed and when the war structurally recomposed the entirety of this country. According to Filipović (2004), one reason for this failure and the inability of sociology to anticipate or to point out these matters and sociopolitical turbulences was,

> Since we had no single institute which deals with the fundamental and applied sociological research and that the created para-scientific institutions, in the form of some centers and

institutions, where the service organ of the authority and the politics, the trend of the sociological research strengthening did not continue, and sociology experienced a collapse at the universities [...] (p. 21).

The public activity of this academic and his effort to establish sociology as a scientific discipline that needs to be beyond dominant political ideologies and practices and beyond abstract theories and dogmatisms made him a highly prominent intellectual in Bosnia and Herzegovina. This is an example that sociology needs to be flexible, critical, and fluid in its interpretations and applications. It is not a science of abstract truths and final explanations of human society and its history; we are not dealing with the 'final vocabularies' (Rorty, 1989) on social organisations, structures and social transformations. This is an example that the efficiency of sociology in civil society, in the public sphere, in politics and its valorisation in public opinion can be reached by some intellectuals who are not primarily sociologists and, in contrast, there are sociologists in the sense of their formal education, who are sterile and who treated sociology as a hermetic form of abstract knowledge of the social world without any reflection to concrete social phenomena, transformations and states.

6.5 The Creative Power of Sociology?: An Academic Sociologist as a Politician and One Example of the New Explanation of the Role of Contemporary Sociology

There is another and more concrete example of the interference between academic sociology and politics. Ivo Komsic is a sociologist and university professor; at the same time, he was an active participant and witness of the political processes that had a crucial role in Bosnia and Herzegovina at the end of the 1980s and the beginning of the 1990s, during the war. He served as a member of the Presidency of Bosnia and Herzegovina, and he also had an active role in the creation of alternative political options regarding the political and historical position of Croat people in Bosnia and Herzegovina. He was also a participant in all peace negotiations that determined the character and destiny of Bosnia and Herzegovina, including the Dayton Agreement in 1995. He also served as a mayor of Sarajevo. Komsic is an example that, first, knowledge of sociology can have a significant role in societal processes and transformations and, second, that this experience can generate new theoretical insights into sociology through which the logic of social reality would be explained more effectively and more adequately. The theory of *social pulsation*, as an idea of this sociologist, attempts to show that social reality is not only an expression of continuous and evolutionary processes, that is to say, states that are well-established and consensually acceptable. The other face of this reality reveals the violent methods and psychotic actions of certain individuals who convert and transform their intentions, aspirations, and mental states into valid and binding social facts. Social pulsation as a theoretical explanation of social ontology and phenomenology is the result of an individual sociologist's activity in reality that was faced with limited situations in the sense of Karl Jaspers. It shows the possibility of the redefining status of sociology toward the new role that this science could have not only within the experience of Bosnia and Herzegovina in the post-war and post-socialist period but also the role that sociology could gain in understanding social reality in general. This sociologist and politician introduced the phrase *social pulsation* through which he explains the various modes in which social actors shape the social space. Sociology, therefore, is a fundamental science since it has the capacity to act and to understand social reality, as well as to transcend certain theoretical and methodological dichotomies by offering a new sociological explanation of society primarily based on the experience in which Bosnia and Herzegovina was found in the early 1990s.

> Then, something happened in Bosnia and Herzegovina that rarely happened in the history of any other society—the collapse of the social structure with its independent elements entering into conflict with one another, as well as the absence of a value system that previously permitted and directed the social activities and the social actors. The social practice had the carpet pulled from under its feet and lost its head as well. In that sense, the nature of the Bosnian-Herzegovinian conflictuality, in all its forms, has become a historical experience for the world (Komsic, 2017, p. 3).

Therefore, this example and excursus point out not only an attempt to introduce a new sociological theory that could be capable of transcending a dichotomy between the social structure and the social action but, more importantly, it is an argument that the experience of sociology and sociologist in transformative and quite extraordinary situations (political, economic, cultural and structural transformations through which Bosnia and Herzegovina passed in the post-socialist era, including the war) may have played a significant role both at the level of political action and political practice and at the level of the sociological imagination and redescription of society.

As Nijaz Ibrulj (2017 in Komsic, 2017) pointed out:

> Ivo Komsic, unlike many of his contemporaries in Bosnian sociology, has chosen the more difficult road to explicate his ideas, conceiving his research, entitled A *Theory of Social Pulsations*, *as a tractatus* that transcends/plunges into *the case study*. Thus, he truly *resorts to a theory* of (the social) world in which concepts are homologized from the *wholly innovative sociological standpoint* of the author while simultaneously *avoiding theorizing* which neglects (social) cases, (social) facts, (social) states of affairs, (social) reality. The form of the *tractatus* is exacting because it demands of the author, aside from the homologization of propositions by turning them into axioms, also their argumentative granulation into lemmas, theorems, and definitions. However, *the case study* enables entry into the *semantics of the concrete* and offers material/sensual evidence of theoretical utterances. This *semantics of the concrete*, according to Komsic, always functions as an *illumination* of the contradictory reality of Bosnian society (p. 92).

However, it is questionable to what degree and to what extent sociologists as individuals have the power to influence transformative processes in a given society. Again, it depends on whether they have a role in political processes (Komsic was a politician, and not just a sociologist) in political epistemology and what is the degree and effect of such a role. In contrast, such scientific-political interdependency can have positive and negative consequences.

6.6 The Role of Sociology in a *Contradictory-Based Society*

To analyse one particular social and state *structure*,[5] we have to be directed to particular modes of the sociopolitical constructions of particular structures (social and state structures) and the way through which these sociopolitical constructions have certain theoretical reflections. A sociology of the *contradictory-based society* must count on these facts. Concretely, this means that sociology must understand a wide range of social facts and actions that have their genesis in a violent rupture of one particular kind of sociopolitical reality (social order, state institutions, ideology, values and norms, history) that culminates with war (conflict level) and the establishing of a new sociopolitical order based on the Dayton peace agreement in 1995 (consensual level), which we are witnessing even today. This is the new 'social site'. These sociopolitical constellations are social facts, actions, and social relations that could be explained through the specific modes of selectivity crucial for the construction, deconstruction, and reconstruction of social relations. Structural, discursive, technological, and agential modes of selectivity (Sum & Jessop, 2013)[6] are the modes through which we can understand the behaviour and mechanisms of social relations and the way in which these social relations are transformed. Sociology must necessarily operate with these modes in a dialectical sense: as a social science that is formed through these modes of selectivity and as a science that is critically and reflexively oriented towards understanding the nature of social and state organisation through these modes of selectivity. These interdependencies and interferences of selectivities shape everyday life, so every social science is more effective and better copes with social reality if it takes into account these issues. Sociologists operate within the network of structural conditions and possibilities, with the technological sets of properties that can be accommodated with the present social realms. In the sense of discursivity and its 'intertextual, interdiscursive and contextual fields' (Sum & Jessop, 2013, p. 215) and its connection with the concept of agency, sociology needs to be capable of grasping all these dimensions, which is, even more, a matter of urgency and necessity when we are dealing with the role of sociology in transformative processes in the specific context of Bosnia and Herzegovina. It is even more obvious when we set up these modes of selectivity within the social framework of Bosnia and Herzegovina. As Schatzki (2002) pointed out: 'The social site is the site of human coexistence. [...] Lives hang together, then, through practical intelligibility, mentality, activity, and settings' (p. 147). However, what about the fact that this 'coexistence' and these four dimensions of 'forms of sociality', constructed by the modes of selectivity, are *intentionally and deliberately fragmented* in order to be *sociopolitical and cultural parallelisms* (with the intention to create, to impose, to disseminate and to *naturalise* parallel and mutually excluded social, cultural, political and mental entities)?

---

[5] By the term structure I understand 'structural principles', 'structures', and 'structural properties' as Giddens (1984) has pointed out.

[6] For a distinctive view of what is meant by the four modes of selectivity, see Sum and Jessop (2013).

Sociological agency and its reflection on various and mutually excluded types of agencies within the Bosnian society is a significant and basic fact, according to Schatzki (2002):

> [...] that human activity holds special causal, prefigurational, and constitutive significance for human life in general and social existence specifically. From the beginning, however, it must be stressed that the unique richness of human agency is neither necessary nor metaphysically significant. It is contingent in a double sense: It is a feature of the world as things happen to be *and* as far as we know how things happen to be' (pp. 192–193).

Sociology is crucial in the demystification and revelation of these social facts and relations since there is a tendency of political ideologies to name all these current social and political positions (contradictions and parallelisms) as natural and implicit things and facts.

6.7 Sociology as a Collaborative Activity and Its Role in the Construction of Social Reality

> In the social sciences, the 'real' is indeed external to and independent of knowledge, but it is itself a social construction, a product of past struggles which, at least in this respect, remains at stake in present struggles. (This becomes clear, even in the case of history, as soon as one tackles events which are still issues at stake for contemporaries). So a constructivist vision of science has to be combined with a constructivist vision of the scientific object: social facts are socially constructed, and every social agent, like the scientist, more or less successfully constructs and seeks to impose, with more or less strength, his individual vision of reality, his 'point of view'. That is why sociology, whether it wants to or not (and mostly it does), is an actor in the struggles it describes. Social science is, then, a social construction of a social construction (Bourdieu, 2004, p. 88).

Thus, contrary to different interests, strategies, technologies, and hegemonies within the very structure of Bosnian society, sociology needs to be imperatively coherent in its agential, structural, discursive, and technological modes of selectivity in the sense of coherent reflexivity and *possible practicability*. However, for me, it is doubtful (and it is a matter of discussion) to what extent sociology is capable of this universal, coherent, and objective task (Sociological *Beruf*) in correspondence to the basic human and existential facts of the Bosnian past and present-day historical and sociological facts, and to what extent it is a part of certain and particular political ideologies and interests. This second position is partly 'narcissistic' (Bourdieu, 2004, p. 89) and also one kind of rationally and intentionally calculated instrumentality with a specific legitimisation and 'objective' characterisation of certain political and historical goals.

The central role of sociology is to point out this *Bosnian social site* and to act in a specific interdisciplinary and transdisciplinary manner with other social sciences, humanities, and all other disciplines and activities that could be able to illuminate and understand this sociopolitical ontology and to be much more active and effective in both, the process of education of students and individuals[7] in general and active in the process of shaping the reflexive and critical public opinion. By doing so, sociologists need to be active in imposing their methodological and analytical tools and positions when it comes to understanding and illuminating social reality, and it is more a matter of challenge and obligation in the case of Bosnia and Herzegovina.

> A realist analysis of the functioning of fields of cultural production, far from leading on relativism, allows us to move past the alternative of antirationalist and antiscientific nihilism, on the one hand, and the moralism of the glorification of rational dialogue, on the other, toward a genuine *realpolitik of reason*. Indeed, I think that short of believing in miracles, we can expect the progress of reason only from a political struggle rationally oriented toward defending and promoting the social conditions for the exercise of reason, a permanent mobilization of all cultural producers in order to defend, through continuous and modest interventions, the institutional bases of intellectual activity (Bourdieu, 1998 [2001], pp. 139–140).

It is questionable to what extent and scope this 'realpolitik of reason' can act autonomously on the one side and to what extent this *realm of reason* can be effective and potent in regards to the *realm of realpolitik* and powerful nation-states and their geopolitical interests, constellations and mutual struggles. On the other side, reason without humanity and ethics (without entering here into different ethical perspectives and points of view that can also be problematic and contextual; I meant ethical in a basic, almost transcendental meaning) is a mere normative illusion and its neutral position, and universality can be equally problematic and potentially dangerous.

My colleague from Slovenia, Borut Rončević, spoke, as part of the *ESA RN 36 Midterm Conference* and *tenth Slovenian Social Science Conference*, about the four ideal-type roles of sociology in society ('activators', 'voyeurs', 'fellow-travellers', and 'marginals'). Methodologically, these four ideal types differ both in terms of their intensity and activity, as well as in terms of their autonomy. It seems to me that these roles, viewed normatively, give a clear picture of the current modes of action of sociology and sociologists in the social world and point to the

---

[7] The question remains open to what extent sociology and the critical engagement of sociologists is possible if we take into account the diverse and mutually exclusive ideal type positions of sociologists, their view of the world, and in general, their view of Bosnia and Herzegovina , and if we take into account what can be called 'convergent political religions' that shape a good part of what we can call public opinion and some sort of collective representations.

'In Bosnia and Herzegovina, as well as in neighboring transitional societies, we are witnessing action of a convergent political religions in a rigid and in the boundary sense. Convergent political religions build a social ontology in a way that "normal social conditions" are always and necessarily identified as a "state of exception." In these societies, we are always dealing with the "breaking and constituting moments," these societies are based on incompleteness and high insecurities. In such societies peace is maintained only by continuous threat of war and suffering and precisely by political and religious leaders' (Tadić, 2021, pp. 265–266).

In addition to this, I argue that a fragmented intelligentsia, as well as the domestic policymakers and international community (both of which are also fragmentations in themselves, with diverse and often mutually exclusive political interests and strategies) are responsible for such a state of affairs.

possibility of speaking about the 'strong' ('activators' and 'fellow-travellers') in relation to a 'weak' role ('voyeurs' and 'marginals'). However, when it comes to trying to apply these epistemic constructions to the level of the empirical world, my understanding has a less optimistic outcome. Probably the reason for this is my sociocultural background and the depressing status of the social reality of the country from which I come. This type of less optimistic view of the world in the sense of talking about the role of sociologists is not derived only from the Bosnian reality and its contradictions but from the overall global trends and tendencies in which the discrepancy between what Weber called 'formal' versus 'substantive rationality' reaches the most intense proportions. Even if we talk about the fact that these sociological roles are not fixed but can change over time, depending on sociocultural and sociopolitical arrangements, I do not see enough empirical confirmation and operative verification that the roles of sociologists are dichotomously constructed as *active* versus *passive*, *strong* versus *weak*, *autonomous* versus *dependent*. Rather, I think that these roles have a *relative, dependent, and relational character*, with a less established idea of sociologists as researchers who, in their scientific centres (institutes, incubators, faculties, academies, etc.), construct certain social theories in an independent and absolutely autonomous manner through the objective and universal way of explanation, viewpoints, attitudes, research results and 'semiotic practices'. Here, I am more inclined to Bourdieu's understanding of science and scientific research, to which, of course, sociologists are not immune.[8] 'Activators' are equipped with a 'good institutional infrastructure', well-funded and do not influence the direct transformation of society or the direct questioning of the previously unquestioned status of the dominant discourse. I do not believe that it is possible to talk about the total autonomy of research work when, on the scene, we have obvious differences between the recognition and recognition of 'scientific truths' that were created at private, prestigious universities and research centres, compared to those that are not. Some are often implicitly treated as prestigious, very well scientifically organised and financially stable compared to others who have an ephemeral status. It is also necessary to ask the question of whether research is completely objective or whether it depends on certain strategies that have to do with incentives and funds and the expected presentation of 'scientific truths'. It is questionable to what extent sociologists create certain 'semiotic practices' that can lead to some political transformations (in collaboration with political scientists, legal scientists, political decision-makers, economists and other stakeholders) if they are not strong enough to exert some kind of pressure on representatives of a dominant discourses and political practices. Do sociologists (in cooperation with other holders of 'expert systems') create alternative discourses, and do they have any resonance and effect at all at the operative level (on various political decision-making, on the level of potential social transformations,

---

[8] For example, Bourdieu argues about the practices in research activities in which there are obvious differences between the things that a scientist had 'written' (in his research analysis, scientific conclusions, scientific facts and truths) and the things that the scientist had 'meant' (see Bourdieu, 2004, pp. 23–28).

etc.) or is there an effect if sociologists institutionally have some connection with the bearers of political subjectivities? Sociologists can support the existing discourse or create alternative ones with faith in the potentiality and possibility of social transformation, but this largely depends on their recognition and the current positions they have as individuals in a given society and in specific decision-making circles. They can influence the educational quality, the strengthening of reflexivity and critical autonomy of individuals and public opinion, but I consider the talk about the indirect possibility of social transformation to be questionable. Rather, it is about the individual achievements of certain sociologists and their recognition in the academic, scientific, and cultural space. We should not ignore the fact that sociologists operate with epistemic and not ontological statuses of social reality and that these epistemic constructions can be mutually exclusive. The effect of these constructions is again related to the place and role that the sociologist occupies in a certain social structure, and this means that these constructions manifest certain sources of 'symbolic power' that depend on prestige, on the dominant political, social or cultural discourse, and, among other things about the nationality of some sociologists in relation to others. 'Semiotic practices' are always connected with some degree of 'symbolic power'. In contrast, 'symbolic power' illuminates 'social doxa', and the position of 'semiotic practices' can be supportive and can go along with the dominant discourse(s), or it can have an alternative, but in most cases, ephemeral and incidental role. In the case of Bosnia and Herzegovina, it can be even more obvious and less sophisticated. We can talk about specific achievements, but the effects (direct and indirect) are extremely questionable. Sociology can illuminate social contradictions, but its 'use value' in terms of indirect influence on political and social transformations in Bosnia and Herzegovina is marginal and sometimes has a voyeuristic character. If we talk about the consensual character of the sociologists of Bosnia and Herzegovina (viewed hypothetically), the concrete possibilities of constructing 'semantic practices' that would influence the construction of new social and political transformations in the direction of prosperity and stability that the European population of Bosnia and Herzegovina should have analogous to the stability of the state and social structures that other European countries have (so that we do not go beyond this geographical, economic, cultural and political space) are questionable.

6.8 Conclusion

The role of sociology in societal transformations of Bosnian society is directly dependent on the social and political organisation (hence, it is dependent on political actors on national and international levels) and the current position of science, research, and critical reflection in general. There are individual cases, individual achievements and individual engagements that have the character of individual recognition and enthusiasm. Researchers of social phenomena are atomised and fragmented, and the recognition of some kind of national strategy (if by that we mean the sociological activism of Bosnia and Herzegovina and not the strategy at the level of three nations and their three national determinations) does not exist.

There is no single institutionally organised sociological activity that deals with the problems and challenges of the post-socialist transitions, except in situations in which sociology has its applicability through some projects that are not organised, coordinated, financed, and cultivated at the level of Bosnia and Herzegovina as a state or as a form of national sociological associations, etc. Instead, we are witnessing the personal activities and capacities of sociologists as university professors, public intellectuals or politicians through which sociology had some microscopic impact on the Bosnian society and the ability to illuminate the complex and quite unpredictable or 'unintended consequences' of Bosnian modernity and its transformations.

Unfortunately, the current sociopolitical and socioeconomic state of Bosnia and Herzegovina reflects the position and the role of sociology. Sociology needs to have an imperative, active and critical role in these unpredictable societal transformations in a sense to illuminate the current state, the state of the "collective representations" (Durkheim, 1995) and political constellations. To do so, sociology needs to have institutionally recognised associations and institutes analogous to ex-Yugoslavian countries and other functionally organised countries in general, but this issue is closely linked with the political ontology of Bosnia and Herzegovina and its fragmentation, ethnoreligious quarantines, and the political and ideological interventions into autonomy of science. To have an active and critical role, sociology needs to accent its capacity to transcend these political dominations and needs to eliminate its own fragmentation that corresponds with the fragmentation of Bosnian society in general. At the level of its scientific and public activity, there is no unique and single national/institutional strategy, no institutionally established organisations and institutes with projects, coordination, practices, and other such activities. What is important to note, and which often affects researchers in stable countries of the world, is a kind of habit, implicitness, observation of social constructions as natural facts, like those Malešević talks about; namely, that we observe organisations, institutions, bureaucratic apparatuses and their rationalising background naturalistically and that they are gradually and totally accepted as such, as a kind of naturally given. In this sense, ideology acquires its ultimate status, and sociology figures as a descriptive activity of talented constructors of social terms and their phenomena, or else figures as a critique whose influence is limited and ephemeral and implies a whole set of different social and political variables that determine that position and its characterisation.

If we omit individual cases and sociologists who had public engagement or/and political activity and sociologists that are at the universities, it can affect future generations to strengthen the status and the role of sociology in their country, to make this position better toward the critical analysis, activities and active participation in public debates that could have echoes to individual and collective identities and political decisions, each other activity is reduced to the following: 'What is happening with science in general also happens with sociology. [...] exists only as a general abstract knowledge about society and nothing more' (Filipović, 2004, p. 23).

Competing Interests The author has no conflicts of interest to declare that are relevant to the content of this chapter.

References

Bourdieu, P. (1990). *The logic of practice*. Polity Press.
Bourdieu, P. (1998 [2001]). *Practical reason*. Polity Press.
Bourdieu, P. (2004). *Science of science and reflexivity*. Polity Press.
Cvitković, I. (2010). Zašto nam je potrebna sociologija. (Why we need Sociology). *Posebna izdanja ANUBIH. (Special edition of the Academy of Arts and Sciences of Bosnia and Herzegovina)*. Accessed Jun 15, 2023, from https://publications.anubih.ba/bitstream/handle/123456789/58/Mjesto%20i%20uloga%20sociologije.pdf?sequence=1&isAllowed=y
Durkheim, E. (1995). *The elementary forms of religious life*. The Free Press.
Filipović, M. (2003). Bosna i Hercegovina u okovima nacionalizma (Bosnia and Herzegovina in the Chains of Nationalism). Svjetlost (Bilioteka Refleksi).
Filipović, M. (2004). Status sociologije kao nauke u današnjoj Bosni i Hercegovini i neki primjeri koji se odnose na to pitanje. (The status of sociology as a science in the present Bosnia and Herzegovina and some examples related to this issue). *Pregled, 1–2*, 3–23.
Fischer, M. (2007). Bosnia's Challenge: Economic Reform, political transformation and war-to-peace transition. In M. Fischer (Ed.), *Peacebuilding and civil society in bosnia-herzegovina-ten years after dayton* (pp. 448–449). LIT-Verlag. Accessed Jul 18, 2019, from https://www.academia.edu/24654760/Bosnias_Challenge_Economic_Reform_Political_Transformation_and_War_to_Peace_Transition_by_Martina_Fischer_in_Martina_Fischer_ed_Peacebuilding_and_Civil_Society_in_Bosnia_Herzegovina_Ten_Years_after_Dayton_Berlin_Lit_Verlag_pp_441_470_Online_at_www_berghof_foundation_org_
Giddens, A. (1984). The Constitution of Society. *Polity*.
Ibrulj, N. (2008). National dogmatism or the logic of consociation. *Pregled: časopis Za društvena Pitanja/Periodical for Social Issues, 4*(4), 195–231.
Ibrulj, N. (2017). Phenomenology of anomalous causality. In I. Komsic (Ed.), *The theory of social pulsation* (pp. 89–136). Peter Lang.
Komšić, I. (2012). Socijalna moć uma. Uvod u teoriju socijalne pulsacije (The Social Power of Mind. *Introduction to the Theory of Social Pulsation*). Svjetlost.
Komsic, I. (2017). *The theory of social pulsation*. Peter Lang.
Krleža, M. (1935). *Evropa danas (Europe Today)*. Zora.
Malešević, S. (2010). *The Sociology of War and Violence*. Cambridge University Press.
Rorty, R. (1989). *Contingency, irony, and solidarity*. Cambridge University Press.
Schatzki, T. R. (2002). *The site of the social: A philosophical account of the constitution of social life and change*. Pennsylvania State University Press.
Schutz, A. (1967). *The phenomenology of the social world*. Northwestern University Press.
Smith, A. D. (1991). *National identity*. University of Nevada Press.
Sociological Society of the Republic of Srpska. (n.d.). Accessed Jul 13, 2023, from https://www.sociolog.rs/istorijat.html
Sum, N.-L., & Jessop, B. (2013). *Towards a cultural political economy: Putting culture in its place in political economy*. Edward Elgar.
Tadić, T. (2021). *Ecclesia Leviathana. Sociogeneza konvergentnih političkih religija. (Ecclesia Leviathana. Sociogenesis of a convergent political religions)*. Academia Analitica.
Touraine, A. (2007). *A new paradigm for understanding today's world*. Polity Press.
University of East Sarajevo. (n.d.-a). Accessed Jul 14, 2023, from https://www.ues.rs.ba/o-univerzitetu/istorijat/slava-univerziteta/
University of East Sarajevo. (n.d.-b). Accessed Jul 14, 2023, from https://www.ues.rs.ba/la/2017/11/01/obiljezeni-dan-i-krsna-slava-pravnog-fakulteta-uis-a-2/

University of East Sarajevo. (n.d.-c). Accessed Jul 14, 2023, from https://www.ues.rs.ba/la/2019/05/22/obiljezen-dan-i-krsna-slava-filozofskog-fakulteta-2/

Zupcevic, M., & Causevic, F. (2009). *Case study: Bosnia and Herzegovina*. Centre for developing area studies, McGill University and the World Bank. Accessed Aug 20, 2022, from https://www.academia.edu/41880037/CASE_STUDY_BOSNIA_AND_HERZEGOVINA

Vedad Muharemovic is an Associate Professor of Sociology at the Department of Sociology (Faculty of Philosophy in Sarajevo). He graduated in Philosophy and Sociology in 2006, then MA in Sociology in 2010 and PhD in Sociology in 2014. He teaches several subjects: Sociology of Nationalism, Social and Political Theories, Cultural Sociology, Political Ideologies, Migration studies and Sociology of Knowledge and Science. His main research interests include social and political theory, comparative policy analysis, migration processes, sociology of nationalism, EU and nation-states, sociology of knowledge and science.

Chapter 7
Sociology as Factor of Change: Reflections on the Bulgarian Experience

Nikolai Genov

7.1 Introduction

The profound post-socialist social changes in Central and Eastern Europe are a unique historical experience. They have become a true laboratory for developing and testing explanatory conceptual frameworks. The tests started with the widely used concept of transition (Genov, 1991, 2021), which was borrowed from the studies on political transitions from dictatorships to democratic political arrangements in Latin America and the south of Europe. Contrary to expectations, the concept turned out to be inefficient in the attempts to explain simultaneous changes in all economic, political, and cultural institutions in Central and Eastern European societies. One of the major reasons for the explanatory deficits of the concept was its inherent link to a definition of the point of departure and the situation resulting from the transition. It turned out that the task was extremely difficult or practically 'mission impossible' due to the large variety of specific path-dependency and path-shaping conditions (Sum & Jessop, 2013, p. 37) in Central and Eastern European societies.

The disappointments with the explanatory potential of the transition concept paved the way for discussions about the causes, processes, and effects of societal transformations. The productive use of the concept in explanations notwithstanding, it soon became clear that the focus on the transformation of separate societies had in-built limitations in the context of the current globalisation (Genov, 2016). Nevertheless, the concept remains widely used as guidance for reflections on the continuing societal transformation in the region of Central and Eastern Europe.

N. Genov (✉)
Freie Universität Berlin, Berlin, Germany
e-mail: genov@zedat.fu-berlin.de

In sharp contrast to the intensive sociological studies on post-socialist transformations, the impact of sociology on these transformations has only exceptionally been a subject of analysis and discussions. Moreover, the rare exceptions have mostly come from Western European authors who had no hesitation in expressing freely normative opinions about what could and should happen to make social sciences more efficient in designing post-socialist institutions and in supporting their establishment in the course of the societal transformations in Central and Eastern Europe (Elster et al., 1998).

The disparity between the overwhelming impacts of societal transformations on the sociological analysis and argumentation and the hardly disputed impacts of sociology on the transformations is striking. Sociology appeared as a science with the ambition to develop and apply strategies for studying *and* steering social dynamics. However, the ambitious project of combining cognitive and practical tasks of sociology designed by Auguste Comte (2016) and developed in detail by early American sociology (Ward, 1906) could not thrive under all social and intellectual conditions. That is why the idea of a pro-active orientation of sociology and sociologists was later replaced by the Weberian strategy of distancing sociological studies from involvement in designing and applying social technologies or in social engineering guided by visions of desirable future situations in social life (Burawoy, 2016). The strong methodological focus on the cognitive tasks of sociology, together with the systematic underestimation of its practical relevance, has been the strategic orientation of mainstream American and American-influenced sociology in other countries during the second half of the twentieth century. The theoretical or methodological specifics of the leading sociologists notwithstanding, most of them used to follow and still follow one common rule: sociologists can successfully describe, explain, and partly forecast social processes but should be very careful as engineers of social change since the effects might be rather disappointing or directly disastrous (Hadnagy, 2011).

In this context, the effort to develop and apply sociology as a guiding factor of social development in Central and Eastern Europe is a particularly intriguing phenomenon. After the Second World War, Marxists in the region were eager to see the dreams of Comte and Marx about scientifically based rational design, building, and management of societal change being realised in the practice of the societies representing 'real socialism'. Immediately after the war, the scientific basis for the rational steering of social processes in the region had to be provided by the philosophical theory of historical materialism. In the area of the Soviet Union's ideological dominance, sociology was declared to be non-scientific, like genetics. However, the supposed rational guidance of the new society by historical materialism turned out to be inefficient and, in some cases, harmful. In the 1960s, the disappointments brought about the understanding that the de-legitimisation of both genetics and sociology was a mistake. The conclusion was that the scientific basis of the decision-making in socialist societies had to be mostly offered by the social science of sociology or by sociology-like conceptual constructions. This was a risky decision. The success of this vision of practically potent sociology in the management of social processes in Central and Eastern Europe would imply the legitimation of sociology as a crucially important factor of social change. However, the failure of the endeavour would imply questioning the vision of sociology as a relevant factor in the guidance of social change indeed.

How did these cognitive and practical processes take place in Bulgarian society? The following will be dedicated to answering the question by analysing the changes in the cognitive and practical relevance of sociology in the management of social development during the socialist and post-socialist periods of this specific national case. The open questions are numerous: What was the real impact of the Marxist vision of scientifically (in the given context—sociologically) guided social change in socialist Bulgaria? What was and remains the impact of sociology on the profound post-socialist changes in Bulgarian society? What might be the realistic theoretical, methodological, and pragmatic conclusions from the collected rich experience about the role of sociologists and the sociological community in the management of the post-socialist transformation of Bulgarian society?

7.2 Sociology in the Steering of Bulgarian Socialist Society

Now, scholars may take advantage of the historical distance in their efforts to objectively study the extent to which Marxism influenced values, norms, institutions, and behaviour in Bulgarian society after 1945. The situation could be tentatively described in the sense that Marxist ideas and related practices were less questioned in Bulgaria than in any other Central and Eastern European country under Soviet dominance. This had ideological and political implications for sociology. Decades after the Second World War, it was understood as a competitor to historical materialism by most ideologues in the Soviet Union and, consequently, in Bulgaria. Moreover, sociology was politically interpreted as part of the ideology of the Cold War's enemy of socialism.

Against this ideological and political background, the rapid institutionalisation of sociology in Bulgaria was a striking achievement of a small group of dedicated social scientists. The achievement became possible as a result of intensive ideological battles with uncertain and potentially dangerous outcomes for the would-be sociologists. The controversial ways in which the monograph of Zhivko Oshavkov (1958) 'Historical Materialism and Sociology' was received was indicative of the open future of sociology and sociologists in the country at that time. The would-be sociologists had some strong arguments, however.

First, the enthusiastic pioneers of Bulgarian sociology could be ideologically and politically trusted by the regime. Some of them had records of participation in the resistance against the pro-Nazi regime. All of them had records of having worked as party functionaries at various organisational levels.

Second, the founding fathers of modern Bulgarian sociology sincerely wanted to develop an objective non-philosophical social science to serve the practical needs of the socialist society. The argument was attractive in the context of the disenchantments with the performance of the socialist economy and state administration after the first decade of building 'real' socialism. New ideas and practices were needed to refresh the Marxist social engineering in socialist Bulgaria. Sociologists came with the promise to offer the remedy.

Third, it was the time to sincerely confess some ideological mistakes. In the new historical context, it was possible to argue that the negation of genetics and sociology was a mistake with negative scientific and practical consequences (see Dobriyanov et al., 1978, pp. 11–24).

The core of the argumentation was the clear social-technological orientation of Bulgarian sociology already in its *statu nascendi*. From its very beginning, it was guided by the rationalist social-technological engagement of social science knowledge, as argued by Comte and Marx. This vision about the unity of cognitive and practical (socio-technological) tasks of sociology was explicitly formulated by one of the first sociologists in the country, Niko Yahiel (1976, p. 19): '[…] sociological research […] cannot be considered complete unless it leads to certain conclusions, proposals and recommendations, to the formulation of long-term and short-term objectives and the anticipation of social prognoses as a basis for concrete decisions and practical action'.

This action-oriented interpretation of the aims of sociology was not just a matter of Marxist ideological indoctrination. Yahiel knew the need for objective information as a sound basis for rational decisions and actions, as well as how to use the information, since he was well established in the very centre of centralised decision-making. Zhivko Oshavkov, who is the recognised intellectual and organisational founding father of the so-called Bulgarian sociological school, had worked at the Central Committee of the Communist Party before becoming director of the newly established Institute of Sociology at the Bulgarian Academy of Sciences in 1968. His successor, Stoyan Mihailov, became Secretary of the Central Committee in the very sensitive area of ideology. Before taking the position, the following directors, Velichko Dobriyanov and Krastyo Petkov, were employed by the same institution. Yet another founding father of Bulgarian sociology, Chavdar Kyranov, used to work at the State Council, which functioned as the presidency of the country.

The point raised here has two major dimensions. *First*, the founding fathers of sociology as a social science in Bulgaria were dedicated and productive scientists and left valuable examples of ambitious theorising and methodologically sound empirical research (Koleva, 2005, pp. 136–170). Oshavkov (1976) developed his original concept of the sociological structure of society as a framework for the definition of the subject matter of sociology and applied the concept in nationwide empirical studies. Mihaylov (1973) opened the way for modern sociological research in the country. After valuable contributions to sociological theory, Dobriyanov (1995) carried out a respectable content analysis on revelations of the famous foreteller Vanga. Petkov (1985) was a recognised specialist in the field of sociology of work. *Second*, all of them were sincerely concerned about the practical relevance of their theorising and empirical research. In most cases, they intentionally oriented their theoretical work and empirical studies towards outcomes which might help improve the management of social interactions and structures. For them, the scientific steering of society was not just wishful thinking. They knew well that the intellectual products of a state-dependent sociology could help the rationalisation of all walks of social life but the functioning of the party-state first. They were also aware of the specifics of the historical situation. Only the economic, political, and cultural resources of the centralised socialist state could make it possible to establish academic and applied sociology in the country and support it with resources in the long run. This was the reason for the strategic preoccupation of the founding fathers of modern Bulgarian sociology with nationally representative studies.

Thus, step by step, it became a widely shared point of view that sociological ideas and institutions really matter as instruments for managing guided social change in Bulgarian society before 1989. The process of the institutionalisation of the discipline moved rapidly forward after the political green light was given. University courses and specialisations in sociology were introduced at the University of National and Global Economy and at the Sofia University in the mid-1960s. Together with the establishment of the academic Institute of Sociology in 1968, the academic journal *Sociologicheski problemi [Sociological Problems]* was also founded. Chairs of sociology were set up first in Sofia and later at universities in the provinces. The teaching of sociology quickly spread to all other universities. New legal regulations made the professionalisation of sociology, the study of the discipline, the practising of the acquired knowledge and skills and the practical relevance of sociology undeniable.

One example may make the point concerning the social-technological orientation and relevance of sociology during the period of socialism clearer. In 1975, the State Council commissioned a national study on the Bulgarian family to the Institute of Sociology of the Bulgarian Academy of Sciences. The topic was very well chosen with a view to the looming demographic crisis in the country. Fertility was declining, particularly among the population of Bulgarian ethnic origin. Mortality was growing in parallel with the ageing of the population. Given the conditions of a very generous pension age of 55 for women and 60 for men, the ageing of the population was already a serious threat to the pension system. So, well-designed and implemented policies supporting family and fertility were urgently needed to stabilise and possibly improve the demographic situation of Bulgarian society.

Therefore, the study became some kind of a litmus test for the viability of sociology as a technologically relevant social science. Professor Chavdar Kyuranov took the leadership of the study with a clear idea about its significance. He was not academically trained as a sociologist, but he had broad knowledge about social life and the ends and means of sociology. Borrowing theoretical ideas from Talcott Parsons, he developed a multidimensional conceptual model of the modern family and consequently operationalised it. The field study was very well planned and organised. The research project enjoyed the support of all relevant institutions, and the field study did not meet organisational handicaps. The academic outcome was the scientific monograph 'The Contemporary Bulgarian Family' (Kyuranov, 1987). However, socially more relevant was the large number of suggestions for legal and institutional changes based on the results of the study. Legal decisions were taken for prolongation of maternity leave, for focusing child benefits on the second child, for special support to single mothers, and for measures to improve the legal status of the

Bulgarian family, among others. As seen from the present-day point of view, the study and its social-technological effects might be regarded as very well embedded in the economic and political environments of Bulgaria during the 1970s and 1980s. The study convincingly exemplifies the possibility of uniting the cognitive theoretical and empirical tasks of sociology with its contribution to resolving complex social-technological tasks by rationally guiding social change.

The practical impact of Bulgarian sociology was multiplied by legal regulations opening workplaces for sociologists at economic enterprises and various political and cultural organisations. Because of the rapid expansion of this component of the sociological community, the congresses of the Bulgarian Sociological Association used to attract 800–1000 participants and were covered by mass media in detail. The dissemination of sociological knowledge functioned through the regular publication of sociological monographs and edited collections. The Institute of Youth Studies became a leader in the carrying out of theoretically and methodologically sound research. Its outcomes were widely used in the decision-making on issues concerning the development and accomplishments of young people in the country. Another centre of valuable sociological research was the Institute of Trade Union Studies. Centres of applied sociology functioned at political, educational, medical, military, and other institutions and strengthened the recognition of sociology as a discipline with the potential to substantially contribute to the scientific steering of the socialist society.

How important sociology was regarded in cognitive and practical terms could be seen from the state support to the international activities of Bulgarian sociologists. One may wonder what the very young Bulgarian sociology could offer to the international sociological community by organising the Seventh World Congress of the International Sociological Association in 1970. Nevertheless, the congress remained the only one that took place in an Eastern European country and left lasting impacts on the development of the discipline in Bulgaria and in the region.

Another telling example of the generous state support to the development of Bulgarian sociology was the funding for the participation of sociologists in scientific events abroad. In 1986, a delegation of 36 Bulgarian sociologists took part in the Eleventh Congress of Sociology in New Delhi on state costs despite the looming economic, political, and value-normative crisis. Indeed, academic sociologists enjoyed the prestigious status of scientists. Applied sociologists were regarded as a privileged group because of their professional closeness to decision-makers.

The generosity of the ruling party and the Bulgarian state to sociology was a matter of political calculation. After 1956, the authoritarian regime preferred ruling mostly by offering carrots and less by applying sticks. As a result, sociologists were fairly well integrated into the political system, like all other groups of the Bulgarian intelligentsia. Conformity dominated the research, the interpretation of the findings, the diagnoses, and the prognostication of social processes. The political integration of sociology had far-reaching implications for its cognitive content and social relevance. Fundamental problems of ownership, inequality, freedom of speech, quality of health care, crime, addictions, and similar issues could only be studied under various political restrictions. The much-needed technologies for innovations in these and many other areas remained out of the academic debates and from the motivation of sociologists themselves. The secret services were well-informed about the public activities of sociologists. However, objectivity requires adding that the sociological community and the professional activities of sociologists have not been subject to serious political repression for the majority of the period. The contribution of sociologists to this relatively peaceful coexistence of a strong repressive apparatus and predominantly academic sociology was substantial. They managed to present their visions for social change as focused on the improvement of socialism as it existed but not as projects for replacing it with another organisation of economic, political, and cultural life.

The reasons for the conformity of Bulgarian sociologists with the authoritarian regime were basically twofold. *First*, the regime managed to develop and apply efficient policies for the political and ideological integration of intellectuals. Only approaching the end of the 1980s did sketchy talks about desirable fundamental changes attract sociologists under the impact of the Soviet *perestroika* policies. However, even in times of deepening value-normative and institutional crises, the ruling party was able to mobilise financial and organisational resources to buy the active or passive cooperation of sociologists. *Second,* another, form of conformity, was the self-censorship. Paradoxically enough, among the outstanding professional sociologists, it was Chavdar Kyuranov who had to suffer repressions just before the changes started in 1989. Because of regime-critical comments, he had to spend some time demoted to life in the provinces. However, real dissidents with alternative projects for the development of the country were practically missing among Bulgarian sociologists before 1989.

After the changes initiated by the ruling party started, sociologists were able to publish everything they could not publish before. It was refreshing to observe that no one sociologist published any previously prepared visions about the desirable state of the economy, politics, and culture after the period of state socialism. The effects of this distancing from truly alternative social projects became obvious very soon. The speed of unexpected changes caught sociologists (like the whole Bulgarian society) by surprise. It was no longer the improvement of the existing societal organisation but its radical change that came as the urgent task. Sociologists did not have ready-made social-technological suggestions for resolving such an ambitious task. The judgment about sociology in socialist Bulgaria saying that it has already become 'a useful instrument for self-understanding of society and for rationalisation of social activities' (Mihaylov, 2003, p. 47) was questioned by the sharp turn in the development of Bulgarian society. What followed were reactive sociological improvisations on the topic 'What is going on and how to adapt to it with the least damage?' The topic 'How to help organise change in order to rationally move forward' was not on Bulgarian sociologists' agenda at the beginning of the post-socialist societal transformation.

7.3 Sociologists in the Management of Profound Changes

Unlike the situation in Poland or Hungary, on the eve of the profound changes which started in November 1989, there was no well-organised and influential opposition in Bulgaria in general and among sociologists in particular. The small circles of critical younger sociologists were involved in discourses about esoteric topics and were unprepared for any kind of practical opposition to the regime despite its heavy loss of legitimacy. It was a paradoxical situation that the young critical sociologists did not have any sound sociological utopia for guiding the efforts to establish the desirable better organisation of Bulgarian society. What could be heard was the general argument that Western European and North American societies had efficient economies, dynamic politics, and pluralist cultures: everything that was missing in Bulgaria. Greece was the most natural case for comparisons, with rather unfavourable outcomes for the Bulgarian side. Given the speed of the changes in the international arena after November 1989, it was too late to prepare and apply a social-technological program for step-by-step changes. Even a year later, there was nothing like 'Plan Balcerovicz' for Bulgaria. Bulgarian politicians just copied the Polish model, which did not work efficiently in Poland itself. As a result, major economic, political, and cultural reforms in the country during the last decade of the twentieth century were initiated or directly guided by agencies from abroad. This humiliating situation had its simple explanation in the fact that the reformers did not follow any comprehensive national strategy for the transformation of Bulgarian society. Reforms were mostly determined by processes outside of the country or were directly initiated by the missions of the World Bank, the International Monetary Fund, and later by the European Union.

In this context, no specific expectations were focused on Bulgarian sociology and sociologists for developing guidance for action in a situation of high uncertainty and profound risks concerning the future of groups, national regions, and the nation. Under these extraordinary conditions, the majority of academic sociologists opted for a 'wait and see' professional strategy and continued the 'business as usual' in desktop studies and university teaching. Their reserved reactions followed the most traditional pattern of passive adaptation of the Bulgarian intelligentsia to precarious situations in critical times. It is true that, contrary to all talks about the depoliticisation of science, the founding of the opposition Union of Democratic Forces (UDF) took place in the facilities of the Institute of Sociology. This was part of the politics of the old regime, which had a clear strategy: opposition had to be skilfully cultivated and domesticated. The old secret services were still able to use their large networks for the purpose. How strong these networks were in the sociological community became known later with the publication of names of collaborators of the former State Security Agency.

The rank-and-file sociologists at the enterprises, in the state administration, and at various organisations had a different attitude to the changes than the academic sociologists. The first discussions about forthcoming reforms immediately provoked existential fears among the people involved in applied sociology. These fears were soon confirmed. This professional group fell victim to the first waves of personnel layoffs. Many applied sociologists joined the growing group of unemployed people together with sociologists from dissolved research institutions, such as the Institute of Youth Studies.

Under these conditions of uncertainty and intensive risks, some academic sociologists and sociological practitioners greeted the changes sincerely and enthusiastically. They expected rapid and substantial improvement in the critical economic situation in the country as a result of massive financial, material, and logistic help from abroad. The background of the high expectations and related enthusiasm was the belief that Bulgaria was about to join the group of affluent societies with a well-balanced market economy, functioning democratic political systems, and a pluralist culture. Other sociologists rushed to join the anti-socialist political forces after careful calculation. They expected that a tremendous redistribution of the national wealth was forthcoming and planned ways for joining the 'winners'. The simplest and most efficient way to attain the goal was active political participation in decision-making about the reforms at various structural levels. Therefore, many reasons for sociologists to influence and actively manage the reform processes exist. How did sociologists, as individuals, take the opportunity to apply their sociological knowledge in steering the transformation at various structural levels of Bulgarian society?

Contrary to many expectations, only a few cases of sociologists' active and publicly visible personal involvement in the management of the transformation occurred. The political activity of Professor Chavdar Kyuranov after 1989 is an impressive case in the context. Due to his professional experience in economic sciences and sociology, his recognised work in the state administration and international organisations, he had the respect of the leftists in the country. He also had the records of a dissident who had suffered reprisals. Few representatives of the anti-socialist opposition forces in the early 1990s could justify their political orientation with this type of dissident activities and with the repressions he had suffered. Kyuranov managed to use this capital of social recognition and respect from both sides of the political spectrum in his activities in the Great National Assembly, which prepared and passed the constitution of post-socialist Bulgaria.

In this turbulent situation, the proposal of the Socialist Party to elect Chavdar Kyuranov President of the Republic of Bulgaria, was a promising one. Only several votes of members of the Great Assembly prevented the positive outcome of the election. This was a loss for the emerging democracy in Bulgaria. Kyuranov's diplomatic experience and negotiation skills, together with the commonly shared public respect for him, could have been very useful in managing the divisions and confrontations during the difficult start of the post-socialist transformation of Bulgarian society. After his candidacy for president of the state failed, Kyuranov continued to be very active in shaping the future of democratic Bulgaria through intensive involvement in law-making.

A few other sociologists had the potential, the desires, and the opportunities to take key positions in transformation management. Professor Krastyo Petkov had the best prospects to be successful in this role. At the end of the 1980s, he was a rising star in the party nomenclature. He had headed the Institute of Trade Union Studies and later the Institute of Sociology at the Academy of Sciences. In the historical autumn of 1989, he willingly accepted the position of the head of the still party-dominated trade unions. The traditional trade unions had to be reformed in the sense of keeping them close to the Socialist Party but no more in the previous manifest way. This was tremendously important for preserving the public support for the party. The task was rather difficult to resolve since the emerging opposition forces also recognised the political relevance of the trade unions and started to develop their own unions. The anti-socialist trade union 'Podkrepa' followed the pattern of the Polish 'Solidarność' and became a strong political force after having received large financial and organisational support from abroad.

Professor Petkov managed the complicated task. He skilfully guided the transformation of the rigid, over-centralised socialist Trade Unions into the flexible, decentralised Confederation of Independent Syndicates in Bulgaria (CISB). The syndicates re-focused their activities toward the typical tasks of trade unions and attracted younger and better-qualified people to the leadership of the branches and in the central bodies of the confederation. Most importantly, Krastyo Petkov managed to develop and spread the new image of politically independent syndicates. The successful mission of Prof. Petkov in the reformation of the socialist trade unions made him the most eminent Bulgarian sociologist, having personally contributed to the reform process in the country in a lasting way.

However, the success backfired. To make the independence of the trade unions visible and recognisable, Petkov emphasised their distance from the political parties too often and too loudly, which made his relations with functionaries of the Socialist Party difficult. The consequence became clear in the moment he decided to return to party politics. It turned out that it was practically impossible to arrange the return via the Socialist Party. He had no other choice but to establish his own Bloc of Labor Party by using the resources of the reformed trade unions. The newly-born party did not succeed in the harsh political competition. To enter parliament, Krastyo Petkov and his party needed a coalition with the Socialist Party. He accepted this solution as temporary. However, once he had left the parliamentary coalition led by the Socialists, he could not find any other organisational vehicle to bring him to the top of Bulgarian politics. Despite his strong political ambitions and abilities to shape the future of democratic Bulgaria, he remained a professor of sociology who had very limited impact on the ongoing transformation of Bulgarian society via the mass media.

Several other intellectuals professionally related to sociology joined the anti-socialist opposition and influenced the political landscape of the post-socialist transformation of Bulgarian society. During the first years of reforms, the most prominent and promising among them was Petko Simeonov. He used to be an Associate Professor at the Institute of Sociology of the Bulgarian Academy of Sciences. The rise of the anti-socialist opposition against the regime and the ruling party at the very end of the 1980s came as an existential opportunity for him. He joined the opposition Union of Democratic Forces. His enthusiasm, rhetorical skills, and friendships with well-known intellectuals made him one of the central figures in the propaganda campaigns of the inion in its romantic phase of oppositional solidarity. He was the major organiser of the participation of UDF in the first democratic elections in 1990 and a very active member of the elected Great National Assembly. However, the phase of optimism, enthusiasm, and solidarity in the political mobilisation of opposition forces was rather short-lived. What followed was harsh competition between persons and factions in the democratic forces for positions in the new power structures, for participation in the re-distribution of wealth and complicated negotiations between political actors about the strategy of reforms. Simeonov did not have the skills and endurance to effectively cope with the new challenges.

Quite disenchanted by the new elites, he was pressed by the radical anti-socialist forces to leave active politics. This might have been a positive development since he wrote a highly intriguing book on the controversial establishment of the Union of Democratic Forces and its propaganda campaigns (Simeonov, 1996). The book contains the most impressive first-hand information about the motives and actions of the leaders of the new right-wing political organisations, their elites, and controversial cooperation in the coalition of the UDF. The book is a significant source of information about the large-scale involvement of foreign governments, foundations, and international organisations in the steering of the transformation of the post-socialist Bulgarian society.

Only a few other sociologists made direct and relevant contributions to the management of the post-socialist transformation of Bulgarian society. Professor Peter-Emil Mitev was a member of the Great National Assembly, which passed the democratic constitution of the country. Professor Georgi Fotev took the position of Minister of Education and Science in a caretaker government. There were deputy ministers with sociological backgrounds. The present author served as Secretary of the President of the state. Exactly as in other former socialist countries, sociologists took the challenge of being active actors in the management of profound changes. However, there were only very rare attempts by sociologists to offer strategic visions about the management of the transformation of Bulgarian society or of some sectors of it. The reasons for this disengagement of sociologists from strategic solutions to the vital tasks of society were and remained manifold. During the first decade of the transformation, Bulgarian society was so divided that all suggestions for strategic action were immediately met with ideological and political uproar. After the years of intentional or non-intentional destruction of the Bulgarian state, the statement 'The consolidation of state institutions is the key to solving social and economic problems' (Genov, 1995, p. 8) and the suggested measures for the purpose were interpreted and criticised as an appeal for a return to the authoritarian state or at least as a strong deviation from the libertarian vision of a night-watchman state which was regarded as only legitimate.

The objective difficulties in making a sociological diagnosis of the rapidly changing economic, political, and cultural situation notwithstanding there were some isolated cases of this type. As a rule, they were accompanied by visions of desirable future state of affairs. Tanya Chavdarova used her international experience to discuss the situation of the informal (shadow) economy and the measures needed to reduce its large share in Bulgarian society (2001). The authors of an informative collection of studies on major events and processes in Bulgarian economic and political life in the course of the post-socialist transformations attempted to connect the critical diagnosis of the economic and political parasitic networks building with visions about the desirable future and organisational measures needed for attaining it (Chalakov, 2008). Temenuga Rakadzhiyska suggested legal regulations for better functioning of the labour market (2010). Maria Zhelyazkova put international experience under scrutiny in order to suggest policies for dealing with inequality under Bulgarian conditions (2011). Using the results of a series of empirical studies and their theoretical generalisations, Yantsislav Yanakiev (2013) suggested decisions fostering the efficiency of the management of the increasingly diverse personnel of military organisations.

7.4 Collective Sociological Actors in the Societal Transformation

The major sociological institution in Bulgaria before and after the changes that started in 1989 was the Institute of Sociology at the Bulgarian Academy of Sciences. During the socialist period, the institute managed to carry out several large-scale research projects relevant to strategic societal steering. Not less important was the position of the institute in supporting the growing community of academic sociologists and sociological practitioners. Together with the Bulgarian Sociological Association, the institute was the core of a broad network uniting sociologists from research centres and universities with sociologists at enterprises, political, and administrative bodies. Both the cognitive and practical relevance of academic and applied sociology in social steering were publicly known and respected.

Some specifics of the Bulgarian post-socialist transformation are easily recognisable in the fate of sociology as a science and as a factor of social change at the national level. The situation has several dimensions. Sociology at the Bulgarian Academy of Sciences followed the organisational troubles of the Academy itself. Its funding shrunk sharply at the very beginning of the transformation and remained miserably low thereafter. The public prestige of science and scientists declined dramatically. Finally, research institutes were united with the major intention to demonstrate reforms. The former well-established Institute of Sociology became part of the new Institute for the Study of Societies and Knowledge. The Institute for the Study of Youth and other sociological research centres were dissolved.

Under these conditions, it is unrealistic to expect a high level of organisational mobilisation for high-quality fundamental and applied research with a serious impact on the multidimensional transformation of Bulgarian society. Nevertheless, it is good to notice that some studies on poverty and impoverishment, changing social structures and conditions of labour, science and technological innovations, and life-long learning have been carried out according to European standards and some of them in comparative international projects. However, regardless of the gains in the freedom of research and publication, accessibility of information, international cooperation, and others, the profound social changes did not make sociology at the Bulgarian Academy of Sciences truly relevant in the steering of social processes.

Essentially, the same holds true for the academic sociologists at the universities. Practically relevant publications by university teachers are rarities. Certainly, one may counter that the spread of knowledge by academic teaching is in itself practically very important in the long run. The argument is valid and might be the major reason why one could be somewhat optimistic in the assessment of the social impact of academic sociology at the universities in the country. Moreover, as this is the case in all post-socialist societies, the number of universities and university students increased tremendously. In all 52 universities, sociology is taught in one way or another. It is indicative of the public perception of sociology that the study of sociology at Sofia University was in third place in the preferences of future students among all disciplines in the 2017/2018 academic year. The attractiveness of the university studies of sociology is at least partly due to the improvement of the teaching itself. Attractive and practically relevant courses on 'Labor Markets and Human Resources Development', 'Labour Markets and Informal Employment: Cross-cultural Management', 'Sociological Studies on Organised Crime', and others were introduced. The methods of teaching also improved in many respects. However, the needs of the national economy, politics and culture of professionally educated and trained sociologists are not properly known. The professional success of young people who have received university diplomas in sociology is not precisely known either. Sociologists have given up the steering of their own discipline (Slavkova & Mitev, 2012). As seen from the point of view of sociology at universities, the broader diagnosis of the present-day situation of Bulgarian sociology is even more challenging: 'the disunited community and the lack of strict professional criteria and ethical norms belongs to the reasons which spread a lasting negative public image of sociology and sociologists' (Mitev, 2012, p. 31). Given this recent experience, one may realistically consider the critical assessment of social engineering via higher education in socialist Bulgaria (Boyadzhieva, 2010).

What is publicly best known about Bulgarian sociology at present is its relevance in measuring *and* influencing public opinion, mostly by results of studies on electoral preferences. This type of activity became the new professional heaven for sociologists. Moreover, the strong focus on the study of electoral preferences opened the door to prime-time debates on the most influential mass media. This is definitely the major and fundamental change in the status of sociology and sociologists after 1989. This is also a major change in the role of sociology as a factor influencing the post-socialist societal transformation in Bulgaria. Sociologists from dissolved institutions, such as the Institute of Youth Studies, university teachers in sociology and related disciplines, or just entrepreneurial individuals recognised the rapidly rising relevance of public opinion in an emerging democratic society and established a number of agencies for studies of public opinion and marketing. Foreign capital and organisational experience were also instrumental in this purpose. Some of the agencies failed, but roughly one dozen, including Gallup International, Alfa Research,

Trend, and others, survived and prospered. In the turbulent times of the early years of the transformation, their activities, diagnoses, and prognoses were generously rewarded by rich and powerful interest groups.

This development came about at the cost of the theoretically and methodologically sound academic sociology. For the vast majority of Bulgarian voters, academic sociologists do not exist since they are hardly visible on TV. Instead, the eloquent researchers from the agencies for public opinion polls are regarded as knowledgeable interpreters of the economic, political, and cultural situation of the country and of the electoral attitudes of the Bulgarian population. However, the widespread perception of the public sociologists from the agencies as advocates of political and economic interest groups sheds a shadow on the legitimacy and prestige of sociology as a serious academic science. In 2016, Krastyo Petkov presented the situation bluntly:

> Another responsible factor [besides the mass media] for manipulative impacts on public mind and electoral preferences is para-sociology. I mean the commercial agencies which abuse the label 'sociology'. In reality, they work as clients of parties, which act under the slogan: 'I pay you to produce data favourable for my candidates'.

Before 1989, the division between academic and applied branches of sociology was represented by sociologists at research institutes and universities on the one side, and applied sociology represented by numerous sociologists at the state-owned enterprises, at political and cultural organisations and at the state administration, on the other. Applied sociology in this form practically disappeared in the course of the societal transformation. Since academic research is publicly funded, it suffered financially during the transformation period and could hardly be a serious factor influencing the transformation. In contrast, the so-called sociological agencies managed to grab the opportunity and develop a lucrative business. If sociology could be defined as a factor influencing the post-socialist transformation in Bulgaria, there were and are private sociological agencies for public opinion research, which would deserve this characteristic mostly. Some of these agencies publish valuable diagnoses of the economic, political, and cultural situations that have essentially sociological content and have their impacts on the decision-makers (Gallup International, 2017).

The picture is more complex and complicated. The booming market of studies on public opinion has been substantially supported by funding from abroad. A major part of this funding was channelled through organisations specially established for this purpose, like the Center for Liberal Strategies, the Center for the Study of Democracy, the Soros Foundation, and others. They were designed as foreign-funded think tanks focusing on key issues in the development of Bulgarian society. The foreign investors, sponsors or donors funded and continue funding surveys and other activities like conferences, workshops, travelling support, support for publications, and others. For instance, the Centre for the Study of Democracy and the affiliated Vitosha Research agency were established with foreign funding and carried out practically oriented research studies on corruption, minorities, cross-border migration, integration of immigrants, and others. No generalisation about the motivation and the impacts of these sociological or sociology-related activities on the transformation of Bulgarian society is possible. The only visible and undeniable effect of this institutional development is that a relevant part of the sociological community in Bulgaria existentially depends on the specific interests of institutions that are not Bulgarian.

Another crucial issue concerns the role of these think tanks as promoters of the policy of their donors wrapped up as the transition to democracy. It turned out that this policy faced substantial difficulties in Central and Eastern Europe in general and in Bulgaria in particular (Lavern, 2010).

7.5 Conclusion

Bulgarian society went and partly still is going through a period of extraordinarily deep and intensive post-socialist transformation. It involves all actors in the country, changes their relations profoundly and includes highly controversial processes of integration and disintegration, rationalisation and de-rationalisation, constructive and destructive individualisation, and others. This is a challenging environment for sociological theorising and research as well as for testing the capacity of sociology and sociologists to influence the all-embracing post-socialist reforms. Given the complexity of the situation, the assessment of the strengths and weaknesses, achievements, and failures in the adaptation of Bulgarian sociology and Bulgarian sociologists to the process of transformation should be well balanced. The most general conclusion is that sociology and sociologists only partly met the requirements for high-quality scientific reflection on the accelerated profound change (Genov, 2002, p. 402). Due to weak explanatory models and the general disorganisation of the sociological community, the social-technological potentials of Bulgarian sociology remain underdeveloped, inefficiently used, or not used at all. However, given the overwhelming trend of the rationalisation of organisations, one may expect that the return of sociologists to the need to strengthen the practical relevance of their professional work will once more become a key issue in sociological discussions and activities.

Competing Interests The author has no conflicts of interest to declare that are relevant to the content of this chapter.

References

Boyadzhieva, P. (2010). *Socialnoto inzhenerstvo. Politiki na priem vav visshite uchilishta prez komunisticheskiya rezhim* [The social engineering. Politics of allowance to higher education institutions during the communist regime]. CIELA (in Bulgarian).
Burawoy, M. (2016). Sociology as a vocation. *Contemporary Sociology, 45*(4), 379–393.
Chavdarova, T. (2001). *Neformalnata ikonomika* [The non-formal economy]. Lik (in Bulgarian).

Comte, A. (2016 [1853]). *System of positive polity, or treatise on sociology. Vol. 3: Instituting the religion of humanity; Containing social dynamics, or the general theory of human progress.* Forgotten Books.

Chalakov, I. (2008). *Mrezhite na prehoda. Kakvo vsashtnost se sluchi v Balgariya sled 1989 [The networks of transition. What actually happened in Bulgaria after 1989].* Iztok-Zapad (in Bulgarian).

Dobriyanov, V. (1995). *Fenomenat Vanga [The phenomenon of Vanga].* Sofia University Publishing House (in Bulgarian).

Dobriyanov, V., Stavrov, B., & Genov, N. (1978). *Savremennata sociologiya v Balgaria [Contemporary Sociology in Bulgaria].* Bulgarian Sociological Association (in Bulgarian).

Elster, J., Offe, K., & Preuss, U. (1998). *Institutional design in post-communist societies: Rebuilding the ship at sea.* Cambridge University Press.

Gallup International. (2017). *Politicheskiyat process i obshtestvenoto mnenie v Balgariya–2016 [The political process and public opinion in Bulgaria in 2016].* Ciela (in Bulgarian).

Genov, N. (1991). The transition to democracy: Trends and paradoxes of social rationalization. *International Social Science Journal, 128*, 131–141.

Genov, N. (1995). Man in a society undergoing transition. In N. Genov (Ed.), *Bulgaria human development report 1995* (pp. 1–13). UNDP.

Genov, N. (2002). Sociology—Bulgaria. In M. Kaase & V. Sparschuh (Eds.), *Three social science disciplines in Central and Eastern Europe: Handbook on economics, political science and sociology* (pp. 386–404). Social Science Information Centre.

Genov, N. (2016). Eastern Europe as a laboratory for social sciences. In S. Eliaeson, L. Harutyunyan, & L. Titarenko (Eds.), *After the soviet empire: Legacies and pathways* (pp. 135–163). Brill.

Genov, N. (2021). Societal transformation: Eastern European experience and conceptualization. *International Area Studies Review, 24*(1), 3–17. https://doi.org/10.1177/2233886592110055589

Hadnagy, C. (2011). *Social engineering: The art of human hacking.* Wiley.

Koleva, S. (2005). *Sociologiyata kato proekt: Nauchna identichnost i socialni izpitaniya v Balgariya 1945–1989 godina [Sociology as a project: Scientific identity and social trials in Bulgaria during the years 1945–1989].* Pensoft Publishers (in Bulgarian).

Kyuranov, C. (1987). *Dneshnoto balgarsko semeystvo [the contemporary Bulgarian family].* Nauka i izkustvo (in Bulgarian).

Lavern, D. (2010). Ekspertite na prehoda. Balgarskite think-tanks i globalnite mrezhi za vliyanie |M. (2012)). Educational integration of refugee and asylum-seeking children, country report Bulgaria. In A. Nonchev & N. Tagarov (Eds.), *Integrating refugee and asylum-seeking children in the educational systems of EU member states* (pp. 108–136). CSD.

Mihaylov, S. (1973). *Empirichnoto sociologichesko izsledvane [The empirical sociological survey].* Partizdat (in Bulgarian).

Mihaylov, S. (2003). *Sociologiyata v Balgariya sled Vtorata svetovna voyna [Sociology in Bulgaria after the Second World War].* M8M (in Bulgarian).

Mitev, T. (2012). Problemi na sociologicheskite profesii v Balgariya: Usloviya za vazmožnost i zavisimost ot izminatiya pat' [problems of the sociological professions in Bulgaria: Conditions for possibility and dependence from the past experience]. *Sociological Problems, 3–4*, 7–40.

Oshavkov, Z. (1958). *Istoricheskiyat materializam i sociologiyata [Historical materialism and sociology].* Nauka I izkustvo.

Oshavkov, Z. (1976). *Sociologicheskata struktura na savremennoto balgarsko oshtestvo [The sociological structure of the contemporary Bulgarian society].* Bulgarian Academy of Sciences (in Bulgarian).

Petkov, K. (1985). *Sociologiya na truda [Sociology of work].* Profizdat (in Bulgarian).

Petkov, K. (2016).*Stagnirashta ikonomika, degradirashta politika, electoralen populizam.* [Stagnating Economy, Degrading Politics, Electoral Populism]. (2016). *Българи* [Bulgarians] Accessed Nov 16, 2016, from http://bolgari.org/stagnirashta_ikonomika_degradirashta_politika_elektoral_populizam-el-2435.html. The cited text belongs to section "Elektoraln iyat populizam sledstvie, a ne prichina" [The electoral pluralism–a consequence, not the cause].

Rakadzhiyska, T. (2010). *Pazar na truda. Socialno-ikonomicheskoto pole mezhdu darzhavata i pazara [Labor market. Socioeconomic field between the state and the market]*. Stopanstvo (in Bulgarian).

Simeonov, P. (1996). *Golyamata promyana: 10.XI.1989–10.VI. 1990: Opit za document [The Great Change: 10.XI.1989–10.VI. 1990: An Attempt at Document]*. Otechestvo (in Bulgarian).

Sum, N., & Jessop, B. (2013). *Towards cultural political economy: Putting culture in its place in political economy*. Edgar Elgar.

Ward, L. F. (1906). *Applied sociology: A treatise on the conscious improvement of society by society*. Ginn & Company.

Yahiel, N. (1976). *Sociology and social practice: A sociological analysis of contemporary social processes and their interrelationship with science*. Pergamon Press.

Yanakiev, Y. (2013). *Horata v otbranata. Edinni v mnogoobrazieto [People in the defense. United in the plurality]*. Publishing House of Sofia University.

Zhelyazkova, M. (2011). *Neravenstva i politiki. Distantsii mezhdu Balgariya i Evropeyskiya sayuz [Inequalities and policies. Distances between Bulgafria and the European Union]*. ALYA (in Bulgarian).

Nikolai Genov is a Professor Emeritus at the Free University in Berlin. He has received his PhD from the University of Leipzig. His research fields include sociological theory, societal transformations, global trends and cross-border migration. He has been Research Fellow and Visiting Professor at the Universities in Berkeley, Berlin, Bielefeld, Lund, Moscow, Rome, Seoul and Warsaw. He is the author of more than 360 scientific publications in 28 countries. He has been Director of the Institute for Eastern European Studies of the Free University Berlin, vice-president of UNESCO's Management of Social Transformations Program and Vice-President of the International Social Science Council (Paris). His recent monographs include Global Trends in Eastern Europe (2016); Challenges of Individualization (2018) and The Paradigm of Social Interaction (2021).

Chapter 8
Sociology in Post-transition Transformations of Croatian Society

Jasminka Lažnjak

8.1 Introduction

The objective of this analysis is to explore the possible role of sociology in post-transition transformations of Croatian society. The impact of the scientific discipline and profession may be visible on the level of the specific expertise that might have been useful or necessary in different types of policy-making or might emerge as an intended or unintended consequence of individual political, public or civil society activist engagement of sociologists. This chapter is focused on the discursive selectivity in four acting types: favouring, selection, retention, and reinforcement of specific discourses in which sociology might have taken part in the past three decades. The proposal initiates important aspects in the relationship of social science with society in transition and opens the issue of a sociologist as an observer or as an active participant in social processes. Michael Burawoy's Presidential Address to the American Sociological Association (2005) marked the entire decade with discussion about public versus policy and professional sociology as the answer to sociology in crisis (Calhoun, 2005; Turner, 2005; Clawson et al., 2007; Nichols, 2011; Matić, 2017). His claim that the sociological profession should actively promote the human values that are embodied in the sociological standpoint gave rise to public sociology globally. Discussion for and against public sociology and related debate about the lost social impact of our discipline, because it became increasingly invisible and irrelevant despite its popularity among students, has been ongoing ever since (Holmwood, 2007; Boyns & Fletcher, 2005).

Jessop's (2004; Jessop & Oosterlynck, 2008) new cultural turn with his concept of cultural and political economy shed light on some neglected aspects of discourse

J. Lažnjak (✉)
Faculty of Humanities and Social Sciences, University of Zagreb, Zagreb, Croatia
e-mail: jlaznjak@ffzg.unizg.hr

creation and exploration at the theoretical and conceptual levels. In Croatia, empirical research that would specifically address dominant social discourses could not be found; so, in this sense, a certain arbitrariness arises in the labelling of dominant discourses. For this reason, the assessment of the relationship of sociology in this chapter is based on some arbitrarily assumed dominant discourses of Croatian society post-accession. Croatia shares with other post-socialist societies discourses of economic transition, marketing and privatisation, and political transition to liberal democracy, but in the specific context of the war for independence, the dominant discourse is also increasing nationalism (Dryzek et al., 2002; Massey et al., 2003).

The starting point in the analysis is the proposition of the marginal role of contemporary sociology in post-transition transformations of Croatian society.

The role of sociology as a scientific discipline in terms of scientific and professional expertise production that would influence or shape the dominant transition discourses has been insignificant in Croatian sociology. It has also been marginal in terms of the participation of sociologists in the new political elite at individual and professional levels. The analysis of the impact on the individual level might be problematic since it implies that it is possible on the conceptual and methodological level to identify and single out when a particular sociologist manages his or her acts in the professional role using sociological knowledge in shaping and entailing some particular discourse of social transformation.

In the search for the arguments that would support our thesis, the analysis draws on the institutional perspective using the concept of path dependency in disciplinary development. The path dependency concept refers to the tendency to rely on past practices. It has been widely used within historical institutionalism (Kay, 2005; Hay, 2002), explaining an institutional change as following a certain trajectory, that is, processes are affected by the initial order in which they happened. According to Mahoney (2000, p. 507):

> […] path dependence characterizes specifically those historical sequences in which contingent events set into motion institutional patterns or event chains that have [got] deterministic properties.

However, this does not mean simply accepting that history is important and that the past influences the future. Post-socialist transition as unique political and cultural convergence of societies cannot be understood in terms of the common 'transition culture' of all former socialist countries but in a specific case-historical context (Blokker, 2005). The analysis of Croatian sociology in the post-transitional context follows the above understanding of path dependence.

The status and role of sociology in the post-transition Croatian society cannot be entirely understood without the reflection on the renewal and re-establishment of discipline in the 1960s. The position has always been between embeddedness in concrete social, political, and ideological systems upon which depends its very subject as well as by institutionalisation and financing and, on the other side, in the critical aspect toward the very same ideology. The marginality of sociology is partly the consequence of previous historical periods. The crisis of discipline and a missed opportunity for a more significant impact on political and social life are discussed in the context of two permanent parallel roles, legitimating and criticising the social system. During the socialist period, sociology was labelled a subversive scientific discipline due to the criticism of dogmatic Marxism and regular alerts to dysfunctional elements of the self-management system. After the change of system, Croatian sociology retained the same label of subversion but this time due to insufficient 'national orientation'.

In the first decades of transition, Croatian sociology was mostly a parochial discipline marked by crisis, with inadequate funding of research, captured in a peripheral position within the national science system and within global sociology (Štulhofer et al., 2010; Baćak, 2011). In the new millennium, after the homeland war and international isolation of Croatia during late President Tuđman's era, sociology had started its way toward more internalisation through more extensive participation in the European Union's (EU) research funds (framework programme) and increasingly publishing internationally.

This chapter is organised in the following way: after the introduction, a short historical outline is given of the development of sociology since the first department and institute were established in the 1960s. In the following section, the marginal role of sociology is explored from the analyses based on content analysis of sociological publications and publicly financed research projects. In the next section, a short overview of the professional development is given, followed by a conclusion.

8.2 Between Ideologisation and Professionalisation (1963–1990)

Sociology as a scientific discipline has two origins: as an academic discipline and as a discipline that deals with emerging social problems. Sociology as a scientific discipline arose in response to the processes and the major structural social changes that took place in the eighteenth and nineteenth centuries: the Enlightenment, modernisation, the Industrial Revolution, secularisation, and urbanisation. The transition from traditional rural to modern industrial society did not happen without social turmoil and crises. The dissolution of traditional communities with their customs and values raised questions about what would replace them, what the moral order would be, and what cohesive forces and type of social solidarity would enable survival, that is, the creation of a new social fabric. From the beginning, the social-historical and political context, particularly the relation to the power and power elites (i.e. the ruling ideology), has defined sociology (Županov & Šporer, 1985).

After the Second World War and the socialist revolution, the status of social sciences changed in accordance with the ruling ideology of Marxism, which served as the foundation for all social sciences. Followed by a period of dominant historical materialism, sociology was proclaimed a bourgeois discipline and completely rejected. After the conflict with the Informbiro, the Stalinist interpretation of Marxism was replaced by a different humanistic understanding of Marx's works and turned to his 'Early Writings' or Praxis philosophy (Gruenwald, 2015). It was the time of introducing the idea of self-management as the basis for the creation of democratic socialism and the opening of the SFR Yugoslavia to the West that opened the space for discussion of the relation of sociology as a positivist, empirical bourgeois discipline and Marxism characterised by a humanistic, scientific orientation. Socioeconomic changes toward the liberalisation of the economy and the development of workers' self-management in the conditions of scientific and technological change opened the space for a critical review of the functioning of the social system of self-management socialism. The departure from dogmatic Marxism and its interpretation of social development made it possible to articulate the ideas of freedom of critical thought, which created the preconditions for the renewal of the institutionalisation of sociology.

Sociology as a discipline emerged in the 1950s through dialogue with Marxism, when the conflict with Stalin opened space for dialogue between humanistic, democratic Marxism within Praxis philosophy and sociology as the primary bourgeois discipline of the time. That is the reason why the newly born sociology was perceived as philosophy's 'younger sister'. The discipline created in the process (or as a result of political conflict) had the latent ideological function to explore and justify the new model of society and be the ideological support for change. Also, it was often used for political purposes by supporters of 'solid' options but also by reformers. Political leaders were acting and using it in the political struggle in any crisis or in changes in society, which gave it the label of 'extended arm of politics'. Despite these circumstances, there were phases when the ideologisation of sociology was replaced by professionalisation (Šporer, 2006).

8.3 The Crisis of Sociology in the Period of War and Transition

The lack of a significant impact of Croatian sociology in the post-transition transformation requires a perspective from the unique social and historical context. It was the period of radical change of the social system, announced by the fall of the Berlin Wall, carried on the already started liberalisation of late socialism on the one side and the coming disintegration of the former Yugoslavia with rising nationalism and increasing power of Slobodan Milošević in Serbia on the other side. Although we will not go deeper in the analysis of the transition in the 1990s, it is necessary to briefly describe the socio-cultural context that situates sociology outside the sphere of significant political participation (at the individual level as well as the discipline) without the possibility of influencing the construction of political discourse. The disintegration of Yugoslavia in the war conflict between Croatia and Serbia took place when Croatian sociology was in the phase of re-ideologisation by 're-Marxisation' and in the remission of the golden age of professionalisation. At that moment, it received the stigma of being a 'Yugo-nostalgic', leftist, and insufficiently nationally oriented discipline. The inherited roles of legitimation and critical discourse, interchangeable phases of more ideologisation, or more professionalisation tendencies had left sociology on the margins. In many aspects, still, within Marxist critical discourse, the main issues were the critical analysis of rising nationalism, so-called tycoon privatisation, and rent-seeking political capitalism.

The illustration of one of the best early sociological analyses of transition processes is the work of Josip Županov, a famous Croatian sociologist and author of the most important theoretical concept in Croatian sociology, 'Egalitarian Syndrome Theory' (Županov, 1977), who writes about weak sociology due to the specific transition that has resulted in political capitalism, tycoon privatisation, and the re-traditionalisation of society. According to Županov, the transition in the former socialist countries did not take place as the construction of capitalism from the ground, ab ovo. In his opinion, within these societies, a political class formed in socialism is part of political capitalism, in which the modi operandi are privileges, robbing the state property, and working in the shadow economy. Jowitt (1992) defines political capitalism as the economic activity that takes place within an administrative hierarchy rather than a market; the ethos of such economic activity is the uncertainty caused by the arbitrariness of the political sponsor rather than the greater predictability of impersonal market regulation; and the primary agents are fiscally oriented corporations instead of individual entrepreneurs.

Croatian transition is characterised by political rather than entrepreneurial capitalism (Županov, 1995, 2011). The basic characteristics of political capitalism are social (state) ownership, fragmented market, politically fake market (monopolies), with political rather than professional managers as the main actors, the state as the shield (against market competition) and 'nanny' (keeping jobs for employees), and a large part of GDP redistributed to state channels. The internal contradiction of such a system, which threatens its existence, is that securing illegally acquired wealth would require a change in the system, and radical change would jeopardise the position of those same existing elites that had arisen in political capitalism. The contradiction was resolved by the anti-communist revolution in which the proto-capitalist elite of the political class (managerial and administrative) legitimised their real wealth in the processes of privatisation. The self-management system as the backdrop of political capitalism helped to dismantle socialism by territorial decentralisation, which made it easy to replace class ideology with national ideology. Social disaggregation occurred before the formal break-up of socialism. Due to the planned market model, a more open economy and more liberal political regime facilitated the transition to wild capitalism. Under the influence of transitional changes, political capitalism from that initial phase has been modified but with strongly present elements of state intervention and the welfare state. The ruling of the new governing elite took place through four processes: de-industrialisation, re-traditionalisation, de-scientisation, and bureaucratic regression. De-industrialisation is the process of disappearing industrial enterprises on an 'empty shell' principle, in which new owners maintained only empty shells with no productive economic activity and new capitalists were dominantly rent-seeking and not profit-seeking. The re-traditionalisation of society most obviously took place as de-secularisation and de-scientisation as the process of continuous financial starvation of the science system (despite a 'knowledge society' being declared, allocations for science have not exceeded 1% of the GDP).

The example of Županov's critical analysis of transition and privatisation illustrates how the subversive role of sociology has been re-established. In a period of turmoil and change in social and political context, sociology was repositioned without gaining the role of social legitimisation. The marginalisation of mainstream sociology and lack of participation in the new political elites can also be partly explained by a new divide in the sociological community that occurred with the establishment of a new institute and department of Croatian studies: a clear-cut and clean start of new Croatian sociology.

8.4 Post-transitional Shaping of Sociological Discourses

Very few Croatian sociologists wrote explicitly about the role of sociology in the transition period. Ivan Cifrić (1995), in his article 'Sociology in the New Social Context', considers recent societal changes as a challenge to sociological science that requires questioning of its identity and new (self-)reflexivity. These changes are, on the one hand, global social change, for example, the ecological crisis and the North and South conflicts, and change in societies in transition on the other hand. The transitional social context raises new questions of modernisation in technological and social terms that sociology should not ignore. His pleading for sociology as practical sociology concludes with the statement that politics should accept the results of sociological analysis and research.

Peračković (2004) explores the new transition sociology as a discipline and analyses different theoretical and conceptual approaches to transition from economic and political aspects to the wider socio-cultural transformation of societies.

The lack of literature explicitly dealing with the sociology of transition or sociology in transition proves how a discursive approach might be much more useful in this analysis.

The post-transition period for the sociological profession was marked by crisis. Within the sociological community, post-transitional sociology was portrayed as insufficiently visible in Croatian society (Tomić Koludrović, 2009). The reasons for the unsatisfactory state of the discipline were attributed to the lack of well-developed theoretical and methodological tools to address the complex processes of social transformation during that period. Inga Tomić Koludrović identified the root cause in the historical role of sociology as a legitimizing force during the socialist era. This means that sociology was not able to position itself in the legitimising role in the new social system on ideological grounds because it was not sufficiently professionally developed and was not able to offer expertise and knowledge as it potentially could have.

The crisis of sociology in the first transition period was a widely accepted diagnosis among the professional community and intellectuals. Under new circumstances due to the dissolution of Yugoslavia, such as political instability, war, and the rise of authoritarianism and nationalism, Croatian sociology, together with other social sciences, went through institutional, ideological, and conceptual transformations that made a significant impact in terms of unfavourable conditions for social research. Some sociologists suggested that sociology reacted insufficiently and overly slowly to some key social processes (Cosovschi, 2017).

The reaction to the political context was either opposition or legitimation (for a part of the sociological community), forcing the opposition to fight for the survival of old institutes and studies in competition with the newly established without burdening Marxist heritage. The early 1990s brought organisational and institutional changes that had consequences in some imbalances in financing of research institute projects and quotas for student enrolment at sociology departments. It is important to emphasise that the political pressure was not coming directly from the members of the sociological community or within professional associations that, despite the ideological polarisation, kept mutual professional respect and tolerance, which enabled their 'cohabitation'.

Inga Tomić Koludrović (2018) divided the post-transitional development of sociology into four phases based on the analysis of keywords in sociological publications. The first phase, from 1990 to 1995, was marked by different discourses and concepts of the post-socialist transition. One discourse focused on socialism as an authoritarian system and glorifying freedom and democracy. Another discourse was a kind of modification of the first one but dealt with the criticism of both socialist and nationalist totalitarianism. Some authors point to the lack of elaborated theoretical perspectives that would be able to explain the consequences of a socialist legacy in the new society. Some sociologists emphasised the missing actors of the new social system in civil society, social movements, and engaged intellectuals. Another approach stressed the lack of values necessary for a liberal democratic transition.

In the context of looking for relevant actors, there was a concern about forming a new entrepreneurial class as a key to transition to a market economy. The key question for the establishment of a market economy came forward: Was it possible without radical privatisation based on corruption and plunder of public property and business companies? Some texts questioned the naïve belief that political pluralism and the market economy would automatically lead toward progress. In sum, sociology in the early transition period was marked by the use of inconsistent and underdeveloped concepts that were very critical toward socialism and, at the same time, pessimistic about future development.

In the second phase, from 1995 to 2000, the debate about transition continued with a focus on socialism as a quasi-modern, traditional, authoritarian, and totalitarian type of society with suspended political freedom, political domination over the economy, and a collectivist, egalitarian value system. At the same time, the description of capitalism was as a desirable system that includes the rule of law, freedom, pluralism, democracy, and market economy. Some key words from that period were 'efficiency', 'rationality', 'modernism', and 'individualism'.

The third phase, in the decade from 2000 to 2010, indicates the opening of Croatian sociology to international academia, higher participation in international research projects, and stronger international institutional cooperation. The Croatian

Sociological Association renewed its professional engagement and returned to regular activities, organising national congresses and international conferences. The association became more active and recognised in international sociological associations that impacted the internationalisation of sociology. New discourses emerged together with more diverse research themes that had moved away from immediate local social issues due to new directions in research from international organisations, sponsors, and academia. The system of research financing increased and became more stable nationally through the new funding scheme of the Ministry of Science and internationally by participation in EU framework programmes, non-governmental organisations, and private and public organisations. Together with private companies as new clients, newly founded opinion poll agencies brought the spirit of commercialisation to sociological research. All these processes resulted in more diversity of themes and subjects of sociological research. As transition processes progressed, the optimistic prognoses were replaced by more critical assessments of neoliberal capitalism using terms such as 'transnational capitalist class', 'corrupted elites', 'international monetary institutions', and similar. This discourse uses concepts of clientelism and wild capitalism to denote a specific type of transition capitalism that might be outlined as the deviation from the more acceptable, normative Western European type. In this decade of more stable and diverse funding resources, sociology gained more professional autonomy, but at the same time, the Bologna reform in higher education, the national system of financing, and the selection of research themes, university programme accreditation, opened the space to more political influence on shaping sociological paradigms.

In the last period, after 2010, among a younger generation of sociologists, a left-oriented critical discourse has arisen. The focus of their work is a critique of capitalism as a normative system combining neo-Marxist and post-structural approaches. The arguments against capitalism are based on the consequences of neoliberal politics exploring the consequences of the commercialisation of education and public services, criminal privatisation of companies, and the flexibilisation of work legislation. Several theoretical frameworks are used, including world system theory, dependence theory, and new Marxism, often by non-academic activist circles.

From the right/conservative side, the second line of criticism appeared with the criticism of new Western imperialism and its political, economic, and cultural consequences, loss of political sovereignty, and national identity. They are accompanied by anti-feminism, gender ideology, anti-LGBT movement, and clericalism.

The focus of mainstream academic sociology is the social consequences, transition costs, labour market flexibility, job insecurity, the social position of women, growing social inequalities, low social mobility, and urban transformation. Identity issues, value orientations, problems related to certain social groups (e.g. young people, women, LGBT communities), environmental issues, new forms of political and civic participation, new forms of work organisation, organisational culture, phenomena such as globalisation, and European integration were also raised in the focus of sociological interests. In the analysis of structural change, a new concept of class emerges, with the addition of neo-Marxist and neo-Weberian concepts of class and new concepts of analysis such as those of Bourdieu.

This analysis is supported by the study of the ten most frequent keywords of articles published in the period from 1990 to 2023 in *Croatian Sociological Review*, which clearly showed how the focus of sociology has changed from immediate consequences of war such as migration and refugees, economic and political transition in the first decade to more structural problems and conceptual sociological themes of globalisation, nationalism, identity, and human rights in the second decade. The 5-year period confirms the thesis of entering a more mature phase of post-transitional development of Croatian sociology. The focal point has turned to the problems of specific groups (youth, women, etc.) and to theoretical and methodological issues. The last period reflects some of the issues in Croatian society: growing socioeconomic differences, gender inequalities, education reform, and family transformations. It is important to consider that published articles reflect editorial policy at the time and the themes of the major research projects in sociology in given periods. They are not representative of the Croatian sociological publication record.

Another aspect of the relatively weak position of Croatian sociology indicates the number and thematic structure of research projects. Public funding of research projects is one of the more powerful levers of focusing sociology on desirable and dominant topics defined by the ruling elite. Programmes and calls to the social sciences (together with the humanities) must only rely on the theme of identity, which was a key national theme in the application process, along with European and international guidelines on sustainable development, the knowledge society, and entrepreneurship.

Based on the list of publicly funded projects of the Ministry of Science and Technology and the Croatian Science Foundation from the Croatian Science Foundation (CSF) and Croatian Scientific Bibliography (CROSBI) database, a small thematic analysis has been made. A total of 49 projects were in the sample, divided into 6 thematic units (Table 8.1). Most projects tackle the themes of quality of life, health, sexuality, sustainable development, tourism, and rural and urban development, followed by identity, ethnicity, and multiculturalism. In the third place are culture, media, and multiculturalism. Some core subjects for sociology, such as social structure and mobility, poverty, social cohesion, knowledge, innovation, and entrepreneurship, are less represented. This clearly shows how sociology was far more in a position of retrieving and adapting to dominant discourses than it could impose them.

Perhaps sociology was able to reinforce the dominant discourses of identity nation-building, which was entailed by public funding schemes for research projects as the main source of funding. Counterbalance factors were EU funds that reinforced issues from the European core in framework programmes and Horizon 2020 priorities and funding from foundations such as Open Society, Friedrich Ebert, Heinrich Böll, and Konrad Adenauer with their agenda. The most significant contribution to oppositional discourse to authoritarian and nationalist discourse during the first decade of the Tuđman era was provided by Soros' Open Society Foundations

Table 8.1 Top ten keywords of articles in *Croatian Sociological Review* (*Revija za sociologiju*)

1991–2000(n = 599)		2000–2010 (n = 590)		2010–2015 (n = 280)		2016–2023(n = 443)	
Keywords	n	Keywords	n	Keywords	n	Keywords	n
Croatia	29	Croatia	16	Croatia	4	Socioeconomic status/differences/inequality; economy	17
Research	16	Identity	7	Youth	4	Gender	13
Refugees	10	Globalisation	5	Class	3	Croatia	12
Sociology of migration	9	Nationalism	5	Bourdieu class theory	2	Education	11
Forced migration	8	Sociology	4	Ethnicity	2	Child(ren)	10
Economic sociology	7	Authoritarianism	3	Feminism	2	Sex	10
Europe	7	Discourse	3	Citizenship	2	National(ism)	9
Democracy	6	Ethnic distance	3	Ideology	2	Family	8
Post-communism	6	European Union	3	Cosmopolitanism	2	Inequality	7
Transition	6	Human rights	3	Qualitative research	2	LGBTQ/gay	7

Source: 1991–2015 data from Latinac (2017); 2016–2023 data by author

Table 8.2 List of research projects in sociology funded by the Ministry of Science and Education (2007–2013) and the Croatian Science Foundation (2014–2023) (CSF and CROSBI database)

Project themes	No. of projects
Quality of life, health, sexuality, sustainable development, tourism, rural and urban	21
Identity, nation, religion, and ethnic minorities	13
Culture, media, and multiculturalism	10
Social structure, class, mobility, elites, institutions, corruption, and gender	7
Knowledge society, science technology development, innovation, and entrepreneurship	6
Social exclusion, poverty, and cohesion	2
Integration and disintegration in the European Union	1

for conferences, book publishing, and scholarships. Its primary role of boosting civil society development turned to the role of life support for many intellectuals, sociologists included (Table 8.2).

8.5 Professional and Institutional Development

The Croatian Sociological Association is a professional non-profit association of sociologists with approximately 300 members, founded in 1959 as the Sociological Association of Croatia that, until 1991, acted as a member of the Yugoslav

Association for Sociology. The association's current name dates from 1992, when the association became a member of the International Sociological Association and also joined the European Sociological Association since its beginnings. Today, the Croatian Sociological Association has 11 specialised sections covering broad areas and social domains and two regional branches in Zadar and Split.

Sociology as an academic discipline has a long tradition in Croatia. The first chair for criminal studies and sociology was established in 1906 at the Faculty of Law at the University of Zagreb as the first sociology chair in the Austro-Hungarian Monarchy. The first professional sociological association was founded in Zagreb in 1918. The society defined its mission as 'to nourish social sciences, study social and economic circumstances of our people, and on the basis of such research, act with the aim of educating the public, providing moral cultivation, and working in the area of social and political issues' (The Statute 1918 in Batina, 2006, p. 33). The first president of the society was Adolf Mihalić, the vice-president Albert Basala, and secretary Juraj Andrassy, who published the first report on the work of the Sociological Society in Zagreb in 1923 in the international journal *Revue internationale de sociologie* (Geneva). In the report, Andrassy wrote about the many conferences and lectures organised by the society and reported that the society has 160 members. The society was active until 1932. It is interesting to mention the role of Baltazar Bogišić in the early institutionalisation of world sociology. In 1888, he became the first president of the newly founded International Institute of Sociology, the predecessor of the World Society for Sociology, today the International Sociological Association (Batina, 2008). The current sociological association, as well as sociology after the Second World War, did not draw on the tradition of the previous period in any aspect.

The institutional structure during the socialist era consisted of two university departments and a few research institutes. After the establishment of the first department of sociology at the Faculty of Humanities and Social Sciences at the University of Zagreb in 1963, the second department was founded in Zadar in 1976 as part of the Faculty of Philosophy in Zadar. The Institute for Sociological Research, founded in 1964, soon changed its name to the Institute for Social Research at the University of Zagreb; it was the central research institution for sociological research, along with the later established Institute for Migration and Ethnic Studies and Institute for Development and International Relations. The status of sociology as an obligatory subject in all higher education syllabi ensured that many sociologists found their academic careers and enabled the development of applied sociologies on different chairs for social sciences in many other faculties.

The transition brought institutional changes in the establishment of a new Institute of Applied Social Research and a new study programme of Croatian studies, which in a few years transformed into the new parallel study programme of sociology, journalism, history, and Croatology at the University of Zagreb. Sociology has been institutionalised and programmatically diversified. With the establishment of new departments at universities, the number of students significantly increased and academic sociology has certainly strengthened. The establishment of new sociology studies at several Croatian universities manifests institutional empowerment.

Currently, in Croatia, there are six departments for sociology at five public universities. Three postgraduate and doctoral programmes are being held at the University of Zagreb, Croatian Catholic University, and the University of Zadar. Diversification of sociology has traditionally been conducted through the sociology chairs at other faculties, such as Law, Economics, Medicine, or Mechanical Engineering. Some applied sociologies also remain in the programmes of other studies. The main research institutes are public research institutes, the Institute of Social Sciences Ivo Pilar, the Institute for Social Research Zagreb, the Institute for Migration, and the Institute for Development and International Relations.

8.5.1 Availability of Funding for Social Research

Since the 1990s, the funding of social research has gone through several phases as the legislative frameworks have changed.

The financing of research in the social sciences in the post-transition period in Croatia is characterised by continuous financial starvation characteristic of the total scientific research area. Social sciences generally account for about 9% of total funding. Public funding has been a major source of funding throughout this period.

Science policy in Croatia is the horizontal policy type that encourages the equal development of all scientific disciplines without emphasis on selected thematic areas, and the basic paradigm of scientific development is a linear model, which, while considered outdated in relation to the interactive model, ensured the continuity of the scientific community in the era of transition. Nevertheless, this type of science policy neglected the need for more intensive internationalisation and greater competition between researchers, institutions, and projects. Consequently, the lower quality of research has led to the 'mini' scientific reforms in 2013 (Švarc et al., 2019).

Another important factor is the prolonged period of Croatia waiting to join the European Union, which has resulted in reduced participation in framework programmes. The late joining of the European Research Area and delaying the reforms of the scientific system created an atmosphere of insufficiently competitive, low-quality scientific projects, which resulted in an atmosphere of discontent with the domination of the interterritorial local science, which was internationally unrecognised.

The reform of the scientific system in 2013 brought new financial restrictions that hit the social sciences in particular. The latest decisions by the Ministry of Science and Education for multi-year funding for scientific activities with different coefficients (ponders) for science fields to promote STEM fields are taking a new hit for social sciences (1.2 for SSH, STEM 2.6 on average).

Sociological projects were few and underfunded. Funding went through the Ministry of Science and Education in 2013. In the last cycle of such funding for scientific projects from 2007 to 2013, social sciences received approximately 1.5 million euros (about 9% of the total budget).

To date, the Croatian Science Foundation has funded (including projects that have just started) a total of 22 projects. For 13 projects after 2013, funding data are available, and they amount to approximately 1,088,000 euros.

8.5.2 Availability of Relevant Empirical Data for Social Research

Croatia joined the European Value Survey in 1999 and participated in three rounds (1999, 2008, and 2017/2018), but the institution that had supported it was the Faculty of Theology and Catechism at the University of Zagreb with a few sociologists in the team.

Croatia was not continuously included in the European Social Survey. First, it was affiliated with the Institute of Social Sciences Ivo Pilar, and since 2019, the Faculty of Humanities and Social Sciences has been the coordinator for Croatia.

Social research mostly relied on the data collected through research projects, and although within sociological associations, there were initiatives to enable access to empirical data to members of the wider sociological community, it never succeeded in becoming fully accessible.

Furthermore, some improvement has been made in the previous decade in cooperation with the Croatian Bureau of Statistics to open its databases for social research.

It can be said that since we are not a large research community, the use of empirical or statistical databases remained in the small circles of a few researchers. The so-called Big Data sociology has not become a regular praxis in Croatian sociology despite some valuable analyses that have been made within research and evaluation policy projects.

8.5.3 Professional Ethics and (In)Dependence from Political Influence

Plagiarism, as the most common violation of professional ethics in academia, has been an issue in Croatia in recent years, but the most controversial cases were not related to sociology. These cases have been highly politically influenced and were part of public discussion about academic corruption that stirred the scientific circles because they were linked to the vice-rector of one university and former government ministers. Two cases of plagiarism in the sociological community provoked debate about efficient mechanisms of sanctions for violating the professional code of ethics due to unclear institutional jurisdictions. One case has been resolved without serious consequences, and the other case of plagiarism of doctoral theses lasted for years because the university and Faculty of Humanities and Social Sciences, a member of the university where the doctorate had been obtained, could not decide whose responsibility it was to revoke the doctorate. Professional ethics in sociology thus far has succeeded in being independent of political influence, but what is still missing is the coordination between professional code and legislation that should act upon it.

8.5.4 The Role of Sociologists from Diaspora

In a period of last 100 years, Croatia has had a large diaspora. Within this population, there were merely a few sociologists. The best-known sociologist from the diaspora is professor Dinko Tomašić, a professor at Indiana University, USA, who left the Kingdom of Yugoslavia in 1941 for scholarship but was not able to return during the Second World War to the 'Independent State of Croatia' (puppet Nazi regime) nor to the socialist Yugoslavia. Croatia within the Socialist Federative Republic of Yugoslavia did not have a large intellectual diaspora, with some exceptions of Croatian nationalists after the 'mass movement' in 1971. The reason that sociologists (and social scientists) were not among that group lies in the history of sociology as a discipline whose founding fathers were mostly philosophers and psychologists belonging to the Praxis philosophy. The members of the Praxis group were Marxist intellectuals who based their theoretical work on Marxist social theory. They were critical of the official system and the ruling communist party, but they were loyal to ideas of critical Marxism, humanism, and democratic socialism.

Essentially, they never distanced themselves from the core ideas of the system and stayed within the system, often (self-)marginalised but in the country.

The sociological diaspora in the post-transition period may be divided into two types: one type is decedents of the old diaspora (emigrants from the past periods) that came to Croatia as soon as democratic changes started, and the second type is a sociologist who went abroad because of war or professional engagement and returned to Croatia. From the first type, there is only one sociologist who became a public figure due to his activism in the pro-life and gender ideology movement connected to the Croatian Catholic Church. His public appearances were not related to the local sociological community, nor did he declare himself as a member of this community.

The sociologists in academia from the diaspora have not become public figures nor played any significant role in the public/political sphere outside academia despite their extensive research on phenomena like post-socialist transition, ethnic conflicts, nationalism, and war in the former Yugoslavia (Sekulić, Meštrović). Their interest was a sociological approach to actual phenomena, such as ethnic conflict and cleansing, war, and nationalism, but their engagement in the academic world never resonated in Croatian society. According to Malešević (2002), the former Yugoslavia has never had a real (strong) intellectual diaspora as most other socialist countries did.

Yugoslavia was much more successful in developing its own organic intellectuals than the rest of the communist world; it never had proper dissidents, and it simultaneously laid the foundations for the metamorphosis of Marxist intellectuals into ethno-nationalist warriors. (p. 75)

The reasons are in the specific type of socialism and because intellectuals took Marxist ideology much more seriously than in other countries in the Eastern bloc. The Praxis tradition of the founding fathers of Croatian sociology, together with the already developed professionalisation processes, made an impact on the anti-nationalistic orientation of sociologists, which put them in the 'marginal' position in society with very few exemptions.

8.6 Conclusion: From Marginality to Internationalisation and Excellence

In this chapter, we have attempted to give an overview of the development of post-transition Croatian sociology, with reference to the role of discipline in shaping, selecting, or favouring particular dominant discourses. Unlike many common approaches to the relationship between sociology and the social context in which it operates, this approach does not analyse how sociology responds to societal challenges but rather starts with the question of how sociology acted in shaping some of the hegemonic discourses of post-transitional transformation.

In the analysis, we have used the path dependence theory to confirm the thesis that the marginal position of sociology in post-transition is the result of a series of specific social and historical circumstances in which it developed. A legacy from this period marked sociology in transition as a leftist, Marxist science and also as insufficiently nationally oriented. Critical thinking, as its basic tool, again gave it the stigma of subversive discipline, resulting in its marginal position in terms of political and social power.

In the past three decades, Croatian sociology did not contribute (except in very few individual cases) to the reinforcement of dominant discourses or the selection of particular ones. Since sociology was never a monolithic discipline, it was not able to act in terms of selection, imposition, or retention of specific hegemonic discourses in society. The same divided situation was actual again, this time between the old leftist and new nationally oriented sociology, but neither was strong enough to provide mechanisms for privileging or reinforcing dominant discourses in a significant manner. It was only in the position to influence a certain kind of selective recruitment in academia and raise research funding within its own institution, which is not easy to differentiate from the usual recruitment practice in academia. On the individual level, very few professional sociologists actively participated in political power as ministers in government (two) and higher positions such as special advisers to presidents (two).

Despite the fact that the Croatian sociological community has never been ideologically politically homogeneous (depending on the social and historical context, closer or further from active participation in government institutions), perhaps because it never possessed significant political power, it succeeded in maintaining professional solidarity and mutual professional respect during the whole period of transition, even in the first period during war time when intentions to dismantle the old sociological institutions, as in the case of Institute for Social Research, were retracted. It might be expected that with the process of institutional diversification, distinct sociological communities will emerge, reflecting worldview and ideology orientations; for instance, a department of sociology is established at Croatian Catholic University, which might be the seed of a stronger Catholic sociological community in the future.

It is at the core of sociology that its research results, theories, findings, and knowledge about society in general could and should make the change in solving problems shaping the future social and other public policies. At the same time, Croatian sociology has not been very successful in the efforts to convince the decision-makers, politicians, and power elite of the usefulness and benefit of sociological expertise for society. It was not able to employ the mechanisms to effectively shape dominant discourses.

According to the classification of transformative roles of sociology in a society (Rončević in this volume), Croatian sociology in the post-transition period has evolved from the role of 'voyeurs' toward an activist role in contemporary Croatian society. Croatian sociology has a respectable research and educational infrastructure; it has strengthened institutionally and certainly tends to participate more strongly in social transformations. However, its role has not yet reached a turning point where we can talk about the effect of selection or retention of the dominant discourse or playing a key role in the transformation of society.

From a temporal perspective, Croatian sociology went through a period of crisis in the initial phase of the transition, when its role was marginal in order to establish itself as a discipline in the mode of service science (Rončević, in this volume). As already described, during the socialist period, Croatian sociology had already passed the path from an ideologised to a professionalised discipline, but this professionalisation was stopped in the late 1970s.

The crisis of Croatian sociology in the first decades of the post-transition period was replaced with more favourable trends. A new generation of sociologists has turned to internationalisation by participating in EU research projects and publishing, keeping pace with world sociology. The generation shift has brought a higher quality of methodology and a more mature theoretical level that has opened the way to more professional and policy sociology. Croatian sociology is now in the same boat as world sociology, for better or for worse, considering the continuous discussion about the future of sociology threatened by increasing interdisciplinarity/cross-disciplinarity.

Competing Interests The author has no conflicts of interest to declare that are relevant to the content of this chapter.

References

Baćak, V. (2011). Bauk internacionalizacije u hrvatskoj sociologiji (the spectre of internationalization in Croatian sociology). *Revija za sociologiju, 41*(2), 239–245.
Batina, G. (2006). *Početi sociologije u Hrvatskoj (The Beginnings of Sociology in Croatia)*. Kultura i društvo.
Batina, G. (2008). Hrvatska sociološka tradicija prije Drugog svjetskog rata–Ružno pače poslijeratne hrvatske sociologije (Croatian Sociological Tradition before World War II–The Ugly Duckling of the Post-war Croatian Sociology). In D. Krbec (Ed.), *Hrvatska sociologija: Razvoj i perspektive: zbornik radova* (pp. 39–58). Hrvatsko sociološko društvo.
Blokker, P. (2005). Post-communist modernization, transition studies, and diversity in Europe. *European Journal of Social Theory, 8*(4), 503–525. https://doi.org/10.1177/1368431005059703
Boyns, D., & Fletcher, J. (2005). Reflections on public sociology: Public relations, disciplinary identity, and the strong program in professional sociology. *The American Sociologist, 36*(3/4), 5–26.
Burawoy, M. (2005). 2004 presidential address: For public sociology. *American Sociological Review, 70*(1), 4–28.
Calhoun, C. (2005). The promise of public sociology. *British Journal of Sociology, 56*(3), 355–363.
Cifrić, I. (1995). Sociology in a new social context. *Društvena istraživanja: časopis za opća društvena pitanja, 4*(2–3), 241–264.
Clawson, D., Zussman, R., Burawoy, M., Misra, J., Gerstel, N., Stokes, R., Anderton, D. L., & (Eds.). (2007). *Public sociology: Fifteen eminent sociologists debate politics and the profession in the twenty-first century*. University of California Press.
Cosovschi, A. (2017). *Sociologija u tranziciji: Kritička analiza hrvatske sociologije ranih 1990ih godina (Sociology in transition: Critical analysis of Croatian sociology in early 1990s)*. Unpublished manuscript.
Dryzek, J. S., et al. (2002). *Post-communist democratization: Political discourses across thirteen countries*. Cambridge University Press.
Gruenwald, O. (2015). Praxis and democratization in Yugoslavia: From critical Marxism to democratic socialism? In R. Taras (Ed.), *The road to disillusion: From critical Marxism to post-communism in Eastern Europe* (pp. 175–196). Routledge.
Hay, C. (2002). Political analysis. A Critical Introduction. Basingstoke: Palgrave
Holmwood, J. (2007). Sociology as public discourse and professional practice: A critique of Michael Burawoy. *Sociological Theory, 25*(1), 46–66.
Jessop, B. (2004). Critical semiotic analysis and cultural political economy. *Critical Discourse Studies, 1*(1), 1–16.
Jessop, B., & Oosterlynck, S. (2008). Cultural political economy: On making the cultural turn without falling into soft economic sociology. *Geoforum, 39*(3), 1155–1169. https://doi.org/10.1016/j.geoforum.2006.12.008
Jowitt, K. (1992). *New world disorder: The Leninist extinction*. University of California Press.
Kay, A. (2005). A critique of the use of path dependency in policy studies. *Public Administration, 83*(3), 553–571. https://doi.org/10.1111/j.0033-3298.2005.00462.x
Latinac, M. (2017). *Development of sociology through analysis of Croatian sociological re-view*. Unpublished paper.
Mahoney, J. (2000). Path dependence in historical sociology. *Theory and Society, 29*(4), 507–548.
Malešević, S. (2002). From 'organic' legislators to 'organicistic' interpreters: Intellectuals in Yugoslavia and post-Yugoslav states. *Government and Opposition, 37*(1), 55–75.
Massey, G., Hodson, R., & Sekulić, D. (2003). Nationalism, liberalism and liberal nationalism in post-war Croatia. *Nations and Nationalism, 9*(1), 55–82.
Matić, D. (2017). The calling of sociology: Beyond value-detached professionalism and partisan activism. *Revija za sociologiju, 47*(2), 177–205.
Nichols, L. T. (2011). *Public sociology: The contemporary debate*. Transaction publishers.

Peračković, K. (2004). Sociology of transition: Structural, socio-cultural and neo modernisation approach. *Društvena istraživanja, 14*(3), 487–504.

Šporer, Ž. (2006). *Između profesionalizacije i ideologizacije–razvoj sociologije u nas (Between professionalization and ideologisation—Development of our sociology)*. Hrvatsko sociološko društvo.

Štulhofer, A., Baćak, V., & Šuljok, A. (2010). A parochial status of Croatian sociology? *Revija za sociologiju, 40*(1), 103–108.

Švarc, J., Čengić, D., Poljanec-Borić, S., & Lažnjak, J. (2019). Academic researchers on the 2013 reforms of the Croatian science policy: A critical analysis. *Politička misao: časopis za politologiju, 56*(1), 7–38.

Tomić Koludrović, I. (2009). A view of the future: Sociology as a multiparadigmatic, reflexive and public science, presidential address. *Revija za sociologiju, 40*(3–4), 139–181.

Tomić Koludrović, I. (2018). *Roundtable discussion: 100 years of first Croatian sociology association*. Croatian Sociological Association.

Turner, J. H. (2005). Is public sociology such a good idea. *The American Sociologist, 36*(3–4), 27–45.

Županov, J. (1977). *Sociologija i samoupravljanje (Sociology and Self-management)*. Školska knjiga.

Županov, J. (1995). *Poslije potopa (After Flood)*. Globus.

Županov, J. (2011). Hrvatsko društvo danas—Kontinuitet i promjena (Croatian society today—Continuity and change). *Politička misao, 48*(3), 145–163.

Županov, J., & Šporer, Ž. (1985). Sociologija na raskršću (Sociology on Crossroad). *Revija za sociologiju, 15*(1–2), 53–65.

Jasminka Lažnjak is a full professor at the Department of Sociology at the University of Zagreb where she teaches Society and Technology, Sociology of Work and Organisation, and Economic Sociology. She holds an MA and PhD in sociology from the University of Zagreb and held a scholarship at Indiana University, Bloomington, USA. Here primary areas of research are science, technology and society studies, sociology of innovation, economic sociology, and sociology of work and organisation. She has participated in the national and EU projects dealing with innovation culture and S&T and innovation policy analysis. From 2015 to 2019, she was the president of Croatian Sociological Association. Also, she was Editor in Chief of Croatian Sociological Review (Revija za sociologiju; 2006–2008) and currently is a member of editorial board of Social Research (Društvena istraživanja).

Chapter 9
Czech Sociology and Transformation

Ladislav Cabada

This chapter is the result of Metropolitan University Prague research project no. 110-1 'Political Science, Media and Anglophone Studies' (2024) based on a grant from the Institutional Fund for the Long-term Strategic Development of Research Organizations.

9.1 Introduction

If we observe over time the Czech public and political debates about the legacies of the pre-Communist period, as the two most visible characteristics of Czech society, the early modernisation and urbanisation and development of the stable industrial platform based on good (predominantly technical/engineering) knowledge will be stressed first and the democratic, egalitarian, and pragmatic nature of the nation second (cf. Cabada, 2003; Nikodým, n.d.; Müller, 2002; Skovajsa, 2006; Večerník & Matějů, 1999). This self-perception adoring the period of the so-called Masarykian First Czechoslovak Republic and selected older historical periods was and is also deeply rooted in Czech social sciences. The First Republic is almost equated with Tomáš Garrigue Masaryk, the first Czechoslovak President (1918–1935) and also the founder of Czech sociology.[1] Masaryk, promoting the struggle against obscurantism and prejudices and emphasising democratic pluralism based on mod-

---

[1] The professional association of Czechoslovak and later Czech sociologists had already included his name in the official title as the 'Masarykian Sociological Association' (*Masarykova sociologická společnost*) already in 1925, that is, during his life; since 1993, after the dissolution of

---

L. Cabada (✉)
Department of Political Science and Anglophone Studies, Metropolitan University Prague, Prague, Czechia
e-mail: ladislav.cabada@mup.cz

© The Author(s), under exclusive license to Springer Nature Switzerland AG 2024
B. Roncevic, T. Besednjak Valič (eds.), *Sociology and Post-Socialist Transformations in Eastern Europe*,
https://doi.org/10.1007/978-3-031-65556-2_9

ern civil society, became a symbol of the specifically Czech way of development. His concept of the so-called de-Austricisation (cf. Cabada, 2019) became one of the most influential narratives of inter-war Czechoslovakia, underscoring the importance of the 'small work' of every member of the nation, anti-elitism, and humanitarianism (Masaryk, 1968, 1990a, 1990b). He and many other influential authors, including some important Czech sociologists, stressed the path dependency of such Czech national characteristics and the 'symbolic centres of Czech political culture' (cf. Havelka, 1995a, 2002), such as the Hussite period (fifteenth century), the so-called Veleslavín period at the turn of the sixteenth and seventeenth centuries culminating during the reign of the Roman Emperor Rudolf II who resided in Prague, and last but not least the period of national revival (late Enlightenment and liberalisation) in the nineteenth century. In all these periods, the Czech nation was supposed to demonstrate its democratic character and important differences in comparison with other Central European nations: Hungarians, Poles, Austrians, and, primarily and naturally, Germans. Such a narrative even survived the Communist period when Czechoslovakia became the 'display window of socialism' (according to the official rhetoric of the Communist regime in the country) and, together with Poles and Hungarians, the evidence of a deeply democratic nature (according to the dissent opposition based on anti-Communist uprisings and revolts in all mentioned countries; cf. Wandycz, 1992).

The described processes and mentality also strongly influenced the way Czech thinkers, social scientists, and politicians contemplated the first transformation steps in late 1989, and later, Czechoslovakia (and even more the Czech Lands) should be well prepared for a short and painful transformation, and soon after the nation would join the (West) European nations; one of the most influential mottos of the Velvet Revolution in the country was the slogan 'Back to Europe'. It was expected that the Communist legacy would be quickly fought off and the nation would follow up with the (extensively idealised) tradition of the First 'Masarykian' Republic. Indeed, the three decades of democratic development evince next to many visible successes also problematic issues that are often (and mostly) related to the societal transformation and negative aspects of the Communist past (post-Communism) or even older legacies. Especially in the societal frame, the Czech transformation seems to be unfinished or 'semifinished', which encourages analysis, reflection, and prognosis for further development.

The aim of this chapter is to assess the development and role of Czech sociology during this period and specifically to examine the influence of Czech sociology on the transformation process after 1989. We will focus on the issue based on five basic questions asked in the introductory chapter of this book:

1. How did Czech sociology contribute to processes of variation of discourses and practices in the past 30 years, which may lead to a variety of alternative paths?
2. How did sociology contribute to the selection of particular discourses?

Czechoslovakia, the Masarykian Czech Sociological Society was (re-)established. In 2016, the name of Masaryk was again excluded from the official title.

3. Did Czech sociology contribute to the retention of specific resonant discourses?
4. Did Czech sociology contribute to the reinforcement of dominant discourses?
5. Did Czech sociology contribute to selective recruitment, inculcation, and retention by privileging those individuals that correspond with dominant discourses?

As the basic frame for our analysis, we use the following timeline. In the first part, we will present the development of Czech(oslovak) sociology before the beginning of the democratic transition, specifically during the period of Communist supremacy after 1948. As the most important fact, we will stress the discontinuity of the discipline during the four decades before the democratic transition and the institutional and personal weakness of sociology as a scientific discipline at the beginning of the transformation. As far as one of the most important determinants and/or limits for the active inclusion of Czech sociology and/or sociologists in the transformation processes, the condition of the discipline should be accentuated; such a 'historical' chapter seems very important for our analysis and argumentation. Based on the contemporary knowledge of the above-mentioned condition of the discipline before and at the start of the transition, we formulate the main hypothesis, namely, that Czech(oslovak) sociology was personally, institutionally, and also, regarding the content and knowledge, very weak and not able to compete with the most developed social science of the Communist period, namely, the (national) economy. Such a weakness of sociology (and the predominance of economy) determined the transition as the starting phase of the long-term process of transformation. During the following decades, Czech sociology recovered and created a vital source of discourses, practices, and advice. Nevertheless, the impact of this knowledge is strictly determined by the political sphere. This is why, in searching for answers to the above-listed set of research questions, we will specifically focus on the interconnectedness of Czech sociology and politics and, in a more general way, the role of Czech sociology in society. For this purpose, we will divide our contribution into several subchapters covering the periods coinciding with the important changes in the political development of the Czech Republic.

9.2 Czech(oslovak) Sociology Before the Transition

The so-called bourgeois pseudoscience sociology was restricted and prohibited in Communist Czechoslovakia after 1948 and, like other social sciences, was replaced by 'scientific communism'. Only in the first half of the 1960s, at the beginning of the liberalisation period that culminated in 1968 in the processes of the Prague Spring, did the floor open for the awakening and revitalisation of sociology in the country. Indeed, such revitalisation was limited by the small number of institutions tolerated by the Communist leadership and (of course) the standing ideological control over the whole revitalisation process. In this sense, many authors stress the role of individual persons or institutions and, conversely, the elimination of these persons and institutions after the Soviet occupation in August 1968, and Czech(oslovak) sociology was again suppressed and/or strongly subordinated to political and ideological control, pressure, and (self-)censorship.

Jiří Musil (2004, pp. 581–582), one of the most visible Czech sociologists after the transition and also the Rector of Central European University, perfectly describes and analyses the challenges and limits for the revitalisation of sociology in the second half of the 1960s. As the main issue for the discipline, and more generally for the plethora of humanities and social sciences in the country, he formulates the question, 'How do we emancipate sociology from ideology?' He positively evaluates the first steps of the reinstitutionalisation of Czech(oslovak) sociology in 1965 when the Czechoslovak Sociological Society (Československá sociologická společnost) was established with the full consent of the Communist Party leadership, departments of sociology were established at the universities, the Sociological Institute at the Academy of Sciences was created, and the independent *Czech Sociological Review* was established. Musil emphasises the role of Jaroslav Klofáč and Vojtěch Tlustý in the second half of the 1960s in the restoration of sociology and, in a broader sense, also related social sciences in Czechoslovakia (Musil, 2004, p. 583; cf. Šanc, 2009, p. 38).

Specifically, Musil stresses the competition between the two officially recognised professional teams associated with the Central Committee of the Communist Party: the first one on the reform of the political system led by Zdeněk Mlynář and the second focusing on the utilisation of the science-technical revolution led by Radovan Richta. Within the second team, the futurological role of sociology was also developed for the first time. Nevertheless, despite all positive changes, Musil concludes sceptically: 'Indeed, the critical sociology demystifying the official positions towards the socialist society was almost missing. Some elements might be observed only in the study focusing on the social stratification prepared by the team led by Pavel Machonin' (Musil, 2004, p. 582). This critical position is also related to the significant fact that influential persons and institutions evolved out of the Communist past. Let us mention as an example the Institute of Social and Political Sciences under the leadership of Pavel Machonin, which was established with the transformation of the Institute of Marxism-Leninism for universities (Koudelka, 2004, p. 627). Nevertheless, after 1964, sociology was newly offered as a study programme at selected Czech(oslovak) universities and, despite the occupation, also after 1968. Specifically, in the first years, the new generation of sociologists was educated in Prague, Brno, Olomouc, and Bratislava and succeeded in maintaining the continuity of the revitalisation process, although only at a very limited level. Sociology was usually offered in combination with other social sciences or humanities, mainly with philosophy and economy. Moreover, this motivates us to study Czech(oslovak) sociology in the broader frame of social sciences; in other words, many important actors balanced between two and even more disciplines, and to include them in or exclude them from sociology is also the issue of context, membership in a specific epistemic community, and others.

The occupation of Czechoslovakia terminated the liberalisation period, and soon, the country was led into the period of so-called normalisation, that is, a revitalised (semi)totalitarian regime dominated by the rigid Communist leadership balancing between autocracy and totalitarianism. After the occupation, 'the Sociological Institute at the Academy of Sciences was eliminated and changed into part of the Institute for Philosophy and Sociology led by Radovan Richta [...] approximately 45 members of the former Institute were released' (Sedláček in Brokl et al., 2004, p. 698). Illner (Brokl et al., 2004, pp. 711–712) specifies that almost two thirds of all scholars were eliminated. This development presents only the tip of the iceberg; similarly, the ideological and political cleansing also struck other newly born sociological institutions and teams. The normalisation and the self-censorship produced the situation of ideological taboos in sociological work. An important segment of sociologists tended towards the research where the risk of being accused of ideological diversion was smaller, especially in the sphere of methodology (Potůček in Brokl et al., 2004, p. 723).

Sociology was therefore tolerated in Czechoslovakia after 1968 (let us mention the important difference with political science that did not exist before the transition (Šanc, 2009, pp. 214–220)) but grew weak. Musil (2002, p. 22) stresses that Czech sociology was much more isolated before 1989 than that of its Polish or Hungarian counterparts (and let us also add Slovak sociology) and was painfully searching for new knowledge on new themes. Among such themes, he mentions national identity, nationalism, nation-states within the integration processes, the role of media in democratic societies, changes in labour in contemporary risk societies, the role of education, and the role of culture, including the changing values and traditions. In his other work, Musil (2004, p. 591) emphasises that after the Soviet occupation, sociology survived mainly in large state firms in which sociological and/or analytical departments existed. We will later mention the most visible and influential of such institutions.

The new situation segmented the Czech sociologist and discipline into very different environments and groups; naturally, this also contributed to the general weakness of the discipline. In this sense, Musil (2004, p. 574) recognises five different actors, groups, and perspectives within the Czech(oslovak) sociology during the Communist period:

1. Official interpretation of Marxist ideology based on the conformity with the Communist rulers
2. Marxist revisionists attempting to accommodate the official ideology based on the observed mistakes and failures
3. Sociologists critical towards Marxism but attempting to 'survive' at the discipline's periphery, that is, in the institutions applying empirical sociology
4. Sociologists rejecting Marxism who engaged in the discipline but did not publish (eventually were writing 'to the drawer')
5. Active dissidents organizing translations of sociological works, publishing illegal publications, etc.

9.3 Dissidents That Were Active Based on a (Semi-) Illegal Platform

Let us add that Groups 1 and 2 did not communicate officially with the last three groups and that many visible members of Groups 4 and 5 decided for exile, which again made Czech(oslovak) sociology weaker. As regards the general theme of our analysis (i.e. the influence of Czech sociology on the transformation processes), we will focus on Groups 3 through 5, although at least one person balancing between Groups 1 and 2 seems to be important for the first phase of transformation. This person is Oskar Krejčí, who studied sociology and philosophy at Charles University from 1969 to 1974 and was a member of Communist nomenclature. Between February 1989 and December 1990, Krejčí acted as the advisor to the last Czechoslovak Communist Prime Minister, Ladislav Adamec, and his successor, Marián Čalfa. Krejčí actively supported the negotiations between the Communist rulers and opposition, supporting the 'transition through transaction' model and reform-style regime change, rejecting the direct turnover towards capitalism and liberal democracy (Šanc, 2009, p. 307; Krejčí, 2014). Nevertheless, neither the sociological community nor Krejčí himself understands his role as 'sociological'.

Krejčí's example serves as a perfect illustration of how difficult it might be to 'define' a sociologist based only on formal education. In other words, in the Czech Republic before and after the transition, we can observe a distinctive interdisciplinary crossover and the inclusion of persons without formal education. In this sense, Czech sociology emphasises the role of different institutions applying empirical sociology, as mentioned in Group 3, as defined by Musil. Often and repeatedly, as one of the most important such institutions and structures, the prognostic divisions and sections for complex planning are mentioned. For example, Illner (Brokl et al., 2004, pp. 738–739) underscores the sociological character of Czechoslovak prognostics and 'complex prognostic planning' produced in Sportpropag, a scientific-technical society, and the Research Institute of Work in Bratislava; specifically, he mentions Miloš Zeman, Martin Potůček, Josef Alan, and Fedor Gál. As Zeman and Potůček will play very important roles in Czech politics and sociology after 1989 and during the transformation, let us briefly present their activities during the 1970s and 1980s.

From 1965 to 1969, that is, exactly during the period of culminating liberalisation, Zeman studied (national) economy planning at the Prague University of Economics and Business (Vysoká škola ekonomická). His final thesis focuses on perspectives of prognostics. Zeman and his teacher and colleague Ota Šulc (in 1969, they published together the book *The Dictionary of Futurology* (*Futurologický slovník*)) remained close to Richta's team (see above). Both cooperated within the research institute at the University of Economics; later, they tried to join the Political Science Institute that had been established at the Academy of Sciences in 1969. After the occupation, the institute ceased to exist (Kopeček, 2017, pp. 18–21).

As one of the first futurologists, Zeman stressed the interdisciplinary nature of this approach. This is why he also flirted with sociology. His short discussion contribution was published in the *Czech Sociological Review* (*Sociologický časopis*) (Zeman, 1969), but more important was his coexistence with the sociologists in state companies related to organised sport activities and their promotion. At the beginning of the 1970s, an important centre of analytical sociology was the state-organised sporting firms Noctua, Technosport, and Sportpropag (Machonin, 2004, p. 645). The centre of technical services in Noctua was led by Pavel Machonin and, after his removal provoked by the Communist secret police, by Zeman under the name the Department of Complex Forecasting Modelling. 'Outside the official state institutions, the centre of semi-official research in social sciences was born' (Kopeček, 2017, p. 24). Among others, Bohuslav Blažek, Jiří Kabele, and Potůček worked in this centre; Potůček was the deputy director and Machonin and Gál as the 'permanent core of externists [external collaborators]' (Kabele, 2011, p. 19). After 1983, Potůček left the department, searching for a more institutionalised and academic environment for the Institute of Social Medicine and health system organisation (Kabele, 2011, p. 33). Indeed, this period also coincides with the power intervention against the department and the forced removal of M. Zeman.

All mentioned persons became key figures in Czech sociology and often politics after the transition. Kabele (2011, p. 29) points out that the department lived in the convictions typical for the contemporary leading ideology of knowledge, at that time, an 'information society'. The Department of Complex Forecasting Modelling should be one of the 'islands of positive deviations' in Communist Czechoslovakia (cf. Bútora et al., 1989; Kabele, 2011, p. 17).

As the second of such 'islands', the department of sociology in Brno is often mentioned. Before 1989, 'the development in Prague and Brno was distinctively different. Brno survived the normalisation period somewhat better than the department of sociology in Prague' (Petrusek in Brokl et al., 2004, p. 707). A sociological symposium was organised in the second half of the 1980s by a key person of the Brno sociological group, Ivo Možný. The title 'Socialist Life Style as Reality' illustrates the official production of the regime-friendly Sociological Institute at the Academy of Sciences (Možný, 2004, p. 621; Petrusek, 1997, pp. 498–490). Petrusek (2004, p. 605) notes that, based on Možný and his collaborators' activities, the sociological department in Brno recovered much better and sooner than in Prague and other cities and regions after the transition. Last but not least, we have to stress that Slovakian sociology was more liberal than the Czech one. 'Under the cover of the Slovak "reformist" Communist centre, the "federalist", "ethnocentric", "prognostic", "Perestroika" projects and discourses were started and outcomes published that would never have had any chance in Prague' (Macháček, 2004, p. 633).

Directly from the above-mentioned 'islands of positive deviations', Czech(oslovak) sociology developed after 1989 and attempted to influence the transformation processes. In the next part, we will focus on this 'liminality period' of late Perestroika and the first steps following the democratic transition.

9.4 Czech(oslovak) Sociology and Transition

The Czechoslovak Perestroika started later than in Communist countries with more autonomous development, such as Hungary and Poland, and due to the strong influence of conservative leaders installed after the occupation, this process was, in general, very moderate and passive. The regime was trying to (re)start the economy in the first place; this is why, in 1984, the Prognostic Institute at the Academy of Sciences was established, based on the Soviet example. The institute, subordinated directly to the Central Committee of the Communist Party, was meant to develop economic transformation model(s) compatible with the Communist regime. Paradoxically, the institute became the cradle of post-1989 prominent neoliberal economists and politicians (Holman et al., 2015, p. 510). As the institute did not produce any public outcomes, we do not have enough information about its activities.

Nevertheless, not only from this institution, Communist leadership gained information about the growing dissatisfaction within society, as well as the middle Communist cadre. Some authors emphasised decreased motivation (Vodička & Cabada, 2011, pp. 136–143). For example, noted sociologist Lubomír Brokl (Brokl et al., 2004, p. 733) recalls that during his experience in the 1980s, the technocrats felt unsatisfied with development in the country. The directors of state-owned firms 'were in the 1980s again at the same turning point as their predecessors in the 1960s. Again, they were in clash [sic] with the county committees of the Communist party and apparatchiks'. As Možný (1991) demonstrated in his excellent analysis focusing on the collapse of the Communist regime in Czechoslovakia with the clear title 'Why so easy?', the group of dissatisfied citizens included a large majority of the population, but the most important and driving group were economically motivated persons and groups, both from the official and semi-official structures. In this sense, homo economicus had already dominated *homo sovieticus* before the transition.

As shown in the example of Brno sociological symposium(s) in the 1980s, sociology also recognised important problems, challenges, and defects of the socialist state and society. Nevertheless, more influential were the books and movies that presented (some of them very critically) the difference between the official rhetoric and social reality. As the most important themes, we can mention the estrangement of the young generation, violence in the stadiums, strengthening of the grey economy and its influence on justice and politics, power games of prominent Communist figures, or a combination of some of or all of them. With all respect to the outcomes of the Czech sociological community, these and other similar works played a very important role towards society, diminishing the official canons of the Communist leaders.

As regards the sociological contribution to the critics of the regime and appeals for reform and even transformation, as the most visible and influential, we should mention the article 'Prognostics and Perestroika' presented in autumn 1989 in 'Technical Magazine' (Technický magazín). Its author, Zeman (1989), openly criticised the regime for an insufficient or missing reform/transformation: 'The central cause of our long-term and speeding stagnation is the failure of decision-making and managing sphere in the society, i.e. the non-efficiency of the societal decision' (p. 6). Zeman presented three different development scenarios: catastrophic, exogenous, and evolutionary. He believed in the evolutionary scenario, based on the positive role of islands of positive deviations and the creation of a horizontal information network among these islands and diffusion of the specific knowledge of these islands into the society. Conversely, regarding the exogenous scenario, he was rather sceptical, stating: 'The changes that do not arise from its internal development needs and are violently introduced from outside, might traumatise the society and lead towards the loss of its identity' (Zeman, 1989, p. 8).

As regards sociologists, the community naturally recognised the coming 'wind of changes' and strengthened its activities. In 1988, the debate on the document 'Sociology of the Slovak Republic in the Context of Perestroika' brought criticism against the apologetic function of sociology, dogmatism, sterility, and over-politicisation. In September 1989, a group of Slovak sociologists wrote a letter to Czechoslovak President Husák, asserting that society was at a crossroads: 'either it finds the power for fundamental structural socioeconomic and political changes, or it definitely drops out from the society of developed nations' (Macháček, 2004, p. 640). This criticism is in full harmony with Zeman's aforementioned article and shows personal interconnections.

In 1989, the *Sociological Forum* (*Sociologické fórum*) was established and had already initiated structural and institutional changes in Czech sociology before November 1989 (Potůček in Brokl et al., 2004, p. 725). The forum was attempting to participate actively in the first phase of the post-1989 transition and gain enough space in the public debate on the social and societal dimensions of the transformation and political positions. At the break of 1989/1990, 'the group of Prague sociologists' (Nešpor, 2006, p. 19) wrote to the newly elected President Havel and stressed the danger connected with the 'unreserved application of neo-classical or neoliberal reform steps' (Nešpor, 2006, p. 19). The 'Declaration of Sociologists (Letter to the President)' (Prohlášení sociologů, 1990/1997) from the beginning of 1990 was signed by Josef Alan, Jiřina Šiklová, Martin Bútora, Miloslav Petrusek, Fedor Gál, Martin Potůček, Jiří Kabele, Jiří Večerník, and Jiří Musil. The authors mention the Masarykian tradition and underscore the 'social issue' provoked by their 'civic and professional responsibility'. They appraise the first 6 weeks of democratic transition, criticising the absence of a social dimension of transformation next to the economic and political ones: 'Social policy must not be only complementary mechanism to soften the undesirable effects of market or compensation of so-called unpopular measures.' The declaration is one of the first critical comments on the 'Klausian' neoliberal approach: 'We can and intend to admire the precision of neoliberal economy tools. Nevertheless, as sociologists, we know that many hard paradigms get drowned in seemingly soft social reality, and the inattention towards their diversity many times led to the best intentions into the deadlock.'

Many of the mentioned persons were connected with the Civic Forum as the most important political actor of the first transformation phase; next to this activity, they also contributed to the revitalisation of the Sociological Institute at the Academy of Sciences and the Faculty of Arts at Charles University and especially in the constitution of the new Faculty of Social Sciences at this university. Nevertheless, as regards their political aspirations, with minor exceptions (Bútora as the advisor of President Havel in 1990–1992; later, after 1998, esteemed diplomat of the Slovak Republic), they did not win power positions to realise their visions. As mentioned above, outside Prague, sociology seemed to be stronger, but the strong centralisation disqualified Brno, and, because of the problematic relations between the Czech and Slovak units of the federation, Bratislava became a prospective centre of sociological influence of Czechoslovak transformation.

Within the Civic Forum, the sociologists also attempted to develop the social dimension of the movement's programme, including the proposal to create the Social Council related to the federal government next to the Economic Council and Legislative Council (Potůček, 1997, pp. 240–245). The main question seemed to be how to solve the issue of the 'socialist welfare state' (Cabada, 2014, p. 25), and the clear sociological answer was the 'traditional welfare state' known from Western Europe after WWII. Nevertheless, after the first parliamentary elections (May 1990), the Civic Forum was overruled by the neoliberal stream, and a group of economists led by Klaus and the social dimension of the programme was suppressed by the economic one. In the first half of the 1990s, neoliberal policies stressing the minimal state and opposing the inclusion of the West European type of welfare state clearly dominated Czech politics. Potůček, an active member of the Czech Social Democratic Party (ČSSD) with both academic and political ambitions, was among the most visible critics of Klaus, as can be observed in their mutual polemics in the review *Sondy* (cf. Potůček, 1997, pp. 77–82). Such arguments between the prime minister and scholar clearly show that the opposition political parties did not offer any fundamental and knowledge-based critiques and/or alternatives.

Also 'politically' weak were the Czech sociologists living in and at least partly returning from exile. Czech(oslovak) sociologists and social scientists in exile often played an important role in the global scientific community. Of the most wellknown, we should mention Karl Deutsch, Ernest (Arnošt) Gellner, and Friedrich (Bedřich) Loewenstein, all coming from the Czech-German-Jewish community in inter-war Prague. Despite their relatively advanced ages, the last two mentioned offered lectures and expertise at the newly established Central European University in Prague (until 1994) and also at Charles University. Nevertheless, they did not join the public debate on the transformation and focused predominantly on the education process.

More active were the next generation's younger Czech social scientists living in exile; among them were Václav Bělohradský and Miroslav Novák. Bělohradský became one of the most visible prophets of liberalism and globalisation in Czech media and public debate, while Novák was the most important person establishing political science at Charles University in Prague after 1989. Moderately older is Erazim Kohák, the 1990s' one of the most active proponents of ecologic discourse in Czech philosophy and social sciences. Bělohradský and Kohák actively cooperated with left-wing parties (ČSSD), including an influence on the programmatic debates. Pragmatically evaluated, their postmodern approach failed in confrontation with the dominant intra-party discourse coming from the traditional class and national-socialist positions. With the exception of Novák, these personalities also did not influence the institutional structure of Czech sociology and more general social sciences (Petrusek, 2011).

Simply speaking, the neoliberal economic concept of transformation almost 'totally' occupied the public debate. Last but not least, we also have to mention that the Czech society (including the so-called interested public, that is, the intelligentsia from other scientific branches) and media did not evince any deeper interest in sociological knowledge and even less in domestic sociology. As Machonin (1995, p. 358) clearly noted, 'Expressions of Czech sociologists about the society did not evoke extraordinary interest not even in Czech educated and societally active public.' Similarly, Miloš Havelka (1995b) shows in his editorial to the special issue of the *Czech Sociological Review* that the main and almost general stance was that there were insufficient reasons to develop a 'Czech' way in sociology as secondary important characteristics; he underscores the resistance towards biographical and generally qualitative sociology both in the public and also within the discipline:

> The specific set of problems is presented by the unclear expectations and disappearing social demand for domestic expert knowledge. Such matters of fact might have more trivial and strictly pragmatic reasons in the transforming society: the simple orientation on already existing and time-proved know-how. (p. 254)

This development may have also brought many sociologists into the private sphere. Specifically, research agencies are oriented on public opinion surveys, media, and others.

Let us conclude that in the middle of the 1990s, (at least part of) Czech sociology felt depressed by the small role of the discipline within the transformation that was internally, but also from external institutions (e.g. International Monetary Fund, World Bank, European Union), evaluated as very successful. This frustration was illustrated in the debate provoked by Petr Matějů (1995), firstly stressing the weakness of Czech sociology caused by the Communist regime:

> Ideological, power and moral devastation of Czech sociology, which began by grasping the power by Communists and lasted with short breaks all forty years […] At the beginning of the post-communist transformation Czech sociology found itself in a much worse situation than the Polish and Hungarian one. (p. 256)

Further, he attempted to explain why the economy and economists overruled the transformation in the Czech Lands:

> Being weak, Czech sociology was not able to brave with the onset of extremely strong liberalism playing in our country the role of dominant ideology of the transition towards market economy […] Czech political elite recruited mostly from the economists brought up on recently forbidden liberal literature, was very hostile towards the possibility of opening the debate about social impacts of economic transformation […] Politically stigmatized sociology was pushed back by the economically approached transitology '[a]s the economic transition was rather successful, the voices asking for a sociological explanation of the problems and social tensions related with the reform were infrequent. (Matějů, 1995, p. 256)

Other influential sociologists tried to oppose this extremely sceptical evaluation. Kabele (1995, p. 263) assumed that Matějů started to retrospect too early. He stressed that the new Czech political elite was recruited mostly from economists, not by accident. They knew the contemporary works going beyond the economy, that is, towards traditional spheres of law, politics, and sociology. 'Since the very beginning, the issue of 'social capability' was included into their own conception and influencing their strategies and tactics [...] In the state budget, the sums appointed for social policy were the most dynamically growing.'

Machonin (1995, p. 337) emphasised the successes of economic sociology: 'The perennial star of Czech sociology became the excellent level of economic sociology with its permanent analyses of income difference, economic behaviour of the households and social policy conception.' Specifically, he depicted Czech sociology as the first to reject the 'linear' model of transformation, that is, the assumption of repetition of Western countries' step-by-step development:

> Among the sociologists from former socialist countries, we first explicitly rejected the interpretation of post-communist development as a normatively determined transition towards some ideal situation of the society, among the first we beforehand warned before relying on a certainly eufunctional and harmonic impact of market mechanism and democratic system. In advance, we also stressed the eventuality of development complications. (p. 337)

Regarding the clear dominance of the economy in the Czech transformation in the period 1990–1997, these attempts to stay positive and consider the glass 'half-full' clearly targeted primarily the doubting and maybe even hopeless part of Czech sociology. Nevertheless, the economic and institutional crisis in 1997 opened the floor not only for a new ruling party but also for sociology.

9.5 Decade of Sociologically Based Transformation? (1997–2007)

Despite all the mentioned problems and obstacles, Czech sociology developed relatively well during the 1990s. Academically, it was stabilised in traditional centres (Prague, Brno, and Olomouc), and in some subdisciplines and areas, it offered good first results. Petrusek (2002, p. 9) mentions above all two important discourses within Czech sociology in the 1990s: the dispute about the middle class and about the transfer of Czech Germans after WWII. As regards the first issue, an important role was played by the activities of Matějů and Večerník as the most visible proponents of a knowledge/information society and the specific role of the middle class in the democracy stabilisation. Next to them, the co-authors of the Freedom Union's (Unie svobody, US) party manifesto and also Možný must be mentioned as important sociologists stressing the issue of social capital. As a member of parliament (1998–2002) and vice-chairman of US, Matějů became one of the most visible sociologists. Indeed, after 2002, he left the party and later accepted a more neoliberal approach and started to cooperate with the Civic Democratic Party (ODS). Matějů acted as the Vice-Minister for Education (2006–2007) and then President of the Czech Science Foundation (2008–2014). Matějů, promoting the 'Anglo-Saxon' style of scientometrics became the highly controversial *éminence grise* of Czech science (Štětka, 2009). Based on our personal evaluation, after 1998, Matějů developed basically as a politician, not fully respecting the multiparadigmatic nature of science.

Indeed, the case of Matějů serves as a good example of recognition that Czech sociology will be capable of influencing politics (including the continued transformation) only when it develops direct ties towards politics. Naturally, the interconnection with the most important political actors seems to be the preference. This is also why we evaluate Potůček and the research and policy institute he created after 1999 as the most influential sociologists and institutions. Since the transition, Potůček tended towards left-oriented actors and, after 1993, logically towards the ČSSD led by his former collaborator and superior Zeman. We already presented Potůček's polemic with the economists and Czech Prime Minister (1992–1997) Klaus in the first half of the 1990s. After 1998 and the creation of the new government led by Zeman and created solely from ČSSD members, Potůček became an important actor in the process of including sociological knowledge in decision-making processes. As the most important outcome of such a new partnership, Machonin (2002, p. 49) observes the elaboration of the 'consensual proposal of the Social Doctrine of the Czech Republic'. The Social Doctrine was presented in September 2001 (Sociální doktrína ČR, 2001). The document, influenced by the (neo-)Keynesian thought (Kubů, 2011, p. 57), was prepared and discussed for almost 3 years under the aegis of Minister of Social Affairs Vladimír Špidla. Among the team members, distinguished sociologists might be found, such as Pavel Machonin, Tomáš Sirovátka, Jiří Musil, and, last but not least, Martin Potůček as the scientific guarantor of the document.

Potůček's ties with the government (and in the first place towards Špidla) also helped in the creation of the Centre for Social and Economic Strategies (CESES), established in October 2000, approximately in the middle of Zeman's government term. As the main goal for the first 3 years, a state-of-the-art analysis was presented and, in particular, the (futurological) vision for the Czech society (CESES, 2017). As the main outcome of the team led by Potůček, three books were presented:

1. *Vision of the Czech Republic Development until 2015* (*Vize rozvoje České republiky do roku 2015*; Potůček et al., 2001), which was presented as the first analysis of debates and discussions organised by the Council of the Czech Government for Social and Economic Strategy (Rada vlády ČR pro sociální a ekonomickou strategii). The council was founded by Zeman's government in May 1999 (Usnesení vlády České republiky č. 421, 1999); among its members, we can find future scholars from CESES (Martin Potůček, Antonín Rašek, and Milan Sojka).
2. *Guide through the Land of Priorities for the Czech Republic* (Průvodce krajinou priorit pro ČR, 2002).

3. *Voyage through the Czech Future* (Potůček et al., 2003), which develops the previous analysis and offers an alternative road towards the future.

CESES was also cooperating with the Slovak government of Mikuláš Dzurinda and inspired the Slovak Institute for Public Issues (Inštitút pre verejné otázky, IVO) to prepare the study *Vision for the Slovak Republic's Development until 2020*.

After the parliamentary elections in June 2002 and the creation of the new coalition government led by Social Democrat Špidla, the role of strategic projection, CESES, and Potůček grew rapidly. After 1998, Potůček was a member of Špidla's advisory team at the Ministry of Social Affairs; after the 2002 elections, Potůček served as the advisor of prime minister until 2004, and again he acted in this position from 2014–2017 on the team of Prime Minister Bohuslav Sobotka when he was also the Chair of the Expert Commission for the Pension Reform. In 2002, Potůček was discussed as the candidate for ČSSD for the office of the President of the Czech Republic. Indeed, in the intra-party plebiscite, Zeman was selected, while Potůček won only minimal support from four candidates (Kopeček, 2017, p. 181).

In 2005, CESES started the research project *Vision and Development Strategy of Czech Society within the EU*; from the expected 6 years, it was prolonged to 7. During this period, tens of books and scientific articles were produced, but more popular outcomes were achieved, including the rich media presentation. CESES also started publishing its own scientific review in English—*Central European Journal of Public Policy* (CEJPP)—in 2007 (since 2016, the CEJPP has been published in partnership with de Gruyter Open/Sciendo). The security research continually strengthened within CESES, becoming dominant after 2010. CESES also became the most important academic centre for education in public policies in the Czech Republic as well as the 'cadre reservoir' for the Czech governments led by Social Democrat prime ministers searching for (ideologically close) experts. Critically observed, the outcomes are prepared mostly with excellent quality, but the public presentations of CESES (and personally Potůček) also include an ideological/party frame. For example, in the *Annual Report for 2007* (i.e. about 1 year after the creation of the right-wing government of Mirek Topolánek), Potůček mentions that he and his co-workers changed the title of one book from *Strategic Governance in the Czech Republic* to *Strategic Governance and the Czech Republic*, which seemed to them 'more realistic'. Even more critical was he in the period of Petr Nečas' government in 2010–2013; in the annual reports for 2011–2013, Potůček repeatedly uses the same rhetoric: 'Many decisions of the political and administrative elite in our country were grounded rather in shallow knowledge and visions or even in poor crutches of ideological clichés than in slid analyses and prognoses of future long-term impacts of corresponding decisions on people's lives.'

The importance of CESES and its production was growing and sinking with the political interest dedicated by the political elite. As shown, during the periods of governments led by Social Democrats, the importance of CESES grew, and Potůček and his co-workers were included in the knowledge-based debates on (some) policies. In the periods of governments led by ODS (2006–2013), such interest sank or (better expressed) was reoriented towards more economically based positions and strategies rooted in the neoliberal approach. All this demonstrates that the role and position of sociology and its influence on transformation were strengthened after 1997 but not fully stabilised, while one of the most important reasons is the ideological/party background of (some) sociologists. In other words, the political sphere tends to use sociological knowledge and sociology as an affirmative science.

Indeed, approximately 15 years after the transition, sociology attempted to (re-) evaluate its role and position. In 2002 and 2004, the *Czech Sociological Review* presented a broad debate that included dozens of sociologists. Let us present briefly the most important positions. As the dominant discourse, fully in scope with the position of social democratic governments and general criticism of the 'Klausian' period, the market reductionism critique was presented. This should be the main cause for the deformation of the first phase of transformation (Potůček, 1997; Frič & Potůček, 2004, p. 425). Evaluating the transformation, Frič and Potůček (2004, pp. 423–424) observe as the most dramatic controversy the debate on the development orientation of Czech society, that is, the contradiction 'between its orientation on economically super-performing turbo-society and orientation on the quality of life'. In the first decade, the first approach definitely predominated based on the programme of catching up with the West. The authors put forth two presumptions behind this choice: first, economic growth will produce a better quality of life automatically; second, the social relations, norms, and values will also automatically adapt to new conditions. Generally, the transformation was criticised as 'one-dimensional', that is, with the supremacy of the economy. Thus, Machonin (2000, p. 424) criticises the underestimation of law and its importance, ecology, health protection, consumer protection, fight against criminality, and other factors.

While in 1995, Matějů seemed to be the most critical towards the discipline, in 2002, this role was adopted by Večerník (2002, p. 65–66). In his opinion, in the 1990s, the Czech social sciences failed. Sociology should have much more strongly opposed the purely economic approach towards transition and underscored the societal nature of capitalist values. Similarly, Keller (2002, p. 32–33) appeals for more assertiveness for sociology vis-à-vis the economy, especially within the discussions about the social state, its crisis, and prospects. 'Transformation was conceptually contained mainly as economic. Its schoolbook became the neo-classical economy, not based on the choice from the variants offered, but based on its clear actual dominance in [the] developed world' (Večerník, 2002, p. 63). Sociology should also clearly distinguish itself from public opinion surveys and show 'how shallow and changeable is the public opinion'. Similar to Havelka in 1995, Večerník (2002, p. 59) criticises the insufficient interest of social sciences and partly also the political sphere in the study of transformation.

Similar to 1995, Machonin (2002, p. 50) seemed to be the most positively based sociologist. Against the critics emphasising the small engagement of sociology within the transformation, he underscores the necessity of keeping a distance from political and ideological conflicts in the first two thirds of the 1990s. The sociologists did not engage prematurely and usually did not risk their reputation by offering any apologetic and non-critical statements. Symbolically, after the year 2000, 'the sociologists do need to inflict on media—media are searching them alone.' Against this positive picture of Czech sociology, we have to argue that staying out of the political and public debates did not make the position and reputation of Czech sociology better. On the contrary, we agree with the positive evaluation of the sociology-media nexus. For example, if we analyse the activities of CESES, next to research, we can observe the important popularising activities in media. Finally, we have to mention that such personal activity towards media was repeatedly the basis for the transfer into politics (Petr Matějů, Ivan Gabal, and Jan Keller).

The repeated debate on the state of the art of Czech sociology in the mid-2000s showed again the unclear position towards its own development. While Petrusek (2002, pp. 13–14) positively evaluates the sociological analyses of transformation (as well as the development of gender studies, but leaving out cultural studies), Machonin (2002, pp. 52) presents better knowledge of post-socialist transformation as the basic mission of Czech sociology. Some sociologists found strong ties with politics to be the best instrument for the implementation of sociological knowledge, while others criticise such an interconnection as making adequate critique impossible (Nešpor, 2006, p. 22).

9.6 New Challenges for Czech Sociology and Study of Transformation?

At the beginning of our contribution, we asked five questions related to Czech sociology's impact on the transformation and the internal transformation of the discipline. As shown in our analysis, the starting point of Czech sociology in 1989 was much more complicated than in the Hungarian or Polish case. While Polish, Hungarian, or Slovene sociologists strongly contributed to the development of the discipline, including the theoretical reflections of the specifics of (post-)socialist societies, Czech sociology was with difficulties searching for its position in the family of social sciences in its own country as well as abroad and above all within Czech society. If we observe the development based on the questions asked, we can observe a mostly defensive position of Czech sociology attempting to protect the idea of the welfare state against the neoliberal economic discourse of the 'market without attributes'. Czech sociologists had warned before the 'one-dimensional' economic path of the transformation at the beginning of 1990 but lost against a much better prepared (and unscrupulous) economist originating in the Communist-organised Prognostic Institute.

Indeed, especially in the second period we indicated after the transition (1997–2007), we can observe visible successes. Sociology helped in the prevention of violent nation-building in the Czech-German and Czech-EU relations; in the sociological community, the support for EU membership was almost unanimous, again unlike the economists. Nevertheless, such a positive evaluation cannot be expressed regarding the feelings of a large part of Czech society towards foreigners, especially migrants. Here, the traditional xenophobia was awakened by populist politicians, and sociology did not find a remedy.

As regards particular discourses, with the fall of Prime Minister Klaus in 1997, the debate on the welfare state was restarted in cooperation with ČSSD and other parties (Christian Democrats). For the first time, Czech sociology played a dominant role among the social sciences, and this was repeated after 2009 and the outbreak of the financial crisis in the EU (cf. Cabada, 2014). With the broader issue of the welfare state, particular issues such as labour and precarity, the middle-class role, transformation towards an information society, and globalisation are also related, including both opportunities and risks. Specifically, the sociology of family should be stressed since the Czech Republic was also affected by the negative trends observed since the 1960s in the West. A strong focus might be observed in gender studies but without reasonable success in public policies.

As demonstrated, Czech sociology and several persons originating from the sociological community were able to push through some of their ideas. Again, we have to underscore the adoption of the Social Doctrine in 2001, although this text is touching on its content very vaguely. A similar role was played by Czech sociology in protecting the extremely egalitarian pension system (in both cases, the role of Potůček was crucial). Let us emphasise that the issue of pension system reform was symbolically 'returned' to the economists by the recent government of Andrej Babiš; the Commission for Just Pensions (Komise pro spravedlivé důchody) established in January 2018 is chaired by the economist Danuše Nerudová. In contrast, in research policy, we can still observe the strong influence of Matějů with his emphasis on scientometrics, quantification, and the full internationalisation of research outcomes.

Reflecting on the four ideal types presented in the initial exploratory analysis in this book, we have to stress that at the beginning of the transition towards democracy and multilevel transformation in 1989, Czech sociology was institutionally weak, personally limited, and not offering a robust platform of contemporary knowledge and expertise. Indeed, this was the situation of all social science branches, with the partial exception of economists, who were strongly preferred by the Communist Party and clearly overruled the first period of transformation. In the first 5 to 7 years after the transition, sociologists were balancing between the ideal types of 'marginals' and 'voyeurs'. During this period, the Czech sociological community caught up with the actual issues, trends, and theories, and institutionally, it boosted distinctively. As early as 1998, we can observe the shift towards a more autonomous position: (some) Czech sociologists presented themselves as 'activists'. Furthermore, as we showed in our analysis, in connection with the different political parties (above all, the Social Democrats), some Czech sociologists became 'passengers'. Depending on the actual political situation and ruling majority, the positions of 'activists' and 'passengers' may alternate.

We should definitely stress that Czech sociology strongly contributed to the preservation (perhaps, we can use the term 'conservation') of extremely egalitarian health and education systems (health care and education with any charges/tuitions). Furthermore, this might be one of the reasons that sociology (and related social sciences and humanities) is repeatedly criticised as an incubator of leftism and a group isolated from reality (Nešpor, 2006, p. 22). The criticism is coming from politicians but also important representatives of the technical and natural sciences (this group is among the most visible supporters of the ANO 2011 movement established by Babiš). Here, the dominant discourse, stressing the knowledge society based on technical and natural scientific education, interconnects the contemporary political elite and business leaders (which might be and often are the same persons) and goes against the mainstream in Czech sociology. This is why we conclude in a rather pessimistic manner, observing that after 2015, the role of sociology is again weakening.

Competing Interests The author has no conflicts of interest to declare that are relevant to the content of this chapter.

References

Brokl, L., et al. (2004). Česká sociologie v letech 1965–1989 (round table; transcription prepared by M. Skovajsa). *Sociologický časopis/Czech. The Sociological Review, 40*(5), 695–740.
Bútora, M., Krivý, V., & Szomolanyiová, S. (1989). *Positive deviation: The career of a concept and the epidemiology of a phenomena in Czecho-Slovakia in the late eighties*. Mimeo.
Cabada, L. (2003). Aspekte der tschechischen politischen Kultur. In G. Erdödy (Ed.), *Transformationerfahrungen: Zur Entwicklung der politischen Kultur in den EU-Kandidatenländer* (pp. 47–69). Nomos Verlaggesellschaft.
Cabada, L. (2014). Neo-liberal, neo-Keynesian or just standard response on the crisis? Clash of ideologies in Czech political, scientific and public debate. *Politics in Central Europe, 10*(1), 25–51.
Cabada, L. (2019). Entösterreicherung als kulturelles Fundament und politisches Programm? Zur Symbolischen Verräumung österreichischen Symboleud Österreichs in Tschechien. In L. Cabada & C. Walsh (Eds.), *Imaginäre Räume in Zentraleuropa: Kulturelle Transformationen, politische Repräsentationen und trans/nationale Identitätsentwürfe* (pp. 111–149). Gabriele Schäfer Verlag.
CESES. (2016). *Annual report of center for social and economic strategies for the year 2015*. Accessed Feb 9, 2020, from https://ceses.cuni.cz/CESES-9-version1-vyrocni_zprava_15.pdf
CESES. (2017). *Annual report of center for social and economic strategies for the year 2016*, Retrieved February 9, 2020 from https://www.ceses.cuni.cz/CESES-462-version1-vyrocni_zprava_16.pdf
Frič, P., & Potůček, M. (2004). Model vývoje české společnosti a její modernizace v globálním kontextu. *Sociologický časopis/Czech Sociological Review, 40*(4), 415–431.
Havelka, M. (1995a). *Spor o smysl českých dějin 1895–1938*. Torst.
Havelka, M. (1995b). Úvodem k diskusní výzvě Petra Matějů "Posttotalitní trauma české sociologie". *Sociologický časopis, 31*(2), 253–254.
Havelka, M. (2002). *Smysl a dějiny: Akcenty a posuny české otázky 1895–1989*. NLN.
Holman, R., et al. (2015). *Dějiny ekonomického myšlení* (3rd ed.). C.H. Beck.
Kabele, J. (1995). Trauma sociologie a české čekání na druhý dech. *Sociologický časopis, 31*(2), 263–266.
Kabele, J. (2011). Sportpropag—nepravděpodobné místo pro studium společnosti: Osobní pohled. *Sociální studia, 8*(1), 17–35.
Keller, J. (2002). Deset témat pro českou sociologii. *Sociologický časopis/Czech Sociological Review, 38*(1–2), 25–35.

Kopeček, L. (2017). *Miloš Zeman: Příběh talentovaného pragmatika.* Intelektuál válčí s intelektuály. Barrister & Principal.
Koudelka, F. (2004). Česká sociologie na Palackého univerzitě v Olomouci v letech 1962–1970. *Sociologický časopis/Czech Sociological Review, 40*(5), 623–630.
Krejčí, O. (2014). *Sametová revoluce.* Professional Publishing.
Kubů, E. (2011). Obraz české transformace v zrcadle sociologického výzkumu. *Historická sociologie, 3*(1), 41–62.
Macháček, L. (2004). Slovenské aspekty rozvoja sociológie v Československu. *Sociologický časopis/Czech Sociological Review, 40*(5), 631–642.
Machonin, P. (1995). K důkladnější analýze příčin problémů české sociologie. *Sociologický časopis, 31*(3), 357–361.
Machonin, P. (2000). Teorie modernizace a česká zkušenost. In L. Mlčoch, P. Machonin, & M. Sojka (Eds.), *Ekonomické a společenské změny v české společnosti* (pp. 97–218). Karolinum.
Machonin, P. (2002). Je čas k zásadní diskusi. *Sociologický časopis/Czech Sociological Review, 38*(1–2), 49–54.
Machonin, P. (2004). K sociologii v období normalizace. *Sociologický časopis/Czech Sociological Review, 40*(5), 643–650.
Masaryk, T. G. (1968). *1968.* Ideály humanitní.
Masaryk, T. G. (1990a). *Problém malého národa.* Melantrich.
Masaryk, T. G. (1990b). *Česká otázka.* Svoboda.
Matějů, P. (1995). Posttotalitní trauma české sociologie. *Sociologický časopis, 31*(2), 255–258.
Možný, I. (1991). *Proč tak snadno?* SLON.
Možný, I. (2004). Brněnská anomálie? Brněnská sociologie 1963 až 1989—subjektivní historie. *Sociologický časopis/Czech Sociological Review, 40*(5), 609–622.
Musil, J. (2002). Zamyšlení nad soudobou českou sociologií. *Sociologický časopis/Czech Sociological Review, 38*(1–2), 17–24.
Musil, J. (2004). Poznámky o české sociologii za komunistického režimu. *Sociologický časopis/Czech Sociological Review, 40*(5), 573–595.
Müller, K. (2002). *Češi a občanská společnost. Pojem, problémy, východiska.* Triton.
Nešpor, Z. R. (2006). Ideologie, rétorika a realita české transformace jako sociologický problém. In Z. R. Nešpor & J. Večerník (Eds.), *Socioekonomické hodnoty, politiky a instituce v období vstupu České republiky do Evropské unie* (pp. 19–24). Sociological Institute at the Czech Academy of Science.
Nikodým, L. (n.d.). *Role neformálních institucí v procesu ekonomické transformace.* Retrieved January 8, 2020 http://www.vsfs.cz/prilohy/konference/kd_2014_nikodym_lukas.pdf
Petrusek, M. (1997). Jubileum sociologa sršatého a moudrého. K 65. narozeninám profesora Iva Možného. Sociologický časopis/Czech. *The Sociological Review, 33*(4), 487–490.
Petrusek, M. (2002). Poučení ze zcela nekrizového vývoje české sociologie let 1989–2001. *Sociologický časopis/Czech Sociological Review, 38*(1–2), 7–15.
Petrusek, M. (2004). Výuka sociologie v čase tání a v časech normalizace (1964–1989) (Kapitola o vztahu vědění a moci, vědy a politiky, reality a mýtotvorby). *Sociologický časopis/Czech Sociological Review, 40*(5), 597–607.
Petrusek, M. (2011). *České sociální vědy v exilu.* SLON.
Potůček, M. (1997). *Nejen trh. Role trhu, státu a občanského sektoru v proměnách české společnosti.* SLON.
Potůček, M., et al. (2001). *Vize rozvoje České republiky do roku 2015.* Gutenberg.
Potůček, M., et al. (2003). *Putování českou budoucností.* Gutenberg.
Prohlášení sociologů (dopis prezidentovi). (1990/1997). M. Potůček, Křižovatky české sociální reformy (pp. 237–239). SLON.
Průvodce krajinou priorit pro ČR. (2002). *Gutenberg.*
Sociální doktrína ČR. (2001). Retrieved February 11, 2020 from http://www.sds.cz/docs/prectete/e_kolekt/soc_dokt.htm
Skovajsa, M. (2006). *Politická kultura.* Karolinum.

Šanc, D. (2009). *Česká politologie—etablování oboru*. University of West Bohemia.
Štětka, J. (2009). *Liberál na deseti židlích*. Ekonom. Retrieved February 25, 2020 from https://ekonom.ihned.cz/c1-38943930-liberal-na-deseti-zidlich
Usnesení vlády České republiky č. 421, o zřízení Rady ČR pro sociální a ekonomickou strategii. (1999). Retrieved February 25, 2020 from https://kormoran.vlada.cz/usneseni/usneseni_webt-est.nsf/0/68F9FEB13040756BC12571B60070BB7A
Večerník, J. (2002). Výzkum společenské transformace a česká sociologie. *Sociologický časopis/ Czech Sociological Review, 38*(1–2), 55–77.
Večerník, J., & Matějů, P. (Eds.). (1999). *Ten years of rebuilding capitalism: Czech society after 1989*. Academia.
Vodička, K., & Cabada, L. (2011). *Politický system České republiky: Historie a současnost* (3rd ed.) Portál.
Wandycz, P. S. (1992). *The price of freedom: A history of east Central Europe from the middle ages to the present*. Routledge.
Zeman, M. (1969). Futurologie v přítomnosti. *Sociologický časopis, 5*(1), 70–73.
Zeman, M. (1989). Prognostika a přestavba. *Technický magazín, 8*, 6–9.

Ladislav Cabada is a Full Professor and the guarantor of MA and PhD Programme Political Science and also the Vice-Rector for the Research, Quality and Development at the Metropolitan University Prague. In 2005, together with Šárka Waisová, he cofounded the international scientific review Politics in Central Europe and was working as the editor of this journal till 2024. He served as President of Czech Political Science Association (2006–2012) and Central European Political Science Association (2012–2018). Since May 2021, he acts as one of the 12 members in the Executive Committee of European Consortium for Political research (ECPR). He focuses mainly on comparative politics of East-Central Europe, regionalism and development studies, Europeanisation, Euroscepticism, and political anthropology.

Chapter 10
Sociology and Sociologists During the 30 Years of Estonia's Post-socialist Transformation

Mikko Lagerspetz

10.1 Introductory Remarks

The three decades (and a few years more) starting from 1987 witnessed fundamental change in Estonia, the northernmost country in what now is usually referred to as Central Eastern Europe (CEE) and the smallest (population 1.3 million) of the three Baltic countries. They were all incorporated by the Soviet Union in 1940, after two decades of independent statehood. The year 1987 marks the beginning of the so-called Singing Revolutions in Estonia, Latvia, and Lithuania, which led to the restoration of their political independence in 1991. The decades that followed brought forth a redefinition of the polity by means of the citizenship legislation enacted in September 1992 and enforced in July 1993; the end of Russian military presence in 1994; the country's membership in various international organisations, notably in the Council of Europe (CoE; in 1993), the European Union (EU), and the North Atlantic Treaty Organization (NATO; both in 2004); and the consolidation of capitalist class society and liberal democracy. A deep change affected CEE societies in all spheres of life: in the political and economic systems and in their culture and social structure. Citing the manifold contents of the process, Claus Offe (1991) has referred to it as a 'triple transition'.

One should note, however, that the term 'transition' is problematic, as it associates with a movement between two clearly defined conditions: 'communism', 'state', or 'real socialism' and 'capitalism' or 'liberal democracy'. It thus presents the process as teleological and its result as more or less self-evident and unambiguous (Haerpfer, 2002, p. 3). In reality, however, the previously real socialist countries' populations and decision-makers did not have just one model of capitalism

---

M. Lagerspetz (✉)
Åbo Akademi University, Turku, Finland
e-mail: mlagersp@abo.fi

and democracy, but several to choose between (and in some countries, the resulting regime is today not even recognisable as democracy). Obviously, the political choices to be made called for debate and self-reflection, besides just a recognition of inevitabilities. Sociology, as a discipline and a profession, has, in Western modernity, often been assigned the task of informing and even initiating such debate. In the following, I will discuss whether and in which ways Estonia's sociological community succeeded in that.

10.2 The Roles of Intellectuals in Real and Post-socialism

In the post-socialist systemic change of the late 1980s–early 1990s, intellectuals played a prominent role. The election of Václav Havel as the first President of the Czech Republic in 1993 is probably the most well-known example. The first President of re-independent Estonia, elected in 1992, was the writer and filmmaker Lennart Meri. The development resonates with Karl Mannheim's (1936/1946, pp. 137–139) vision of intellectuals as a 'socially unattached' stratum, relatively independent of the interests of other classes more immediately connected with processes of economic production. While the dominating state and Communist Party bureaucracies retreated, and while other social classes and interest groups were still nascent, intellectuals continued to be in possession of both efficient networks and authority. Their authority was at least in part independent of the old power structures: it was based on professional activity, not on formal position in a rapidly eroding hierarchy.

However, it is not sufficient to discuss just 'intellectuals' *tout court*. There is reason for distinguishing at least between intellectuals within arts and humanities and within science and engineering. The two groups' possibilities for expressing dissent differed. 'Dissident', as Havel (1978/1992, pp. 173–175) powerfully argues, was a label attached by power holders to people in conflict with the regime for varying reasons. A dissident career possibly began just from 'an attempt to do your work well' and ended with 'being branded an enemy of society'. In sociological terms, we could discuss being 'a dissident' as a sort of secondary deviance produced in the interchange between the subject and the mechanisms of normative control. In the case of the Estonian Soviet Socialist Republic, the latter dealt much more harshly with the technological intelligentsia. Many participants of the outright dissident movement had an education in engineering or natural sciences (Kukk, 1991, p. 238), while the option of a kind of semi-legal opposition was open mainly for intellectuals within humanities. When in trouble with authorities, an engineer had few chances of continuing a career. Meanwhile, a writer, an artist, or even a historian could often count on some lobbying activities from the state-sponsored 'Creative Unions'. If the conflict remained unresolved, it would first result in an 'inner exile', during which the artist, writer, or scholar would perform less visible teacher or translator jobs outside the gaze of the public or the authorities. Eventually, there was the chance of regaining one's former position when political moods changed (Lagerspetz, 1996,

p. 104f). Some of the creative and humanitarian intellectuals had become (with the help of state-sponsored media and publishing houses) prominent public figures, and works of their authorship stood on the bookshelves of many ordinary citizens.

Despite the thorough changes that have taken place since the 1980s, some basic determinants of the position of the group of intellectuals remain. First, the group's or profession's degree of autonomy continues to play a role; what matters here is not just the administrative or financial independence from the state or from the business. The relative autonomy of the Writers' Unions of the Soviet republics was not due to formal legal guarantees (even when they formally existed), any more than today's social science departments of state-run universities or market research institutes can rely solely on them (whatever any constitution says about the freedom of scientific research). An institution's, a group's, and a discourse's autonomy vis-à-vis political decision-makers or the business arises from the existence of some additional power base. Both popular or media appeals and successfully established academic authority may serve as such a power base.

Second, a group of intellectuals may adopt different positions as to what it counts as its public. Its focus may be on professional activities, which makes fellow intellectuals of the same profession one's primary addressee. In contrast, there may be prominent members of the profession who choose to address a more mixed public of decision-makers, movement activists, and/or citizens in general. These two dimensions and the positions resulting from them are summarised in Fig. 10.1.

The model bears some resemblance to Michael Burawoy's (2004) now-famous interpretation of different kinds of sociological practice and to Borut Rončević's (in this volume) typology of the roles of a sociologist in society. However, Burawoy focuses on the type of knowledge produced (instrumental or reflexive) and not the autonomy of the profession, while Rončević divides between 'strong' and 'weak' roles, not between different publics addressed.

To summarise, when assessing an intellectual profession's role and position in society, I propose that we consider two dimensions: the professionals' autonomy from political decision-makers and business and their willingness and capability to

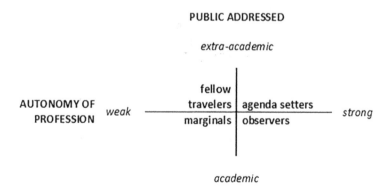

Fig. 10.1 Possible social positions of an academic profession, by autonomy and by the public addressed

address either the general public or a more confined academic audience. The two dimensions combine to form four different actor positions. Returning to the examples discussed above, we can attempt to place them in the appropriate categories. If this analysis of the relative autonomy of engineers and writers in the Estonian SSR is correct, we can now understand why those writers banned from the publicity became rather 'observers' than 'marginals', why engineers were in a contrary situation, and why writers and intellectuals within humanities became important agenda setters when political censorship of the media was gradually abandoned during the final years of the 1980s (Lagerspetz, 1996, p. 84).

10.3 Basic Trends of Development

The role of the sociological profession in Estonia's post-socialist transformation and beyond is, of course, not reducible to the political activities of its individual members. Above, I suggested some more general outlines for its interpretation. As an introduction to the discussion to follow, it is useful to state some basic trends of development of both the discipline itself and its relations to other actors and discourses. In order to understand them, I find the following worth considering:

A development from social statistics to sociology, with all that it includes for the potential role of the discipline.
The emergence of clearer distinctions between and within social science disciplines, accompanied by continuous close cooperation.
Media's and decision-makers' interest in 'facts', not in their interpretation.
The profession's relationship with politics has turned from intimate to strained and unclear.

There are no thorough overviews of the development of sociology in Estonia; the issue has, however, been treated in a few book chapters over the years (Titma, 2002; Lagerspetz & Pettai, 2003; Opermann & Vihalemm, 2017). Moreover, the discipline's recent history and development have been discussed with some regularity at conferences organised by the Estonian Union of Sociologists and by the social science units of the universities in Tartu and Tallinn.

10.4 From Social Statistics to Sociology

The view of what actually counts as 'sociology' has changed over time. To define the discipline is, of course, no easy undertaking. Dag Østerberg (1989) has suggested that sociology is about issues concerning societies, communities, interaction, and so on: that is, about issues that cannot be reduced to the level of individuals. Accordingly, studies about, for instance, living conditions, consumer preferences, or attitudes, if they build merely on aggregate data on individuals, would fall outside the definition of sociology. His preferred term for research of that type is *social statistics*. Sociological research can be identified by its use of theories concerning society, community and group interaction, and concepts such as norms, values, culture, roles, and identities. Aggregate data on individuals becomes sociology inasmuch as it is interpreted with the help of such theories and concepts.

The perspective of the present chapter is not philosophical or methodological but mainly historical. Instead of attempting to define sociology from today's point of view, we must discuss those research practices that have been called sociology by their contemporaries. Sociology, as it was understood during the Soviet regime and still some years after that, was larger than it is today as to its empirical foci, with less clear boundaries towards demography, social policy, consumption studies, media research, and political science. 'Sociology', as the name of a professional practice, was used as an umbrella concept to depict all kinds of social research with an empirical and mainly quantitative approach. Disciplinary boundaries between sociology and other social sciences have become clearer only with the emergence of academic study programmes from the 1990s onwards. The Estonian Union of Sociologists, founded in 1990, initially hosted as its members (and still to some extent does) researchers from a wide array of social science disciplines. At the same time, sociology lacked many of the research questions rooted in the sociological theory that defined the discipline in the West, or that define it now.

Undergraduate academic curricula in sociology were created first in 1990–1997 (Rämmer et al., 2015; Lagerspetz & Pettai, 2003, pp. 64–65). The older generation of sociologists received their basic university education in some other discipline (e.g. psychology, history, philosophy, mathematics, or journalism) and continued with specialised studies within a research group, leading to the Soviet Candidate's degree (roughly corresponding to the doctoral of today). From the mid-1960s onwards, research groups emerged for youth studies, media research, family studies, the study of living conditions, and so on. Thus, the disciplinary background of sociologists varied, and they seldom moved beyond their own research field of specialisation. The fields all had their own specific approaches. Sociology was not defined through a shared theoretical tradition but as a research practice in which some typical methods of data collection and analysis were used (questionnaires, content analyses, observation). In Østerberg's terminology, much (even if by no means all) of that research could more suitably be called social statistics. An Estonian translation of parts of Elisabeth Noelle's (1967) German textbook on survey research was published in 1967. The original book's term *Demoskopie*, or population survey, was translated simply as 'Sociology'.

In the Soviet society of the 1960s, sociology emerged as an answer to a demand for information of a certain kind: numeral feedback from society. During the Khrushchev 'Thaw' period, the rulers became aware of a need for mechanisms of economic and political steering that were subtler than those employed by Stalin's regime. Economic and social statistics produced by state agencies and state-run enterprises were unreliable because of the ways in which they were collected. The data-providing agencies had a vested interest in displaying successful performance even when there was none (Ruutsoo, 1991). Sociology offered the option of receiving information directly from the population instead of relying on misleading statistics. Paralleling similar developments in the West, survey research became an instrument in the creation of a modern consumer society of the Soviet type. Sociology was given the role of a helping hand in social engineering, providing the decision-makers with data otherwise not available.

Likewise, the rulers received no political feedback because of the lack of democracy, public debate, and independent organisations. Sociology should help to answer questions such as the following: How are the living conditions, in fact? Are people happy with their lives? How are the relations between people of different nationalities? How do people relate to mass media? Are they aware of issues that the decision-makers consider important? At the same time, researchers had to keep themselves within the confines of the ruling ideology. Any discussion of general trends of development was not what the decision-makers expected of sociology. Conclusions critical of the regime had to be 'hidden in the tables': visible to the trained eye rather than spelt out.

Since the 1990s, important institutional changes influencing the sociological profession have taken place. First, reliable statistics on the economy and society have become available. At the same time, enterprises dealing with opinion polls and market research have emerged, some of them before Estonian independence. The emergence of university curricula in sociology (1990–1997) has strengthened the discipline theoretically, defined it more clearly vis-à-vis other social science disciplines, and made sociologists more aware of different research fields and methodological approaches. This created a new institutional context in which the discipline became defined through specific theories and types of research questions. International contacts and participation in European research projects have become part of an academic sociologist's everyday work. There has been a general change in the role of intellectuals: they no longer need to function as substitutes for democratic institutions and civil society. Unlike during the Soviet regime or during the revolutionary period, there exist both political parties, democratic elections, uncensored media, and interest groups in favour of one or another policy. Thus, both the numeral and the political feedback functions have been handed over to specialised institutions.

Consequently, there has been a development towards more 'sociological' ways of defining research questions. For example, research in deviant individuals has given way for research in subcultures and control policies; research in household income has developed into more refined research in economic coping strategies and in the structural determinants of life chances. In all, sociologists see their topic of research more as the agency embedded in the social environment and less as the behaviour and characteristics of atomised individuals.

10.5 Sociologists in the Political Process

The Marxist-Leninist ideology legitimated itself, among other things, with the claim of being scientific. On the one hand, this meant that researchers within social sciences and humanities were supposed not to openly divert from the official truths of the ideology and at least pay it lip service by quoting Marxist-Leninist classics. On the other hand, scientific experts were bestowed with considerable authority. From 1986 on, this balance was affected by the reform policies known as *perestroika* and by the liberalisation and gradual removal of censorship known as *glasnost*. Political change started to seem plausible and desirable; possibilities for its public discussion opened. Initially, mass media was expected to remain loyal to the prevailing political and economic system. 'Glasnost also means criticizing errors. But it does not mean undermining Socialism, our common socialist values', as General Secretary Mikhail Gorbachev put it in 1987 (Lagerspetz, 1996, p. 84). However, it did not take long for a criticism of the system's ideological foundations to surface. At the same time, science and scientific experts continued to hold high esteem, even higher now, when large-scale social restructuring was at stake, and old power hierarchies were rapidly losing their significance.

Scientists, including sociologists, became instead important critics of the system. This is illustrated by a content analysis of claims on social problems made in the leading official newspaper, *Rahva Hääl* (The Voice of the People) (Lagerspetz, 1996, p. 91, 99). During the initial years of the Singing Revolution, the share of academic experts making such claims went up dramatically. In 1988–1989, 42 and 45%, respectively, of such claims were made by 'specialists' (persons presented in the newspaper with their scientific degrees and employees of universities and research institutes). In 1975–1984, their share was a mere 16% and, in 1992, again just 12%. The political debate of the revolutionary period was also characterised by a gradual widening of the range of problems discussed. Such new issues as environmental problems and relations between different nationalities were lifted to the fore. Less controversial issues, such as alcoholism or low labour efficiency, were first debated within the frameworks of individual attitudes or organisational performance, but those problems also became associated with fundamental shortcomings of the entire economic and political system by 1988 (Lagerspetz, 1996, p. 97f).

In Estonia, the revolution was triggered by environmental concerns. In February 1987, a popular television programme informed the public about the all-Union authorities' plan to expand the mining industry in the region, and a large social movement was born practically overnight to protest against its potential environmental effects (Lagerspetz, 1996, p. 58). The protest soon found its proper addressee in the administrative mechanisms that subjugated local interests to those of the all-Union economy. In September 1987, the regional newspaper *Edasi* (Forward) published an article in which a programme aiming at Estonia's economic independence from the rest of the Soviet Union was proposed (Lagerspetz, 1996, pp. 57–60; Lieven, 1994, p. 221). The four authors were all social scientists, and two of them, Mikk Titma and Edgar Savisaar, had, at the time, a close relationship with sociology. Titma was heading the Sociology Section of the Institute of History of Estonian SSR's Academy of Sciences, and Savisaar became in 1988 the Research Director of the consultation centre *Mainor*, which carried out voluminous opinion surveys. Savisaar, along with the sociologist Marju Lauristin, was soon among the leading figures of the Popular Front movement founded in April 1988.

The prominent position of sociologists in the revolutionary process was no mere coincidence on the level of individuals. They did not contribute to the movement as activists only but to its strategic thinking as well through research-based theoretical and empirical work. Until 1991, the Popular Front remained the most efficient mobiliser of the Estonian quest for economic autonomy and, gradually, for full political independence. Two more movements, the openly anti-Communist and nationalist Movement of Estonian Citizens and the counter-revolutionary Interfront movement, were born in early 1989 (Lagerspetz, 1996, p. 60). During what is usually considered an aborted coup d'état in August 1991 in Moscow, the Supreme Soviet of the Estonian SSR issued a declaration of independence. The Soviet Union was dissolved at the end of 1991.

In the parliamentary democracy of independent Estonia, social movements gave way to a spectrum of political parties. Politics shaped around a competition between movements gave way to a parliamentary contest. Whereas the authority of movement leaders was based on their professional credentials or on their assumed personal integrity as intellectuals or 'dissidents', that of being a political personage in a liberal democracy is more intimately linked to their capability of catering to different groups of voters and lobby groups.

Savisaar, at one time, the Mayor of Tallinn and the Chairman of the Centrist Party, preserved his political significance for a long time, not because of his background partly in sociology, but by his appeal to groups of voters dissatisfied with the prevailing 'nation-liberal' (Lagerspetz & Vogt, 2013, p. 66f) policies. Due to both deteriorating health and serious accusations of corruption, he finally resigned from his political duties in 2017 and died in 2022. Another person with strong ties to both sociology and politics, Professor Ülo Vooglaid, served two full election terms in the Estonian parliament in the 1990s but left it in 2004, shortly after the beginning of a third term, with a disappointed protest against his own party (then the conservative-populist Res Publica) (Postimees, 2004). Professor Marju Lauristin, in contrast, is the possibly only example of a person who has been successful in combining the roles of an academically active sociologist and of a leading politician. In the early 1990s, she became the country's first Minister of Social Affairs and had to develop its social policy essentially from scratch. For some years, she served as the Chairwoman of the Social Democratic Party and was later elected Member of the European Parliament. In the 2000s, few sociologists have openly aligned with political parties, and (with the exception of Lauristin) none has gained a prominent political position.

Lauristin's accomplishment is, in many ways, exceptional; there is no longer any direct pattern from academic excellence to political leadership. Even the 'movement society' of the late 1980s that originally lifted her to key political positions was exceptional in many senses. For one thing, Estonians' political fight for sovereignty was not considered a divisive effort but one uniting Estonians of different political stances (then only emerging). The party politics that was introduced along with parliamentary democracy instead tended to stress political divisions and to present politics as a zero-sum game. In the public consciousness of both the Soviet and the present times, a scientist's authority is based on his or her assumed objectivity. That very objectivity is thought to be compromised by open support of any political creed. Thus, the legitimacy of a scientific expert and that of a political leader now seem to be based on mutually exclusive foundations. (Of course, one can imagine situations where it would not be so: in a society with a less confrontational political culture and with a view of science that recognises its basis in 'standpoint epistemologies'; see Harding (1991, pp. 138–163)).

After independence, the most important occasion when a group of prominent sociologists, together with other social researchers, collectively took a stance on major trends of social development was the open letter by 26 social researchers published in 2001 in a major daily newspaper (Postimees, 2001, reprinted in Vetik, 2002). The letter claimed that:

> The power elite has become alienated from ordinary people to the extent that it is appropriate to talk about two different Estonias. Two thirds of Estonian children grow up in poverty, people lack even elementary security, and many young people would like to leave the country. Egotism and lack of ethics are nowadays accepted as self-evident in everyday political practice, and the very concept of responsibility has become blurred. Major economic and strategic decisions are made without any analysis of their social effects. [...] The depth of the bifurcation is shown by public opinion polls, in which more than half of the people are against, and a third do not care about Estonia's future direction, i.e., about the question of joining the EU. [...] As long as we lack objective scientific analysis of what, in fact, is going on in Estonia, it remains impossible to encounter the negative processes.

At the same time, the signatories were careful to distance themselves from any political ideologies, wishing to shroud themselves in the role of experts. The letter stated:

> We do not want the present political opposition to use this letter for its own advantage, interpreting it merely as a criticism of the government coalition. Most of our conclusions apply to Estonian politics in its entirety. It is not a question of names but of the system and its principles.

The letter gained rapid resonance on the highest political level. The authors were invited to meet with members of parliament (Riigikogu) for discussion, and later, the prime minister formed a working group to prepare a report on the issues at stake (Marmei, 2001). No concrete measures followed. The government's press releases did, however, manage to create the misleading impression that a major programme of financing applied social research had been initiated, from which some commentators later inferred that precisely the wish to receive more funding had been the hidden motive behind the open letter in the first place (as quoted by Proos (2002, p. 62)). In any case, it succeeded in establishing the term 'Second Estonia' as a household word in the political debate for several years to come. Five years later, the political scientist Tõnis Saarts (2006) summarised some of the debate in a newspaper column. In his opinion, the letter did prepare for a political shift 'to the left', away from orthodox neoliberal economic policies, but also contributed to the spectacular rise in the 2003 parliamentary elections of the new right-wing Res Publica party. The latter's electoral appeal was largely based on a populist, anti-establishment sentiment (Lagerspetz & Vogt, 2004, p. 68), but after a devastating result in the European elections next year, the party merged with the conservative Isamaa ('Fatherland') party in 2006.

The episode is instructive in many senses. There was (and, to some extent, there still is) a trust in open letters as a means of resetting the public agenda. The letter discussed social issues that had been neglected, but it also made a connection with the political elite's most favoured project, EU accession (and, indirectly, with the coming referendum). The signatories' scientific credentials certainly played a role. At the same time, initiators of such action ostensively distanced themselves from party politics. Even then, they remained an easy target of accusations about having party political or their own narrow interests in mind. Although there are recent examples of sociologists and other social scientists who publicly take word in, for example, alcohol policies, sociologists have, in general, preferred to influence political development in the narrower role of experts.

10.6 Sociologists as Experts

Almost all government cabinets since the restoration of Estonia's independence have been strongly committed to ideas of economic liberalism and minimal state, at least as to their rhetoric. However, these principles are easier to preach than to practice. The task of transforming the entire economic, political, and administrative system has required the state's active involvement in creating market relations and liberal democracy 'by design' (cf. Hoen, 2001). The 1990s and early 2000s were a period of rapid modernisation from above, with Western societies as role models. Its aims matched with a scholarly view on the post-socialist 'transition' as essentially a modernisation (or post-modernisation) process, then influential within Western sociology (e.g. Fukuyama, 1992; Bauman, 1993). At the same time, the development was also both in Estonia and generally in CEE, seen as 'a return' to a social model prevalent before real socialism. There is no contradiction here: there was a way of combining the perspectives of modernisation and that of the return. The countries of CEE could be shown as returning from the Russian sphere of influence to 'the West' and to the modernity it represented (Lagerspetz, 1999, p. 388f).

In Estonia, a seminal edited volume on the country's transition was published in 1997 by Marju Lauristin and her co-workers and carried the telltale title *Back to the Western World* (Lauristin, 1997). The collection of articles introduced a perspective of Estonia's development both as a process of modernisation and as one of realignment with the 'West', especially with the Nordic countries (Scandinavia and Finland). Democratisation and marketisation were presented as embedded in the 'civilisational context' discussed by Huntington (1996), and their outcome was essentially shaped by it through such mediating factors as the political and entrepreneurial culture and the population's motivation to rejoin the West (Lauristin, 1997, pp. 25–40). If one can talk about any macrosociological paradigm's dominance within Estonian sociology of the 1990s and 2000s, it was the view of the country's development primarily as modernisation and (re-)Westernisation. In fact, this view was the very same that the government acted upon. Since the beginning of independence, the main political goal of every government cabinet was to prepare the country for eventual membership in the EU and NATO. Both goals were finally reached in 2004.

In particular, the objective of joining the EU called for an enormous amount of legislative and organisational work. When harmonising existing legislation with that of the EU or creating new regulations where there previously had been none, parliamentarians felt a need for sociological impact analyses of the bills. In 1995, the Riigikogu Chancellery established a Department of Economic and Social Information with the task of gathering and analysing data for use in the legislative process. In 1998, the chancellery organised an international seminar around the use of socio-economic studies in parliamentary work. In her opening speech, Ms Krista Kilvet, MP and Deputy Chair of the Foreign Affairs Committee, indicated a very straightforward connection between the need for social research and the process of joining the EU (Society…, 1999, p. 10):

> Speaking of Estonia and other Central and Eastern European countries joining the structures of the European Union, I, as a member of parliament, think that the time of general political discussions (slogans) is coming to an end—different delegations to negotiations need concrete empirical data and comparative analyses in order to discuss the problems and solutions of concrete fields of life. You cannot do without social-economic studies here.

While the hurried pace of legal and administrative reform certainly created a demand for information possible to be referred to in negotiations about various fields, it did not encourage dialogue on policy development. 'In this environment, it is remarkable', commented a research group who investigated linkages between research and policy-making in the three Baltic states, 'that any other policy initiatives were possible' at all than those which were aimed at meeting the demands of the acquis communautaire, that is, the EU's common regulative framework (Purju et al., 2005, p. 17).

During the 1990s and early 2000s, a number of new channels opened for the financing of both policy development and policy-relevant research. The Soros-financed Open Estonia Foundation was set up in 1990 (OEF, 2018). Its focused areas of policy development and research included open and transparent governance, equal opportunities, and civil society. Other important financers eventually became the Nordic Council of Ministers, the European Economic Area (EEA) and Norway Grants, and the European Commission.

Lauristin, as already mentioned, served as Minister of Social Affairs in 1992–1994. In a private discussion, she recently recollected that she had organised regular seminars for the ministry staff, where Esping-Andersen's (1993) treatise on capitalist welfare regimes was discussed. In 2005, the Ministry of Social Affairs was reported as one of the two ministries that possessed their own research and analysis departments (Purju et al., 2005, p. 5 (fn. 5)).

Among all policy fields, the sociologists' impact has probably been most visible within minority policies. Close to a third of Estonia's population speaks Russian as their first language. The restoration of Estonian independence did not include any ethnic violence, but it clearly introduced a 'nationalising state' (Brubaker, 1996). With the Citizenship Act of 1992, most of the Russians suddenly found themselves without any citizenship whatsoever, as they were now redefined as first- or second-generation immigrants from the Soviet Union. Along with the introduction of formal requirements of proficiency in the Estonian language in many vocations, this led to a rapid weakening of the minority's socio-economic position (Pettai & Hallik, 2002, pp. 515–519). Estonia's treatment of its minorities was regularly met with criticism by European organisations, notably the Organization for Security and Co-operation in Europe (OSCE). This, in turn, was obviously a signal that the EU took into account when assessing Estonia's readiness for membership (Johns, 2003). In 1998, a parliamentary document was adopted called 'The Integration of non-Estonians [sic] into Estonian Society' and, subsequently, in 1999, a national programme for integration. This was preceded in 1996 by the establishment of an interuniversity research team of sociologists (with the acronym VERA) by the Minister of Education, Professor Jaak Aaviksoo. The documents were largely based on the conclusions and advice of the VERA team (Heidmets & Lauristin, 2002, pp. 323–324). Later, integration policies and minority issues have been regularly monitored by sociologists (see Kallas et al. (2013)), and these studies tend to receive media attention.

Another attempt to influence an emerging policy field was sociologists' participation in initiatives around relations between civil society and the state. Partly inspired by the British and Canadian Compacts between governments and civil society organisations (CSOs) (see Liiv (2001)) and financially supported by the UN Development Programme and the Soros foundations, a series of roundtables and workshops started in 1998 to draft a document explicating the joint principles guiding such relations (Ruutsoo, 2012, pp. 75–78). A group of sociologists actively participated as experts. Consultations between civil society organisations (CSOs), political parties, and experts resulted in a draft document. However, as Ruutsoo (2012, 88) points out, the bill was finally adopted in December 2002, as The Estonian Concept for the Development of Civil Society became heavily altered during the process. As proposed by the parliamentary group of the neoliberal Reform Party, it played down CSOs' roles in advocacy and interest representation; avoided mentioning concrete activities that might lead to financial responsibilities for the government; and omitted some terms that were thought of as belonging to a left-wing discourse (such as 'social capital' and 'social inclusion'). Unlike the sociologists' vision, politicians decided to treat non-governmental organisations more as actors in a market and less as representatives of civil society (for a general overview, see Rikmann (2012)).

In communicating social research to decision-makers and to the public, the most well-established channel is the annually published Human Development Report (Opermann & Vihalemm, 2017). The series was started in 1995. Published in both

Estonian and English and freely available on the Internet, the reports account for the United Nations Human Development Index and give overviews of some key areas of social development. In recent years, they have been published by a state-owned foundation close to the Chancellery of the President of the Republic and have grown in both volume and visibility. Despite often being critical of economic policies leading to growing economic inequality, the reports are usually treated as non-partisan by the politicians and the media.

10.7 The 'Expert' Role Challenged?

As to the role of social researchers as experts consulted by politicians, Purju and his co-workers (2005) pointed out a paradox: there were numerous formal and informal contacts between researchers and decision-makers, but the results of the research did not seem to have much impact. As already noted, one reason was the preparation for EU membership, which left little space for real decision-making. However, the research group also pointed at other, more intriguing reasons related to a persisting legacy from the Soviet period. They referred to a prevailing view of the function of social research: it is seen as providing the decision-makers with facts, not with analysis. Research is expected to be exclusively empirical, not theory-based. Referring to their case study on the processes of introducing new family benefit schemes in Estonia and Latvia, the research group suspected 'that politicians continue to believe that policy-making in the end does not need evidence—especially when the policy in question is purely domestic and does not need to be justified to partners (e.g., the EU)' (Purju et al., 2005, p. 25).

This instrumentalist and suspicious view of social sciences that still prevails has its roots in the Soviet ideology and practice of government. However, there are some disquieting signs of its appeal among proponents of more recent ideologies. Over the past few years, the nationalist-populist wave sweeping over Europe has become part of the Estonian political debate. There are attempts to delegitimise research on issues that belong to the core of sociological research, such as diversity of values and interests, different life chances of social groups, the processes of social construction underlying norms and institutions, and mechanisms of power. Instead, the 'people' and the 'nation' are presented as sharing the same interests and values, and the society is void of other than spurious conflicts. A privately financed think-tank set up in 2016 and calling itself the Institute of Social Studies (MTÜ Ühiskonnauuringute Instituut) easily finds media coverage for its press releases conforming to a populist agenda, but professional sociologists have questioned both its expertise and its political motives (Ott, 2019). There is at least one other recent example of politically motivated but less than professionally made effort of social research by a government-financed private foundation (Pärli, 2023).

It is not only the populist ultranationalists but also politicians within the right-wing mainstream who sometimes seem to prefer an idealised nationalist narrative to empirical analyses. In 2011, the then Minister of Defense, Jaak Aaviksoo of the

Fatherland-Res Publica Union (later and until 2020, Rector of the Tallinn Technical University), published a remarkable speech on what he called a state's 'right for informational sovereignty' (Aaviksoo, 2011). He stated that:

> [...] psychological defense is a crucial part of every conscious carrier of identity and for that reason, it is also needed for the defense of the Estonian state, people, culture and language. [...] We must accept the position, that God or Darwin—again, depending on your worldview—did not give us self-consciousness and intelligence in order to serve the Truth (as until this day is claimed by some people grossly misled by the Reformation and the Enlightenment), but in order to survive. [...] Consider, why we have pictures of weddings and newborn babies in our albums of family photos, but almost never [...] pictures of family quarrels or domestic violence. Families have the right to choose the pictures they want to display, and a similar right must be granted to the state and the people.

10.8 Conclusions

To put it concisely, during the three decades discussed above, Estonian sociologists have held the positions of both agenda setters, fellow travellers, and observers. Some recent tendencies in politics might even push them into a more marginal role. During the revolutionary period of the late 1980s and early 1990s, sociologists could influence both public debate and social movements, as a relatively visible group among other intellectuals. From later periods, there are just a few examples of sociologists making open efforts to influence politics, and not all of them were successful. More typically, they have found themselves in the narrower roles of policy consulting or academic experts. Sociologists have preferred to distance themselves from party politics, even if their research has sometimes directly pointed at shortcomings of prevailing economic, social, or minority policies. At the same time, most of them have shared with the political elite the basic goals of modernisation, liberal democracy, and accession to Western-based international organisations. Estonian sociologists' criticism of the political decision-makers has been an internal criticism from within a larger common framework.

Above, I quoted two examples of relative success in influencing politics. Some obvious reasons for their success can be pointed out. As to the VERA research project of 1996 and the subsequent policy documents on minority integration, one could say that sociologists were needed in order to spell out what almost every politician knew but what none of them wanted to say aloud. That is, Estonian nationalist politicians' hope of solving the minority issue by changing the demographic ethnic balance in favour of the Estonians never had any real chance of success; there was no need for new symbolical acts of national pride, but for realistic policy measures to accommodate the large Russian minority. Moreover, the EU had made it clear that accession was contingent upon the new members' acceptable treatment of their minorities. It is interesting that sociologists have since preserved a central role in minority policies. Despite integration in the form of the Russians' growing fluency in the Estonian language, one can argue that their integration in the Estonian public sphere remains incomplete. Partly resulting from deliberate negligence, partly from active efforts by the government, and partly from the minority's internal heterogeneity, it has no visibly active interest groups or any institutionalised representation. In essence, Estonian minority politics have remained a strictly top-down enterprise (Lagerspetz, 2015). Thus, issues such as attitudes towards integration, trust towards government institutions, identity, and loyalty continue to be something that survey research must inform decision-makers about. In this policy field, sociology has preserved some of its Soviet-era function of compensating for the lack of democratic feedback mechanisms.

The open letter of 2001 caught the attention of both politicians and the media. It pointed to serious mistrust between decision-makers and the 'Second Estonia' of ordinary people. One can argue that the letter did have some, albeit partly, unintended consequences for the development of Estonian politics (Saarts, 2006). Again, sociologists spelt out issues which politicians were well aware of but unwilling to discuss. As in the case of minority integration, the putative gap between political elites and 'Second Estonia' had the potential to hinder the country's EU accession.

From one point of view, this chapter could be ended with a positive note. In the very heart of sociological discourse, there is a commitment to modernity and equality, as corollaries of reason, and to democratic pluralism, as a corollary of empirical observation. As 'democratisers', 'modernisers', and 'Westernisers', Estonian sociologists could note with content that most of what they recommended over the years has come true. They used to warn about excessive inequality, discrimination against minorities and women, and so on; some policy measures have emerged, and with Estonia's EU membership, at least some of the problems they pointed at may also be further tackled and moderated by European regulations. From a less rosy perspective, however, we will note that the demands for minority integration, equality, and bridging the gaps between research and politics, and between the ordinary people and the elite, gained passing momentum because of the EU accession process, with its conditionality and scrutiny of progress reports (Raik, 2003). After that, politics has nevertheless not become evidence-based, and there is a fashionable new way of thinking that openly questions the very need for expert knowledge or seeks to replace it with 'alternative expertise'. Estonian sociologists have hitherto avoided taking openly party political stances; but with the rise of nationalist populism, they may finally see themselves forced to do exactly that.

Competing Interests The author has no conflicts of interest to declare that are relevant to the content of this chapter.

References

Aaviksoo, J. (2011, March). Infokonfliktid ja enesekaitse. *Diplomaatia*. https://www.diplomaatia.ee/artikkel/infokonfliktid-ja-enesekaitse/.
Bauman, Z. (1993). *Intimations of postmodernity*. Routledge.
Brubaker, R. (1996). *Nationalism reframed: Nationhood and the National Question in the new Europe*. Cambridge University Press.
Burawoy, M. (2004). For public sociology: 2004 presidential address. *American Sociological Review, 70*(February), 4–28.
Fukuyama, F. (1992). *The end of history and the last man*. Hamish Hamilton.
Haerpfer, C. W. (2002). *Democracy and enlargement in post-communist Europe: The democratisation of the general public in 15 Central and Eastern European countries, 1991–1998*. Routledge.
Harding, S. (1991). *Whose science? Whose knowledge?* Open University Press.
Havel, V. (1978/1992). The power of the powerless. In I. V. Havel (Ed.), *Open letters: Selected writings 1965–1990* (pp. 125–214). Vintage.
Heidmets, M., & Lauristin, M. (2002). Learning from the Estonian case. In M. Lauristin & M. Heidmets (Eds.), *The challenge of the Russian minority: Emerging multicultural democracy in Estonia* (pp. 319–332). Tartu University Press.
Hoen, H. W. (2001). *Good governance in Central and Eastern Europe: The puzzle of capitalism by design*. Edward Elgar.
Huntington, S. P. (1996). *The clash of civilizations and the remaking of world order*. Simon & Schuster.
Johns, M. (2003). 'Do as i say, not as i do.' The European Union, Eastern Europe and minority rights. *East European Politics and Societies, 17*(4), 682–699.
Kallas, K., Mihkelsoo, I., & Plaan, K. (2013). *Integrating Estonia 2000–2011: An analysis of integration monitoring surveys*. Institute of Baltic Studies.
Kukk, M. (1991). Poliitiline opositsioon Eestis Nõukogude perioodil. With a summary in English. Dissent in Estonia during the soviet period. *Proceedings of the Estonian Academy of Sciences/Social Sciences, 40*(3), 229–248.
Lagerspetz, M. (1996). Constructing post-communism: A study in the Estonian social problems discourse. *Annales Universitatis Turkuensis*. http://users.abo.fi/mlagersp/Constructing%20Post-Communism.pdf.
Lagerspetz, M. (1999). Post-socialism as a return: Notes on a discursive strategy. *Eastern European Politics and Societies, 13*(2), 377–390.
Lagerspetz, M. (2015). When formal and informal rules meet: The four sets of rules of the Estonian language and minority regime. In A. Mica, J. Winczorek, & R. Wiśniewski (Eds.), *Sociologies of formality and informality* (pp. 127–148). Peter Lang.
Lagerspetz, M., & Pettai, I. (2003). Estonian sociology of the 1990s: In search of an identity. In M. F. Keen & J. L. Mucha (Eds.), *Sociology in Central and Eastern Europe: Transformation at the dawn of a new millennium* (pp. 61–72). Praeger.
Lagerspetz, M., & Vogt, H. (2004). Estonia. In S. Berglund, J. Ekman, & F. H. Aarebrot (Eds.), *The handbook of political change in Eastern Europe* (2nd ed., pp. 57–93). Edward Elgar.
Lagerspetz, M., & Vogt, H. (2013). Estonia. In S. Berglund, J. Ekman, K. Deegan-Krause, & T. Knutsen (Eds.), *The handbook of political change in Eastern Europe* (3rd ed., pp. 51–84). Edward Elgar.
Lauristin, M. (1997). Contexts of transition. In M. Vihalemm, P. Vihalemm, K. E. Rosengren, & L. Weibull (Eds.), *Return to the Western world: Cultural and political perspectives on the Estonian post-communist transition* (pp. 25–40). Tartu University Press.
Lieven, A. (1994). *The Baltic revolution: Estonia, Latvia, Lithuania and the path to Independence*. Yale University Press.
Liiv, D. (2001). Koostöökokkulepped Suurbritannias ja mida meil on neist õppida. *Riigikogu Toimetised, 3*, 261–266.

Mannheim, K. (1936/1946). *Ideology and utopia: An introduction to the sociology of knowledge*. Kegan Paul, Trench, Trubner & Co.
Marmei, K. (2001, May 21). *Prime Minister quizzes social scientists on social programs*. Central Europe Review.
Noelle, E. (1967). *Sotsioloogilised küsitlused [partial translation of Umfragen in der Massengesellschaft. Einführung in die Methoden der Demoskopie]*. Eesti NSV Ajakirjanike Liit.
OEF. (2018). *About Open Estonia Foundation*. Retrieved July 22, 2021, from https://oef.org.ee/en/about-us
Offe, C. (1991). Capitalism by democratic design? Facing the triple transition in East Central Europe. *Social Research, 58*(4), 865–892.
Opermann, S., & Vihalemm, P. (2017). Meedia ja ühiskonna seose uurimine Eesti sotsioloogilise traditsiooni kontekstis. In P. Vihalemm, M. Lauristin, V. Kalmus, & T. Vihalemm (Eds.), *Eesti ühiskond kiirenevas ajas: Uuringu 'Mina. Maailm. Meedia' 2002–2014 tulemused (pp. 24–59)*. Tartu Ülikooli kirjastus.
Østerberg, D. (1989). The challenge of contemporary knowledge: Social statistics, social research, and sociology. *Studies of Higher Education & Research, 4*, 10–17.
Ott, M. (2019, January 25). Teaduspesu. *Sirp*. Retrieved July 22, 2021, from https://www.sirp.ee/s1-artiklid/c21-teadus/teaduspesu/
Pärli, M. (2023). Isamaa foundation conducts unethical survey on behalf of Tartu university. *ERR News*, Retrieved September 27, 2023 from https://news.err.ee/1609060589/isamaa-foundation-conducts-unethical-survey-on-behalf-of-tartu-university
Pettai, V., & Hallik, K. (2002). Understanding processes of ethnic control: Segmentation, dependency and co-optation in post-communist Estonia. *Nations and Nationalism, 8*(4), 505–529.
Proos, I. (2002). Avaliku dialoogi võimalikkusest poliitikute ja ühiskonna analüütikute vahel. In R. Vetik (Ed.), *Kaks Eestit: Artiklite, ettekannete ja analüüside kogumik* (pp. 58–62). Rahvusvaheliste ja Sotsiaaluuringute Instituut.
Postimees. (2001, April 22). Sotsiaalteadlaste avalik pöördumine. Retrieved August 02, 2024, from https://arvamus.postimees.ee/1863213/kirjad
Postimees. (2004, February 27). *Ülo Vooglaid*. Res Publical puudub kompass. [Interview] Retrieved March 12, 2018, from https://www.postimees.ee/1400665/ulo-vooglaid-res-publical-puudub-kompass
Purju, A., Pädam, S., Müür, M., Vanags, A., Alasheyeva, J., Kalnins, V., Vitola, K., Chandler, M., Kvedaras, V. (2005). *Research policy linkages in the Baltic States: Comparative analysis of a natural experiment. Final report (revised)*. Baltic International Centre for Economic Policy Studies. Retrieved July 22, 2021, from https://www.biceps.org//assets/docs/izpetes-zinojumi/Bridging-Research-and-Policy_Baltic-States.pdf
Raik, K. (2003). *Democratic politics or the implementation of inevitabilities? Estonia's democracy and integration into the European Union*. Tartu University Press.
Rämmer, A., Kalmus, V., & Käärik, H. (2015). Academia sociologicae 25. *Tartu Ülikooli ajaloo küsimusi, 42*, 8–39.
Rikmann, E. (2012). *Construction of civil society in Estonia: Discursive and institutional changes*. Institute of International and Social Studies.
Ruutsoo, R. (1991). Miten neuvostotilastoja on luettava? *Tiede ja Edistys, 1991*(2), 132–136.
Ruutsoo, R. (2012). Kodanikuühiskonna ülesehitamine. In R. Vetik (Ed.), *Eesti poliitika ja valitsemine 1991–2011* (pp. 67–107). Tallinna Ülikool.
Saarts, Tõnis (2006, April 25). Kiri, mis muutis Eestit. *Postimees*. Retrieved March 12, 2018, from http://epl.delfi.ee/news/arvamus/tonis-saarts-kiri-mis-muutis-eestit?id=51037268.
Society... (1999). Society, parliament and legislation. *Proceedings of the international seminar*. Department of Economic and Social Information of the Chancellery of the Riigikogu.
Titma, M. (2002). Estonia. In M. Kaase, V. Sparschuh, & A. Wenninger (Eds.), *Three social science disciplines in central and Eastern Europe: Handbook on economics, political science and sociology (1989–2001)* (pp. 425–436). GESIS/Collegium Budapest.
Vetik, R. (Ed.). (2002). *Kaks Eestit: Artiklite, ettekannete ja analüüside kogumik*. TPÜ Kirjastus.

Born and educated in Turku, Finland, Mikko Lagerspetz has been active as a sociologist in Estonia since 1989. Until 2008, he taught at various Estonian universities; he finally worked at Tallinn University as Professor of Sociology and Director of its Centre for Civil Society Study and Development. He served as the President of the Estonian Union of Sociologists in 1998–2003. In 2017, he authored the first comprehensive textbook in Estonian on the methodology of social research. From 2006, he has been Professor of Sociology at the Åbo Akademi University in Turku. His research interests include the sociology of knowledge, civil society and social diversity, and social change in Central and Eastern Europe.

Chapter 11
Hurried Professionals: Sociology in Latvia

Emils Kilis

11.1 Introduction

Publications dealing with the sociology of sociology have illustrated the manifold impacts that social factors and institutional arrangements have had on sociology and social thought. The converse (the impact of sociology on society) has historically been given less attention. However, Michael Burawoy's (2005) call for public sociology rekindled reflection regarding the impact of sociological research on society and the influence of sociologists on public discourse. Furthermore, the reaction to Burawoy's call revealed a number of internal tensions within the discipline. The responses ranged from support for Burawoy's call to cautious reflection on the complexities attendant to combining academic research and social activism. In short, reactions were based on both philosophical and practical considerations regarding the active public stance of the sociologist and the societal impact of sociology.

Such tensions are equally evident in the Latvian context, and sociology in Latvia has a number of features that make it an interesting case study for illuminating the impact of sociological knowledge and research on societal transformation while paying attention to the conditions that shape the conduct of sociologists and influence their ability to contribute to public debate and challenge dominant discourses about their areas of expertise. Firstly, sociology in Latvia has historically been an applied discipline with limited attention given to theoretical reflection. Even though researchers draw upon a range of theoretical sources to inform their work, publications focusing on theoretical questions are rather scarce, even among academic articles. Furthermore, the bulk of sociological work is applied research motivated by practical interests, rather than academic curiosity. Secondly, even though

---

E. Kilis (✉)
Baltic Studies Centre, Riga, Latvia
e-mail: emils.kilis@bscresearch.lv

sociology in Latvia is primarily applied, the impact of sociologists on public discourse and policy has been limited, which raises the question of whether there are specific reasons for this. Thirdly, sociologists in Latvia emphasise the role of professional competence and professionalism in general, which suggests that sociologists generally see themselves as members of a professional group, rather than politically engaged commentators or public intellectuals.

In view of the above, Latvia can serve as an illustrative case study of the way an emphasis on professional virtues and applied research shapes the impact of sociological inquiry on public discourse and societal transformation.

This chapter draws on a number of different data sources. The historical background is mainly based on the accounts provided in Socioloģija Latvijā[1] (Tisenkopfs, 2010) and a book on the history of the Faculty of History and Philosophy (Keruss et al., 2010). The analysis of the presence of Latvian sociologists in local print media is based on information obtained from the national publication database, accessed via the National Library of Latvia. In addition, interview data from 2012–2013 and 2018 are employed.[2]

This chapter is divided into three parts. The first provides a brief overview of the historical development and current state of sociology in Latvia. The second part looks at Latvian sociology, emphasising the contributions of Latvian sociologists to public discourse (understood broadly). Finally, I conclude by suggesting that financial uncertainty and a commitment to professionalism have significantly shaped the ability and willingness of sociologists to actively engage in public discourse and drive societal transformation, making them both passengers and voyeurs.

11.2 Historical Preliminaries

In the early days of Latvian sociology, the discipline had an intimate connection to philosophy. The first department of sociology was established in 1977 in the faculty housing history and philosophy. Close links with philosophy also meant that the generation of sociologists educated in the Soviet Union studied side by side with philosophers, and the professional status of sociology and sociologists was a matter of practical concern for the faculty (Keruss et al., 2010). Furthermore, the historical connection between sociology and philosophy is still evidenced by the fact that the Institute of Philosophy and Sociology is still a major research centre in Latvia.

Nonetheless, the association with philosophy did not make sociology a theoretical discipline. Sociology in Latvia has historically been an applied discipline, rather than an exercise in theory and conceptual innovation. As Aivars Tabuns suggests, this is mainly due to the historical circumstances surrounding the emergence of

---

[1] Hereafter, *Sociology in Latvia*
[2] The interviews were carried out in Latvian.

Latvian sociology. Sociology was tolerated because it was seen as a practical way of managing society (Tabuns, 2010, p. 108).

11.2.1 Sociology in the 1990s

Tisenkopfs (2010) argues that the 1980s saw the rise of theory. Nonetheless, the persistence of applied sociology was once again evident after the dissolution of the Soviet Union, which has been noted as having had a significant impact on research (Graham, 1998). The most visible aspect was the sudden disappearance of public funding for academic research and, consequently, the dissolution of several research centres (Tabuns, 2010, p. 113). The public funds that were made available for sociological research in the 1990s were limited, and researchers were growing increasingly reliant on international funding. This, in turn, led to a peculiar situation whereby the experts assessing grant applications to the Latvian Council of Science also considered the potential to attract funding from other sources (Tabuns, 2010, p. 113).

Despite the precarious financial situation, the infrastructural foundations were laid in the 1990s. For example, funding and educational opportunities obtained through a programme called 'Social Development and Social Security' were used to lay the foundations for social science in Latvia, develop tools for dealing with issues of social development and social security, create a research infrastructure and participate in various international research projects (Tabuns, 2010, pp. 114–115). The Latvian Sociological Association was also revitalised but mainly served an informative and community-building function. Overall, Aivars Tabuns concludes that the funding made available to sociology was sufficient to sustain it, but the financial requirements of sociological research meant that the available funding was insufficient for sociology to develop.

Concurrently, Latvian sociologists honed their skills both abroad (at conferences and Western research centres) and locally (as researchers). In the 1990s, social research projects were diverse, and most were short, which meant that sociologists had a general understanding of many topics but were not specialists in any area in particular. Furthermore, Tabuns' account indicates that Latvian sociologists often used research tools developed in Western research centres. This mainly included methodological tools, which allowed Latvian researchers to produce internationally comparable data (Tabuns, 2010, p. 118).

Nonetheless, Talis Tisenkopfs argues that the 1990s was a period of privatisation and disintegration of the discipline. There are several reasons for this. Firstly, while the generation educated in the 1970s and 1980s was interested in sociological theory, the practical needs of the 1990s meant that sociologists had to focus on applied research. Much like sociologists in some other post-socialist countries, Latvian sociologists became involved in applied research (often market research). This became the main form of sociological research and the prime way of justifying the utility of the sociological profession. Secondly, most applied research was carried out by recently established private research centres rather than academic units. This disrupted the connection between teaching and research, and teaching was hampered by heavy workloads and limited access to well-regarded data analysis software (Tabuns, 2010, p. 122).

One positive development was the creation of a separate undergraduate programme in sociology (in 1990), which was followed by postgraduate programmes in 1996. However, the separation of research and teaching had a profound impact on sociology in Latvia. For example, there was a considerable gap in terms of people receiving doctorates in sociology. While several prominent members of the academic community received their doctorates prior to the dissolution of the Soviet Union, the first doctoral dissertation after Latvia regained independence was defended in 2003 (by Dagmāra Beitnere).

Nonetheless, one should be careful when making a distinction between the old generation and the new generation. For example, several researchers who received their doctorates after 1990 had already concluded their undergraduate studies during the Soviet period. In addition, researchers with considerable professional experience did not seek to translate their competence into academically recognised forms of capital immediately. Once funding was made available, however, there was a rapid increase in the number of sociologists with doctorates (with 2010–2014 being especially productive[3]).

11.2.2 Sociology Since 2000

The Faculty of Social Sciences was established at the University of Latvia in 2000. The newly established faculty had a Department of Sociology, which meant that sociology had moved away from philosophy. The creation of a separate department was followed by the establishment of social research institutes at various Latvian universities (e.g. University of Latvia, Daugavpils University).

As regards the people populating these institutions, Tālis Tisenkopfs notes that the early 2000s was characterised by individual survival strategies that grew out of the fragmentation of the 1990s (Tisenkopfs, 2010). Individual researchers or research collectives had built international connections. While he emphasises that this was not necessarily a negative development, it did perpetuate the separation of teaching and research.

Public funding for fundamental research remained low, and some areas of research could develop largely as a consequence of the availability of European Union (EU) funding and grants from other international funding schemes (see Šūmane (2010)). For example, the last reports from the Latvian Council of Science, where sociology is listed as a separate discipline (in 2010), show that funding for

---

[3] A total of 35 sociologists received doctorates at Latvian universities between 2010 and 2021, with 26 of the doctorates being granted between 2010 and 2014.

sociology is negligible, and Aivars Tabuns published an opinion piece (Tabuns, 2009) around the same time emphasising the very same point. Furthermore, even though public funding for science in Latvia is low in general, social science and humanities funding compares unfavourably to the amount granted to other branches of science (Kunda, 2013; Kunda et al., 2016).

At the same time, researchers strengthened collaboration with colleagues from other countries. As noted by Pal Tamás (2002), researchers from post-socialist countries, for a long time, were in a subordinate position. They were tasked with carrying out case studies and identifying local analogues for issues and topics raised by their senior colleagues in Western academic or research centres, and this seems to be the case in Latvia as well, at least in the 1990s. Even though international contacts were established, and local sociologists participated in international projects, only recently have Latvian sociologists been engaged as senior partners or leaders of work packages. Concurrently, towards the end of the 2000s, there was a gradual increase in the number of publications in international peer-reviewed journals that are indexed by respected databases (e.g. Scopus), suggesting that Latvian sociologists are becoming increasingly integrated into the international research community.

Several universities grant degrees in sociology. The most prominent is the University of Latvia, but other universities also offer courses in sociology and have research units dedicated to social research. Furthermore, research centres conduct research that could be classified as sociological, but a considerable portion is applied research for public and private organisations.

However, even though it is present at various universities and research centres, sociology in Latvia remains a minority discipline. For instance, the conclusion of the 2013 research assessment exercise was that little of Latvian social science research falls into the established disciplines of economics, political science and sociology, and many traditional disciplines (including sociology) are minority disciplines (Technopolis, 2013). A related point was made in the subsequent research exercise of 2020, with the panel noting that very little basic research is undertaken in the traditional social science disciplines (Technopolis, 2021). Some of this can be explained by the fact that many studies are hybrid in nature and involve researchers from different backgrounds. However, it should also be noted that much social research lacks significant theoretical content that could be tied to a specific academic tradition. Nonetheless, the report on the social sciences from 2013 recommended promoting units in political science and sociology, where there are small numbers but good potential.

11.2.3 Publications and Areas of Research

With few exceptions, publications tend to be applied in nature, even if they are published in academic outlets. There are no clearly identifiable theoretical preferences, which would allow one to define the main theoretical frameworks in use among

Latvian sociologists. Researchers tend to be opportunistic as regards theories and methods, largely basing their choice on the specific goals of the project and topic in question.

The overview of research areas provided in *Sociology in Latvia* shows that a considerable amount of research output is in the form of various reports. This should not lead to the conclusion that academic publications are scarce, however, and there are local outlets for sociological work (e.g. *Humanities and Social Sciences*) and publishers of academic publications (e.g. University of Latvia Academic Press, Zinātne). Furthermore, it should be noted that there has been an increase in the number of articles published in peer-reviewed journals in the previous decade, though the number of social science publications, as a share of all publications by Latvian researchers, remains low (Technopolis, 2017).

As regards prominent research topics, Tabuns' historical account of sociology in the 1990s mentions ethnicity as the main area of inquiry with a significant group of researchers working on it (Tabuns, 2010, p. 118). Ethnicity, national identity and social integration remain the most prominent areas of research, and research reflects upon various aspects of ethnic relations that characterise cultural and political life in Latvia. Other significant areas of research activity include rural sociology, sociology of youth, sociology of culture and migration. Rural sociology is well-represented in international academic outlets, and social studies of culture and migration have recently enjoyed media exposure. In the case of migration, this is arguably a result of the growing awareness that current demographic and migration trends are unsustainable. In the case of the sociology of culture, reports on cultural consumption have attracted attention and even stimulated an exchange regarding the interpretation of sociological data with representatives of the arts (see below). It is worth noting that *Sociology in Latvia* (Tisenkopfs, 2010) also contains three chapters dedicated to the social study of work and entrepreneurship, albeit with different emphases, suggesting that these topics are also prominent in Latvia.

The contrast between *Sociology in Latvia* and *Social change in Latvia* (Tabuns, 1998) should be noted in the context of a discussion on social transformation. While both books provide an overview of social research in Latvia, the focus of the latter volume is on social change and transformation, rather than sociology. The topics covered in the book include the stability of democratic institutions, civic values, the formation of a new political elite, poverty and cultural shifts as a result of the transition to capitalism. Even though the topics are pertinent for a discussion of social transformation, the tone of the publications is measured and generally aims for descriptive adequacy, rather than critical intervention.

A prominent example of a publication aimed at stimulating public discourse is the *Human Development Report* (HDP). The beginnings of this publication can be traced back to the United Nations *Human Development Report*. However, since 2004, the publication has been taken over by the Advanced Social and Political Research Institute of the University of Latvia, and sociologists have taken an active role. The report is published biannually, and the institute has published seven reports as of 2019. The reports aim to provide a multifaceted understanding of the chosen topic and include recommendations for resolving the identified problems. The intended audience goes beyond governmental institutions, and the reports also contain recommendations for NGOs and individuals. In the interviews I carried out at the beginning of 2018, it was referred to as an example of public engagement. Topics the reports have addressed include:

1. Regional identity and regional sustainability
2. Social and political accountability and responsibility
3. Threats to social sustainability (e.g. poverty, inequality, population drain)
4. Development of human capital (e.g. improved public health care and education)
5. National identity and social integration

The most recent HDP (published in 2019) addressed the issue of public goods and the safeguarding of collective resources.

Among the most controversial is the 2001 iteration of the HDP, still published under the auspices of the United Nations. The topic of the report was the public policy process, and it was edited by Tālis Tisenkopfs. The content of the report provoked commentary from then Prime Minister Andris Bērziņš, who challenged the conclusion of the report that business interests play a significant role in politics. Tālis Tisenkopfs responded that Latvia has a secretive public policy process and that private financial interests take precedence over public interests (BNS, 2001).

11.3 Sociologists as Agents of Social Transformation?

As part of my doctoral studies, I interviewed several Latvian sociologists in 2012 and 2013. I observed that they did not locate the value of sociology solely in the academic realm. Indeed, the list of functions of sociology and the future challenges for sociology outlined by Tālis Tisenkopfs in *Sociology in Latvia* includes academic components and extra-academic components, suggesting that sociology is perceived as an active participant in social transformation. Nonetheless, some of my informants found it difficult to articulate their opinion as to the role and function of sociology outside the realm of research, and the impact of sociology on public discourse.

11.3.1 Sociologists as Professionals

According to Michael Burawoy (2005), professional sociology designates forms of sociology whose intended audience is other academics and researchers. For the purposes of avoiding confusion, in my interviews I referred to this as 'academic sociology'. I believed that this better captured what Burawoy meant and clearly differentiated between academic and applied sociology—a distinction of great importance in the Latvian context. Nonetheless, the reflections of my informants on applied sociology are also revealing and worthy of mention.

Specifically, several researchers were adamant that keeping research findings and critical, evaluative statements separate and refraining from the use of loaded language was crucial. Such arguments were often related to the idea of professionalism and the ability to keep one's personal views in check, which was treated as a hallmark of skill, quality and commitment to the integrity of the scientific process. Even when the distinction between observation and evaluation was not made explicit, it was argued that one should attempt to separate and clearly distinguish between the arguments based on research data and the researcher's own personal views. In other words, sociologists are free to express disapproval of policies and produce and report politically inexpedient findings or challenge the way a particular issue is framed, but such moves are subject to careful management and professional constraints. Indeed, it was argued that neutrality and professional restraint were prerequisites for successfully articulating a critical response.

Concurrently, my informants described sociology as a mirror, and this metaphor was invoked on a number of occasions. Presumably, the mirror metaphor is supposed to convey the idea that sociological work shows us what we as a society actually look like. Read this way, mirroring inevitably leads to questions of representation and portrays sociologists as passive observers. A more active role was suggested by an informant who compared sociologists to photographers, emphasising skill and the choices to focus on some things rather than others. Thus, while at first glance the photographer is simply an extension of the mirror metaphor, it reveals the political, or even partisan, dimension of sociological work and gives the sociologist a more active role in depicting her object.

However, respondents reacted with unease to my questions regarding the political dimension of sociological work. Some of my respondents expressed concerns that derived from equating politics with ideological support for a particular party. This elicited a specific take on scientific integrity and the role of sociological knowledge in relation to political matters. Specifically, my informants argued that sociologists study the world, but they have no business trying to alter it. Indeed, this was even framed as one of the preconditions for being able to give critical feedback. However, when I qualified my question by saying that I did not mean preferences as regards political parties, the responses indicated a situation that was similar to the relationship between descriptive and evaluative statements, and it was acknowledged that sociological work exhibits certain political preferences.

This opinion, however, was not dominant, and the discussion concerning neutrality elicited a series of ambivalent responses. For example, some acknowledged that sociological knowledge could change how we perceive certain phenomena. Furthermore, these aspects of social life are usually value-laden, which means that sociological research is situated in the midst of normative struggles. This leads us to the issue of responsibility because such research can be used for myriad different purposes. Thus, the question 'for whom' becomes very important, and this was acknowledged by my respondents.

> Who would use this information? Let's say we're finally able to understand how a certain group thinks, and how to alter their way of thinking… And who do you think will use this information? Those self-same members of society, or some sort of corporate faction…or an

ideological group? Who will be the first to use it? If you look at it this way, I'm not at all grieved that sociology everywhere is slowly dwindling away.

11.3.2 Sociologists as Critical Academics

It was clear that Latvian sociologists doubted that pure academic sociology was a vital component of Latvian sociology. The reasons for this would appear to be simple: the majority of work done by Latvian sociologists consists of research reports, rather than academic publications. There are certainly publications that would be primarily of academic interest, but these do not form the backbone of sociological work in Latvia. Furthermore, there was pervasive scepticism as to whether the situation would improve significantly in the near future. Consequently, while my respondents believed that academic work is of great value and a desirable form of existence for sociology, the prospects for academic sociology in Latvia were unclear.

The scarcity of academic output has consequences for what Michael Burawoy calls 'critical sociology'. According to Burawoy (2005), critical sociology grows out of disaffection with dominant trends and assumptions in professional sociology. Given, however, that the academic dimension of sociological work is not pronounced in Latvian sociology, critical sociology in Burawoy's sense is elusive in Latvia. That is to say, any discussion of critical sociology is moot largely because there is no academic consensus in the Latvian context, other than an emphasis on professionalism and the ability to carry out applied research. Nonetheless, there were glimmerings of critical sociology in the responses of Latvian sociologists.

> Those so-called government-commissioned studies degrade the sociological market. We'll give money to him, but we won't fund him etc.

The above quote hints at a kind of internal tension within sociology whereby there are perceived differences between the goals and interests of those funding research and the interests of sociologists and sociology as a whole. This, according to Burawoy, is a common characteristic of critical sociology, which expresses fears associated with sociology becoming an inward-looking and overly technical discipline with little to offer to the non-specialist and with minimal regard for the goals of sociological inquiry.

11.3.3 Sociologists and the Policy Process

In Michael Burawoy's division of sociological labour, policy sociology is a form of instrumental knowledge that refers to sociological research that has been carried out for a client. He discusses the use of sociological research in the context of policy-making.

On the whole, the impact of sociological research on government discourse in Latvia is a potentially contentious issue. For example, Tālis Tisenkopfs contends that sociology has been of little use to policymakers, even though it is generally applied in nature (Tisenkopfs, 2010). Similar issues have been raised about the appreciation of the social sciences and humanities more generally: they are undervalued in Latvia. Social surveys are routinely commissioned by public institutions, and sociologists are involved in various important research projects and advise public institutions. However, much social research is innocent of specific disciplinary ties and discursive perspectives.

These reservations notwithstanding, Tabuns notes that sociologists cooperated with several line ministries in the 1990s. However, he also notes that sociologists had difficulty dealing with several state institutions and municipalities, though he singles out Vladimirs Meņšikovs and his cooperation with the municipality of Daugavpils as an exception to this rule. Furthermore, in the first decade of the twenty-first century, sociologists were engaged as part of the preparation of long-term planning documents (e.g. Latvia 2030). Tālis Tisenkopfs was a member of the Strategic Analysis Commission and edited (together with Baiba Bela) a volume dedicated to an in-depth understanding of quality of life (Tisenkopfs & Bela, 2006), which was published under the auspices of said commission. More recently, Inta Mieriņa has been consulted as an expert on matters pertaining to migration.

In my conversations with sociologists working in Latvia, the overall view was that sociological knowledge should, indeed, play a role in policy-making and any kind of decision-making that concerns large groups of people. The reasons for this mostly derived from my informants' belief that political decision-making and policies would simply have a greater chance of success if they were based on sound information. In other words, rather than assuming that they know best, politicians and state bureaucrats would be wise to consult experts with potentially useful suggestions and solutions. The responses were, therefore, in line with Michael Burawoy's thesis that policy sociology is an instrumental form of knowledge.

However, even though my informants believed that sociological knowledge should play a part in decision-making, they were cautious and sceptical as to whether it had any actual impact on the decisions and policies that were implemented. As an illustration, in their overview of research on ethnic integration, Evija Kļave and Brigita Zepa provide a complex picture. Ethnic integration is one of the more contentious policy issues in Latvia and a topic to which considerable sociological attention has been devoted. However, the extent to which sociologists have succeeded in challenging dominant assumptions is difficult to estimate. On the one hand, Kļave and Zepa suggest that in the 1990s research on citizenship was used as part of social integration policies (Kļave & Zepa, 2010, p. 218). On the other hand, they indicate that much research on education was funded by the Soros Foundation, rather than government institutions (Kļave & Zepa, 2010, p. 207). This would suggest limited interest from state institutions in research of this sort, even though education is an important aspect of ethnic integration. Furthermore, it also resonates with a point made in passing during the interviews. Specifically, sociologists could often effect change in a research capacity via studies commissioned by international organisations (e.g. Soros Foundation, World Bank).

Consequently, it is not surprising that the overall impression of the research-policy nexus depended on the professional experience of my informants. Those who were working or had worked for research centres with a history of being commissioned by the State Chancellery of Latvia, line ministries or NGOs were generally quite optimistic. However, my informants repeatedly suggested that the perception of credibility and competence was tied to specific researchers who had established professional relationships. Collaboration did not lead to trust in the discipline as a whole. In addition, informants who had professional experience working for government institutions acknowledged that not all of their research had the desired effect. Sometimes this was because the findings conflicted with the current political climate, while at other times there was simply a change of staff at the institution in question.

One should also bear in mind that sociological work in Latvia is reliant upon the ability to attract competitive funding. This financial uncertainty, in addition to affecting the production of academic sociology (e.g. books and journal articles), also hampers the possibility of critical interventions on policy matters. In addition to international research projects, much of social research in Latvia is contract-based, which means that sociologists are often in a position in which they are providing a service. Presumably, this means that their livelihood depends upon maintaining a good working relationship with clients. Consequently, financial insecurity hampers the freedom of the sociologist to voice dissenting opinions without concerns regarding long-term financial repercussions. In response to this, my informants argued that a prerequisite of sociological critique was financial independence.

Furthermore, my informants suggested that their clients generally want instrumental rather than reflexive knowledge. Even if sociological research is commissioned and carried out, it may simply be a matter of ticking a box and satisfying official requirements: in other words, it is done only to keep up appearances. This means that there are certainly research projects or surveys, but they fail to make much in the way of difference or impact. A related point has been made by Latvian sociologist Anda Laķe (2012), who looked at evaluation research as an example of the research-policy nexus. She argued that communication between researchers, bureaucrats and politicians is often hampered by different conceptions of the value of social research and discrepant forms of rationality guiding their actions. Thus, while sociologists themselves might see the value of their work in terms of the insights it provides, their clients are more interested in strategically deploying the simple fact that research was carried out. Their interest is purely instrumental, with little regard for the reflexive value of research.

Overall, there was a definite belief among the sociologists I interviewed that sociology is and should be part of the decision-making process. The actual role of sociological research, however, was framed in instrumental, means-to-an-end terms, which is somewhat at odds with the reflexive and horizon-expanding narrative that I encountered when talking about the value of sociological knowledge. This may simply be a matter of genre. That is to say, policy sociology is different in kind to public sociology and critical sociology. The latter are reflexive about the needs sociology serves and the realities it enables, whereas policy sociology is not. I want to suggest an alternative explanation, however, that has to do with the practical realities of Latvian sociology. Specifically, the precarious financial situation of researchers means that time has to be devoted to professional commitments (e.g. teaching, research, writing project proposals). Consequently, little time can be devoted to public pronouncements, critical commentary and challenging dominant policy discourses.

11.3.4 Sociologists in Public

A report on the ecosystem of the social sciences and humanities in Latvia was published in 2016. This document was prepared for the Ministry of Education and Science. The overall conclusion was that the social sciences and humanities contribute significantly to society and public institutions. However, the report also notes that social scientists and humanities scholars often find it difficult to communicate their contributions and do not devote enough attention to 'selling' themselves (Kunda et al., 2016). Consistent with this assessment, my informants considered the communicative dimension in general and public sociology in particular to be a sore spot. However, a closer analysis reveals a nuanced picture of the historical contribution of sociologists to public discourse.

11.3.4.1 Presence in the Media

Aivars Tabuns argues that in the 1990s sociologists were among the most popular politically unaffiliated 'talking heads' on television. However, as other disciplines became more prominent towards the end of the 1990s, sociologists gradually faded from public discourse. This is consistent with my examination of printed media sources. After analysing the output provided by the national publication database, observations can be made regarding the current media presence of sociologists and the media profile of several prominent academic sociologists.

Overall, sociologists provide commentary on a range of different topics, but the most frequent are questions dealing with political life. By far the most prominent sociologists, judging by the number of appearances, are Arnis Kaktiņš and Aigars Freimanis. They are both regularly featured in newspapers and provide commentary on the results of recent opinion polls and topical political issues. Each of them heads his own social research centre that provides commercial social research services. While both of them appear regularly, Freimanis has an edge in terms of commenting upon matters that pertain to the political elite, and he was an adviser to the former Prime Minister of Latvia, Māris Kučinskis. Kaktiņš became more prominent during the COVID-19 pandemic, providing commentary on the results of recent public opinion surveys.

Upon closer inspection, it is also evident that the identity of the sociologist is frequently unclear. Anthropologists (e.g. Aivita Putniņa and Roberts Ķīlis) are occasionally referred to as sociologists, though this may have something to do with the fact that social/cultural anthropology is treated as a subfield of sociology. In other cases, researchers with a doctorate in sociology are identified with a different area of expertise (e.g. Signe Mežinska as an expert on bioethics and Anda Rožukalne as a media and communications expert). A boundary case is Dagmāra Beitnere-Le Galla whose institutional affiliation (Institute of Philosophy and Sociology) often took precedence over her educational qualifications.

In terms of thematic coverage, the range is quite wide, though publications associated with transformative events do not stand out. Publications dealing with accession to the EU appeared sporadically in the second part of the 1990s and early 2000s. Though there were occasional publications dealing with the transition to a market economy in the early 1990s, economic issues and welfare became much more prominent during the economic crisis of 2008–2009. The contributions of sociologists to public discourse regarding the European refugee crisis have been limited. This was confirmed in the interviews I conducted in 2018, as informants did not recall any particular media activity associated with these issues. Again, anthropologists (e.g. Ieva Raubiško) have been more prominent in attempting to challenge dominant discourses in the media. Finally, ethnicity and integration are topics that have a constant presence in public media and happen to be areas of considerable research activity in Latvia. While sociologists have sought to provide a more nuanced understanding of ethnic relations and impediments to integration, the extent of their contribution is difficult to gauge.

As regards individual sociologists, Pēteris Laķis was the most prominent sociologist in the 1990s. He published articles in various media outlets intended for different audiences; he even published in a magazine aimed at teenagers. While the thematic scope of his publications was broad, he mainly focused on issues pertaining to education, cultural life and the political situation, providing critical commentary. At the beginning of the 1990s, there were more publications on poverty and social stratification.

Aivars Tabuns was also active in the 1990s. Like Laķis, he wrote and published opinion pieces in publications aimed at different audiences. The bulk of his publications were about political life, intellectuals and science (e.g. funding). He published less frequently after 2000. The situation is similar in the case of Vladimirs Meņšikovs, who published both in Latvian and Russian in the 1990s and early 2000s but has since focused on research and publications in academic outlets.

Another prominent sociologist, Brigita Zepa, generally speaking, provides commentary as an expert or researcher. She is considerably less likely to publish opinion pieces, though her conversations with journalists are available in the media. Most of her publications deal with the results of recent studies. Consequently, she most closely resembles an expert or an external observer, rather than a public commentator.

Tālis Tisenkopfs comments on a broad range of topics, broader than those of Tabuns and Laķis. A distinctive characteristic of Tisenkopfs' output is the comparatively high number of essays published in the magazine *Rīgas Laiks*. He published rather frequently up until 2007–2008, and his non-academic output has subsequently declined, though he still occasionally publishes in the newspaper *Ir*.

Overall, it appears that academic sociologists had a greater media presence in the 1990s and early 2000s and the number of publications written by sociologists has subsequently diminished. The old generation gradually became less active, and representatives of the new generation appeared in the media only sporadically, with Arnis Kaktiņš and Aigars Freimanis taking over as sociologists in the media.

There are, however, several examples of academic sociologists contributing to a more nuanced form of public discourse. Firstly, Dagmāra Beitnere-Le Galla has consistently been prominent in the media since the 1990s and provides commentary on a diverse range of topics. In most cases, she is engaged as someone knowledgeable about social and cultural life (e.g. identity, patriotism) in general, which moves her closer to the status of an intellectual or commentator. Furthermore, her output has actually increased since the early 2000s. Secondly, while Baiba Bela and Līga Rasnača have published sparsely in non-academic outlets, they made a significant contribution to public discourse in the context of the 2017 tax reform. In particular, they published articles (e.g. Rasnača and Bela (2017)) and gave radio interviews, commenting on the impact that the tax reform will most likely have on economic inequality and issues of social equity in general, thus challenging the official position that the tax reform would reduce economic inequality.

Other prominent recent contributions of sociologists to the public debate have mainly been in the area of migration (e.g. the work of Inta Mieriņa and Aija Lulle). Sociologists attempt to provide a more nuanced understanding of the causes of migration, thus challenging simplistic analyses. While the impact of these publications and interventions is difficult to gauge, they do suggest that the relevance of sociological research to issues of migration is acknowledged.

11.3.4.2 Use and Misuse of Sociological Data in the Media

An important theme that emerges upon inspection of newspaper and magazine publications is the use and misuse of sociological data (e.g. survey results during election periods). This usually involves sociologists explaining the nature of social data and their limitations in response to a perceived public failure of sociology (e.g. failure to predict election outcomes).

Specifically, the nature of social surveys is an issue that periodically attracts attention in the media. Latvian sociologists have engaged in written exchanges with members of parliament who have suggested a temporary ban on publishing survey results (Tabuns, 1994). Sociological research has been condemned as propaganda (see Ivanovs (2006)); there have been televised discussions, and sociologists are routinely asked to comment on surveys. Furthermore, the role of social surveys in the context of elections (be they municipal or general) often figures in the media.

The first instance I would like to highlight was a professional objection of the Latvian Sociological Association in 2010. As part of their pre-election campaign, the political party Unity commissioned the market research company GfK to conduct a public opinion poll. The poll was about people's preferences for the future prime minister. The choice was between the candidate put forwards by Unity (Valdis Dombrovskis) and the candidate put forwards by their (presumed) main rivals Harmony Centre (Jānis Urbanovičš). The Latvian Sociological Association challenged the validity and reliability of the poll, accused GfK of committing numerous methodological mistakes and argued that the poll was a form of political technology, rather than a sociological survey. In this case, the attempt was to disassociate the activities of GfK from what actual sociologists do in order to preserve the integrity of the sociological enterprise.

> They renamed it. Now it is a simple poll. That's it. Without the word 'sociological.' At least that much we could get across don't go about putting on our 'coat.' Anyone can do a poll. A journalist can do a poll, a street sweeper can do a poll, but… don't go about discrediting our 'coat.'

Nonetheless, this dispute had to be appropriately managed so as to prevent developments that would actually be damaging to sociology.

> Over there, nobody's thinking about GfK, nobody knows that it's [mainly] economists… managers. Everyone will think it's sociologists… again… forging data. You know, making a muck of it. They'll never make the distinction.

The integrity of sociology and social surveys was also at stake in relation to the municipal elections of 2017. The results of pre-election social surveys predicted a composition of parties in Riga City Council that deviated considerably from the actual results, with the incumbent parties maintaining a majority position after the election. The survey results featured prominently in the media. This discrepancy between survey results and the actual outcome caused some to refer to one of the major social research centres as a purveyor of fake news (Ozols, 2017), which, in turn, motivated a piece on the limitations of sociological data and research (Buholcs, 2017), which mimicked the content of several publications dedicated to this topic going back to the 1990s.

A more recent public exchange touched upon the way sociological research is understood. On 1 December 2017, Arno Jundze, a writer and culture journalist, published a comment in a local newspaper's online version expressing his confusion as to the seemingly contradictory results of different studies on cultural consumption (see Jundze (2017)). Within a week's time, two sociologists published a response suggesting that, upon careful inspection, the findings of the various studies are actually consistent (Daugavietis & Leiškalne, 2017). They went on to argue that complex findings require careful engagement with the actual conclusions of the study in question—a point often raised regarding the ability of journalists to represent sociological insights.

11.3.4.3 Ignorance of Sociology

Aivars Tabuns notes that towards the end of the 1990s, sociologists gradually stopped publicly commenting upon topics that fell outside their areas of competence. The causes were manifold. For example, representatives of other disciplines became more involved in public discourse. However, a common complaint that I came across in my interviews was that sociology was equated with questionnaires and public opinion polls, or that sociologists were treated as experts who could comment upon a vast range of social and political topics. In short, media representatives and the public had a poor appreciation of what sociologists could offer.

My informants noted that communication with journalists was complex because the result would usually be an article that summarised a sociologist's comment in a simplistic manner. Sociologists were also worried that journalists would simplify nuanced remarks and pay scant attention to the qualifications that accompany most comments or mainly focus on shocking findings. This was a particular point of concern since journalists were, at the University of Latvia at least, educated just a few doors down the hall, at the Department of Communication Science.

Policymakers and politicians, more generally, were also perceived to have a limited understanding of the value of sociology. My informants suggested that politicians assume that they can achieve their goals without input from social scientists. Consequently, even though the emphasis on applied research characteristic of sociology in Latvia would appear to be conducive to sociological input in the policy process, the perception of sociology as an unnecessary and politically contentious form of knowledge prevents this.

Further still, sociologists argued that communication with the public is hampered by the fact that there is simply too little in the way of interest and understanding about what sociologists actually do. Consequently, communicating sociological knowledge to the public is exceedingly complicated, although there have been attempts to address this. A textbook and dictionary of sociological terms aimed at high school students were published in the 1990s (Zepa & Zobena, 1996; Zepa & Zobena, 1997).

Finally, it was suggested in the interviews that professional sociologists do not necessarily see themselves as public intellectuals. Rather, they see themselves as researchers and professionals with a specific set of skills. This raises the possibility that additional funding would not necessarily lead to increased public presence. Furthermore, while it would be inaccurate to generalise about the non-academic publications of the old generation, a cursory examination suggests that sociologists took a more critical or provocative tone in the 1990s and early 2000s, whereas the new generation appears to be more measured.

11.4 Conclusions

The sociological community in Latvia is small, although the last decade has seen a considerable increase in the number of researchers with a doctorate in sociology. Concurrently, Latvian researchers have become increasingly involved in international research projects and publish more regularly in international peer-reviewed journals.

Latvian sociologists participated in public conversations on key topics (e.g. transition to a market economy, accession to the EU) in the capacity of both researchers and public intellectuals, and academic sociologists published opinion pieces in the 1990s and early 2000s. However, since then the old generation has appeared in the media only sporadically, while the new generation is generally less active. Consequently, the most prominent sociologists in the public arena are the heads of two research centres, which perpetuate the idea that social surveys and sociology are interchangeable. There are other publicly active members of the sociological community, such as Dagmāra Beitnere-Le Galla and, more recently, Baiba Bela and Līga Rasnača, but Aigars Freimanis and Arnis Kaktiņš are the most prominent sociologists in the public media space.

While this relative absence of academic sociologists from public discussions can be explained by a lack of appreciation for sociology as a pertinent form of knowledge, the practical realities of research in Latvia play an equally important role. Sociology is a minority discipline with a small number of practitioners. In the 1990s, the need to build a research infrastructure was the focus of many sociologists, though certain prominent members of the sociological community published regularly in non-academic outlets. More recently, the preparation of publications and project proposals simply limits the time available for critical interventions in public discourse.

In *Sociology in Latvia* (2010), Tālis Tisenkopfs articulated a vision of the main future challenges for sociology, which draws on the position that sociology is a politically engaged discipline that can and should contribute to the welfare of society. This vision of sociology was shared by many of my informants, and one can identify contributions to social transformation. There have been contributions in relation to politically sensitive topics, such as ethnic integration and migration. Research in rural sociology and sociology of youth addresses policy-relevant issues. Sociologists have participated in (and continue to do so) research projects initiated by international organisations. Nonetheless, the overall influence of sociology and sociologists on societal transformation has been sporadic, and sociologists in Latvia can be regarded as either passengers or voyeurs. The applied nature of sociological work, the need to attract competitive funding and the emphasis on practical skills and competence have created a variant of sociology that focuses on professional commitments and integrity and has limited the public forms of sociology. Indeed, as Tālis Tisenkopfs notes, sociology in Latvia has historically been applied, busy and in a hurry (Tisenkopfs, 2010, p. 23). Challenging dominant ways of framing issues or providing alternative lenses through which to interpret social phenomena, other than in a research capacity, has seldom been part of the agenda.

Competing Interests The author has no conflicts of interest to declare that are relevant to the content of this chapter.

References

BNS. (2001). *Premjers pārmet pretrunas ANO attīstības pārskatā*. Retrieved Accessed 25 August 25, 2021. https://www.delfi.lv/news/national/politics/premjers-parmet-pretrunas-ano-attistibas-parskata.d?id=1576607

Buholcs, J. (2017). *Vēlētāju aptaujas—publiskais viedoklis, klusēšana un politika*. Retrieved August 25, 2021, https://www.lsm.lv/raksts/arpus-etera/arpus-etera/janis-buholcs-veletaju-aptaujas-publiskais-viedoklis-klusesana-un-politika.a239869/

Burawoy, M. (2005). For public sociology. *American Sociological Review, 70*(1), 4–28.

Daugavietis, J., & Leiškalne, A. (2017). *Grāmatas Latvijā tiešām nelasa trešdaļa pieaugušo; atbilde Arno Jundzem*. Retrieved August 25, 2021, https://nra.lv/viedokli/janis-daugavietis-anna-leiskalne/230929-gramatas-latvija-tiesam-nelasa-tresdala-pieauguso-atbilde-arno-jundzem.htm

Graham, L. R. (1998). *What have we learned about science and technology from the Russian experience?* Stanford University Press.

Ivanovs, I. (2006). Sociologu pētījumi kā politiskā propaganda: [par pētījumu ticamību]. *Rītdiena, 53*.

Jundze, A. (2017). *Kam ticēt, kam neticēt*. Retrieved August 25, 2021, http://nra.lv/viedokli/arno-jundze-9/230270-kam-ticet-kam-neticet.htm

Keruss, J., Lipša, I., Runce, I., & Zellis, K. (2010). *Latvijas Universitātes Vēstures un filozofijas fakultātes vēsture padomju laikā: personības, struktūras, idejas (1944–1991)*. University of Latvia Academic Press.

Kunda, I. (2013). *Metris country report: Humanities and social science in Latvia, 2012 Report*. Retrieved June 22, 2015, from http://www.metrisnet.eu/metris//fileUpload/countryReports/Latvia_2012.pdf

Kunda, I., Ozoliņa, E., Rolle, K., & Daugavietis, J. (2016). *Sociālo un humanitāro zinātņu ekosistēmas analītisks apraksts*. Retrieved August 25, 2021, from https://www.izm.gov.lv/lv/petijumi-0/shz_ekosistemas_apraksts1_1.pdf

Kļave, E., & Zepa, B. (2010). Etniskā integrācija Latvijā—pētnieciskais diskurss. In T. Tisenkopfs (Ed.), *Socioloģija Latvijā* (pp. 201–219). University of Latvia Academic Press.

Laķe, A. (2012). Evaluation research as a society's expression of rationality, its utility in policy making in Latvia. In *Summary of doctoral thesis*. Riga Stradiņš University.

Ozols, O. (2017). *Pašmāju viltus ziņu ražotāji—premjera padomnieka firma, LNT un citi*. Retrieved August 25, 2021, from https://www.delfi.lv/news/versijas/otto-ozols-pasmaju-viltus-zinu-razotaji-premjera-padomnieka-firma-lnt-un-citi.d?id=48924583

Rasnača, L. & Bela, B. (2017). *Kurus aizstāv nodokļu reforma?*. Retrieved August 25, 2021, from https://www.delfi.lv/news/versijas/liga-rasnaca-baiba-bela-kurus-aizstav-nodoklu-reforma.d?id=48783219

Šūmane, S. (2010). Eiropas Savienības Lauku attīstības pētījumu ieguldījums Latvijas socioloģijā. In T. Tisenkopfs (Ed.), *Socioloģija Latvijā* (pp. 420–432). University of Latvia Academic Press.

Tamás, P. (2002). Followers or activists? Social scientists in the reality shows of transformation. In M. Kaase, V. Sparschuh, & A. Wenninger (Eds.), *Three social science disciplines in central and Eastern Europe: Handbook on economics, political science and sociology (1989–2001)* (pp. 376–385). Informationszentrum Sozialwissenschaften.

Technopolis. (2013). *Latvia: Research assessment exercise. Panel report: Social sciences.* Retrieved August 25, 2021, from https://www.izm.gov.lv/lv/media/5149/download

Technopolis. (2017). *Izvērtējuma ziņojums.* Retrieved August 25, 2021, from http://www.esfondi.lv/upload/Petijumi_un_izvertejumi/izvertejuma-zinojums_22122017.pdf

Technopolis. (2021). *International evaluation of scientific institutions activity. Panel report: Social sciences.* Retrieved August 25, 2021, from https://www.izm.gov.lv/lv/media/10717/download

Tabuns, A. (1994, March 17). Kam traucē socioloģiskie pētījumi. Diena.

Tabuns, A. (Ed.). (1998). *Sabiedrības pārmaiņas Latvijā.* Jumava.

Tisenkopfs, T., & Bela, B. (Eds.). (2006). *Dzīves kvalitāte Latvijā.* Zinātne.

Tabuns, A. (2009). *Sociālās zināšanas kā slogs.* Retrieved August 25, 2021, from https://www.delfi.lv/news/versijas/aivars-tabuns-socialas-zinasanas-ka-slogs.d?id=28294383

Tabuns, A. (2010). Socioloģija Latvijā: divdesmitais gadsimts. In T. Tisenkopfs (Ed.), *Socioloģija Latvijā* (pp. 81–124). University of Latvia Academic Press.

Tisenkopfs, T. (Ed.). (2010). *Socioloģija Latvijā.* University of Latvia Academic Press.

Zepa, B., & Zobena, A. (1996). *Cilvēks un dzīve socioloģijas skatījumā.* Cathedra of Sociology, University of Latvia.

Zepa, B., & Zobena, A. (1997). *Socioloģijas skaidrojošā vārdnīca.* Cathedra of Sociology, University of Latvia.

Emils Kilis is a senior researcher at the Baltic Studies Centre. His research interests include the sociology of knowledge, interdisciplinarity and social studies of science and technology.

Chapter 12
The Contribution of Sociology to Post-communist Restoration in Lithuania

Zenonas Norkus and Vaidas Morkevičius

12.1 Introduction

This contribution aims to analyse changes in the professional status and social role of sociology as a social discipline in Lithuania since the early beginnings of post-communist transformation (in 1987–1988) up to the early 2020s, applying the conceptual framework of cultural and political economy (very broadly conceived; cp. Jessop & Oosterlynck, 2008; Sum & Jessop, 2015). Instead of a generic (and nearly empty) concept of transformation, we are using that of restoration to describe the overall character of social change in Lithuania since the late 1980s, drawing on our earlier (Norkus, 2012) and recent research (Norkus, 2023a, b).

The point is that post-communist developments in Lithuania (and other Baltic countries) were marked by the domination of the restorational orientation in the discourses and social imaginary during the exit from communism. These developments encompassed the ternary restoration of the independent nation-state, capitalism, and democracy, involving the attempted return to the status quo as of 1940, the date of the Soviet occupation and annexation of the Baltic States. There was no such clear status quo date in the formerly communist countries of Central and Southeastern Europe because, before the communist takeover, they were exposed to the

---

Z. Norkus (✉)
Faculty of Philosophy, Institute of Sociology and Social Work, Vilnius University, Vilnius, Lithuania
e-mail: zenonas.norkus@fsf.vu.lt

V. Morkevičius
Faculty of Social Sciences, Arts and Humanities, Kaunas Technology University, Kaunas, Lithuania
e-mail: vaidas.morkevicius@ktu.lt

aggression of Hitler's Germany and Mussolini's Italy (e.g. Poland, former Yugoslavia) or were their allies (Bulgaria, Hungary, and Romania). We will show that the prevalence of restorational thinking also strongly influenced the post-communist developments of academic institutions, which are the natural harbours of sociology as a profession.

In fact, to make its mark during the post-communist restoration, sociology had to exist before its start in the late 1980s. Therefore, we start with a description of the sociological landscape in Lithuania during the late Soviet time in the first section. After introducing institutions created during the Soviet times and their agenda, we continue with the depiction of their transformation after the restoration of independence. Conceptually, this analysis is guided by Michael Burawoy's (2005) famous differentiation between professional, critical, policy, and public sociology. We also use this work in the next two sections, combining it with the proposal of Borut Rončević (see the introductory chapter of this volume) to differentiate the dimension of the status of sociology as a profession in a society (autonomous versus dependent) and that of sociology's role in society (strong versus weak).

We apply the joint Burawoy-Rončević framework in the second section to trace the trajectory of Lithuanian sociology during the previous three decades, starting with its meteoric rise to an activist role during the last years of Soviet occupation, continuing with the movement to a passenger role during the first decades of post-communist restoration, and its current situation, which continues since 2004–2011.[1] By this time, the academic sector was exposed to shock caused by the opening of the Lithuanian study market to international competition (since 2004) and then by the economic (from 2009 to 2011) and demographic crisis in Lithuania, which intensified competition for resources and students between social scientific disciplines. In this competition, sociology lost.

Since this time, the role of sociology remains weak, and its situation can be described as the struggle against ultimate marginalisation. During the episodes when sociology succeeds in this struggle, it enjoys the voyeur's status. The third and last section attempts to explain the failure of Lithuanian sociology to preserve a strong role, drawing on Burawoy (2005) again. We conclude with a recapitulation of the main points and a confession of the limitations of this study, pointing to tasks of further research.

We focus on institutional developments and general trends, moving on the macro level. However, where appropriate, we extend our analysis by zooming in to the micro level, highlighting the role of some significant individual actors. Along with other sources of information, we drew on the work of Gaidys and Vosyliūtė (1994), Vosyliūtė (2002, 2003a, 2010), Vaicekauskaitė (2013), Leonavičius (1999), and Leonavičius (2002). We also used several collections of conference materials dedicated to making sociology in Lithuania (Leonavičius, 1991, 1992, 1994a, 1994b, 1996a, 1996b; 1999; Vosyliūtė, 1996, 1999, 2000, 2001a, 2001b, 2003b) and

---

[1] In fact, our analysis closes with 2020, which is the year of the outbreak of the COVID-19 pandemic (see Conclusion).

memoirs (Matulionis, 2011, 2021; Grigas, 2011, 2020). Of particular value was the unpublished doctoral dissertation by Liutauras Kraniauskas (2001) because its author was able to interview crucial actors in the late Soviet and early post-Soviet sociological scene, including those who have since passed away.

12.2 The Rise of Sociology as a Profession in Lithuania

The history of sociology as a social science discipline in Lithuania can be traced back to the times of the inter-war Republic of Lithuania in 1918–1940. Sociology was taught at its first and only university in Kaunas. It was founded in 1922 and called 1930 Vytautas Magnus University to honour the greatest ruler of the medieval Grand Duchy of Lithuania, Vytautas (1350–1430). The teaching also continued after its only professorship for sociology (at the Theology and Philosophy faculty) was abolished in 1932 (Leonavičius, 1996c, p. 166). Several sociology textbooks and other publications bearing the word 'sociology' in their titles were published until 1940 when Lithuania was occupied and annexed by the Soviet Union.

The new start or rebirth of sociology in Lithuania was part of the new grounding or renaissance of sociology as an autonomous social science discipline in the Soviet Union in the 1960s (see, e.g. Yadov (1998)). Lithuanian developments just followed or reproduced trends launched in the metropolitan centres of the Soviet empire because, at this time, it was not possible to open new research centres or change higher schools' curriculum without explicit permission from Moscow offices supervising research and higher education (Kraniauskas, 2001).

In 1964, the Section of Sociology and Law was established at the Institute of Economics of the Lithuanian Academy of Sciences (LAS). The following year, the Sociological Research Laboratory was grounded at Vilnius University, followed by the establishment of another Sociological Research Laboratory in 1966 at the Kaunas Polytechnic Institute (now Kaunas Technological University). In 1969, the Section of Sociology and Law was moved from the Institute of Economics to the Institute of History of the LAS, where the Division of Philosophy, Sociology, and Law was established with separate sections for philosophy, sociology, and law.

In 1977, it was transformed into the Institute of Philosophy, Sociology and Law of the LAS with 96 staff positions (Bagdonavičius & Katinaitė, 1997, p. 9); only a third of them belonged to the sociology division. Its researchers had no formal education or training in sociology, being recruited from very different professions, ranging from economics and history to physics and radio-electronic engineering. Nevertheless, the founding of this institute marked the arrival of sociology as a profession in Lithuania: the emergence of a community of full-time employed experts with a prestige hierarchy, reproduction system, and specialised periodical publishing outlets.

Describing the situation of sociology under Soviet communism in terms of the influential metasociological analysis by Michael Burawoy, we conclude that at this time, sociology was incomplete, lacking essential parts of its disciplinary identity.

According to Burawoy (2005, p. 11), there are two fundamental questions about sociology: 'Knowledge for whom?' and 'Knowledge for what?' Responses to the first question differentiate between two audiences of sociological knowledge: academic and extra-academic. Responses to the second question draw the demarcation line between reflexive knowledge and instrumental knowledge (see Table 12.1).

Instrumental knowledge is about how to solve internal problems (puzzles) of theory-driven research, interesting only for sociologists themselves (professional sociology) or external problems proposed by policymakers (policy sociology). Reflexive knowledge is about the ends of society, involving dialogue with the extra-academic public and discussion about the directions of change in a society where sociologists live and work (public sociology) or about the foundations of the sociology itself (critical sociology).

During the Soviet era, the field of critical sociology was occupied by the dogmas of the Marxist-Leninist social philosophy (historical materialism). Under a totalitarian regime, the practice of public sociology was possible only in the degenerate form of propaganda. Otherwise, it amounted to dissident activities, which were prosecuted. While dissident public sociology was present in some Central European countries with civil society in the making (first of all, in Poland and some former Yugoslavia republics), it was totally absent in Soviet Lithuania.

Therefore, in Soviet Lithuania, only professional and policy sociology thrived. Important research output was produced in five research areas, which can be associated with five names referring to leaders of researcher groups in the respective fields: social planning at the 'socialist enterprise', encompassing issues of industrial sociology, such as job satisfaction and the microclimate of the team (Romualdas Grigas b. 1936); workers' leisure (Alfonsas Mitrikas b. 1932); the professional orientations of youth (Arvydas Matulionis b. 1946); the prestige of profession (Meilutė Taljūnaitė b. 1952); and the research on students' and lecturers' time budgets (Juozas Leonavičius (1927–2008)). With the exception of Juozas Leonavičius (employed by Kaunas Polytechnic Institute), all other researchers worked at the Institute of Philosophy, Sociology and Law of the LAS.

With no competencies in non-Marxist-Leninist critical and public sociology, late Soviet and early post-Soviet sociology could only contribute during the times of 'extraordinary politics' (1988–1992) to the retention of specific resonant discourses as well as to reinforcement of dominant discourses generated or disseminated by intellectuals with a background in philosophy, economics, history, and other humanities. Tellingly, the leader of the Lithuanian Reform Movement (Sąjūdis), Vytautas Landsbergis (b. 1932), was an expert in the history of Lithuanian music.

We will discuss these contributions in the next section. Before that, we will continue with post-Soviet developments and the current condition of sociology in

Table 12.1 Composition of sociological labour according to Michael Burawoy (2005)

	Academic audience	Extra-academic audience
Reflexive knowledge	Critical	Public
Instrumental knowledge	Professional	Policy

Lithuania. In the Soviet era, the dogma of historical materialism as Marxist sociology did the most harm to the rise of sociology as a profession by blocking the establishment of study programmes in sociology. Only at Moscow and Leningrad universities (but also at Latvian University in Riga) were there minor studies in 'concrete sociological research' for major studies in 'scientific communism' (in Leningrad and Moscow) or philosophy (in Riga). Only during the brief Mikhail Gorbachev era were the first study programmes with a major in sociology started, and several faculties of sociology were even opened.

Vilnius University planned to host one of them, but by this time, the national communist government of Lithuania was already so self-assertive that it changed Moscow's directive on its own, opening its Faculty of Philosophy in 1989 instead. This was the preference of the Lithuanian public, also voiced by the Lithuanian Reform Movement (Sąjūdis). This collision may provide a curious illustration of the power of restorative orientation in the Lithuanian social imaginary at this time: the main reason to prefer the Faculty of Philosophy to the Faculty of Sociology was that philosophy faculties were closed by the Soviets in 1940. Meanwhile, it was reputed to be the oldest faculty of Vilnius University. So, according to the restorers' argument, a university cannot claim to be a 'real university' without a faculty of philosophy as its part.

In the same year, the Sociology Department was established at the restored Faculty of Philosophy, which was 410 years old[2] at its restoration year, according to its official history (see Jakutienė et al. (2009)). During the first years, its main responsibility was to launch BA, MA, and then PhD study programmes in sociology. In the next years, the supply of such programmes was quickly expanded by Vytautas Magnus University in Kaunas, another prominent case of post-communist restorations in Lithuania. It was (re)-established simultaneously with the Faculty of Philosophy as a continuator of inter-war Vytautas Magnus University in Kaunas, which was closed by the Soviets in 1950.

However, one difference was neglected by the restorers of Vytautas Magnus University. In fact, its closure involved the reorganisation, dividing it into Kaunas Medicine Institute and Kaunas Polytechnic Institute. Both institutes could claim the legacy of Vytautas Magnus University, too, whose 'real' restoration would have meant their reunification. Kaunas Polytechnic Institute (renamed to Kaunas Technology University) also launched sociology studies (see Jucevičienė (2010)). Next, another two players entered the field in Vilnius: Lithuanian Educology University, which launched BA and MA study programmes in sociology and political science, and Mykolas Römeris Law University, opening a BA programme in sociology and MA programme in 'welfare sociology'.

However, as of 2023, only sociology study programmes at Vilnius University were surviving, with admissions barely exceeding minimal threshold requirements (15 students for the BA programme, 10 students for the MA programme) for the

---

[2] Vilnius University was established in 1579 by Jesuits to fight against Reformation, which was nearly victorious in Lithuania at that time.

conduct of studies. In 2018, Lithuanian Educology University was closed together with its social science departments. At Vytautas Magnus University, sociology studies did survive but only as part of a joint study programme encompassing both sociology and anthropology. Sociology programmes were outcompeted by management, public administration, law, economics, politics, and other social science programmes, which were perceived as more promising in terms of professional careers by the graduates of secondary schools. Arguably, this is a misperception because the surveys of the graduates of sociology programmes conducted as part of their assessment and re-accreditation procedures provide evidence that the majority of the graduates find employment according to competencies and skills acquired during studies.

Marketing and opinion research firms are important employers. The first of them were successors of the applied research centres that were privatised in the early 1990s. In this way, the two oldest and most authoritative commercial market and opinion research firms 'Baltijos tyrimai' (Baltic Surveys; directed by RasaAlišauskienė) and 'Vilmorus' (directed by Vladas Gaidys) emerged, the first descending from the Sociological Research Laboratory at Vilnius University and the second from the Public Opinion Research Center of the LAS. They were followed by the subsidiaries of the transnational companies (e.g. AC Nielsen, Norstat, Taylor Nelson Sofres [TNS], Growth from Knowledge [GfK]) and new ventures launched by the graduates of the master's and doctoral sociology programmes (e.g. Spinter Research, Social Research Centre [SIC], and Rait Research). Over time, many of them expanded service supply through consultation and assessment research, which became highly demanded after Lithuania's accession to the European Union (EU) by various applicants for EU structural funds money. Parts of the applied research done by these firms can be attributed to policy sociology, although commercial research firms do not make public the data they collect and conduct only limited scientific analyses.

We will attempt to answer the question of why sociology failed in the competition with other social scientific disciplines after such a promising start in the last section. In the next section, we will explore the contribution of sociology to post-communist restoration in Lithuania, using as the guideline the proposal of Borut Rončević to differentiate between the dimension of the status of sociology as a profession in a society (autonomous versus dependent) and that of sociology's role in society (strong versus weak).[3] We aim to trace the overall trajectory of Lithuanian sociology in terms of Rončević's four ideal types of the role of sociology in society: activist, passenger, voyeur, and marginal.

---

[3] See further details in the introduction of this volume.

12.3 From Activists and Passengers to Voyeurs and Marginals: The Tale of the Brief Glory and Decline of Lithuania Sociology

Because dissident public or critical sociology was absent in Lithuania until 1989, Lithuanian sociology could not contribute to processes of variation of discourses and practices, which may lead to a variety of alternative paths or to a selection of particular discourses at the initial phase of post-communist transformation. Nevertheless, we would claim that sociology played an activist role during this time. However, the time of its activism was very brief indeed, encompassing the period from May 1989 to October 1992. After highlighting its contribution during this 'epic' period, called the era of the 'rebirth of the Lithuanian nation' in contemporary Lithuanian historical textbooks, we will proceed to the discussion of its contribution to the retention of specific resonant discourses and to its role in the retention and change of dominant discourses. We will personalise this discussion, showing the role of some influential individuals and their fates in the wake of the reconfiguration of the dominant discourses.

We will claim the activist role on behalf of Lithuanian sociology in 1989–1992 because of the extraordinary impact of the first representative surveys of mass opinions conducted by Lithuanian sociologists. The survey data became, for some time, the real focus of political life. Reformist (national communist) leaders of the Lithuanian Communist Party (seceding from the Communist Party of the Soviet Union in December 1989) were extremely sensitive to changes in public opinion trends and adjusted their policies according to the findings of sociologists in order to prevent the ratings of the party falling back below the ratings of the Lithuanian Reform Movement (Sąjūdis). Curiously, reformist national communists partly succeeded in this 'rating contest'. While the majority of the population preferred Sąjūdis to reformist communists, their leader, Algirdas Brazauskas, was mostly more popular than the leader of Sąjūdis Vytautas Landsbergis (see Gaidys and Tureikytė (2015)).

Somewhat unexpectedly to sociologists, the proclamation of the restoration of independence of Lithuania on 11 March 1990 heralded the sunset of this nostalgically remembered time (Gaidys & Tureikytė, 2015, p. 9). When polls detected the decreasing popularity not only of Sąjūdis leader Landsbergis but also of Sąjūdis as such, sociological surveys and pollsters came under attack in the pro-Sąjūdis mass media, claiming that the pro-Sąjūdis majority in the parliament represented the 'true' public opinion. In reaction, during the period of most intense confrontation between pro-Moscow and pro-independence forces in January–late August 1991, Lithuanian sociologists removed the questions about the popularity of competing political leaders and political forces to avoid accusations of playing into Moscow's hands (if the poll findings occasionally would turn out to Lithuania's government dislike) (Gaidys & Tureikytė, 2015, p. 88). In terms of Rončević's typology, this can be described as the move from the activist (in 1988–1991) to the passenger's role (1991–1992).

The sensitive questions came back to questionnaires only in late 1991. By this time, the independence of Lithuania had been internationally recognised, including by the USSR itself (after the failure of the August 1991 putsch, ushering into its ultimate dissolution after a few months). According to polls, the popularity of Sąjūdis continued to decrease, while that of the ex-communist Lithuanian Labour Democratic Party (under Brazauskas) increased. Findings provoked a new wave of disbelief and attacks against sociologists by Sąjūdis leadership and Sąjūdis-dominated mass media. The new parliament election in October 1992 could become the ultimate vindication of Lithuanian sociology, as its outcome (with 44% of the votes in the first run, it was won by ex-communists, while Sąjūdis collected 21.2%) closely corresponded to the survey-based prediction (42% for ex-communists and 22% for Sąjūdis (Gaidys & Tureikytė 1997, p. 122)).

However, pro-Sąjūdis media malignantly (mis)represented it as sociology's ultimate fiasco, because it deviated from the prediction of the Sąjūdis victory, made on election day by foreign pollsters based on exit polling. In fact, it was a clear case of a 'spiral of silence' (Noelle-Neumann, 1984) in action, because few ex-communist subalterns (mainly would-be losers of the market reforms) dared to disclose their real voting, exposed to the heavy pressure by dominant pro-Sąjūdis nationalist discourse (Gaidys, 1995). However, the pro-Sąjūdis media used the election debacle of foreign pollsters to marginalise Lithuanian sociology. This is indeed the role to which Lithuanian sociology has been gravitating since 1992. This drift could be stopped and partially reversed by the move to a voyeur position in 2004–2014 thanks to the temporary improvement of the research funding in Lithuania during the first two (2004–2006 and 2007–2014) EU financing periods.

It took several elections to teach the Lithuanian elite the usefulness of the representative polls while conducting election campaigns. By the end of the first post-communist decade, survey monitoring of the popularity of political parties and their leaders became a firmly established routine in the workings of Lithuanian democracy, as in other post-communist countries. In mass perception, sociology remains firmly associated (if not identified) with public opinion research (cp. Daujotytė, 1997, p. 26). The director of the Vilmorus company, Vladas Gaidys, remains the most famous Lithuanian sociologist since the epic times of 1989–1991 when he was an oracle loudly speaking out the vox populi.

However, although Gaidys remains the most publicly visible Lithuanian sociologist, he is now perceived as a weather forecaster or sports events commentator (broadcast in real time) rather than a living personification of 'people's mind'. Therefore, it is problematic to place him squarely into the public sociology field, where new discourses are forged to fight for dominance or to find popular resonance at the very least. Because the polling industry is at least nominally independent from government funding, this secures sociologists like Gaidys a modicum of autonomy. However, the self-limitation to tracing the changes in public opinion weakens the status of this kind of sociology. Because of this limitation, the overall trajectory of the sociology associated with public opinion polling can be described as the movement from activist to voyeur sociology.

12 The Contribution of Sociology to Post-communist Restoration in Lithuania

Among Lithuanian sociologists of the first (now oldest) generation, Romualdas Grigas (b. 1936) made perhaps the most sustained effort to promote activist sociology in Lithuania by establishing himself as a powerful public intellectual (see Voverienė (2009, pp. 171–181)). Arguably, he was one of the most successful sociologists of the Soviet period. He was the first (in 1980) to defend the 'doctoral' dissertation in sociology, which was the Soviet equivalent of the 'habilitation thesis' still surviving in some Western countries. Then, he was the head of the social planning section at the sociology division of the Institute of Philosophy, Sociology and Law of the LAS and director of the advisor council on social planning at the government of Soviet Lithuania. A gifted stylist, he published several works of fiction, a 'sociosophic poetry' book (Grigas, 2010), and very interesting and open memoirs (grounded in his diary) (Grigas, 2011, 2020).

During the post-Soviet time, he remains one of the most important voices of the Lithuanian conservative nationalist discourse. He published many books about the Lithuanian mentality and its roots in the ancient Baltic worldview and on the harm done to Lithuanian culture and people's morals by Soviet occupation, among other topics. He also pleaded for the 'Lithuanisation' of sociology, resisting the intellectual colonisation and self-colonisation of Lithuanians. The titles of his books speak for themselves: *Cain the Loser* (1991); *Self-defence of Nation* (1993); *The Fate of Nation* (1995); *Prolegomena: For a Politician and for a Citizen* (1997); *Fields of Social Tensions in Lithuania: A Critical Sociological Panorama Closing 20th Century* (1998); *Sociological Self-Reflection: Specifics, Methods, Lithuanisation* (2001a); *National Self-Reflection* (2001b); *The Drama of the Survival of Lithuanian Nation* (2013); and others (Grigas, 2004, 2009, 2016, 2017; Grigas & Ružas 2007).

In 1992–1994, Grigas organised and directed the Independent Centre of Strategical Investigations (Nepriklausomas strateginių tyrimų centras), supervising the evaluation of the new Constitution of Lithuania (adopted in 1992), reform of the public administration system of Lithuanian, the draft of the law on Lithuanian municipalities, and others. These evaluations contained criticisms targeting reforms implemented under the ex-communist government of Lithuania in 1992–1996. However, he did not succeed in associating with the leadership of the anti-ex-communist opposition around the former leader of Sąjūdis Vytautas Landsbergis, who came back to power in 1996. In 2001–2003, Grigas presided over the Forum of Lithuanian civic organisations, and in the next year, he ran (unsuccessfully) for a seat in the Lithuanian parliament as a candidate of the Peasant and New Democracy party. With no political backing, the influence of Grigas remained limited.

Another prominent Lithuanian sociologist during the Soviet period, the director (in 1989–1997) of the Institute of Philosophy, Sociology and Law, Arvydas Matulionis, was appointed the chief advisor of the ex-communist leader Brazauskas, who was elected Lithuania's President (for the 1993–1998 term). His area of responsibility was education, culture, science, and religion. Seemingly, this position provided a good opportunity to broker competing discourses, supporting discourses articulating heterodox alternatives to the complementary hegemonic nationalist and neoliberal discourses. In fact, ex-communists remained completely passive and sterile ideologically, leaving the public sphere under the control of their political opponents.

The most important attempt to upgrade sociological labour to activist sociology occurred in 2007 when young intellectuals attempted to launch Lithuania's New Left 95 movement. Led by philosophers Andrius Bielskis and Nida Vasiliauskaitė, this group included three sociologists of the younger generation (Jolanta Aidukaitė, Rasa Baločkaitė, and Tadas Leončikas). However, focusing on the issue of the rights of sexual minorities instead of broader problems of social inequality and exclusion or the plight of the losers of the post-communist transformation, this group did not become a real social movement with a distinctive agenda. In fact, the issue of sexual minority rights was already claimed by the influential Lithuanian Gay League (LGL), enjoying strong international support, as its monopolist social responsibility domain.

The work done by a few Lithuanian sociologists on feminist and gender issues (Giedrė Purvaneckienė, Artūras Tereškinas, and Alina Žvinklienė) contributed to the retention of sexual minority rights discourse, which still did not have strong resonance in this rather culturally conservative country. Some members of the New Left 95 (most notably, Bielskis) attempted to ally with the ex-communist party, which since 2001 has been named the Lithuanian Social Democratic Party. This attempt failed because, by this time, Social Democrat leaders conceived their party as a centrist 'catch-all' party, expecting to remain politically competitive by building the reputation of the technocratic expertise and preserving neutrality concerning all 'politically correct' discourses (excluding radical left and radical right, which they of course condemned).

Thus, Lithuania remains in the grip of nationalist and neoliberal discourses. Since the early 1990s, the main bulwark of 'market bolshevism' in Lithuania remains the Lithuanian Free Market Economy Institute (Lietuvos laisvosios rinkos institutas), expounding libertarian ideology, grounded in the work by Ludwig von Mises and Friedrich von Hayek. Arguably, it is the best-funded and most active 'think-tank' in Lithuania, whose activities significantly contribute to the continuing dominance of the neoliberal discourse in Lithuania. However, it concentrates its attention on economic policy. In the sphere of broadly conceived cultural policy, also encompassing ideas of the 'good life' (what people do when not working or sleeping), nationalist discourse preserved its hegemony but split into two varieties: conservative nationalism and liberal or pro-European nationalism. Then, the intellectuals of Grigas cast were marginalised by the exponents of a more liberal or 'pro-European' version of nationalist discourse, with the tale of 'Lithuania's return to Europa' as a master narrative.

The tension between two varieties of Lithuanian nationalist discourse was latently present during the era of the 'national renaissance' in the late 1980s–early 1990s. There was much talk about the 'return to the West'. However, there was no reason for conservative nationalists to worry about the opportunity cost of this return until the Soviet and then Russian Army (until September 1993) remained in Lithuania. Western help was the only hope during the dramatic time of standoff against Moscow and the restoration of independent Lithuania. However, when

Lithuania's joining the EU became a real option, this tension became manifest, leading to polarisation between the two varieties. Liberal nationalist discourse did become hegemonic by the year 2000.

Its first promoters in the 1990s were scholars and public intellectuals supported by the George Soros Foundation. Then, it was supported just by the Lithuanian government, which funded much public relations work to educate Lithuanian populations about the advantages of Lithuania's membership in the EU (this was the mission of a special ministry established in 1996). Again, philosophers and other scholars in humanities were most prominent in producing variations in this discourse, with sociologists and other social researchers providing for resonance and contributing to its retention.

Two historians, Alfredas Bumblauskas (b. 1956) and Edvardas Gudavičius (1929–2020), were the most famous mouthpieces or trumpets of the liberal nationalist discourse, along with philosophers Leonidas Donskis (1962–2016) and Nerija Putinaitė (b. 1971). Among sociologists, Vytautas Kavolis (1930–1996) was about to become a leading exponent in Lithuanian public sociology, promoting a liberal variety of nationalism. Kavolis was an American Lithuanian who defended a doctorate in the sociology of art at Harvard University (in 1960) and made his mark in the sociology of culture and comparative civilisation studies, publishing both in English and Lithuanian (Kavolis, 1968, 1972, 1986, 1991, 1992, 1993, 1994, 1995a, 1995b, 1996, 1998). He returned to Lithuania in 1992.

Significantly, he was the trusted confidant of another influential American Lithuanian, Valdas Adamkus (b. 1926), who was elected Lithuanian president for the 1998–2003 and 2004–2009 terms. Kavolis' authority among post-Soviet Lithuanian intellectuals was enormous. Predictably, Kavolis could become Adamkus' key advisor, who probably would have been more successful in realising sociology's transformative potential (or the public visibility, at the very least) than Matulionis could achieve in a similar role under Brazauskas.

Sadly, Kavolis' career in Lithuania was terminated by an untimely death. While in Lithuania, he preferred the company of scholars in human studies, associating himself with the Department of Lithuanian Literature of the Philology faculty of Vilnius University (Viliūnas, 2004, p. 180). However, he made a lasting contribution to the education of Lithuanian sociologists as a top advisor of the large translation programme 'Open Lithuania Book' of Western literature in the humanities and social sciences, sponsored by the George Soros Foundation. As a result, not only part of the work of classical sociologists (including Emile Durkheim, Alexis de Tocqueville, Max Weber, and Georg Simmel) but also that of influential contemporary sociologists (Benedict Anderson, Zygmunt Bauman, Daniel Bell, Peter L. Berger, Pierre Bourdieu, Rogers Brubaker, Manuel Castells, James S. Coleman, Ralf Dahrendorf, Gerard Delanty, Louis Dumont, Norbert Elias, Harold Garfinkel, Anthony Giddens, Ernest Gellner, James Gilligan, Erving Goffman, Jürgen Habermas, Bruno Latour, David Matza, Marshall McLuhan, Robert A. Nisbet, Karl Polanyi, Robert D. Putnam, Lawrence A. Scaff, Don Slater, Anthony Smith, John Tomlinson, Frank Webster, Wolfgang Welsch, and Robert Wuthnow) is accessible now in Lithuanian.

Furthermore, Kavolis decisively influenced several sociologists of the younger generation, including Marius Povilas Šaulauskas (b. 1961), who pioneered information society studies in Lithuania, and, most importantly, Algimantas Valantiejus (1958–2016). They both considered themselves Kavolis' pupils. Valantiejus made a path-breaking contribution to the emergence of critical sociology (in Burawoy's sense) in Lithuania, publishing two books discussing metasociological issues (2004, 2007a). He founded (in 1997) and edited the journal *Sociology: Mintis ir veiksmas* (*Sociology: Thought and Action*), with the distinctive mission to promote sociological theory in Lithuania.

Valantiejus succeeded as a teacher, instructing social science students in Klaipėda and Vilnius universities in the arcana of contemporary sociological theory. However, because of his choice to publish only in Lithuanian, his highly sophisticated and original contributions to social theory and metasociology found limited reception because there are very few readers in Lithuania able to appreciate and even understand them. After Valantiejus's death, the very survival of critical sociology is in danger. Only the first volume of his monumental and profound history of sociology (Valantiejus, 2007b) could be published.

12.4 Why Did Lithuanian Sociology Lose a Strong Role in Lithuanian Society?

All considered, the situation of Lithuanian sociology since 1992 can be described as a ceaseless struggle against marginalisation, the major driving force of which has been underfunding: an endemic problem in Lithuanian research and higher education since 1992, when the contraction of the Lithuanian economy together with neoliberal economic reforms severely reduced the revenue of the state budget. At public universities, state funding was not sufficient even for paying teaching staff salaries. Struggling for survival, higher education institutions expanded the admission of students, accepting nearly all applicants able and willing to pay for their studies. The outcome was a huge expansion (boom) of higher education in Lithuania by the end of the first post-communist decade, with circa 50% of graduates from secondary schools continuing their studies at the universities.

However, universities typically did not use the funds made in this way for research, spending them on 'hard' infrastructure development and renovation projects. Researchers could get funding only by working as local under-labourers in international research projects or competing for the meagre state grants distributed by the Lithuanian Research Council, whose funds were very small before Lithuania joined the EU.

After Lithuania's accession to the EU in 2004, the situation improved for some time. Although the distribution of the EU structural funds was heavily biased in favour of natural and technological sciences, they also allowed to create and expand the 'soft' infrastructure as a necessary condition for making Lithuanian professional sociology (along with 'professional' parts of other social sciences) internationally visible and competitive. Lithuanian sociologists could join academically driven cross-national surveys (European Social Survey (ESS), International Social Survey Programme (ISSP), Survey of Health, Ageing and Retirement in Europe (SHARE)) producing cross-nationally comparable data about their country. The Lithuanian Academic e-Library (eLABa), which is a national aggregated open access (OA) repository, was started at the end of 2006. The virtual digital infrastructure LiDA (Lithuanian Data Archive for Social Sciences and Humanities) was launched in 2012, where researchers can deposit, search, browse, and download social sciences and humanities data sets.

Simply put, the arrival of the EU funding in 2004 rescued Lithuanian academic sociology from marginalisation, securing for it a modicum of independence and so a voyeur status. However, after 2004, Lithuanian sociology repeatedly moved from voyeur to marginal status. Its oscillation between voyeur and marginal roles is synchronised with the EU budgeting periods: it is a voyeur when the EU funds are flowing in but slips into a marginal position for years between financing periods. More specifically, the happy voyeur period 2004–2014 was interrupted by the utterly marginal existence period 2014–2016, which was the pause between the two EU budgeting periods.

However, importantly, the EU funding could not help to solve all existential problems of Lithuanian sociology. Specifically, it could not offset the impact of the demographic crisis, which has been felt since 2010. It was caused by the drop in the birth rates since the early 1990s and huge emigration, reducing the population of Lithuania by more than 20% since 1990. The crisis sharply increased competition between universities and study programmes for students. Since 2004, this competition also has an international dimension, as Lithuanian high school graduates (first, those with well-to-do parents) started in increasing numbers to opt for university studies abroad, while the overall number of graduates sharply decreased.

In this competition, sociology was a loser. In the pending downsizing or fusion of Lithuanian universities, the sociology departments should be the first victims. Sharply increasing defence spending in the wake of the Ukrainian crisis (since 2014), the Lithuanian government has no funds and political will to compensate for the decrease in demand for teaching by expanding opportunities for research. Consequently, the very existence of sociology is endangered in contemporary Lithuania, with the very real prospect that after some 10 years, there will be no more BA, MA, and PhD study programmes in sociology and no sociology departments.

That said, we still owe to provide an explanation for Lithuania's sociology failure to contribute significantly to the variation of resonant discourses and practices after the 'epic' phase of post-communist transformation. Why was it able only to reinforce dominant discourses or contribute to the retention of non-hegemonic discourses, which were selected by other actors? Why is sociology losing the competition for study admissions to other social scientific disciplines?

Answering these questions, we will take guidance from Burawoy's penetrating analysis: 'Economics, as we know it today, depends on the existence of markets with an interest in their expansion, political science depends on the state with an interest in political stability, while sociology depends on civil society with an interest in the expansion of the social' (Burawoy, 2005, p. 24). This does not mean that civil society is the sole subject matter of sociology. Civil society is just the standpoint of sociological study: studying politics sociologically means an examination of the social preconditions of politics or the politicisation of the social, while economic sociology is interested in the social foundations of the market. Even more importantly, the standpoint of civil society commits sociology to the defence of the social: 'In times of market tyranny and state despotism, sociology—and in particular its public face—defends the interests of humanity' (Burawoy, 2005, p. 24).

Taking inspiration from Burawoy's argument, we would argue that the marginal role (lack of autonomy and weak impact on society) of sociology in Lithuania is the consequence of the triumph of neoliberalism in Lithuania, creating an exemplary case of post-communist neoliberal capitalism. We will only add to the list of its distinctive features (see Norkus (2012, pp. 242–269)) concluding and critically important attribute: weakness of civil society (cp. Howard, 2003; Laurėnas, 2017, pp. 283–309). In fact, civil society can be weak in different ways. Civil society can be weak because of totalitarian control of the state, although it was not totally absent during the late Soviet period, according to findings of recent research (see Kavaliauskaitė and Ramonaitė (2011)). It blossomed shortly during the epic times of the mobilisation of Lithuanian Sąjūdis in 1989–1991 ('national renaissance'), with the first representative mass opinion survey serving as its voice.

The ensuing contraction of the Lithuanian economy, putting the majority of the Lithuanian population under severe stress, precluded its consolidation. It enabled the supervisors of Lithuanian economic transformation to impose on this country a political-economic model, providing an absolute edge of bargaining power to private capital. With no time for civil society to come to maturity, which may have been provided under the transition to capitalism in the gradualist mode, the tyranny of the state was swiftly replaced with that of the market.

In fact, experts in comparative political economy describe the political system of Lithuania (along with other Baltic countries) as 'simple polity' (Kattel & Raudla, 2013; Raudla, 2013; Raudla & Kattel, 2011; Reinert & Kattel, 2014), opposing polity of this type to 'compound polities' (cp. Schmitt, 2008, 2010).[4] In these polities, corporatist structures, social partnerships, and veto players are involved in the decision-making. In compound polities, civil society partners, political parties, and government agencies are engaged in coalition-building, negotiation, or coordination. In this way, multiple authorities participate in the governing, while in simple polities, a single authority channels the governing activity, insulating itself from social partners in policy-making. In the Baltic countries, 'it is difficult to name even one policy area where the government is engaging in significant coalition-building, negotiations, or coordination with the opposition, unions, or civil society partners' (Thorhallsson & Kattel, 2013, p. 95).

---

[4] Schmidt classifies as simple polities most 'adversary democracies' (cp. Lijphart, 1984, 1999), with the exception of the USA, which is 'compound polity'.

Nominally, such partners exist; one can find in Lithuania, as in other Baltic countries, trade unions, writers' organisations, environment activists, and gay and lesbian activists, but most of them are decorative institutions co-opted by the power elite which used to exclude non-compliant players from access to mass media or funding or just demonises them as foreign (Russian) 'influence agents'. It is important to note that many non-governmental organisations were founded as entrepreneurial projects to get financial assistance from international organisations or EU structural funds distributed by local government agencies (cp. Laurėnas, 2017, p. 303–304; Howard, 2003). Dealing only with the co-opted or corrupted civil society players, the power elite does not take them seriously, engaging them only in make-believe mode to demonstrate its democratic credentials. Political communication proceeds in persuasive mode, with no real public discussions on the real issues taking place (cp. Kattel & Raudla, 2013, p. 441). The exponents of 'politically incorrect' opinions are muzzled and discredited by declaring them as unpatriotic or just bullied.

With only slight exaggeration, Lithuanian political culture can be described as a 'bullying culture', as bullying is the only reaction the representatives of the dissenting opinions can expect. With the number of civil society forces that can provide inputs to national policy-making limited to a few selected actors representing business and especially banking interests, there is usually in the Lithuanian mainstream mass media and on public TV only one causal story or policy narrative concerning economic development, social situation, and foreign policy presented. Real communication is replaced by propaganda, by which the political elite seeks to persuade the public of the necessity and appropriateness of existing neoliberal policies.

With tamed, co-opted, or colonised civil society, sociology in Lithuania lacks its empowering backing and is nearly superfluous. Lithuania's 'simple polity' needs lawyers, managers, and economists to run the economy; graduates from the political science and public administration to staff central and local government agencies; and social workers to control dropouts from the labour market and schools. Furthermore, it needs an increasing number of psychologists to assist employers in selecting the best applicants for employment and to console (if they can afford to pay for their services) those who lose in the market competitions or win but suffer from psychological traumas. In fact, psychology BA and MA programmes attract the most applicants in social sciences, with the annual number of freshmen in all BA in psychology programmes approaching 400–500. These are very large numbers for a country with a population of 2.8 million by 2023.

Next, the neoliberal capitalism of the Baltic type needs experts in crime control; the recently launched programme in the criminology BA studies at Vilnius University was a huge success. The brighter side of the story is that it also needs increasing numbers of experts in mass entertainment, with the study programmes in 'creative industries', 'creative communications', and others being stunning but probably brief success stories. This indicates that the Baltic model of capitalism did not fail economically: despite emigration, the number of consumers who can afford to pay more than only for the bare necessities of life is increasing. However, this model has no significant demand for experts in social criticism and innovation of the social imaginary, which is the best service that sociology can supply.

12.5 Conclusion

We applied Michael Burawoy's analysis of the varieties of sociological labour and the typology of sociology roles in society, crafted by Borut Rončević, to the analysis of the development of sociological knowledge in Lithuania. Our main finding was that Lithuanian sociology was able to play a strong and autonomous (activist) role in Lithuanian society during the period of 'extraordinary politics' (Balcerowicz, 1995) in 1988–1991. In 1991, it accepted a passenger role, and since 1992, it has had to struggle against marginalisation. Lithuania's accession to the EU secured for sociology the voyeur's role, except for periods between the EU budgeting periods, when the slipping towards a marginal role resumes again. The availability of EU funding since 2004 enabled it to preserve the voyeur role for the most time. However, sociology lost competition to other social scientific disciplines: study programmes in sociology attracted fewer students. We consider the weakness of civil society in post-communist Lithuania as the ultimate cause of the weak and dependent role of sociology in this country.

The application of Rončević's typology of the sociology roles in society to Lithuanian sociology in the late Soviet and post-communist time has demonstrated its heuristic value as a tool in national sociology history writing. Book series published by the Springer Group includes the series *Sociology Transformed* (editors are John Holmwood and Stephen Turner). It is published by Palgrave/Macmillan, which is now one of Springer's trademarks.[5] This series is conceived as a collection of sociology histories in particular countries. It started in 2014 with a book by Kirsten Harley and Gary Wickham (2014) on the history of sociology in Australia. Currently, the series closes with a volume on Mexico (Zabludovski Kuper, 2023). However, only a few Eastern European countries are covered: Serbia (Spasić et al., 2022), Hungary (Karády & Nagy, 2019), the Czech Republic (Skovajsa & Balon, 2017), Russia (Titarenko & Zdravomyslova, 2017), and Poland (Bucholz, 2016). Even the history of sociology in Slovenia remains unwritten.

We believe that studies collected in this volume may be very useful for authors working on further volumes in this series. In particular, our study may be expanded into the history of sociology in Lithuania, applying the Burawoy-Rončević framework to earlier historical periods (first of all, inter-war Lithuania). Such elaboration should also include its application to developments since the global outbreak of COVID-19 in 2020, continuing with the transformation of the hybrid Russian-Ukrainian war (since 2014) into an ordinary or open war in February 2022. The changes brought by these two events have been so deep that we need time to wait

---

[5] See https://link.springer.com/series/14477

and see how sociology in Lithuania and other countries will answer these challenges and opportunities. Our suggestion is that in this situation, demographic, economic, energetic, food, and epidemiological resilience of the restored independent state, capitalist economic system, and democratic regime should move into the focus of Lithuanian sociology (cp. Norkus, 2023a, 2023b).

Because of space limits, we close with this suggestion without further elaboration. This is a limitation of our study. However, this is the price for making our study more focused on its proper subject: sociology's role in the context of post-communist transformation in the strict sense. In fact, it can be argued that in most formerly communist countries, post-communist transformation ended in 2004 because their admission to NATO and especially the EU amounted to their certification as normal Western countries (Norkus, 2012). Our finding that the admission of Lithuania to the EU did help Lithuanian sociology's ultimate marginalisation prompts us to ask the question of how much the situation of sociology differs in the 'new' and 'old' West.

Are there Western countries where sociology permanently preserves the activist role? Is not, instead, the passenger's or voyeur's role a normal situation for contemporary sociology? Can recent crises related to the COVID-19 pandemic and the failure of diplomacy to preserve peace in Europe have an impact on sociology's role? What are the implications of rapid progress in work on artificial intelligence for the role of sociology in society? How will the pending transformation of sociology into 'digital sociology', based on the application of artificial intellect and 'big data', influence sociology's received roles? These are research questions that should be answered in further research, applying Rončević's scheme beyond the context of post-communist transition (or transformation) studies in the strict sense.

Acknowledgments We thank the anonymous reviewer for advice how to align our draft with other contributions to this collection.

Competing Interests The research of Zenonas Norkus for this publication has received funding from the Research Council of Lithuania (LMTLT), agreement No. S-VIS-23-15.

References

Bagdonavičius, V., & Katinaitė, P. (1997). Lietuvos filosofijos ir sociologijos instituto darbai ir dienos. *Lietuvos mokslas, 5*(15), 3–27.
Balcerowicz, L. (1995). *Socialism, capitalism, transformation.* CEU Press.
Bucholz, M. (2016). *Sociology in Poland. To be continued?* Palgrave Macmillan.
Burawoy, M. (2005). For public sociology. *American Sociological Review, 70*(1), 4–28.
Daujotytė, V. (1997). Žvilgsnis į sociologiją iš šalies, arba žvilgsnis į bendrą erdvę. *Sociologija: Mintis ir veiksmas, 1*, 26–31.
Gaidys, V. (1995). Political preferences in Lithuania: Why the 1992 election was a surprise. In M. Taljūnaitė (Ed.), *Lithuanian society in social transition* (pp. 8–15). Institute of Philosophy, Sociology and Law.

Gaidys, V., & Tureikytė, D. (1997). Visuomenės nuomonės tyrimai. *Sociologija: Mintis ir veiksmas, 1*, 115–124.

Gaidys, V., & Tureikytė, D. (2015). *Visuomenės nuomonės tyrimai Lietuvos istorinio lūžio laikotarpiu. Viešosios nuomonės tyrimų centro tyrimai 1989-1993 metais*. Lietuvos socialinių tyrimų centras.

Gaidys, V., & Vosyliūtė, A. (1994). Main features in the development of Lithuanian sociology. In M. F. Keen & J. Mucha (Eds.), *Eastern Europe in transformation: The impact on sociology* (pp. 149–155). Greenwood Press.

Grigas, R. (1991). *Pralaimėjęs Kainas: (kritinė istoriosofinė apybraiža)*. Okto-Piligrimas.

Grigas, R. (1993). *Tautos savigyna*. Academia.

Grigas, R. (1995). *Tautos likimas (sociologinė apybraiža)*. Rosma.

Grigas, R. (1997). *Prolegomenai: politikui ir piliečiui*. Rosma.

Grigas, R. (1998). *Socialinių įtampų Lietuvoje laukai*. Vilnius Pedagogical University Press.

Grigas, R. (2001a). *Sociologinė savivoka. Specifika, metodai, lituanizacija*. Vilnius Pedagogical University Press.

Grigas, R. (2001b). *Tautinė savivoka*. Rosma.

Grigas, R. (2004). *Savasties ieškojimas arba laiškai Amerikos lietuviams*. Margi raštai.

Grigas, R. (2009). *Senieji lietuviai: tapatybės bruožai ir jų likimas*. Vilnius Pedagogical University Press.

Grigas, R. (2010). *Akivarų atspindžiai: sociosofinės mintys eilėmis*. Vilnius Pedagogical University Press.

Grigas, R. (2011). *Dienoraščio langą pravėrus: 10 mano jaunystės metų (1956–1965)*. VKnygų kelias.

Grigas, R. (2013). *Lietuvių tautos išlikimo drama*. "Diemedžio" leidykla.

Grigas, R. (2016). *Lietuvių tapatybė ir Europa: istoriosofinis aspektas*. Versmė.

Grigas, R. (2017). *Nutylėtų tiesų sakymas*. "Diemedžio" leidykla.

Grigas, R. (2020). *Dienoraščio langą pravėrus. Antroji knyga, Mano brandos metai (1966–2012)*. Versmė.

Grigas, R., & Ružas, A. (2007). *Lietuviškieji "...izmai*. Gairės.

Harley, K., & Wickham, G. (2014). *Australian sociology: Fragility, survival, rivalry*. Palgrave Macmillan.

Howard, M. M. (2003). *The weakness of civil society in post-communist Europe*. Cambridge University Press.

Jakutienė, V., Norkus, Z., & Šopaitė-Šilinskienė, G. (Eds.). (2009). *Vilniaus universitetas, Filosofijos fakultetas 1579–1989–2009*. Vilnius University Press. Retrieved July 19, 2023, from https://www.fsf.vu.lt/dokumentai/Mokslas/filosofijos-fakulteto-istorijos-bruozai.pdf

Jessop, B., & Oosterlynck, S. (2008). Cultural political economy: On making the cultural turn without falling into soft economic sociology. *Geoforum, 39*, 1155–1169.

Jucevičienė, P. (Ed.). (2010). *Kauno technologijos universiteto socialinių mokslų fakultetas: istorinės ištakos ir 20 metų kelias*. Technologija.

Karády, V., & Nagy, P. T. (2019). *Sociology in Hungary: A social, political and institutional history*. Palgrave Macmillan.

Kattel, R., & Raudla, R. (2013). The Baltic Republics and the crisis of 2008–2011. *Europa-Asia Studies, 65*(3), 426–449.

Kavaliauskaitė, J., & Ramonaitė, A. (Eds.). (2011). *Sąjūdžio ištakų beieškant: nepaklusniųjų tinklaveikos galia*. Baltos lankos.

Kavolis, V. (1968). *Artistic expression: A sociological analysis*. Cornell University Press.

Kavolis, V. (1972). *History on art's side; social dynamics in artistic efflorescences*. Cornell University Press.

Kavolis, V. (1986). *Sąmoningumo trajektorijos: lietuvių kultūros modernėjimo aspektai*. Algimanto Mackaus knygų leidimo fondas.

Kavolis, V. (1991). *Epochų signatūros*. Algimanto Mackaus knygų leidimo fondas.

Kavolis, V. (1992). *Moterys ir vyrai lietuvių kultūroje*. Lietuvių kultūros institutas.

Kavolis, V. (1993). *Moralizing cultures*. University Press of America.
Kavolis, V. (1994). *Žmogus istorijoje*. Vaga.
Kavolis, V. (1995a). *Kultūrinė psichologija*. Baltos lankos.
Kavolis, V. (1995b). *Civilization analysis as a sociology of culture*. E. Mellen Press.
Kavolis, V. (1996). *Kultūros dirbtuvė*. Baltos lankos.
Kavolis, V. (1998). *Civilizacijų analizė*. Baltos lankos.
Kraniauskas, L. (2001). *Sociologinio diskurso raida Lietuvoje (1960–2000 m.)*. PhD dissertation: social sciences, sociology. Vilniaus universitetas.
Laurėnas, V. (2017). *Spartėjančios visuomenės politinis režimas. Lietuvos politinės sociologijos studija*. Klaipėda University Press.
Leonavičius, J. (Ed.). (1991). *Sociologija Lietuvoje. Praeitis ir dabartis. D.1*. Kauno technologijos universitetas.
Leonavičius, J. (Ed.). (1992). *Sociologija Lietuvoje, Praeitis ir dabartis. D.2*. Kauno technologijos universitetas.
Leonavičius, J. (Ed.). (1994a). *Sociologija Lietuvoje, Praeitis ir dabartis. D.5, kn.1*. Kauno technologijos universitetas.
Leonavičius, J. (Ed.). (1994b). *Sociologija Lietuvoje, Praeitis ir dabartis. D.5, kn.2*. Kauno technologijos universitetas.
Leonavičius, J. (Ed.). (1996a). *Sociologija Lietuvoje, Praeitis ir dabartis. D.6, kn.1*. Kauno technologijos universitetas.
Leonavičius, J. (Ed.). (1996b). *Sociologija Lietuvoje, Praeitis ir dabartis. D.6, kn.2*. Kauno technologijos universitetas.
Leonavičius, J. (1996c). Sociologija Lietuvos aukštojoje mokykloje tarpukario metais. In J. Leonavičius (Ed.), *Sociologija: praeitis ir dabartis. Tarptautinės konferencijos pranešimų medžiaga. D.6, kn.1* (pp. 164–167). Kauno technologijos universitetas.
Leonavičius, J. (Ed.). (1999). *Sociologija aukštojoje mokykloje*. Kauno technologijos universitetas.
Leonavičius, V. (2002). Sociologijos diskursas ir sociologijos studijos Lietuvos aukštosiose mokyklose. *Filosofija. Sociologija, 1*, 24–29.
Lijphart, A. (1984). *Democracies: Patterns of majoritarian and consensus government in twenty-one countries*. Yale University Press.
Lijphart, A. (1999). *Patterns of democracy: Government forms and performance in thirty-six countries*. Yale University Press.
Matulionis, A. (2011). Lietuvos sociologijos centrų formavimasis ir raida. In A. Bagdonavičienė (Ed.), *Šiuolaikinis mokslas visuomenei: Lietuvos mokslo sektorių apžvalgos, T. 2* (pp. 1–40). Lietuvos mokslų akademija, Lietuvių katalikų mokslo akademija.
Matulionis, A. (2021). *Mano pasaulio žmonių autografai*. Utenos Indra.
Noelle-Neumann, E. (1984). *The spiral of silence: Public opinion, our social skin*. University of Chicago Press.
Norkus, Z. (2012). *On Baltic Slovenia and Adriatic Lithuania. A qualitative comparative analysis of patterns in post-communist transformation*. CEU Press.
Norkus, Z. (2023a). *The great restoration: Post-communist transformations from the viewpoint of comparative historical sociology of restorations* (International comparative social studies, 56). Brill.
Norkus, Z. (2023b). *Post-communist transformations in Baltic countries: A restorations approach in comparative historical sociology*. Springer Nature.
Raudla, R. (2013). Fiscal retrenchment in Estonia during the financial crisis: The role of institutional factors. *Public Administration, 91*(1), 32–50.
Raudla, R., & Kattel, R. (2011). Why did Estonia choose fiscal retrenchment after the 2008 crisis? *Journal of Public Policy, 31*(2), 163–186.
Reinert, E. S., & Kattel, R. (2014). Failed and asymmetrical integration. The Baltics and the non-financial origins of the European crisis. In J. Sommers & C. Woolfson (Eds.), *The contradictions of austerity: The socioeconomic costs of the neoliberal Baltic model* (pp. 64–86). Routledge.

Schmidt, V. A. (2008). Discursive institutionalism: The explanatory power of ideas and discourse. *Annual Review of Political Science, 11*, 303–326.
Schmidt, V. A. (2010). Taking ideas and discourse seriously: Explaining change through discursive institutionalism as the fourth "New Institutionalism". *European Political Science Review, 2*(1), 1–25.
Skovajsa, M., & Balon, J. (2017). *Sociology in The Czech Republic: Between East and West.* Palgrave Macmillan.
Spasić, J., Pešić, J., & Babović, M. (2022). *Sociology in Serbia: A fragile discipline.* Palgrave Macmillan.
Sum, N. L., & Jessop, B. (2015). *Towards a cultural political economy: Putting culture in its place in political economy.* Edward Elgar.
Thorhallsson, B., & Kattel, R. (2013). Neo-liberal small states and economic crisis: Lessons for democratic corporatism. *Journal of Baltic Studies, 44*(1), 83–103.
Titarenko, L., & Zdravomyslova, E. (2017). *Sociology in Russia: A brief history.* Palgrave Macmillan.
Vaicekauskaitė, A. (2013). The features of the history of sociology in Lithuania. *Social Transformations in Contemporary Society, 1*, 223–234. Retrieved July 19, 2023, from https://silo.tips/download/the-features-of-the-history-of-sociology-in-lithuania
Valantiejus, A. (2004). *Kritinis sociologijos diskursas: tarp pozityvizmo ir postmodernizmo.* Vilnius University Press.
Valantiejus, A. (2007a). *Socialinė struktūra: nuo makro prie mikro modelių.* Vilnius University Press.
Valantiejus, A. (2007b). *Sociologijos istorija: teorinės idėjos, problemos ir sąvokos. T.1 Sociologijos filosofija.* Vilnius University Press.
Viliūnas, G. (2004). Literatūros mokslas. In G. Viliūnas (Ed.), *Lietuvos humanitarinių ir socialinių mokslų plėtros problemos* (pp. 177–185). Lithuanian Institute of History Press.
Vosyliūtė, A. (Ed.). (1996). *Iš Lietuvos sociologijos istorijos: straipsnių rinkinys. Kn. 1.* Lietuvos filosofijos ir sociologijos institutas.
Vosyliūtė, A. (Ed.). (1999). *Iš Lietuvos sociologijos istorijos: straipsnių rinkinys. Kn.2.* Lietuvos filosofijos ir sociologijos institutas.
Vosyliūtė, A. (Ed.). (2000). *Iš Lietuvos sociologijos istorijos: straipsnių rinkinys. Kn.3.* Lietuvos filosofijos ir sociologijos institutas.
Vosyliūtė, A. (2001a). Lietuvos sociologijos orientacijos amžiui baigiantis. In A. Vosyliūtė (Ed.), *Lietuvos sociologija amžių sandūroje* (pp. 21–31). Socialinių tyrimų institutas.
Vosyliūtė, A. (2001b). *Lietuvos sociologija amžių sandūroje.* Socialinių tyrimų institutas.
Vosyliūtė, A. (2002). Sociology–Lithuania. In M. Kaase, V. Sparwschuh, & A. Wenninger (Eds.), *Three social science disciplines in Central and Eastern Europe: Handbook on economics, political science and sociology (1989–2001)* (pp. 467–483). Informationszentrum Sozialwissenschaften. Retrieved July 19, 2023, from http://nbn-resolving.de/urn:nbn:de:0168-ssoar-278699
Vosyliūtė, A. (2003a). Lithuanian sociology, 1990–2000. In M. F. Keen & J. Mucha (Eds.), *Eastern Europe in transformation: The impact on sociology* (pp. 97–106). Greenwood Press.
Vosyliūtė, A. (Ed.). (2003b). *Iš Lietuvos sociologijos istorijos: straipsnių rinkinys. Kn. 4.* Lietuvos filosofijos ir sociologijos institutas.
Vosyliūtė, A. (2010). Sociology and society: Towards diversity. In *Nation and language: Modern aspects of socio-linguistic development. Proceedings of the 4th international conference* (pp. 112–118). Technologija. Retrieved July 19, 2023, https://files.eric.ed.gov/fulltext/ED513739.pdf
Voverienė, O. (2009). *Žymieji XX amžiaus Lietuvos mokslininkai.* Mokslo aidai.
Yadov, V. A. (Ed.). (1998). *Sociologiya v Rossii* (2nd ed.). Publishing House of the Sociology Institute of the Russian Academy of Science.
Zabludovski Kuper, G. (2023). *Sociology in Mexico: An intellectual and institutional history.* Palgrave Macmillan.

Zenonas Norkus, PhD (1984), Sankt-Petersburg University (USSR), is a professor of Comparative Historical Sociology at Vilnius University, Lithuania. He was a fellow at the Institute of Advanced Studies, Berlin (1998–1999), and Fulbright research fellow at the Institute of Slavic, East European, and Eurasian Studies at the University of California, Berkeley (2003–2004). His book publications include Max Weber and Rational Choice (2001), Which Democracy, Which Capitalism? Post-communist Transformation in Lithuania from the Viewpoint of Comparative Historical Sociology (2008), On Baltic Slovenia and Adriatic Lithuania (2012), Two Twenty-Year Periods of Independence: Capitalism, Class and Democracy in the First and Second Republics of Lithuania from the Point of View of Comparative Historical Sociology (2014), An Unproclaimed Empire: The Grand Duchy of Lithuania (2018), and The Great Restoration: Post-communist Transformations from the Viewpoint of Comparative Historical Sociology of Restorations (2023).

Vaidas Morkevičius, PhD (2006) in sociology, is a professor at the Faculty of Social Sciences, Arts and Humanities, Kaunas University of Technology, Lithuania. He also works as the coordinator of the Lithuanian Data Archive for Social Sciences and Humanities. His main academic interests are political communication and elite research, social stratification studies, survey research, text analytics, as well as the curation and management of social sciences and humanities data.

Chapter 13
Sociology in Macedonian Society in Transition

Konstantin Minoski and Antoanela Petkovska

> This chapter is prepared based on the paper 'Sociology in Dialogue: Macedonian Sociology In-between Surviving and Internalization' presented at the Fourth ISA Council of National Association Conference held in Taipei, Taiwan, on May 8–11, 2017.

13.1 Introduction

People have always endeavoured to understand the world around them and the changes taking place within it. The Industrial Revolution, as well as the French and October Revolutions, caused major social changes in European societies. Various thinkers have made serious efforts to understand and explain the direction of these 'great transformations' of their economic, political, and social lives (Comte, Spencer, Marx, Durkheim, Weber, and Polanyi). Thus, Jary and Jary (1991, p. 577) have noted that 'if it is true that sociology has always studied the social changes of one or the other in other words, then it is also true to say that sociology itself is a child of social change'. In this context, we can accept the definition that social change is 'the difference between the present and the past state of any chosen aspect of a social organisation or structure, such as family, voting patterns, religious beliefs, economic activity, etc.' (Jary & Jary, 1991, p. 577).

Nowadays, social change can be considered an omnipresent and intense phenomenon: a normal state of contemporary societies. We can understand modern societies as unstable dynamic systems that constantly, or even more precisely, asymptotically, strive to achieve stability. The tendency for stability is reflected through the action of the internal elements of the system but also through the interaction with other, external, similar systems or their elements. Of course, the basic elements of any social system are people, their actions (individually and in groups), and the social forms that occur as a result of their actions (Minoski, 2011, p. 356).

K. Minoski (✉) · A. Petkovska
Institute of Sociology, Faculty of Philosophy—Skopje, Ss. Cyril and Methodius University in Skopje, Skopje, North Macedonia
e-mail: konstantin@fzf.ukim.edu.mk; antoanela@fzf.ukim.edu.mk

© The Author(s), under exclusive license to Springer Nature Switzerland AG 2024
B. Roncevic, T. Besednjak Valič (eds.), *Sociology and Post-Socialist Transformations in Eastern Europe*,
https://doi.org/10.1007/978-3-031-65556-2_13

Social change can manifest in different ways. They can be long-lasting, but they can also be sudden and short-lived social processes. Craig Calhoun distinguishes cumulative social change from the universal, procedural aspect of overall social life. He points out that both sociologists and historians study the latter by focusing on those dynamic processes through which the social lives of certain individuals and groups can change, even though global patterns remain relatively constant. However, individual processes of social life may undergo longer-term transformations. According to Calhoun (1993), 'these transformations in the nature, organisation, or results of the processes themselves are what are commonly studied under the term "social change"' (p. 391). Cumulative social change is one that shapes human social history, for example, the creation of the modern state but also the invention and spread of the handshake as a form of greeting (Calhoun, 1993, p. 391; Minoski, 2011, p. 356).

Some extreme societal changes identified in contemporary societies have recently been researched in social theories and marked with the expression 'social trauma' and 'cultural trauma' (Sztompka, 2004, 2008; Alexander, 2012). It seems it is the case with all the so-called transitional societies (mostly former socialist states), including the Macedonian society after 1991, having a 'transitional' impact on sociology as a social science. To present Macedonian sociology in the transition period, we need to look back in history because the main reasons for its establishment as a science, and even more for the topics that are the subject of the recent sociological research, reflect the social processes that took place on its territory during its history. Thus, we will start with a brief historical overview of events that we consider to be significant.

Large empires and civilisations, as well as smaller kingdoms, were born and disintegrated on its territory from antiquity to the twentieth century, which left a lasting civilisational mark on its development. During the Second World War, the foundations were laid for the establishment of the federation of the Yugoslav peoples (Slovenes, Croats, Serbs, Montenegrins, and Macedonians): the Democratic Federal Yugoslavia in 1943, Federal People's Republic of Yugoslavia in 1945, and the Socialist Federal Republic of Yugoslavia (SFRY) in 1963. This political form lasted until 1991 when four republics seceded (Slovenia, Croatia, Bosnia and Herzegovina, and Macedonia) from SFR Yugoslavia, and the same year saw the start of the military conflicts that lasted 10 days in Slovenia and up to 1995 on the territories of Croatia, Bosnia and Herzegovina, and Serbia. The Republic of North Macedonia managed to gain independence peacefully, but in 2001, a short-lived war broke out, mainly spilling over from Kosovo, which (under external political interference) changed the constitutional character of the country with the well-known Ohrid Framework Agreement.

Saints Cyril and Methodius created the Glagol alphabet; that is, the alphabet was used to translate the Bible and other church books into the language of the Slavs, but it was also used in church schools and for administrative purposes on this territory in the ninth century. This encouraged a civilisational leap towards the emancipation of the Slavic peoples and their own cultural development. On this territory, in Ohrid, the last cathedral before the schism in Christianity was built: St. Sofia. Furthermore, at some point in the tenth century, the Bogomil movement appeared, which soon became not only a critique of the Christian church but also a social movement against feudalism. Kosta Racin describes the Bogomils and their teachings as forerunners of the Enlightenment, that is, 'those rebels from the XVII century, who spoke of a "natural right" of man, of equality of all people, and wanted a "stateless" order of the world' (Racin, 1987, pp. 135–136). One of the most consistently humanistic thoughts expressed in these parts of the world is that of the Macedonian revolutionary Goce Delchev, who said, 'I see the world as a field for cultural competition between nations'. In 1903, as a revolutionary act against the Ottoman Empire, the Krushevo Republic was established (lasting 10 days). The Krushevo Republic and the French Republic were the only republics in Europe at that time.

Macedonia, as a geographical area of exceptional strategic, economic, and political importance, was the target of the political aspirations of the great powers. However, such aspirations especially intensified after the weakening of the political power of the Ottoman Empire in the nineteenth and early twentieth centuries. With the division of the territory of Macedonia between Greece, Bulgaria, Serbia, and in small part Albania, after the Balkan Wars at the Bucharest Peace Conference in 1913, assimilation propaganda became the official policy of these countries, to a greater or lesser extent surviving to this day.

After the conflict with Stalin, the Inform Bureau, and the period of etatism, the era of building a socialist self-governing system (the only one of its kind in the world) began within the Yugoslav federation. During this period, significant progress was made in the fields of economics, culture, education, science, art, and other spheres of social life for a relatively short period of time, and one of the main driving ideas was the 'versatile man' and the development of 'brotherhood and unity'.

The collapse of SFR Yugoslavia and the declaration of independence in 1991 marked the last transitional period of Macedonian society into political pluralism and 'democracy'. Unfortunately, these 'democratic processes' accompanied by the creation of a multi-party political system, and especially the process of privatisation of social capital without fully developing the appropriate institutions that would manage the transition of Macedonian society, did not meet citizens' expectations for the benefits of democracy, causing severe cultural and social trauma in the country.

13.2 Proto-sociological Thought

The development of Macedonian social thought can be traced back in history, in the period of the national renaissance in the nineteenth and early twentieth centuries, with the increased discourse about the uniqueness of the Macedonian people and their cultural features: language, culture, identity, and political autonomy. The first linguists, writers, jurists, self-taught revolutionaries, and historians in their works dealt with topics related to the national identity of the Macedonians but also with other aspects of social life.

For example, we can recognise naïve, intuitive, or proto-sociological thought in the works of Gjorgija Puleski[1] (1817–1893). According to Puleski, 'People who are of the same family (origin), who speak the same language, who live and socialize with each other, who have the same customs, songs, and festivities are what we call a nation and the land where these people live can be called their fatherland. Thus, the Macedonians are a nation, and their land is called Macedonia' (Puleski, 1875, p. 49).

Another important figure from the late nineteenth and early twentieth centuries is Krste Petkov Misirkov (1874–1926). Rightfully, some historians, philologists, and other representatives of the social sciences and humanities in Macedonia consider him one of the most important Macedonian figures of the twentieth century as well as the most complete Macedonian Slavist with a wide range of scientific interests (Ristovski, 1991, p. 43).[2]

Misirkov (1903), in his most important work, *On Macedonian Affairs*,[3] elaborates on the position of the Macedonian people in the context of the political, economic, and cultural situation in Macedonia and the Balkans at that time. In the last part of the book entitled *A Few Words on the Macedonian Literary Language*, Misirkov proposes the formation of a standard literary Macedonian language based on the central dialects. Of great importance is the fact that Misirkov uses the alphabet that is the basis for today's Macedonian Cyrillic alphabet. Analysing the situation in the Balkans in 1903, when referring to the Macedonian literary language, Misirkov clearly expresses his opinion that the Macedonians should give up the spring uprising and start a new cultural struggle prioritising the issue of nationality and national-religious development. Language, national literature, and national education were to be considered important (Misirkov, 1903, p. 133). In his analysis of the social, political, and cultural processes in the Balkans concerning the national and cultural emancipation of the Macedonian people, he approaches his topic studiously by applying an appropriate scientific methodology in the argumentation of his views, allowing his works to abound in sociological elements. We concur with Tasheva's (2021) standpoint:

> Misirkov had fully accepted the theses of the modernist theory of the nation—that the nation is a modern phenomenon, conditioned by the needs of the modern organization of a

---

[1] Gjorgija Puleski (1817–1893) was a self-taught revolutionary leader, poet, historian, ethnographer, textbook writer, and grammarian.

[2] Krste Petkov Misirkov (1874–1926) is considered to be the most complete Macedonian Slavist with a wide range of scientific interests, codifier of the modern Macedonian literary language and orthography, author of the first book *On Macedonian Affairs* (1903) and the first academic literary magazine published in the modern Macedonian literary language *Vardar* (1905), the first national philologist, historian, ethnographer, folklorist and publicist, revolutionary, and national activist (Ristovski, 1991, p. 43). He lived and was educated at a time when Greek, Bulgarian, and Serbian propaganda were the strongest in Macedonia, where they often clashed competing for greater influence.

[3] Misirkov published his most important work, the book *On Macedonian Affairs* in Sofia in 1903 (printed at the so-called Liberal Club).

society, including the inevitability of establishing mechanisms for providing its unity. (p. 407–408)

13.2.1 The Beginnings

The beginnings of sociological science in Macedonia can be traced to the 1920s and 1930s, when Macedonia was a part of the Kingdom of Yugoslavia. In 1920, the Faculty of Philosophy was established in Skopje as part of the University of Belgrade. According to Petre Georgievski, in the 1930s, sociology became part of the curriculum of the Department of Philosophy. He quotes Boris Arsov's statement, published in the newspaper *Vardar* from June 26, 1936, that a sociology course was taught by 'the great scientist and professor Prvosh Slankamenac at the Faculty of Philosophy and that so far several generations of students had had the opportunity to be educated in this young science' (Georgievski, 2005, p. XV).

Georgievski points out that Boris Arsov (1906–1954) was the first Macedonian sociologist. He completed his doctoral dissertation entitled 'The Economic Life of Macedonia in the XIX Century' at Sorbonne University in Paris in 1936. The thesis was published in the edition 'Publication contemporariness France-Balkans: Paris'. The focus of his research was the problem of the peasants in Macedonia and the Balkans and their position in the social structure (Georgievski, 2005, p. XV; 2012, p. 76).

The second critically important Macedonian scholar who dealt with sociological issues, especially the analysis of national issues in Macedonia, the Balkans, and Europe, was Kosta Veselinov (1908–1942), although he worked and lived in a different social environment.[4] In 1938, he founded the National Scientific Library 'K'lbo' (Globe) and authored the book *National Enslaved Peoples and National Minorities* (scientific sociological essay). In 1939, he published the book *The Rebirth of Macedonia (Ilinden)*, and in 1940, he published the booklet *Fighters for the People's Freedom* (Veselinov, 1938; Ristovski, 1990, p. 458, 2009, p. 269).

In its beginnings, sociology was born from the attempt to explain mainly two essential social problems: social inequality and the disadvantageous position of the peasantry in the social structure and the actualisation of the national question about the uniqueness of Macedonians and the need for the formation (restoration) of an independent Macedonian state.

---

[4] Kosta Veselinov (1908–1942) mainly lived and worked in Bulgaria.

13.2.2 Macedonian Sociology in SFR Yugoslavia

In 1948, after Tito and Stalin parted ways, the Socialist Federative Republic of Yugoslaviac (SFRY) split from the Stalinist ideology of the USSR. As early as 1950, workers' self-government was being introduced in the economy, and from 1952, it continued to be introduced in the government. Such reforms in the economic and political governance of former Yugoslavia allowed the emergence and recognition of sociology as a social science that would contribute to a scientific approach to building a new self-governing socialism (Petroska, 1985, p. 193; Nikodimovski, 1985, p. 218).

Studies in sociology were first established in 1959 at the Faculty of Philosophy in Belgrade and a year later in Zagreb and Ljubljana (Georgievski, 2012, pp. 96–97).

After Second World War, Macedonia became a federal unit of SFR Yugoslavia. Sociology was considered a bourgeois science and was banned due to ideological reasons from 1946 (when the Faculty of Philosophy in Skopje was reinstated with teaching in the Macedonian language) until the end of the 1950s (when dogmatic Stalinism was the dominant ideology in socialist countries).

Instead of sociology, other subjects considered part of orthodox Marxist doctrine were taught, such as dialectical materialism and historical materialism, along with political economy. A 'Foundations of Marxism' course was introduced in numerous faculties. At the Faculty of Philosophy in Skopje, the Department of Marxism was established in 1977/1978, despite the presence of a Study Group for Philosophy and Sociology (Kepeska, 2003, p. 502).

Slavko Milosavlevski was the first to teach a course in sociology at the Faculty of Law at UKIM in Skopje from 1961 to 1974 and published the first textbook in sociology: *Introduction to Sociology* (Georgievski, 2014).

In 1965, Blaga Petroska (one of the dominant figures in Macedonian sociology and one of the founders of the Institute of Sociology at the Faculty of Philosophy—Skopje) became the first doctor of sociological sciences in the Republic of Macedonia within SFR Yugoslavia at the Faculty of Philosophy in Skopje.

Sociology studies were established in 1975/1976 at the Faculty of Philosophy in Skopje (Study Group and later Institute of Sociology). Previously, in post-war Macedonia, sociology courses were taught at the Faculties of Philosophy, Law, Economics, Natural Sciences, and other faculties.

The most prominent sociologists in this period were Slavko Milosavlevski (1928–2012), Blaga Petroska (1931–2021), Desanka Miljovska (1918–2013), and Petre Georgievski (b. 1940).

Slavko Milosavlevski[5] criticised the official political ideology in his works from the 1960s and 1970s, including *Revolution and Democracy* (1967), *Election System*

---

[5] Born near Tetovo in 1928, Slavko Milosavlevski completed his undergraduate studies at the Faculty of Law in Skopje in 1957. He then pursued a graduate degree at the Department of Political Science at the Institute of Social Sciences in Belgrade until 1960. In 1961/1962, he studied at the University Institute of European Studies in Turin, where he was introduced to the ideas of

and Elective Democracy in Practice (1968), *Revolution and Antirevolution* (1972), and his doctoral dissertation, 'The League of Communists of Yugoslavia in the System of Socialist Democracy in Yugoslavia', which he defended at the Faculty of Law in Skopje in 1965. He also implemented and developed progressive ideas of Eurocommunism, which he became familiar with during the academic year of 1961/1962 while studying at the Institute of European Studies at the University of Turin.

Milosavlevski's *Introduction to Sociology* was published in 1967 and became a textbook for students studying at the Faculty of Law in Skopje. The book aimed to go beyond the simplistic interpretation of Marxist thought and offered a comprehensive overview of social thought from ancient times to the rise of Marxism. It covered a variety of topics, such as the characteristics of nations, the specificities of European nations, and Yugoslavia's national question. The book also delved into political and legal aspects, cultural aspects, economic aspects, and national minorities, along with theoretical elaborations by the author (Minoski, 2014, p. 51). He co-initiated the establishment of the Institute for Sociological, Political, and Juridical Research.

Desanka Miljovska[6] was appointed Full Professor of General Sociology at the Faculty of Philosophy in Skopje (where she was also the Dean from 1963 to 1965) in 1970. She participated in study visits in Paris from 1954 to 1955 and in Boston from 1962 to 1963, where she became acquainted with the methods of sociological research. She has published over 50 scientific papers in sociology and Macedonian history (Kantardziev et al., 1976, p. 76). Miljovska was mostly focused on researching the economic foundations of the social structure of Macedonian towns in the second half of the nineteenth century. Finally, more general conclusions are given about the character of the economic-social changes that the Macedonian towns went through in the second half of the nineteenth century (Miljovska, 1963, pp. 51–52).

Blaga Petroska[7] received her doctorate in Sociological Sciences after she defended her thesis on 'Family Types in the Tetovo Region (Polog)' in 1965 at the

---

Eurocommunism and the Italian Socialist Party of Pietro Nenni. Milosavlevski actively participated in the National Liberation War from 1941 and was a long-time member of the Communist Party of Macedonia (and Yugoslavia). He held senior political positions in the Republic of Macedonia (and SFR Yugoslavia) but was compelled to resign from all political positions in the League of Communist of Macedonia (and Yugoslavia) in 1974 due to his 'liberal' Marxist political beliefs that were in opposition to the official political ideology. He was subsequently 'expelled' from academia and remained excommunicated and isolated until the early 1990s when the process of political pluralism and secession from the Yugoslav federation began. Milosavlevski passed away in 2012.

[6] Desanka (Desa) Miljovska (1918–2013) was born in Prizren. She enrolled in the pedagogical programme at the Faculty of Philosophy in Skopje in 1937 and graduated from the Faculty of Philosophy in Belgrade after the Second World War in 1948. She acquired a doctorate on 'Class forces of the national revolutionary movement of the Macedonian people in the second half of 19th century' in 1962 at the Faculty of Philosophy in Belgrade. She was the President of the Education Council of the People's Republic of Macedonia (PRM) and the President of the Culture Council of the PRM.

[7] Blaga Petroska (1931–2021) completed her primary and secondary education in her native town Bucharest where she started her university studies. She continued her studies and graduated from

Faculty of Philosophy in Skopje. It was the first doctoral thesis in sociological sciences that had been defended in Macedonia. In 1976, she became a full professor in the field of general sociology. Her academic and research interest was in the field of general sociology, sociology of the family, as well as sociological aspects of women's issues in Macedonian society (Mladenovski, 2013, pp. 8–12).

Petre Georgievski (1940) is also one of the founders of the Institute of Sociology at the Faculty of Philosophy in Skopje. He graduated from the Faculty of Philosophy in Belgrade in 1965 and received his master's degree in 1971 and doctorate in 1981 at the Institute for Sociological, Political, and Juridical Research in Skopje (Kantardziev et al., 1976, p. 76). On several occasions, he was the head of the Institute of Sociology and was also Vice-Dean and Dean of the Faculty of Philosophy in Skopje. He taught the basics of Marxism, sociology, methodology of sociological research, and sociology of education. He participated in a dozen research projects (as a researcher or as a project manager) on topics related to the social structure and mobility in the Republic of Macedonia, as well as topics related to educational issues. He retired in 2006.

Some sociology professors taught at other faculties or worked in research institutions before joining the Faculty of Philosophy or other universities. The Institute for Sociological, Political, and Juridical Research in Macedonia hired few sociologists with undergraduate degrees in sociology, leading to limited employment opportunities in related fields. Since its establishment, Macedonian sociology was integrated into SFR Yugoslavia through participation in international scientific conferences and congresses organised by the Yugoslav Association of Sociology, publishing papers in Yugoslav sociological journals, like *Sociology* and *The Sociological Review*, and participating in sociological research conducted at the federal level in Yugoslavia. Additionally, Yugoslav sociologists participated in conferences organised by the Institute of Sociology at the Faculty of Philosophy (Georgievski, 2012, pp. 108–109).

13.3 Establishing Academic Studies in Sociology and the Profession of Sociologist

Along with the academic and institutional establishment of sociology in the 1960s, incentives for the scientific research of sociologists were made, and social research institutes were founded in Belgrade, Ljubljana, and Zagreb.

Given the need to create research staff in the field of sociology and political science in Macedonia, an Institute for Sociological, Political, and Juridical Research

---

the Faculty of Philosophy in Skopje in 1954. Her academic career began at the Faculty of Philosophy in Skopje in 1956 as an assistant lecturer. On several occasions, she was the Head of the Institute of Sociology and Dean of the Faculty of Philosophy in Skopje. She retired in 1996. She was a member of the SFR Yugoslavia Parliament and was the author of a TV series on the most influential woman in the political life of SFR Yugoslavia.

was established. It started working in the 1967/1968 academic year and was involved in academic research implemented at the Yugoslav level in the field of sociology and political science (Georgievski, 2012, pp. 96–97; Borota Popovska et al., 2015, pp. 7–8).

At the institute, research was directed towards the study of social structures, transformations of the village, employment conflicts, social background of high school youth, religion and religiousness of the rural population, electoral systems in Macedonia and England, and class being in the Yugoslav society, among other topics.

Several years later, it became possible to establish a university level of education in sociology in Macedonia. Sociologists in Macedonia were inspired by recent sociological research and by the already-established studies in sociology in almost all republics of former SFR Yugoslavia. Georgievski notes that taking into consideration the experience from Belgrade, Zagreb, and Ljubljana, where the sociological studies were established at the faculties of philosophy, but also because of the engagement of the sociologists that were part of the faculties, the decision was made that the studies in sociology should be established at the Faculty of Philosophy. First, in 1973, the Department of Sociology was established at the Faculty of Philosophy to create conditions for starting undergraduate studies in sociology (Georgievski, 1978, pp. 100–101).[8]

13.3.1 Institute for Sociological, Political, and Juridical Research at Ss. Cyril and Methodius University in Skopje

In 1965, the University Council of 'Ss. Cyril and Methodius' University in Skopje established the Institute for Sociological, Political, and Juridical Research (ISPJR) with the objective: 'to scientifically study the sociological, political and legal phenomena in the country, to encourage and organise the study of issues from a sociological, political and legal aspect, to develop and improve the research methods in social sciences' and other research-related and educational activities (Borota Popovska et al., 2015, p. 8).

In the beginning, the institute established two scientific research divisions: for sociological and political research. The research work in the Division for Sociological Research was organised into several scientific groups, for example, general sociology, rural sociology, sociology of the city, sociology of culture, social pathology, and scientific research methodology (Borota Popovska et al., 2015, p. 12). The expertise and the activities of the institute created the need for the formation of new scientific research organisational units: the Centre for Human Resource Management; the Centre for Ethnic Relations; the Centre for Applied Policy and Public

---

[8] The members of the Department were Desanka Miljovska, Blaga Petroska, and Petre Georgievski, and they had to provide teaching, create curricula, and establish a library, among others.

Administration; the Centre for Criminology; the Centre for Communications, Media and Culture; and the Centre for Human Rights (Borota Popovska et al., 2015, p. 13). The institute developed its research activities in several scientific fields: sociology, political science, law, organisational sciences (management), communication, and a number of interdisciplinary research areas (Borota Popovska et al., 2015, p. 13).

Since 1967, the institute organised postgraduate studies in sociological and political sciences. Research and education (postgraduate and doctoral studies) are the two main activities of the institute. Since 2011, the Institute for Sociological, Political and Legal Research has been organising third-cycle study programmes: doctoral studies in the field of social sciences, in the following fields: democracy in the context of globalisation, organisational sociology, environmental sociology, as well as organisational sciences and management, in cooperation with the Faculty of Economics—Skopje and the Institute of Economics—Skopje (Borota Popovska et al., 2015, pp. 15–16). The Institute cooperates with several other scientific, educational, and other institutions in Macedonia and abroad.

Currently, at the ISPJR, several sociologist professors are working in the field of sociology.[9]

13.3.2 Institute of Sociology at the Faculty of Philosophy at the Ss. Cyril and Methodius University in Skopje

The Institute of Sociology was established in 1973 as a Study Group in Sociology at the Faculty of Philosophy in Skopje. In October 1975, undergraduate studies in sociology began for the first time in Macedonia. The establishment of the Institute of Sociology (at that time the Study Group for Sociology) at the Faculty of Philosophy in Skopje and, thus, the institutionalisation of sociology in Macedonia were achieved with a special contribution from distinguished colleagues Desanka Miljoska, Blaga Petroska, who was also the first Head of the Institute of Sociology, and Georgievski. Tasheva, M. and Mladenovski, Gj. (then a teaching assistants) were the implementers of the first curriculum of sociology, also (Petroska, 1985, p. 58; Mladenovski, 1996, p. 99).

The curriculum in sociology was a result of the effort of the teaching staff (from the beginning of the studies in 1975/1976 until today, 2023) to remain acquainted with the newest achievements in sociology and other social sciences and to implement them in research and teaching. Various modules were introduced and removed from the curriculum in sociology, primarily due to the problems with the employment of sociologists. It is important to emphasise that because of the need to harmonise the Macedonian higher education system with the European environment, in the academic year 2004/2005, 4-year undergraduate studies in sociology by the

---

[9] Jorde Jakimovski, Emilija Simoska, Petar Atanasov, Slavejko Sasajkovski, Ruzica Cacanovska, and Ganka Samoilova Cvetanovska.

European Credit Transfer System (ECTS) were introduced. This programme brought back sociologists for research and education, but now also for responding to the challenge of the European integration processes and the cultural processes, which are becoming increasingly visible in the process of transition of Macedonian society. Upon completion of the studies, in addition to the diploma for completed studies, students could have received a diploma supplement that describes narrower specialisations (Mladenovski, 2006, p. 121; Georgievski, 2012, p. 100; Minoski, 2020, pp. 299–300).

The most radical and rather ambitious curriculum was developed at the Institute of Sociology in 2017. The first-cycle studies last 4 years or eight semesters, have 240 ECTS credits and were organised into six modules: population and sustainable development, policy and communications, European integration, research and analysis, culture, and sociology of ethnic groups, and the final exam is the defence of a diploma thesis (Mladenovski, 1996, pp. 95, 98; 2006, p. 121; Minoski, 2020, pp. 299, 303–304). In contrast, there is an effort to respond to the challenges arising from the dramatic social changes that have affected the whole world and Macedonia and to educate staff that will successfully deal with these new challenges. Highly qualified staff is being developed to be ready to work in education, science, culture, social services, public administration, and civil society, as well as in other institutions and organisations in the private sector.

The need for a second cycle of studies (i.e. master's studies) at the Institute of Sociology was recognised in the 1980/1981 academic year, but due to the lack of teaching and scientific staff, they could not have been introduced until 1992. Thus, at the beginning of 1992, the Institute of Sociology at the Faculty of Philosophy in Skopje introduced a 2-year magisterium study programme in sociology[10] (Master of Arts in Sociology) (Mladenovski, 1996, pp. 101–102; 2006, p. 123; Georgievski, 2012, p. 103; Minoski, 2020, p. 305). The students acquired a degree in Magister in Sociological Sciences after defending their magisterium thesis. After introducing the European Credit Transfer System, the second cycle became 1 year (two semesters for 60 ECTS credits). Today, students can choose between three offered modules: Culture and Religion, Economics and Human Resources Development, and Modern Macedonian Society. The final exam is the preparation and defence of a magisterium (master's) thesis, which gives the student the title of Magister (master's) in Sociological Sciences. The main goal of these studies is for students to expand and deepen their knowledge in certain narrower areas of sociological research or disciplines close to sociology.

The final exam is the preparation and defence of a master's thesis, which gives the student the title of Master in Sociological Sciences.

European Integration Studies is another second-cycle study offered by the Institute of Sociology. These interdisciplinary studies were introduced in 2001 as 2-year (four semesters) European studies in Integration and Communication. Since

---

[10] Thus far, more than 229 students have received a master's degree in the two study programmes of the second cycle of studies: in Sociology and European Integration Studies at the Institute of Sociology at the Faculty of Philosophy in Skopje (Minoski, 2020, p. 307).

the introduction of the European Credit Transfer System, these studies last 1 year (two semesters) and have 60 ECTS credits. Students acquire the title of Master in European Integration Studies after a successful defence of the master's thesis. Since the beginning, the purpose of these studies has been to form highly educated staff with in-depth knowledge of the European Union and its institutions. Particular attention has been paid to the economic, political, security, and cultural institutions of the European Union, which are extremely important given the Macedonian strategic commitment to membership in the European Union (Mladenovski, 2006, pp. 123–124; Minoski, 2020, p. 306).

The doctoral studies in sociology offered by the Institute of Sociology are an integral part of the School for Doctoral Studies at St. Cyril and Methodius University. School for Doctoral Studies was established on December 1, 2011, and replaced the previous practice of studying and preparing a doctoral thesis solely with mentoring. These third-cycle sociology studies typically last 3 years and are worth 180 ECTS credits. Once completed, students will receive a Doctor of Social Sciences degree in Sociology. To date, 66 doctoral candidates have successfully completed their doctoral dissertations at the Institute of Sociology and St. Cyril and Methodius University's School for Doctoral Studies (Minoski, 2020, pp. 306–307).

Colleagues[11] from the 'Ss. Cyril and Methodius' University and other units of the Faculty of Philosophy in Skopje were involved in teaching sociology. It is important to note that professors from the University of Belgrade[12] contributed to the teaching activities of the Institute of Sociology and its development (Mladenovski, 1996, p. 99; 2006, p. 122; Georgievski, 2012, pp. 102–103; Minoski, 2020, p. 307).

Previously, the activities of the members of the Institute of Sociology had not focused solely on teaching but, to a considerable extent, on research and applied activities. These activities resulted in several scientific papers being published in academic journals, academic yearbooks, various national and international conference proceedings, special monographs, translations, and others, according to the scientific interest of the members of the Institute of Sociology. Along with university textbooks, some of the members of the Institute of Sociology published textbooks for courses in primary and secondary education.

The research activities at the Institute of Sociology started immediately following its establishment at the Faculty of Philosophy in Skopje. It is noted that since 1980, the institute has appeared as a participant in research projects that sought to investigate and explain the social life and changes that occurred in Macedonia but also in Yugoslavia, Europe, and other societies. At that time, the members of the

---

[11] Dr Lazar Nikodimovski, Dr Ljupco Arnaudovski, Dr Jakim Sinadinovski, Dr Stefan Kostovski, Dr Vlado Popovski, and Dr Jorde Jakimovski. Many colleagues from the Institutes of Philosophy, History, Psychology, Pedagogy, Social Work and Social Policy, Security, Defense and Peace Study, History of Art and Archaeology, and Gender Studies, from the Faculty of Philosophy—Skopje, participated in teaching courses in their academic disciplines in order to supplement and enrich the knowledge of sociology students from related disciplines.

[12] Prof. d-r Vladimiri Milic, Prof. d-r Vladimir Milanovic, as well as Prof. d-r Aleksandar Todorovic and Prof. Vladimir Nesic.

institute participated in research projects organised or conducted by fellow sociologists from other universities in the former SFR Yugoslavia, as well as in international projects (Mladenovski, 1996, p. 101; 2006, p. 124; Georgievski, 2012, pp. 103–104). We would like to mention some of the projects led by Blaga Petroska: 'Low and high birth rate among the Macedonian population—continuity or change' and 'Some aspects of the family life of Macedonians who immigrated to Canada (Toronto)'.

The members of the Institute of Sociology participated in the Macedonian Academy of Sciences and Arts (MANU) project for developing terminological dictionaries in the Macedonian language. These activities were coordinated by Blaga Petroska, and other participants from the Institute in the multi-year project were Marija Tasheva, Ilija Aceski, Jovan Korubin, Nelko Stojanovski, Antoanela Petkovska, Ilo Trajkovski, Eleonora Kalajlieva, and Vasil Pluskovski. Many young sociologists[13] were engaged in the realisation of the research project. The final output was the *Dictionary of Sociological Terminology*, published for the first time in the Macedonian language by the Institute of Sociology, the Faculty of Philosophy, and MANU.

To date, the Institute of Sociology has realised several research projects of fundamental importance for Macedonian science and society, including 'Sociological aspects of ethnic coexistence in the Republic of Macedonia' (1993–1998, led by Marija Tasheva), 'The problems faced by emigrants from Macedonia–the family life of Macedonian emigrants in Canada and their ethnic identity' (1995–1996, led by Blaga Petroska), 'Changes in the social structure in the Republic of Macedonia with special focus on higher education' (1995–1998, led by Petre Georgievski), 'Macedonian society in transition' (1995–1997, led by Ilija Aceski), 'Drug abuse and other psychotropic substances in Macedonia' (led by Nelko Stojanovski, 1999–2002), 'Children and youth development/basic youth trends' (2001–2003, headed by Antoanela Petkovska), 'European values among the citizens of the Republic of Macedonia' (2010–2012, led by Antoanela Petkovska), as well as the international research projects 'Innovative Sociology. Transformation of the Societies in South-East Europe' (1999–2004, led by Jovan Korubin) and 'European Values Study' (2008–2012, 2017, led by Antoanela Petkovska).

An important aspect of the research activities is sharing research experience and conference participation on national and international levels. Some of the conferences were organised by the Institute of Sociology, and some were arranged in cooperation with other academic institutions and attended by fellow sociologists from the country and abroad. Gjorgje Mladenovski noted that the first scientific conference was held in 1984 in Skopje on the topic 'Sociology and economy' (Mladenovski, 1996, p. 102). The conferences that followed were 'Durkheim and

---

[13] Some of the students were in the final years of undergraduate studies; some of them were graduate sociologists, as well as postgraduate students and doctoral students. For some of them, this was the first time to be involved in the practical application of methodological and theoretical knowledge, some expanded the experiences gained during their postgraduate and doctoral studies, and some worked on their master's and doctoral theses.

contemporary sociology' held on October 8–9, 1998, in Skopje; 'Max Weber: Understanding the changes in modern society' held on November 23–24, 2000, at the Faculty of Philosophy in Skopje for the 25th anniversary of the Institute of Sociology at the Faculty of Philosophy in Skopje; 'Contemporary American Sociology: Robert K. Merton in focus' held on October 7–8, 2004, at the Faculty of Philosophy in Skopje; 'Sociology and social change–30 years of studies in sociology at the Faculty of Philosophy in Skopje' held on November 18–19, 2005, in Skopje; 'Sociology and the challenges of the global age: 35 years of the Institute of Sociology—80th Birthday of Professor Blaga Petroska' held on June 13–15, 2011, in Skopje and Ohrid; 'Facing social trauma: A challenge for sociological research 40 Years of the Institute of Sociology' held on April 23–24, 2015, at the Faculty of Philosophy in Skopje for the 40th anniversary of the establishment of the Institute of Sociology; and 'The new challenges of the sociological imagination (in honour of Charles Wright Mills 1916–2016)' held on November 25–26, 2016, at the Faculty of Philosophy in Skopje organised with the Association of Sociologists of the Republic of Macedonia.

It should be noted that this conference was also attended by eminent sociologists and the main speakers were Frank Velz, from the University of Innsbruck, President of the European Sociological Association, Sari Hanafi from the American University of Beirut, Lebanon, Vice-President (current President) of the International Sociological Association, and Professor Gerard Delanty of the University of Sussex, UK (Mladenovski, 1996, p. 102; Georgievski, 2012, pp. 112–113; Minoski, 2020, pp. 311–312). Some texts from conferences have been published in the peer-reviewed journal *The Sociological Review* since 1994, while others have been published in special conference proceedings.[14]

In 1978, the Jagiellonian University Institute of Sociology in Krakow and the NNSG for Sociology at the Faculty of Philosophy in Skopje (UKIM) established a cooperation to organise biannual sociological seminars in Skopje and Krakow[15] (Georgievski, 2012, p. 109). The seminars covered various topics related to sociology and social life, including industrialisation, urbanisation, socialism, self-government, socio-economic and cultural changes, transition, European integration, and identity issues. A total of 12 seminars have been held thus far (Georgievski, 2012, pp. 110–111; Mladenovski, 2006, p. 102; Minoski, 2020, pp. 312–313). The Institute of Sociology collaborated with the Department of Sociology of the Faculty of Philosophy in Sofia on the 'Innovative Sociology. Transformation of the Societies from South-Eastern Europe' project (1999–2004), which was led by Georgi D. Dimitrov from the Department of Sociology (later Department of European Studies) at the Faculty of Philosophy at Sofia University Kliment Ohridski and Jovan Korubin from the Institute of Sociology at the Faculty of Philosophy—Skopje

---

[14] The Association of Sociologists of the Republic of Macedonia founded *The Sociological Review* in 1994, and the Institute of Sociology has been a co-publisher since 2010.

[15] This cooperation was established in 1978 on the initiative of Vladislav Kwasniewicz, Director of the Jagiellonian University Institute of Sociology in Krakow in collaboration with Petre Georgievski, Head of the NNSG for Sociology at the Faculty of Philosophy in Skopje.

(Ss. Cyril and Methodius University in Skopje). The project involved professors and students from both institutions who participated in guest lectures and coordinated joint students' educational research activities. An important outcome of the project was the book *Innovative Sociology* (Иновативна Социология), edited by Georgi D. Dimitrov and published in 2007 by St. Kliment Ohridski University Press in Bulgarian, with the participation of some faculty members from both institutions.

It is important to mention the Institute of Sociology at the Faculty of Philosophy—Skopje's cooperation with Tilburg University's Department of Sociology for the European Values Study (EVS). The institute joined the project during the fourth survey wave in 2008 and later became a full member in the fifth wave from 2017 to 2020. The National EVS team has had a productive working relationship with Tilburg University and the EVS consortium, which organises workshops and conferences annually on comparative analysis of the survey results.[16] The Faculty of Philosophy also signed an Erasmus Agreement with Tilburg University, and the Institute of Sociology has cooperated with other universities[17] as part of the Erasmus Student and Teaching Mobility Program.

Today the Institute of Sociology consists of nine members/nine full professors: Antoanela Petkovska, Mileva Gjurovska, Zoran Matevski, Vesna Dimitrievska, Ilo Trajkovski, Anica Dragovic, Konstantin Minoski, Marija Drakulevska-Chukalevska, and Tatjana Stojanovska Ivanova. Retired professors participate in the third-cycle studies: Marija Tasheva, Amalija Jovanovich, and previously Petre Georgievski, Gjorgje Mladenovski, Nelko Stojanoski, and Ilija Aceski.

13.3.3 Sociology at Other Higher Education Institutions in Macedonia

The Institute of Sociology at the Faculty of Philosophy in Skopje and ISPJR have produced specialists who conduct sociological research and education in various higher education institutions, including private ones. Approximately 20 accredited higher education institutions in North Macedonia now offer sociology courses.[18]

---

[16] The National EVS research team (Prof. Antoanela Petkovska, National Project Manager, Prof. Ilo Trajkovski, Prof. Konstantin Minoski, Prof. Mihajlo Popovski from the Institute of Psychology, Prof. Aleksandar Jovanoski from the University St. Kliment Ohridski Bitola', Bitola, and d-r Marija Dimitrovska former Ph.D. student at the Institute, now a Ph.D. in Sociology) has a fruitful working cooperation with Prof. Loek Halman, Prof. Ruud Luijkx, and other members of the Secretariat of EVS.

[17] The Pantheon University in Athens, Greece, the Institute of Sociology of the Faculty of Social Sciences at the University of Ljubljana, the Department of Sociology of the Faculty of Philosophy at the University of Novi Sad, the Department of Sociology at Tilburg University, and others.

[18] Sociology is taught at the Institute of Sociology at the Faculty of Philosophy, Ss. Cyril and Methodius University in Skopje, at all levels (undergraduate, master's, and doctoral studies), and at the Institute of Sociological, Political and Juridical Research (master's and doctoral studies). They are also taught at the Faculty of Philosophy of the State University in Tetovo.

13.4 The Transition Period: The Recent State of Affairs

Balkan societies are undergoing a process of transition from socialism to capitalism, or rather to democracy. There are opposing opinions on whether the transition is complete or remains ongoing. In our opinion, the transition process in Macedonian society is still ongoing and, accompanied by the EU integration process, seems like a 'never-ending story'.

The transition process started with high enthusiastic energy and trust in the forthcoming democracy and well-being to be achieved with the support of the trusted 'mentors' (i.e. EU, USA, IMF, and World Bank) that were the main advisors for the political and economic transformation of the society.

In fact, what happened with the idea of transition was an evident development of authoritarianism. Instead of the expected reforms in line with the progress of political organisations, state institution services, economic development and growth, education and science, culture, and civil society organisations, we are facing unemployment, increased crime rates, high corruption, increased poverty, politicised civil society organisations, 'governed' non-governmental organisations, eroded educational and healthcare system, partisan state and public institutions, and a politicised judiciary system, among other issues. Thus, our society has transformed into an anomic one, with a governing elite with very low (or better to say without) responsibility and a political system qualified as an authoritarian regime. This kind of transformation resulted in a certain disorientation and anomie in the social values area that affected ordinary people's increasing distrust, apathy, and nostalgia (i.e. retro-socialistic values). The main side effect is an increased rate of youth emigration (brain drain) but also emigration of skilled workers.

The social changes that took place in our country after the disintegration of Yugoslavia and with the return of the sovereignty of the Republic of North Macedonia affected, to a great extent, all aspects of social life. The radical changes occurred in the social organisation, most apparently in the change of the political system into a democratic and multi-party one, the process of the privatisation of social ownership, the pluralisation of the mass media, and so on. The processes of democratisation of society became the primary goal of both political parties coming out of the reformation of the former League of Communists and other socio-political organisations and of the newly created political parties. Parallel with these processes, ethnic and religious differences in Macedonian society came to the foreground as an outcome of its ethnic composition, and all this was charged with the

---

Various courses are taught at 'University St. Kliment Ohirdski Bitola, the Goce Delcev University in Stip, the University of Information Science and Technology 'St. Paul the Apostole' in Ohrid, University American College Skopje, FON University in Skopje, International Slavic University 'G.R. Derzavin' Sv. Nikole—Bitola, and Southeast European University in Tetovo/ BUS Balkan University (list of professors teaching sociology in other university institution, outside the Faculty of Philosophy: Emilija Simoska, Ganka Samoilova, Gjorgji Tonovski, Strasko Angelovski, Hasan Jashari, Pere Aslimoski, Zlatko Zoglev, Ljupco Pecijareski, Sase Gerasimoski, Daniela Jakimovska, Ali Pajaziti, Aleksandar Jovanoski, Kire Sharlamanov, and others).

burden of historical circumstances (as well as the traumatic clash of the value systems). Thus, politics becomes an inevitable segment of our daily life, essentially linked to all fields of existence. The turbulent events in Macedonian history have left, to a great extent, their stamp on the relations of the Macedonian nation and state with the neighbouring nations and states, on the relations with Europe and especially on the interethnic relations inside the Macedonian state.

The right of people to self-determination, related to the right of people to live in peace, is excluded at that moment when one tries to separate these two rights from one another. In other words, the former remains within the framework of the humanistic dimension, and the latter within the framework of political pragmatism, explained by the principles of contemporary democracy.

In Western countries (and more recently in post-socialist countries), the focus on individualistic beliefs versus collective values is increasingly pronounced, which is especially evident among young people. As has already been pointed out, the evolution of postmodern society has brought about changes in value systems, and the old values, norms, and rituals were replaced by those of civil society. Instead of two opposing ideologies, a series of small ideologies and movements of different provenance emerged but tended to fit into the universal world ideology of civic culture, carried out by the meticulous methods of cultural imperialism of economically and militarily superior civilisations in the modern world (Petkovska, 2009, p. 166).

The fall of socialism and the disappearance of the 'iron curtain' between the two worlds imposed a sense of a historical turning point and a sense of breaking the modernist paradigm. The information age, or the age of the rule of knowledge, has caused the most concrete restructuring of the world with the greatest impact on young people and their life determinants but generally on all generations affected by the transition (with a sense of 'captivity' between two worlds, one known and the other full of puzzles and questions about the further destiny and existence). If we have marked above the general framework of paradigm shifts in the existence of individuals and groups in such a world, we can now specify these phenomena or their value syndromes in post-socialist countries (Petkovska, 2009, p. 167).

Again, here, we face our contemporary environment as an age in which politics is a major argument for the change of the social order. As the source of true power, the power of manipulation, hypocrisy, and ambiguity, politics on behalf of designing 'new' civil society and its virtues, such as scientism, technophilia, globalisation, neoliberal economy, and ideological quasi-democracy, permanently and persistently achieves social engineering. The urgent need for a social articulation of a new cultural identity in relation to contemporary existential challenges is again placed under the temptation to change the old 'classical' values with a new, imposed with the politics of cultural imperialism. In reaction to this political and cultural aggressiveness and ethnocentrism of developed countries in the world, new particularistic concepts are born, placed in a position to fight for their own cultural identity, allowing the old, good, historically tested recipe: *divide et impera* (Petkovska, 2009).

The intention of the leading nations that the whole world needs to fit into the 'new world order' is achieved through the newly imposed values of popular culture, mass media, and education. The pursuit of the postmodern culture to 'reconcile' the popular and the high cultures, human rights movements, conflict resolution theories (ethnic, social, racial, gender), building a culture of peace, multiculturalism or interculturalism, civil education, civil democracy, and liberal economy are a result of the modified circumstances and cataclysmic visions for the future of our civilisation, as they are constructed ideological concepts whose ultimate goal is meticulously designed political domination. Marshall McLuhan concluded that the awareness of our era bound to our environment attempts to bridge the values of the old world that is not programmed and the new one that belongs to the sphere of programmed existence. The question which arises again is whether this 'strictly controlled' project is just a vulgar expression of the power of technologically superior civilisations or an ethnocide, which, according to Pier Paolo Pasolini, confronts us with a new, the worst and most repressive totalitarianism, such as the culture of consumption. This culture allows for 'bridging' the cultural, ethnic, class, individual, and gender differences to build a new principle of collectivism vis-à-vis individualism, irrationality, and chaos that lead to new rationality and a new order of things (Gillo Dorfles, 1991): in short, achieving a postmodern society whose unprogrammed and non-conceptual being hides a hard concept of latent authoritarianism (Petkovska, 2009).

Macedonia is a rather complex but distinctive example of a country in a situation to protect and complete its cultural identity and integrity in the context of the coexistence of different cultures while building mechanisms for selection and buffering external influences. Moreover, this position is further complicated by the fact that Macedonia was exposed to several social systems only in this century, which expectedly created a source of conflicts in the sphere of cultural values:

1. Traditional, historically developed mentality, especially regarding existential circumstances
2. Sociorealistic, ideologically and politically constructed and imposed model of thinking and evaluating current social reality, whose main goal is the displacement of the interest and needs of the individual towards the interests and needs of society as a whole, thus camouflaging the inability and unwillingness of the socialist political and economic system to solve the basic problems of the individual
3. Current, contemporary, arising from the needs of today; challenges to our civilisation, driven towards material values and consumer mentality; turning to the world, globalisation of values that have a universal character; information boom; penetration of the postmodern cultural model, tolerance in selecting the values as a response to the repressive mechanisms, especially of contemporary culture, deletion of cultural, national, and state borders, respect for cultural differences as a mode for simultaneously achieving both ethnic and individual integrity and identity; for that purpose re-escalation of ethnic, religious, and cultural conflicts; new more treacherous types of assimilation (Petkovska, 2009)

The resultant conflict between these three value systems is confusion and lack of a clearly defined cultural model burdened by the pressures for self-promotion of the differences and their erroneous articulation in creating the current political interests despite acknowledging historically long, rich, and relevant cultural tradition.

Furthermore, it turns to ethnic and religious features and differences of social groups living on the territory of Macedonia, vis-à-vis the deep economic and existential differences and consequent problems. Building a culture of poverty, on the one hand, and a culture of snobbery, on the other, in conjunction with the uncritical adoption of civic culture virtues beyond the sensibility of the Macedonian national mentality, followed by the need for new types of authoritarianism. Consequently, the disproportion between needs and possibilities, the impact of foreign media cultures, and information about the 'civilised' way of life only deepen the contradictions in the current value system. In this way, Macedonia and many other countries have transformed their social and cultural concept and are facing, in a brutal way, the reality of an eclectic culture or postmodern culture (Petkovska, 2009).

13.5 Sociology and Civic Education in the National Education System

The independence of the Republic of Macedonia brought about changes in the education system, including the introduction of a new worldview and value system among citizens, particularly youth. Civic education was debated in primary and secondary schools, with cooperation from academic institutions and organisations from both Macedonia and abroad.

The Faculty of Philosophy in Skopje, along with the Pedagogical Institute, initiated and implemented a project for civic education. The project manager was Ilo Trajkovski, and it resulted in the collection of texts titled *Civic Education in the Republic of Macedonia: Education for Civil Society—Book I*.

The discussion during the debate showcased a range of opinions regarding the importance and role of civic education in the Macedonian educational system. The course covers various fields of social sciences and humanities, but the majority agreed that it should include predominantly sociological aspects.

The public debate centred on the proposed integration of civil society education in primary and secondary schools in the Republic of Macedonia. Sociologists, historians, philosophers, psychologists, and lawyers all noted the importance of educating young people about modern society, its structure, institutions, and rights, as well as the need for civic participation and social change.

In the next period, sociologists were excluded from teaching the course civic education despite the fact that the course content is fully covered in the curriculum of sociology at the Institute of Sociology of the Faculty of Philosophy in Skopje. The course was introduced in secondary vocational schools and could be taught by other social science and humanities professionals, which diluted its importance in developing democratic tendencies during the transition period.

In the later period, Professors Marija Tasheva and Dimitar Mirchev from the Institute of Sociology at the Faculty of Philosophy in Skopje were involved in the reform of civic education.

However, the recent reforms in the education system, particularly in primary education, have significantly integrated civic education with the history and geography courses, further endangering the status of sociologists in the education process.

13.6 The Role of the Association of the Sociologists of the Republic of Macedonia

The Association of the Sociologists of the Republic of Macedonia promotes sociology in Macedonian society, connects Macedonian sociologists with the international sociological community, and promotes Macedonian sociology abroad. Macedonian sociologists were active members of the Sociological Association of SFRY, founded in 1954. The Macedonian section was established soon after (Petroska, 1985, p. 194). It was re-established after the country's independence in 1990/1991. The association carries out activities related to education, science, publishing, the recognition and improvement of sociologists' status, and the promotion of sociologists in the labour market.

13.7 Contemporary Conditions: Instead of a Conclusion

There have been many debates about the competencies and position of sociologists in society since the institutionalisation of sociology in former Yugoslavia. The 'struggle' to position the profession on the 'labour market' in Macedonian society has continued since 1991. To improve this problem, a letter was sent to public institutions, NGOs, and businesses in April 2010, detailing the competencies of graduate sociologists to include the profile of sociologists on the labour market. The competencies were systematised by Prof. Gjorge Mladenovski, and the importance of sociologists for the functioning of all segments of the social system was pointed out. Today, studies in sociology enable students to acquire knowledge of basic concepts and theoretical orientations in sociology.

Students are gaining a deep understanding of sociology and learn critical thinking, data analysis, and effective communication. They also develop cultural sensitivity and are introduced to the EU, as well as European and Balkan societies and cultures.

Graduates of sociology can work in various institutions, such as public and private organisations, schools, research institutions, and international bodies. This includes roles such as teachers, analysts, researchers, and administrative staff.

The rebuilding and further development of the Macedonian sociological community requires secure financial support from institutions responsible for science, research, and higher education, such as the Ministry of Education and Science, the Ministry of Finance, the government, the Ministry of Culture, and the Ministry of

Economy. However, the scientific community, particularly in the field of social sciences, is currently experiencing a lack of financial support for research activities, including funding for sociological research projects from the Ministry of Education and Science and from 'international community' representatives located in Macedonia such as various NGOs and foundations that 'distribute' financial support from various foreign state institutions.

Due to insufficient financial support for research, Macedonian universities have exceeded their capacities by increasing undergraduate, postgraduate, and doctoral programmes. This has led to the emergence of interdisciplinary studies and a decline in the number of sociologists working in higher education. The number of sociologists working in higher education has been steadily decreasing in recent years due to a lack of government employment opportunities. State universities receive government funding, but there are two quotas for students: the first quota with a participation fee of €200 per year and the second quota of €400 per year. The costs are mainly covered by the parents of the students, but scholarships are also available.

Sociologists have considerable independence from the government in their teaching and research pursuits. They conduct research in various fields, including sociology of culture, ethnic groups, education, religion, value orientation, politics, media, and poverty. However, research funding limitations affect the quantity and quality of research activities.

The development and affirmation of sociology in Macedonia is undoubtedly related to the teaching and scientific activity of the Institute of Sociology at the Faculty of Philosophy in Skopje. For 45 years, the institute has been educating young people who need to apply their knowledge in our society, in the public and private spheres, especially in education. Macedonian society has been studied for the same number of years, and efforts have been made and are still being made to explain the challenges of social life in different periods of our society in the context of profound social changes followed by fierce conflicts and serious risks to the very survival of Macedonian society. In particular, the recent years of the transition of the Macedonian society and the desire for integration into the wider European space have awakened the 'ghosts of the past', which are becoming our traumatic reality. In this social context, sociologists are still fighting for their place in society and for the 'recognition and appreciation' of sociological activity. The Institute of Sociology, with its scientific, educational, and even wider public activities, has constantly been highlighting the importance of the sociological profession for our society. However, even in the field of higher education, the domain of sociology is narrowing, as its parts are becoming 'interdisciplinary' and 'de-sociologised'. The same thing is occurring in secondary and primary education. What the Institute of Sociology has achieved with its scientific research activity is for Macedonian sociology and Macedonian sociologists to be recognisable on the international sociological scene and to be able to collaborate and communicate with colleagues from around the world on the same level. However, what lies ahead in the next period is intensified activity in our society in relation to improving the social position of one of the most promising professions, that is, the profession of a sociologist. This requires, in addition to other provisions, employment of the graduates of the Institute of Sociology at the Faculty of Philosophy, for which neither institutions of the system nor institutions of the private sector have not shown interest, commitment, or funding.

Despite the existence of sociology in Macedonian society for over five decades, sociologists are barely recognisable in the labour market in the Macedonian economy. The 'older' and more established, or rather 'prestigious', social sciences like law, economy, pedagogy, and others 'take up' most of the vacancies in the civil service, social services, organisational activities, and education. Even though sociologists are still present in secondary education (less so in primary education), their status is still uncertain.

Sociologists are mainly employed in education, the civil service, and NGOs, and to a lesser degree in private companies, but recently, various other jobs have become available. There is a lack of available data on how many sociology graduates are able to find a job after graduation, but the process is certainly longer than 3 years. Currently, more than 130 sociologists are unemployed and are active job seekers.

Competing Interests The authors have no conflicts of interest to declare that are relevant to the content of this chapter.

References

Alexander, J. C. (2012). *Trauma: A social theory*. Polity Press.
Borota Popovska, M. et al. (Ed.). (2015). *50 years Institute of Sociology, Political and Juridical Research, St. Cyril and Methodius University Skopje 1965–2015*. Institute for Sociological and Political-Legal Research, University "Ss. Cyril and Methodius," Skopje.
Calhoun, C. (1993). Nationalism and social change. In V. Vazquez De Prada & I. Olabarri (Eds.), *Understanding social change in the nineties: Theoretical approaches and historiographical perspectives* (pp. 389–420). V Conversaciones Internacionales de Historia.
Dorfles, G. (1991). *Praise for disharmony*. IP Svetovi.
Georgievski, P. (1978). Development of sociology at the Faculty of Philosophy in Skopje. *The Sociological Review, 8*(2–4), 100–108.
Georgievski, P. (2005). 85th anniversary of Faculty of Philosophy—Skopje. In *Annual Proceedings*. Faculty of Philosophy at the University "St. Cyril and Methodius" – Skopje.
Georgievski, P. (2012). *Sociology as a critique of social, educational and cultural change*. Matica Makedonska.
Georgievski, P. (2014). A brief reflection on the life and the professional journey in the field of sociology of professor Slavko Milosavlevski. *The Sociological Review, 15*(2), 7–24.
Jary, D., & Jary, J. (1991). *Collins dictionary of sociology*. Harper Collins Publishers.
Kantardziev, R., Andonov-Poljanski, H., & Dimeski, D. (1976). *Faculty of philosophy 1946–1976*. Faculty of Philosophy, Skopje.
Kepeska, J. (2003). Report on the 25-year activity of the Department of Humanities. *Annual Proceedings of the Faculty of Philosophy, 38*.
Miljovska, D. (1963). Economic basis of the social structure of Macedonian Cities in the Second Half of the XIX Century. *Annual Proceedings of the Faculty of Philosophy, 15*. Faculty of Philosophy, Skopje.
Minoski, K. (2011). The social changes in Republic of Macedonia from 1991 until 2005: From nation-state to bi-national state? In *Sociology and Social Changes: 30 years Studies in Sociology at the Faculty of Philosophy in Skopje*. Faculty of Philosophy, Skopje.

Minoski, K. (2014). Minorities in the work of Professor Slavko Milosavlevski. *The Sociological Review, 15*(2).
Minoski, K. (2020). Institute of Sociology. In R. Duev (Ed.), *Faculty of Philosophy 1920–2020: A century of higher education, a century of state-building*. Ss. Cyril and Methodius University in Skopje, Faculty of Philosophy.
Misirkov, P. K. (1903). *On Macedonian meters*. Liberal Club Printing House.
Mladenovski, G. J. (1996). *Institute of Sociology. In Faculty of Philosophy 1946–2006*. Faculty of Philosophy, Skopje.
Mladenovski, G. J. (2006). Institute of Sociology. In *Faculty of Philosophy 1946–2006*. Faculty of Philosophy, Skopje.
Mladenovski, G. J. (2013). A portrait of Blaga Petroska: Towards a history of Macedonian sociology. In *Proceedings from the International scientific conference Sociology and the Challenges of the Global Age - 35 years of the Institute of Sociology, 80th Anniversary of Prof. Dr. Blaga Petroska*. Faculty of Philosophy, Skopje.
Nikodimovski, L. (1985). The place and role of sociology in self-management labor. In *Annual Proceedings of the Faculty of Philosophy* (Vol. 38, pp. 217–221). Faculty of Philosophy, Skopje.
Petkovska, A. (2009). *Essays on sociology of culture*. AZ-BUKI.
Petroska, B. (1985). Sociology and the profession of sociologist in our society. In *Annual Proceedings of the Faculty of Philosophy* (Vol. 38, pp. 191–198). Faculty of Philosophy, Skopje.
Puleski, G. J. (1875). *Trilingual* (Dictionary of three languages Macedonian, Albanian and Turkish). Belgrade.
Racin, K. [1987] (1939). *Prose and journalism*. Nasa kniga.
Ristovski, B. (1990). *Portraits and processes from the Macedonian literary and national history, III*. Kultura.
Ristovski, B. (1991). *Krste P. Misirkov, selected writings*. Misla.
Ristovski, B. (Ed.). (2009). *Encyclopedia Macedonica*. Macedonian Academy of Sciences and Arts, Lexicographical Centre.
Sztompka, P. (2004). The trauma of social change: A case of Postcommunist societies. In J. Alexander, R. Eyerman, B. Giesen, N. Smelser, & P. Sztompka (Eds.), *Cultural trauma and collective identity* (pp. 155–195). University of California Press.
Sztompka, P. (2008). The ambivalence of social change in Post-Communist Societies. *Kultura i Politika: zeszyty naukowe Wyższej Szkoły Europejskiej im. Ks. JózefaTischnera w Krakowi, 2*(3), 131–153.
Taševa, M. (2021). Rereading Misirkov: The nation as a factor of unification. In R. Duev (Ed.), *Science and society: Contribution of humanities and social sciences* (pp. 407–418). Faculty of Philosophy.
Veselinov, K. (1938). *National–Enslaved peoples and national minorities (scientific sociological essay)*. K'lbo.

Konstantin Minoski is a Full Professor at the Institute of Sociology, Faculty of Philosophy at the 'Ss. Cyril and Methodius' University in Skopje, Macedonia. Born in 1964 in Skopje, he studied sociology at the Institute of Sociology, Faculty of Philosophy in Skopje, where he graduated in 1991. He completed his postgraduate studies in sociology—sociology of politics—in 1998 at the same institute and defended his doctoral dissertation in 2005. Since 1993, he has been working at the Institute of Sociology, Faculty of Philosophy in Skopje, first as a research assistant and at present as a full-time professor. His scientific research interests are sociological theories, the sociology of ethnic groups, the sociology of nationalism, and the sociology of sport. He has participated in national and international scientific research projects and has presented papers as an author or co-author in national and international scientific meetings and conferences. Currently, he is the President of the Association of Sociologists of the Republic of Macedonia and Vice-President of the Macedonian Centre for Culture and Arts.

Antoanela Petkovska, Ph.D. in Sociology, is a Full Professor at the Institute of Sociology, Faculty of Philosophy, 'Ss. Cyril and Methodius University' in Skopje. Her main fields of interest are the sociology of culture, sociology of art, sociology of youth, sociology of Macedonian culture, European civilisation, gender, and society. She was a member of several scientific projects: Macedonian Literature and Art in the 20th Century, Macedonian Academy of Sciences and Arts; Mapping of the Cultural Industries in the Republic of Macedonia, Ministry of Culture of RM and BC in Macedonia (2007–2008); and European Value Survey, International project (national project manager), financed by the Faculty of Philosophy and FIOM (2007–2009 and also in 2019). Her most important publications are in 2009, 'Essays on Sociology of Culture', AZ-BUKI, Skopje; 1998, 'Sociology', (co-author), textbook, Studentski zbor, Skopje; 1997 'Sociology of the Macedonian Fine Arts (1945–1980)', Makedonska civilizacija, Skopje; and 1995 'Macedonian Sociological Terms Dictionary', (co-author), Institute of Sociology, Faculty of Philosophy—Skopje and MASA, Skopje. Petkovska is a former president of the Macedonian Sociological Association and a current Chair of the General Assembly of European Value Survey.

Chapter 14
Moldovan Post-socialist Transformation: The (Un)successfulness of Sociology

Victor Cepoi

14.1 Introduction

The transformation of the geographical boundaries in Eastern Europe has resulted in significant changes in the newly emerged countries. The fall of the USSR led to the emergence of 15 independent republics and initiated a transition process not only in these newly established republics but also in the countries of the post-socialist block. This transition process brought about not only the transition from authoritarian regimes to democracies but also the need to embrace the market economy and adapt to the new realities of the post-socialist transformations in Eastern Europe. Nevertheless, these changes also triggered problems. The moment the social model disappeared, the void it left created several crises (cultural, structural, economic, social, and ideological), which are ongoing (Želvys, 2017).

At the same time, the concept of 'transition' essentially implies a temporary state between two fixed positions: the point of departure and that of arrival (Bridger & Pine, 1998). As a result, the socialist symbolic, which was for many decades the sole symbol in the region, started to be replaced with those of the free market, democracy, free elections, civil society, and many others. The post-socialist transformation implies not only technical changes, but rather changes of culture, identity, and traditions (Verdery, 1999). Therefore, the process of re-territorialising started, which requires new or adapted processes of legitimating and validating new conceptualisations of power (Graham, 2000).

The new order is established by different actors through different means. As Sum and Jessop (2013) highlight, semiosis enables interpreting and explaining the logic of capital accumulation and its relation to the social formation in which it is

V. Cepoi (✉)
Faculty of Information Studies, Novo Mesto, Slovenia
e-mail: victor.cepoi@fis.unm.si

embedded with the help of the concepts and analytical tools that it provides, pointing at the role that semiosis plays in understanding the institutionalisation of regional economies (Jessop & Oosterlynck, 2008). Therefore, it can be stated that both history and institutions matter in the process of transition and resetting national strategies and visions in post-socialist countries.

The complexity of the new realities is differentiated into subsystems considered to be simultaneously interdependent and autonomous (Makarovič et al., 2013, p. 7). The new realities imply social, economic, and political relations and identities (Paasi, 2002). Once a strategic-relational approach is adopted, the focus is on the issue of complexity reduction. In this regard, this process is about discursively selective imaginaries and structurally selective institutions. Nevertheless, the role of imaginaries and institutions should be delimited. Imaginaries can be considered to be semiotic systems, which have the role of providing the foundation for the lived experience of the complex world. Additionally, institutions embed the lived experience in broader social relations and interpret it across various social spheres (Jessop & Oosterlynck, 2008, p. 6). Fictions (imaginaries) create a world of their own, thus a space for possibility of imaginations and thought is present and experience a different reality. This reality can differ from the 'real reality' (Beckert, 2010, p. 5). In an economic context, fictions motivate actions in the real world. The assumption is that what is something imaginary will turn into something existing at a later point in time (Beckert, 2010, p. 11). Even more, this fiction is open to adaption and vulnerable to contradictory experiences in the real world. The role of the economic imaginary is to identify, privilege, and seek to stabilise some economic activities from the totality of economic relations. Furthermore, these economic relations are transforming into objects of observation, calculation, and governance (Sum & Jessop, 2013, p. 66). The case of the USSR can be regarded as an eloquent example. This process was instituted by the communist government, by which the communist imaginary was brought to its absolute and began its erosion, starting in the 1980s. In other words, we can deliberate that this process included both the semiotics and the institutional part. In other words, institutions became inefficient because of their corruption. Moreover, it contributed to an alienated public discourse, characterised by flaws and a lack of 'sacrality'. As such, we have a transition process, which can be seen as a way of finding and relaunching the national path through the Cultural Political Economy.

Building a new nation with new perceptions of statehood was a common challenge for the Eastern European, post-Soviet, and post-socialist countries. It implies building a new community and a new social system (Wilkinson, 1970, p. 312). The transformation is dynamic; some orders are inherited, and others are created. The degree of ambiguity and system volatility of the time only makes one wonder: what forces shape the new imaginaries? The chapter will focus on analysing a practical case study concerning the role of sociology during the early stages of transition and developing a new political, social, and economic system in the Republic of Moldova. This research is the first attempt to understand the role of Moldovan sociology in the framework of the post-socialist transformation. Following the Cultural Political Economy (CPE) model, the research will attempt to understand the role of the

Moldovan sociology academic group during the post-socialist transition. The research focuses on analysing and comparing the perceptions of Moldovan sociologists, active or knowledgeable, of the volatile situation of Moldova in the early 1990s.

14.1.1 Cultural Political Economy: Foundation of Understanding the Post-socialist Transformations

The importance of the Cultural Political Economy lies in the evolutionary mechanisms of social systems in the analysis of path-dependent and path-creative semiotic and extra-semiotic aspects of political and economic systems. Moreover, CPE enables conceptualising and analysing the path-shaping potential of strategic documents and practices (Makarovič et al., 2013). The role of CPE is to contribute to the understanding of new regionalism because it integrates semiotic factors in the analysis of the institutionalisation of regional economies (Jessop & Oosterlynck, 2008, p. 4). CPE involves exploring the semiotic and extra-semiotic mechanisms involved in selecting and consolidating the dominance/hegemony of some meaning systems and ideologies over others (Jessop & Oosterlynck, 2008, p. 5). These mechanisms can facilitate two lines of investigation of relevance to economic, political, and cultural geography (Jessop & Oosterlynck, 2008, pp. 2–3). The aim is to avoid the assumption of social constructivism, which sees social reality as only the participants' meanings and understandings of their social world. It is important to address the complex aspects of semiosis and explore the discursive and material mechanisms. These mechanisms shape how 'ideas matter' in the political economy (Jessop & Oosterlynck, 2008, p. 30).

The Cultural Political Economy approach has three essential features. The first distinctive feature is that history and institutions matter for CPE, unlike the more usual generic studies of semiosis (Jessop & Oosterlynck, 2008, p. 3). The second characteristic of CPE is that it takes cultural turns seriously, focusing on the complex relations between meanings and practices. Like variants of cultural materialism, but unlike the institutional political economy, the description, understanding, and explanation of economic and political conduct result from the production of intersubjective meaning (Jessop & Oosterlynck, 2008, p. 4). Thirdly, the authors speak about the co-evolution of semiotic and extra-semiotic processes and their impact on the constitution and dynamic of capitalist formations. Following this line of argument, the authors highlight that this feature results from focusing on the first and second features as a ground building.

Meanwhile, compatible and competitive discourses, mutual overlapping combinations of localities, states, or regions (sub-/supranational or macro), coexist (Makarovič et al., 2013, p. 6). If semiosis is regarded as a concept, then a discourse indicates particular types of semiosis (e.g. forms of discourse, codes, genres, styles, and representations of self-identities and alterity) (Sum & Jessop, 2013, p. 153). Nevertheless, as the authors mention, CPE also considers social practice, which can constrain the non-semiotic features of social structure and by inherently semiotic factors.

In this regard, CPE integrates four general evolutionary mechanisms, variation, selection, retention, and reinforcement, into semiotic analysis. Moreover, existing political economies are triggered by the path-dependent co-evolution of the semiotic and extra-semiotic. These aspects make CPE different from other approaches, with the help of the cultural turn (Jessop & Oosterlynck, 2008, p. 2).

14.2 Post-socialist Transformation in Moldova

As in the case of other former socialist countries, with the collapse of the Soviet Union, Moldova, a new in-formation state, faced many challenges that had to be solved. As a result, within Moldovan society in this period, various institutions started to appear, which were nascent (Colatchi, 2011). These institutions had to learn how to 'play by the new rules' and to work together. The socio-cultural dynamic of the Moldovan society is triggered by new transformations, which affect both the political and economic processes. As a result, the newly formed state did not have the luxury of choosing a long, smooth transition; rather, the new political elite understood that the transition from totalitarianism to democracy and the consolidation of democracy itself were processes that had to occur simultaneously (Colatchi, 2011, p. 114). As such, Margarint (2004) points out that the transformation process started with reforming the political system in 1984. It lasted until 1989 and was characterised by changes within the system, though retaining the existing social arrangement. Next, from 1989 to 1991, the period was characterised by changes in the old political elite and the rejection of the old regime. As a result, from 1994 to 2004, the new period focused on social transformation, emphasising the redistribution and privatisation of property (even without a consensus among the political elite) (Margarint, 2004, p. 47).

The formation of the Republic of Moldova state had four main stages, each an important milestone. The first phase (1990–1994) includes the declaration of independence and the first parliamentary elections and ends with the constitution's adoption (Varzari, 2018, p. 153). This period is also known as the period of institutionalisation and the formation/consolidation of the newly appeared state through the help of essential legislative acts.

The second period of the post-socialist transformation starts with the adoption of the constitution and ends in the year 2000 with its modification and the switch to a parliamentary form of government and the election of the president by the parliament. In this period, as Varzari (2018, p. 155) emphasises, there were three main discourses:

- The development and consolidation of the Republic of Moldova as a state
- Unification with Romania (either immediate or gradual)
- Unification with Russian Federation or accession to the Russia-Belarus Union

The 2001–2009 period constituted the third period of the transformation. Additionally, it was called the period of 'pseudo-democracy'.

Lastly, from 2009 to the present day, Moldova is in the fourth period of its transformation (Varzari, 2018, p. 156). It is characterised by reforms, which are meant to bring to 'normality' the functionality of the state institutions. Thus, in this period, the main promoters of public opinion were/are the party leaders. Moreover, their role in this period can be summarised as follows: as symbolic actors, as staff for the political elite, and the role of political directors and crisis politicians. Nevertheless, as a common characteristic for the transition countries, these political actors have the role of 'saviours' of the nation.

In accordance with the practice of modernising post-communist states for almost three decades, the mechanism of democratic transformations here has both common aspects and differences. Compared with other former socialist countries, Moldova has encountered some similarities in the democratic transformation with these. As Saca (2016) mentions, these similarities are on several levels. Firstly, most of the actors involved in the transition process were representatives of the old regime, and at the same time, despite declaring themselves partisans of the new reform, they lacked the knowledge for this transition. This aspect results in the second characteristic: deficits of experience and skills that the modernisation projects need. Third, we speak about modernisation reforms that had to be done by stakeholders with a polarised mentality (authoritarian-democratic). These stakeholders were directly involved in the decision-making process of the reforms. The lack of experience led to another characteristic: the inconsistent adjustment to national conditions of foreign experience. Lastly, a lack of consistency in the logic in the activity of promoting reforms from one stage to another of modernisation is considered a common trait for the former socialist countries.

Saca (2016) highlights that this mechanism of socio-political modernisation in the post-communist space has some problems. For example, it lacks integrity of content. An eloquent example is the lack of stakeholders' knowledge in 'to know, to be skilled, to act'. The moment there is a mismatch between these crucial processes, the process of social reformation makes the modernisation mechanism incoherent. Thus, in Moldova, it resulted in the procrastination of the reform process.

Additionally, when we put Moldova in the context of the modernisation mechanisms, these are misused by the national elite, thus influencing and creating an obstacle to the modernisation of the state (Saca, 2016). Thus, the political elite simulated the capacity to adapt to what is new because this elite does not take sufficient account of the national specificity. As a result, the available modernisation mechanisms become deficient.

14.3 The Role of Sociology: Moldovan Case Study

A knowledge society can be considered as an example of an imaginary, which Jessop considers as becoming a powerful economic imaginary. It can influence the policy paradigms, strategies, or policies across many various fields of social practice. Moreover, privileging certain forms of political, economic, or cognitive actions can increase the benefits of the actors over others (Makarovič et al., 2013, p. 9). Sociologists can be seen as one who shapes different discourses, especially in a transition period.

The post-socialist space offers a unique opportunity to study the transition to a new economic imaginary. The appearance of different discourses materialised into different successful strategies, but sometimes, it disintegrated the illusions of the new societies in Central and Eastern Europe. For example, Moldova can be considered a case in which sociologists, or sociology as such, did not play an important role in shaping dominant discourses in society, according to their primary role. In order to sustain this argument, the study focuses on the CPE's mechanisms (variation, selection, retention, and reinforcement of discourses) in the context of sociology's role in Moldova's post-social transformation. This theoretical framework will enable obtaining insights into understanding the rationale of the Moldovan post-socialist transformation.

Moldova's geographical position throughout history made it the crossroads of clashes between Western and Eastern 'worlds'. Located as such, Moldova's history had the co-influence of the European and Russian streams, which left an impression on the development of sociology. Therefore, the two schools are differentiated in the methodological approach. This differentiation offers a unique possibility for sociologists to consider both perspectives in analysing and explaining the post-socialist transformations that occurred in the 1990s, immediately following the collapse of the Soviet Union. Nevertheless, the development of sociology in Moldova started long before the collapse of the post-socialist transformation. As Bulgaru and Cheianu (2005) indicate, there are five stages of sociology's development in Moldova as a science:

1. 1934–1940, development within the Romanian Social Institute
2. The 1960s, within the Soviet Socialist Moldovan Republic
3. The 1970s, aiming the recognition of the theoretical dimension in developing new theoretical models, which would explain the general characteristics of society
4. The 1980s, sociology as an independent science
5. The 1990s, the transition period

Nevertheless, considering the new realities, Moldovan society needed a reinvention or change of the Soviet realities. Following this line of argument, every segment of the daily routine had to be reshaped with the help of the available tools. Did sociology or sociologists contribute to the creation of new discourses? Did they influence the development of necessary change?

Until the 1990s, in Moldova, sociology did not have the possibility to grow and train its own sociologists, and the main topics of academic research were focused on rural research. Therefore, the qualitative evaluation of the sociologic outcome from 1934 to 1990 pointed to three key characteristics of the sociological development in the Republic of Moldova (Bulgaru & Cheianu, 2005, p. 13):

1. Moldovan sociologists were prepared outside the country because of a lack of an institutional framework for preparing specialists in the domain.
2. Social science specialists re-profiled themselves to sociology, thus contributing to the creation of new sociologists' generations and creating institutions that develop new specialists.
3. Rural sociology is the main topic of research.

With the fall of the socialist system, the economic imaginary had to be radically redefined. Even more, the semiotic systems provide the framework for the real economy. One of the sociologists with whom the interview was carried out, for the purpose of this research, pointed that there was a shift toward new realities. Namely, the participants mentioned that:

> The '90s was a period of citizens' education, including that of political leaders, including that of the decision factors regarding the importance and utility of conducting sociological research.

The beginning of the post-socialist transformation determined the creation of a 'sociologist class', in which philosophers, psychologists, or journalists became sociologists. The aim was to change the Marxist-Leninist paradigms to contemporary sociology. As a result, the absence of sociology as a science determined this intradisciplinary approach toward creating a sociological movement in the country. Additionally, the intradisciplinary approach was sometimes more force-driven than will-driven. Nonetheless, this determines the need for future intradisciplinary cooperation between sociology and other social sciences.

Within the last decade of the twentieth century, several studies were conducted with a special emphasis on pension reform, the impact of privatisation, or even agriculture reform (e.g. Pohl (1997), Young (1997), Csaki et al. (1997), Gorton (2001)). Another milestone was the year 1998, when the first public opinion barometer was published (BOP, 1998). It was a breakthrough contributing to the appearance twice per year of a national public opinion survey allowing access to the analysis of the society's preferences on various topics. Even so, the impact of the sociology did not impact the creation or shaping of the new realities. Additionally, sociology is lacking attention even in the present. For example, sociology is still not perceived as a science or vocation. Even more, we can deliberate that this can be considered inertia from the past, where there was little trust toward institutions. Thus, the semiotic has denigrated both sociological institutions and political studies but also their reputation in the common imaginary. This led to them being seen as vocations or rational decisions. Therefore, society and the political elite did not acknowledge the importance of sociology in shaping different aspects of society's daily interaction. One of the participants in the study highlighted that state institutions also neglect sociology's role, the role that could help in promoting national strategic interests:

> There's probably no interest in… I don't know how this happens in other countries, but in Moldova… basically, the state doesn't finance research, the institutions don't finance research.

Nevertheless, the first decade of 2000 brought a small change, by which the opinion of sociology was considered, but on a narrow aspect, not only to the electoral campaigns but also the implementation of important reforms in priority areas such as education, health system, or others.

Sociological research is done with the help of grants from abroad. At the same time, the research focuses firstly on the donors' interests. Additionally, we can understand, from what the participants in the study pointed, that the recommendations that come from these studies are considered; meanwhile, at the national level, the suggestions are rarely considered:

> We can make a parallel. If we are to conduct a study for an international organisation (I'm referring to the business field here), then surely, they will take into account all or at least most of sociologists' recommendations. But, if we're speaking about governmental institutions, then here maybe… it rarely happens for them to take these recommendations into account.

Nevertheless, within the interviews with the Moldovan sociologist, we found that some of the topics overlap with what is primordial for Moldovan authorities. For example, because of a massive population exodus, the topic of migration became popular among sociologists:

> Regarding migration, there were plenty of studies conducted. But, again, this was done due to pressing made by international organisms that've seen this necessity.

14.4 New Economic Imaginary and the Role of Sociology

To date, as has been emphasised, the role of sociology has not been highly explored in the context of the post-socialist transformation. Even if it was, it was highly dependent on the international donor, who set their own agenda of interest. Considering CPE as an analytical tool will enable an understanding of the role of sociology from the perspective of the CPE's approach. CPE offers four evolutionary mechanisms of particular imaginaries (variation, selection, retention, and reinforcement), which are integrated into semiotic analysis (Jessop, 2010).

The first mechanism is the variation in discourses and practices that appear during a crisis or when an opportunity arises. Nonetheless, it does not mean that each of them will succeed, being considered a discursive process (Makarovič et al., 2013, p. 9). The presence of a continuing variation in discourses redefines sites, subjects, and stakes of action, articulating innovative strategies, projects, and visions. All these are done intentionally or unintentionally (Jessop & Oosterlynck, 2008, p. 12). Because of the lack of long-term consequences for overall social dynamics and the short lifespan of the variation, particular semiotic innovations are selected. There are two main reasons that this process appears. It occurs because of the discursively resonating of the semiotic innovations with other actors and social forces. In addition, they are reinforced with the help of different structural mechanisms. Regarding discourses, Jessop and Oosterlynck (2008) say that they become more powerful, operating across sites and scales. Also, they can encompass a hegemonic project by connecting or establishing local hegemonies.

The changes in the political and economic arenas made society to be perceived as a result of these changes. The numerous reforms were fragmentally reflected in several doctoral dissertations or international reports. As experts, there were selected people from countries that finance different projects or national-level experts from the NGO sector. Therefore, from the discussions with the Moldovan sociologists, we can acknowledge that the national academic sector was mostly neglected. At the same time, sociologists have the right to tackle important issues, but if the problem is in the decision-making phase and can affect the political actor's image, then sociologists' input faces hostility in order to be considered.

> We do have freedom of speech in Moldova, and it's a time when anyone can publish a study can even reach a level of conversation with institutions to discuss decision factors; they are receptive. But the actual direct decisions are made at a political level. And so, if the politician or party X or Y is willing and believes to gain political advantage in this matter, then they will take the recommendations into account. But if the recommendations affect, in any way, their image, then it becomes so much harder to implement a particular reform based on sociological research or sociologists' recommendations.

Consequently, there are discourses in various fields within the public space, including the economic imaginary, but the task is to materialise these discourses. As a result, these changes were found in some fields, but not always. A possible explanation is how Moldova was clothed from exposure to non-communist countries. Therefore, the first decade of independence was tied to the old symbolism with a Soviet understanding of the economic imaginary. This can be explained by the presence of a social discourse, which is negatively oriented toward any process of social analysis. Thus, it generates from inertia the previous semiotic concept.

The selection of particular discourses is considered the second CPE mechanism, which can be privileged or disapproved (Makarovič et al., 2013, pp. 9–10). Discourses rely not only on semiotics but also on other factors, including material to be noticed by the relevant onlookers. In this regard, discourses can resonate in broader debates (Makarovič et al., 2013, p. 10).

Starting in 1990, there was a huge possibility to launch programmes for changes in the political, economic, and social sectors. These programmes could diminish the problems of the transition. Nevertheless, in the period of post-social transformation in Moldova, things changed unpredictably and fragmentally. As the participants in the interviews pointed, there was no formulated plan, therefore allowing the transition to develop by itself:

> Things have developed chaotically and fragmentarily. The frequent changes of the Government, the lack of consecutiveness in the implementation of development projects and strategies, the degree of corruption in the state's superior hierarchy, the lack of 'brakes'

in the moral behaviour of the new Moldovan elite in the transition period all together had a negative impact on the population.

Even more, as one of the participants mentioned, the economic discourses available at that time were described as a '[…] a sentiment which was interiorised concerning the agricultural field'. As a result, the discourses focused on the economic imaginary as an agricultural state, and the society should follow this dimension. Nevertheless, even in the present, the preconception remains, contributing not to focusing on the invention of new discourses but rather on reinventing agriculture. As a result, even if the economic field attempts to change the direction of the discourses, backed by research data, resistance is present from the political perspective. There was a resistance force, mostly representing the political perspective's unwillingness to hear the change's necessity.

Retention, the third mechanism, implies that discourses can be found in actors' habitus, hexis, and personal identity. Nevertheless, they have the property to constitute official or unofficial organisational routines and rules or even become part of the environment.

The mid-1990s was characterised by the crystallisation of the dominant discourses in Central Europe, especially those related to national identification. At the same time, during this period in Moldova, there was a crucial need for self-identification in the discourses provided by the academic and political elites. On the one hand, neither the political elite nor the academic sphere or society emphasised national identification. On the other hand, one of the processes that was at the forefront was the crystallisation of embracing 'European principles and values' but only, as the participant mentioned, if it was something that the society wanted and demanded:

> This is when, in Moldova, the European principles and values were crystalised, to a point where this became a condemned topic within the society… But these issues were crystallised precisely because it was a desire and aspiration of the population, and it was adopted.

The crystallisation of European principles and values within the political and sociological discourses happened after the year 2000. Moreover, the political discourses, relying on sociological research, materialised during the electoral campaigns.

Poverty is another topic included in the political discourse, which is part of the economic imaginary. The need to retain this particular discourse about being the poorest country in Europe was mainly because of the presence of international reports emphasising this aspect. However, if the programmes of the left- or right-wing parties/candidates are compared, these do not differ (Pisica, 2013).

Reinforcement is the last mechanism. It highlights the possibility of privileging certain discourses with semiotic or material mechanisms. This mechanism can be considered as an added value for the selective recruitment control. Moreover, remembering by particular social groups and institutions, among others, is also present. After being discursively reproduced, incorporated into individual routines, and institutionally embedded, the discourses will be retained at the moment discourses guide structural transformation and reorganise the balance of forces.

As discussed, most of the discourses that appeared and reinforced in the society are because of the conducted research for international institutions (International Monetary Fund, World Bank, UNICEF, or Soros Foundation). At a later stage, these institutions could pressure the government to include these particular issues on the agenda. As a result, several topics were reinforced, which even led to the creation of state institutions with the help of foreign donors to tackle the particular problem, as in the case of Barometrul Opiniei Publice, which provided means to tackle important issues. Nevertheless, in most cases, it was neglected by the decision-making, creating a gap of mistrust between society, sociologists, and politicians. At the same time, after conducting the interview, we found that the lack of trust in the state institutions convinced people to be more open through bringing direct contributions and to prefer to support something specific:

> ... people are more open to bringing their direct contribution, because they lack trust. This matter is the trust in our state's institutions and politicians. And during the last years, this issue has grown significantly. And people prefer to support something specific, to offer these resources and see the result themselves, because they do not trust the state institutions or their capacity to do something.

Although the role of academia or sociologists had to be amplified, especially during the process of retention and reinforcement, in Moldova, this did not happen. In the first decade of Moldova's independence, both political and academic spheres had the urgent need to focus on the self-identification discourses rather than on the economic ones, as it was in other countries. Even when the discourses were shifted to other topics, we can say that it was due to external pressure and created an even greater misunderstanding between all actors.

14.5 Foreign Aid as a Tool for the Development of Sociology

As emphasised, international organisations stimulated the development of sociology in Moldova or at least increased its importance in shaping and retaining particular discourses. The national mechanisms for sociological research do not exist; meanwhile, the private sector cannot perform complex research studies without additional help. Therefore, the presence of foreign donors constitutes a positive aspect of the development of sociology as a science in Moldova; however, sometimes, these organisations are 'pushing' their agenda to increase their influence in Moldova.

Another important feature is the aspect of internationalisation. Because of the absence of sociology, this is being formed through those who have obtained university degrees abroad. Studying abroad, these students not only received knowledge on the theoretical level but also had a preparation in being trained from a methodological perspective. However, the participants pointed that the issue is that good specialists never remain in academia but end up in international organisations.

> Globalisation was also felt within Moldova, or the opening of the possibility for Moldovan sociologists to move to other markets.

Transnational knowledge sharing is almost absent because usually only the managers of the institutions benefit from the international cooperation. At the same time, the foreign academic environment seems to be closed to outsiders lacking training.

Additionally, non-governmental organisations (NGOs) are at the forefront because most sociological research studies are done through grants and foreign funds. As a result, the NGOs have the skills and resources to write and attract international projects.

14.6 Conclusions

The post-socialist transformation intended to change the existing imaginaries and offer a reinvention of the social, economic, and political imaginaries. Sociology had the opportunity to lead the change within the Moldovan society by shaping the dominant discourses. Nevertheless, the role of Moldovan sociology in the post-socialist transformation was, at a minimum, related to its impact on the ongoing changes taking place in society. Thus, it created a void in the processes of variation, selection, retention, and reinforcement of discourses. As a result, researchers from other fields had to assume the role of sociologists to explain and promote new discourses that were vital at that period. Unfortunately, the absence of specific training for experts and the unwillingness of the local political elite to consider the recommendations hindered the reputation of sociology as a science. Even if some of the studies materialised into policies, it was only because the international donors persuaded the state to consider work carried out by sociologists. At the same time, we can say that international help addressed the consequences of the problem and then the problem itself. In this manner, the role of sociology remains unnoticed.

This arduous process can be partially caused by the system inertia mentioned in previous chapters. A possible explanation for the importance of this inertia was the presence of mistrust in society. In turn, this great mistrust was caused by the inefficiency and disability to retain the transition process on a smooth path.

Considering the above-mentioned, sociology had the opportunity to lead the change within the Moldovan society by shaping the dominant discourses. Nevertheless, the role of Moldovan sociology in the post-socialist transformation was shattered due to its non-existence, or at least its underdevelopment, in Moldovan society. As a result, researchers from other fields had to assume the role of sociologists to explain and promote new discourses that were vital in that period. Unfortunately, the absence of specific training for experts and the unwillingness of the local political elite to consider the recommendations hindered the reputation of sociology as a science. Even if some of the studies did materialise into policies, it was only because the international donors persuaded the state to consider work carried out by sociologists.

In comparison to other societies from Western countries where sociology and research affiliated with it are considered and regardless of whether it is done in a political context or not, sociology and research constitute the framework for any action. Meanwhile, in Moldova, the academic community must put great effort into ensuring that the recommendations are transposed into specific actions with evident outcomes. Additionally, after the independence, the issue of nationality remains vivid. Sociologists would be at the forefront of starting the debate and articulating a consensus. However, the inability of sociologists' mobilisation and their lack of decision-making hinder their ability to create vital discourses for the Moldovan society.

Furthermore, the effort consists in linking the academic area with the society. The relationship lacks an intermediary who would facilitate the communication between the two. As it appears, in Moldova, the actors are in a position of 'bowling alone' rather than a team effort in identifying the main problems of society and, most importantly, solving them.

At the same time, the Ukrainian-Russian war also affected Moldova on several levels, from the risk of political (e.g. Ciobanu and Ciobanu (2002)) and energy (e.g. Platon and Vieru (2022)) security to Moldova's integration to the European Union (e.g. Cebotari (2023)), as starting 2022 Moldova alongside Ukraine obtained the candidate status. Another topic of interest has also arisen for the Moldovan scientific community: the Ukrainian refugee crisis (e.g. Gorobievschi (2023)). The multiple crises simultaneously required the state to make important decisions, though many were considered difficult to address. Thus, these crises, especially the refugee one, must be considered as important as the other, as it changes the core foundations of society and its processes. Following this line of argument, sociology in Moldova has a new opportunity to reaffirm itself as an important study, but even more important is having real-life opportunity to be the forefront actor contributing to the variation, selection, retention, and reinforcement of discourses in society.

Acknowledgements Special thanks go toward those that provided valuable insights on the role of sociology in post-socialist Moldova. Additionally, thank you to Prof. Rončević, who provided the interview guide that helped me in having prolific discussions with sociologists from Moldova and to obtain a better understanding about the role that sociology has for Moldovan society.

Competing Interests The author has no conflicts of interest to declare that are relevant to the content of this chapter.

References

Beckert, J. (2010). How do fields change? The interrelations of institutions, networks, and cognition in the dynamics of markets. *Organization Studies, 31*, 605–627. https://doi.org/10.1177/0170840610372184

Bridger, S., & Pine, F. (Eds.). (1998). *Surviving post-socialism local strategies and regional responses in Eastern Europe and the former Soviet Union*. Routledge.

Bulgaru, M., & Cheianu, D. (2005). *Dezvoltarea științei și învățământului sociologic în Moldova*. CEP USM.

Cebotari, S. (2023). *Relațiile Republica Moldova – Uniunea Europeană În Contextul Războiului Din Ucraina*. Consolidarea Instituțiilor Statului Și Buna Guvernare. Chișinău, Moldova, 27 Septembrie 2016.

Ciobanu, N., & Ciobanu, I. (2002). Cadrul Legal Și Instituțional Pentru Realizarea Politicii Securității Naționale A Republicii Moldova Versus Riscuri Și Provocări Actualizate. *Conferința Științifică Internațională Strategia Securității Uniunii Europene În Contextul Metamorfozelor Relațiilor Internaționale, II*, 41.

Colatchi, A. (2011). Criza Politică Și Consolidarea Democrației În Republica Moldova. *Moldoscopie, 1*(LII), 109.

Csaki, C., Lerman, Z., & Nucifora, A. (1997). *Land reform and private farming in Moldova*. Report number: EC4NR Agriculture Policy Note 9 Affiliation: World Bank, Natural Resources Management Division, Country Department IV, Europe and Central Asia Region. Retrieved from https://www.researchgate.net/publication/304936403_Land_Reform_and_Private_Farming_in_Moldova

Gorobievschi, S. (2023). The quality of life and the migration of people in the Republic of Moldova. *Strategia Securității Uniunii Europene În Contextul Metamorfozelor Relațiilor Internaționale, II*, 41.

Gorton, M. (2001). Agricultural land reform in Moldova. *Land Use Policy, 18*(3), 269–279.

Graham, J. R. (2000). How big are the tax benefits of debt? *The Journal of Finance, 55*(5), 1901–1941.

Institutul Opiniei Publice. *Baromentrul Opiniei Publice*. (1998). Accessed 18.10.2023, from https://ipp.md/old/lib.php?l=ro&idc=156&year=&page=2

Jessop, B. (2010). Cultural political economy and critical policy studies. *Critical Policy Studies, 3*(4), 336. https://doi.org/10.1080/19460171003619741

Jessop, B., & Oosterlynck, S. (2008). Cultural political economy: On making the cultural turn without falling into soft economic sociology. *Geoforum, 39*(3), 1155–1169.

Makarovič, M., Šušterič, J., & Rončević, B. (2013). Is Europe 2020 set to fail? The cultural political economy of the EU grand strategies. *European Planning Studies, 22*(3), 610–626.

Margarint, A. (2004). Etapele evoluției elitei politice posttotalitare din Republica Moldova. *Moldoscopie, 2*(25), ISSN 1812-2566 /ISSNe 2587-4063.

Paasi, A. (2002). Regional transformation in the European context: Notes on regions, boundaries and identity. *Space and Polity, 6*(2), 197–201. https://doi.org/10.1080/1356257022000003626

Pisica, G. (2013). *Reflecții privind sistemul pluripartidist din Republica Moldova* [Reflections On the multiparty system in the Republic of Moldova]. Muzeul Național de Istorie a Moldovei.

Platon, N., & Vieru, T. (2022). *The specific risks of the energy market of the Republic of Moldova in times of crisis*. Conference paper - Conferința "Competitivitate și inovare în economia cunoașterii" 26, Chișinău, Moldova, 23–24 septembrie 2022, https://doi.org/10.53486/cike2022.07

Pohl, G. (1997). *Privatization and restructuring in central and Eastern Europe: Evidence and policy options*. World Bank Publications.

Saca, V. (2016). *Mecanismul Și Ritmurile Modernizării Sociopolitice A Republicii Moldova În Contextul Proceselor Integraționiste*. Retrieved September 23, 2023, from https://ibn.idsi.md/sites/default/files/imag_file/189-194_0.pdf

Sum, N.-L., & Jessop, B. (2013). *Towards a cultural political economy: Putting culture in its place in political economy*. Edward Elgar Publishing.

Varzari, P. (2018). *Considerente Privind Evoluția Statului Republica Moldova*. Moldoscopie.

Verdery, K. (1999). *The political lives of dead bodies. Reburial and post-socialist change*. Columbia University Press.

Wilkinson, K. P. (1970). The community as a social field. *Social Forces, 48*(3), 311–322.

Young, J. T. (1997). *Economics as a moral science*. Edward Elgar Publishing, number 842, September.

Želvys, R. (2017). Education systems in times of multiple crises: The case of post-socialist transformations. *Iranian Journal of Comparative Education, 1*(1), 45–61.

Victor Cepoi, PhD, is a researcher at the Faculty of Information Studies, Novo Mesto. He has experience working in various national and international projects as a researcher and project manager: Interreg Danube Region and Erasmus+, among others. He is a holder of a Jean Monnet Module 'Technology and Innovation Communities 2030'.

Chapter 15
Sociology as a Witness to the Value Dormancy of Post-socialist Society or Ideological Subjugation

Vladimir Bakrač and Predrag Živković

15.1 Introduction

It is possible to find a connection with the mentioned title in the manuscripts of the French writer Michel Houellebecq (2015), who, through vivid and often apocalyptic predictions, speaks about unsolved conflicts and civilisational, religious, and cultural outwitting from the not-so-distant French past, as well as the identity submission in the name of artificial acceptance of a multicultural structure, which has been changing the appearance of its republican tradition for decades. Relying on the literary tradition helps sociology to recognise the peculiarity of the spirit of an epoch and its 'value nature', which certainly gives this paper the legitimacy to construct and explain 'the semantics' of post-socialism, stimulated by undoubted theoretically significant views from the world of literature because three decades of painful transformation of society carry 'the burden of the past' and catharsis of redemption due to the attempt to change 'the soil of its origin' forcibly thus becoming societies that do not have their own traditions. The announcement of this research review, observed in the mentioned literary achievement, obliges its authors to be cautious when analysing the defined research subject. Therefore, a more detailed elaboration of the sociological discourse, which requires a critical review of the sociological presence in the period of the post-socialist transformation of Montenegrin society, is needed, as well as calling its responsibility before 'the court of the scientific public' and assessing its value narrative about the future development of the mentioned society. Perhaps this conception is both pretentious and belated if one considers a 'value dormancy', which occurred during neoliberal

V. Bakrač (✉) · P. Živković
Department of Sociology, Faculty of Philosophy, University of Montenegro, Podgorica, Montenegro
e-mail: vladimir.b@ucg.ac.me

nihilism. However, the authors persist in the belief that any response to the coming crisis is the hour of responsibility of scientists, especially those who represent the tradition of sociology and its step towards independence and the boldness of studying society in a time of ideological and revolutionary upheavals.

We have to be precise in the theoretical approach, as well as in panoramic presentation. Studies of this type, which emphasise the consideration of chronology of the thematic events, do not represent glorification and advocacy for only one reference social system (because it is questionable whether it even exists) but a credible and objective presentation of an endangered social situation observed through sociological, anthropological, economic, religious, ecological, cultural, geopolitical, and ethnomethodological frameworks faced with existing atavism and insufficiently prepared and often premature encounters with the challenges brought by the transition to a new 'system yard'. However, no matter how 'painful' and demanding the research subject of sociological science was, one cannot escape the impression that with each encounter with social changes, it became more and more diverse, thematically gifted so that particular points of view proudly began to emerge from it, thus forming a sovereign scope of research and pleading for its independence. That has often led to issues of discussion and questioning of philosophical, epistemological, and methodological approaches within the sociology of science (see Wettersten (1993)).

The emergence of postmodernism attracted the particular attention of sociological science, for which it was necessary to create a new world of meaning to construct a suitable theoretical apparatus for analysing recent social phenomena. By emerging in multiple spheres, postmodernism has provoked zealous sociological theorists to 'a public class' and debate regarding the supplementation and reconstruction of 'sluggish narratives'. Postmodernism did not become a monolithic feature and an epochal deed only of Western society (as was thought for a long time), carried away by the dream and belief about its chosenness. We must admit that Western society has opened the door to technological progress; however, in recent decades, it is increasingly being said that in its desire to set 'sails' to the shores of 'the end of history', it simply sank and got lost in the realisation that there is a historical alternative on the other side of the world. The end of history was bought at the public auction of resurrected civilisations. It was necessary to retouch the image of a unipolar world. We will leave the phases of restoring trust in alternative historical outcomes for the following chapters of this paper. Here, we will present and prepare the ground for observing a chronological movement of (post-)socialist societies, their system changes, religious buildings, anthropological positives, and geopolitical beliefs, as well as their general culture of memory (Kuljić, 2006), without losing sight of our insistence to present institutionalisation of sociological science most faithfully. Perhaps we are not up to that task since we are witnessing the daily eruption of new worlds and social changes, the enigmatic nature of which disarms any attempt to establish objective and rational scientific communication. Neven Cvetićanin also agrees on this when being 'enthralled' by Baudrillard's Fatal Strategies points to the need for a new perception of the irrational and mythological sphere that opposes the scientific spirit that has taken over the Western Hemisphere (see more in Cvetićanin (2008, p. 446)). Although it cannot be said that we are witnessing 'the peaceful harbours' of postmodernity and postmodernism, as the quote interpreted above literally sounds, they still represent 'a new social zone' that sociology has yet to examine. That does not diminish the importance of previous knowledge and the cognitive accumulation of gnoseology. However, we refer to those 'chess squares' that remained uncovered by the moves of analytical observation. We have referred to the postmodern world because it would be too immature and naive to search for the necessary answers in explaining frequent social phenomena and not to refer to the epoch in which they emerged. Therefore, sociology also had to adapt to 'the spirit of the times', not in the context of conformist approval of the mentioned epoch but in examining and preparing the ground for the coming invasion of all those plagues it brought with itself.

15.2 Conceptual Course of Sociological Science in the (Post-) Socialist Period

We believe we have given sufficient motives and valid reasons on the basis of which the diligent reader would pay attention. No matter how much the topics authorised to be discussed in our research plead for the independent characteristics of the societies in which analytical discourses are formed, we cannot take them out of the context of global social events and changes. We say this because sociological science in the areas of former Yugoslavia, that is, in those university centres where it was independently studied, focused its direction of search on the study of new social changes that occurred under the mantle of postmodernism. Through the chronology of the theoretical and empirical orientations of Montenegrin researchers, we will present their affirmation by studying the mentioned epoch through different spheres of its reflection on the following pages of the paper so, for now, it will suffice to become acquainted with the conceptual focus around which the relevant empirical edifices have been built. In Montenegro, as in other university centres and scientific institutes, the gathering centre of scientific thought relied on the conflicting tradition in sociology (Marinković, 2008) based on the Marxist legacy (see Brdar (2005)). Such orientation also represented an intimate desire of the official socialist establishment to constitute, according to its beliefs, a scientific environment that would remind but also maintain an atmosphere of memories of the former revolutionism. Marx's works had to gain greater appreciation than the usual memory of his intellectual engagement. Regarding this remark (which should not be understood as a form of devaluation of Marxist creativity), warning signs pointing to not-so-hidden and secret desires for indoctrination of public opinion should be heeded. As to Montenegro, the first imprints of the Marxist-type academic demonstration had to follow the theoretical and ideological tenacity of the other Yugoslav centres. Socialist agitprops should not allow the outlines of possible alternatives to be seen next to their generally valid theoretical platform. For this reason, political decisions suppressed the looming images of other social spheres (cf. Bernik, 1994). That has been especially visible in relation to religion and everything that had religious characteristics. Marx focused his theoretical criticism on social position and life, believing that by correcting social conditions, the need for people to believe in the illusions offered by religion would reduce so that the causes of religious beliefs would gradually disappear. The communist idea would relativise the social basis of religion, people would stop believing in God, and atheism would be the natural ideology of communist society (Mekgrat, 2022). Sociological expertise in Montenegro exuded that spirit and ideological provenance in the study of religion and religiosity, first through very modest studies of religiosity from that period and then through empirical verification of conducted atheism in the state and the secular order in society (Vrcan, 1990). Marx encountered misunderstanding even in the political establishment of that time; he was wrongly understood and accepted. He was accepted in the way others wanted, at least the way Marx imagined the future world, and all this made a significant impact on the then-sociological establishment, which deeply wrapped its theoretical and empirical review in its understanding of the Marxist idea. Clearly, the following was needed:

> Normative neutralization (ideological, political) of science is a condition for its institutionalization and professional differentiation, even in the case of the most favourable external political environment. The exclusion of non-scientific issues is a sign of real and not just declarative institutionalization to the point of autonomizing one's problem field and scientific ethos. That means a scientific career can no longer be made at the expense of ideological orientation—as in Marxism and socialism. (Brdar, 2005, pp. 342–343)

That empowered the programme content and the first teaching programmes implemented at the Department of Marxism and Socialist Management in Montenegro (Vukićević, 1998a). In our case, the source revealed a much more layered ideological desire and the later barrenness and impossibility of realising the integral scientific knowledge of the governing bodies in the Socialist Federal Republic of Yugoslavia (SFRY), which wanted to be embodied in Marxist doctrine and its implementation in the sphere of education. No matter how much the competent aspirations had the character of a worldview, they could not count on their ideological application for a long time because social cries became more and more frequent, specifically, demands that were the result of newly emerging social needs for engaging and 'abrasing' subtler professions (Vukićević, 1998a). As a witness to the necessary institutional changes in Montenegro at the time, Slobodan Vukićević presented a factual analysis of events.

> The Department of Marxism and Socialist Self-Management transformed after ten years of work into the Department of Philosophy and Sociology with two courses: a philosophy course and a sociology course. From 1988 to 1992, the first two years of study at the Department were common to both courses, while they were separate courses in the third and fourth years of study […] Since 1992, the curricula of both courses at The Department of Philosophy and Sociology have been separated in the first year of study. Since then, we can talk about an integrally based study of philosophy and an integrally based study of sociology in Montenegro. (Vukićević, 1998a, pp. 150–153)

We can conclude that from that moment, sociological thought gained its importance, especially if we consider that it was a time of shocking social changes (the 1990s) that included not only the eruption of civil unrest but also confrontation in the field of social sciences. At the 'eclipse of the twentieth century', new topics are emerging in the sociological lobby, but above all, there are a need and necessity to find answers to the coming crisis, as well as the direction towards finding solutions and cultivating a democratic culture in the post-socialist environment. That will also require a new orientation of sociological science. It will first be necessary to point out new solutions for overcoming the socialist climate and the glorified walk into the uncertain corridors of post-socialism, which will turn out to have simulated social changes all along (Vukićević, 1998b). However, the wave of euphoria will soon subside because the post-Yugoslav societies will find themselves in 'disoriented areas' from which they are still trying to get out and find a way out of the general crisis. Here, it is necessary to point out a peculiarity of the transitional period, manifested in the so-called simulating of social transformation (Vukićević, 1998b, 2016).

The space for greater visibility of sociology in Montenegrin society emerged with its separation from philosophy. The possibility for the crystallisation of three groups of sociological activism in society opens up with the independence of sociology at the university. Sociologists in science stand out: mostly university professors or associates who study Montenegrin society from a sociological paradigm. It is about the academic elite that engages in empirical research and monitors social trends in contemporary Montenegrin society. That does not mean that sociologists are directly involved in creating social reality. However, in cooperation with other related scientific disciplines, political science, economics, etc., they follow the process of society's transition. Then, sociologists in education do not have an active role in society in the sense that they scientifically contribute to monitoring the trends of social changes. Since they are, to a large extent, graduated students and sociology professors in secondary schools, their role is more in the educational context, educating secondary school-aged children about society and social movements. Sociology enables each individual to recognise, understand, and explain the mechanisms of social phenomena in order to contribute to life in the community and recognise and find their role in it. It also affects mastering the competencies (knowledge, skills, and attitudes) needed for life and participation in a democratically organised multicultural, multi-confessional society, as well as facing numerous challenges in Montenegrin and then global, modern society. With the sociology programme, it will not only be possible to emphasise the significant results of insight into the historical context of all developmental, political, economic, cultural, and other processes in the educational process and to perceive the global contemporary society from that and other positions, but as a subject programme, it will open numerous options, analyses, interpretations, and explanations of Montenegrin society. In that manner, concreteness is ensured because reflection on social phenomena will not be trapped and burdened by academic theoretical study. Students are provided with the vitality of an animated, dynamic, and attractive scientific discipline and the in-depth applicability of the so-called sociological imagination to the current and active challenges of the present, as well as a futuristic approach to the humanistic goals of society. Finally, sociologists without influence are individuals who engage in public opinion research within some political parties or institutions without any impact on social movements in Montenegro.

We should emphasise that Montenegro not only represented a time-space paradigm for playing out these fictitious metamorphoses. That applies not only to the other republics of the (SFRY) but also to the largest socialist bloc: the Union of Soviet Socialist Republics (USSR). Although the answer imposes from the previous understanding of social reality, due to theoretical and methodological precision, we will rely on the research material of the already mentioned sociologist Slobodan Vukićević who, with his works, has initiated the study of social transformation in Montenegro and beyond. One of the pioneering studies guided by the motives of discovering the secret desires of all those actors labelled as 'leaders or pioneers' of creating new social changes is the study 'Simulation of a Change/Transformation of Socialism'. Its author, aware of the need to publish a credible study of that period that would not represent an ode to instrumental and indoctrination-shaped research in a sociologically correct way, introduced a balanced set of theoretical approaches into the discussion, of which we should single out, in particular, the tradition of functionalism and Sorokin's social and cultural dynamics (see Tartalja (1976)), in order to study the pulse of post-socialist transformation in Montenegro on the basis of such a theoretical and analytical apparatus, not losing the sight of external influences and historical development of socialism (Vukićević, 1998b). The key finding of this study, which cannot be considered exclusive when it comes to a phenomenon that wanted to stand out with this sociological edifice, corresponded to many other phenomena close to it that chose the spaces of the newly formed states as the place of their emergence. How clear the finding of the study shows the fact that it remains relevant today in the advanced phase of social transformation of post-socialist societies, whose establishments propagate their success, both in the selection and implementation of reforms, all intending to be able to speak and justify in principle the hour of determination that has led to the decadence of socialist *etatism* (cf. Stojiljković, 2017).

Even though post-socialist societies very easily rid themselves of the ghosts of socialism (proudly denying its ideology but keeping some relics that also appeared in the period of social transformation), they could not even imagine what would await them on the first page of the new 'socio-economic contract'. In their desire to approach the splendour of liberal-democratic societies, imitatively creating liberal constitutionalism (Zakarija, 2004), they embraced neoliberalism, making itself a home in their backyard (Bakrač et al., 2019). Before the onslaught of the devastation of the economic environment, the country suffered strong shocks and economic decadence. The widely known syntagm 'shock doctrine' promised post-socialist societies the development achieved in military dictatorships. Incorporating the neoliberal doctrine, the newly formed classes propagated and resolutely preserved the portrait of neoliberalism on the one hand; on the other, they strove daily to banish any memory of the leftist ideas (cf. Дугин, 2013).[1] Day by day, the state became weaker and hid behind the intrusive voices of neoliberal theorists. At this point, the door has opened to a wider debate about two economic schemes: the regulatory state and the developmental state, which, according to Nebojša Katić, is still taking place. The first model of the regulatory state is closer to market-oriented theorists, who see in it the function of creating a strong institutional order and, as far as possible, a neutral arbitrator who will not harm and cause panic in the market (Katić, 2015). Such a model of the state remains in the domain of secret desires of post-socialist societies because its emergence requires an appropriate historical climate:

> On the other side of this division is the developmental state, which is trying to escape poverty through its activism, especially its insistence on accelerated industrial development. A developmental state is always interventionist, but not every interventionist state is necessarily developmental. (Katić, 2015, p. 68)

Aware of the challenges in theoretical debates, this eminent economist, who leans slightly towards the dirigiste economy of Asian countries, resorts to a syncretic answer in the model of the 'thinking state' when postulating the correct answer. The quote fits our theoretical approach.

> The thinking state is primarily developmental; it is regulatory, where it suits it, and the dynamics that suit it. Such a state does not ignore reality or fight battles it cannot win, and it makes concessions slowly, hard, and only when it has to. Such a country adapts to new conditions on the fly; it is not afraid of experiments and failures as long as the number of hits exceeds (by number and/or importance) the number of misses. (Katić, 2015, p. 71)

Can post-socialist societies be said to strive to evolve into a 'thinking state'? The answer is given in the daily activities and tensions in which the modern state awakes.

15.3 Epistemological Experience of Sociological Science in Montenegro

Based on the above-mentioned absorbed knowledge, significant sociological studies were published in Montenegro over the previous decade, some of which had a comparative character. In cooperation with the national academy and other scientific institutions, attention was paid to the demographic trends of Montenegrin society, and issues of cultural policy, official social policies, economic models imposed by post-socialism, confessional climate, urban policies, issues of entrepreneurship, the establishment of macro- and microeconomic stability, socio-pathological

---

[1] We will pay more attention to the phenomenon of national leftism in those segments relating to the awakening of religiosity and nationalist folklore in post-socialist societies. In several theoretical papers, we have described in detail all the theoretical directions of the (neo-)left wing in Europe. Therefore, we believe it is sufficient here to emphasise those phenomena visible and integrated in the sociological studies of post-socialism. As a more comprehensive manuscript in which it is possible to become acquainted with neo-leftist trends, we cite Živković and Bakrač; Самарџић and Живковић; etc.

phenomena, neoliberalisation of the social milieu, as well as other parameters that appear in sociological discourse (see more in Vukićević (2012, 2016) and Bakrač et al. (2019)). It will be enough to introduce the scientific public to the study results, which had a national character and appeared as Montenegro in the Era of Competitiveness, within which several exemplary studies were created. The study 'Demographic and Population Problems in Montenegro/Society, Family', freed from the propagated monitoring, embodied in the slogan "the successfully travelled" path of Montenegrin society in post-socialism, disclosed a significant medium that does not correspond to the reports presented to the public. Unfavourable demographic growth, mass migrations, low level of citizens' trust in the institutional order, and mixed sensibility of survived conservatism with introjected liberalisation of society are just some of the features of the dysfunctionality of Montenegrin society (see more in Vukićević (2012)). This study has become the basis for a comparative study of post-socialism in Montenegro and Russia (post-socialism), within which an extensive study of the phenomenon of post-socialist transformation in these two countries was carried out. The study dealt in detail with the problems of entrepreneurship and entrepreneurial culture in Montenegro and Russia and many other sociological, anthropological, and economic phenomena. The relevant conclusion of this study could be summed up in the remark by Ratko R. Božović:

> With the introduction of democracy in the post-socialist period, little thought is given to creating and establishing democratic institutions, without which there is no democracy, civil society or political culture. The ruling parties, as only nominally transformed communists, do not like such an ordered society because it goes against establishing an authoritarian government and opens up the possibility of losing elections, changing the government, and controlling unlimited power. Creating the democratic institutions, the validity, and implementation of their jurisdictional regulation is important so that every government would not turn into tyranny. (Božović, 1995, pp. 139–140)

We need to be careful in this analysis. Post-democracy is one of the phenomena that has been gravitating in the social sciences and has increasingly attracted the attention of sociologists and political scientists in the previous two decades (cf. Krauč, 2014). We can say that the study post-socialism, following the voice of Colin Crouch, pointed to the stages of the reduced presence of democratic myths in the twenty-first century, which await post-socialist societies on their path to democratisation (Krauč, 2014). Interestingly, these societies combine some elements from the post-democratic environment. A detailed introduction to the elaboration of post-democratic principles would lead us away from the ultimate goal of this study, so here we will explain its content in a few theoretical steps.

> The idea of post-democracy helps us to describe the situation when frustration, boredom, and disillusionment take the stage after the introduction of democracy, when the interests of a powerful minority become far more effective than the mass of ordinary people in establishing a political system that works in their favour; where political elites have learned to manage and manipulate the demands of the people; where people have to be convinced to vote in 'top-down' campaigns. (Krauč, 2014, p. 33)

If we follow the conclusion of Colin Crouch, we will inevitably find ourselves in the sociologically related discourse of Sheldon Wolin. When this political philosopher describes, in Crouch's terms, 'the lack of democratic capacities' in the modern world, especially in the USA, he uses two dominant models of democratic folklore. Centrifugal and centripetal forces are at issue, where the centrifugal forces refer to the fragmentation of the collective through the emergence of various social movements, both irredentist and minority social movements, while centripetal forces refer to the power of the corporate centres of Western society (Volin, 2007; Живковић, 2017). Although they remain in the phase of primordial forms of democracy, the governments and elites of post-socialist societies are increasingly dependent on the reflections of corporate interests. Due to ineffective deregulation, they are becoming increasingly attractive to pervasive multinational corporations who see them as a flexible model for cultivated corruption. Those activities maintain and imperially service the state of the periphery of those countries that emerged from, in their opinion, 'someone else's socialist story'. Contemporary sociological thought also had to count on the redefinition of some previous theories that described 'imperial brutes' and the colonial past, thus arriving at the knowledge that postcolonial studies, as well as post-socialism itself, after the Cold War, must have an exogenous and introvert time for looking at its past (see more in Chari and Verdery (2009)). In this area, too, sociology waged a fierce struggle with other social sciences to win a place and role as a witness of social changes. Successfully avoiding 'the vanity of natural sciences' (Волин, 2007) and their establishment in a modern technological civilisation, sociological science managed to point out the angle of events and warn the scientific thought about the coming invasion of not-so-peaceful social changes.

The emergence of the revitalisation of religion not only in the areas of the former Yugoslavia but in all areas that were part of the socialist camp marked post-socialism at the end of the 1980s. Sociologists in Montenegro were faced with the widespread phenomenon of religiosity on its territory. Bearing in mind that Montenegro also followed and adhered to 'secular religiosity' (Dugandžija, 1980) and renewed the expulsion and stigmatisation of believers, mass religiosity in the 1990s was a challenge when creating a scale of sincerity and a spirit of trust in primal values. That also meant re-examining the new identity models of the believing (Berger, 2003; Davie, 2007) and a marble slab on which future national features will be imprinted, reviving the forgotten myths (cf. Дугин, 2013). In recent years, in 'the sociological corner', the study 'Religion and Youth or Religiosity of the Youth in Montenegro' was published (Bakrač, 2013), which was accepted as a kind of contribution to the sociology of religion and epistemological expertise of religiosity. The religious landscape in the spiritually depleted Montenegrin society changed at the beginning of the 1990s. Specifically, with the collapse of the socialist regime that was a form of 'secular religion' and numerous events that followed as a result of the collapse of socialism, such as the collapse of the SFRY and the secession of the former republics from the SFRY, religion returned to the social stage, and the desecularisation of society happened. Religion was returning to the social scene burdened by relapses of the collapsed political and ideological contrast, followed by social limitation and the clergy's frustration with the long-term rule of real socialism. All this affected the public activity of religion, which was burdened by tradition and nationalism, where the church appeared as the pivot and guardian of value and identity. Empirical records testify to the return of religion and the desecularisation of society. That is especially visible in the Orthodox-dominant areas and, therefore, in Montenegro. Revitalised religion had a special impetus among the youth population. To summarise, the analytical and empirical demands of the study led the authors to those sources that awakened feelings of a return to religion and to those that supported the legitimacy of official socialist atheism a couple of decades ago. On the basis of these theses, we could start a narrative about national leftism, which was accompanying but also a denying phenomenon of the socialist bloc, especially in the USSR, whose 'archetypal torches' were lit in the corridors of their religious consciousness. We must emphasise that it was not a native phenomenon (only in the territory of the former Soviet Union), which was preceded by an archaic and long-suppressed tradition. As we have announced, we can also link this phenomenon with the national-leftist movements widespread in most socialist countries. The essence is the suppression and suffocation of the national ethos (Дугин, 2013). As the distinguished Russian sociologist Aleksandr Dugin proves, the national-leftist narrative was expressed shyly in post-socialist societies because the national paradigm that absorbed the mythological legacies of pre-socialist societies was latently imprisoned (Дугин, 2013, p. 53). Synthesising local features, as Dugin says, national leftism was established on internal mythological motivations (Дугин, 2013, p. 56)

> ... in the emergence of national-leftism, we are dealing with Marxism modified in the spirit of archaic eschatological expectations, deep national mythology related to the expectation of 'the end of time' and the return of 'the golden age' (cargo cults, chiliasm). The thesis about justice and 'the state of justice,' on which the socialist utopia is built, is perceived religiously, which awakens the fundamental tectonic energies of ethnos. (Дугин, 2013, p. 56)

Although Dugin mainly dealt with this movement within the political discourse of the USSR and the current Russian Federation, his conclusions and findings were compatible completely with leftist movements that had or were created on latent national tendencies in the former Yugoslavia.

In recent years, we have observed a significant number of epistemological analyses based on the study of geopolitical movements and the place of Montenegro within the two ruling geopolitical discourses between the Western and Eastern Hemispheres (Дугин, 2004; Živković & Bakrač, 2017), which contributed to the publication of reference scientific works and studies. Interpreting the contemporary geopolitical movements of the former Yugoslav republics, above all, the involvement of Slovenia and Croatia in the North Atlantic Treaty Organization (NATO) alliance, the Montenegrin establishment attempted to reach the level of influence of the thalassocratic centre as soon as possible without first considering its historical experience, which can cause strong shocks in public opinion. The findings and warnings of geopolitical strategists, sociologists, and philosophers were ignored because the desire was to manifest the state of apparently completed democratic reforms through integration into the North Atlantic bloc. The narrative about European Union (EU) integration and the NATO alliance itself is usually profiled as an indispensable step towards the gates of progress, sometimes ignoring 'the voices of repentance' that have been heard more and more often since the world economic crisis. That does not represent the stigmatisation of Western values but an attempt to create a healthy scientific environment that will base its conclusions on the analysis of the confessional provenance that forms the very core of the North Atlantic and (Neo)Eurasian bloc, especially when considering Christian provenances, Orthodoxy, Catholicism, and Protestantism that form particular types of civilisations, with a particular analysis of Asian civilisations, but also focusing on perceived spaces that can serve as a ground for future proxy wars on behalf of corporate capital (see Gross (1979)). The problem of modern online wars can be seen here (Савин & Дугин, 2018). Thanks to the researchers' findings, sociological science warned at national and international conferences about the emergence of another threatening phenomenon in the Balkans. We are talking about neo-Ottomanism, which used its imperial experiences from past centuries, or rather a relic of the past, to renew and prepare the paths of Turkish influence in these areas, especially through the doctrine of strategic depth (cf. Tanasković, 2010; Давутоглу, 2014). This kind of revitalisation of neo-Ottomanism has been implemented through cultural and corporate influence in recent years, thus making the areas/states of the Balkans new or old colonies.

After the fall of the Berlin Wall and the most powerful socialist bloc, the USSR, a climate of conformism prevailed in the social sciences, which wanted to renounce and declare their previous literary heritage as pseudo-literature, all for the sake of adapting to an alienated stage of historical continuity, which was recognised in the periodically adopted syntagm 'the end of history'. External conformity is nourished by an internal confrontation with the socialist past. The former members of the SFRY were eager to demonstrate their power on spatial features as soon as possible. This discourse was included in the comparative research *Transition Transformation of the Capital Cities of Zagreb and Podgorica as Systems of Settlements* (Svirčić-Gotovac & Šarović, 2016), and within it, the monograph *Symbolic Texture of Post-Socialist Transformation of Urban Space* (Podgorica-Zagreb) (Samardžić & Živković, 2016), where 'the abdication' of the symbols of Titoism was proven. What we are pointing to grew out of the not-so-distant past, when new nations were created, and the past was violently overcome in the areas of the former Yugoslavia (Kuljić, 2002, 2006). Vigilant sociological expertise did not miss the events surrounding the Law on Freedom of Religion in Montenegro, which resulted in a peaceful change of multi-decade government in this country. The then-political regime adopted the law which, according to the opinion of the clergy and believers, discriminated against the Serbian Orthodox Church and its believers. The church responded to the Law on Freedom of Religion, adopted by the Parliament of Montenegro, with processions, that is, peaceful and quiet resistance to the mentioned law. The law was opposed by a large number of citizens, who expressed their dissatisfaction with a peaceful walk. People were revolted not only by the Law on Freedom of Religion but also by political, social, and economic issues. In the political sense, the multi-decade rule of a political oligarchy, actually a political party, called into question democracy while the democratic transition of power stopped. Relatively low wages compared to the developed countries of the West and an unenviable social position only contributed to the citizens' dissatisfaction. In short, all this could have been the reason for the people's dissatisfaction, which culminated in the Law on Freedom of Religion. The first processions were held on 31 December 2019 and were continuous for 2 days a week. In all cities, processions were led by priests and believers. The epilogue of the persistent protest was a peaceful change of government in the elections on 30 August 2020. Subsequently, the new government adopted amendments to the Law on Freedom of Religion on 17 December. Amendments to the Law on Freedom of Religion implied the deletion of disputed articles of the existing law that referred to the property of the Serbian Orthodox Church, which greatly provoked the people and caused a revolt of the Serbian Orthodox Church (Bakrač, 2022).

From a sociological aspect, the hot topic of religious, linguistic, and ethnic identity in Montenegro and the possible political influence on these issues are analysed. The impact of politics on the ethnic distinctiveness of Montenegrins became especially active at the beginning of the twenty-first century; therefore, this time frame represents an essential period for problematising this topic. Since the difference between the Montenegrins and the Serbs is highly ambiguous in terms of ethnic, linguistic, and religious distinctiveness, one of the hypotheses problematised by sociological expertise is that politics appears as the main factor that dictates the differences between these two peoples in Montenegro. Accordingly, the hypothesis problematised by contemporary sociological thought in Montenegro is that the political differences between Serbia and Montenegro are broader, the gap between ethnic Montenegrins and Serbs is widening, the number of Serbs is increasing, and the number of Montenegrins is decreasing (Bakrač & Blagojević, 2023). After reviewing the chronology of sociological thought in Montenegro during the period of social transformation, more precisely, its vitality to replace, scientifically correct, and reject the recklessness that emerged after the incorporation of imposed modernisation solutions or the so-called shock therapy, the consequences of which remain noticeable in Montenegrin society because it gravitates between the influence of the East and the West, not realising the need for the necessary selection and adoption of compatible values, once pointed out by Rene Guenon (2022) and Gorazd Kocijančič (2021), we can say that sociological science, as well as the sociological profession in Montenegro, persistently but correctly, testifies and points to socio-economic models that would be attractive as well as helpful in overcoming the imposed neoliberal capitalism. As evidenced by the texts of sociologists, post-socialism in Montenegro took place as a simulacrum renegade and simulacrum actor of neoliberal ideology, simultaneously applying ornamentation and relapses of socialist practice and neoliberal policies. It is interesting that in the Montenegrin research community, the left-wing liberal tradition was the most prominent, which brazenly rejected the possibility of applying and implementing what can be considered 'right-wing thought' and the consideration of such research conclusions as 'distributivism' and 'moral frameworks of the market economy', about which the political philosopher Miša Đurković wrote argumentatively (see more in Ђурковић (2021)). It is questionable how the Montenegrin elite, if it is even possible to talk about the emergence of the political elite in the post-socialist transformation of our society, applied imposed values under the pretext of 'Western values'. However, as political sociologist Zoran Stojiljković says, 'European vesture is necessary for the march to power' (Stojiljković, 2017, p. 50), which is a narrative about European and Western values. The party monopoly that was in force in Montenegro for almost three decades can be compared to the post-October elite in Serbia, which Stojiljković accused of violent 'neoliberal economic policies' that cost Serbia society in the EU (Stojiljković, 2017, p. 54). That is why we say that Montenegrin society was closer to neo-leftist ideas and interpretations of the present modernisation than to more conservative or right-wing thinking due to compatibility with its tradition. Thus, we received a neoliberal Leviathan that gravitated with the tide of socialist etatisation, that is, the influence and control of the political elite in decision-making processes and the masking of the democratisation of society and the new 'capitalist oligarchy' (a term used by many theorists and that has remained universal for most post-socialist societies), which controlled the courses of privatisation.

It seems that sociological thought recognised 'The time for an upheaval, a new thought revolution, an anarchic dispersal of existing thoughts, ways of speaking and writing, dying deposits of non-spiritual thought' and started the analysis of the pandemic situation and the recognition of a new capitalist passage. The period that encompassed or was marked by the emergence of the COVID-19 pandemic represented, due to its increasingly noticeable planetary dispersion, the reminiscence of the observed Foucauldian biopolitical characteristics that served sociologists to intone the increasingly visible problems of manipulation and abuse of vaccination but also the emergence of transhumanism (cf. Fuzaro, 2022). That narrative about biopolitics with a strong scientific contribution has also been visible in Montenegro, more precisely as an enticing scientific and epistemological result that, in the emergence of the mentioned pandemic, also observed epiphenomena that were somewhat obscured and not so engaged and that have been considered legacies of Badiou's and Baudrillard's philosophical and sociological tradition. Namely, the results obtained by sociologists in Montenegro in cooperation with their European colleagues revealed glimpses of those social phenomena that concerned, we can freely say, the imagological image of the Other, of course, observed from the point of view of the already extracted postmodernists and especially the theory of Jean Baudrillard (see more in Han (2015)). More precisely, the mentioned research revealed the application of the patterns of 'the disciplinary subject' and bio- and nanotechnologies as apparent examples of pandemic-narrative manipulation, but also of the phenomenon of death, which in this 'therapeutic capitalism' (Fuzaro, 2022) lost its sacredness and became a kind of market raw material (Раконяц et al., 2022). The research on the pandemic situation that was published (Раконяц et al., 2022) highlighted important research categories such as 'the (self) efficient subject' (Han, 2015) and traces of 'the logic of capital and the ontology of profit' (Badiou, 2008; cf. Vladušić, 2012) involved in the memory of COVID-19 but also the proposal to abandon the apology of neoliberal capitalism whose anti-humanist memories became more visible in the disrespect and neglect of primary human needs during the pandemic (Раконяц et al., 2022). As Раконяц et al. (2022) conclude, it served as specific and geopolitical literature or a form of confirmation or anticipation of new geopolitical strategies, especially with the emergence of the so-called immunological prophylaxis that served as a membrane and a wall of resistance against the potential geopolitical carrier of the virus (see also Han (2015)). We must say that the above-mentioned lines about newly discovered or confirmed sociological and philosophical sentences are within a new culture whose portrait is presented in our paper. Namely, it is about the so-called necroculture, which can be considered a conduit for therapeutic capitalism.

We should emphasise the confirmation of identical results that were published later in other research centres. We especially highlight the study of the Italian philosopher Diego Fusaro, whose scientific results correspond with the research results of Montenegrin sociologists. Namely, noting the already mentioned biopolitical admixtures, Fuzaro (2022) characterised the pandemic situation as 'therapeutic capitalism'. Why do we single this out? Precisely for the reason that the quality of sociological research on the COVID-19 pandemic by Montenegrin sociologists revealed and suggested the so-called primordial forms of new capitalism named 'therapeutic', as will be confirmed in Fusaro's studies. That is how a new 'capitalist clinic' was created, of which Fusaro says:

> Drugs, therapies, virologists, and the medical lexicon lead to a massive exit from the hospital stricto sensu environment to occupy the entire social space, now redefined as a clinic for patients who must submit to the authority of the doctor and his/her imperatives, presented as the only possible salvation. For this reason, within the new techno-sanitary Leviathan, there are no longer autonomous citizens, subjects of law who…, decide upon their own existence: instead of citizens subject to the law, there are patients who need to be treated, upon whose lives decide experts in white coats. (Fuzaro, 2022, p. 48)

The pandemic has deep roots in ancient myths and biblical texts in which it is used as the voice of God's punishment, but 'the war metaphor is, according to Susan Sontag, effective in the narrative presentation of the epidemic because it is […], the only state in which people are ready for anything, in terms of economic and social sacrifice, just to save their own life' (Fuzaro, 2022, p. 119). Apparent examples of the interpretation of what the COVID-19 pandemic announces to us is a new transhumanist era in which therapeutic capitalism has initiated the process of 'regulating and administering the body' (Brajdoti, 2016), but also increasingly popular biotechnological enhancements point to the world of social surveillance (Đurković, 2021, pp. 186–187), whereby the results of Montenegrin sociologists are affirmed and recognised through these comparative studies.

15.4 Conclusion

At the very end of this, not only a chronological but also a theoretical review of sociological science in Montenegro, we are obliged to say that, even though it often lacks the understanding of the political establishment, it has managed to restore the social thought that was in crisis but also to point out the constant need to coexist with social volition. In recent years, government projects have bypassed sociological studies. One of the reasons is that the official elites are sensitive to sociological studies, which often reveal the latent motives of their actions. That secret confrontation, however, did not succeed in derogating from the continuity of the institutionalisation of sociology in Montenegro. Redirecting more and more to empirical research, the sociological and scientific centre in Montenegro managed to connect with relevant regional and world sociological centres, institutes, and universities, and it managed to open the door to comparative studies based on which it offered possible paths of social development of post-socialist societies. From the first steps of social transformation, sociological thought in Montenegro confirmed its presence through those spheres in which the light of description and explanation fell on those phenomena that networked the disciplinary viewpoints with their emergence. By analysing research findings, sociology developed and enriched its disciplinary world and pedagogical and didactic mission. As it understood the world of postmodernity in time, sociology gathered theoretical forces from the world of social sciences to communicate, in a conceptually understandable way, to a modern individual his/her role in a world in which he/she is losing conceptual and anthropological identity. We can freely conclude that the Department of Sociology developed alongside the processes of post-socialism. Namely, as a relatively young department at the Faculty of Philosophy, sociology matured with the transition processes in Montenegro. This could explain why the society in the transition process, which was marked by the non-transparent privatisation of the social sector, was somewhat denied a critical review of sociological thought. What contemporary sociology suffers from in the world is also the case in Montenegro, and it is unclear, when it comes to the influence of politics on sociology, how much influence sociology has on politics and how significant the contribution of other social sciences is in the analysis of social movements in transitional processes and the cooperation of these sciences in the overall process. Also, the period of transition cannot boast of some empirical research in the field of sociology. In this, it lags behind the other republics of the former Yugoslavia. During the transition period, Montenegrin society was deprived of the wider and more detailed influence of sociology in all social events. Future sociological thought should address whether transition is only a form of social change and what its dimensions of society are, as well as verify whether there is room for the sociology of transition as a separate sociological discipline and which would be its specificity. As we live in a world of global, ecological, and economic crises, we expect that sociology in Montenegro will have a much more significant role and a better positioning in society.

Competing Interests The authors have no conflicts of interest to declare that are relevant to the content of this chapter.

References

Badiou, A. (2008). *The meaning of Sarkozy*. Verso.
Bakrač, V. (2013). *Religija i mladi / Religioznost mladih u Crnoj Gori*. Narodna knjiga.

Bakrač, V. (2022). Church and state in Montenegro: From the Serbian orthodox church to the Church of Serbia. *Occasional Papers on Religion in Eastern Europe, 42*(9), 38–52. https://doi.org/10.55221/2693-2148.2394

Bakrač, V., & Blagojević, M. (2023). Religious, ethnic, and linguistic distinctiveness in political context. *Religija i tolerancija, XXI*(39), 21–33. https://doi.org/10.18485/rit.2023.21.39.2

Bakrač, V., Živković, P., & Saggau, E. H. (2019). Some sociological aspects of religiosity (religiosity in contemporary societies between neo-liberalism and globalization). In M. Blagojević & D. Todorović (Eds.), *Traditional and non-traditional religiosity: A thematic collection of papers of international significance* (pp. 114–135). IDN – Junir.

Berger, P. L. (2003). Orthodoxy and the pluralistic challenge. *Greek Orthodox Theological Review, 48*(1–4), 33–41.

Bernik, I. (1994). Politics and society in postsocialism. *International Journal of Sociology, 24*(2/3), 45–60. Retrieved from http://www.jstor.org/stable/20628412

Božović, R. R. (1995). *Preživljavanje politike*. Unireks.

Brajdoti, R. (2016). *Posthumano*. Fakultet za medije i komunikacije.

Chari, S., & Verdery, K. (2009). Thinking between the posts: Postcolonialism, postsocialism, and ethnography after the Cold War. *Comparative Studies in Society and History, 51*(1), 6–34. Retrieved from http://www.jstor.org/stable/27563729

Cvetićanin, N. (2008). *Epoha s one strane levice i desnice / O levici, desnici i centru u političkom polju Evrope o građanskom i antigrađanskom shvatanju politike o postideološkoj politici u 21. veku*. Službeni glasnik / IDN.

Davie, G. (2007). *The sociology of religion*. Sage.

Dugandžija, N. (1980). *Svjetovna religija*. NIRO Mladost.

Đurković, M. (2021). *Mračni koridori moći*. IES / Catena Mundi.

Fuzaro, D. (2022). *Globalni udar / Terapeutski kapitalizam i Veliki reset*. Akademska knjiga.

Genon, R. (2022). *Istok i Zapad / Premošćavanje razlika*. Zlatno runo.

Gross, B. (1979). The contradictions of socialism and capitalism. *India International Centre Quarterly, 6*(1), 12–19. Retrieved from http://www.jstor.org/stable/23001591

Han, B. C. (2015). *The burnout society*. Stanford University Press.

Katić, N. (2015). *Iz drugog ugla*. Catena Mundi.

Krauč, K. (2014). *Postdemokratija / prevod Milana Đurašinov*. Karpos / Binder.

Kuljić, T. (2002). *Prevladavanje prošlosti*. Helsinški odbor za ljudska prava.

Kuljić, T. (2006). *Kultura sećanja / istorijska objašnjenja upotrebe prošlosti*. Čigoja štampa.

Marinković, D. (2008). *Uvod u sociologiju / Osnovni pristupi i teme*. Mediterran Publishing.

Mekgrat, A. (2022). *Sumrak ateizma: uspon i pad neverja u modernom svetu*. Biblos Books.

Samardžić, O., & Živković, P. (2016). Simbolička tekstura postsocijalističke transformacije urbanog prostora (Podgorica-Zagreb). In A. Svirčić Gotovac & R. Šarović (ur.), *Tranzicijska preobrazba glavnih gradova Zagreba i Podgorice kao sustava naselja* (pp. 167–200). Institut za društvena istraživanja u Zagrebu.

Stojiljković, Z. (2017). *Srbija traži vođu*. Službeni glasnik, Vukotić media.

Svirčić, G. A., & Šarović, R. (ur.) (2016). *Tranzicijska preobrazba glavnih gradova Zagreba i Podgorice kao sustava naselja*. Institut za društvena istraživanja u Zagrebu.

Tartalja, S. (1976). *Skriveni krug / Obnova ciklizma u filozofiji istorije*. PKSSO.

Uelbek, M. (2015). *Pokoravanje / prev. Vladimir D. Janković*. Booka.

Vladušić, S. (2012). *Crnjanski, Megalopolis*. Službeni glasnik.

Volin, S. Š. (2007). *Politika i vizija – kontinuitet i inovacija u zapadnoj političkoj misli / prev. Slobodan Damjanović*. Filip Višnjić.

Vrcan, S. (1990). Omladina, religija i crkva. In V. Iličin (Ed.), *Ogledi o omladini osamdesetih* (pp. 111–150). IDIS.

Vukićević, S. (1998a). *Mit o nauci i obrazovanju / preispitivanje*. Institut za filozofiju i sociologiju Filozofskog fakulteta u Nikšiću.

Vukićević, S. (1998b). *Simuliranje promjene / transfromacija socijalizma*. Univerzitet Crne Gore.

Vukićević, S. (prir.) (2012). *Demografski i populacioni problemi u Crnoj Gori / Društvo, porodica, omladina*. CANU.

Vukićević, S. (prir.) (2016). Постсоциализм (Черногория—Россия 1990–2015). МГУ имени М.В. Ломоносова - Социологический факультет / Институт социологии и психологии Философский факультет Университета Черногории.

Wettersten, J. (1993). The sociology of scientific establishments today. *British Journal of Sociology*, 44(1), 69–102. https://doi.org/10.2307/591682

Zakarija, F. (2004). *Budućnost slobode – neoliberalna demokratija kod kuće i u svetu*. BDan Graf.

Živković, P. (2017). Intelektualac – izgubljena riječ u prevodu i/ili sjenka izgubljenog raja. Letopis Matice srpske, 193, (1–2), 89–99.

Živković, P., & Bakrač, V. (2017). Evroazija – idejna nužnost ili ideološka privlačnost. *Sociološka luča*, XI(2), 50–61.

Брдар, М. (2005). *Узалудан позив / Карл Манхајм и социологија знања као саморефлексија друштвених наука*. Stylos.

Давутоглу, А. (2014). *Стратегијска дубина / Међународни положај Турске / превод Сенка Ивошевић Ипек*. ЈП Службени гласник.

Дугин, Г. А. (2004). *Основи геополитике / Геополитичка будућност Русије / превод Сава и Петар Росић*. Екопрес.

Дугин, Г. А. (2013). *Четврта политичка теорија / превод Сава Росић*. МИР Publishing.

Коцијанчич, Г. (2021). *Између истока и запада / четири прилога екстатици*. Bilbos Books.

Раконяц, М., Живкович, П., Раделич, Б., & Бакрач, В. (2022). Анализ социальных явлений, связанных с пандемией COVID-19. *Вопросы филосо-фии, 2022*(3), 64–70.

Савин, В. Л., & Дугин, Г. А. (2018). *Мрежни ратови: аналитички извјештај Александра Дугина [[и] Леонид В. Савина] уз учешће Валерија Коровина и Александра Бовдунова / превод Слободан Стојичевић*. Авала пресс.

Танасковић, Д. (2010). *Неоосманизам / Повратак Турске на Балкан / Доктрина и спљнополитичка пракса*. ЈП Службени гласник / Службени гласник Републике Српске.

Vladimir Bakrač was born in Montenegro. After completing his graduate and postgraduate studies in 2009, he applied for doctoral studies at the Faculty of Philosophy at the University of Belgrade, in the Department of Sociology. He defended doctoral thesis titled 'Religiosity of the Young in Montenegro' at the Faculty of Philosophy in Belgrade. He has been engaged in teaching at the Faculty of Philosophy, University of Montenegro, as a professor of Sociology of Religion, Politics and Religion, and Sociology of Politics. Currently (since 2022) he works as associate professor at the University of Montenegro, Faculty of Philosophy, Political Science. He is the author of many scientific papers, articles, and reviews, mainly in the field of religion, and a participant in national and international scientific conferences. In addition to the papers he has published in scholarly journals, he has published a monograph Religions and Youth, as well as a Glossary of Monotheistic Religions. He is the head of the Department of Sociology at the Faculty of Philosophy, University of Montenegro.

Predrag Živković is a professor at the Faculty of Philosophy, University of Montenegro. He also taught at the Faculty of Architecture, University of Montenegro. He is actively engaged in sociological research, as demonstrated by his participation in the implementation of national and international scientific projects, studies, and monographs. The specific fields of his scientific-theoretical interest and research are sociology of politics, political philosophy, geopolitics, sociology of international relations, memory culture, thanatopolitics, thanatosociology, necroculture, and sociology of culture. As a scholarship holder for specialist doctoral studies, he studied at the Faculty of Sociology of M. V. Lomonosov Moscow State University.

Chapter 16
Polish Sociology and the Post-socialist Transformation

Agnieszka Kolasa-Nowak

The fall of communism in Poland marked the beginning of a long-term, complex process of social reconstruction and reformulation of fundamental principles. The transformation was seen as a challenge for the whole of society. The new governing elites had to develop and implement a broad project involving new economic and political rules. For ordinary people, it meant the necessity to adapt to new conditions. It also created a new situation for sociology: in addition to usual tasks, such as observing, monitoring, and gathering data, it was also supposed to provide an understanding and evaluation of the on-going processes. Although, in view of the extraordinary situation of deep societal change, a specific role for sociological studies seemed obvious, it is difficult to determine their actual impact on the course of transformation. Nevertheless, there are some aspects for which the role of Polish sociologists could be noticed.

From the very beginning, sociologists have taken up the transformation as the main subject of their field. It remained the dominant framework at least until Poland's accession to the European Union in 2004. Sociological reflection has developed in four subsequent stages: the discourses of transition, post-communism, European integration, and critical approach. All these issues have been considered essential to society's development. Sociologists in Poland see themselves as part of the intellectual elite, whose role has traditionally been identified as leaders of a society that needed to compensate for its historical backwardness. In the times of the Solidarity social movement, sociologists played an important role as providers of the general picture of social conflict and the analysis of the delegitimisation of the system. Their prominent position at the time defined the expectations in the

A. Kolasa-Nowak (✉)
Institute of Sociology, Marie Curie-Sklodowska University, Lublin, Poland
e-mail: agnieszka.kolasa-nowak@mail.umcs.pl

period of transformation, which is why it is worth starting with a description of the role of Polish sociology in the socialist era.

16.1 Polish Sociology in Socialism

Poland has a long sociological tradition, reaching back to the beginnings of the modern Polish state in 1918. The establishment of communist rule after the Second World War resulted in the Stalinisation of all spheres of life, including academia. In 1948, sociology, recognised as a 'bourgeois science', was eradicated from all universities. The chairs of sociology were abolished, and sociology courses closed. Luckily, this did not last long; after 1956, the trend was reversed. Sociologists regained their academic positions, and sociological studies shortly became one of the most popular among students.

From then on, there has been a stable development of academic sociology, marked by strong international connections. This was reflected in the constant reception of Western theories and the international presence of Polish sociologists in the International Sociological Association (see Bucholc, 2016). Polish sociology quite swiftly returned to its pre-war position as a regional leader in the discipline (Keen & Mucha, 2004, p. 128). One of the reasons was its strong methodological tradition and theoretical achievement. Significant developments occurred in many aspects of sociological expertise. Since the 1970s, sociology has been taught at the seven biggest public universities. The first opinion poll centre in Soviet-dominated Eastern Europe was established in 1958 at the Polish public radio service. In the 1960s and 1970s, over 400 industrial facilities employed in-house sociologists who were supposed to contribute to effective management by using their sociological expertise and methodology in practice (Kwaśniewicz, 1994, p. 66). The Polish Sociological Association, established in 1956, was a large and relatively independent professional organisation (see Sułek, 2011).

The dissemination of new Western sociological theories and research methods was possible as a result of contacts with universities in the United States through Ford Foundation scholarship programmes, which started in 1957. This contributed to a relatively early opening of Marxist sociology to contemporary trends. Poland was the window to the West for many scholars from communist countries (Mucha & Krzyżowski, 2014, p. 409). This Westernisation of Polish sociology gained a new dimension in the late 1970s and 1980s when sociologists became involved in anti-communist opposition. After 1980, most sociologists supported the Solidarity social movement (Bucholc, 2016, p. 52; Kaźmierska et al., 2015, p. 252). Their most direct involvement was participation in the circle of experts during the strike at the Gdańsk Shipyard in August 1980. At the time, Polish society was the only one massively contesting the socialist system. Simultaneously, the country had a well-developed academic sociology. This resulted in a large body of research on the on-going social conflict. Although, under the conditions of censorship, these analyses were published in a very limited number of copies, their influence on Polish public opinion was quite considerable, thanks to the practice of 'oral sociology' (Sułek, 1987). The discipline had the ambition to 'spread social self-awareness' by making people realise their aspirations in socialist reality (Lutyński, 1987). In a society deprived of free access to information and the circulation of ideas, sociologists saw themselves as 'a medium giving voice to social moods, attitudes, and aspirations' (Ziółkowski, 1987, p. 20). In 1986, the Warsaw branch of the Polish Sociological Association prepared an expert opinion and a radical programme of change (Sułek, 2011, p. 159). The next year, a report by Stefan Nowak, calling for urgent, deep social and systemic reforms, was published in a sociological journal (Nowak, 1988). Social scientists were involved in the process of pre-transformation negotiations known as the Round Table talks. By the time of the systemic breakthrough in 1989, Polish sociology had the experience of participating in the creation of a new reality. It was a unique occasion for academics to explain society to itself directly and interactively as the events unfolded. Moreover, international attention to an unprecedented situation in the Soviet bloc created particular interest in Polish sociological studies (Bucholc, 2016, pp. 52–53). It was a unique moment for Polish sociologists: their interpretations were important for local and foreign audiences alike. They provided Poles with a language to describe the on-going social conflict. For external observers, the Solidarity social movement was an example of civil society in action. At the time, Polish sociology was a kind of 'a two-way exhibition window', providing East European sociologists with an insight into the world achievements of the discipline and presenting an image of the problems of communist Europe to Western sociologists (Kwaśniewicz, 2005, p. 248).

16.2 Breakthrough and Transition

The unexpected and surprising end of 'real socialism' found researchers busy with the issues of its disintegration but unprepared for coping with the problems of building a new system. One must agree with Claus Offe's (1995) statement that post-communist transformation was 'a revolution with no revolutionary theory' (p. 16). In Poland, it was seen as a 'neo-traditionalist' exercise, 'a revolution in the name of [a] return to normality', the old, tried, and tested rules and social forms (Rychard, 1995, p. 5; Staniszkis, 1992, p. 32). This was why sociologists' attention was focused not so much on the content of the reforms and their direction as on their possible social blockades and future long-term effects on society. They believed that 'normal' (which meant Western-like), spontaneous, bottom-up processes of social adaptation would be stimulated by the new rules of market economy and political democracy. The expected ease of transition to the free market and democracy was based on the conviction that the implemented model not only met the expectations and aspirations of Poles but was also rational and promising. There was very little consideration of options other than neoliberal ones, especially those that took into account the interests of employees who had lost their position in the labour market (e.g., Kowalik, 1991). Academic interest was mainly focused on overcoming the burden of socialist residue.

Sociologists took an active part in the transition mainly as experts, although at the first stage, they were also involved in the government: for some time, two ministers and three deputy ministers in the same cabinet were academic sociologists (Sułek, 1992, pp. 22–23). A clear proof of the importance of their professional expertise was the project called 'The President Asks the Questions—The Sociologists Give Their Advice'. In the third year of transformation, a hundred renowned Polish intellectuals were asked fundamental questions about Poland's most needed actions and policies, the most salient dangers, and the most difficult issues at the time. Among them, there were 14 leading sociologists, mainly from Warsaw academic institutions. In their opinion, transformation had created a unique opportunity to enter the European community and overcome the barrier of historical backwardness. However, the openness to imitating Western models should have been accompanied by protective mechanisms. They pointed out the social costs of the change: growing disorientation of people, declining confidence in the reforms, lowering living standards, and 'neoliberal insensitivity'. The academics also expressed concern about the first signs of social polarisation and division between 'winners' and 'losers' (Kurczewska, 1992). Sociologists, as part of the intellectual elite, approved of the premises of the reforms and even felt responsible for the intellectual and political quality of the project of transformation. They saw themselves as mediators between the wide social strata and the political elite. Their strong belief in the significance of sociological expertise in the transition was the consequence of their engagement in the Solidarity social movement.

At this point, it seemed that the Polish case would be similar to the transition from dictatorship to democracy known from Latin America or Spain and Portugal. Such an image of a swift passage, however, appeared insufficient and simplistic for sociologists, although it had been widely accepted.

The change was set in motion by new, officially introduced rules, which required adaptation of individual reactions. The ensuing result was bound to include a mix of intended and unintended changes. According to sociologists, the gradual dissemination of new institutional rules had been restrained by old habits (Rychard, 1993). A configuration of group interests inherited from the old system was a factor motivating people to defend themselves in the free-market environment. This was identified as the reason that made it difficult for new types of interests to emerge. One of the popular claims was that the era of socialism had destroyed social ties and resulted in deficits in social capital. This was supposed to be counterproductive to the creation of an expected civil society and active citizens (Sztompka, 1999). 'Civilisational incompetence' meant the absence of individualistic, future-oriented attitudes, which were much needed in the projected democratic public sphere (Sztompka, 1993). The term 'homo sovieticus', referring to a type of mentality unconducive to the new order, gained wide currency (Świda-Ziemba, 1994) and was frequently used as an explanation of attitudes seen as dysfunctional or irrational from the point of view of the aims and objectives of transformation. Consequently, the assumption was that reforms had to rely on a yet non-existent 'theoretical interest' of the middle class

(Staniszkis, 1991, 1992; Mokrzycki, 1991, p. 57). The workers came to be portrayed as a group threatening the success of reforms due to their socialist mentality (Krzemiński, 1993). In 2002, the weaknesses of the democratic system were still explained by the persistence of influential interest groups, mainly workers from large industrial plants (Mokrzycki et al., 2002). In the country of the Solidarity social movement, there was a quick shift in perception of the role of society, especially its lower strata. In the 1980s, society was seen as the main actor of social change; in the next decade, it became 'the subject of concern' (Morawski, 1996, p. 170). According to an external observer, the marginalisation of Polish workers was 'one of the most unusual phenomena in the history of political sociology' (Ost, 2005, p. 52). In the liberal discourse of the 1990s, there was no room for the articulation of their interests, especially in economic terms. Instead, it was replaced by a conflict of historically defined identities.

As a project designed from above and aimed at accelerated modernisation, the process of departure from communism showed marked similarities with the introduction of the system after the Second World War. But this 'social engineering of democratic transformation' was mentioned very rarely (Narojek, 1993) and became the subject of sociological analysis only in one aspect. The phenomenon of 'liberalism after communism' as a peculiar transfer of liberalism to the alien social environment of Eastern European countries came to be critically studied by Jerzy Szacki (1995). In post-communist countries, liberalism was becoming 'constructivist' and served primarily as a justification for social engineering, whose objective was the rapid building of capitalism. In Poland, it took the form of 'state liberalism', a hybrid formed by a clash of top-down implementation and grassroots resistance in the name of egalitarian ideas (Morawski, 1993; Wnuk-Lipiński, 1996, p. 61). However, this critical analysis of the ideological foundations of transformation had limited influence outside academia.

Apparently, the intellectual atmosphere of the 'end of history' was not conducive to raising new questions, and sociologists no longer shaped the discussion on the prospects of Poland as they had before 1989 (Szacki, 1993, p. 175). They were rather perceived as technocrats and professionals whose task was to deliver reports on the current situation, indicating the difficulties and obstacles to the transformation. The sociological discourse was in accord with the dominant narrative of the first stage of transformation. The on-going change was about a complete eradication of all remains of socialism in order to create a neoliberal market economy and democratic public sphere.

16.3 Post-communism: Critical Analysis of Stabilisation of the New System

With time, attention was drawn to the evolutionary nature of change. The metaphor of the breakthrough and transition gave way to images of a gradual transformation of the whole system. It slowly became evident that the social order was governed by two different types of rules: one originating in the past, in real socialism, and the other, new, stemming from market and democratic reforms. From the second half of the 1990s, the idea of a temporary and transient nature of the current social reality was replaced by the recognition of a new system which had been gradually rooted in everyday activities (Marody, 1996, p. 274).

This new phase was described as incomplete and open. The change evidently lost its pace. The term post-communism was used with the undertones suggesting that the modernisation project had taken a different course than expected. Intended to stress the distinctiveness of this transitory period, the term gained popularity in public debate. Sociologists drew the attention of the public not only to the problematic nature of the rapid transition but also to the characteristics of the new stage. In broad terms, the post-communism of the 1990s was characterised by a domination of hybrid forms of ownership, increasing polarisation of social structure, and the weakness of the middle class. Sociologists were concerned about the premature consolidation of the system and its incompleteness resulting from unfinished institutional changes (Rychard, 1996; Staniszkis, 1994, 2001 Marody, 2004; Mokrzycki et al., 2002).

The systemic change in its daily course was seen as a confrontation of top-down elite design with grassroots strategies of individuals. The project of institutional reform was subject to constant modification through contact with values and interests on the individual level. The 'new reality' emerged, therefore, by trial and error, and its shape was difficult to predict. Three levels of institutional change were distinguished. The basic one was the level of new constitutional rules. The second was the level at which operational rules of state administration and law-making in specific issues were produced. Since they were subject to political games, this level was where systemic uncertainty and ambiguity were generated. Finally, the last one was the level of spontaneous grassroots institutionalisation, identified as the environment in which individual strategies of social actors forged the beginnings of social order. New institutionalism became an inspiration to Polish sociologists at the time: it enabled an analysis which was closer to reality and blurred the radical nature of the transformation, intertwining old and new elements. In this perspective, the intentionality and linear character of change as an implemented reform project were diminished (Rychard, 1996).

Sociologists were looking for signs of stabilisation of the new system. They tracked the progress of its legitimation in everyday strategies of social actors. With time, they focused on assessing the social consequences of transformation, mainly the negative ones. A new field of study was that of emerging divisions in Polish society.

Apart from institutions typical of democratic systems, some sociologists noticed new informal solutions, which they referred to as 'the second' (i.e., concealed) stage of democracy (Mokrzycki et al., 2002) or its backstage. According to the most far-reaching interpretations, it was the environment of real power and interests reproduced from socialism by hidden interest groups (Zybertowicz, 2005). This served as an argument in a growing political conflict between conservatives and liberals. Criticism of the course of transformation was one of the most important political weapons in this attack. The attention of social scientists was also focused on pathologies of the new system, such as corruption, clientelism, or informal networks (Gadowska, 2002; Jarosz, 2001; Kamiński, 1997; Kamiński & Kamiński, 2004). Their proliferation was seen as proof of the faults of the transformation project. However, one of the most important negative effects of systemic change was that Poland became an increasingly divided country. Indeed, sociologists began to wonder whether there emerged 'two different societies: those taking part in the transformation and those left out, whose resources were devalued in new circumstances' (Marody, 1997, p. 17; Adamski & Rychard, 1998).

The division between 'winners' and 'losers' indicated the most often experienced aspect of the change. These notions had become very frequently used in critical comments about transformation in public discourse. This involved a different pace and rhythm of development and different developmental prospects of the two groups. The neoliberal model introduced by the reforms not only created new lines of inequalities but also deepened the existing divisions. For years, sociologists have been warning against the progressing polarisation or 'the Matthew effect' (Słomczyński & Janicka, 2008, p. 125; see also Słomczyński et al., 2007). The ongoing change was seen as resulting in the emergence of two almost separate parts of society, also in the sphere of mentality. One was characterised by optimism, individualism, and self-reliance. The other was described as the 'authoritarian syndrome' (Ziółkowski et al., 2001, p. 256). Later, the phenomenon came to be known as 'a society of two vectors', with growing social differentiation (also regional) pushing it apart in opposite directions. The issue was also conceptualised as a split between traditional and modern Poland, with the former lagging behind the pace of progress of the latter. 'A journey between Warsaw and a village in north-eastern Poland is a journey in time' (Giza-Poleszczuk, 2004, p. 265). The growing social divisions were gradually seen as related to regional differences of durable historical origins.

16.4 Accession to the European Union

Around the year 2000, a new subject emerged both in academic studies and in public discourse: the place of Poland in the global system and the challenges stemming from opening up to modern global processes. Systemic transformation began to be perceived as a process gradually 'dissolving' in global changes. In this respect, the 'Polish case' became less and less unique and shaped mostly by external factors.

This broadening of perspectives was connected with the forthcoming accession of the country to the European Union. In this context, analyses of 'Polish society in the unifying Europe' became widely popular. The process of integration was approached from the perspective of imitative modernisation, which, this time, had been enriched with the awareness of growing regional diversity and the impact of history.

This is why sociological studies gained a comparative dimension, including not only the post-communist countries but also the rest of Europe or the world. Sociologists began to reflect on the range of possible trajectories of development (see Kochanowicz, 1998), and the future was no longer as obvious and clear as it had been so far. The post-communist transformation was placed in the long-term perspective. This meant a need for a macro-systemic approach and the search for the historical factors that shaped separate developmental paths. Regional variations were seen as examples of different stages of modernisation processes. There was a growing awareness that the barriers to 'catching up' with Europe were quite difficult to overcome for relatively backward eastern regions. Eastern Europe entered the era of globalisation while experiencing a confusion of historical epochs and 'time compression'. Such a perspective implies a coexistence of elements that belong to different stages of the development of capitalism, ranging from those typical of highly developed regions to ones characteristic of peripheral areas, including post-communist countries with their imitative modernisation (Ziółkowski, 1998).

After a decade, it was widely acknowledged that transformation was a process dependent on history. Path dependence was an inseparable component of the interpretation of change. In analyses of regional differentiation, the eastern regions of Poland were generally characterised as the most underdeveloped areas with the lowest development potential. In the dominant discourse of modernisation, eastern Poland appears as a model opposite of strong, rapidly growing regions. In addition to this, it is an example of a region where the influence of the past appears to be the strongest and virtually impossible to overcome. This historical burden is not restricted to economic infrastructure but also pertains to the mentality of the population. The lack of expected patterns of behaviour and modern attitudes is explained in terms of a burden of pre-modern tradition rather than such present structural features as unemployment or poverty (Gorzelak, 2001; Jałowiecki & Szczepański, 2002).

The perspective of the *longue durée* in Eastern Europe exposed the burden of the distant past. The project of integration with Europe could be seen as a chance to overcome it and make a leap towards a rich, modern welfare society. Sociologists turned their attention to dependency theory and Immanuel Wallerstein's world-system theory (Kochanowicz, 1998; Sosnowska, 1997). There were interpretations of the Polish post-1989 change as yet another example of a top-down attempt to break away from the backward position of Eastern Europe (Sosnowska, 2004; cf. Leszczyński, 2013). The issue of backwardness and underdevelopment has spread outside academia, and the problem of the durable peripheral position of Poland penetrated the public debate. From this perspective, entering the European Union and opening to globalisation processes were not seen as an opportunity but as a threat. The peripheral capitalism of the post-communist region could lead to the petrification of backwardness in new hierarchies of the global market (Staniszkis, 2003).

A new interpretative framework involved the idea of transition from a Soviet province of 'the Second World' to a periphery of the world capitalist system, as well as the notion of concluding the process of modernisation, which followed the selective modernisation introduced by 'real socialism'. At this point, however, the polarisation of discourses began. It followed the previous split between the optimistic view of the transformation as a chance for individual entrepreneurship and a critical approach stressing negative consequences for individuals and the national community. There was an increasing difference between the two kinds of explanations. While one was based on the conventional modernisation paradigm, the other stressed traditional local values, sometimes opposed to the cosmopolitan modern values of the European Union. A practical dilemma was whether to apply solutions that worked in the Western context or look for homemade, indigenous ones. Since the conflicting visions of Poland's place in the global system are one of the main reasons for the controversy, attitudes to its peripheral status have been identified as an important factor dividing the political scene in the country.

16.5 Critical Sociology

With time, sociological studies conducted in the spirit of the modernisation model have come under increasing criticism owing to their distinctly normative standpoint and arbitrary, paternalistic tone towards society. The point was that 'the enchantment of Polish sociology with the theory of modernisation' had excluded other approaches for years (Sosnowska, 2004, p. 14). Critics also pointed out that analyses following the paradigm of implementing Western patterns lacked originality and overlooked important areas of sociological study. As identified, their principal fault was the outside perspective taken by sociologists, who adopted foreign standards imposed by the logic of modernisation (cf. Bukraba-Rylska, 2004). Critics also stressed the abstract and unrealistic character of the adopted model of modernity. From the conservative point of view, a strong cultural identity enables a successful combination of local tradition and modern requirements. Some elements of Polish tradition could be seen as a useful resource for coping with global challenges (Krasnodębski, 2003, p. 221).

In recent years in Polish sociology, there has been a growing interest in the consequences of the centre-periphery division. This may be seen as an approach critical to the mainstream understanding of modernising efforts related to EU accession. The main point is that the imposition of categories taken from the dominant discourse of well-developed, wealthy Western societies deprives peripheries of their own voice. Consequently, they are unable to define themselves in terms other than those expressed in the alien language of peripherality and necessary imitation (Said, 1978). This sets an important task for sociologists: a search for a new, better-tailored approach to express particular Polish problems. Sociologists are becoming aware of the public function of social sciences as a source of imagery and interpretations which provide an alternative perspective. The political role of such knowledge is manifested in discursive games. Recently, critical analysis has been applied to the study of the mechanism of constructing images of Eastern Europe and the functioning of the ideology of 'Eastness' as an effect of the process of Orientalisation (Zarycki, 2014). It is based on Pierre Bourdieu's theory and postcolonial perspective, both of which are very popular in Poland. The latter seems to be especially useful for rethinking the transformation, as confirmed by translations of major works of postcolonial theory and a continuing discussion over its suitability for Polish problems (Buchowski, 2006; Domańska, 2008; Kołodziejczyk, 2010; Skórczewski, 2013). It functions as a conceptual framework in the attempts to rethink and criticise the idea of imitation of the Western path, which was the main principle of the neoliberal project in Poland. It has also created a theoretical context for a new and growing object of study: the role of the intelligentsia and intellectual elites, including sociologists, in understanding and diagnosing the peripheral status of Poland. They 'function as an intermediary transmitting the patterns of Western modernity and as a peculiar guarantee that the country remains a part of Western civilization' (Zarycki, 2009, p.116). Being a Polish intellectual, then, necessarily entails adopting a Western perspective of modernisation, which consequently makes it difficult to recognise the essence of local differences. This approach is marked by a patronising and arbitrary attitude towards society. Polish mainstream social sciences become key providers of academic and intellectual discourse legitimating neoliberal reforms. The notion of the 'comprador service sector', initially applied to local managers of global corporations (Drahokoupil, 2008), has been turned to the 'comprador elite' (Bukraba-Rylska, 2004, p. 157). Moreover, the Polish sociological field is also interpreted as a structural reflection of the political field, 'which rather than being structured by the left vs right logic may be seen as divided between pro-and anti-centre poles' (Warczok & Zarycki, 2014). In this perspective, a fundamental framework of sociological discourse, the division between 'winners' and 'losers', which repeats the divisions between modern and traditional, European and anti-European, is a legitimation of the privileged status of the winning elites. It also implies that the position of the 'loser' results from one's own misguided choices, hiding the fact that it may be an effect of structural injustice.

Analyses of the special position of intelligentsia are based on the conception of its compensatory role as 'cultural capitalists' in Eastern Europe (Eyal et al., 1998). Critical sociology in Poland must ultimately turn to a self-diagnosis of its own representatives. A deep understanding of the social situation of intellectual elites is more important in peripheral societies. The popularity of the critical approach has increased, particularly among young researchers seeking a new key to understanding the social processes in Polish post-transformation society (Kolasa-Nowak, 2015). However, in peripheral conditions, it is not easy to determine in whose name and from what viewpoint critical analysis is conducted.

In recent years, sociologists in Poland have become even more interested in practices of meaning production and the formation of collective imaginations (Hałas & Maslowski, 2021). There are many new popular subjects, including discourses about Eastern Europe, regional imaginaries of community formation, the origins of contemporary collective identities, and the functioning of the Polish public sphere. In these studies, history and path dependency plays an important role. Historical sociology has recently become very popular in Poland, as well as memory studies (Kolasa-Nowak & Bucholc, 2023; Kończal & Wawrzyniak, 2018). Taking up historical topics, sociologists join current Polish public debates, as is the case of the renewed discussion on the peasant roots of Polish society (Leszczyński, 2020; Rauszer, 2020; Pobłocki, 2021). This need to rethink the legacy of the pre-communist past is, in my opinion, a delayed effect of transformation. This all gives rise to yet another new thematic field in Polish sociology, which is about the global knowledge production system and the historical sociology of social science in a peripheral context (Zarycki, 2022a). Inspired by Bourdieu's sociology of science, these researchers explore the effect of homology between the changing field of power and the main axes of dispute in scientific debates in Polish historiography, linguistics, and sociology (Behr, 2021; Zarycki, 2022b). Thus, a critical sociology of the social sciences developed, which is a part of the broader question of the role of elites in post-transformation Eastern Europe.

At present, almost 35 years after the fall of communism, sociology in Poland is a mature science, rich with various research trends and interpretation styles. Alongside the mainstream of increasingly specialised research on topics common to all EU societies, critical and historical sociology is developing. In its theoretical pursuit, it goes beyond the framework of post-communism and constructs new interpretations focused on a separate, semi-peripheral path of development of Eastern Europe.

16.6 Conclusions

For years of social change, the sociological discourse in Poland played different roles depending on the stage of transformation. In the beginning, sociological studies fully supported the mainstream neoliberal discourse of imitative modernisation. It is important to stress that after 1989, no new ideas were sought, recognising the obviousness of the direction and purpose of the change. The atmosphere of the 'end of history' was not, however, accompanied by intellectual ferment (Szacki, 1993, p. 170). Scientific diagnoses were supposed to reveal the reasons for the difficulties in introducing new rules. The first years passed in the atmosphere of 'a revolution in the name of a return to normality'. According to their earlier findings, sociologists recognised that for Poles, transformation meant a chance to meet the expectations and aspirations expressed in the 1980s. From the role of committed social critics before 1989, researchers have come closer to the role of technocrats and agents of change. It was widely accepted that the transition was an attempt to follow tried and tested Western solutions with the necessary acceleration of a 'latecomer'. Society was described as a collective actor, and its actions were studied mainly in the context of the assumed goal of transformation. It was not discussed whether this kind of transition was necessary or possible in Polish conditions. It seemed that a new 'historical necessity' was again to be fulfilled in Poland (Sułek, 1995, p. 12). The prevailing tone of public discourse was strengthened by sociologists who added such notions as civilisational incompetence, socialist residues, and the 'homo sovieticus' syndrome. The propagation of the idea of civil society as an imperative of modern democratic society also affected sociology. There was a considerable effort to reformulate this general concept into empirically detectable indicators to measure its so highly anticipated development (see Szczegóła, 2017).

Soon enough, however, the initial enthusiasm gave way to disappointment stemming from the prolonged transitional period, the unfinished shape of the institutional system, and the slowing down of the pace of change. The most important question concerned the causes of this situation. Sociologists began to diagnose individual strategies and grassroots activities in which people assimilated new rules and institutions. The gradual adaptation resulted in a new social reality at the micro- and meso-levels. Its shape was difficult to predict. Inspirations from new institutionalism have been adjusted to explain these processes. In this perspective, individual actors regained their agency and autonomy. However, it was the idea of post-communism as a period of hybrid forms and the incomplete shape of the social system that attracted public attention. The social costs of transformation, pathologies, and deviation from the linear path of transition dominated public discourse in Poland. These issues entered the dictionary of political polemics. Critical analyses of the modernisation project and its top-down implementation have started. The social imaginary was enriched with a metaphor of new divisions, cracks, and even the growing polarisation of Polish society. They were spotted in different dimensions: structural, regional, and mental. The division between 'winners' and 'losers' became the most popular image of the costs of transformation. It was frequently used in political struggles, as with years, the project of transformation came under growing criticism.

After Poland's accession to the European Union, sociological studies gained a comparative and historical dimension. There was a growing awareness of the legacy of the pre-socialist past of the backward region of Eastern Europe. That was the point from which the modernisation paradigm was criticised. The imaginaries taken from dependency theory, world-system theory, or postcolonial studies have penetrated the public debate. They have been adapted to the local context and inspired sociologists to search for original, indigenous interpretations. These new concepts drew on the achievements of critical sociology and focused on discourse analysis. One interesting direction of development is a study of Polish elites as managers of the discursive space. They are presented as responsible for implementing the project of transformation. This also involves criticism of sociological diagnoses for their distinctly normative standpoint and their arbitrary, paternalistic tone towards society. Social scientists have been accused of showing a lack of sensitivity to their own cultural context and an inability to invent local categories to express the unique, post-socialist experience (Csepeli et al., 1996), which resulted in neglecting important issues. Once again, like in the 1980s, the role of sociology is to expose hidden mechanisms and take up issues that are absent in public discourse.

The status of the sociological profession is quite strong in Poland. This academic community seems to be quite independent and autonomous. It has a long genealogy, which started with the beginning of the modern Polish state after 1918. It had managed to create a strong institutional infrastructure and stable funding in the academic system. In communist times, it maintained relative autonomy from the political system and intellectual independence from official ideology. With time, the role of sociology diminished similarly to the position of academia in new capitalist and free-market reality, but sociologists have maintained their aspirations as leaders and experts in important issues of public discourse in Poland. In general, the main role of Polish sociologists comes closest to being activators (see Chap. 1), but it is more complex when seen from close.

The second dimension, which is the transformative role of sociology, is much more difficult to assess in the Polish case (Chap. 1). Sociologists play many roles as experts and consultants, academic researchers, and active participants in public debates. However, in the Polish context, the most important transformative aspect of sociology is connected with the role of public intellectuals engaging with wider audiences. The evolution of Polish sociology shows the durability of its public function and constant engagement in fundamental public debates. Shaping public discourse has been the most important way in which sociology influenced the Polish transformation. The standpoint of the discipline has changed from being affirmative of the transformation project to standing on the side of society and fulfilling the role of a 'guardian of democracy' to having an increasingly clear critical role. The sociological agenda during the entire post-war period stretched between the project of organised development and the idea of a return to normality (Kolasa-Nowak, 2017). Of course, it is impossible to determine precisely the strength of the influence that sociological interpretations had on the course of change in the Polish public sphere, although it does not seem to be particularly big considering the complexity and the variety of factors shaping social transformation in Poland. There are also some quite surprising side effects of this involvement with the project of change. By recognising the entanglement of the role of the sociologist as an engaged citizen, our discipline developed reflexivity on a previously unknown scale.

Recently, in the context of the global historical sociology of knowledge, the trajectories of Polish intellectuals are being theorised using the thesis of the dominant position of the cultural elite in the field of power. There is a growing awareness that sociologists are involved in the process of creating collective imaginaries, which are directed at strengthening national identity. Sociology then could be seen as having a clear political aspect. In the vein of critical analysis, it can be seen with other social sciences as one of the 'tools for defending the autonomy of the national fields of power in a global context' (Zarycki, 2022a, p. 473). This results in social scientists having a dichotomy of orientation. There are two quite separate arenas in which they can receive recognition. One is obviously an international academia, but the other, which is equally or even more important, is the national field of power. This multi-positioning is typical for intellectual elites in Poland as peripheral ones. In their academic trajectories, they have to combine the duties of a scholar with those of a public figure with moral obligations in regard to the national community. This situates them in the position of activists, able to introduce alternative discourses in the public sphere and participate in the selection and retention of these discourses. However, they share this role with other social scientists. Sociologists give way here to historians, whose position in the Polish public sphere as creators and guardians of the social imaginary seems to be unchallenged so far (Kolasa-Nowak & Bucholc, 2023).

Competing Interests The authors have no conflicts of interest to declare that are relevant to the content of this chapter.

References

Adamski, W., & Rychard, A. (1998). Zakończenie [Conclusion]. In W. Adamski (Ed.), *Polacy '95. Aktorzy i klienci transformacji* [Poles 1995: Actors and beneficiaries of transformation]. Wydawnictwo IFiS PAN.

Behr, V. (2021). *Powojenna historiografia Polska jako pole walki. Studium z socjologii wiedzy i polityki* [Post-war Polish historiography as a battlefield. A study in the sociology of knowledge and politics]. Wydawnictwa Uniwersytetu Warszawskiego.

Bucholc, M. (2016). *Sociology in Poland: To be continued?* Palgrave Macmillan.

Buchowski, M. (2006). The specter of orientalism in Europe: From exotic other to stigmatized brother. *Anthropological Quarterly, 79*, 463–482.

Bukraba-Rylska, I. (2004). Socjolog czasu transformacji – Portret z negatywu [Sociologists of the transformation period: A reverse portrait]. In M. Marody (Ed.), *Zmiana czy stagnacja? Społeczeństwo polskie po czternastu latach transformacji* [Change or stagnation? Polish society after fourteen years of transformation]. Scholar.

Csepeli, G., Orkeny, A., & Scheppele, K. L. (1996). Acquired immune deficiency syndrome in social science in Eastern Europe. *Social Research, 63*(2).

Domańska, E. (2008). Obrazy PRL w pespektywie postkolonialnej [Visions of communist Poland in a post-colonial perspective]. In K. Brzechczyn (Ed.), *Obrazy PRL. O konceptualizacji realnego socjalizmu w Polsce* [Visions of communist Poland: Conceptualisation of 'real socialism' in Poland]. Oddział IPN.

Drahokoupil, J. (2008). The rise of the comprador service sector: The politics of state formation in Central and Eastern Europe. *Polish Sociological Review, 162*(2), 175–189.

Eyal, G., Szelenyi, I., & Townsley, E. R. (1998). *Making capitalism without capitalists: Class formation and elite struggles in post-communist Central Europe.* Verso.

Gadowska, K. (2002). *Zjawisko klientelizmu polityczno-ekonomicznego. Systemowa analiza powiązań sieciowych na przykładzie przekształceń sektora górniczego w Polsce* [The phenomenon of political and economic clientelism: An analysis of network connections on the example of the transformation of the mining sector in Poland]. Wydawnictwo UJ.

Giza-Poleszczuk, A. (2004). Brzydkie kaczątko Europy, czyli Polska po czternastu latach transformacji [The ugly duckling of Europe: Poland's fourteen years of transformation]. In M. Marody (Ed.), *Zmiana czy stagnacja? Społeczeństwo polskie po czternastu latach transformacji* [Change or stagnation? Polish society after fourteen years of transformation]. Wydawnictwo IFiS PAN.

Gorzelak, G. (2001). Przyszłość polskich regionów [The future of Polish regions]. In M. S. Szczepański (Ed.), *Jaki region? Jaka Polska? Jaka Europa?* [What kind of region? Poland? Europe?]. Wydawnictwo Uniwersytetu Śląskiego.

Hałas, E., & Maslowski, N. (Eds.). (2021). *Politics of symbolization across Central and Eastern Europe.* Peter Lang.

Jałowiecki, B., & Szczepański, M. S. (2002). *Rozwój lokalny i regionalny w perspektywie socjologicznej* [Local and regional development in the sociological perspective]. Wyższa Szkoła Zarządzania i Nauk Społecznych.

Jarosz, M. (ed.). (2001). *Manowce polskiej prywatyzacji* [Polish privatisation astray]. Wydawnictwo Naukowe PWN.

Kamiński, A. Z. (1997). Corruption under the Post-Communist transformation. *Polish Sociological Review, 2*, 91–117.

Kamiński, A. Z., & Kamiński B. (2004). *Korupcja rządów. Państwa postkomunistyczne wobec globalizacji* [Corruption of governments: Post-communist states facing globalisation]. Trio.

Kaźmierska, K., Waniek, K., & Zysiak, A. (2015). *Opowiedzieć uniwersytet. Łódź akademicka w biografiach wpisanych w losy Uniwersytetu Łódzkiego* [Academic Łódz in biographies]. Wydawnictwa Uniwersytetu Łódzkiego.

Keen, M. F., & Mucha, J. L. (2004). Sociology in Central and Eastern Europe in the 1990s: A decade of reconstruction. *European Societies, 6*(2), 123–147.

Kochanowicz, J. (1998). Transformacja Polska w świetle socjologii historycznej. Między Trzecim Światem a państwem opiekuńczym [Polish transformation in the perspective of historical sociology: Between the Third World and the welfare state]. *Kultura i Społeczeństwo, 1*, 23–37.

Kolasa-Nowak, A. (2015). Critical sociology in Poland and its public function. *Polish Sociological Review, 3*(191), 381–399.

Kolasa-Nowak, A. (2017). Polish sociology between the project of organised development and the idea of a return to normality. *State of Affairs, 13*, 67–92.

Kolasa-Nowak, A., & Bucholc, M. (2023). Historical sociology in Poland: Transformations of the uses of the past. *East European Politics and Societies, 37*(1), 3–29. https://doi.org/10.1177/08883254211057908

Kołodziejczyk, D. (2010). Postkolonialny transfer na Europę Środkowo-Wschodnią [Postcolonial transfer to Central-Eastern Europe]. *Teksty Drugie, 5*, 22–39.

Kończal, K., & Wawrzyniak, J. (2018). Provincializing memory studies: Polish approaches in the past and present. *Memory Studies, 11*(4), 391–404.

Kowalik, T. (1991). Zmiana ustroju – Wielka operacja czy proces społeczny? [The change of the system: A major operation or a social process?]. In R. Gortat (Ed.), *Społeczeństwo uczestniczące, gospodarka rynkowa, sprawiedliwość społeczna* [Participant society, market economy, social justice]. ISP UW.

Krasnodębski, Z. (2003). *Demokracja peryferii* [Democracy of the peripheries]. Wydawnictwo Słowo/obraz terytoria.

Krzemiński, I. (1993). Ideały i interesy: świadomość społeczna zakłopotana. Szkice do obrazu [Ideals and interests: A confused social awareness. A sketch]. In M. Grabowska & A. Sułek (Eds.), *Polska 1989–1992. Fragmenty pejzażu* [Poland 1989–1992: Fragments of the landscape]. Wydawnictwo IFiS PAN.

Kurczewska, J. (1992). The president asks the questions – The sociologists give their advice. *The Polish Sociological Bulletin, 3/4*(99/100), 197–364.

Kwaśniewicz, W. (1994). Dialectics of systemic constraint and academic freedom: Polish sociology under socialist regime. In M. F. Keen & J. L. Mucha (Eds.), *Eastern Europe in transformation: The impact on sociology*. Greenwood.

Kwaśniewicz, W. (2005). Socjologia Polska (1945–89) [Polish sociology, 1945–1989]. In *Encyklopedia socjologiczna. Suplement* [Encyclopedia of sociology. Supplement]. Oficyna Naukowa.

Leszczyński, A. (2013). *Skok w nowoczesność. Polityka wzrostu w krajach peryferyjnych 1943–1980* [A leap into modernity: Growth policy in peripheral countries, 1943–1980]. Krytyka Polityczna.

Leszczyński, A. (2020). *Ludowa historia Polski. Historia wyzysku i oporu. Mitologia panowania* [A people's history of Poland. A history of exploitation and resistance. Reign mythology]. WAB.

Lutyński, J. (1987). Niektóre uwarunkowania rozwoju socjologii polskiej i ich konsekwencje [Some developmental conditions of polish sociology and their consequences]. *Studia Socjologiczne, 2*, 127–141.
Marody, M. (Ed.). (1996). *Oswajanie rzeczywistości. Między realnym socjalizmem a realną demokracją* [Taming the reality: Between real socialism and real democracy]. Instytut Studiów Społecznych UW.
Marody, M. (1997). Post-transitology or is there any life after transition? *Polish Sociological Review, 1*, 13–21.
Marody, M. (Ed.). (2004). *Zmiana czy stagnacja? Społeczeństwo polskie po czternastu latach transformacji* [Change or stagnation? Polish society after fourteen years of transformation]. Scholar.
Mokrzycki, E. (1991). Dziedzictwo realnego socjalizmu, interesy grupowe i poszukiwanie nowej utopii [The heritage of real socialism, interest groups and the search for a new utopia]. In A. Sułek & W. Wincławski (Eds.), *Przełom i wyzwanie. Pamiętnik VIII Ogólnopolskiego Zjazdu Socjologicznego* [Breakthrough and challenge: Proceedings of the 8th Polish Sociological Congress]. Wydawnictwo Adam Marszałek.
Mokrzycki, E., Rychard A., & Zybertowicz, A. (Eds.). (2002). *Utracona dynamika? O niedojrzałości polskiej demokracji* [A lost dynamics? On the immaturity of Polish democracy]. Wydawnictwo IFiS PAN.
Morawski, W. (1993). Zmiana społeczna jako wyzwanie cywilizacyjne [Social change as a civilisational challenge]. In M. Grabowska & A. Sułek (Eds.), *Polska 1989–1992. Fragmenty pejzażu* [Poland 1989–1992: Fragments of the landscape]. Wydawnictwo IFiS PAN.
Morawski, W. (1996). Społeczeństwo i jednostka. Dwa typy podmiotowości [Society and the individual: Two types of subjectivity]. In A. Jasińska-Kania & J. Raciborski (Eds.), *Naród – Władza – Społeczeństwo* [Nation, authorities, society]. Scholar.
Mucha, J., & Krzyżowski, Ł. (2014). No longer between east and west: Dialectics and paradoxes in polish sociology. In S. Koniordos & A.-A. Kyrtsis (Eds.), *Routledge handbook of European sociology*. Routledge.
Narojek, W. (1993). Tworzenie ładu demokratycznego i rynku: inżynieria społeczna demokratycznej przebudowy [Shaping the democratic order and the market: Social engineering of democratic transformation]. In A. Rychard & M. Federowicz (Eds.), *Społeczeństwo w transformacji. Ekspertyzy i studia* [Society under transformation: Studies and expert reports]. Wydawnictwo IFiS PAN.
Nowak, S. (1988). Społeczeństwo polskie drugiej połowy lat 80tych. Próba diagnozy stanu świadomości społecznej [Polish society in the second half of the 1980s: A tentative diagnosis of the state of social consciousness]. *Studia Socjologiczne, 1*, 23–55.
Offe, C. (1995). Projektowanie instytucji w krajach Europy Wschodniej w okresie przemian [Designing institutions in East European countries in the time of changes]. In J. Hausner (Ed.), *Narodziny demokratycznych instytucji* [The birth of democratic institutions]. Wydawnictwo Akademii Ekonomicznej.
Ost, D. (2005). *The defeat of solidarity: Anger and politics in post-communist Europe*. Cornell University Press.
Pobłocki, K. (2021). *Chamstwo* [Rabble]. Wydawnictwo Czarne.
Rauszer, M. (2020). *Bękarty pańszczyzny. Historia buntów chłopskich* [Bastards of serfdom. History of peasant revolts]. Wydawnictwo RM.
Rychard, A. (1993). *Reforms, adaptation and breakthrough*. Wydawnictwo IFiS PAN.
Rychard, A. (1995). Ludzie i instytucje – Kto tworzy nowy ład? [People and institutions: Who makes a new order?]. *Studia Socjologiczne, 1–2*, 5–15.
Rychard, A. (1996). *Czy transformacja się skończyła? Powstawanie nowego ładu w perspektywie socjologii zmiany instytucjonalnej* [Is the transformation over? The shaping of the new order from the perspective of the sociology of institutional change]. Instytut Badań nad Gospodarką Rynkową.
Said, E. (1978). *Orientalism*. Routledge and Kegan Paul.

Skórczewski, D. (2013). *Teoria, literatura, dyskurs. Pejzaż postkolonialny* [Theory, literature, discourse: A postcolonial perspective]. Wydawnictwo KUL.
Słomczyński, K., & Janicka, K. (2008). Dychotomie w strukturze klasowej: o efekcie świętego Mateusza i pogłębiających się nierównościach społecznych [Dichotomy in the class structure: On the Matthew effect and deepening social inequality]. In J. Mucha, E. Narkiewicz-Niedbalec, & M. Zielińska (Eds.), *Co nas łączy, co nas dzieli?* [What unites us and what divides us?]. Oficyna Wydawnicza University of Zielona Góra.
Słomczyński, K., Janicka, K., Shabad, G., & Tomescu-Dubrow, I. (2007). Changes in class structure in Poland, 1988–2003: Crystallization of the winners-losers divide. *Polish Sociological Review, 1,* 45–64.
Sosnowska, A. (1997). Tu, tam – Pomieszanie [Here, there, confusion]. *Studia Socjologiczne, 4,* 61–85.
Sosnowska, A. (2004). *Zrozumieć zacofanie. Spory historyków o Europę Wschodnią (1947–1994)* [Understanding backwardness: Historical controversies about Eastern Europe, 1947–1994]. Trio.
Staniszkis, J. (1991). *The dynamics of the breakthrough in Eastern Europe.* University of California Press.
Staniszkis, J. (1992). Ciągłość i zmiana [Continuity and change]. *Kultura i Społeczeństwo, 1,* 23–41.
Staniszkis, J. (1994). *W poszukiwaniu paradygmatu transformacji* [In search of paradigm of transformation]. ISP PAN.
Staniszkis, J. (2001). *Postkomunizm. Próba opisu* [Post-communism: An attempted definition]. Słowo/obraz terytoria.
Staniszkis, J. (2003). *Władza globalizacji* [The helm of globalisation]. Scholar.
Sułek, A. (1987). Przeciwko socjologii oralnej [Against oral sociology]. *Kultura i Społeczeństwo, 31*(4), 227–229.
Sułek, A. (1992). Zmiana ustroju w Polsce a zmiany w życiu polskiej socjologii [Change of the political system in Poland and change in the life of polish sociology]. In B. Synak (Ed.), *Społeczeństwo polskie: Dylematy okresu transformacji systemowej* [Polish society: Dilemmas of systemic transformation]. Gdynia Victoria.
Sułek, A. (1995). Inauguracja Zjazdu [Inauguration of the congress]. In A. Sułek & J. Styk (Eds.), *Ludzie i instytucje: Stawanie się ładu społecznego. Pamiętnik IX Ogólnopolskiego Zjazdu Socjologicznego* [People and Institutions: The emergence of the social order: Proceedings of the 9th Polish sociological congress]. Wydawnictwo UMCS.
Sułek, A. (2011). *Obrazy z życia socjologii w Polsce* [Pictures from the life of sociology in Poland]. Oficyna Naukowa.
Świda-Ziemba, H. (1994). Mentalność postkomunistyczna [Post-communist mentality]. *Kultura i Społeczeństwo, 1,* 35–50.
Szacki, J. (1993). Sociology at the turning points of polish history. *Polish Sociological Review, 3,* 167–176.
Szacki, J. (1995). *Liberalism after communism.* CEU Press.
Szczegóła, L. (2017). Uwagi o roli i ewolucji polskiej refleksji wokół społeczeństwa obywatelskiego [Remarks on the role and evolution of Polish reflection on civil society]. *Roczniki Historii Socjologii, 7,* 35–55.
Sztompka, P. (1993). Civilizational incompetence: The trap of post-communist societies. *Zeitschrift für Soziologie, 22*(2), 85–95.
Sztompka, P. (Ed.). (1999). *Imponderabilia wielkiej zmiany. Mentalność, wartości I więzi społeczne czasów transformacji* [Imponderabilia of the period of great change: Mentality, values and social ties of the transformation period]. Wydawnictwo Naukowe PWN.
Warczok, T., & Zarycki, T. (2014). Bourdieu recontextualized: Redefinitions of Western critical thought in the periphery. *Current Sociology, 62*(3), 334–351.
Wnuk-Lipiński, E. (1996). *Demokratyczna rekonstrukcja. Z socjologii radykalnej zmiany społecznej* [Democratic reconstruction: On the sociology of rapid social change]. PWN.

Zarycki, T. (2009). Socjologia krytyczna na peryferiach [Critical sociology on the peripheries]. *Kultura i Społeczeństwo*, *1*, 105–121.

Zarycki, T. (2014). *Ideologies of Eastness in central and Eastern Europe*. Routledge.

Zarycki, T. (2022a). *The polish elite and language sciences: A perspective of global historical sociology*. Palgrave Macmillan.

Zarycki, T. (Ed.). (2022b). *Polskie nauki społeczne w kontekście relacji władzy i zależności międzynarodowych* [Polish social sciences in the context of power relations and international dependencies]. Wydawnictwa Uniwersytetu Warszawskiego.

Ziółkowski, J. (1987). Przemówienie inauguracyjne Przewodniczącego PTS [The opening speech of the chairman of the polish sociological association]. In E. Wnuk-Lipiński (Ed.), *VII Ogólnopolski Zjazd Socjologiczny. Materiały* [Proceedings of the 7th Polish Sociological Congress]. Polskie Towarzystwo Socjologiczne.

Ziółkowski, M. (1998). O różnorodności teraźniejszości. Pomiędzy tradycją, spuścizną socjalizmu, nowoczesnością a ponowoczesnością [On different varieties of the present: Between tradition, socialist heritage, modernity and postmodernity]. In A. Sułek & M. S. Szczepański (Eds.), *Śląsk – Polska – Europa. Zmieniające się społeczeństwo w perspektywie lokalnej i globalnej: Xięga X Ogólnopolskiego Zjazdu Socjologicznego* [Silesia, Poland, Europe: Changing society in a global and local perspective. Proceedings of the 10th Polish Sociological Congress]. Wydawnictwo Uniwersytetu Śląskiego.

Ziółkowski, M., Zagórski K., & Koralewicz J. (2001). Wybrane tendencje przemian świadomości społecznej [Selected tendencies in the changes of social mentality]. In E. Wnuk-Lipiński & M. Ziółkowski (Eds.), *Pierwsza dekada niepodległości. Próba socjologicznej syntezy* [The first decade of independence: Towards a sociological synthesis]. Wydawnictwo ISP PAN.

Zybertowicz, A. (2005). Antyrozwojowe grupy interesu. Zarys analizy [Anti-developmental interest groups: An outline of an analysis]. In W. Wesołowski & J. Włodarek (Eds.), *Kręgi integracji i rodzaje tożsamości Polska Europa świat* [Integration circles and types of identity: Poland, Europe and the world]. Scholar.

Agnieszka Kolasa-Nowak works at the Institute of Sociology of the Maria Curie-Sklodowska University. Her specialty is historical sociology, sociology of science, and analyses of post-communist transformation. Currently, she studies the role of the past in Polish contemporary sociology and rising popularity of historical sociology. She is a Board Member of the European Sociological Association Research Network 36 Sociology of Transformations: East and West. She is also the Chair of Section of Sociology of Science in Polish Sociological Association.

Chapter 17
From Past to Present: An Overview of the History of Sociology in Romania

Sorana Constantinescu and Gabriel Bădescu

17.1 Introduction

The influence that sociology has had on Romanian society will be historically contextualised following shifts in the political evolution of the country. This analysis will focus on four distinct historical phases:

1. Between the late nineteenth century and 1947, when sociology was constituted as an autonomous academic discipline with its own educational and research institutions.
2. 1948–1989, the communist period, during which sociology was first banned as a 'bourgeois science', reinstated as a 'Marxist-Leninist science' starting with 1959, and then, once more, pushed out of academia starting with 1977.
3. 1990–2007, the post-communist transition, during which sociology was reconstructed as an independent academic field, closely following Western standards.
4. 2008–present, after Romania joined the European Union and the financial crisis of 2007–2008 hit international as well as national markets, Romanian sociology has seen a shift in the topics that have been pursued and a change in the way the Romanian sociologist networks across the world have been developing.

This historical division of sociology in Romania presented here is, for the most part, the one traditionally recognised by Romanian sociologists, which is most comprehensively developed by Zamfir and Filipescu (2015). The notable distinction is the fourth additional phase, covering the very recent past, which usually falls outside the purview of previous histories of Romanian sociology. The discussion around this phase will track the notable theoretical and institutional changes that

S. Constantinescu (✉) · G. Bădescu
Babeș-Bolyai University, Cluj-Napoca, Romania
e-mail: sorana.constantinescu@ubbcluj.ro; gabriel.badescu@ubbcluj.ro

sociology underwent in Romania after the end of the post-communist transition, as the country became a European Union (EU) member state undergoing recession and austerity politics (Ban, 2014).

This division into historical phases is not unique to the Romanian situation, as both the institutional framework and the theoretical perspectives that characterise the disciplinary environment of sociology within a nation-state often follow or react to the ideas, values, and imperatives of the political and social atmosphere of different periods (Halsey, 2004). In this sense, the institutions and research programs of Romanian sociology are historically informed both by the general ideological consensus of their day and the limitations that each era placed on what should be studied.

Moreover, due to the discipline having its institutional groundwork repeatedly destroyed and reconstructed, sociology in Romania has had a historical dependence on key researchers who pushed for the foundation and development of the academic institutions necessary for the existence of sociology (university departments, research centres, journals, etc.).

This has shaped the social impact of sociology in two main ways. First, sociologists had to repeatedly formulate discourses around the social necessity of sociology, adapted to the sensibilities and constraints of each period. This has led to a consistent casting of sociology as a socially engaged science and, in turn, to the prescribing of particular social tasks that sociology in Romania was expected to fulfil during each stage of its history. Second, because of the presence of major foundational figures for a better part of its history, Romania has had a history of sociologists with a considerable public presence and political influence: Gusti during the interbellum, Constantinescu during the communist regime, as well as a number of sociologists with high-ranking positions during the post-communist transition, whom we will focus on later.

17.2 Pre-communist Sociology

This period follows, for the most part, standard patterns of development, with early works being devoted to social theory articulated by researchers in other social sciences or humanities. We can place the actual institutional starting point for the discipline in the founding of two sociology chairs at each of the two major universities (in Iași and Bucharest), in 1910, and with the creation of the Romanian Social Institute (initially the Association for Science and Social Reform) at the end of World War I.

While frequently overlooked in the history of sociology in Romania, there is a parallel development of sociology in Transylvania, within the framework of Austro-Hungarian academia. After the war, with the integration of Transylvania into the Romanian kingdom, the Hungarian/Magyar social scientists did not have a similar unitary framework to that of the Gustian school but were instead working within associations centred around religious institutions (Negru & Pop, 2002).

Another ignored group in the history of sociology in Romania were the women involved in sociological research, who were contributors to the field research that laid the groundwork of Romanian sociology. As Văcărescu (in Natasă-Matei, 2016) explains, although they were involved in sociological research, as well as the work of institution-building, their roles were either overlooked entirely or diminished to barely relevant assistant work. What recognition they did achieve was mostly in fields deemed 'suitable for women', such as social work.

While the initial landscape of Romanian social theory and research is more heterogeneous, the principal figure of Dimitrie Gusti dominates all discussions pertaining to the period, both due to his position as an institutional figurehead and to his role in setting the agenda and wider outlook of sociology in the interbellum period. During this period, either Gusti personally, or his disciples, held key positions in academic institutions, conducted the major research work of the period, and were politically active, either in influential party positions or as members of the state apparatus. Moreover, his disciples would later be the principal architects in the reconstruction of sociology during communism, cementing Gusti's influence beyond his immediate historical epoch.

Furthermore, the Gustian conception of sociology as a socially involved science that participates in formulating projects and directions for community and national development granted sociology a key place within society and will remain a recurring model for Romanian sociologists. Lastly, Gusti's legacy was used in attempts by Romanian sociologists to rebuild a continuity that had been 'broken' by the communist regime as a legitimising narrative. In this regard, the history surrounding the Gustian School and its descendants offers a longstanding local tradition that has been simultaneously well-connected to Western trends in sociology. Casting themselves in the trail of the Gustian school not only allows Romanian sociologists to stake a claim to a century-long history as a separate academic field but also places their transition-era assimilation of mainstream Western sociological theories and methods within a longer history of scientific exchange and assimilation, thus putting them, at least discursively, on equal footing with their Western counterparts.

The principal unifying features of the Gustian school of sociology lie more with their methodology and ultimate goals of sociology rather than with social theory. While a certain theoretical outlook of Gusti himself can be described, it does not extend to his disciples in the school, whose political views and theoretical backgrounds are often intertwined and remarkably diverse: from Leninists to social-democratic Austro-Marxists, to various corporatists or neoliberals in tone with the social and economic policy of the last stage of the monarchy, and to far-right legionnaires. This ideological and theoretical mix can probably be best exemplified by three of Gusti's disciples who were later crucial to the communist reconstruction of sociology: Miron Constantinescu, Henri H. Stahl, and Traian Herseni. Prior to the regime change, the three had been, respectively, a Leninist, a social democrat, and a member of the far-right (Guga, 2015; Bosomitu, 2011; Zamfir & Filipescu, 2015).

From a theoretical point of view, Gusti's attention to social issues, especially pertaining to the lower strata of Romanian society, the focus of his sociological outlook on the nation as a larger organicist unit, and his treatment of communities as both the building blocks of the nation, as well as subordinate to the needs of this nation, show his immersion in the ideological environment of his time and his sociological theory having at least some common ground with the divergent paradigms of economists like Mihail Manoilescu or Virgil Madgearu (Ban, 2014; Costinescu, 2018).

The first period of Romanian sociology also marks the beginning of its long relationship with social work, which develops as a separate field of study and practice in relation to sociology, and usually with sociologists being among the first generation of theorists, educators, and practitioners.

17.3 Sociology During Communism

After the end of World War II, Romanian sociology entered a period of crisis, as the new People's Republic, following the Soviet model, denounced sociology as a bourgeois pseudo-science (Greenfeld, 1988; Bosomitu, 2011; Zamfir & Filipescu, 2015).

The Soviet Union's relationship to sociology is complicated. While Marx appears in the line of foundational thinkers for sociologists, as Marxist sociology and, more generally, conflict theories remain relevant approaches in the field, the development of Soviet social science hinges upon a very restrictive interpretation of Marxist theory, known alternatively as dialectical materialism, historical materialism, or Marxism-Leninism. According to Greenfeld (1988), this results in a rejection of the criterion of scientific objectivity put forth by Western sociology as being illusory and accusing sociologists of obfuscating a class bias inherent in their endeavours; by contrast, what later becomes Soviet or socialist sociology is subjected to the principle of partisanship, which places research in service of the Party (and, at least officially, of the class it claims to represent).

The banning of sociology in the USSR started in 1924 and was completed in 1929 with the declaration of sociology to be a 'bourgeois pseudo-science' that is associated with the positivist project of Auguste Comte. This decision would be the groundwork for the rejection of sociology in all Eastern Bloc states, regardless of the way in which it developed, or its relationship with early positivist sociology (Greenfeld, 1988; Bosomitu, 2011).

Nonetheless, some sociological or quasi-sociological research does take place in the USSR, under the cover of neighbouring disciplines such as ethnology (which is seen as 'esoteric and inoffensive' by state authorities), political economy, literary theory (an entire sociology of literature developed in the tracks of 1920s formalists), and similar (Greenfeld, 1988). This trend is also present in Romanian research, where the disappearance of sociology is supplemented by research done within anthropology, psychology, urbanism, in economics, social work, or public health institutions or by empirically oriented philosophers and also by former sociologists, usually of their own initiative (Zamfir & Filipescu, 2015).

The reinstating of sociology in the USSR in the 1950s finally made it possible for its reinstitution in other East European countries. In 1955, the Soviet Union sent a delegation of researchers to the International Sociological Association, opening up towards sociology, but in a peculiar way, motivated primarily by Cold War competition with the West, as well as the need for more empirical data to work with. The other countries quickly followed suit; Poland was the first to reestablish its university programs in 1956 (it had the strongest sociological tradition out of the Eastern Bloc countries, and still maintained individual contacts with international organisations), while other states followed a slower pattern of reestablishing sociology, formation of national organisations, the establishment of university departments and research institutions, and the emergence of specialised sociological publications. This process started in 1959 in Romania, 1963 for East Germany and Hungary, 1964 for Czechoslovakia, and 1967 for Bulgaria (Bosomitu, 2011).

In Romania this process took on different characteristics. It can be argued that Soviet sociology was probably the most important foundation for East European sociologies, not only establishing the criteria for ideological acceptability but also providing the frame that drew East European sociologies together as part of the same field of study (Bosomitu, 2011). Nonetheless, the geopolitical calculations of the Romanian regime led to both an openness to Western sociology, as well as a gradual reduction of Marxist-Leninist references, and a recuperation of previous, more nationalist tendencies in the social sciences and humanities. This would later provide the seeds for the recovery of Gustian sociology and for Romanian sociology's reimagining of its own history during the post-communist transition (Zamfir & Filipescu, 2015).

After sociology became an acceptable field of study in Romania, it slowly recreated its institutions, with a series of research facilities being formed in the 1960s, as well as sociology departments in Bucharest (1966), followed by Cluj and Iasi (1968). After a slow start, the newly established discipline exceeded its prewar peak output, despite the fact that new sociologists were not trained until the early 1970s, research being thus dependent on older sociologists as well as experts from neighbouring fields. Starting with the 1970s, postgraduate programs in the USA, Great Britain, France, and other Western countries were offered to sociologists, which led to the large-scale import of concepts and methods from Western schools of sociology (Zamfir & Filipescu, 2015).

The Gustian heritage makes itself felt, both due to its adherents being the primary professional sociologists present at the beginning of this period and due to its mostly descriptive character, lacking in any serious theoretical commitment and thus open to being coopted by the new regime's ideology. Also, by focusing on descriptive aspects, researchers could avoid the risk of an ideological misstep by engaging in discussions over theory and interpretation. However, the monographic method of the Bucharest School was only present in the 1950s and early 1960s and suffered drastic alterations over time, as its multidisciplinary teams were replaced by teams of sociologists, and the more complex analysis of social phenomena was replaced with standardised methods like surveys. During the peak of sociological development during socialism, the major studies were devoted either to identifying the degree to which society assimilated the attitudes, behaviours, and values of the socialist project or to specific data-finding problems for state institutions (Zamfir & Filipescu, 2015).

To a degree, sociology was not only used in the ideological competition for prestige with the West but also as a tool for data collection and social monitoring, albeit less so than in its more ambitious program, which aimed towards a sociology that would catalogue and interpret the phenomena of a rapidly changing society, confront this data with party-planning, predict future social developments, identify social problems and formulate potential solutions: a social science that would help build and consolidate socialism (see Zamfir & Filipescu, 2015; Cistelecan & State, 2015). This introduced two issues. First, there was an ambiguity as to whether sociology was an autonomous scientific field or merely a scientific instrument of governance: a complex data-finding tool, in other words. Second, this introduced a tension with other data-collecting institutions of the State, specifically the party bureaucracy.

The 1970s represented not only the peak development of sociology during communism but also marked the final period of sociological progress during communism. The June Theses of 1971 reversed the opening of the dictatorship that started a decade earlier, and independent social researchers came under threat. With the death of Miron Constantinescu in 1974, a veteran communist, sociologist of the Gustian school, and the main promotor of sociology in the upper party ranks, sociologists were left without any serious advocates in the central circles of the party. While sociology did not suffer an official ban, in 1977, the university departments of sociology were closed, and sociologist positions in state companies were eliminated. For the next decade, sociologists would linger on the fringes of academia.

Returning to the issue of the status of sociology in socialist regimes, Greenfeld (1988) argues that Soviet sociology constitutes a different, albeit related, field of study to what we consider sociology as a social science:

> Soviet sociology, as defined by those who practice it, is a utilitarian discipline with clearly political goals, in which one can distinguish two relatively independent parts: theory and research. The purpose of theory is to defend and propagate the message of Marxism-Leninism. The purpose of research is to obtain information relevant to the 'strategic goals' of the party. (p. 114)

Thus, Soviet sociology can be said to be a separate theoretical endeavour from Western sociology, which does not have a clearly differentiated identity from other social sciences and humanities and is not seen by its theorists and practitioners as being identical or parallel in its development to Western sociology, as it adopts neither the discoveries nor the conceptual framework of its Western counterpart. Lastly, criticism of 'bourgeois sociology' is seen as crucial to Soviet or socialist sociology, as well as the grounding of this sociology in historical materialism, understood as a proper science of its own. In this sense, it often resembles a technology as much as it does a science (Greenfeld, 1988).

This appearance of an instrument of data collection was also gladly assumed by sociologists themselves, as they considered it would shield them from ideological criticism. However, this introduced a tension between the sociologist experts and the party bureaucrats, as to who was responsible for gathering information about the state of society, while also posing ideological problems relating to the processing and interpretation of this information. In Soviet-style communist regimes, the ruling party insisted on holding a privileged knowledge of history due to its being the representative of the subject of history: the working class. This claim to knowledge would always come into conflict with its actual need for concrete empirical knowledge about the society it governed. Moreover, this would put the bureaucracy at odds with social scientists, as the latter investigated society with its own mechanisms of data collection, its own scientific methodology, and its own conceptual instruments of interpretation, whereas the members of the state apparatus, holding themselves as democratic representatives of the people, would lay claim to a direct relationship with the population and an intimate, practical knowledge of its situation and grievances (Zamfir & Filipescu, 2015; Cistelecan & State, 2015).

To give an example of this, at the beginning of the regime, studies conducted by social workers were at one point shut down after their data pointed to the existence of homeless people, vagrants, sex workers, and beggars, all of which was considered impossible in the ideal socialist state (Zamfir & Filipescu, 2015, p. 111).

An interesting aspect to note concerning the communist legacy for sociology is the tendency of post-communist readings of this period towards minimising the Marxian dimension, as either never consolidating into a proper scientific project (Zamfir & Filipescu, 2015) or being simply a cosmetic aspect, lip service paid to the Party (Bosomitu, 2011). While this helps build up the legitimising narrative of post-communist sociology, it does not paint a fully accurate picture of Romanian socialist sociology, which not only contains a project for Marxist sociology but also actual sociological research using Marxist concepts and analytical methods, as evidenced, for example, by Stahl's work during the socialist regime (Guga, 2015). This unwillingness to assume any Marxist influence shapes both the way in which Romanian sociologists interpret their own intellectual tradition and their assimilation of Western sociological traditions, which are, in hindsight, not only purged of any Marxist references but also recast as a unified set of ideas instead of a field of competing theories and modes of interpretation (Bosomitu, 2011; Zamfir & Filipescu, 2015; Guga, 2015; Cistelecan & State, 2015).

17.4 The Transition to Democracy (1990–2007)

The revolution of 1989 gave sociology a new start. While at this point the body of experts was slim due to a decades-long gap in sociological education, most sociologists, being veteran researchers that had survived in the shrinking research institutions, have their status bolstered by the prestige of belonging to a discipline marginalised under the dictatorship. Under this atmosphere of reconstruction, sociologists attempted to assume what they saw as their social role as scientists who could contribute to the drafting of a project of national development based on rational scientific methods of analysing and interpreting the needs and demands of the population and drafting and implementing policy, even as they were conscious of their institutional weaknesses.

If not always visible, sociologists have occupied important positions in political parties, government, cabinets and presidential councils as well as being important actors in the newly formed organisations of civil society and in business, as they held key roles in the fast-growing branch of market research. While less influential than legal scholars or economists in the policy making of the transition, they still played an important part (Zamfir & Filipescu, 2015).

The main initial challenge faced by sociological research institutions that had survived for decades on state funding alone was that of transitioning to a research grant system of financing. However, the explosion in the number of university sociology departments, public and private research institutions, as well as the massive increase in publication output (nearly two thirds of all academic publications from the appearance of sociology in Romania to the present day having been published in the past three decades) suggest that sociologists have managed to adapt quite successfully to the new market structure (Zamfir & Filipescu, 2015).

The major debate in the beginning of the 1990s did not so much concern the direction in which society should develop (free market capitalism and parliamentary democracy), as much as the speed and method with which society should progress. To simplify, the main ideological discussions of the period were between the ideas of a more gradual transition towards capitalism opposed to that of a more rapid 'shock therapy'. Sociologists were aware of the potential social costs of a mismanaged transition out of communism and of the dangers of rushing into reform plans without a clear picture of the social reality that was being acted upon and raised their concerns in public debates (Pasti, 2006; Zamfir & Filipescu, 2015).

However, it is, as of yet, difficult to say what the general consensus was regarding the direction of the post-socialist transition. While Zamfir et al. (2015) claim that the sociologists, for the most part, agreed to a gradual transformation of society, converging with the developed West, by building democratic consensus and minimising social costs, the very short-term transition plans they cite, the presence of sociologists across party lines, as well as the rapid adaptation of sociologists to the new market conditions, suggests a more complex reality.

Moreover, sociologists were subject to the same integration into Western expert communities as experts from other fields, from academia to politics, which led, to a certain degree, to adopting some aspects of Western projects for Eastern Europe and Western attitudes towards the transition (Ban, 2014, 2016): that is, internalising the perception of themselves and the members of their communities as political children unaccustomed to the demands and logic of the developed world (Buden, 2012). While it could be speculated that Western sociologists' more critical positions towards Western projects of development might have complicated Romanian sociologists' image of themselves and the political trajectory of their society, we would nevertheless face the additional challenge of identifying who among these critical sociologists actually occupied important decision-making or influence positions, since this critical approach was not needed in the transition process.

As previously noted, while individual sociologists have played important parts in politics, civil society, business, and so on, the profession as a whole seems to assume it is marginalised in the decision-making around the direction of national development (Zamfir & Filipescu, 2015). Certainly, sociology may not hold the same level of prestige at a wider social level as other academic disciplines since it still holds a marginal place in pre-university education (during the transition, only around 10% of high schools offered optional sociology courses). During the post-communist transition period, there was also the issue of a lack of major cross-disciplinary initiatives, beyond individual efforts, to propose large-scale policy plans close to Romanian sociology's self-prescribed ideals. While important sociological research centres have been formed, many of them have not made the transition to organised think tanks, for example, that would be required in order to promote sociologically based plans for social development.

After communism, the professional activity of Romanian sociologists can be split into three main areas: research, political activity, and activism, areas which occasionally overlap or complement each other. This marks a departure from the previous era, as the strict state control of the communist government prevented the formation of independent (legal) activist action. These areas of activity were styled after Western models of institutional organisation, action, and financing. Each of these areas will be explored separately in order to provide a more detailed picture of transition-era sociology.

17.5 2008–Present

The accession of Romania to the EU in January 2007 and the financial crisis that hit the global markets in 2007–2008 changed the situation for sociology in Romania significantly. The social impact that these events gave the ideas and work of sociologists more weight and the integration of the institutional structures of Romanian sociology into those of the European Union marked a new phase in the history of sociology in Romania.

On the one hand, sociologists began to tackle with increased interest themes such as class, inequality and precarity, or the situation of vulnerable groups, not only as academic pursuits but also as activist issues and topics for policy intervention. On the other hand, the opening of EU grants and funding meant a reorientation of Romanian sociology towards the focus topics of EU priority axes, simultaneously giving researchers and activists a larger degree of freedom from their previous dependence on less stable sources of funding in the form of foundations and private donors.

As Romania became an EU member state, sociologists were given access to Structural and Cohesion Funds, forms of financing granted by the EU for regional-level action to limit economic and social inequalities and increase opportunities for poor, marginalised, and vulnerable segments of society. These forms of funding covered, directly or indirectly, all the various forms of activity that sociologists in

Romania undertook, supporting academic research projects, targeted activist action, as well as social policy implementation at the different levels of public administration. They were essential, both in thematically orienting the work sociologists do and in bureaucratising this work to a larger degree than before by introducing standardised practices in applying for funding and in administrative work while simultaneously establishing clearly targeted lines of funding with predictable time frames.

The EU funding priorities for sociologists after 2007 came in two phases: during the 2007–2013 funding period, these were convergence, regional competitiveness and employment, and European territorial cooperation, while for the 2014–2020 period, they were promoting social inclusion, combating poverty and any discrimination, and investing in education, training, and vocational training for skills and lifelong learning. Moving to the present, this increased focus on issues concerning social welfare and social mobility in the aftermath of the financial crisis and slow recovery is also reflected in the reorientation of Romanian sociologists to these topics.

All these changes determined a shift in how sociologists in Romania perceived their role in society. They became increasingly sensitive to issues of social inequality, while at the same time moving towards a more grassroots approach towards politics and activism, in contrast with the previous generation (Ban, 2015). Moreover, younger generations of sociologists came into a completely different field than those of the 1990s, with already established university departments, research institutions, and NGO networks. These younger sociologists also entered a discipline where international academic exchange had been normalised, many of them undergoing academic training in the West and some occupying positions in foreign universities, creating transnational networks of Romanian sociologists.

Although, as Ban (2015) points out, ideological differences between newer generations of sociologists and their predecessors who rebuilt the field during the post-communist transition can account for part of this transformation, we should not ignore the role played by the institutional changes that sociology underwent after Romania's EU integration. After the revolution of 1989, sociologists comprised a small number of highly trained intellectuals, relative to the rest of the population, who relied on networking with political elites to influence public policy. On the eve of the financial crash hitting Romania, however, sociologists were already an established professional category, with numerous graduates across the country and beyond, many working in lower-level bureaucratic positions. This has changed not only how activist-sociologists operate but also how sociologists see themselves as political agents, as well as the topics and directions of their research.

17.6 The Role of Sociology in Romanian Society

17.6.1 Research and Academia

The main task for sociology as an academic discipline during the post-communist transition was reconstruction. With most university departments and research institutions closed down during the last decade of communist rule, rebuilding the institutional structures necessary for sociological research was imperative. In 1990, sociology departments were opened in Bucharest, Cluj, Iasi, and Timisoara, with an additional 12 departments founded in universities around the country in the next 4 years. By the time Romania joined the EU, it had 28 sociology departments in both public and private universities (Zamfir & Filipescu, 2015). Hungarian-language departments were also created in universities in Cluj, Oradea, and Miercurea Ciuc.

Outside the universities, a number of research institutes emerged immediately after the revolution, starting with the reconstitution of the Romanian Academy of Science's Sociology Institute and the foundation of the Research Institute for Quality of Life (ICCV), also as a part of the Romanian Academy's network of research institutions, as well as a growing number of private research institutions. Zamfir and Filipescu (2015) count at least 14 major private sociological research institutions founded in the period between 1990 and 2007.

This large private sector of sociological institutions has also produced a shift in the types of research conducted by sociologists. While polling had already been developed and was widely used by Romanian sociologists as a methodological tool during the 1960s and 1970s, the goals of this sort of research changed drastically with the transition to a market economy and multiparty system. In addition to purely academic work or research aimed at the amelioration of social issues, which were the hallmarks of sociological work both before and after World War II, market research for firms and opinion polling for parties became major focuses for sociological study after 1990. This introduced a new role for Romanian sociologists to fulfil, expanding labour market possibilities for graduates of sociological programs and helping support the field's growth.

In terms of academic research, the transition period saw a rapid expansion in publication. As well as publishing research in international journals and publishing houses, local journals focused on sociology appeared, printed either by teams within public research institutes or by university departments. Overall, the output of Romanian sociologists increased significantly: compared to the interbellum peak of 247.2 works published, on average per year (between 1936 and 1940), and the peak during communism of 288.3 works published, on average per year (between 1966 and 1971), the post-communist transition saw an average of 773.1 works published per year (between 1990 and 2010), with a peak of 1387 published works in 2007 (Zamfir & Filipescu, 2015).

After the financial crisis of 2008, sociology saw a change in the topics being pursued and a change in the way the Romanian sociologist networks across the world developed. The increased ease with which Romanian sociologists could participate in international (mostly Western) academic life was also a contributing factor. The internal pressures of growing social inequalities and the threat of precarity, combined with the external growing convergence with Western sociology departments in terms of methods and ideas, allowed sociologists to discuss more openly and confidently issues of social inequality and bring back elements of class analysis that had previously been marginalised in the public sphere and in academic research through their association with the previous regime's ideology (Ban, 2015). The protest wave of the early 2010s also helped bring these ideas into public discussion, in a sense legitimising the research work that sociologists had started to do and confirming that it was indeed relevant and connected to local realities and not merely another wave of 'importing' theoretical frameworks and topics from outside academic environments.

The transformation that brought back social class as an important object of academic study was not limited to sociology. However, it was sociologists from departments in the major universities, and researchers working with the Research Institute for Quality of Life, who had done important pioneering empirical work in this regard in the second half of the 2000s and the early 2010s. While Ban (2015) notes that there seems to be a stronger emphasis on critical class analysis with sociologists at the Babeș-Bolyai University in Cluj-Napoca than in other major universities, such as the ones in Bucharest, the strong presence of Bucharest social scientists in the early party-building of a left-leaning group such as Demos seems to indicate a wider embrace of class-oriented approaches than previously assumed.

This openness towards class analysis can be also traced back to the growing number of sociologists educated in Western universities, where these ideas did not encounter the opposition they faced in post-communist countries. The opportunities to become accustomed to these theories and to express ideas, disseminate research, and receive feedback unburdened by ideological taboos about topics, such as social inequalities, the economic marginalisation of minority groups, and social analyses of class division, were crucial factors in allowing sociologists to address social class and economic disparities more adequately.

17.6.2 Politics and Civil Society

The political activity of sociologists after 1989 differs significantly from previous eras. Contrasted to the communist period, the emergence of party pluralism and the opening of the public sphere to ideological conflict and debate has allowed sociologists to become more easily involved in politics, which was previously heavily conditioned on ascending through the ranks of the single party. Furthermore, due to the differences in the structure and operation of political parties between the pre-communist and the post-communist periods, contemporary sociologists played different political roles to their interbellum counterparts. As consultancy has begun playing an important formalised role in party life, both in terms of developing electoral campaign strategies and drafting public policies, Romanian sociologists have started to impact political life without necessarily occupying important positions in the parties or in public office.

Nonetheless, sociologists have also affected politics by occupying official positions, albeit with less prominence than academics from other fields (such as economy or law). For example, Cătălin Zamfir held the position of minister of labour in the early 1990s, Vasile Dîncu has been the minister of regional development and public administration as well as deputy prime minister, while Sebastian Lăzăroiu has been a presidential advisor as well as minister of labour. Outside of these positions in the executive branch, a few other high-level officials had backgrounds in sociology.

In an analysis of the legislatures between 1990 and 2004, Culic (2006) has shown that only a negligible number of members of parliament (MPs) had degrees in sociology, despite the number of MPs with degrees in social sciences seeing an increase across the 1990s. A growing number of these MPs had degrees in 'national security studies', an academic field with some elements of sociology, with many of them obtaining postgraduate degrees from the National Defence College, which replaced the Stefan Gheorghiu Academy, the university previously responsible for training communist party officials. Nonetheless, outside of degrees from technical universities, domains like economics, political science, and law remained the more popular areas for graduate and postgraduate education for politicians. For example, out of the roughly 10% of MPs in the 2000–2004 Parliament who had acquired a postgraduate degree, almost half specialised in economics, a third in political science, and a sixth of them in law (Culic, 2006). Sociology does not seem to have been seen as an avenue of training for public office during the post-communist transition.

The activist work done by sociologists in Romania was influenced significantly by funding, more precisely by what topics and issues were considered relevant by the donors and institutions that were open to financing the nascent Romanian civil society. This was mainly due to the lack of a continuous tradition and institutional structures with established practices and resources. Like with every other area of their activity, sociologists in Romania had to build the infrastructure for activism from the ground up. Also important in this regard was the fact that the attention of sociologists was divided between multiple projects (academic, political, etc.).

As Ban (2014) points out, in this context, the more lucrative topics for activists to focus on after the revolution were human rights, justice reform, civic education, and the construction of political parties, as these were the areas that Western backers considered to be crucial for the immediate success of the transition to democracy. Issues surrounding ethnic tensions were also a focus, especially with the violent breakdown of Yugoslavia looming in the background (Ban, 2014). That being said, as the second half of the 1990s came about, the end of the Bosnian and Croatian conflicts, the decrease in ethnic tensions within Romania itself, and the electoral victory of the Romanian Democratic Convention (CDR) CDR in 1996 led to a loss of interest on the part of donors. For the rest of the transition, financing would shift to issues of public policy and economic reform, limiting the role that activist sociologists could play (Ban, 2014).

Nonetheless, some financing networks still involved themselves in supporting activist work surrounding social topics. In 1993, the Soros Foundation for an Open Society started its activities in Romania, providing funding that encourage sociologists to work on topics, such as minorities, gender issues, ethnic relations, and democratic rights. The first president of the foundation, between 1990 and 1999, was Alin Teodorescu, a sociologist who also held a top position in the Social Democrat Party between 2004 and 2008, after serving as councillor to the Social Democrat prime minister between 2003 and 2004.

The Soros Foundation also supported the development of the first feminist NGO with an activist agenda, The Filia Center (Centrul Filia). The centre's members were also associated with the first academic program (MA) in Gender Studies in Romania (Bucharest, 1998), at the present moment named Politics, Gender, and Minorities. This is somewhat emblematic of a wider shift in the social sciences, as the country's academic curricula increasingly started dealing with minorities and oppression. Central figures in feminism during this period are Mihaela Miroiu and Laura Grunberg, who is one of the founders of the Society for Feminist Analysis (Societatea de Analize Feministe AnA), that started its activity in 1990 and that was, for the first decade of the transition, one of the only explicitly feminist organisations (Grunberg, 2000).

Between 1990 and 1994, approximately 25 groups devoted to women's issues were identified by the Catalogue of Non-Governmental Organisations (NGOs) in Romania edited by the Soros Foundation, out of a total of 1034 NGOs, with the number climbing up to nearly 60 towards the end of the 1990s (Grunberg, 2000). While these numbers were reasonably high, the reality is that many had few members, lacked permanent financing, had very little activity, and were often disconnected from the needs and issues facing Romanian women in their daily lives (Grunberg, 2000). These organisations also suffered from underfinancing and an inability to publicise their activities and construct their public image in a way that would ensure their efficiency. Moreover, they tended to frame women's rights within a more generic 'human rights' paradigm, rather than in the explicit term of feminism, a signifier which was often met with misunderstanding, if not outright hostility (Grunberg, 2000).

The situation of NGOs dealing with women's rights portrays, at a smaller scale, the problems arising from the poor state of sociology in the early 1990s and its (lack of a) relationship with the society at large. Due to these organisations' limited professional expertise in the social issues they tackled, as well as their narrow influence over policy makers, their efforts often went towards particular instead of structural issues and solutions. Moreover, their outlook lacked the more solid theoretical underpinnings that their Western counterparts had and had a general anti-political view of civil society that other Central European intellectual environments had been cultivating since the 1980s (Grunberg, 2000). The organisations that overcame these limitations were often staffed or led by academics with a background in social science; however, they too suffered early on from the lack of developed sociological institutions that dealt with academic and social work and that could sustain and support the activities of these NGOs (Grunberg, 2000).

Activism around gender issues can be seen as exemplary of the activist work that sociologists have done throughout the post-communist transition. The involvement of sociologists in civil society has relied heavily on university departments to provide personnel and leadership for NGOs, in large part due to the issues of financing facing these organisations. Relying more heavily on foreign sources for their financial resources, NGOs in Romania concerned with social issues often conducted their work in precarious circumstances and rarely had the means to train their own experts. Moreover, the marginal status of the Romanian civil society meant that activists relied more heavily on politicians to have their issues brought to the fore, as they lacked sufficient grassroots support to put these topics on the public agenda by themselves.

This mirrors similar developments in other post-communist countries. As Regulska (1998) points out, the fact that Western donors set the agenda for local activist groups discouraged them from engaging in mass grassroots movement building, by introducing generic topics for activism that disregarded local realities. Additionally, the reliance of civil society organisations on foreign aid sources induced competition between these organisations and hampered the formation of more robust activist networks (Regulska, 1998; Nimu, 2018).

These limitations meant that the sociologists who played a role as activists had to supplement these activities with academic work and some level of political involvement. Thus, the various roles played by sociologists in Romania ended up overlapping and complementing each other. It also meant that, as activists, Romanian sociologists could not operate only as members of NGOs but also had to fulfil the function of public intellectuals, bringing social issues into the public sphere through whatever media presence they had available.

Perhaps the most visible fruit of this activism was the presidential report commissioned by the centre-right president Traian Băsescu in 2009. This was one of several policy papers to have some impact on how social issues are being handled by policymakers and can be seen as the result of the two decades of coordinated activist and academic work done within Romanian sociology, as the coordinator of the report and most of its contributors are sociologists from the Romanian leading universities and research institutes, covering a wide array of social issues.

The impact sociology had during the early stages of transition was through a small number of prominent social scientists who had been educated during the 1960s and 1970s and who had managed to accumulate some degree of importance either within the former state apparatus or the newly developing civil society. They often served as ministers, councillors for high-ranking politicians, or leaders of NGOs and used their influence in the drafting of public policy or in the construction of the social and institutional networks required by the new democratic society. This last role was fulfilled especially through the training, mentoring, and promotion of a new generation of sociologists. To this end, the activity of these sociologists in the reconstitution of sociology departments, in the founding of public or private research institutions, and in establishing the bridge between academic and activist work was crucial.

In terms of the political involvement of sociologists, little has immediately changed after 2007. Activism through NGOs has still remained the main source of public participation on the part of sociologists, as they've had little success in increasing their presence at the level of party politics. Out of roughly 400 ministers that have held various positions in governments after 1990, only four have had backgrounds as active sociologists. Furthermore, there has been a general decline in the quality of MPs' university diplomas in the parliaments after EU accession, with Romanian politicians padding out their resumes with master's or doctoral degrees from less competitive universities that often do not offer sociology degrees (Muntean & Preda, 2016).

This limited success in occupying positions of power has left sociologists with two strategies for political involvement. One has been continuing their consultancy roles both within parties and institutional structures, as well as pushing for policy change from the outside, by producing reports and policy recommendations on social issues from academic and activist groups.

The other path to politics has been achieved by involving themselves in party-building for the newer generation of political parties, with mixed results, most of these parties not surviving beyond one election cycle (e.g. Democracy and Solidarity Party Demos).

The increased attention paid to social inequality and the emergent reintroduction of the concept of class in sociological analysis (Ban, 2015) has led to an increasing number of NGOs that focus less on 'generic human rights', moving towards a more nuanced approach, mixing single issue-campaigns with wider structural critiques, and introducing a sensitivity to class division in their target groups. The foundations for this change were established by the fact that the work on legal rights had already been done for the most part during the post-communist transition. This new direction meant activists could tackle topics such as violence towards women, the inclusion of the Roma minority, opposition to austerity politics and additional privatisation, housing rights, marriage equality, among others.

In contrast, the changes in NGO financing after Romania's EU accession have led to a decrease in private Western funding sources and an increased reliance on EU funds. While these have been considerably more predictable, with clearer goals and guidelines, they are also more bureaucratically taxing and competitive. In practice, this has favoured larger organisations with longer histories to flourish, and inequities between large and small NGOs began to develop. As many sociologists rely on NGOs both as activists and frequently for aid in research work, the tendency of EU funding to favour NGOs with bigger bureaucratic structures and longer established histories has perhaps reduced the speed at which changes in ideas and practices in activism are taking hold.

A similar effect has been observed in other post-communist countries that have pursued EU accession. As Korolczuk (2014) observes, there has been a tendency towards the consolidation of more bureaucratised and depoliticised NGOs, primarily focused on their own institutional survival, rather than massive social change. Furthermore, as Hann and Dunn (1996) mention, the more influential members of the well-established first wave of post-communist civil society organisations operated more akin to managers than grassroots leaders, leading to a disconnect from local communities. While this also meant the initial promotion of unpopular issues in conservative Eastern societies (e.g. minority rights), this had been done to a large degree without the involvement of members of these communities and without any sort of mass movement building around the issues.

Nevertheless, the standardisation brought about by financing through EU funds has led to some degree of coalition building among NGOs working on similar topics (Korolczuk, 2014). Also, with the advent of online media, activist organisations have gained additional platforms to reach target groups of particular campaigns directly, without having to go through the intermediation of already entrenched actors. This has allowed younger generations of more grassroots-oriented, class-conscious activist sociologists to extend beyond the reach that would have been afforded to them by their influence and institutional weight.

Of course, this activism did not emerge in a vacuum and received a boost from protest activities that had started flaring up once again in the early 2010s, after largely dying down in the 2000s. The 2012–2013 protests that had erupted in the general backdrop of the post-crisis period of recession not only pushed for single issues but also allowed for the emerging discourse surrounding social inequality and class analysis to break out of purely academic and activist environments into the wider public discourse (Ban, 2015). With the austerity politics of the immediate post-crisis period being reversed towards the mid-2000s, later mass protests were more oriented towards issues, such as corruption and graft; however, issues of inequality and social welfare have retained their place in the public sphere, marginal as it may be.

The COVID-19 health crisis has been described as an unprecedented natural experiment. Among many other things, it tested the capacity of various types of experts to assess the problem and shape policies and public opinion. Within the Romanian context, there were numerous cases of researchers, policymakers, activists, and politicians trained as sociologists who played significant roles during this health crisis. To our knowledge, there is no systematic assessment of who and what shaped various policies dealing with COVID-19 in Romania. However, the fact that in terms of excess mortality measured since January 2020, Romania is currently in the 16th place in the world, and 16 of the top 20 countries have an ex-communist past (The Economist, 2022), which suggests that the impact of expertise provided by specialists, including sociologists, had been minimal at best.

The political and social impact of Russia's war against Ukraine has been profound. Since the end of February 2022, around 3.5 million Ukrainians have fled to Romania via various border crossings, and, to date, more than 100,000 refugees have remained in Romania. Drop-in centres were set up at border crossings, train stations, and airports, many run by associations and NGOs. Since a large share of sociology graduates are employed or volunteers in the NGO sector, we can safely assume that training in sociology played a significant positive role. At the same time, the only top politician who is widely known in society as a sociologist, Vasile Dincu, the Defence Minister at the time of the crisis, was forced to resign in October 2022 after saying that Ukraine's only chance for peace would be negotiating with

Russia, since his comments went against Romania's official stance as a NATO member.

17.7 Conclusions

Over the course of time, the role of sociology in Romanian society has undergone significant transformations. Initially, sociology played a crucial role in understanding and analysing the social structures, norms, and dynamics within the country. As Romania experienced various sociopolitical changes and transitions, including the fall of communism and integration into the European Union, the focus of sociology evolved accordingly. It has not only adapted to the shifting societal landscapes but also actively contributed to shaping public discourse on issues such as identity, inequality, and cultural diversity.

1. Between the late nineteenth century and 1947, we can see sociology emerging as a discipline, with its role understood by the Gustian school to be the same as the general role of science: to be the basis for social change (Văcărescu in Văcărescu, 2022). Therefore, the explicit goal of sociology in this period is to influence politics and society as a whole. We can think of sociologists of this period as aiming to be 'sociologists and activists' (see Chap. 1), even if the field was still developing in Romania.
2. The period between 1948 and 1989 cannot be included in the four ideal types of the role of sociology in the society as the communist regime had banned sociology for most of the time. Moreover, during the period when the field is allowed to exist, the few sociologists that did manage to pursue their research were marginalised even within the academic community.
3. The period between 1990 and 2007 is the post-communist transition, during which sociology reconstructs itself as an independent academic field closely following Western standards. In this period, sociology was characterised in Romania as a being dependent of external financing, as we have shown earlier, so even if sociology attempted to play different roles in Romanian society, we can say that the sociologist as fellow traveller has been the most prominent type.
4. During the period between 2008 and the present, after Romania joined the European Union and the financial crisis of 2007–2008 hit both international and national markets, Romanian sociology has seen a shift in the topics that are being pursued and a change in the way in which networks of Romanian sociologists across the world develop. Sociologists aim to be activists, with conglomerates of clear agendas. The funding is present, but the sources are mixed; therefore, we can talk about a mixture of 'activists', 'voyeurs', 'fellow travellers', and 'marginal' (see Roncevic in Introduction) types of sociologists, depending on the institutional ties, the funding they are able to lock as independent researchers, and so on.

In conclusion, the role of sociology in Romanian society has undergone a turbulent evolution across distinct historical periods. This intricate evolution underscores the adaptive nature of sociology in Romania, mirroring and responding to the sociopolitical and economic dynamics shaping the nation over time. We see the field of sociology having to reestablish itself multiple times as the country undergoes regime changes and historical ruptures, with sociologists attempting to tie their discipline to the various social roles it can serve, both in order to gather the resources required for their work and to justify the necessity of their field in the face of the vagaries of history.

Competing Interests The authors have no conflicts of interest to declare that are relevant to the content of this chapter.

References

Ban, C. (2014). *Dependență și dezvoltare: economia politică a capitalismului românesc.* Editura Tact.
Ban, C. (2015). Beyond anticommunism: The fragility of class analysis in Romania. *East European Politics and Societies, 29*(3), 640–650.
Ban, C. (2016). *Ruling ideas: How global neoliberalism goes local.* Oxford University Press.
Bosomitu, Ș. (2011). In the age of 'misery': The Romanian sociology during the communist regime (1948–1977). In E. Bedreag et al. (Eds.), *New Europe College–Ștefan Odobleja program yearbook 2011–2012* (pp. 43–82). New Europe College-Institute for Advanced Studies.
Buden, B. (2012). *Zonă de trecere: despre sfârșitul postcomunismului.* Editura Tact.
Cistelecan, A., & State, A. (Eds.). (2015). *Plante Exotice: Teoria și practica marxiștilor români.* Editura Tact.
Costinescu, I. M. (2018). Interwar Romania and the greening of the iron cage: The biopolitics of Dimitrie Gusti, Virgil Madgearu, Mihail Manoilescu, and Ștefan Zeletin. *Journal of World Systems Research, 24*(1), 151–187.
Culic, I. (2006). From amateur revolutionaries to professional politicians: The transformation of the Romanian political elite, 1990-2004. *International Journal of Sociology, 36*(1), 69–92.
Greenfeld, L. (1988). Soviet sociology and sociology in the Soviet Union. *Annual Review of Sociology, 14*(1), 99–123.
Grunberg, L. (2000). Women's NGOs in Romania. In S. Gal & G. Kligman (Eds.), *Reproducing gender: Politics, publics, and everyday life after socialism* (pp. 307–336). Princeton University Press.
Guga, Ș. (2015). *Sociologia istorică a lui Henri H. Stahl.* Editura Tact.
Halsey, A. H. (2004). *A history of sociology in Britain: science, literature, and society.* Oxford University Press.
Hann C. and Dunn E. (1996). Civil society : challenging western models, Routledge, London
Korolczuk, E. (2014). Promoting civil society in contemporary Poland: Gendered results of institutional changes. *VOLUNTAS: International Journal of Voluntary and Nonprofit Organizations, 25*(4), 949–967.
Muntean, I., & Preda, M. (2016). Why does Romania have a negative selection in parliamentary elections? An analysis of the recruitment and selection system during the last three legislative terms. *Transylvanian Review of Administrative Sciences, 12*(48), 84–103.
Natasă-Matei, I. (2016). Eveniment academic sau interes politic? Participarea germană la lucrările Congresului Internațional de Sociologie de la București din 1939, „Revista română de sociologie", serie nouă, anul XXVII, no. 5–6, p. 469–484, București.

Negru, A., & Pop, E. (2002). *Sociologia clujeană interbelică: Repere teoretice și empirice*. Argonaut.

Nimu, A. (2018). Surviving mechanisms and strategies of gender equality NGOs in Romania and Poland. *VOLUNTAS: International Journal of Voluntary and Nonprofit Organizations, 29*(2), 310–332.

Pasti, V. (2006). *Noul capitalism românesc*. Polirom.

Regulska, J. (1998). Building local democracy: The role of Western assistance in Poland. *VOLUNTAS: International Journal of Voluntary and Nonprofit Organizations, 9*(1), 39–57.

The Economist. (2022). *The pandemic's true death toll. Our daily estimate of excess deaths around the world*. Updated on September 11th. Retrieved from https://www.economist.com/graphic-detail/coronavirus-excess-deaths-estimates

Văcărescu, T. (2022). Contribuțiile mișcărilor de emancipare a femeilor la înființarea Institutului Social Român și a Arhivei pentru știința și reforma social. In T. Văcărescu & Z. Rostás (Eds.), *Mărire și decădere. Sociologia gustiană în context central-est-european după Marele Război*. Ekion.

Zamfir, E., Stănescu, S. M., & Arpinte, D. (2015). *Social Work in romania after 25 years: answers to tranzition's problem – selected texts, ed*. Eikon, Cluj-Napoca.

Zamfir, C., & Filipescu, I. (Eds.). (2015). *Sociologia Românească. 1900-2010. O istorie socială*. Eikon.

Sorana Constantinescu is a lecturer at Babeș-Bolyai University, Department of Political Science, and a researcher at the Center for the Study of Democracy. Starting 2020, she holds a Ph.D. in Sociology, with a thesis on internalised misogyny and its connection to homophobia and racism. Her academic work focuses on gender studies, education, and democratisation.

Gabriel Bădescu is Professor of Political Science and the Director of the Center for the Study of Democracy at Babes-Bolyai University, Romania. He held a Fulbright Research Fellowship, an International Fellowship of Open Society Institute, and a UNESCO Global Education Monitoring Report fellowship. His publications include five books, five edited collections, and more than 50 articles and book chapters on democratic and economic transitions, social capital, educational policies, research methodology, income inequality, and labour migration. His work has appeared in Humanities and Social Sciences Communications, International Journal of Educational Development, Acta Politica, Higher Education, Communist and Postcommunist Studies, Europe-Asia Studies, East European Politics and Societies, and numerous other journals. He coordinated more than 15 research projects, both national and international. In addition to his academic research activity, Gabriel Bădescu is frequently involved in policy research. He was the president of the Romanian Agency for Governmental Strategies (2009–2010) and a member of the Romanian National Council of Higher Education Statistics and Forecast (2016–2018) and is currently a member of the Romanian National Research Council.

Chapter 18
Sociology in Subaltern Conditions: A Story About Russian Sociology

Elena Zdravomyslova

18.1 Theoretical Introduction

My contemplations are based on the critical studies of knowledge production, combining neo/colonial and anti-authoritarian approaches to sociological practices (Hanafi & Yi, 2020). Recent postcolonial readings have developed the imagery of Russia as a subaltern empire (Morozov, 2015; Makarychev & Morozov, 2013; Etkind, 2011). This seemingly oxymoronic naming means that (1) Russia has been essentially dependent on the West in 'normative terms', and (2) Moscow continues to engage in imperial politics, developing an ideology of the concept of state civilisation (Morozov, 2013, p. 10). This chapter is an effort of theoretical contribution to envisioning Russian sociology as a necessary discursive structure of the subaltern empire, which is currently going through the delayed post-imperial syndrome (Garbuzov, 2023). The subaltern position of Russian sociology is producing a fragmentation and politicisation of the disciplinary field, manifesting in anxious debates and unfriendly relationships between residents of different sociological principalities (camps). At first glance, the subaltern condition is just another wording for sociology from the global (semi) periphery. Partially, this is true. However, I trust that the added value of the concept *subaltern* (as compared to the concept periphery) is connected with professional anxiety, continuous politicisation, and the fragmentation of social sciences and attempts to impose ideological supremacy either in the version of Soviet Marxism or in the version of current civilisational neo-imperialist official discourse.

The subaltern sociologist always has *others* over his/her shoulder. There are at least two others that are envisioned at different levels of knowledge production and

E. Zdravomyslova (✉)
European University at St. Petersburg, St. Petersburg, Russia
e-mail: zdrav@eu.spb.ru

shape the professional practices of Russian sociologists. The *first other* is dogmatic ideology as part of the state apparatus that crucially impacted Soviet sociology. Russian sociologists have a constant concern about authoritarian surveillance and ideological control, which have had an influential legacy in our profession. This *first other* went into the shadows in the early post-Soviet and in the normalising phase of our discipline's history; however, since the strengthening of authoritarian rule and the conservative ideological turn in the 2010s, its figure again became not only visible but also tangibly menacing.

The *second other* shaping the situation of Russia's subaltern sociology is an imagined Western sociology, which is looked upon with ambivalence. On the one hand, the sociological West is envisioned as a collective example of a 'proper knowledge' producer, a container of (post)classic canons from which Russian scholars may more or less responsibly choose the pattern to follow and reproduce as good students or junior partners. On the other hand, a lack of local theoretical insights and an uncritical borrowing of methods and approaches are seen as the unfavourable effects of a hegemonic sociological core. As a result, the disciplinary field is marked by the constant tensions between international and local orientations in the field of sociological knowledge production (Hanafi & Yi, 2020, p. 34; Sokolov & Titaev, 2013; Guba & Tsivinskaya, 2021).

The hybridity of the field and tense fragmentation caused by the dual subaltern position are long-term structural features of Russian sociological discourse. According to the neocolonial approach (Spivak, 1988), the subaltern hybrid position results in a subjectivity that fails to project an independent voice. In a similar fashion, researchers of post-Soviet social science reveal syndromes of public muteness and aphasia, preventing the development of theoretical insights in Russian intellectual discourses (i.e. Vakhtin & Firsov, 2016; Oushakin, 2009). Subaltern sociology eagerly imports existing disciplinary practices that rely on theories and methodologies of the sociological core while simultaneously reproducing discontents over its peripheral status and attempts at indigenous breakthroughs.

The voices that attempt to oppose the double subaltern position of Russian sociology in knowledge production are political and ideological antagonists. Neo-Westernisers (often called 'universalists', 'liberals', or 'assimilators') fight for the international integration and normalisation of Russian sociology, for sociology without borders. They argue that learning, financial investments, and academic freedoms are necessary prerequisites helping to transgress the subaltern situation. Neo-Slavophiles (conservatives, localists), under the slogan of 'fight for justice', present imperialist Russian civilisation discourse as indigenous historiosophical knowledge. This discourse is currently supported by the official ideology of the Russian state.

In the following sections of the chapter, the idea of the dual subaltern situation of Russian sociology is unfolded in different political contexts.

18.2 Subaltern Sociology of the Late Soviet Authoritarianism

The brief review of the deeply studied period of the revival of sociology in the late 1950s helps to show how the dual subaltern condition emerged and became a long-standing feature of Russia's sociology.

Russian sociology entered the global sociological community as a latecomer. This step became possible because of the shift in Cold War politics, the launch of the international Containment policy, and the enactment of the Doctrine of Peaceful Coexistence of two sociopolitical systems. A new course on sociology was adopted during Khrushchev's thaw when the official road for its uneven and non-coherent institutionalisation was opened within strict boundaries: (1) to be a scholarly instrument of state socialism, (2) to be theoretically founded on the official version of historical materialism and scientific communism, and (3) to be limited to the concrete empirical research of social policy issues. Not without support of the International Sociological Association, the first institutions were established, and the reformist wing of the Communist party gave the go-ahead to the new profession. Exactly at that time, the orthodox consensus in global sociology gave prevalence to the structural-functionalist paradigm in sociological theorising, and empirical research methods were rapidly developing mainly in the form of mass surveys, the final target of which was social engineering inspired by scientific, managerial spirit (Shalin, 1979; Shlapentokh, 1987).

The first step to institutionalise sociology was the creation of the Soviet Sociological Association (SSA) in 1958. The government decree that constituted the association required its members to promote the virtues of Marxist sociology at international conferences (Chernysh, 2016). Soon, pilot research institutions were established: the Sociological Laboratory at Leningrad State University and the Section for the Study of New Forms of Labor and Leisure at the Institute of Philosophy of the USSR Academy of Sciences. From the 1960s to the 1970s, sociological research institutions were opened in large industrial cities and university centres: Moscow, Leningrad, Sverdlovsk, and Novosibirsk, among others. The establishment of the Moscow Institute of Concrete Social Research (ICSR) in the Academy of Sciences USSR in 1968 was a significant event in the institutionalisation process. The first soviet sociological journal, Sociological Studies, was established in 1974. In this period, the partial institutionalisation of sociology as the field of concrete empirical research and middle-range theorising took place (Titarenko & Zdravomyslova, 2017).

The mission of the new profession was to promote scientifically based social management of the socialist system (Batygin, 1998). Nevertheless, the motivations of the young cohort of sociologists were more ambitious; they wanted to be scholarly, modern and up-to-date in the global scientific world, looking for integration into the academic community globally, and open to progressivist spirits. Although they shared the basic truths of the Soviet doxa, they believed in the possibility 'to build socialism with a human face'. Sociology, for them, was a technology of state socialist modernisation. Thus, they contributed to the reformist discourse on state socialism. Their naïve hope was to implement a dual professional role: to be advisers of Genghis Khan (as Boris Grushin said) and to share their professionally obtained social knowledge with the publics. They dreamed that in the near future, public opinion surveys would be the major practice of the profession (Shubkin, 1996).

> Pioneering sociologists had to learn how to conduct empirical studies from scratch. One of the most honourable of the first cohort of late-Soviet sociologist Vladimir Yadov confirms, 'all pioneers of sociology [...] had to study new profession as [...] distance learners, from textbooks (mainly in English), which were difficult to obtain and, therefore, had to be distributed by 'samizdat'—carbon copies with the translations. Communication with sociologists from Poland, where the sociology profession was firmly established as an academic discipline, despite the 'iron curtain', was vital [...] I was lucky to be engaged in close communication with Jan Szczepański, while Zygmunt Bauman educated me in theory, and Stefan Nowak spent many hours explaining all the nuances of field research'. (Yadov, 2013, p. 10)

Theoretical and methodological dependency has been an inevitable 'normal' feature of the novel profession; the student status was recognised and enjoyed optimistically, and this is typical for any subaltern subjectivity. The most important for the first generation of Soviet sociologists at that time was the fight for professional autonomy. They sought liberation from the tenets of historical materialism and scientific communism and wanted to minimise the ideological control of sociological research practices; they advocated sociological openness, specifically the availability of research results for the broader publics. Later, they expressed bitterness and disappointment caused by the inferior status of the profession, the lack of professional recognition, and the deficit of skills and knowledge of autodidacts. Igor Kon, Gennadii Osipov, Tatyana Zaslavskaya, Rozalina Ryvkina, Boris Grushin, Andrei Zdravomyslov, Vladimir Shubkin, Leonid Gordon, and Eduard Klopov 'were part of a loose network of Soviet sociologists who promoted honesty in research, freedom of discussion, and openness to the world' (Chernysh, 2016, p. 33).

Structural selectivity in an authoritarian regime manifests itself in the habitual professional practice of an applied research project implemented under the supervision of the ideological curator from the Communist Party committee. Hierarchical communication with curators from the party ideological apparatus required diplomatic skills from sociological administrators and, if not successfully carried out, resulted in the failures of the project and sanctions to the research collective. The results of empirical studies were addressed to the managing authorities in the form of solid academic reports; they were hardly available to the broader public and had very limited professional circulation. The structure of such reports included the core content surrounded by two ritual sections: the first contained ideological standpoint with reference to the canon Marxist-Leninist authors and recent ideological directives of the party congresses. The last section was a required list of recommendations addressed to the management (of different levels) targeted on the melioration of different aspects of life and narrowing the gap between ideological declarations and research results.[1]

These practices shape two normative roles of applied sociologists. The first role was that of a mediator in the communication between the state and citizens, representing the needs (voices) of people in the results of their research; the second role was that of the advisers of the Soviet ideological management bodies. These roles presumed dependency on ideological control; in my view, they fit the type of *fellow traveller* described by Borut Rončević but have a servile flavour in an authoritarian context.

The reformist hopes of the Soviet sociologists failed when, with the new authoritarian turn in the 1970s to the 1980s, sociology was 'normalized [...] as an almost secret tool of authorities' (Chernysh, 2016, p. 33). People did not hear them, and authorities did not listen to them (Shubkin, 1996). Soviet ideological apparatchiks were aware of the subversive potential of sociological findings: the results of empirical research revealed the devastating gap between ideological declarations and real conditions of poverty and inequality. Blowouts and 'soft repressions', caused by the conflicts with controlling bodies, are vividly discussed by the Soviet sociologists in their memoirs and interviews (Alekseev, 2005; Doktorov, 2013; Firsov, 2012; Kon, 2008; Zaslavskaya, 2007). Public lectures on sociological theory delivered by Prof. Yuri Levada in 1969 became immediate provocation for one such repressive attack; they were classified as ideologically revisionist, and Levada was fired; in 1972, the Central Committee of CPSU and the Academy of Social Sciences issued a directive that sociological discussions should remain outside the political domain (Yadov & Grathoff, 1994). However, the critical and reformist ambitions of Soviet sociology endured. A significant spasm of ideological pressure was connected with the analytical report written by Aganbegyan and Zaslavskaya known as the 'Novosibirsk Manifesto', which described the systemic crisis of industrial relations in the Soviet society and demanded radical economic reforms (1983). The report's leak to foreign media became the trigger for the persecution wave throughout sociological institutions in the country. In the mid-1980s, Vladimir Yadov and later Boris Firsov had to leave the Institute for Socio-Economic Problems in Leningrad, and the authors of the 'Novosibirsk Manifesto' were ostracised. Later, pioneer sociologists confirmed that authoritarian rule was detrimental to the development of open and rich sociology (i.e., Firsov, 2012; Shlapentokh, 2015).

The position of sociologists during the late Soviet authoritarian regime can be characterised as a subaltern in a dual way: First, academic freedoms were limited by ideological control. Sociology functioned as a transmission belt for the ideology of the party state (Burawoy, 2021, p. 45) and existed mainly in the form of servile policy-oriented research. Second, in empirical research, sociologists relied on Western theories and research methodologies. However, the oppositional (i.e.

---

[1] Another genre of sociological writing revealing the subaltern situation was the critical review of the Western sociological literature on the relevant issues. This practice contributed to the learning of Western sociology and to the positioning of the Soviet Marxism in critical stance towards the core of global knowledge system.

anti-subaltern) current and commitment to public openness was also important in the Soviet sociological landscape. Sociologists were asserting their right to provide independent expertise and to be public intellectuals. Sociological findings contributed to the criticism of the hypocrisy of the regime, which later became an important aspect of post-Soviet discourse. Pioneering sociologists expanded the field of social sciences, introducing research practices of a democratic nature. I believe that empirical sociological research is founded on democratic communicative practices: asking questions and seeking answers concerning policy issues and everyday life are research instruments that contribute to civic consciousness-raising and the formation of a public sphere.

Though the position of Soviet sociology was subaltern, its professional practices exercised influence on journalists and on mass culture. Soviet-censored media adopted sociological skills, and documentaries on non-securitised issues and social problems were sociologically informed (on family issues, on drinking habits, housing problems, work attitudes, and youth strategies). Thus, sociological practices in authoritarian systems are ambivalent. On the one hand, they are tools of party-state management; on the other, they contain democratic critical potential.

In the short, enthusiastic *period of perestroika* (1985–1991), the pioneers of Soviet sociology (no longer young) had a new chance in the final institutional breakthrough. The democratic reforms of *glasnost* opened opportunities to implement their lifelong dream of establishing an autonomous profession. Much later, in the 2000s, Boris Doktorov (2013) collected and published the life stories of the first generations of sociologists that became a chronicle of the development of sociology in Russia.

In 1988, the CPSU Directive on the Reinforcement of the Role of Sociology in the Solution of Social Problems symbolised official recognition of the transformative role of sociology in the reforms of glasnost and democratisation. That same year, sociology was included in the nomenclature of scholarly disciplines; the Institute of Sociological Research (affiliated to the Academy of Sciences) was renamed the Institute of Sociology. One of the liberal father-founders of Soviet sociology, Vladimir Yadov, became the head of this institute; in Leningrad (soon renamed to St. Petersburg), the branch of the Institute of Sociology was established headed by the reformist Boris Firsov. At that time, the first state independent pollster agencies were established: All-Union Centre for Public Opinion Research (VCIOM), headed by Tatyana Zaslavskaya and Yuri Levada, and the Vox Populi-Public Opinion Institute, headed by Boris Grushin).

In the context of the final institutional breakthrough and politicised public atmosphere, the range of sociological roles expanded. Sociologists became university teachers; new departments, however, were hobbled by the lack of professionally trained faculty and the deficit of literature. At the same time, sociologists enthusiastically engaged in political life as activators of democratisation; several sociologists became political consultants; others actively participated in the grassroots democratic initiatives and emergent political parties. Thus, the only female academician in the Soviet time, Tatiana Zaslavskaya, was elected President of the Soviet Sociological Association (SSA) (1986–1991) and a deputy of the 1989 Congress of

USSR People's Deputies. Galina Starovoitova was elected deputy of the Supreme Soviet and later adviser to President Yeltsin. Activities in the SSA became vivid and enthusiastic again. The professional Codex of Sociologists establishing priority of academic freedoms was adopted; the discussion on the mission of sociology in the transformation took place, and sociological education in high school was returned to the agenda. In 1989, the Russian Society of Sociologists (RSS) was established and, after the breakup of the USSR, became the legal successor of the SSA and a collective member of ISA.

Qualitative methods became an innovation in research practices; action research and sociological intervention expanded the toolkit of empirical studies. Sociologists shared the belief that their mission was not only to produce scholarly knowledge about social reality but that they strive to be activators (in terms of Rončević) and to 'influence the movement of social planets', as the charismatic Vladimir Yadov said. He insisted: 'If we sociologists will limit ourselves to writing books, we will not fulfil our civic duty' (in Chernysh, 2016, p. 34; see also Zaslavskaya, 1996; Zdravomyslov, 2006).

Not surprisingly, rapid institutionalisation and political enthusiasm were accompanied by the fragmentation of the field along ideological, administrative, and methodological lines. *Glasnost* and democratisation reforms resulted in the breakdown of the hegemony of Marxist Orthodoxy and triggered an open confrontation between the two emergent camps that reproduced the long-known Russian confrontation between Slavophiles and Westernisers[2] (Uspenskii, 1999). Neo-Westernisers were oriented to international universal standards of knowledge production, which emphasised the autonomy of sociology and ideological disengagement. The neo-Slavophile trend claimed that sociology had to implement an ideological normative function, helping to revive Orthodox Christian values as the foundation of the Russian national idea. Both camps had their supporters and made political allies; such politicisation is quite typical for the subaltern condition of sociology (Pogorelov & Sokolov, 2005).

Noteworthily, the democratisation of *perestroika* gave the profession new impetus. The civic commitment of the sociologist came to the fore of professional awareness. Finally, the institutionalisation of sociology was complete, and ideological tenets were broken; it seemed that, at last, the discipline had been emancipated from a subaltern status shaped by ideological surveillance.

---

[2] 'The process of modernisation (in Russia) was deeply divisive, and its significance and effects were debated in the nineteenth century by 'Westerniser': intellectuals, who favoured modernisation, and their 'Slavophile' opponents, who idealised the Muscovite past. In the post-Soviet period, as Russians attempt to reconstruct their national identity after the experience of seven decades of state socialism, aspects of this debate have been revived' (Perrie, 2006, p. 7).

18.3 Post-Soviet Ups and Downs of Subaltern Sociology

The controversial 1990s are usually described in professional and popular discourses as a stormy period of a *protracted multidimensional transformational crisis*. In this decade, Russian social science underwent radical changes, which have had controversial results. On the one side, researchers consensually recognise that rapid institutionalisation and budget cuts resulted in the financial starvation of new and old sociological institutions. The effects of economically 'poor science' and brain drain hit Russian academia hard in this period (Radaev, 2008). Another conclusion is that the field of sociology in the 1990s totally disintegrated as a result of the diversity of economic bases, the lack of state control, and opposing political standpoints (Sokolov, 2018; Gudkov, 2006).

On the other side, quite generous international support helped institutions, individuals, and research collectives to continue and even advance professional activities. Beneficiaries of the academic grant economy concentrated in the new institutions and younger generations; politically, they were neo-Westernisers and methodological universalists. They wanted to overcome the subaltern legacies of Soviet sociology and develop professional partnerships in the regional and global arenas. However, the majority of Soviet social scientists became the losers in the emergent academic market and felt acute resentment.

Below, I would like to contribute to the positive, creative imagery of the sociological 1990s, underlining several modernising and innovative aspects of sociological knowledge production.

- *The emancipation of sociology from ideological control* gave way to academic freedoms. Ryvkina (1997) confirms that sociologists started to enjoy the freedom of choosing research themes, scientific exchange and international communication, freedom of speech and theoretical pluralism, and freedom to use and collect any information they needed. These freedoms, however, were available only to the part of a community that mastered the not-necessarily-fair rules of the emergent academic market.
- *Theoretical pluralism* replaced domination of dogmatic historical materialism. With the financial support of international foundations, sociological classics and neoclassics, handbooks and readers were translated and published. In the absence of ideological taboos, a wide range of new topics and research fields were discovered and cultivated (e.g. religion, gender, social movements, ethnic conflicts, migration, corruption), equipping new generations of sociologists with the ideas and tools that helped them investigate Russian society and the challenges it faced.

One good example of a new publicly engaged research branch that appeared in the late *perestroika* period is the field of gender studies, which was established due to the efforts of academic feminists and the international community that provided financial, organisational, and intellectual support to gender projects. At the beginning of the 1990s, women's groups emerged at the grass-root level and were later registered as noncommercial and nongovernmental organisations. In these activities, gender enlightenment and feminist education played an important role (Anastasia Posadskaya, Valentina Uspenskaya, Irina Tartakovskaya, and Olga Shnyrova. The very term 'gender' has gradually become common for academic and public discussions. In the 1990s, gender studies included both feminist critical methodology and the conventional 'adding women' in education and research. Russian academic feminists focused on the deconstruction of the soviet policy of gender equality, the crisis of masculinity, gender economic gaps, and women's movements. Gradually, gender studies were incorporated into the academy and in university education in the form of elective courses and research centres (Temkina & Zdravomyslova, 2015). Academic feminists tried to adjust theoretical gender concepts to the Russian context, collect empirical data, and interpret it within a new methodological framework, focusing on the public concern related to anti-discrimination and gender equality. When institutional domestic and international support declined, gender studies became more homogenous; the critical commitment of researchers became more articulated. In the 2000s, the conservative turn in Russian state ideology provoked a fundamentalist attack on gender studies. As a result, the ideological climate for academic feminism has become unfavourable, if not hostile. Current gender research is focused on issues of care, binary gender differences, and inequalities in the spheres of health, labour (both public and domestic), political participation, and the like. Overall, although gender studies and feminist theories have taken their niche in Russian social sciences, there are constant attempts to marginalise their scholarly standing.

Institutional building. New sociological institutions (state and nongovernmental) restructured the professional field and produced new divisions and hierarchies. In the realm of higher education, new universities made serious differences. The state research university, the Higher School of Economics, was founded in 1992, and the non-state Moscow School of Social and Economic Sciences (Shaninka) opened in 1995;[3] the European University at Saint Petersburg was established in 1994. These institutions were designed as research universities and declared that their mission is to be leading centres of social science research and education by international standards. Nongovernmental agencies conducting empirical research and pollsters created separate segments of the field. For example, the Centre for Independent Social Research (CISR) in St. Petersburg was established in 1991; the noncommercial Foundation of Public Opinion was founded in 1991; the Levada Centre, an independent, nongovernmental polling and sociological organisation, named after its founder, founded in 1987, became quite famous in the 1990s (CISR and Levada Centre are currently classified as 'foreign agent' organisations.) Several gender studies centres were registered as nongovernmental organisations (NGOs) (Moscow, Tver, Samara, Ivanovo, Saratov).

---

[3] The first rector of 'Shaninka' was Prof. Teodor Shanin, a renowned sociologist, research in peasant studies and informal economy, and professor at the University of Manchester (see Shanin, 1999); the first rector of European University at St. Petersburg was Prof. Boris Firsov, well-known for his studies in mass communication and research in the history of Soviet sociology (Firsov, 2012).

The institutionally fruitful 1990s provided opportunities for innovative sociological organisations with great ambitions. The founders of these institutions were charismatic academic entrepreneurs who formulated the professional course of international integration of Russian social sciences. The optimistic projects of the 1990s were full of hopes for a better future and full-fledged professional recognition in all four modes of sociological knowledge production: professional, critical, policy, and public sociology (Burawoy, 2021). These modern institutions attracted younger cohorts of social scientists. Western-oriented internalisation trends in education and research were manifested in student and faculty exchanges and joint projects.

Later in this chapter, I will give an overview of the troubled lives of these new sociological institutions in the transition to authoritarianism. Their manifested independence and internationalisation strategies make them vulnerable players in the current situation; they have been constantly under the scrutiny of security bodies and undergo regular checks of various controlling agencies, including the prosecutor's office. At the same time, their competence has been used by authorities running national welfare programs and by civic organisations promoting human rights agendas.

The public visibility of sociology extensively increased. Post-Soviet society expressed a wide interest in sociological research, mainly in public opinion polls, media studies, marketing, and political public relations. Opinion polls became recognised as a primary sociological practice and the most important sociological contribution to democratisation (Shlapentokh, 2015).

Sharing the arguments of Sokolov and Titaev (2013), I claim that the liberal political climate of the 1990s harmonised with academic *Europeanisation*, which in principle leads to the dependency of Russian sociology on the Western sociological core (see also Makarychev & Morozov, 2013). However, in the 1990s, the subaltern position of new Russia's sociology on the global arena was not problematised in the professional community. The major perceived menaces were a *lack of professionalism and funding starvation*. Sociologists considered authoritarian pressures on academic autonomy nonexistent and were confident that the normalisation of sociological practices was coming (Lapin, 2007; Radaev, 2008).

18.4 Normalisation and Professional Debates in Subaltern Sociology

From the 2000s to the 2010s, young cohorts of Russian sociologists started to work in the international regime of so-called 'normal science' with its hierarchies and troublesome neoliberal management. Western foundations significantly diminished their financial support to Russian scholars (because of economic and political reasons); however, international research collaboration developed and was financed by both Russian and international grants.

The 'depoliticised authoritarianism' (Savelyeva & Rogov, 2023) of this decade launched a knowledge policy based on the hegemonic neoliberal principles of science management that were adopted as the most advanced and meritocratic. The goal of this policy was 'to catch up' and integrate Russia's academia into the global knowledge production system as a soft power in the international arena (Kuzminov & Youdkevich, 2022). The key direction of Russia's academic nationalism was the Europeanisation of knowledge production (Makarychev & Morozov, 2013, p. 15). Russian sociologists participated in international panel projects: World Values Survey, International Social Survey Program, European Values Study, European Social Survey, and the International Survey of Russian Elites. Comparative research between two countries (e.g. Russia and Germany, Russia and China) became common. Involvement in the activities of the international research networks provided the access of Russian sociologists to huge databases and advanced methodological tools and helped to bring Russian theoretical and empirical findings to the global community of sociologists.

This academic policy on the manifest level was counter-subaltern: it presumed significant budget financial investments in the increase of national human capital. Thus, the '5/100' program of the Ministry of Education and Science formulated the goal of getting five Russian universities into the top 100 of global university rankings. Publications in professional journals indexed in international databases became the primary criteria of academic assessment. Russian sociologists became increasingly published in English in high-impact peer-reviewed journals; Russian journals also started publishing articles written in English.

In the years of normalisation, policy-oriented sociology had a place. Social reforms and new regulations on urban development, healthcare, maternal capital, elderly care, migration, gender equality, and other policy issues were accompanied by sociological expertise.[4] However, economists were more welcomed by authorities in the role of advisers.

The public presence of sociology also grew. Mostly, public sociologists were engaged in traditional roles performing in media as policy experts and opinion survey presenters. As a novel format of publicity, sociological popular enlightenment projects found their niche in social media (e.g. Post Nauka, Arzamas).

At the same time, ideas of organic public sociology oriented on the issues of civil society resonated with the professional ambitions of new generations (i.e. Romanov & Yarskaya-Smirnova, 2008). Post-Soviet sociologists have asserted that empirical research must engage with citizens and grassroots initiatives and NGOs that raise the issues of human rights violations, inequalities, and injustice.

Media (traditional and virtual) played an increasingly important role in the transmission of simplified sociological knowledge and its visibility. A political split in Russia's sociological field expressed itself in the media. Even for oppositional critical public sociologists, there has been a reliable niche comprised of agencies that

---

[4] Clients (*zakazchiki*) of expertise could choose from an apologetic or critical pool of the sociological community.

were ready to work with them, including the Echo of Moscow radio channel, the Novaya Gazette newspaper, and several online resources. However, with the tightening of authoritarian rule, the public realm has gradually shrunk (Yaroshenko & Zdravomyslova, 2022).

It seemed that, at last, sociology had reached the position of being a normal profession. In the first decade of the twenty-first century, there were 35 faculties, 25 branches of faculties, and 85 departments of sociology at different Russian universities, and almost 8000 young sociologists graduated every year (Radaev, 2008, p. 24). By 2015, sociology was taught in more than 150 universities, and almost 4000 students graduated as sociologists. There were about 20 professional sociological periodicals (Toschenko & Romanovsky, 2013).

Interestingly, in the phase of normalisation, 'local' theories emerged at the intersection of different social science disciplines and became important in the sense-making of transformations and their controversial effects. The examples are theoretical models of Soviet etacratic stratification (Radaev and Shkaratan), administrative markets (Kordonskii and Naishul), violent entrepreneurship (Volkov), and the model of Homo Sovieticus (Levada Centre).

Professional debates of normalisation phase. One of the active critics of the state of the art in Russian sociology observed that as soon as 'post-Soviet childhood of the social sciences was over, an almost obsessive, hyper-reflexivity has replaced decades of unreflective thinking' (Vakhshtayn, 2012a, p. 41). Discussion was a symptom of subaltern discontent; it was vivid in the 2000–2010s and then abated.[5] The most divisive issues of discussions are three: assessment of the crush of the Soviet system and following reforms, professional vocation and political engagement, and attitude to the subaltern condition of sociology. Let me unfold these criticisms below.

Polarisation in the assessment of the crush of the Soviet system and following reforms is based on divisive historiosophical legacies that revived in the current search for the Russian national identity ('Russian path'): the schism between conservatives/neo-Slavophiles and liberals/neo-Westernisers. For conservatives, the mission of sociology is to be the agency of authorities and an instrument of national ideology. They established a separate association (Union of Sociologists of Russia) and, at its third congress, accused liberal neo-Westernisers of instigating 'orange revolutions'. Viktor Vakhstayn (2012b) calls their position neo-Soviet 'with its distinct sociolect, codes, mechanisms of reaching an understanding, shared axiomatic

---

[5] The professionalisation and normalisation of sociological practices inevitably generated critical debates in the disciplinary field. Russian sociologists to a large extent share the worries of sociologists elsewhere, including those belonging to the core of the global knowledge production system. Commodification, university crises, fragmentation, debates between professional purists, and engaged sociologists in the right and left wings—all these issues are widely discussed in the professional realm. However, as subaltern sociologists (from semi-periphery), they have a specific agenda: they continue to worry about lack of indigeneity, economic and theoretical poverty, unequal integration into global sociology and neoliberal management of science, and menaces of authoritarian pressure. Politicisation of the divided field does not make Russian sociology unique, but it is a feature of a subaltern empire living through the crisis of identity.

and the logic of tautology'. Another camp is the liberals; for 18 years, their annual symposium, Russian Pathways, expressed solidarity with neo-Westernisers/universalists. They believe that sociology should be oriented on public values and the democratic modernisation of Russia and follow international professional standards. Both neo-Westerners and neo-Slavophiles focus on Russian cultural patterns as important factors of social change and the Russian historical trajectory. If Westernisers emphasise the totalitarian legacy and old Russian traditions of despotism and autocracy that hinder democratic transition (Gudkov, 2004), neo-Slavophile circles claim that indigenous Russian values uncontaminated by the corrupt technocratic Western influences guarantee a bright civilisational future of Russia (Dugin, 2014). This neo-Slavophile civilisational discourse is currently held by the Russian authorities. To a large extent, however, post-Soviet empirical sociologists distance themselves from macro-historiosophical discourse as they habitually limit their theorising to middle-range models and inductive conclusions based on empirical data.

Debates on vocation and public sociology divide purists and engage sociologists. Academic purists loudly voice for academic sovereignty and demand that sociologists withdraw from political standpoint/civic participation and focus on professional refinement, meaning theories and research (Gabovich, 2008; Zdravomyslov, 2006; Voronkov, 2008; Zdravomyslova, 2008; Filippov, 2000). Academic neutrality became the widely shared ideal role for Russian sociologists because this standpoint openly confronted the Soviet sociological legacy and the gradual strengthening of ideological control. One of the leading figures of the Association of Professional Sociologists, Nikita Pokrovsky, claims, 'in today's world the future of sociology is seriously endangered by external and internal risks. While 'external danger stems from society's denial of rational and scientifically-based analysis of the present situation', the second menace comes from those who see sociology as 'a sort of broad social movement for a better society' (Pokrovsky, 2011). He continues, 'We can and should contribute to changing the world by maintaining our professional scholarly objectives and also by increasing sociological culture and awareness within our societies through education and mass media. This alone is the 'public mission of sociology' (Pokrovsky, 2011). The role of a professional observer whose scholarly expertise is available on demand is presented here as the implementation of the disciplinary ethos.

Another vision is promoted by the researchers that reproduce the patterns of Soviet policy sociology; they strongly oppose disengagement, but their understanding of the public role of sociology is limited to its traditional version. Discussing the roles of sociologists, Mikhail Gorshkov, the former director of the Institute of Sociology (Russian Academy of Science, Moscow), asserts that 'in certain way sociologists inherit the mission of philosophers, poets and thinkers of the past who (like Plato in Syracuse or Machiavelli in Florence) often sought to play the role of the adviser of the prince'. Gorshkov acknowledged the dependent (subaltern) position and fellow traveller's role of sociologists; he laments that the wishful role of the activator is hardly attainable when authorities remain deaf to the scholarly diagnoses. He openly declares the state orientation of the important segment of the Russian sociological community he chairs: 'experience of the past convinced us that sociology is a language of power and is unseparable from the political process [...]' The conclusion verified by practice is that the relationship between sociology and power have to be based on the principles of partnership and tolerance (Gorshkov, 2011, p. 17). His position is that of a traditional public sociologist addressing a 'thin' public easily manipulated by authorities.

The solid positions of academic neutrality and policy-oriented sociology (voyeur and fellow-traveller imageries of professional roles) are challenged by the younger leftist colleagues inspired by Michael Burawoy's project on public sociology. The Manifesto of the research collective named the 'Public Sociology Lab' (founded in 2011) states: 'political engagement of sociologist becomes inevitable when people suffer daily from the lack of freedom, being exiled, imprisoned and tortured [...] Political standpoint—the fight against inequality, for political and academic freedoms and democracy—becomes the answer for the political invasion of authoritarian state and its conservative ideology into academic life' (Public Sociology Lab, 2015).

As I will show later in this text, in the course of the politicisation of authoritarianism and conservative turn in official discourse, the possibilities for sociologists to abstain from political judgements are gradually dwindling.

Quality debates are indicative of the subaltern position of Russian sociology. Global and national inequalities have become significant issues of concern. Members of the fragmented community criticise the peripheral status of Russian sociology in the global arena, the imposed neoliberal academic management neglecting local conditions of knowledge production, and the resulting inequalities between sociologists.

In Russia, as in many developing countries (see Connell, 2013), the teaching load of the faculty is heavy, and salaries are relatively low, so university staff usually have two or three jobs to provide a decent standard of living for their families. Critics have observed that intensive teaching prevents involvement in research that would demand substantial amounts of field research or knowledge of recent foreign literature (Yadov, 2007). A large part of professional work could not largely meet international standards. The Higher School of Economics and private universities are exceptions in this gloomy picture: good funding and adherence to scholarly standards encourage high-quality research and attract the best professionals.

Internal inequalities were revealed by the research on the structure of the Russian peripheral sociological field divided into provincial, internationally oriented, and nationally oriented segments. Research has documented a huge gap between the small sociological elite with relatively high international publication records and the majority of sociologists who publish mainly in Russian professional journals. The scholars on the top of the ranking scale mostly studied abroad, belong to the liberal community of Russian sociologists affiliated with new non-state institutions, and participate in international events. The sociology community became conscious of the abuses of sociological analysis in the interests of market and political clients and growing plagiarism in publications (Guba & Tsivinskaya, 2021). In 2007, a student protest at the MSU Faculty of Sociology raised the issues of poor teaching standards, nondemocratic relationships between faculty and students, and corrupt practices. An independent commission (organised by RSS) supported the students' demands, and some administrative changes at this faculty were made.

Perhaps the most contested were *debates on* 'theoretical poverty' and the epigone character of theorising and methodology. In particular, critics emphasise the fruitlessness and lack of explanatory capacity of the 'transition paradigm' as applied to the Russian case (i.e. Gudkov, 2004, p. 455; Shlapentokh, 2015). The reasons for the poor state are the legacy of the soviet patterns of doing sociological work in servile, imitative, non-creative ways and the impact of an authoritarian neoliberal regime that underestimates sociological research, reducing it to the manipulative survey data. A robust civil society is seen as a prerequisite for the development of insightful theoretical sociology (Dubin, 2009, 2010; Shlapentokh, 2015).

Sociologists in many countries of the world have been confronted with similar challenges in their professional work (Patel, 2010; Hanafi & Yi, 2020; Hanafi & Arvanitis, 2019). Sociology and ideology, state control, methodological dependency, and complex of inferiority vis a vie more sociologically advanced societies—these issues are discussed in the sociological (semi)periphery (Blagojević & Yair, 2010), and we consider them indicators of troublesome 'sociological normality' and of orientation to the advancement of professionalisation. A specific Russian feature of the debates is their acute politicisation and resulting polarisation of the community. In the normalisation period, sociological Westernisers prevailed, and neo-Slavophiles were seen as marginal in the empirically based discipline.

18.5 Politicised Authoritarianism and Its Consequences for Sociological Work

The trend of normalisation (though troubled) of sociological work started to break about a decade before 24 February 2022, with the enactment of conservative official discourse and the hyper-politicisation of authoritarian rule (Østbø, 2016; Savelyeva & Rogov, 2023). Conservative ideology has shifted to the centre of official discourse in the wake of the massive protests against electoral fraud in 2011–2012. The subaltern empire 'began to portray itself as a state civilisation, with a historical mission to defend authentic Christian traditions from the Western "genderless and fruitless tolerance" emanating from the US and the EU'. In the course of the conservative attack, the focus of political discourse in Russia has gradually moved to the issues of demographic nationalism (family, gender, sexuality, childbirth). The legal core of the conservative turn was repressive laws that took a serious toll on civil society. More specifically, conservative jurisprudence (Muravyeva, 2021) manifested itself in the 'Gay Propaganda' (2013) and the 'Foreign Agents' laws (2012).

Authoritarian pressure, both ideological and legal, is felt differently in different segments of the sociological field. The most vulnerable has been the NGO segment of sociology, which is tightly connected with civil society (including human rights organisations and independent media) and deeply involved in international communication. The repressive laws restrict the freedom of speech and criminalise the LGBTQI+ community. It has contributed to the straightjacketing of gender studies in Russia. The Foreign Agents' law initially targeted NGOs involved in political activism and receiving international grants. Research and scholarly events on security topics became qualified as political activities. Human rights organisations and nongovernmental research institutions, such as Memorial, the Levada Centre, the Centre for Independent Social Research, and gender studies centres, were the first organisations listed as 'foreign agents' (FA). The costs of this 'toxic' status are often insurmountable barriers to social research, narrowing scholarly cooperation, financial austerity, and bureaucratic expenses (Skibo, 2020). Most NGOs have sought to avoid this stigmatising status and have chosen the strategy of self-liquidation. (Many gender studies centres have closed.) Few 'FA' NGOs have continued their activities, carrying out a self-imposed experiment for survival.

Self-censorship has become another popular strategy for researchers and journalists who are trying to continue 'business as usual' under stifling conditions. While the official media channels have restricted contact with FA, social media have started to constitute an alternative public realm for open discussions. However, the 2010s marked only the first stage of the 'special operation' launched against Russian civil society and the sociologists associated with it.[6]

Since 24 February 2022, the opportunities for safe public critical professional expression have been reduced even further. A new series of repressive laws has shut the door on public debate and criminalised critical speech. The 'fake news' laws, amendments to the law on 'foreign agents', and the new legal statuses of 'undesirable organisation' and 'unfriendly country' have expanded the circle of persecution and undercut efforts to engage in international scientific cooperation. Independent critical media were wiped out from the public scene. Under these conditions, public intellectuals can easily be classified as 'foreign agents' and join the ranks of the marginalised. This can happen even to those who demonstrate academic neutrality. The number of 'foreign agents' constantly grows.

Conservative pressure of official discourse was reinforced by the Presidential Decree on Traditional Values (9.11.2022). The administrative implementation of this ideological guidance resulted in the inclusion of the new mandatory course 'Foundations of Russian Statehood' (Osnovy rossiskoi gisudarstvennosti) in the curricula of higher education. The declared aim of this course is to introduce the official ideology with its focus on Russia's civilisational mission, as opposed to the corrupt West, its adherence to traditional values, and an official version of Russian history.

Researchers recognise isolationist trends in social knowledge production manifested in the so-called *cancel culture* effects, especially visible on the institutional

---

[6] COVID-19 has contributed to the deepening depoliticisation of the population by shifting public attention to health threats. The authorities have given a new legitimacy to policies restricting public gatherings. The role of the pandemic in preparing for the special military operation in Ukraine and the destruction of civil society has yet to be fully analysed.

level. 'After the outbreak of war, and especially after the Russian rectors' letter of support for the war, universities in many countries ceased institutional cooperation with Russian institutions. In contrast, there has been a breakdown in relations on the part of Russian universities, which are afraid to be blamed for 'cooperation with the enemy' (Yudkevich, 2023).

In this atmosphere, the political polarisation of loyal and oppositional sociologists received a new impetus. Soon after the start of the war, representatives of both sides expressed their opposing positions either in open letters of support for the military operation or in antiwar statements. As a result, many open opponents of the special military operations were forced to leave their institutions and/or leave the country. However, they are the minority. Silent opponents remain at work. What tactics can sociologists employ when academic freedoms are being curtailed and public sociology is being stifled?

Most professionals continue to do what they normally do: teach, research, and supervise. They consider it their duty to sustain the trend of professional 'normalisation' launched at the end of the 1990s–beginning of the 2000s. Many emphasise teaching responsibilities, corporate solidarity, the importance of helping students and colleagues overcome feelings of confusion or frustration, and the need to preserve institutions and jobs for professionals. These tactics, however, require serious professional compromises. Educators change curricula according to the ideological directives; researchers avoid toxic topics (such as gender or political activism) and collaborations with 'foreign agents', 'unfriendly organisations', and colleagues from 'unfriendly countries'. Some believe that it is time for ethnographic descriptions and diaries reporting on the breakdown of our life-worlds. Others turn to historical analysis in search of tools to make sense of the catastrophic social reality. At the same time, social scientists in Russia are directly experiencing the social emotion of fear. Many colleagues have already been afflicted. The security of academic neutrality turned out to be an illusion. Sociologists can sense the growing risks and precarity caused by politicisation from above. These feelings, to a great extent, determine the survival tactics used by those who stay in the professional field. Let us describe some of them using the expressions of our colleagues.

Five Survival Tactics

- *Try and revive the practices of Aesopian language*: turning to doublespeak and quasi-safe topics, searching for loopholes that provide more academic freedom.
- *Stay and keep a low profile*: avoiding publicity and sequestering yourself in your ivory tower.
- *Stay on the captain's bridge*: heroic standing your ground, assuming responsibility, first and foremost, for the security of your colleagues and institution while endangering your personal reputation and manoeuvring in search of a safe track.
- *Stay and to induce safe extraterritorial areas of self-expression*: creating alternative, relatively safe platforms for public discussions in social media and in 'club' or 'workshop' formats, following the script of a late-Soviet *tusovka* (casual get-together).

- *Stay and demonstrate loyalty* to the authorities and the official ideology of Russian path and traditional values.

These are all 'tactics of the weak', full of compromises and moral dilemmas so well-known to the Soviet sociological subaltern. These tactics are inherently built into the professional hierarchy of the insecure disciplinary field permeated by new precarities (see also Skibo, 2020; Dubrovsky & Meyer, 2020; Temkina, 2022; Sokolov, 2023).

It is possible to point out yet another tactic of our colleagues: *stay and procrastinate*. Many social scientists and their students are hopelessly disillusioned with our discipline. They are not ready to quit their jobs, but they realise how inextricably linked sociology is with official politics, authoritative discourse, and the extent to which polls (which are considered sociological work) are tools of political manipulation. In recent years, they have learnt how dangerous it is to engage in organic public sociology and how high the costs of combining professional work and oppositional civic engagement can be. Fear and hopelessness surrounding the prospects of conducting meaningful professional work in Russia engender alienation, contribute to 'discursive paralysis', and are causing promising students to avoid sociology as a professional choice.

The traumatic asphyxiation of public sociology (Yaroshenko & Zdravomyslova, 2022) affects all four modes of sociological knowledge and impacts all sociological roles. This situation reminds us of the Soviet version of subaltern sociology but seems more catastrophic after the years of normalisation, perceived academic freedoms, and internationalisation. Now again, the disciplinary field is under ideological pressure; sociology under authoritarianism is afflicted with a sort of aphasia and public muteness.

We would like to add to this gloomy picture some hopeful comments. Antiwar sociologists are attempting to make their voices heard in Russia and globally. Their strategy is to continue professional work and to raise their voices in the alternative public sphere made available by new information technologies. In this virtual public realm, we hear the voices of sociologists and political scientists who perform the dual roles of experts and public intellectuals. Oppositional sociologists give online lectures and interviews to alternative media; they compete with the propagandist experts who occupy state media channels. Sociologists in exile endeavour to build up informal, open educational platforms in different countries and even conduct empirical research. Sociologists dive into theoretical debates on neo-totalitarianism, violent dictatorship, colonialism, and empire. They are attempting to find a proper signifier for the Russian regime. Many feel responsibility for the catastrophe. They ask: What did we miss? How could we have prevented the war? Why did we fail in our forecasts? What is the future? They wonder why the voices of two or three Cassandras (like Yudin and Gudkov) who warned of the growing threat of imperialist outbursts were not noticed by colleagues and did not reach the public.

18.6 Concluding Remarks: Agential Selectivity, Discourses, and Roles

In the previous sections of this chapter, I attempted to show that there are many problems that make sociological development in Russia controversial, among them its dual subaltern imprint, causing hierarchical fragmentation of the disciplinary field, different conditions of professional work (infrastructure and funding), divide in accordance with the fields of activity, professional roles, political standpoints, state dependency, and support. These institutional differences are manifested in the existence of several professional associations that profess different understandings of the profession and different relationships with the authorities, from collaboration (e.g. VTSIOM) to the status of foreign agents (e.g. Levada Centre). The feudal-like picture of the field explains to some extent why the agential potential of sociology at different levels of discourse production is lower than sociologists themselves would wish.

Below, I present a brief sketch of the sociological map, which allows some conclusions to be made. The major 'sociological principalities' (*knyazhestva* in Russian) (or agents) are the following: the oldest professional territory includes sociological research institutes affiliated with the Russian Academy of Sciences. In the post-Soviet period, they lost their professional monopoly and became weaker actors; their funding is insufficient; they highly depended on the state and followed some 'unwritten rules' to obtain research grants from private and public sources. For a long time, the influx of younger researchers to these institutions was quite low because of financial and infrastructural poverty and insufficient academic mobility. In the course of professional normalisation, we have witnessed the signs of professional modernisation in this segment, but ideological control and self-censorship in the current situation could have detrimental effects on the critical research potential of this part of the sociological community. However, given its relatively low salary level, academic sociology remains active and quite productive. Focusing on the normalisation period, Sokolov calculated that no European country has such 'cheap' social scientists as Russia, considering the number of publications Russian scholars produce for miserable pay (Sokolov, 2018).

Sociological departments of state universities constitute the second principality. Here, the inequality of working conditions at the centre and periphery is quite palpable. While regional state universities (with some exceptions) can hardly meet standards of internationalised social sciences, sociological life at the top of the university hierarchy (the Higher School of Economics and non-state universities) is different; in these institutions, the combination of teaching and research is strongly encouraged, young faculty are supported by comparatively good funding, and neoliberal management operates in its full capacity (Kuzminov & Youdkevich, 2022). Sociologists of these institutions are in demand for policy and politics expertise and participate in designing different national programs and even now continue the internationalisation path (with the change of geographical priorities).

A small state-independent sociological principality comprising nongovernment research centres exists on shaky ground. Their research is focused on the issues of public concern connected with human rights and advocacy initiatives (prisoners, sick people, elderly); in the phase of post-Soviet normalisation, they established strong ties with international foundations. Currently, their situation has worsened drastically for both economic and ideological reasons.

At the top of the professional hierarchy are institutions founded in the 1990s: the flagship of sociological education and public expertise is the prosperous Higher School of Economics and the highly prestigious Shaninka and European University in St. Petersburg. The Levada Centre ('foreign agent') and VTSIOM (pro-state agency) are known to the broader public and political elite for their pollsters and analysis. These institutions are homes for the sociological elite; they have infrastructure and famous names. They obviously have gained sufficient expertise to implement the role of fellow travellers contributing to policy reforms; they initiate new research programmes with the potential to influence the discourses. Polling companies provide public opinion survey data that, in an authoritarian context, are used for international and domestic political legitimation. There is also part of a professional community that prefers the role of a distant observer—the voyeur—and regards this stance as fitting to their professional commitment and safer in the context of the securitisation of sociological work.

I believe that, because of its dual dependency, Russia's subaltern sociology could not have a strong and direct influence on societal transformation and dominant discourses. Russian sociology, however, made a significant contribution to the collapse of the Soviet regime in a subtler way by developing critical attitudes by revealing the gaps between propaganda and everyday life. Its impact is difficult to measure but important to recognise. In the 1990s, sociology was just institutionalised and could hardly take on the role of an independent transformation actor. At the same time, sociologists participated in the consolidation of the oppositional ideological-political camps of liberals (neo-Westernisers) and conservatives (neo-Slavophiles). During the normalisation phase, sociologists became common figures in policy and politics. At the same time, the concerns raised about Russia's social sciences in relationship to the Western core of the knowledge system and promising theoretical models started to ripen.

In the current situation of authoritarian ideological control, we observe the revival of the Soviet legacy of knowledge production in social sciences. Current disposition reminds us of three distinct models of the relationship between Soviet sociologists and the ideological apparatus identified by Boris Firsov (2012). One group of sociologists preferred the absentee-ist strategy. They cut down their creative ambitions and attempted to maintain distance from ideological control. They pretended to neglect ideological surveillance and to be just pure professionals doing high-quality research. They intentionally chose topics peripheral to the core ideological concern. Their role is that of a voyeur (according to the typology of Rončević presented in this volume). The second pattern is presented by social policy sociologists who believe that sociological knowledge should contribute to the amelioration of the regime and its concrete institutions. Such a stance is very stable: it was extremely prominent at the beginning of the sociological revival, revealed itself in the *perestroika* period, and is quite noticeable in the normalisation face. This model presumed an alliance of sociologists with the reformist part of authorities and engagement in moderate social critique. The third pattern represents ideological service sociologists: they saw their professional duty in the legitimation of state ideology and politics. These are also fellow travellers supporting state ideology. They never worried about the lack of professional autonomy and were actively involved in the work of ideological apparatus.

These roles are enacted in today's securitised authoritarian context. Given the pressures on academic freedoms, the activator's role of sociology can hardly be implemented; research oriented on the needs of civil society is being seriously marginalised. The 'foreign agent' title, however, implies that the law enforcement bodies recognise the agential role of sociology connected with the human rights agenda. Under such conditions, policy-oriented empirical sociology and authoritarian servile sociology will prevail in the local professional landscape.

Regarding the discursive impact of sociology, in the course of market transition, liberal economists were real discourse constructors, while the influence of Russia's sociology on dominant transformational discourse was quite low. At the same time, certain ideas developed by sociologists in the post-Soviet period have resonated with publics and are still shaping the controversial politicised discourse on Russia's self-identity. There are several examples of these ideas, but I will focus on the concept of *Homo Sovieticus* (*Prostoi Sovetskii Chelovek*) as part of the broader discourse of path dependency and cultural limitations to democracy. The concept reminds us of the models of 'civilisational incompetence' (Sztompka, 1993) and 'egalitarian syndrome' (Županov, 1969). It was developed by the collective of the Levada Centre (Levada, 1993), was refined in its later publications (Levada, 1999), and received new attention in recent years (Dubin, 2009, 2010; Gudkov, 2004, 2022). Its original version is based on the panel data of national representative mass surveys regularly conducted since the 1990s. According to the Levada group interpretation, these data reveal a specific highly conservative anthropological type of personality producing cultural practices that block modernisation and democratic normalisation; negative personal qualities inherent in the Soviet person are interpreted as adaptive mechanisms for life without freedom. The 'Soviet person' as both a cognitive and (negatively assessed) normative model contains such features as social hypocrisy, paternalism, suspicion and isolationism, inclination to moral corruption, bribery and doublethink, sense of exceptionality state paternalist orientations, and imperial disposition. The attitudes and patterns of behaviour of *Homo Sovieticus* are objects of vivid criticism as the products of Soviet totalitarianism.

Although the explanatory power of this model has been recognised, critics emphasise the moral bias of this analytical lens shaping data interpretation, lack of differentiation and its fundamental essentialism (i.e. Sharafutdinova, 2019; Gabovich, 2008). The discursive influence of this theoretical model is proved by the fact that for more than three decades after its first announcement, it has been widely discussed in professional circles and among public intellectuals; it has had powerful resonance in everyday discourse as expressed in the vernacular pejorative term *sovok*. To my mind, this model is exactly the product of post-Soviet subaltern sociology: it is critical towards the Soviet past and looks forward to the normalities of the democratic West.

As a final note, paradoxically, the attack of imperial authoritarianism has contributed to the gradual growth of professional consciousness. Russian subaltern sociologists have to think about close ties between their professional and political positions, their practices and moral commitments, the dissonance between the ethos of the discipline and the way it is actually being practised, the comfort of loyalty, and the persecution of colleagues who dare to make critical public statements. Reflection on these issues, which could have been avoided previously by adhering to the scholarly principle of academic neutrality, is now awakening a professional and personal *sovest'* (conscience) in our community members.

Competing Interests The author has no conflicts of interest to declare that are relevant to the content of this chapter.

References

Alekseev, A. (2005). *Dramatic sociology and sociological self-reflection*. Institute of Sociology Russian Academy of Sciences.
Batygin, G. S. (1998). Continuity of the Russian sociological tradition. In V. Yadov (Ed.), *Sociology in Russia* (pp. 19–39). Institute of Sociology.
Blagojević, M., & Yair, G. (2010). The catch 22 syndrome of social scientists in the semiperiphery: Exploratory sociological observations. *Sociologija, 52*, 337–358.
Burawoy, M. (2021). *Public sociology: Between utopia and anti-utopia*. Sage.
Chernysh, M. (2016). Vladimir Yadov: A life devoted to an open sociology. *Global Dialogue, 6*(1), 39–41.
Connell, R. (2013). The vocation of sociology. *Global Dialogue, 3*(3), 5–6.
Doktorov, B. (2013). *Modern Russian sociology: History in biographies and biography in history*. European University.
Dubin, B. (2009). Disengagement regime. *Pro et Contra, 13*, 6–19.
Dubin, B. (2010). Special way and social order in contemporary Russia. *Public Opinion Bulletin, 1*(103), 8–19. In Russian.
Dubrovsky, D., & Meyer, I. (2020). Academic freedom or freedom of speech? Russian social scientists' understanding of academic freedom. *Demokratizatsiya: The Journal of Post-Soviet Democratization, 30*(1), 35–57.
Dugin, A. (2014). *Eurasian mission: An introduction to neo-Eurasianism*. Arktos.
Etkind, A. (2011). *Internal colonization: Russia's imperial experience*. Polity Press.
Filippov, A. (2000). Cognition of reality and theoretical communication. *Pro et Contra, 5*(4), 203–208.
Firsov, B. (2012). *History of Russian sociology: 1950–1980*. European University.
Gabovich, M. (2008). On discussion about theoretical legacy of Yu. Levada. *Public Opinion Bulletin, 4*, 50–59.
Garbuzov, V. (2023). For Russia's self-awareness we need knowledge and not mythology Для самопознания России необходимы знания, а не мифы. *Nezavisimaya Gazeta*. Retrieved from https://www.ng.ru/ideas/2023-08-29/7_8812_illusions.html
Gorshkov, M. (2011). Dialogue of Russian sociology with the power and the society: Past experience and future prospects. *Russian Journal of Philosophical Sciences, 4*, 13–25.

Guba, K., & Tsivinskaya, A. (2021). *Ethical ambiguity in the academic periphery: Global versus local science in explaining plagiarism*. Center for Institutional Analysis of science and education, European University at St. Petersburg, St. Petersburg. Retrieved from https://osf.io/preprints/socarxiv/u8qwz/

Gudkov, L. (2004). *Negative identity*. Neprikosnovennyi zapas.

Gudkov, L. (2006). About the situation of the social sciences in Russia (O polozhenii sotsial'nykh nauk v Rossii). *Novoie literaturnoe obozrenie, 77*, 314–339.

Gudkov, L. (2022). *Recurrent Totalitarianism*. Novoie literaturnoe obozrenie.

Hanafi, S., & Arvanitis, R. (Eds.). (2019). *Knowledge production in the Arab world: The impossible promise*. Routledge.

Hanafi, S., & Yi, Ch. (eds.). (2020). *Sociologies in dialogue*. Sage.

Kon, I. (2008). *Eighty years of loneliness*. M. Vremya.

Kuzminov, V., & Youdkevich, M. (2022). *Higher education in Russia*. John Hopkins University.

Lapin, N. (2007). Our sociology became the field of professional research (interview). *Sotsiologicheskii zhurnal, 1*, 143.

Levada, Y. (Ed.). (1993). *A simple Soviet man*. Okean.

Levada, Y. (1999). Homo Soveticus ten years later. *Public Opinion Bulletin, 3*, 10–16.

Makarychev, A., & Morozov, V. (2013). Is "non-Western theory" possible? The idea of multipolarity and the trap of epistemological relativism in Russian IR. *International Studies Review, 15*(3), 328–350.

Morozov, V. (2013). Subaltern empire? Toward a postcolonial approach to Russian foreign policy. *Problems of Post-Communism, 60*(6), 16–28.

Morozov, V. (2015). *Russia's postcolonial identity: A subaltern empire in a Eurocentric world*. Palgrave Macmillan.

Muravyeva, M. (2021). Conservative jurisprudence and the Russian state. *Europe-Asia Studies, 69*(8), 1145–1152.

Østbø, J. (2016). *The new third Rome: Readings of a Russian nationalist myth*. Columbia University Press.

Oushakin, S. (2009). *Past in usage: Post soviet condition as a form of aphasia*. Novoe Literaturnoe Obozrenie.

Patel, S. (Ed.). (2010). *The ISA handbook of diverse sociological traditions*. Sage.

Perrie, M. (Ed.). (2006). *The Cambridge history of Russia*. Cambridge University Press.

Pogorelov, F., & Sokolov, M. (2005). Academic markets, segments of professions and intellectual generations: Fragmentation of Russian sociology. *Journal of Sociology and Social Anthropology, 2*, 110–128.

Pokrovsky, N. (2011). "Patient denied hospitalization" or "in defence of sociology." *Global Dialogue, 2*(2). Retrieved from https://globaldialogue.isa-sociology.org/articles/patient-denied-hospitalization-or-in-defence-of-sociology

Public Sociology Lab. (2015). Sociology in a hostile environment. *Global Dialogue, 5*(3). Retrieved from https://globaldialogue.isa-sociology.org/articles/sociology-in-a-hostile-environment

Radaev, V. (2008). Is a positive program possible for Russian sociology? *Sotsiologicheskije Issledovanija, 7*, 24–33.

Romanov, P., & Yarskaya-Smirnova, E. (Eds.). (2008). *Public role of sociology*. Variant.

Ryvkina, R. (1997). Paradoxes of Russian sociology. *Sociological Journal, 4*, 197–208.

Savelyeva, N., & Rogov, K. (2023). *Between de- and hyper-politicization: The evolution of Russian authoritarianism*. Retrieved from https://re-Russia.net/en/expertise/091/

Shalin, D. (1979). Between the ethos of science and the ethos of ideology. *Sociological Focus, 12*, 175-193.

Shanin, T. (1999). *Informal economy: Russia and the world*. Logos.

Sharafutdinova, G. (2019). Was there a "simple Soviet" person? Debating the politics and sociology of "Homo Sovieticus". *Slavic Review, 78*(1), 173–195.

Shlapentokh, V. (1987). *The politics of sociology in the Soviet Union*. Westview.

Shlapentokh, V. (2015). *Public opinion in a non-democratic society: Lessons from Russian history—The 1960s and 2000s*. Retrieved from https://shlapentokh.wordpress.com/2015/03/19/

Shubkin, V. (1996). *Sociological dreams. Violence and Freedom. Sociological essays*. Institut sotsiologii Rossiiskoi Akademii nauk.

Skibo, D. (2020). *Russia: There will be more foreign agents*. Retrieved from https://cisrus.org/ru/2020/02/25/rossiya-inostrannyh-agentov-stanet-bolshe/

Sokolov, M. (2018). The sources of academic localism and globalism in Russian sociology: The choice of professional ideologies and occupational niches among social scientists. *Current Sociology, 67*(1).

Sokolov, M. (2023). *Is "scientific Putinism" a threat to Russian universities?* Retrieved from https://cisrus.org/2023/01/11/putinizm/

Sokolov, M., & Titaev, K. (2013). Provincial and indigenous science. *Anthropological Forum, 19*, 239–276.

Spivak, G. C. (1988). Can the subaltern speak? In C. Nelson & L. Grossberg (Eds.), *Marxism and the interpretation of culture* (pp. 271–313). Macmillan Education.

Sztompka, P. (1993). Civilizational incompetence: The trap of post-communist societies. *Zeitschrift für Soziologie, 22*(2), 85–95.

Temkina, A. (2022). *The conservative swing and gender studies in Russia*. Retrieved from https://cisrus.org/2022/12/02/gender-study/

Temkina, A., & Zdravomyslova, E. (2015). Gender's crooked path: Feminism confronts Russian patriarchy. *Current Sociology, 62*(2). https://doi.org/10.1177/0011392113515

Titarenko, L., & Zdravomyslova, E. (2017). *Sociology in Russia: A brief history*. Palgrave Macmillan.

Toschenko. Zh., & Romanovsky, N. (2013). On the real state of sociology in Russia: Opposing Vakhshtayn's polemics. *Global Dialogue, 2*(5). Retrieved from https://globaldialogue.isa-sociology.org/articles/on-the-real-state-of-sociology-in-russia-opposing-vakhshtayns-polemics

Uspenskii, B. (1999). Russian intelligentsia as a specific phenomenon of Russian culture. In B. Uspenskii (Ed.), *Russian intelligentsia and Western intellectualism* (pp. 7–19). Moskva-Venetsia.

Vakhshtayn, V. (2012a). *Global Dialogue, 2*(3). Retrieved from https://globaldialogue.isa-sociology.org/authors/victor-vakhshtayn

Vakhshtayn, V. (2012b). 'We have it all. But do we have anything? *Global Express*. Retrieved from https://globaldialogue.isa-sociology.org/articles/we-have-it-all-but-do-we-have-anything-further-confirmation-of-the-lamentable-state-of-russian-sociology

Vakhtin, N., & Firsov, B. (Eds.). (2016). *Public debate in Russia: Matters of (dis)order*. Edinburgh University Press.

Voronkov, V. (2008). *'Rodovaya travma Roissiiskoi sotsiologii'* ['Birth trauma of Russian sociology']. Retrieved from http://www.polit.ru/science/2007/05/08/voronkov.html

Yadov, V. (2007). Theoretical-conceptual explanations of post-communist transformations. In M. Gorshkov (Ed.), *Russia undergoes reform* (pp. 12–23). Institute of sociology.

Yadov, V. (2013). Sociologist as life destiny. *Global Dialogue, 3*, 10–12.

Yadov V., & Grathoff, R. (1994). Introduction. In *Proceedings of the Symposium of Russian Academy of Science* (pp. 3–5). Institute of Sociology.

Yaroshenko, S., & Zdravomyslova, E. (2022). Public sociology in the Russian context. *Global Dialogue, 12*(3). Retrieved from https://globaldialogue.isa-sociology.org/articles/public-sociology-in-the-russian-context

Yudkevich, M. (2023). *Internationalisation's new goals are political, not academic*. University World News. Retrieved from https://www.universityworldnews.com/post.php?story=20230721135638147

Zaslavskaya, T. (1996). Role of sociology in Russian transformation. *Sotsiologicheskie issledovanija [Social Research], 3*, 3–9.

Zaslavskaya, T. (2007). My life: Recollections and contemplations. *Collected Works, 3*. Economika.

Zdravomyslov, A. (2006). Field of sociology in contemporary Russia: Dilemma of autonomy and engagement in the framework of perestroika's heritage. *Obshchestvennye nauki i sovremennost, 1*, 5–20.

Zdravomyslova, E. (2008). Make way for professional sociology! Public sociology in the Russian context. *Current Sociology, 56*(3), 405–414.

Županov, J. (1969). Egalitarizam i industrijalizam. *Naše teme, 14*(2), 237–296.

Elena Zdravomyslova is Professor Emerita in the European University at St. Petersburg (RF) and a leading research fellow at the Center for Independent Social Research (St. Petersburg). She is one of the leading experts in gender studies in the Russian academy, and she published also on the developments of Russian sociology. For 8 years (2000–2008), she was a member of the Executive Committee of the International Sociological Association, and this experience substantially broadened her understanding of sociological knowledge production on the global, regional, and national levels.

Chapter 19
The Role of Sociology in Post-Socialist Transformation in Serbia

Marija Babović, Jelena Pešić, and Ivana Spasić

The chapter 'The Role of Sociology in Post-socialist Transformation in Serbia' is partly based on research material that was also used in the writing of the book *Sociology in Serbia. A Fragile Discipline* (authors: Ivana Spasić, Jelena Pešić and Marija Babović), published by Palgrave Macmillan (Springer) in 2022 as part of the series Sociology Transformed.

19.1 Introduction

The main objective of this paper is to examine the role of sociology in Serbian society over the previous 30 years and how it changed alongside (1) changing global and local social contexts (especially those related to major systemic changes, i.e. post-socialist transformation), (2) shifts in dominant theoretical paradigms and the emergence of new theories and approaches, but also (3) changing status of sociology as a profession. The role or the impact of sociology on the processes of post-socialist transformation can be explored at different levels. Sociology, like other disciplines, has different appearances that can be analytically distinguished: as a science, sociology produces scientific knowledge; as a profession, it builds its own institutional infrastructure and organisational networks; as expertise, it offers applicable knowledge and makes a more or less direct impact on shaping public and other policies. In addition to this emergent level, sociology appears at the individual level: sociologists may act as academics, engaged intellectuals, educators, experts, politicians, journalists, civic activists, and political analysts, among others. As a social formation, sociology, therefore, produces structures but also meanings and interpretations

M. Babović · J. Pešić (✉) · I. Spasić
Faculty of Philosophy, University of Belgrade, Belgrade, Serbia
e-mail: mbabovic@f.bg.ac.rs; jlpesic@f.bg.ac.rs; ispasic@f.bg.ac.rs

of the social world, creating material as well as cultural (ideological) forms (see Jessop, 2009).

The impact of sociology, thus, may arise from all of those appearances, varying in its scope, strength, and significance. Furthermore, the role of sociology in post-socialist transformations may not only evolve over time, invoking an analysis that takes account of its dynamic aspects, but also may vary from society to society, depending on dialectical relations between specific structural (relational, extra-semiotic) and cultural (semiotic) contexts. Nevertheless, due to limited space, the main aim of this paper cannot be to analyse comprehensively all the channels through which sociology can make an impact on the processes of social change. The focus will be on the main discourses sociology in Serbia has produced over the previous three decades (particularly the discourses used in interpreting the new social reality that came into being after the fall of socialism) and how these semiotic imaginaries evolved in a dialectic relation to the structural elements (produced in the field of sociology or arising as external products of the wider social context).

19.2 Theoretical Framework

In analysing the role of sociology in Serbia, we will largely rely on the cultural political economy approach (CPE) (see Jessop, 2009; Sum & Jessop, 2013). The core of our analysis will be devoted to discourses on post-socialist transformation (also encompassing discourses related to current processes of social change that go beyond the notions of transition or post-socialist transformation) that circulated within the two most influential sociological journals in Serbia: *Sociologija* (*Sociology*) and *Sociološki pregled* (*Sociological Review*) and (when needed) in other key works (monographs and edited volumes) of Serbian sociologists, during the period from 1990 until 2018. In accordance with the CPE approach, we will address the issues of selection, retention, and possible reinforcement of certain discourses (construals that potentially have transformative power; see Sum & Jessop, 2013, p. 4) and rejection of other discourses.

Analysis of discourses will thus have to take into account:

- Evolutionary mechanisms of discursive changes (which discourses were 'at the table' as compossibilities; see Sum & Jessop, 2013; whether we could talk about a variety of discourses; why were certain discourses selected and others were not; which discourses, if any, became dominant; how dominant sociological discourses shaped public discourses and policies; etc.)
- To address the issue of a dialectic relationship between semiotic elements (related to specific construals) and those that are being produced within and/or outside the sociological field (representing the 'material force' behind the discourse: who were the people 'behind' certain discourses: what was their institutional position and what was the position of their institutions in sociological and other fields; which discourses were 'imported' and which were endogenous; what was

the role of sociological diasporas in the process of selection/retention/reinforcement of certain discourses; whether sociologists played important roles outside the narrow sociological field, exporting sociological discourses into economic or political fields and shaping public policies; what was the level of autonomy of sociology as a profession in the society, and how this influenced the role of sociology in shaping processes of social change; etc.)

- The main questions that need to be answered by this paper are whether sociology had any role in defining the specific path of Serbia's post-socialist transformation, what its role was (was it predominantly critical towards ongoing processes, passive, supportive, or initiating), and whether the sociological community was homogeneous or heterogeneous in producing certain discourses and practices (and if the latter is correct, whether heterogeneity meant plurality of standpoints that crossed institutional lines or it went hand in hand with clear institutional and/or ideological divisions and construction of competing imaginaries)?

In order to answer some of these questions, we will set an analytical matrix that follows the cultural and political economy approach and evolutionary paradigm. However, first and foremost, we will divide the period of post-socialist transformation in Serbia into two distinctive phases (Lazić, 2011):

1. The phase of 'blocked' post-socialist transformation that lasted from the beginning of the 1990s until the year 2000; this phase was marked by the break-up of the Socialist Federative Republic of Yugoslavia, involvement in civil wars, international isolation, economic breakdown, but also by very slow pace and scope of structural changes and reforms towards market economy and political pluralism.
2. The phase of 'unblocked' transformation, beginning after the fall of Milošević's regime in 2000, was marked by accelerated reform processes towards market economy on the grounds of neoliberalism and political pluralism.

As the main focus of our analysis will be discourses on post-socialist transformation and ongoing processes of social change, the evolutionary paradigm will have to take into account some of the following elements:

1. Variety of discourses: how did Serbian sociology and sociologists see the process of transformation in its initial phase; did they recognise that the process involved major systemic changes; which discourses did they use in order to explain the ongoing processes of change; was there a variety of discourses or not; how did these discourses correspond to major paradigm shifts in sociology in general; who were the proponents of certain discourses; who were 'authorities'; did Serbian sociology produce endogenous discourses or it relied on 'imported' ones; etc.?
2. Selection of discourses: which discourses were privileged over others; did certain discourses become dominant over time; which factors influenced the selection of certain discourses (e.g. political, institutional, and/or professional positions/roles of its proponents); how did the selection of discourses correspond

to changes in pace and direction of post-socialist transformation in Serbia; did dominant discourses shift over time; etc.?
3. Retention of discourses: did certain discourses become regular parts of individual or collective practices, identities, or even state strategies and policies?
4. Reinforcement of dominant discourses: were any of the discourses on ongoing processes of change in Serbian sociology dominant; if yes, how did these discourses correspond to changes in global and local contexts (especially changes related to the difference in the two phases of post-socialist transformation); who were their proponents and what were their institutional positions; were there competing discourses; and, if yes, were they related to local or global sociological schools of thought?
5. Selective recruitment, inculcation, and retention: were the proponents of certain discourses privileged in professional institutions (such as the national sociological association) and academia and also in public administration, state bodies, and media?

The analysis we are proposing will have to take into account a dialectic relationship between semiotic and extra-semiotic elements and the articulation of four different selectivities: discursive, structural, technological, and agential (Sum & Jessop, 2013). Structural selectivity denotes the 'asymmetrical configuration of constraints and opportunities on social forces as they pursue particular projects', which exists only until it has been reproduced through social practices (Sum & Jessop, 2013: 214). They are grounded in the reproduction of basic social forms, institutional orders, organisational forms, and interaction contexts. Structures selectively favour particular agents, interests, and identities, while path dependency limits the scope for path shaping. Discursive selectivity not only frames and limits possible imaginaries and discourses but also frames hegemonies at different levels and is grounded in the enforced selection of sense and meaning in the face of complexity. Technological selectivity involves specific objectivation and knowledge production technologies; it shapes choices and capacities to act and distributes resources and losses. It represents a collection of knowledge, disciplinary and governmental rationalities, as well as mechanisms of intervention. Agential selectivity is grounded in the capacities of specific social agents (or groups of agents) to use structural, discursive, and technological selectivities, which enable them to make an impact, to induce change, to rearticulate discourses, in general, and to 'make a difference' (Sum & Jessop, 2013, pp. 214–219). The analysis of these four selectivities should answer the question of what the role of sociology was in establishing and reproducing the new capitalist system of relations in Serbia after the fall of socialism (on the application of CPE in analysing capitalism; see more in Jessop, 2004).

19.3 Sociology During 'Blocked Transformation' (1990–2000)

The fall of socialism in Yugoslavia was coupled with the dismantling of the (Yugoslav) state, which, for sociologists, also brought about the dismantling of the (Yugoslav) sociological community. Confronting systemic crisis was not new for many of them, as the so-called crisology (i.e. a derogatory term used by Communist Party officials for sociological analyses of Yugoslav society using the notion of 'crisis') was present during socialism, particularly among critical sociologists (Popović, 1982; Rus, 1982; Bolčić, 1982; Golubović, 1988). However, the scope of destruction they faced during the first years of the post-socialist period posed challenges in every sense: to bring in new paradigms, concepts, and discourses that can provide a new frame for understanding the changes, to reconfigure and reconstruct their own professional community, to redefine its roles regarding academic and public spheres, and to use different technologies as affordances had changed. Simply put, the specific path of post-socialist change set a very different scene for the transformation of sociology as a discipline and a community in Serbia in comparison to other (former) socialist countries in Europe.

The dissolution of the state unfolded through fierce wars in Croatia and Bosnia and Herzegovina and later in Kosovo; even though the multiparty system was formally introduced, the rule remained autocratic with power concentrated in very narrow circles around Milošević; the political elite maintained control over economic resources by postponing privatisation (with sporadic 'wild' privatisation) and economic reforms; control over civil society impeded the articulation of autonomous interests and social groups; isolation from the international community and economic sanctions, imposed in May 1992, blocked external transformative influences and the inflow of necessary resources. The social context in Serbia was marked by the destruction of the system, institutions, structures, and relations and the emergence of 'para' institutions (informal economy, informal education, informal social protection networks, etc.) developing in order to enable basic reproduction in the absence of formal system (more in Lazić et al., 1994; Bolčić, 2013). These systemic and structural changes had a major impact on sociological discourses, opening space for 'endogenous' theories and discourses, such as the 'destroyed society' discourse, which were more heuristically fruitful in explaining the changing reality during the first years of post-socialism than typical 'transitology' discourses used elsewhere in Eastern Europe, particularly in Visegrád countries.

19.3.1 Structural Selectivity

To understand how sociology as a discipline and sociological community has been transformed within such a context, it is essential to be aware of the legacies from the socialist period that defined the path-dependent transformation of both discipline and structures. An analysis of the main currents in Yugoslav sociology under socialism (Vuletić, 1995, 1996) argues that the development of sociology as a discipline depended on structural shifts within the ruling Communist Party. As power relations between key factions in the Communist Party were changing, the influence and institutional positioning of different streams among sociologists shifted in consequence.

According to some views (Bolčić, 1993; Lazić, 1993), the institutionalisation of Yugoslav sociology was continuously obstructed because of its immanent critical orientation. Two major strategies used by the political elite to prevent sociology's full institutional development can be singled out: firing professors at the Universities of Belgrade and Ljubljana and replacing the subject of sociology with Marxism in secondary school curricula (on the latter, see Jarić, 2014a). Despite these interventions, the community continued to grow through influential researchers, improving quality standards, and increasing international contacts. Thus, during the last decade of socialism, a core of the professional community was established, consolidating the discipline primarily through quality empirical research. The collapse of socialism and the disintegration of the state disrupted the development of sociology once more. These discontinuities led some commentators to conclude that in Serbia, there is no sociology, only sociologists (Lazić, 1993, p. 68). Weak institutionalisation prevented sociology from influencing politics and policies; sociologists remained outside of power circles and played no substantial role in the reforms undertaken in late socialism (Bolčić, 1993, 2013).

In socialist Yugoslavia, sociology was taught at ten universities,[1] with each constitutive republic and autonomous province having its own sociological association (in Serbia, it was the Sociological Society of Serbia) and the joint Yugoslav Sociological Association (JUS). At the time of the fall of the Berlin Wall, academic sociology was placed in Serbia at the University of Belgrade (as a department within the Faculty of Philosophy), University of Niš (also a department within the Faculty of Philosophy), University of Novi Sad (departments of sociology and philosophy had initially been merged, separating in 1996), and University of Priština (also first as a combined philosophy/sociology department, and since 1994 sociology proper, at the Faculty of Philosophy).[2] In addition, there were several research institutes: Institute for Sociological Research (a research unit of the Department for Sociology at the Faculty of Philosophy, University of Belgrade-ISI), Institute of Social Sciences, Institute for Philosophy and Social Theory (until 1992, part of the Institute of Social Sciences), and Institute for Criminological and Sociological Research (Bogdanović et al., 2009).

---

[1] Belgrade, Zagreb, Ljubljana, Sarajevo, Skopje, Zadar, Niš, Priština, Novi Sad, and Nikšić.

[2] After the 1999 war, (the non-Albanian) part of the University of Priština staff and students were relocated to Central Serbia. In 2001, the Government of Serbia reinstated the University of Priština (with the addendum: 'temporarily displaced') in Kosovska Mitrovica, in northern Kosovo. While the status of Kosovo remains unresolved, the Serbian Sociological Society treats sociologists from the Department of Sociology in Mitrovica as equal members of the professional community.

The Yugoslav Sociological Association ceased to exist in its original form with the dissolution of the Yugoslav state (sociological associations of Slovenia and Croatia left the joint association in 1991, after the outbreak of war).[3] The association was transformed several times along with the state, functioning for years under the name of the Sociological Association of Serbia and Montenegro, though only formally.[4] Two sociological journals have remained the main outlets for placing sociological work: *Sociologija* (*Sociology*), published by the successor(s) to the former JUS, and *Sociološki pregled* (*Sociological Review*), published by the Sociological Society of Serbia.

During the 1990s, the sociological community in Serbia was in institutional and academic isolation. Institutional contacts with international and ex-Yugoslav sociological communities were dramatically reduced. Prior to 1990, the journal *Sociologija*, as the organ of the federal association, had naturally been open to authors from other Yugoslav republics (roughly one-half of articles published during the 1980s were by authors outside Serbia), as well as from other countries, and in the early 1990s traces of this legacy remains. However, later in the decade, the tendency of 'closure' towards authors from outside Serbia became increasingly visible, and references to recent foreign literature dropped significantly in both *Sociologija* and *Sociološki pregled* (Vuletić & Stanojević, 2013). The reasons were suspended international cooperation, severely reduced academic mobility, very sporadic participation in international research projects (only on individual rather than institutional basis), and impoverished libraries. The sociological diaspora was not numerous, and its connections with academics back home were loose and occasional.

The sociological community suffered from a chronic shortage of basic financial resources for research, conferences, and publishing. Despite the dearth of funds, dedication and persistence allowed researchers to carry out an empirical study on the early stage of Serbian post-socialist transformation, providing evidence of unprecedented processes causing societal destruction. The results became available in the volume *Social Change and Everyday Life: Serbia at the Beginning of 1990s* (Bolčić et al., 1995).

---

[3] Thus, the sociological community was partly split along national-republic lines. The JUS presidency and the editorial board of *Sociologija* issued two open letters, in September and December 1991, addressed to the presidents of Yugoslav republics, the military leadership, and the public at large, protesting against violence and destruction, denouncing nationalism and calling for the war to stop immediately. At that moment, the president of JUS was Slobodan Vukićević from Montenegro, while the editor-in-chief of *Sociologija* was Mladen Lazić, a key Yugoslav and post-Yugoslav sociologist who had just moved from Zagreb to Belgrade. Some other republic's associations (e.g. Macedonian) joined the statements. The Croatian association however received these responses coldly, describing them as insufficient and inadequate. The polemical exchange can be found in volume 33, issues 3 and 4 (1991) and volume 34, issue 1 (1992) of *Sociologija*. The 1991 and 1992 volumes of *Sociologija* still contain articles by Croatian and Slovene authors, the latter printed in their original Slovene language, as had been customary.

[4] In 2019, the association was transformed once more into the Sociological Scientific Society of Serbia.

One very important channel for accessing the international scholarly community and literature was the Central European University in Budapest, in which 'transitology' dominated. In addition, the Open Society Foundation was one of the rare sources of funds for sociological research during this decade. Also, towards the end of this period (1999–2002), a significant role was played by summer schools financially supported by the Open Society Fund and coordinated by Mladen Lazić. They gathered scholars from Serbia, the former Yugoslavia, other East European countries, and beyond. This was where junior scholars were professionally socialised into studying post-socialist transition by working with professors from abroad, learning about and exchanging theories, approaches, methods, existing studies, findings, and so on.

The sociological community was divided, and the gap between different streams was widening towards the late 1990s. While more on this will be said in the section on discourses, let us note here just that the community was roughly split into a 'nationalist' and an 'internationalist' faction. The latter, which was not really a unified collective but rather a collection of individuals and groups brought together by their shared characteristic of being critical towards the dominant nationalist ideology and Milošević's authoritarian regime, played rather prominent roles in the turbulent events of the time. It provided a theoretical foundation and a platform for civil activism in different forms: within peace, feminist, and student movements or in NGOs addressing various consequences of blocked transition. During 1996/1997 student and citizen protests, many sociologists gathered around this 'bloc' and joined as active citizens while simultaneously researching the movements themselves, identifying, for example, an 'awakening' of the middle class asking for democratic reforms (Babović et al., 1997; Lazić et al., 1999). Since the university represented one of the strongholds of opposition to Milošević's regime, its autonomy was constantly under attack, culminating in the 1998 University Law.[5] Again, sociologists were active in organising protests, as well as in establishing the Alternative Academic Educational Network (AAEN, or AAOM in Serbian), an incipient parallel academic structure providing university-level courses, where many of the scholars expelled from or persecuted within the university found refuge.

19.3.2 Technological Selectivity

Different technologies were used during this decade to communicate sociological knowledge on the transformation of Serbian society within the professional community and beyond with other groups in the society. As far as the two journals are concerned, their content was shaped primarily by the policies of their

---

[5] The law, for example, stipulated that the government rather than autonomous bodies established by the university appoint university rectors, faculty deans, and administrative and supervisory boards (see *Službeni glasnik Srbije*, 1998). Also, academics were required to sign a new labour contract, with provisions that severely curtailed their intellectual freedom.

editors-in-chief and editorial boards.[6] At a more general level, what must be appreciated is the sheer continuity of publication, as both journals published their volumes more or less regularly: an almost heroic accomplishment under the given conditions.

The same holds for conferences and round tables, which sought to maintain the continuity of communication both within the sociological community itself and with the broader public. The Sociological Society of Serbia held congresses (annually or biannually), as well as round tables, panel discussions, and other meetings, invariably thematising the most topical social issues.[7]

Through various available channels, the Serbian sociologists discussed their thoughts and research findings among themselves and offered them to the public. While they sought to share their knowledge about the dramatic processes taking place in society, this had little effect. The government did not 'need' sociologists; the Milošević regime was even more dismissive of social scientific research as the basis for designing policies than the Titoist and post-Titoist authorities had been.

What public influence sociologists did exert was through their engagement in the civil sector and activism, especially in the anti-war movement. Thus, many sociologists joined the Belgrade Circle, an informal association of intellectuals emerging from the protest against the nationalist and aggressive policies of the Milošević regime and representing what came to be called the 'Other Serbia' (see Čolović & Mimica et al., 1992, 1993). Another, and partly overlapping, activist/intellectual group was the one gathering around the magazine Republika, which started in 1989 as the organ of the Jugoslovensko udruženje za demokratsku inicijativu (Yugoslav Association for Democratic Initiative or UJDI), the last all-Yugoslav political organisation, and after 1991 continued as a magazine published in Belgrade and edited by the sociologist Nebojša Popov.[8] Republika's motto was 'Against the Force of Fear, Hate, and Violence', and it steadily promoted rational, critical, democratically minded, and anti-authoritarian analysis of what was going on in the territory of former Yugoslavia. Sociologists writing for Republika sought to communicate the results of their scholarly inquiries in a more accessible language to a wider audience, thus reaching out beyond the boundaries of their own professional community. A remarkable result of Republika's labours is the massive collective volume *Serbian Road to War* (Popov et al., 1996), examining the political, social, and cultural processes that led to the war.

---

[6] Hence, change of editor could have evident repercussions, as illustrated, for example, by a distinct change of tone between volumes 27 (1993) and 28 (1994) of *Sociološki pregled*.

[7] An early example is the roundtable Society at War, organized by the Society in June 1992, and the proceedings published in issue 1–4/1992 of *Sociološki pregled*.

[8] See: http://www.republika.co.rs

19.3.3 Sociologists as Agents of Social Change

During this decade, sociology as a discipline and its individual members, *qua* sociologists, had virtually no influence on determining the direction of social change. The scope of their impact was limited despite the fact that several sociologists were engaged in politics. There was a curious asymmetry in the sense that more power in the political arena usually went hand in hand with reduced professional repute and vice versa. The most glaring example is Mirjana Marković, the wife of Slobodan Milošević and a powerful shadowy figure, the leader of Jugoslovenska levica (Yugoslav Left), an electorally insignificant party with disproportionate influence as a coalition partner to Milošević's own party (the SPS). Marković, despite being a professor of sociology at the natural science departments of Belgrade University, was effectively not part of the sociological community at all: not doing research, never publishing her work in the main journals, never participating in conferences, never taking up any responsibility in the sociologists' association, and never showing up for any professional meeting.

There were very few sociologists with positions in the government during Milošević's rule, and they belonged to the 'nationalist' strand. The highest office was occupied by Zoran Avramović, a researcher in the sociology of culture, who was deputy minister of education appointed by the ultranationalist Serbian Radical Party (SRS) in the SPS-SRS coalition government that marked the gloomiest and most repressive final years of the Milošević regime (1998–2000). In contrast, some sociologists put their academic careers on hold and joined the political opposition: for instance, prominent sociologist Vesna Pešić was for many years the leader of the liberal, anti-nationalist party Građanski savez Srbije (Civic Alliance of Serbia).[9] Still others retained their professional careers while devoting significant amounts of time and energy to political engagement, as intellectuals affiliated with political parties (e.g. Dragan Radulović in Demokratska stranka Srbije, Democratic Party of Serbia or DSS). However, sociologists' involvement in the civil sector was much more massive, as described previously.

Despite these (weak) links between individual sociologists and different factions of the political elite and counter-elite, sociology as a discipline and sociologists, by institutionally performing their profession, exerted no real impact on decision-making. Their role in shaping policies was nil, unlike economists and legal scholars, who were overrepresented among policymakers during that period. In this sense, sociology remained marginal. Yet this, in turn, enabled it to maintain its independence from political circles, to conduct autonomous research (despite lack of funds), and to remain critical.

---

[9] Pešić had also been a founding member of the most important Serbian anti-war NGO, Center for Anti-War Action.

19.3.4 Discursive Selectivity

During the last decade of socialism, there was a growing body of critical sociological analysis of immanent weaknesses of the socialist system, coming from different streams and circles. What proved to be probably the last joint conference before the end of the socialist Yugoslavia gathered social scientists and academics from different parts of the country, including sociologists, with the aim of discussing the situation.[10] Despite these efforts, the severity of destruction surprised even those who had been very thorough in the analysis of factors leading to the fall of socialism. The sociological community in Serbia entered a period of simultaneous change in structure, institutional settings, approaches, and discourses.

While large-scale societal transformation always makes a fascinating sociological subject, Serbian society, even more than the more fortunate East European countries whose transition did not include war, international isolation, record hyperinflation, dictatorship, and state terror, was a kind of 'live social laboratory': it was a historically unique moment and an example of society inviting sociological study. Therefore, Serbian sociology displayed a huge (and somewhat chaotic) variety of analytical levels and topics in an effort to grasp all the aspects of the rapidly changing social reality. The topics involved issues directly related to the war and societal destruction, as well as broader new subjects stemming from a more 'normal' evolution of the discipline. We may mention the following: re-stratification (Janićijević et al., 1990; Lazić 1994, 1996a, 1996b; Lazić et al., 1994), ethnic and social conflicts (Janjić, 1999; Milosavljević, 1999), religious revival (Blagojević, 1995b), social movements (Davidović, 1995; Lazić, 1996b; Babović et al., 1997; Čičkarić, 1997; Spasić & Pavićević, 1997; Lazić et al., 1999), everyday life, transformation of family, gender relations and identities (Blagojević, 1995a, 1995b, 1998; Tomanović-Mihajlović, 1994; Tomanović, 1995; Milić, 1995a, 1995b), informal economy (Mrkšić, 1994), urban and rural change (Petovar, 1992; Mitrović, 1994; Pušić, 1995; Vujović, 1995, 1997), transformation/destruction of the sphere of work and employment (Bolčić, 1995b; Novaković, 1997), traumatisation and mental health issues (Korać, 1994; Opalić, 1994; Radulović, 1995), gender and family violence (Nikolić-Ristanović, 1994), political party pluralism and elections, public opinion (Gredelj, 1993; Branković, 1996; Antonić, 1998), sociology of law and human rights in particular (Molnar, 1993; Branković, 1996; Antonić, 1998; Mihajlović, 1998), and so on.

Such a background encouraged the proliferation of authentic, endogenous approaches at the expense of borrowed ready-made paradigms subsumable under the label of 'transitology', which prevailed in other East European countries. A deep suspicion against the simplistic optimist account of transition as heading towards an unquestionable 'good' was present from the very beginning. It can also be read as a

---

[10] The conference 'The Crisis and the Bases for Reform' was held in October 1990, organised by the Institute of European Studies and the Consortium of Social Science Institutes of Yugoslavia. The proceedings, including some 20 papers and as many short discussions, appeared in volume 32, issue 4 of *Sociologija*, 1990.

disciplinary matter, pitting (more optimist) political scientists, and economists against sociologists, who have been more attentive to the complexities and social costs of large-scale change. The fact that Serbia's path deviated from the 'model' transition bolstered the relatively stronger position of this skeptical-sociologising view against the optimistic-simplifying one (Vuletić et al., 2011). A good illustration is the 1993 call issued by the editorial board of *Sociološki pregled* to a number of prominent sociologists to take part in a sociological survey, a collective reflection on 'what kind of society we have found ourselves in'. The situation in Serbia, 'which though not at war, has seen the war destroy its basic social and economic institutions that every society rests upon', is described in bleak terms (basic social and economic institutions ruined, flood of decivilisation, leap into the past, anomie, undoing of interpersonal relations, manipulation, regression, hatred, etc.). Sociology is urged to face it and take its own responsibility, lest its very meaning and mission become problematic (see volume 27, issues 1–4 of *Sociološki pregled* (1993), special issue on Serbian Society Today).

Speaking of endogenous discourses thriving in Serbian sociology, one of the most important was the concept of 'destruction of society', attached to the so-called 'Belgrade school,' first proposed by Bolčić (1993; see also Bolčić, 2013) and later elaborated by Lazić et al. (1994).

While in the other Central and Eastern European countries, one of the main debates on the structural changes during post-socialism evolved around theses of circulation versus reproduction of elites, Mladen Lazić proposed the notion of 'adaptive reconstruction of elites', which he subjected to repeated empirical tests. Essentially, it argues that the elites in Serbia were not replaced during the transition, but the ruling elites from the socialist period (what he had dubbed the 'command class'; see Lazić, 2000) instead retained power by adapting to the new circumstances, such as by converting organisational and political into economic capital in the form of private ownership. Related to this is the refutation of the belief that the 'middle class has vanished', which was widespread in a journalistic, publicist, and everyday discourse in the 1990s. Serbian sociologists showed through empirical research (Lazić et al., 1994; Babović et al., 1997) that the middle class by no means disappeared but that its relative status, mode of reproduction, and power were, of course, changing in the emerging social system.

Still, and in parallel with these views, there was also the local variant of 'transitology'. This approach was embraced as well and applied to a range of issues quite comparable to what analyses of transition did in other settings: models of privatisation, winners and losers of post-socialist transformation, new entrepreneurs, and changing organisations, among others. The transition paradigm, coming in from the Central European University or by other routes, served as a major platform for critiquing the deficiencies of Milošević's regime but was never shaped as an integrative and homogenous theoretical paradigm.

Then, the 'totalitarianism' discourse briefly surfaced, for example, in the writings of Mihailo Popović (1991, 1995a, 1995b, 1996), a key figure of Serbian sociology between the 1960s and 1980s and particularly of its professionalised, empirically based variant nurtured at the Belgrade Faculty of Philosophy (the 'Belgrade School' referred to above). In a veritable example of what Todor Kuljić (2001) has called the 'conversion of Yugoslav humanistic intelligentsia', the man who had under communist rule been rather quiescent[11] now turned to examining the common features of 'bolshevism' and fascism. The totalitarian paradigm, however, was contested from the very beginning and never took root.

The 1990s were also the period when feminist discourse, though not unknown previously, became much more salient. In addition to increased frequency, this expansion was manifested in bringing the feminist perspective to bear on a growing and more variegated range of topics that were taken up as subjects of sociological, including empirical research. Novel views of phenomena such as violence, domesticity, parenthood, criminal law, human rights, demography, professions, general social and political theory, and so on were thus provided. This evolution is to be credited primarily to Žarana Papić (1992, 1993, 1997) and Marina Blagojević (1992, 1995a, 1995b, 2000), as well as to Anđelka Milić (1992, 1994), who had pioneered feminism in Serbian sociology. The organisational upshot of these discursive innovations was the launching of the first women/gender studies courses in Serbia at the Sociology Department in Belgrade.

Going back to a theme taken up in a previous section, sociological discourses in Serbia were importantly marked by a cleavage between the 'nationalist' and 'internationalist' camps. The cleavage partly maps onto the division between the two journals, *Sociološki pregled* and *Sociologija*.[12] The latter was steadily antinationalist throughout, broader in the selection of its authors and positions; it was struggling to retain a degree of 'internationalism' in spite of isolation by publishing translated articles, including foreign authors where possible, and publishing in English more than the other journal. *Sociološki pregled*, in contrast, was more obviously 'national', both in an institutional and organisational sense and in the form of political commitment and partiality. It was more welcoming of nationalist positions, from moderate to extremist, and less concerned with maintaining a universalist face.

The difference is visible, for example, in a bifurcation of accounts of the same processes. For example, Bolčić writes about the 'nationalization of social relations' and clearly judges it in negative terms (Bolčić, 1993, 1995a). The phenomenon is treated similarly by Golubović (1993), Milić (1993), or Sekelj (1991). These authors, representing the 'internationalist' discourse, chastise sociology for not paying sufficient attention to rising nationalisms and their destructive potential in Yugoslavia and Serbia prior to 1990. Simultaneously, the same phenomena are described by other writers as Serbian sociology's 'sin' of not being sensitive enough

---

[11] During the political persecution of dissident sociologists and philosophers from the Faculty of Philosophy, who belonged to the so-called Praxis school of humanistic Marxism and were accused by the regime of instigating rebellion among students in 1968 and later, when the harassed professors enjoyed strong institutional and personal support by their department, the faculty, and individual colleagues, Popović was among the few who did not join this defence. The events, evolving from 1968 to 1975, are described in Popov (1989).

[12] The division was tendential rather than absolute: most Serbian sociologists published in both outlets, although clear preference patterns can be observed.

to the plight of 'its own people'. In other words, in the nationalist discourse, Serbian sociology is ascribed an (ethno)national responsibility and found wanting on this count (more on this issue in Spasić et al., 2022).[13]

It must be admitted, though, that the ideological difference was temporarily blurred by the NATO bombing campaign against what was the Federal Republic of Yugoslavia (March–June 1999) that ended the war in Kosovo. Both journals responded in a similar way: protesting the campaign, pointing out its destructive consequences, and appealing to the international sociological community for solidarity.[14] Still, the differences were not totally wiped out, as *Sociologija*, even in this 'black' edition,[15] shunned overt chauvinism, war-mongering, and insulting language; among the articles published in addition to the bombing-related content, some are very critical of Serbian nationalism.

As for discourse selection and retention, the Belgrade Department's institute (ISI) was the site of the only recognisable group-based sociological orientation: the so-called 'Belgrade school' of empirical study of stratification, identified and informally named back in socialist times, was maintained and advanced further in the 1990s. At this key institutional node, several generations of sociologists were socialised and worked, sharing a set of basic theoretical and methodological commitments. This commonality may be recognised in shared concerns, joint research projects and publications, a similar conceptual vocabulary, and a critical distance to political power. Apart from this, no other 'school' that would promote a particular discourse in a sustained fashion may be discerned in Serbian sociology.

19.4 Sociology in Serbia After the Year 2000

The phase of post-socialist transformation in Serbia that started with the regime change in the year 2000 and continued with reforms towards the establishment of a market economy and political pluralism is often called 'unblocked transformation' (Lazić, 2011). This period was marked by the lifting of economic sanctions, acceleration of reforms, and implementation of neoliberal policies (privatisation of state property, restructuring of the financial and banking sector, price liberalisation, the introduction of free trade, turning to foreign direct investments, liberalisation of the labour market, and similar changes) (see more in Uvalić, 2010; Lazić & Pešić, 2012). At the same time, political pluralism and democratic institutions were gradually stabilised. Such developments led to social restructuring, the crystallisation of

---

[13] Thus, Popović (1993) argues that 'Serbian sociologists failed to take seriously enough the Serbian experience in the 2nd World War' and Mitrović (1993), more bluntly, that 'the only responsibility [of sociology and sociologists] that can meaningfully be discussed now is the one to the Serbian people and its destiny and interest'.

[14] See volume 41, issue 3 of *Sociologija* (1999) and volume 33, issue 1–2 of *Sociološki pregled* (1999).

[15] All four 1999 issues of *Sociologija* were printed with black covers, as a sign of protest and grief.

new class relations (Lazić, 2011), and rising social inequalities, reinforced by a system of party clientelism and patronage, which evolved in the meantime (Cvejić et al., 2016). In addition, due to unresolved territorial issues with Kosovo[16] and the relatively slow pace of institutional reforms, Serbia's accession to the European Union remains uncertain. This, in turn, allows political elites to hold power by suspending periodically some of the achieved standards of democratic governance and the rule of law in exchange for maintaining political stability in the region and implementing neoliberal reforms.

While, during the previous decade, Serbian sociologists were predominantly critical towards the system shaped by Milošević's regime and bursting nationalism, systemic changes and reform processes imposed new challenges on sociology: whether to preserve its critical role or to become a socio-integrative social science that provides legitimacy to the new social order. Here, we must bear in mind that the foremost target of sociologists' critique during the 1990s had actually been the slow pace and 'blockade' of post-socialist transformation on capitalist grounds. Discourses that were now 'at the table' necessarily had to be different from those shaped during the first decade of transition since the social context changed and, along with it, the role of sociology, its professional status, structural possibilities, available technologies, and other factors.

19.4.1 *Structural Selectivity*

After the year 2000, the context in which Serbian sociology developed changed in major ways. First and foremost, economic sanctions were lifted, enabling the opening towards international academic communities, participation in international projects, staff exchange, and international institutional cooperation. Structural possibilities expanded, offering diversification of access to institutional resources and academic networks, as well as to new theoretical concepts and paradigms. A much denser, formal, and informal academic communication enabling academic exchange was also made possible by technological development and by the expansion of academic internet networks. In this way, the structural base for the development of sociology in Serbia became very different than in the 1990–2000 period.

Another crucial external (in the sense of coming from outside the sociological field) element changed: namely, the dissolution of the joint state of Serbia and Montenegro in 2006 meant the disappearance of the formal territorial and political base of one of the two existing professional associations: the Sociological Association of Serbia and Montenegro (SASM, successor to JUS). This association remained active only formally as the publisher of the journal *Sociologija* (until 2019, when it transformed into the Sociological Scientific Society of Serbia), while

---

[16] The union of Serbia and Montenegro dissolved in 2006, while Kosovo, de facto not part of Serbia since 1999, proclaimed independence in 2008.

the other association, the Serbian Sociological Society (SSS), acquired legitimacy as the official professional association recognised by the state. The division of the sociological community in Serbia around two professional associations (one being formally recognised by the state and the other existing merely on paper until the recent aforementioned changes) coincided with institutional but also ideological cleavages. Namely, the SASM mostly gathered sociologists from the Department of Sociology at the Faculty of Philosophy in Belgrade, while the SSS had a more diversified structure, with members from three other university centres and research institutions, as well as sociologists working outside academia.

This division, like in the 1990s, had its reflections on the two main journals: *Sociologija* and *Sociološki pregled*. Almost exclusively, the editors of *Sociologija* between 2000 and 2018 were from the Department of Sociology at the University of Belgrade. Although editors and editorial staff of *Sociologija* sought to remain open to international influences, paradoxically, it seems that, in an effort to maintain the exclusive character of the journal and the relatively good quality of the papers, it has become increasingly closed to the rest of the sociological community in Serbia. Conversely, the editors of *Sociološki pregled* had more diversified affiliations, making the journal more open towards sociologists coming from other institutional centres.[17] These structural and agential selectivities were closely related to technological ones. Specifically, 'national' and 'international' strategic orientations of the journals were underwritten by the choice of script used for typesetting: Cyrillic in *Sociološki pregled*[18] (since 1998) and Latin in *Sociologija* (which also kept the tradition of publishing volumes or single texts in English), indicating that the first journal was dominantly oriented towards the domestic professional community, while the other sought to address a wider audience in the region and internationally.

While ideological and institutional divisions within the Serbian sociological community were 'inherited' from the previous phase of blocked transformation, a new one emerged as a response not only to the changes in social order, in general, but also to changes within the sphere of higher education that took place after the reforms were sped up. Let us address the latter issue first. After the year 2000, the reform of higher education, in accordance with the Bologna agreement, was a key one. The reform brought about changed modalities of research funding: the Ministry of Education and Science began granting scientific projects proposed by research institutions through a competitive and selective process. The capacities of different institutions varied: for example, the ISI had managed to sustain the tradition of conducting empirical studies during the period of blocked transformation and was relatively well prepared for the new conditions (the key role was here played by the

---

[17] With three editors coming from the Department of Sociology—University of Novi Sad, and one from each of the following: Institute for Educational Research, Institute of Social Sciences, Department of Sociology –University of Belgrade, and Department of Sociology—University of Priština at Kosovska Mitrovica.

[18] Only in recent years, starting from 2017, has *Sociološki pregled* begun to publish texts bilingually, in Serbian (Cyrillic) and in English.

sociologists gathered around the 'Belgrade school'[19] reinforced by the arrival of Mladen Lazić). Other institutions either had failed to develop recognisable research traditions or, if they had one, struggled to preserve their research capacities in times of scarcity. In a situation in which different institutions now acted as competitors for grants and funds, strategies for ensuring institutional existence varied depending on the resources available. Some institutions acted on the principle of openness towards the international community while simultaneously striving to maintain their elitist character within the national sociological community. Other institutions (or academics working within them) resorted to networking through the professional association and strengthening the official position of the association, sometimes using political connections to that effect. In this manner, they secured not only their institutional status but also the status of individual academics, projects, and journals.

Another line of division within the sociological community was related to the problematisation of the issues arising from the accelerated institutional reforms towards establishing the capitalist system of relations. Although there were no direct proponents of neoliberal reforms among sociologists in Serbia (this discourse was typically present among economists who were involved in creating neoliberal policies and among political scientists who provided the broader legitimacy framework for the reforms), discourses on the ongoing processes of change varied. The line of division was the presence or absence of problematisation, that is, critique of the installation of capitalism on neoliberal grounds and the consequences of this process.

This ideological/discursive division was reinforced by structural, agential, and technological selectivities. The noncritical, non-problematising trend (closely coupled with promoting the development of civil society, state institutions, the rule of law, political pluralism, etc.; see more in Kuljić, 2009) was mostly to be found among sociologists tied to institutions benefitting from the reform processes and from the gradual commercialisation of higher education. In contrast, critique of the reform processes, especially after the 2008 economic crisis, was related to two types of agents: to those whose theoretical positions were not tied to mainstream discourses within academia or research institutions (such as, for example, Todor Kuljić) and to those who were not at all affiliated to academic institutions but worked outside them (mainly activists).

Critiques of the neoliberal reforms were coming from both the right and the left sides of the ideological spectrum. In the first case, the critiques involved the whole set of nationalist and conservative narratives (anti-EU, anti-NATO, anti-US, homophobic, anti-democracy, anti-imperialism, etc.), while in the other case, narratives ranged from academic neo-Marxism and anti-globalisation narratives to the extreme left critique of capitalism, usually coupled with engagement in social protests and direct actions.

---

[19] One of its proponents, Marija Bogdanović, became the University of Belgrade's Rector in the early 2000s. Since she had been the Dean of the Faculty of Philosophy that supported student protests against Milošević in 1996/1997, she was also simultaneously recognised as a symbol of academia's resistance to the old regime.

In parallel with these general ideological and institutional/structural divisions and Serbian sociology's opening to the international community, a thematic, theoretical, and methodological diversification of sociology was underway (Kuljić, 2009). This process was closely related to the depoliticisation of academic sociology, the declining importance and potential of critical discourses, as well as to broader changes in the field of social theory (Kuljić, 2009).

Finally, one important structural element also contributed to the growing plurality of sociological themes and theories, and that is the diversification of funding schemes: in addition to the relatively stable scheme provided by the state, the opportunities for involvement in academic and commercial projects funded by international funders, European Commission and its bodies, local nongovernment organisations, and various state bodies opened up. This diversification, along with commercialisation and a gradual shift to the production of applicable knowledge, led to the selection of research questions and problems being increasingly determined by the demands coming from agents outside the academic field (the state, donors, private companies, etc.).

19.4.2 Technological Selectivity

Technological selectivity reinforced the described institutional and ideological divisions within the sociological community in Serbia: after the year 2000, sociologists started to act increasingly as political analysts, experts working as consultants for the government, nongovernmental organisations or international bodies, policymakers, public opinion researchers, and similar, directly or indirectly providing legitimacy base to the reform processes and to the establishment of the new, capitalist type of social relations. Critics of the capitalist system, in contrast, relied mostly on alternative technological assets, such as blogs, newspaper columns and commentaries, social media, projects supported by various nongovernmental organisations or international funders, direct action, and so on. However, only a few sociologists were directly politically involved, and, to our knowledge, no one was directly involved in creating and implementing reform policies.

Several sociologists, working primarily in academia, still write or used to write regular newspaper columns in leading daily newspapers (Politika and Danas) or prominent media outlets (Peščanik), such as Todor Kuljić, Slobodan Antonić, Vladimir Ilić, Vladimir Vuletić, Jovo Bakić, Nataša Jovanović Ajzenhamer, or Aleksej Kišjuhas. Often, these columns served as a means of public promotion of certain sociological discourses: for example, Marxist or conservative critique of capitalism or the globalisation paradigm as a general framework for legitimating pro-EU policies. However, those sociologists who nurtured critical discourses on the government reform policies became unsuitable and undesirable (although not completely absent) in pro-government or 'neutral' media, especially in the period after the economic and financial crisis in 2008. Discourses fostered by sociologists that 'survived' in the mainstream media were mostly those being ideologically neutral or supporting European integration policies and the inevitability of institutional reforms in order to comply with the demands coming from international institutions.

Nevertheless, although the mechanisms whereby Serbian sociology communicated within and outside the narrow professional circles diversified, dominant channels remained academic: journals, sociological conferences, publishing, and activities of the professional association. Even though the sociological community was involved in publishing and conducting research more than ever before, it was not always recognised by the public or by politicians as relevant in providing interpretations of social reality. The reasons were multiple: sociology did not offer a dominant and non-contradictory discourse on the ongoing processes of change; fundamental divisions within the sociological community discouraged closer professional integration; due to the hermetic communication style of sociologists, the media preferred the interpretations of the daily events put forward by the so-called political analysts to the systematic, empirically, and theoretically based knowledge of the sociologists, etc. (Bolčić, 2011).

The stabilisation of funding schemes, opening towards the international community, involvement in international academic projects, enhancement of institutional capacities by employing young researchers, and the new system of evaluation of academics based on quantitative indicators of academic publications led to a flourishing of professional activities within the sociological community, especially in the second half of the examined time period. Alongside the two previously mentioned journals, *Sociologija* and *Sociološki pregled,* specialised in publishing sociological texts, several other, mainly multidisciplinary-oriented academic journals have also been publishing sociological papers: *Kultura, Stanovništvo, Filozofija i društvo, Teme, Etnoantropološki problemi*, among others. Moreover, almost all faculties and institutes developed their own publishing activities, mainly publishing books (monographs) of the academics working within them.[20]

Domestic and international sociological conferences were held regularly, as well as round tables, open debates, and similar events. In comparison to the previous period, the forms, organisers, occasions, themes, and similar were more diversified, pointing to the expanding capacities of the sociological community but at the same time to its fragmentation. In contrast, visits of internationally recognised sociologists or social theoreticians were often organised by institutions that were not particularly related to sociology and its associations (mostly those who had international connections and financial resources). The fragmented character of the community could be recognised in the fact that sociological debates within the journals (regular during the 1990s[21]) almost disappeared after the year 2000. Therefore, in spite of the increased scope of professional activities, it seems that communication within the

---

[20] However, it has to be said that these books are often published in small circulation and due to the underdeveloped distribution network, the visibility of sociologists and the dissemination of texts often depends on their own initiative and the use of modern technologies (above all, academic networks on the internet).

[21] Some of the participants in those debates in *Sociologija* were Borislav Milić, Vladimir Ilić, Milan Brdar, Srbobran Branković, and later also Aleksandar Molnar, Mladen Lazić, and Vladimir Vuletić.

sociological community tends to be rather quiet, mostly oriented towards narrow (fragmented) audiences, while at the same time being insufficiently open towards other disciplinary areas of social sciences and humanities.

Although sociologists were increasingly involved in international projects and collaborations during the examined period, influential and widely recognisable sociological diaspora that would act as a source or transmission channel of certain discourses failed to develop. Sociologists at international academic institutions coming from Serbia generally maintained individual contacts with academics currently working in Serbia, but consistent cooperation and exchange of discourses did not take place.

Finally, sociology in Serbia has managed to preserve continuity over conducting empirical research and providing reliable data on various aspects of social reality and transformation processes (ranging from the research of social stratification, mobility and inequalities, values, and attitudinal changes to research on the patterns of cultural consumption, survival strategies of households, youth, urban and gender issues, etc.). However, apart from the fact that data gathered through sociological surveys are not publicly available, they are almost never used by various decision-makers and policymakers either in designing the reform processes or in managing and controlling their consequences. In this way, the transformative power of sociological surveys and empirical data remains negligible.

19.4.3 Agential Selectivity: Sociologists as Agents of Social Change

The role of sociology (as a profession, and even as expertise) in Serbian reforms after the year 2000 was rather marginal (Bolčić, 2011): sociology was not invited to provide the legitimacy basis for the new types of social relations (the legitimacy of neoliberal reforms was mainly ensured by economists, political scientists, and legal scholars), although sociologists were or still are active as politicians or as public intellectuals. For example, Slobodan Antonić, president of the SSS between 2009 and 2013 and editor of *Sociološki pregled* 2006–2009, also advanced as an exponent of conservative ideology. Another editor of *Sociološki pregled* (1997–98), Milan Brdar, was for a short time (2004) deputy minister of education under the DSS prime minister Koštunica. Dragoljub Mićunović, once a member of the dissident group expelled from the Faculty of Philosophy in 1975 by the Communist regime, was for years an important figure of the socio-democratic faction within the Democratic Party (DS). The Serbian Progressive Party (SNS), in power since 2012, was publicly endorsed by Zoran Avramović, another ex-president of the SSS and ex-editor of *Sociološki pregled*. Jovo Bakić and Todor Kuljić, acting as engaged intellectuals, were proponents of the leftist critique of neoliberal reforms (together with a number of younger sociologists and left-wing activists not tied to institutional sociology). Two more sociologists from an older generation, belonging to the

'Praxis school' of critical theory, must be mentioned here for their sustained critiques of (Serbian) capitalism from a left-wing perspective: Zagorka Golubović and Nebojša Popov.

Although sociologists served as experts for the governments or NGOs in designing the reforms of certain segments of society (e.g. Marija Babović on gender inequalities, or Smiljka Tomanović and Mirjana Bobić and shaping youth and demographic policies), they were not at the forefront and recognised as prime reformers and ministers in the governments or frontbenchers in the parliament.

Besides Jovo Bakić, who tasted politics as an 'ideologist' of the political party Levica Srbije (the Left of Serbia) in order to withdraw soon after and became active several years later in Partija radikalne levice (Party of Radical Left), one of the most publicly recognisable sociologists acting as politician is the already mentioned former opposition leader Vesna Pešić (former ambassador and member of parliament), who, paradoxically, for many years has not been active within the sociological community (but rather as part of a group of liberal thinkers gathered around the internet portal Peščanik).

19.4.4 Discursive Selectivity

When discursive variety and dominance are concerned, initially, that is, during the first decade of twenty-first-century 'transformation' discourse clearly prevailed over the 'transitology' discourse (Lazić et al., 2000; Lazić, 2002; Bolčić, 2003; Lazić & Cvejić, 2004; Babović et al., 2010; Petrović, 2013b; Pešić, 2017). However, as reforms gained momentum and the new system of social relations was gradually put in place, discussions of transition/transformation gave way to discussions of capitalism (Antonić, 2006; Lazić & Pešić, 2012). Analytical considerations of capitalism were mainly critical, either from the left or the right positions. Critiques of capitalism varied and ranged from rejection of particular aspects of this system to the rejection of the entire system (among leftists, see Vukša & Simović, 2016; Vratuša, 2016) to a (social-democratic) critique of the particular forms of capitalism being established in the periphery (of the so-called crony, wild, neo-patrimonial, etc. capitalism, but not of capitalism as such; see Cvejić et al., 2016). Left-wing and right-wing critiques often borrowed arguments from each other. Discursive selection also occurred through journals: right-wing critique of capitalism was more present in *Sociološki pregled*, while left-wing critique could be found more frequently in *Sociologija*. However, discourses openly advocating for neoliberal reforms were almost absent from sociology in Serbia.

Sociological discourses in this most recent period became more diversified: new topics were broached, and new theoretical approaches were tried out. Feminist discourse was now solidly entrenched (albeit, like in many places, never fully accepted by the mainstream) and with a broader base. Moreover, it was expanded by new takes on LGBT/queer identities, practices, and lifestyles that work with a constructionist understanding of identity (e.g. Jovanović, 2016; Radoman, 2017). The constructionist approach also gained ground in discussions of other forms of collective identity: ethnic, national, religious, and regional, particularly among sociologists from Novi Sad University (Tripković et al., 2006; Lazar et al., 2007; Sokolovska & Marinković, 2012; Ristić et al., 2016). Some other fresh discourses also emerged thanks to authors from Novi Sad, e.g. Foucauldian (Marinković & Ristić, 2013, 2016; Milenković, 2016), or the sociology of science and sociobiology (Škorić, 2010; Škorić & Kišjuhas, 2012). Sociologists from Niš championed innovative approaches to questions of culture, such as taste (Cvetičanin, 2007; Cvetičanin et al., 2012; Krstić, 2014), religious practice (Gavrilović, 2013), or leisure (Đorđević, 2011). Rational choice theory and methodological individualism, largely ignored before, also made their way into sociology, and their proponents were often people originally trained as political scientists (Pavlović, 2014; Dekić, 2013) but not necessarily (Ignjatović, 2016). New forms of social network connectivity through social media and the internet also became an important research area (Petrović, 2013a, 2008). Sociological research was expanded to bordering areas with other disciplines, that is, social policy (Babović et al., 2010; Babović & Vuković, 2014; Vuković, 2017), economic sociology (Mojić, 2014; Cvejić, 2011), and others.

At ISI in Belgrade, the tradition of empirical studies and monitoring changes in social structure, based broadly on the neo-Marxist class paradigm developed by Mladen Lazić, continued, recently enriched by an additional focus on elites (Lazić et al., 2014, 2016). Furthermore, new approaches to social structural issues emerged, like the legacy of Pierre Bourdieu (Filipović, 2011; Spasić, 2013; Birešev, 2014).

Processes of institutional selection can be observed in the dominance of those discourses that enjoy institutional grounding and continuity through projects. The Belgrade ISI provides an illustration, with the group around Mladen Lazić being the carrier of the hegemonic discourse within the institution (Cvejić, 2010; Lazić & Cvejić, 2019), while other groupings include the urban sociology (Petrović, 2014a, 2014b; Backović, 2018; Mirkov, 2018; Vukelić, 2015), gender studies (Bobić, 2003; Bobić & Stanojević, 2014; Jarić, 2014b, 2014c; Sekulić 2014, 2016), sociology of youth (Ljubičić, 2008; Tomanović, 2012; Tomanović et al., 2016; Tomanović & Stanojević, 2015), and so on. There is also growing interest in researching the possibilities for implementing various methods in sociology (Ilić, 2016; Manić, 2017). Generally, groups engaged in empirical studies displayed more discursive coherence than sociologists working individually on their selected theoretical topics (such as Aleksandar Molnar, Milan Vukomanović, Đokica Jovanović, or Jovo Bakić).

Overall, sociology has grown less critical of the system. Simultaneously, there is less self-reflection on sociology's own role in society. Societal reforms currently undertaken are contested very rarely, if ever. In other words, sociology has become largely depoliticised.

Hegemonic discourses have not yet been crystallised in direct relation to problems of reproduction and legitimation of the existing system. However, although sociology as an academic discipline and as expertise is not called upon to provide legitimacy to the new system of relations, this does not hold for the so-called political analysts, whose legitimising discourses are less tied to academic sociology but more to their media engagement.

19.5 Conclusions

Finally, if we want to return to the issues addressed in the first two sections and reach conclusions on the role of sociology and sociologists (in their various social roles) in the processes of transformation in Serbia, they cannot be unequivocal. First, it is hard to make straightforward conclusions because of the existence of two distinct periods in which overall social and disciplinary contexts differed widely. Second, the Serbian sociological community was institutionally fragmented and ideologically and professionally divided, which made it difficult to constitute itself as a community that would be able to defend its professional integrity and interests and to impose itself as relevant in providing answers to key social issues. Although it enjoyed a certain degree of professional autonomy throughout the entire period, due to limited resources and reduced structural opportunities to develop through communication and knowledge exchange with the international community, it remained an academic discipline whose findings rarely served as the basis for policy creation or even for providing legitimacy to the system. There are grounds to conclude that in times when sociology as a profession was marginalised (during the 1990s), potentials for developing subversive and critical discourses were greater; in contrast, as institutional and structural capacities expanded (after 2000), sociology's instrumental character tended to be more pronounced, with a notable decline in its critical edge.

Although several alternative discourses circulated in Serbian sociology, none of them prevailed as the dominant interpretation of social reality (or as the immediate base for the legitimacy of the reforms). Furthermore, since the challenges society was facing in the two phases differed, sociology inevitably had to provide different solutions. If we wanted to address the issue of evolutionary change of paradigms, it would roughly follow the scheme proposed by Rončević (with some modifications due to Serbia's late start of the transformation): the first phase, during and after the fall of socialism, was marked by 'crisology' discourse through which sociologists tended to explain the causes of the system breakdown but also to predict the consequences of the crisis; the second phase was characterised by the search for the 'right' paradigm that would explain Serbia's specific path of transformation (featuring alternative discourses on post-socialist transition/transformation); the third phase was marked not only by the instrumental use of sociology as a socio-integrative science in the context of institutional reforms but also by thematic and methodological diversification (this discursive shift coincided with significant improvements of the structural conditions in which sociology was developing); finally, the fourth phase (which started after the 2008 economic crisis) was characterised by the rise of new critical discourses (this time, the main object of the critique were neoliberal reforms and capitalism: as a whole, or of its specific aspects and modes, such as 'political capitalism').

Finally, apart from academic sociology, sociologists acted during the processes of transformation through various roles. In the first period (during the 1990s), they were dominantly engaged as opposition leaders and politicians, as anti-war and

NGO activists, and as public intellectuals critical of Milošević's regime and prevalent nationalism. After the regime change, sociologists increasingly started to act as political analysts, experts, and policymakers, providing legitimacy to the institutional reforms and processes of European integration. This shift from critical to socio-integrative engagement did not, however, lead to a significant increase in the direct involvement of sociologists in the government and public administration nor to a change in the dominant public perception of sociology as a science that could potentially provide answers to key social problems.

Competing Interests The authors have no conflicts of interest to declare that are relevant to the content of this chapter.

References

Antonić, S. (1998). Stranački i društveni rascepi u Srbiji. *Sociologija, 40*(3), 323–356.
Antonić, S. (2006). *Elita, građanstvo i slaba država*. Službeni glasnik.
Babović, M., & Vuković, D. (2014). Social interests, policy networks and legislative outcomes: The role of policy networks in shaping welfare and employment policies in Serbia. *East European Politics and Societies, 28*, 5–24. https://doi.org/10.1177/0888325413495088
Babović, M., et al. (1997). *'Ajmo, 'ajde svi u šetnju: građanski i studentski protest 96/97*. Medija centar & ISIFF.
Babović, M., et al. (2010). *Izazovi nove socijalne politike. Socijalna uključenost u EU i Srbiji*. SeConS.
Backović, V. (2018). *Džentifikacija kao socioprostorni fenomen savremenog grada*. ISIFF & Čigoja.
Birešev, A. (2014). *Orionov vodič: otkrivanje dominacije u sociologiji Pjera Burdijea*. IFDT.
Blagojević, M. (1992). *Žene izvan kruga: profesija i porodica*. ISIFF.
Blagojević, M. (1995a). Svakodnevica iz ženske perspektive: samožrtvovanje i beg u privatnost. In S. Bolčić (Ed.), *Društvene promene i svakodnevni život* (pp. 181–209). ISIFF.
Blagojević, M. (1995b). *Približavanje pravoslavlju*. JUNIR & Gradina.
Blagojević, M. (Ed.). (1998). *Ka vidljivoj ženskoj istoriji: ženski pokret u Beogradu 90ih*. Centar za ženske studije.
Blagojević, M. (Ed.). (2000). *Mapiranje mizoginije u Srbiji: diskursi i prakse*. AŽIN.
Blagojević-Šijaković, M. (1994). War and everyday life: Deconstruction of self-sacrifice. *Sociologija, 36*(4), 495–514.
Bobić, M. (2003). *Brak ili/i partnerstvo: demografsko sociološka studija*. ISIFF.
Bobić, M., & Stanojević, M. (2014). Procesualnost porodične transformacije i refleksivnost aktera – dijadna perspektiva. *Sociologija, 56*, 445–457. https://doi.org/10.2298/SOC1404445B
Bogdanović, M., et al. (2009). *Sociologija u Srbiji 1959–2009: Institucionalni razvoj. Pedeseta godišnjica Odeljenja za sociologiju Filozofskog fakulteta u Beogradu*. Filozofski fakultet & Službeni glasnik.
Bolčić, S. (1982). Teze za razgovor sociologa o aktuelnim kriznim procesima u jugoslovenskom društvu i društvenim pretpostavkama uspešne političke stabilizacije. *Sociologija, 24*(2–3), 195–201.
Bolčić, S. (1993). Sociologija i „jugoslovenska svakodnevica" početkom devedesetih. *Sociološki pregled, 27*(1–4), 27–37.
Bolčić, S., et al. (1995). *Društvene promene i svakodnevni život: Srbija početkom devedesetih*. ISIFF.

Bolčić, S. (1995a). The features of a "nationalized" society. *Sociologija, 37*(4), 473–483.
Bolčić, S. (1995b). Changing features of the workforce in Serbia in the early nineties. *Sociološki pregled, 29*(2), 149–161.
Bolčić, S. (2003). Blocked Transition and Post-Socialist Transformation: Serbia in the Nineties. *Review of Sociology 9*(2), 27–49.
Bolčić, S. (2011). O skorašnjoj „skrajnutosti" sociologije i sociološke profesije. *Sociologija, 53*(4), 489–496.
Bolčić, S. (2013). *Razaranje i rekonstitucija društva*. Službeni glasnik.
Branković, S. (1996). Još jednom o pitanju levice i desnice u političkom prostoru Srbije. *Sociologija, 38*(2), 315–326.
Čičkarić, L. (1997). Prilog socio-kulturnoj analizi studentskog pokreta 91/92. *Sociologija, 39*(1), 51–71.
Čolović, I., & Mimica, A., et al. (1992). *Druga Srbija*. Plato & Beogradski krug & Borba.
Čolović, I., & Mimica, A., et al. (1993). *Intelektualci i rat*. Beogradski krug & Centar za antiratnu akciju.
Cvejić, S. (Ed.) (2010). *Suživot sa reformama: građani Srbije pred izazovima „tranzicijskog" nasleđa*. ISIFF.
Cvejić, S. (2011). *Društvena određenost ekonomskih pojava*. ISIFF.
Cvejić, S., et al. (2016). *Informal power networks, political patronage and clientelism in Serbia*. SeConS.
Cvetičanin, P. (2007). *Cultural needs, habits and taste of citizens of Serbia and Macedonia*. Committee for Civil Initiative.
Cvetičanin, P., et al. (2012). *Social and cultural capital in Serbia*. CESC.
Davidović, M. (1995). Rat i alternativni ženski pokret u Srbiji. *Sociologija, 37*(2), 133–148.
Dekić, M. (2013). Šta je to analitička sociologija? Ka sociologiji kao 'normalnoj nauci'. *Sociološki pregled, 47*, 327–354. https://doi.org/10.5937/socpreg1303327D
Đorđević, D. (2011). *Kazuj krčmo Džerimo: periferijska kafana i okolo nje*. Službeni glasnik & Mašinski fakultet.
Filipović, B. (2011). Relacionizam Pjera Burdijea: između materijalističkog i lingvističkog strukturalizma. *Sociologija, 53*, 323–344. https://doi.org/10.2298/SOC1103323F
Gavrilović, D. (2013). *Doba upotrebe: religija i moral u savremenoj Srbiji*. Filozofski fakultet.
Golubović, Z. (1988). *Kriza identiteta savremenog jugoslovenskog društva: jugoslovenski put u socijalizam viđen iz različitih uglova*. Filip Višnjić.
Golubović, Z. (1993). Od dijagnoze do objašnjenja „jugoslovenskog slučaja". *Sociološki pregled, 27*(1–4), 39–48.
Gredelj, S. (1993). Šta istražuju istaživanja javnog mnjenja. *Sociologija, 35*(3), 395–401.
Ignjatović, S. (2016). Nasleđe Rejmona Budona. *Sociologija, 58*(1), 32–52.
Ilić, V. (2016). *Posmatranje i analiza sadržaja*. Univerzitet u Beogradu - Filozofski fakultet.
Janićijević, M., Bolčić, S., Topić, L., Davidović, M., & Novaković, N. (1990). *Novi pravci promena društvene strukture Jugoslavije*. Centar za sociološka istraživanja, Institut društvenih nauka.
Janjić, D. (1999). Etnički sukob i kriza identiteta: srpsko-albanski sukob na Kosovu. *Nova srpska politička misao, 6*(3–4), 61–79.
Jarić, I. (2014a). *Javni i skriveni kurikulumi srednjoškolske nastave sociologije: obrazovne reforme u Srbiji (1960–2006)*. Filozofski fakultet.
Jarić, I. (2014b). Pozicioniranje iskustva materinstva unutar socijalne mreže porodičnih odnosa. *Sociologija, 56*, 458–473. https://doi.org/10.2298/SOC1404458J
Jarić, I. (Ed.). (2014c). *Politike roditeljstva: iskustva, diskursi i institucionalne prakse*. ISI FF.
Jessop, B. (2004). Critical semiotic analysis and cultural political economy. *Critical Discourse Studies, 1*, 1–16. https://doi.org/10.1080/17405900410001674506
Jessop, B. (2009). Cultural political economy and critical policy studies. *Critical Policy Studies, 3*, 336–356. https://doi.org/10.1080/19460171003619741
Jovanović, M. (2016). *Identitet, Religioznost, seksualnost: problem identiteta religioznih LGBT osoba u Srbiji*. Mediteran Publishing.

Korać, M. (1994). Representation of mass rape in ethnic conflicts in what was Yugoslavia. *Sociologija, 36*(4), 495–514.
Krstić, N. (2014). Simboličke granice – značaj kulturnih faktora u formiranju, održavanju i menjanju socijalnih razlika i sukoba. *Kultura, 143*, 273–296. https://doi.org/10.5937/kultura1443273k
Kuljić, T. (2001). On the conversion and self-consciousness of the Yugoslav social science intelligentsia. In I. Spasić & M. Subotić (Eds.), *R/evolution and order: Serbia after October 2000* (pp. 369–383). Institute for Philosophy and Social Theory.
Kuljić, T. (2009). Sociološke generacije - hipotetički uporedni okvir. *Sociologija, 51*, 55–64. https://doi.org/10.2298/SOC0901055K
Lazar, Ž., et al. (2007). *Vojvodina amidst multiculturality and regionalization*. Mediterran Publishing.
Lazić, M. (1993). *Sociologija*: između iluzija i stvarnosti. *Sociološki pregled, 27*(1–4), 67–73.
Lazić, M., et al. (1994). *Razaranje društva: Jugoslovensko društvo u krizi 90-ih*. Filip Višnjić.
Lazić, M. (1994). *Sistem i slom. Raspad socijalizma i struktura jugoslovenskog društva*. Filip Višnjić.
Lazić, M. (1996a). Delatni potencijal društvenih grupa. *Sociologija, 38*(2), 259–288.
Lazić, M. (1996b). The breakdown of socialism and changes in the structure of Yugoslav society. *International Review of Sociology, 6*(2), 279–294.
Lazić, M., et al. (1999). *Protest in Belgrade: Winter of discontent*. Central European University Press.
Lazić, M., et al. (2000). *Račji hod*. Filip Višnjić.
Lazić, M. (2002). (Re)strukturisanje društva u Srbiji tokom 90-ih. In S. Bolčić & A. Milić (Eds.), *Srbija krajem milenijuma: razaranje društva, promene i svakodnevni život* (pp. 17–34). ISIFF.
Lazić, M. (2011). *Čekajući kapitalizam*. Službeni glasnik.
Lazić, M., et al. (2014). *Ekonomska elita u Srbiji u periodu konsolidacije kapitalističkog poretka*. ISI FF & Čigoja.
Lazić, M., et al. (2016). *Politička elita u Srbiji u periodu konsolidacije kapitalističkog poretka*. ISI FF & Čigoja.
Lazić, M., & Cvejić, S. (2004). Promene društvene strukture u Srbiji: Slučaj blokirane postsocijalističke transformacije. In A. Milić (Ed.), *Društvena transformacija i strategije društvenih grupa: svakodnevica Srbije na početku trećeg milenijuma* (pp. 39–70). ISIFF.
Lazić, M., & Cvejić, S. (Eds.). (2019). *Stratifikacijske promene u periodu konsolidacije kapitalizma u Srbiji*. ISIFF.
Lazić, M., & Pešić, J. (2012). *Making and unmaking state centered capitalism in Serbia*. ISI & Čigoja.
Ljubičić, M. (2008). Školsko postignuće i resocijalizacija maloljetnih delikvenata: sociološka perspektiva. In D. Radovanović (Ed.), *Istraživanja u specijalnoj pedagogiji*. Fakultet za specijalnu edukaciju i rehabilitaciju.
Manić, Ž. (2017). *Analiza sadržaja u sociologiji*. ISIFF & Čigoja.
Marinković, D., & Ristić, D. (2013). *Nacrt za sociologiju ideologije*. Mediterran Publishing.
Marinković, D., & Ristić, D. (2016). *Ogledi iz geoepistemologije: Prostor – prakse – moć*. Mediterran Publishing.
Mihajlović, S. (1998). Mogućnosti moderne legitimacijske formule u Srbiji. *Sociološki pregled, 27*(3–4), 275–293.
Milenković, P. (2016). *Ogledi iz sociologije savremenosti*. Mediterran Publishing.
Milić, A. (1992). Nove tehnologije i odnosi polova-pogled iznutra na odnose moći. *Sociologija, 34*(1), 5–22.
Milić, A. (1993). Antimoderna društvena svest u postmodernom okruženju. *Sociološki pregled, 27*(1–4), 17–26.
Milić, A. (1994). *Žene, politika, porodica*. Institut za političke studije.
Milić, A. (1995a). Svakodnevni život porodice u vrtlogu društvenog rasula. Srbija 1991-1995. In S. Bolčić (Ed.), *Društvene promene i svakodnevni život* (pp. 135–254). ISIFF.
Milić, A. (1995b). Social disintegration and families under stress: Serbia 1991–1995. *Socioloigija, 37*(4), 455–472.

Milosavljević, O. (1999). Nacionalizam u službi politike moći: tri kontroverze u shvatanjima srpskih intelektualaca početkom i krajem 20. veka. *Sociologija, 41*(2), 125–142.
Mirkov, A. (2018). *Socijalna održivost grada*. ISIFF & Čigoja.
Mitrović, M. (1993). Sociologija i današnje srpsko društvo. *Sociološki pregled, 27*(1–4), 75–88.
Mitrović, M. (1994). Ekologija sela i poljoprivrede. *Sociologija, 36*(3), 325–335.
Mojić, D. (2014). *Organizacije i (post)moderno društvo*. ISIFF & Čigoja.
Molnar, A. (1993). Stanje osnovnih prava čoveka u Jugoslaviji – sociološka perspektiva. *Sociologija, 35*(2), 197–212.
Mrkšić, D. (1994). Dualizacija ekonomije i stratifikaciona struktura. In M. Lazić (Ed.), *Razaranje društva*. Filip Višnjić.
Mrkšić, D. (2000). Restratifikacija i promene materijalnog standarda. In M. Lazić (Ed.), *Račji hod* (pp. 237–292). Filip Višnjić.
Nikolić-Ristanović, V. (1994). Nasilje nad ženama u uslovima rata i ekonomske krize. *Sociološki pregled, 28*(3), 409–417.
Novaković, N. (1997). Radništvo i tranizicija u SR Jugoslaviji. *Sociološki pregled, 31*(4), 425–534.
Opalić, P. (1994). Types of collective irrational phenomena and possibilities for their study. *Sociologija, 36*(4), 431–442.
Papić, Ž. (1992). Telo kao proces u toku. *Sociologija, 34*(2), 259–275.
Papić, Ž. (1993). Novije feminističke kritike patrijarhata: relativizacija univerzalizma. *Sociologija, 35*(1), 107–122.
Papić, Ž. (1997). *Polnost i kultura*. XX vek & Čigoja.
Pavlović, D. (2014). *Teorija igara: osnovne igre i njihova primena*. FPN.
Pešić, J. (2017). *Promena vrednosnih orijentacija u postsocijalističkim društvima Srbije i Hrvatske: politički i ekonomski liberalizam*. ISIFF.
Petovar, K. (1992). Bespravna izgradnja i siva ekonomija – jedna paralela. *Sociologija, 34*(4), 525–538.
Petrović, D. (2008). *U međumrežju – Internet i novi obrasci društvenosti*. Saobraćajni fakultet & ISIFF.
Petrović, D. (2013a). *Društvenost u doba Interneta*. Akademska knjiga.
Petrović, I. (2013b). Promene vrednosnih orijentacija srednje klase u periodu post-socijalističke transformacije u Srbiji. *Sociologija, 55*(3), 375–394.
Petrović, M. (Ed.). (2014a). *Strukturni i delatni potencijal lokalnog razvoja*. ISIFF & Čigoja.
Petrović, M. (2014b). *Društvo i gradovi između lokalnog i globalnog*. ISIFF & Čigoja.
Popov, N. (1989). *Contra fatum: slučaj grupe profesora Filozofskog fakulteta u Beogradu (1968–1988)*. Mladost.
Popov, N., et al. (1996). *Srpska strana rata: trauma i katarza u istorijskom pamćenju*. Republika.
Popović, M. (1982). Uzroci ekonomske i društveno-političke nestabilnosti u Jugoslaviji. *Sociologija, 24*(2–3).
Popović, M. (1991). Totalitarne karakteristike realsocijalizma. *Sociologija, 33*(4), 577–586.
Popović, M. (1993). Zašto sociolozi nisu predvideli surov građanski rat u Jugoslaviji. *Sociološki pregled, 27*(1–4), 57–66.
Popović, M. (1995a). Uporedna analiza boljševizma i fašizma. *Sociologija, 37*(2), 97–117.
Popović, M. (1995b). Da li su boljševizam i realni socijalizam tragična istorijska greška. *Sociologija, 37*(3), 255–275.
Popović, M. (1996). Liberalizacija socijalizma – degeneracija totalitarnog sistema: slučaj Jugoslavije. *Sociologija, 38*(1), 47–68.
Pušić, L. (1995). The (im)possibility of urban society. *Sociologija, 37*(4), 567–574.
Radoman, M. (2017). Biti LGBTTIQ – značenja koja nas oblikuju. *Kultura, 157*, 203–219. https://doi.org/10.5937/kultura1757203R
Radulović, D. (1995). Drug use in post-communist societies. *Sociologija, 37*(4), 575–601.
Ristić, D., Marinković, D., & Lazar, Ž. (2016). *Ogledi o regionalnom identitetu*. Mediterranean Publishing.
Rus, V. (1982). Conflict regulation in self-managed Yugoslav enterprises. In G. B. J. Bomers & R. B. Peterson (Eds.), *Conflict management and industrial relations* (pp. 375–395). Nijhoff.

Sekelj, L. (1991). Realno samoupravljanje, realni nacionalizam i dezintegracija Jugoslavije. *Sociologija, 33*(4), 587–599.

Sekelj, L. (1995). Yugoslavia: Change without transformation. *Sociologija, 37*(4), 421–440.

Sekulić, N. (2014). Društveni status materinstva sa posebnim osvrtom na Srbiju danas. *Sociologija, 56*, 403–426. https://doi.org/10.2298/SOC1404403S

Sekulić, N. (2016). *Kultura rađanja: Istraživanje o seksualnoj i reproduktivnoj socijalizaciji žena.* ISIFF.

Škorić, M. (2010). *Sociologija nauke: mertonovski i konstruktivistički programi.* Izdavačka knjižarnica Zorana Stojanovića.

Škorić, M., & Kišjuhas, A. (2012). *Evolucija i prirodna selekcija: Od Anaksimandra do Darvina.* Mediterranean Publishing.

Službeni glasnik Srbije. (1998). *Zakon o univerzitetu.* Službeni glasnik.

Sokolovska, V., & Marinković, D. (Eds.). (2012). *Regioni i regionalizacija. Sociološki aspekti.* Mediterranean Publishing.

Spasić, I. (2013). *Kultura na delu: društvena transformacija Srbije iz burdijeovske perspektive.* Fabrika knjiga.

Spasić, I., & Pavićević, Đ. (1997). Simbolizacija i kolektivni identitet u građanskom protestu. *Sociologija, 39*(1), 73–93.

Spasić, I., Pešić, J., & Babović, M. (2022). *Sociology in Serbia. A fragile discipline.* Palgrave Macmillan.

Sum, N., & Jessop, B. (2013). *Towards cultural political economy.* Edward Elgar Publishing.

Tomanović, S. (1995). Svakodnevica dece u društvu u tranziciji. In S. Bolčić (Ed.), *Društvene promene i svakodnevni život* (pp. 211–227). ISIFF.

Tomanović, S. (Ed.). (2012). *Mladi – naša sadašnjost: istraživanje socijalnih biografija mladih u Srbiji.* ISIFF.

Tomanović, S., & Stanojević, D. (2015). *Mladi u Srbiji.* Friedrich Ebert Stiftung.

Tomanović, S., Stanojević, D., & Ljubičić, M. (2016). *Postajanje roditeljem u Srbiji: sociološko istraživanje tranzicije u roditeljstvo.* Filozofski fakultet.

Tomanović-Mihajlović, S. (1994). Socialization of the child under conditions of a changed everyday life of the family. *Sociologija, 36*(4), 483–493.

Tripković, M., et al. (2006). *Multikulturna Vojvodina u evropskim integracijama.* Filozofski fakultet.

Uvalić, M. (2010). *Serbia's transition: Towards a better future.* Palgrave Macmillan.

Vratuša, V. (2016). Privatizacija i klasni interesi. *Sociologija, 58*, 467–489. https://doi.org/10.2298/SOC1603467V

Vujović, S. (1995). Urbana svakodnevica devedesetih godina. In S. Bolčić (Ed.), *Društvene promene i svakodnevni život* (pp. 109–134). ISIFF.

Vujović, S. (1997). Grad, spektakl i identit: traganje za modernism kulturnim identitetom grada. *Sociologija, 39*(1), 269–281.

Vukelić, J. (2015). Ko su ekološki aktivisti i lideri ekološkog pokreta u Srbiji? *Kultura, 148*, 123–143. https://doi.org/10.5937/kultura1548123V

Vuković, D. (2017). *Preoblikovanje neoliberalizma. Socijalna politika u Srbiji.* Mediterranean Publishing.

Vukša, T., & Simović, V. (Eds.). (2016). *Bilans stanja - doprinos analizi restauracije kapitalizma u Srbiji.* Centaur za politike emancipacije.

Vuletić, V. (1995). Jugoslovenska sociologija i socijalizam (I deo). *Sociološki pregled, 29*(1), 41–57.

Vuletić, V. (1996). Jugoslovenska sociologija i socijalizam (II deo). *Sociološki pregled, 30*(3), 267–292.

Vuletić, V., & Stanojević, D. (2013). Sociološke teme prve decenije XXI veka – uporedna analiza Srbija i Hrvatska. *Sociologija, 55*, 47–68. https://doi.org/10.2298/SOC1301047V

Vuletić, V., Stanojević, D., & Vukelić, J. (2011). Srpska tranzicija u sociološkom ogledalu. In S. Mihailović (Ed.), *Dometi tranzicije: Od kapitalizma ka socijalizmu* (pp. 327–342). FES.

Marija Babović is Full Professor at the Department for Sociology of the Faculty of Philosophy, University of Belgrade. She has authored or co-authored more than 15 monographs, including Sociology in Serbia. A Fragile Discipline, and a number of papers and chapters in academic journals and edited volumes.

Jelena Pešić is Assistant Professor at the Department for Sociology, Faculty of Philosophy, University of Belgrade. She has authored or co-authored three sociological monographs, including Sociology in Serbia. A Fragile Discipline, and a number of papers and chapters in academic journals and edited volumes.

Ivana Spasić is Full Professor at the Department of Sociology, Faculty of Philosophy, University of Belgrade. She has written extensively on social theory, nationhood, urban identities, and cultural aspects of post-socialist transformation in Southeast Europe. She is also a faculty fellow at Yale University's Center for Cultural Sociology.

Chapter 20
Slovak Sociology and Postcommunist Transformation

Robert Klobucký and Silvia Miháliková

20.1 Introduction

The development of sociology in Slovakia has to be understood on two levels, which are analytically distinct though closely linked. The first is consistent with the trends seen in western Europe in the nineteenth century. The systematic study of society liberated itself from the tutelage of positive law and gradually transformed into independent social science disciplines, with sociology being one of the last to declare its independence in the early twentieth century. The second level of analysis concerns Slovakia's historical experiences and the way that its delayed social and political development, together with the dynamics of nation and state building, determined the trajectories taken by the social sciences, and sociology, in particular, when they embarked on their paths to independence.

The fact that society became the object of intellectual interest was the achievement of a few individuals through whose efforts the study of social phenomena was singled out from the plethora of arts and social sciences. Thinking specific to sociology can be found in the works of our leading thinkers, which we will summarize briefly in the parts of our analysis that follow. These writers' specific interest in explaining how society functioned led them to separate the study of society from the areas to which it had hitherto been assigned (ethics, history, economics, or law). However, it should be emphasized that the first systematic attempts at sociological thinking about society were inspired by contemporary world theories, which were discovered in Slovakia relatively late, only at the beginning of the twentieth century.

This text was created with the support of VEGA grant number 2/0068/22.

R. Klobucký (✉) · S. Miháliková
Institute for Sociology, Slovak Academy of Sciences, Bratislava, Slovakia
e-mail: robert.klobucky@savba.sk; silvia.mihalikova@savba.sk

The subsequent turbulent development of society in Slovakia and the peripeteia of its study within the social sciences and sociology, in particular, present a three-dimensional picture of change affecting not just the political regime but also the entire social atmosphere and the research priorities in the area of social processes and the entire functioning of individual institutions and the social system as a whole.

The three decades since the end of the communist regime in Slovakia have not only transformed mutual relations in Europe through growing globalization and integration but have also enabled a fascinating insight into fundamental social change together with both its limitations and far-reaching effects. Since sociology is often regarded as the "king" of disciplines, characterized by a strong interdisciplinary reach, the following text attempts to prove that in Slovakia, the development of society has been reflected in the peripeteia of sociology's development.

20.2 The Development of Slovak Sociology During the Communist Regime

After the Communist coup in 1948, sociology in Czechoslovakia was declared a "bourgeois pseudoscience" as in the Soviet Union and banned (see, e.g., Vorisek, 2007; Mucha & Keen, 2000). All sociology departments were disbanded, and sociologists were either persecuted by the regime and forbidden to work in any intellectual profession or, at best, had to move to other disciplines (mostly Marxist philosophy). The promising development of Slovak sociology, which in the 1940s in particular had diversified notably both thematically and methodologically, was thereby forcibly interrupted.

In the interwar period, Slovak sociologists actively engaged in public discourse and discussed the most important public questions of the era. For example, we can mention the actual creation of Czechoslovakia after the First World War. The need for a common state of Czechs and Slovaks was justified by Tomáš Garrigue Masaryk, the Czech philosopher, sociologist, and later the first president of Czechoslovakia, by the existence of a Czechoslovak nation, whereby he proved his conviction "scientifically"—with the help of sociology. In Slovakia, the concept of the gradual merging of Czechs and Slovakia was promoted, among others, by Anton Štefánek, Marsaryk's pupil and the first Slovak professor of sociology, who defended the project both as a politician and as an academic: a sociologist (Klobucký, 2011).

The developing sociological tradition of entering into public debate was forcibly suppressed after the communist regime was installed, and in Slovakia, in contrast to the Czech Lands, it was not revived even in the 1960s when the discipline of sociology was reestablished. Unlike their Czech colleagues, Slovak sociologists had no major involvement in the process of liberalizing the communist regime, which culminated in the so-called Prague Spring of 1968 and was later suppressed by the invasion of Czechoslovakia by Warsaw Pact troops. However, the subsequent repression during the "normalization" period also affected Slovak sociologists. The normalization regime was distinctly anti-intellectual as a large part of the reformers, as well as the open critics of the regime, came from the ranks of the intellectuals. These reformers and regime critics were labeled as "self-proclaimed intellectuals" during the normalization period, and a significant proportion of academics from the social sciences and humanities were assigned to this category of regime enemy. This criticism of intellectuals was also linked to the notion that the leading role of the party had been attacked and now had to be guaranteed by the "dictatorship of the proletariat."

The normalization regime intensified the "differentiation" process (the contemporary newspeak for interviewing party members and expelling or "deleting" anyone who did not say the right thing) in 1970. This process was often quite formalistic and affected by personal antipathies. Academics who failed the test found their professional careers made very difficult or, in the worst case, terminated. However, it is important to note that normalization took a more moderate form in Slovakia than in the Czech Lands (a phenomenon studied in detail by Juraj Marušiak in Kmeť and Marušiak, 2003) and whereas 23% of members had to leave the Communist Party in the Czech Lands, it was only 17.5% in Slovakia. In Czech philosophy and sociology departments, 70% of academics lost their party membership, compared to around 30–35% in Slovakia (Szomolányi, 1990). Apart from this, Slovak party members who were not interviewed but merely deleted from the membership records were often able to remain in their profession, though they were obliged to give active proof of their class consciousness and loyalty to the ideology of the time. In the Czech Lands, it was quite common for careers to be terminated completely, whereas in Slovak sociology, this was more of an exception.

Sociology as an academic discipline had to rid itself of its heretical ideas by converging with Marxist-Leninist dogma and adopting historical materialism and "scientific communism." The Czech sociologist Jiří Musil (Musil, 2004) explains that when sociology was revived at the beginning of the 1960s, there was discussion of three modalities between sociology and historical materialism. The first modality connected sociology with historical materialism; the second limited sociology to specific sociological research with its own methodology, while historical materialism remained the overall theory; and the third regarded sociology as an independent science in both theory and methodology. Musil says that when sociology was revived, the Communist Party was inclined toward the second modality, but it soon favored the third modality, and sociology established itself as a relatively independent social science discipline. Normalization was an attempt at regression and returning sociology, and sociological theory in particular, under the protective wing of dogmatic historical materialism. It thus intended somehow to restore and implement earlier ideas about so-called Marxist sociology having its specific place in the system of social sciences in a "socialist" society. In Musil's typology, the beginning of normalization was an attempt to enforce the first and second modalities of the relationship between sociology and historical materialism (although later on, sociology gradually established itself as an independent discipline again).

In general, normalization can be regarded as a time when sociology became, for a long period, an undemocratic science in which academic success or failure was determined by ideological doctrine, politically nominated commissions, and everyday human intrigue. Sociology became an uncritical and subservient mouthpiece for the politics and ideology of the Communist Party. Soňa Szomolányi called the normalization period the "sterilization" of sociology (Szomolányi, 1990, p. 378), with the designation encompassing lack of fertility, dogmatism, and the loss of creativity. One important characteristic of normalization sociology was its deliberate ideologization, which was first and foremost intended to serve the propagandistic and uncritical proclamation of the Communist Party's ideological postulates. In the initial normalization period, sociology did not even accomplish its socio-technical functions: it did not serve the regime as an empirical science that could alert the rulers to various problems. It was limited to pseudo-theoretical, dogmatic, and ideological tracts that supported the current political developments.

Later, in the 1980s, we can observe the division of sociology into empirical and theoretical streams. Theoretical texts were very often tainted by ideology and lacked any reflection on reality, while empirical research suffered from a lack of consistent theoretical underpinning. Soňa Szomolányi (1988, p. 314) draws attention to the fact that academic sociology suffered most from this: "The absence of any confrontation with reality distanced it from the real world more and more and at the same time allowed it a comfortable existence in a world composed of its own constructions." Ján Sopóci (1997) says that most Slovak sociologists managed to carry on throughout the 1960s to 1980s without any defined theoretical or methodological orientation. The majority of sociologists contented themselves with formally endorsing Marxism in their work and had no ambitions to develop theories.

One of the most marked characteristics of the way Slovak sociology functioned during the communist regime was how some themes were discovered as part of a political campaign and became very popular for a certain time, only to disappear almost completely some time later. These included social development and social forecasting, the scientific-technical revolution, and the socialist personality. These themes were implanted into science from Party documents or congresses; by developing them, sociologists were effectively carrying out the wishes of those in power. As a scientific discipline, in this period, sociology, to a large extent, lost the ability to raise and solve problems in society which their knowledge had enabled them to identify. Instead, they were forced to deal with topics which were approved of, or even assigned to them, by the Party apparatus.

20.3 Slovak Sociology at the End of the 1980s

In the second half of the 1980s, sociology's subservience to the normalization regime began to change markedly when some sociologists began to free themselves from their rulers and introduced themes that had previously been taboo. Zora Bútorová and Ivan Dianiška (Bútorová & Dianiška, 1988) wrote about the self-regulation of the academic community, with their text being targeted against the current practice of science being governed by politics. Another example is a polemical article by Pavol Frič, Fedor Gál, and Ivan Dianiška (Frič et al., 1988), which was based on an analysis of articles in the journal *Sociológia* and criticized the inadequate research into real social problems. The text also contained an appeal for the participatory examination of society, that is, a permanent dialog of all concerned parties, coupled with the democratization, complementarity, tolerance, and social oversight of sociology. The text was published in the "Discussion" section of the journal together with critical (but, in essence, factual) comments by reviewers. Soňa Szomolányi (1988, p. 311) extended the earlier criticism to the social context of the functioning of sociology: "[…] sociology is asked to […] fulfil primarily a function that is vulgarly ideological rather than cognitive." This text contains a detailed analysis of the state and development of Slovak sociology, together with criticism of the situation under normalization. Vladimír Krivý adds similar arguments (Krivý, 1988, p. 421), criticizing sociologists' "painstakingly loyal" approach to the political system. He suggests that sociology should have greater autonomy and proposes "the revival of its cultural and historical roots" and "a renewal of its links to world sociology" (Krivý, 1988, p. 423). Probably the most fundamental criticism of normalization effects in Slovak sociology was Soňa Szomolányi's lecture on the history of the Sociology Institute of the Slovak Academy of Sciences. The lecture, which openly referred to all the negative political interference by the Communist regime, was delivered in 1988 but could only be published in 1990, after the fall of the regime (Szomolányi, 1990).

Sociologists were also very active in creating the ecological/social samizdat report "Bratislava nahlas" ("Bratislava Out Loud" 1987). This presented a vision of a more democratic, ecological, and healthy Slovakia and, above all, raised the "quality of life" issue. For example, it contained a chapter about disadvantaged social groups. Of course, the Communist regime vehemently rejected such a critical document and reacted with reprisals against its authors. "Bratislava Out Loud" was of exceptional importance in Slovakia as there had not previously been much significant anti-regime activity. Martin Bútora (2008, pp. 41–43), in a retrospective assessment, highlights the "professional and civic ethos" of "Bratislava Out Loud" and mentions the effect it also had on the period that followed, such as the positive traditions that were later developed within civil society: civic participation, independent civic public discourse, self-organization and networking between civic initiatives and various subcultures, oversight of the exercise of public office and state power, bottom-up social innovation, and participatory research and politics.

The Congress of Slovak Sociologists at the end of September 1989 (just a few weeks before the regime fell) was the culmination of Slovak sociologists' attempts to emancipate themselves. On the evening before the congress, 14 Slovak sociologists wrote a letter to the Czechoslovak president protesting the political trial of a group of Slovak dissidents, and at the congress itself, a number of sociologists who had up to that point been ostracized were politically rehabilitated. At the congress, held in the building of the Slovak Sociological Association, Slovak sociologists made a revolutionary declaration in favor of fundamental social system change just a few days before this actually began to happen.

A number of contributions at the conference came under the theme of modernizing society, as opposed to the immobility of the Communist regime after normalization. This was later strongly criticized by Bohumil Búzik (2000, p. 385), who writes that: "The way that the concept of modernisation, and also civic society, emerged in Slovak sociology can only be described as a revelation. And a revelation in the actual theological meaning of the word." After this critical and ironic introduction, Búzik explains that the use of the concept of modernization had not been preceded by any academic studies in Slovak sociology that attempted to define it scientifically. He felt that this meant the concept was understood in an optimistic and positive sense (e.g., Europeanization, innovation) and for Slovak sociologists offered the prospect of progress for Slovak society at a time when criticism of some of the consequences of modernization was multiplying in western sociology (Búzik, 2000, p. 389). At the end of his analysis, Búzik states:

> Slovak sociology wanted to use modernisation to replace one holistic portrait of society with another one that was just as holistic... Lack of familiarity with the discourse surrounding modernisation, which at that time already existed, was a sign of how backward and lacking erudition Slovak sociology was... It sounds like a paradox, but this lack of knowledge played a significant role in the unity and mobilisation of Slovak sociologists and became the driving force for their radicalisation during the Martin congress in 1989. Would Slovak sociology have been able to make such a significant contribution to what we call the 'Velvet Revolution' if we had known, or if we had adopted a degree of scepticism towards, the optimism and certainties of modernisation and if we had viewed contemporary western society as very uncertain and full of risk? But thanks to our lack of knowledge and orientation in the sort of reflection which was typical of western societies, the energy that came from error and ignorance enabled us to contribute to the overthrow of socialism. (Búzik, 2000, p. 390)

After the fall of the Communist regime, there was no decommunization of Slovak sociology because prior to 1989, there had been no non-Communist and non-Marxist alternative (Búzik & Laiferová, 2003). Slovak sociologists were not divided into members and non-members of the Communist Party, but according to their level of conformity to the regime. However, the communist ideologues and scientific communists who hitherto tried to regulate the development of Slovak sociology did, of course, disappear. In contrast, sociologists who had previously been unable to carry out their profession because the regime did not approve of them were able to start working again.

As we mention in another analysis (Klobucký, 2009), it is extremely surprising that in the 1990s (i.e., in the period after the Marxist hegemony had ended), the only Slovak academic sociological journal, *Sociológia*, did not have a single article framed in a Marxist perspective or defending the principles of Marxist ideology. The Marxist paradigm vanished from Slovak sociology. According to Bohumil Búzik (1997), there are two explanations for the rapid silencing of Marxism: first, before 1989, authors were only using Marxism for tactical reasons, as an essential prerequisite for getting sociology published; second, some authors had an indifferent attitude to any sort of theory. A further explanation could be a generational change in Slovak sociology (Kusá et al., 2002) or the fact that the Marxist paradigm is inapplicable to sociological analysis of society's post-1989 transformation. For example, two leading Slovak sociologists, Róbert Roško and Ján Stena, who in the previous era had been among the few who attempted to develop Marxist sociology theory in an undogmatic and inspiring fashion, started to look at issues of citizenship and civic society after 1989, and there was no noticeable Marxist influence in their work.

Several authors remark on the inadequate theorizing in Slovak sociology in the 1990s and on its low quality (e.g., Sopóci, 1995; Búzik, 1995; Kusá, 1997; Sopóci, 1997; Búzik, 1997). The 1990s in Slovak sociology could, therefore, be characterized as a period of empiricism: work was published that focused mainly on empirical data, and there was far less sociological theory, interpretative schemes, or typologies (Búzik, 1997). There are various explanations for this state of affairs. Bohumil Búzik maintains that it was a result of the traditional division of labor from the period of the common Czechoslovak state when it was mainly Czech sociologists who dealt with theoretical problems and that this tradition, in a way, repeated itself in collaboration with foreign sociologists, where the work of Slovak sociologists was often restricted to translating questionnaires and organizing data collection.

Ján Sopóci (1997) offers the following explanations for the neglect of theory in Slovak sociology: (1) the low professional standard of Slovak sociologists, (2) the quantity and quality of sociology departments and the conditions in which sociologists worked, (3) the quality of training for new sociologists, (4) the standard of academic life in the sociological community, and (5) the failure to master the relationship between the theoretical and political/ideological orientation of sociologists. The history of Slovak sociology provides a further explanation for the undervaluing of theory and the emphasis on empirical research and associated socio-technical functions. In Slovakia, sociology emerged as a means of transforming society in order to assist the national emancipation struggle before the First World War. Later, Marxist sociology maintained this tradition; when sociology was reconstituted in the 1960s, emphasis was laid on the socio-technical opportunities it could provide. Paradoxically, even the anti-totalitarian tendencies before 1989 were linked to socio-technical issues: the idea of "participatory research" mentioned earlier (Frič et al., 1988). It is understandable that given all the ruptures in the development of Slovak sociology, each time it was reestablished, its usefulness and practical applications were considered important, and with every radical change in society, the old theory was criticized (and often identified as ideology), and sociology's socio-technical functions and empiricism were highlighted.

20.4 Themes in Slovak Sociology After 1989: Key Theoretical and Methodological Foci

The change in political regime that resulted from the social processes that started in 1989 brought with it a change in the research agenda. After 1989/1990, we can identify a number of broadly conceived research phases, which in the social sciences concentrated on the process and the effects of economic transformation, the emergence and functioning of democratic institutions, the forming of a democratic political culture, and processes of European (dis)integration (see ESF, 2012). The first phase covers the 1990s, which is sometimes called "the transition period." Emphasis was laid on democratization and economic transformation, and although the fall of communism per se attracted the most attention, comparative studies in this decade focused on analyzing the character of the changes which this brought with it. In economics, discussion concentrated on questions about whether rapid liberalization and privatization in themselves create the conditions for changing people's economic behavior, whether their life strategies and everyday behavior become more commercial and profit-focused and whether institutional changes were the necessary precondition for the emergence of capitalism. At an empirical level, emphasis was placed on the emergence and development of democratic institutions, on the new institutional framework of democracy, on the changes of power elites and their influence on the character of economic and political change, on the relative weakness of civil society, on the social effects of economic changes, and on changes in values and attitudes toward the new regime. In Slovakia's case, it was often said that its citizens had very little previous experience of the functioning of a democratic regime, that civil society was almost nonexistent, and that many democratic institutions had to be built from scratch.

The thematic and methodological focus of Slovak sociology can also be shown by a content analysis of the articles in Slovakia's only academic sociology journal, *Sociológia/Slovak Sociological Review* (Janák & Klobucký, 2014). The results show that purely theoretical or methodological articles are rare. Instead of articles that respond to contemporary western sociological theories, there is more examination of social reality or a search for sociological traditions.

When it comes to thematic focus, one of the most commonly studied areas was the transformation of society, which is understandable given the important social changes that had taken place. However, at the same time, when reflecting on this period in the development of sociology, there have been critical voices who say that articles about transformation are often apologias rather than critical, analytic texts (see, e.g., Kusá et al., 2002). There are also complaints that there is little investigation into the social bases of transformation and, in general, the "uncertainties, pathologies, tensions or crises" that produce modernization (Búzik, 2005, p. 11) and also that there is a "lack of discussion, and the fact that articles are focused primarily on the barriers to transformation, rather than the bearers […] has supported the naturalisation of the transformation to the idea of 'historical necessity'" (Kusá et al., 2002, p. 525). Bohumil Búzik (2005) has also criticized the inadequacy of theoretical definitions and the insufficient citation of relevant foreign texts when using new terms and concepts in Slovak sociology.

This is also linked to the relatively low number of articles from the field of social pathology. Research on a lot of negative phenomena that accompanied the transformation period, such as unemployment, poverty, criminality, drugs, the exclusion of the Roma community, corruption, or anomie, did not appear in the journal. After 1989, Slovak sociology focused mainly on macro-sociological problems connected with transformation and democratization or sometimes on the theme of new interpretative schemes in the field of political sociology. Common themes in Slovakia were citizenship and civil society, and one of the basic principles of democracy—free elections—was also examined quite frequently. The postrevolutionary enthusiasm promoted the need to defend democracy, and negative social tendencies quite understandably escaped greater attention from the Slovak sociological community.

However, in the 1990s, the journal contained a considerable number of articles from the field of political sociology, which was closely connected to the social transformation mentioned earlier and the establishment of new political institutions. A fairly large proportion of articles focuses on issues of nationhood, ethnicity, or identity. Historical tradition played an important role here (as Slovak sociology had been built up around these themes at the beginning of the twentieth century), as did the contemporary social situation, since apart from the division of Czechoslovakia, in the 1990s, a deterioration in Slovak-Hungarian relations and the related situation of national minorities had to be addressed.

The next research period dates from the year 2000 and is sometimes called "the consolidation phase." European integration began to dominate the research agenda, and while in the 1990s, European Union (EU) enlargement only received marginal attention, once negotiations about EU accession started (1997–1999), the topic quickly became the center of attention. Harmonization and consolidation became a central focus for research into political and economic transformation, together with the expectation that the development of the new democracies could be assessed according to their level of convergence with western Europe. In this period, empirical studies began to focus on questions about the different types of capitalism and democracy, migration in Europe, problems of corruption and international crime, ethnic identities, and the relationship of these problems to political consolidation and social justice based on European norms and the reform of social policies in various countries in our region.

From 2014 onward, the research agenda began to shift toward consideration of the future of the EU and democracy not just in Europe but as a global-level threat because of the failure to resolve the migration crisis in EU states, the results of the global financial crisis of 2008 and the growing signs that another financial crisis could occur, the growth of populist and authoritarian political parties and groups in both old and new member countries of the EU, and the expected and unexpected effects of Brexit.

A more detailed overview of the development of Slovak sociology after the fall of the communist regime, focusing on the most important themes and personalities, is presented in a monograph by Eva Laiferová and her team of coauthors (2018).

Because research had hitherto focused mainly on Slovakia, we cannot talk about a clear-cut theoretical and methodological focus. Journal articles, book chapters, monographs, and all other sorts of publications concentrate on collecting, presenting, and interpreting data mainly about Slovakia. Because of the small number of scientists, research is fragmented. It lacks coordination and collaboration. Slovak researchers who speak foreign languages are included in various international research teams in which their research activity largely consists of collecting data, and they are rarely included in theoretical and methodological discussions. They are often inundated with work because they are taking part in a number of projects, to say nothing of their teaching duties and routine administrative tasks. It has to be noted that a large majority of international research projects are realized in a "participatory" form. This means that Slovak researchers carry out the research as members of international teams so that they collect data about various areas of domestic social and political life without doing further analysis.

If we can talk about a fundamental change in Slovakia, then it is the abandonment of Marxism-Leninism mentioned earlier and the shift toward the eclectic and selective use of various concepts and methods such as functionalism, symbolic interactionism, qualitative research methods (the study of national identity, territorial and regional aspects of social development, value orientations and political culture), quantitative studies (electoral behavior, migration, social stratification), and the institutional approach (the study of the education system, organized interests, religion, etc.) All the fields mentioned are characterized by the choice of method, which usually "corresponds" to the theme (chosen by the leaders of the research teams) and has not encouraged debate about methods and paradigms among sociologists in Slovakia. Consequently, in many respects, sociology has remained in the first initial phase of collecting data from various relevant areas, with an absence of constructive discussion about fundamental approaches.

Knowledge and analysis of contemporary societies, politics, economics, and culture require attention to be paid not only to their formal institutional framework but also to their interpretation and to the dominant themes of public discourse and its symbolic character. In societal and political discourse, an important factor is the "timing" of the period under discussion, the extent of critical attitudes toward political actors in the opinion-forming media, the varying intensity of external influences on the nature of internal political discourse, and the way in which the positives or negatives of social and political development are interpreted by politicians, the media, professionals, intellectuals, and academics.

However, despite the previous critical words, we have to state that, at present, the level of Slovak sociology is evaluated very well in comparison with other scientific disciplines in Slovakia. This statement can be evidenced by the evaluation of the workplaces of the Slovak Academy of Sciences, which were evaluated by an international panel of experts, and the Institute of Sociology ranked in the best third of institutions. An even more important indicator is the evaluation of the Ministry of Education "Verification of Excellence in Research 2022," for which sociology, together with cultural anthropology, was evaluated as one of the most successful scientific disciplines in Slovakia because a large part of their outputs was evaluated as achieving significant international quality (Ministry of Education, Science, Research and Sport of the Slovak Republic, 2022; Slovak Academy of Sciences, 2023).

20.5 The Institutional Development of Sociology as a Research Discipline and Subject of Study

Institutional development, meaning the founding of various research and education departments, was the prerequisite for the development of sociology as a scientific discipline. This means that sociology's theoretical and methodological orientation was influenced by the specific features and character of individual institutions and the leading figures working there. It should be emphasized that in Slovakia, there is no dominant paradigm or clear orientation toward any existing paradigm. There are overlapping tendencies which emphasize liberal (often designated "neoliberal") democratic values, while at the same time, there is still a strand loyal to nationalist rhetoric and the protection of vaguely defined national interests. These controversies reflect the picture of political competition in Slovakia and, to an extent, complicate the development of sociology and discussion of the direction in which it is headed.

The Slovak Sociology Society (SSS) at the Slovak Academy of Sciences, created in 1964, is a voluntary association of professional and research workers in the field of sociology. The society's aim is to support the development of sociology as a scientific discipline, to spread sociological knowledge among the public, and to assist the professional and research development of its members. At present, the SSS has over 250 registered members who are involved in the work of 9 specialist sections and 1 regional (Eastern Slovak) branch. Interest in membership increases in proportion to the development of sociology at Slovak universities and research centers.

University departments traditionally link teaching and research, but in the case of sociology, we have to note that Slovakia has a limited number of sociology departments that offer all three levels of study. Apart from this, we need to differentiate between universities and colleges that offer only basic sociology courses as part of the compulsory minimum for social science students and institutions that have sociology as a main discipline so that students graduate with a diploma in that subject. At present, sociology is studied as a main subject at three universities, which at the same time carry out relevant academic research or at least state that they carry it out. One of these universities is Comenius University in Bratislava, which is the leading university in Slovakia; it obtained university status in 1919. Comenius University offers sociology at all three levels (bachelor's, master's, and doctoral) while simultaneously having the accreditation necessary to award the title of professor or associate professor in the academic discipline of sociology. Apart from this, students can take sociology as an independent subject at bachelor's, master's, and doctoral levels at Trnava University and bachelor's and master's levels at Matej Bel University in Banská Bystrica. Both these universities only began to extend the provision of social science programs and set up sociology departments after 1989.

The frantic founding of new universities, colleges, and university departments in Slovakia was not a response to the relatively low number of people with higher education but was rather a result of the battle between the party and intellectual elites after 1989. At the moment, there are 35 universities in Slovakia (20 public, 3 state, and 12 private) for a population of somewhat over 5 million. Over the previous decades, there have been regular discussions, usually in the run-up to parliamentary elections, about the need to reduce the large number of universities and colleges, particularly because of the manifestly low quality of results achieved in teaching, research, and publication at a number of them. However, after the elections, there ceases to be the political will to embark on really disbanding universities, particularly because of strong regional interests and sometimes religious links between parliamentary deputies and representatives of individual colleges. The consequence of this situation is that Slovak universities do not enjoy high prestige, and almost 20% of Slovak university students (which is the highest proportion of OECD countries after Luxembourg) study at foreign universities, especially in the Czech Republic.

The composition of sociology departments in universities and colleges offers a good example of the changes in intellectual elites and the diversity of the teaching staff in various social sciences. There is an acute shortage of sociologists formally qualified to oversee the study of sociology since there have thus far been only three sociology professors in Slovakia. This led to the "buying in" of professors and associate professors from abroad, mainly from Poland and the Czech Republic. A younger generation of home and foreign sociology graduates is gradually replacing faculty who were once employed by the former institutes of Marxism-Leninism and other ideologically based university departments.

However, it can be stated that sociology in Slovakia did not take advantage of the massive increase in university students after 1990. Although the increase in the number of sociology students is obvious, it has been limited mainly to the production of graduates of lower levels of higher education (bachelor's and master's). The number of sociology doctoral students has long been stagnating (in the years 1990–2022, the average number of successful graduates from the year was only 1.5), and therefore, Slovak sociology has not grown significantly institutionally or personally in the long term (unlike other social science disciplines such as political science).

Individual universities differ not only in the way that they teach subjects but also in the whole way the subject is structured. A relatively broad palette of subjects is taught, whereby departments not only offer traditional courses such as the history of Slovak and world sociology, general sociology, methods and techniques in sociological research, sectoral sociology, and similar but also courses for related academic disciplines and a large number of optional courses according to the profile of the department's lecturers.

The direct predecessor of the current Sociology Institute of the Slovak Academy of Sciences was the so-called Department of Social Research, which was in due course renamed the Department of Sociological Research and, in 1963, moved to the Philosophy Institute of the Slovak Academy of Sciences, thanks to the persistence of sociology's enthusiastic supporters. Attempts to create an independent sociological center resulted in the creation of the Sociology Institute of the Slovak Academy of Sciences in January 1965. The focus of the newly established institute was the field of theory and methodology of sociology, as well as teaching and developing domestic and foreign collaboration. Sociological research focused especially on the analysis of the social consequences of industrialization and collectivization in Slovakia.

The existence of the Sociology Institute was often threatened by political events after the Soviet invasion of Czechoslovakia in August 1968. Although it was not abolished, its whole operation in the normalization period was influenced by ideological pressure and personnel purges. The result of normalization on sociology's development can be described as "retarded professionalisation, isolation from the development of the discipline in the world at large […] and a distorting ideologization of thought" (Szomolányi, 1995, p. 161).

In 1975, after the Sociology Institute had existed independently for 10 years, it was merged with Philosophy, and an Institute of Philosophy and Sociology was established at the Academy of Sciences. The sociology section's main focus was research into the social structure of socialist society in Czechoslovakia.

After the revolutionary changes in November 1989, there were changes at the institute as well, and in 1990, the Sociology Institute of the Slovak Academy of Sciences became independent again. At present, it is the center for sociological research in Slovakia and also touches on other social science disciplines. It links research into problem areas in society with the examination of the theoretical and methodological questions of sociological thought.

Cross-sectional work that ensures the accumulation of knowledge is assured by its orientation toward comparative and longitudinal empirical surveys.

The specific relationship between scientific and pedagogical workplaces of Slovak and Czech sociology is documented by Slovak and Czech sociological days in the form of scientific conferences, which have been organized alternately every other year since 2004 by the Slovak and Czech Sociological Societies. As a rule, conferences have a broad thematic focus from various areas of sociology and also enjoy the interest of the professional public and students from related scientific disciplines. The research focus of the institute concentrates on investigating the dynamics of social, economic, and spatial inequalities and their domestic and global dimensions as reflected in public opinion. Projects examine changes in the content and organization of work and political and administrative discourses about employment and unemployment, the research of socio-spatial processes and disparities, and the social aspects of settlement and regional development. Some of the Sociology Institute's most important projects are international comparative research for the International Social Survey Programme (ISSP) and the European Values Study (EVS), in which teams of researchers from the institute regularly take part and make it possible to analyze Slovak society in an international comparative perspective. Research themes are national identity, citizenship, attitudes to work, the role of government, social networks, electoral behavior, and political communication and the pluralism of lifestyles, religious and cultural values, and traditions. The fundamental social, economic, political, and cultural changes which have taken place in Europe since 1990 have led not only to changes in the legal order but also to changes in the value orientation of the population and in the creation of public policies to ensure solidarity. The aim of the projects is to identify the dynamic of change in the basic value orientations of Slovakia's population against the background of the creation of the independent state and the country's integration into European structures and to compare them internationally. When comparing Slovakia in the European and global context, theoretical and methodological concepts are developed, and they are verified to see if they are valid in Slovak conditions.

Researchers also address issues of the institutionalization and legitimacy of representing collective interests, the social responsibility of economic actors and institutions, discourse analysis about questions of public interest in the context of economic globalization and integration into transnational structures, as well as the process of democratization and its reflection in public opinion. Research activity also focuses on changes to the family cycle and lifestyle and how free time is spent within the framework of the sociology of everyday life. Issues such as the causes and consequences of migration, changes in factors influencing family and societal solidarity, and the development of social trust, as well as processes of marginalization and exclusion affecting some groups in the population, are also establishing themselves as urgent topics for research.

Research at the Sociology Institute has been a consistent part of the broad scientific collaboration between sociological centers in Slovakia and abroad. There are interdisciplinary overlaps, and research teams maintain a dialog and create joint research consortia with experts from a number of related academic disciplines within the framework of the Academy of Sciences in partnership with home and foreign universities and research institutes.

Since 2017, the Sociology Institute has been part of the European Strategy Forum on Research Infrastructures (ESFRI) of the European social science data archive consortium (Consortium of European Social Science Data Archives—European Research Infrastructure Consortium (CESSDA-ERIC)), where the Slovak Republic is 1 of the 15 founding members. The Slovak Archive of Social Data, which is run by the institute, is the national service provider in this distribution infrastructure.

20.5.1 The Journal Sociológia

The Sociology Institute of the Slovak Academy of Sciences publishes the bimonthly journal *Sociológia*.[1] The journal has appeared without interruption since 1969, and for the entire period of its existence, it has been the only academic sociological journal in Slovakia. Since 1997, it has appeared four times a year in Slovak and twice a year in English under the title *Sociológia: Slovak Sociological Review*. The journal is indexed in *Current Contents: Social & Behavioral Sciences* (Thomson ISI) and in other databases. The journal publishes original research articles covering a very broad range of sociological research and thinking. It provides a space for

---

[1] See http://sociologia.sav.sk/static.php?id=1153#a1

professional discussion about contemporary social problems in Slovakia, Europe, and the world.

20.5.2 Sociologists in the Public Sphere

When examining the public engagement of Slovak sociologists, we can start in 1989 with the events that led to the fall of the communist regime. One of the leading figures of the "Velvet Revolution" was the sociologist Fedor Gál, who was a founder of Public Against Violence (Verejnosti proti násiliu or VPN), which was the leading opposition force in 1989, and later went on to lead VPN's coordination center and became the movement's chair and a government advisor. After the victory of nationalist Prime Minister Vladimír Mečiar in 1992, he withdrew from politics, moved to Prague, and worked as a writer and independent intellectual who supported civil society and liberal values and fought against political extremism.

Martin Bútora, who had been the initiator of the Slovak sociologists' petition demanding the release of imprisoned Slovak dissidents in the summer of 1989, represents similar values. In November 1989, he was a cofounder of VPN, a member of its coordinating committee, and one of its leading figures. From 1990 to 1992, he worked as a human rights advisor to the Czechoslovak President Václav Havel. In the 1990s, he was the Director of the Institute for Public Affairs, and from 1999 to 2003, he was the Slovak Ambassador to the USA. Since 2014, he has been an advisor to the Slovak President, Andrej Kiska.

Juraj Schenk represents the opposite end of the political spectrum of sociologists who were active in politics. He was a professionally highly respected sociologist who was only the second Slovak professor of sociology, and for many years, he led the most prestigious university sociology department in Bratislava. In the 1990s, he supported Slovak independence and was Minister of Foreign Affairs in the third Mečiar government from 1994 to 1996, but after this short exposure to political life, he returned to academia, and since resigning from politics, he has not been publicly active.

Helena Woleková became the first woman in the Slovak government after the fall of communism when she held the office of Minister for Labour and Social Affairs from April 1991 to June 1992 as a member of VPN. In 1994, she became a ministerial advisor at the same ministry, and from 1995 onward, she has been active in civil society.

Iveta Radičová is a professionally respected sociology professor who, after 1989, worked as an advisor for VPN and, later its successor, the Civic Democratic Union. In 2005–2006, she was Minister of Labour, Social Affairs and the Family, having previously been Director of the Sociology Institute of the Slovak Academy of Sciences. From 2010 to 2012, she was the Prime Minister of the Slovak Republic, having unsuccessfully stood for election as Slovak president in 2009, when she lost in a second-round runoff. After 2012, she returned to academia and has repeatedly refused to return to politics, although she actively participates in public discourse.

The members of the advisory team of the President of the Slovak Republic, Zuzana Čaputová, during her term of office (2019–2024) were sociologist Zuzana Kusá (in 2019) and since 2020 Oľga Gyárfášová.

From this slightly superficial and undoubtedly incomplete overview of the most important sociologists in Slovak politics, we can see that most of them entered politics in the "revolutionary" period between 1989 and 1991 as opponents of the communist regime. Similarly, a large majority of them were involved in liberal, pro-western, and pro-European politics and favored ideas about developing liberal democracy and civil society. It is interesting that none of the most influential figures in sociology established themselves in the conservative, nationalist, or even the left-wing part of the political spectrum. A possible explanation for this is that after the "founding generation" of Slovak politicians who came from the VPN movement, most of the later politicians tended to be lawyers and economists. The usual West European phenomenon of left-wing sociologists engaging in politics is not at all markedly present in Slovakia, which can be explained by the total abandonment of the Marxist paradigm in Slovak sociology after 1989.

Apart from this brief overview of the Slovak sociologists who took part, or still take part, in politics, we will attempt to analyze the broader work of Slovak sociologists in public discourse. For this analysis, we can use the rankings of the most cited experts and analysts, which have been published by different bodies since 2006.

Of the academic sociologists, the most publicly visible have for a long time included Zuzana Kusá, who represents left-wing values and is involved mostly in issues of poverty and social exclusion. Another sociologist who is prominent in the media is Silvia Porubänová, who mainly studies the family and presents fairly liberal views in this field. Oľga Gyarfášová focuses on voting behavior, political attitudes, and associated values.

However, analysis of the rankings of the most influential experts in the Slovak media shows that sociologists are not heavily represented and that lawyers and political scientists tend to dominate. The structure of the most cited sociologists is also interesting. The most publicly visible are representatives of research agencies, who rarely engage in deeper analysis of social processes, and their comments to the media are mostly on the level of talking about election results.

However, we can also bring a positive example from the recent past. The Institute for Sociology was heavily involved in the continuous research of society in the time of the coronavirus pandemic "How are you, Slovakia?" This is a series of Internet-based representative surveys. A number of the institute's staff participated in the development of the questionnaire and collaborated in the publication of 46 press releases from 17 waves of research carried out from 2020 to 2023. The findings from this series of research have received considerable media coverage and have contributed to the Institute's visibility as a center of social science expertise in relation to the pandemic. For their participation in this project, the Institute's staff received the Slovak Academy of Sciences Award for Popularization of Science and Social Applications of Science.

20.6 In Place of a Conclusion

As we have already mentioned, sociology as an academic discipline, whether in the Slovak Academy of Sciences or specialized applied research departments or as a subject of study at universities and colleges, has undergone rather traumatic developments in Slovakia; after 1989, for a variety of reasons, it very quickly began to fragment. In this respect, the most important role was played by the political polarization of the entire society in the 1990s that accompanied the governments of Slovak Prime Minister Vladimír Mečiar from 1992 to 1998. A result of this was the gradual formation of two groups of social scientists in general and therefore also of sociologists, who ceased communicating with each other because of their political and ideological views and were in a permanent conflict that, in some cases, still lasts today. The politics of the coalition then in government led to a situation where a university was founded in almost every provincial town. Slovakia, with its five million inhabitants today, has ten universities where the basics of sociology, if not the subject as an independent degree course, is taught in small, underfinanced, understaffed social science departments. Slovak education has always suffered from a lack of funds, but the current fragmentation entails even more ineffective use of the resources that are available.

A further consequence of this fragmentation is inadequate contact between universities and research centers, with limited communication between sociologists at universities and research institutes. As a discipline, sociology has no tradition of debates on research, although the Sociology Institute of the Academy of Sciences and the Slovak Sociological Society have made huge efforts to act as fora for such discussions. Apart from this, there is a growing danger of duplication. Academics usually teach and conduct research at the university where they themselves studied, and there is nothing to stimulate them to gain professional experience at another university or maybe abroad. The result of this is that very few of them participate in conferences, seminars, workshops, or other similar events organized by their colleagues abroad. Another reason for this, particularly among the older generation of lecturers and researchers outside Bratislava, is a lack of knowledge of foreign languages.

Sociology as a university subject was only fully integrated into the Slovak education system after the fall of communism; previously, there was only one department with a very small number of students. Moreover, in recent years, sociology has not really developed any further in part because of the demographic curve and the declining number of students. The academic community perceives that the interest in doctoral study is in the long term not very high, and particularly at some recently founded universities, the prevailing view is that law and economics are more important than sociology. However, despite all these problems, there are some research centers and university departments that are able to compete at the international level. This is witnessed by the exchange programs and international projects in which they take part.

Therefore, if we take 1989 as the date of the new rebirth of sociology in Slovakia, we can say that the first stage of its existence has been successfully completed: it is respected as an independent subject for university study, the quality of staff available has improved, its university departments and research centers are quite well-established, international collaboration has been developed, there is a well-functioning professional organization, etc. Of course, there are many things that still need to be accomplished, and most of all, we need to consolidate all the positive achievements that have already been made.

Borut Rončević identified four ideal types of the role of sociology in society based on two dimensions: the role of sociology in society and its status as a profession. With such an analytical view, Slovak sociology, especially in the 1990s, can be understood primarily as an activist science that attempted to address current macro-social topics, such as social transformation, building democracy, and civil society.

In the next period after Slovakia's accession to the European Union, however, the level of its activism declined somewhat, and after its more internationalization and fragmentation, its social role came closer to the voyeur ideal type, while paradoxically its critical functions and analysis of social pathologies were simultaneously strengthened.

The whole history and identity of Slovak sociology is connected with the regularly repeated need to prove its necessity and usefulness. At the beginning of the twentieth century, it was supposed to be a pragmatically used tool for improving national emancipation efforts; in the interwar period, it was the scientific apologetics of Czechoslovakism: the idea of the gradual merger of the Czech and Slovak peoples on which the Czechoslovak Republic was founded. The communist regime, following the example of Stalin, first discarded sociology in order to reestablish it in the 1960s as a science that was primarily supposed to help with reforms and partial democratization of society. After the collapse of reform efforts and the occupation of Czechoslovakia by the troops of the Soviet Union and its allies, sociology was at first severely suppressed again, but by the 1980s, it became a haven for nonconformist voices protesting against the communist regime. After the fall of the communist regime, it, therefore, logically became actively involved in building a democratic society.

Recently, however, the issue of social transformation has disappeared from social and sociological discourse, and sociologists have begun to take on the role of critical observers of social processes rather than activism and promoting a concrete vision of the development of society.

Many solutions are entirely in the hands of the academic community in Slovakia, whereas others depend on the goodwill of the state administration and its institutions, on the elected leaders of the country, and also on the assistance and collaboration of foreign colleagues and institutions and international research networks. As an EU member state, Slovakia has the opportunity to make effective use not just of financial stimuli for the development of research, innovation, and technological progress but also for support for developing academic disciplines which contribute to self-reflection in society and which use analytic tools to identify the challenges currently facing society. Sociology is undoubtedly such a science.

Competing Interests The authors have no conflicts of interest to declare that are relevant to the content of this chapter.

References

Bútora, M. (2008). Bratislava/nahlas – odkaz i výzva. In M. Huba, V. Ira, & P. Šuška (Eds.), *Bratislava/nahlas - ako výzva* (pp. 38–52). Geografický ústav SAV.
Bútorová, Z., & Dianiška, I. (1988). Samoregulácia vedeckého spoločenstva. *Sociológia, 20*(2), 141–155.
Búzik, B. (1995). Teoretický pluralizmus alebo eklekticizmus? *Sociológia, 27*(2), 297–300.
Búzik, B. (1997). Od kritiky teórie k empiricizmu. In Ľ. Turčan & E. Laiferová (Eds.), *O kontinuitu a modernu. Predpoklady, možnosti a realita rozvoja sociológie na Slovensku* (pp. 19–30). Sociologický ústav SAV.
Búzik, B. (2000). Zjavenie sa modernizácie v slovenskej sociológii. *Sociológia, 32*(4), 385–390.
Búzik, B. (2005). Od triednej spoločnosti k postkomunizmu: užitočnosť veľkých rozprávaní. In J. Matulník, J. Sopóci, & K. Čukan (Eds.), *Vývoj slovenskej spoločnosti v 90. rokoch a na začiatku 21. storočia – trendy, problémy, perspektívy* (pp. 9–14). Slovenská sociologická spoločnosť pri SAV.
Búzik, B., & Laiferová, E. (2003). In search of its own identity: A decade of Slovak sociology. In F. M. Keen & J. L. Mucha (Eds.), *Sociology in Central and Eastern Europe: Transformation at the dawn of new millennium* (pp. 153–163). Praeger.
ESF. (2012). Forward *look: Central and Eastern Europe beyond transition: Convergence and divergence in Europe.* European Science Foundation. Retrieved from http://archives.esf.org/coordinating-research/forward-looks/social-sciences-soc/completed-forward-looks-in-social-sciences/central-and-eastern-europe-beyond-transition.html
Frič, P., Gál, F., & Dianiška, I. (1988). Profesiová orientácia sociológa vo svetle spoločenských očakávaní. *Sociológia, 20*(1), 71–83.
Janák, D., & Klobucký, R. (2014). Co bychom věděli o sociologii, kdybychom četli pouze Sociologický časopis a Sociológii? Obsahová analýza dvou sociologických periodik od 'sametové revoluce' do současnosti. *Sociologický časopis/Czech Sociological Review, 50*(5), 645–670.
Klobucký, R. (2009). Štyridsať rokov časopisu Sociológia. *Sociológia, 41*(1), 52–82.
Klobucký, R. (2011). Sociologické myslenie Antona Štefánka. In *Anton Štefánek: Vedec, politik, novinár* (pp. 58–83). Sociologický ústav SAV.
Kmeť, N., & Marušiak, J. (Eds.). (2003). *Slovensko a režim normalizácie.* Ústav politických vied SAV.
Krivý, V. (1988). Sociotechnika: možnosti a hranice. *Sociológia, 20*(4), 417–425.
Kusá, Z. (1997). Nechcená kontinuita? In Ľ. Turčan & E. Laiferová (Eds.), *O kontinuitu a modernu. Predpoklady, možnosti a realita rozvoja sociológie na Slovensku* (pp. 155–160). Sociologický ústav SAV.
Kusá, Z., Búzik, B., Turčan, Ľ., & Klobucký, R. (2002). Sociology – Slovakia. In M. Kaase & V. Sparschuh (Eds.), *Three social science disciplines in Central and Eastern Europe: Handbook on economics, political science and sociology (1989–2001)* (pp. 518–535). Social Science Information Centre (IZ) / Collegium Budapest.
Laiferová, E., Mistríková, Ľ., Capíková, S., Lubelcová, G., & Eckerová, L. (2018). *Slovenská sociológia po páde komunizmu - ideové korene, súčasné trendy a osobnosti vedy* (2nd ed.). Univerzita Komenského V Bratislave.
Ministry of Education, Science, Research and Sport of the Slovak Republic. (2022). *Výsledky periodického hodnotenia výskumnej, vývojovej, umeleckej a ďalšej tvorivej činnosti.* Retrieved

from https://www.minedu.sk/33250-sk/vysledky-periodickeho-hodnotenia-vyskumnej-vyvojovej-umeleckej-a-dalsej-tvorivej-cinnosti/

Mucha, J., & Keen, J. (2000). History in the making: Sociology and the transformation of Eastern and Central Europe. *Sociológia, 32*(3), 227–240.

Musil, J. (2004). Poznámky o české sociologii za komunistického režimu. *Sociologický časopis, 40*(5), 573–596.

Slovak Academy of Sciences. (2023). *Regular assessment of the research Institutes of the Slovak Academy of sciences 2016–2021*. Retrieved from https://www.sav.sk/uploads/dokumentySAV/evaluation/Final_SAS_Metapanel_Report_2023.pdf

Sopóci, J. (1995). Hľadanie teórie v slovenskej sociológii. In *Sociológia v meniacej sa spoločnosti* (pp. 21–28). Katedra sociológie FF UK.

Sopóci, J. (1997). Problémy teoretickej diferenciácie v slovenskej sociológii. In Ľ. Turčan & E. Laiferová (Eds.), *O kontinuitu a modernu. Predpoklady, možnosti a realita rozvoja sociológie na Slovensku* (pp. 46–53). Sociologický ústav SAV.

Szomolányi, S. (1988). Pokus o sebareflexiu slovenskej sociológie ako jej problémové a participatívne skúmanie. *Sociológia, 20*(3), 307–318.

Szomolányi, S. (1990). História zrodu a formovania sociologického pracoviska SAV. *Sociológia, 22*(3), 367–382.

Szomolányi, S. (1995). Metareflexia histórie SÚ SAV. Sociológia, 27(3), 158–161.

Vorisek, M. (2007). Ideology that mattered: The debates on historical materialism and sociology in the USSR, Poland, and Czechoslovakia, 1948–1968. In L. Babka & P. Roubal (Eds.), *Prague perspectives II: A new generation of Czech East European studies* (pp. 121–156). National Library of the Czech Republic—Slavonic Library.

Mgr. Robert Klobucký , PhD in Sociology from Comenius University in Bratislava, is the Director of the Institute for Sociology, Slovak Academy of Sciences (2011–2015), and Deputy Director of the Institute for Sociology, Slovak Academy of Sciences (2015–2019, 2023–present). He deals with the history of sociological thought, conspiracy theories and trust, as well as drug policy and other topics. He is the author of the monographs The Hlasist Movement: Nation and Sociology (2006) and Illegal Drugs and Drug Policy in Slovakia (2016). Since 1996, he has been working at the Institute for Sociology of the Slovak Academy of Sciences in Bratislava.

Prof. Silvia Miháliková , PhD in Sociology from Comenius University in Bratislava, is Professor in Political Science and Dean of the Faculty of Social and Economic Sciences at Comenius University (2010–2014). She is a Guest Professor at the Institute for Political Science, Vienna University; a Research Fellow at the Institute for East Europe, Bremen University; a Jean Monnet Professor in European Integration and Bearer of the Jean Monnet European Centre of Excellence; an International Coordinator of the EC 5th Framework project Cultural Patterns of the European Enlargement Process (2002–2005); the President of the Central European Political Science Association (2006–2009); the Head of the Slovak Political Science Association (1994–1998); a Director of the Institute for Sociology, Slovak Academy of Sciences (2015–2019); and a Professor of Sociology at the Faculty of Philosophy, Trnava University, in Slovakia since 2015. Her academic activities comprise comparative research on democratization, political cultures and identities, political symbolism, communication, and minority questions. She is an author of several publications: Zwischen Kreuz und Europastern: Politische Symbolik der Slowakei (Münster, LIT Verlag, 2004) and Miesto politickej symboliky v politickej kultúre Slovenska (Towarzystwo Słowaków w Polsce, 2018).

Chapter 21
The Role of Slovenian Sociologists in Shaping National Imaginary Through Discursive Practices

Tea Golob and Tamara Besednjak Valič

21.1 Introduction

The primary purpose of this chapter is to discuss the impact of Slovenian sociology on the national imaginary, reflecting certain cultural, political, and economic structural settings and articulating particular semiotic orders (cf. Jessop & Oosterlynck, 2008). Leaning on the conceptual tools of the cultural and political economy (Jessop, 2004), it aims to elucidate the role of sociology in the post-socialist transformations in terms of contributing to evolutionary mechanisms of the variation, selection, and retention of privileged discourses. This chapter is primarily focused on the transition period from the end of the 1980s to the beginning of the 1990s, when major structural and semantic changes occurred. However, a narrated national environment can ensue not just in new configurations of genres, discourses, and styles, but it can also be rooted in old semiotic order pertaining to certain path dependency with the former structural settings. While new discourses can become privileged in the era of major transformation, there are also certain discourses ingrained in individual and collective routines and identities (Jessop, 2004). Comprehending Slovenian sociology in the period of transition thus requires a brief consideration of its emergence in the twentieth century, specific developments in the communist period, and, nevertheless, its readiness to tackle the contemporary

T. Golob
Faculty of Information Studies in Novo Mesto, Novo Mesto, Slovenia
e-mail: tea.golob@fis.unm.si

T. Besednjak Valič (✉)
Faculty of Information Studies in Novo Mesto, Novo Mesto, Slovenia

Rudolfovo – Science and Technology Centre Novo Mesto and School of Advanced Social Studies in Nova Gorica, Novo Mesto, Slovenia
e-mail: tamara.valic@rudolfovo.eu

© The Author(s), under exclusive license to Springer Nature Switzerland AG 2024
B. Roncevic, T. Besednjak Valič (eds.), *Sociology and Post-Socialist Transformations in Eastern Europe*,
https://doi.org/10.1007/978-3-031-65556-2_21

challenges and approaches referring to technological expansion and global connectivity.

In order to elucidate Slovenian sociology in the context of the cultural political economy, we will attempt to understand the roles sociologists occupy based on the conceptualization and typology of Borut Rončević (Chap. 1). He elaborates, based on research on the transformative power of sociology, the roles sociologists can play, ranging from the weak status of the profession (marginals to passengers) to autonomic positions (voyeurs to activists).

To understand the roles of Slovenian sociologists fully, this chapter primarily draws on the existing literature and selected secondary data dealing with the history, development, and challenges of sociology in Slovenia. Several interesting articles, overviews, and collections on the topic exist. As Adam and Makarovič (2002) observed, initial considerations were provided by Jogan (1994, 1995), Vičič (1989), and Kerševan (1995), but also by Adam & Rončević (2001), while the reactions of sociologists on the transformations brought by democratization, modernization, and statehood were scrutinized by Adam and Makarovič (2001). A brief overview of relevant publications (Adam & Makarovič, 2002), including the prewar history of sociology (Čas, 1996), has also been provided. The recent and extremely comprehensive work on Slovenian sociology has been provided by Zdravko Mlinar, who has edited the collective monographs on the venture points, challenges, and prospects of Slovenian sociology and sociologists (2016). The first monograph provides valuable information on the topic, as it entails a firsthand overview of sociology provided by its founding fathers and other prominent actors within the field. The literature review and the collection of personal opinions by Slovenian sociologists (in Mlinar, 2016) also inspired the empirical part of this chapter. Its purpose is to provide a view on the chronological density and interrelation of the prevailing topics in two sociological scientific journals, *Teorija in praksa* and *Družboslovne razprave*, published since 1956 and 1984, respectively. The empirical part thus aims to complement the existing studies and literature overviews. It is structured so as to analyze the aforementioned journals in the time span of 30 years (from 1987 to 2017). The year 1987, as a cutoff year, was selected due to its being recognized as the dawn of Slovenian democracy with the 57th issue of *Nova revija* being published. With the help of the Slovenian online library system Cobiss, we were able to collect all entries for both journals in the designated time span. With methods of selection, we secured 445 entries for analysis in the years 1987, 1990, 1991, 1992, 1997, 2007, and 2017. Entries were analyzed in a two-step coding process with the help of predefined codes. In the second step, the codes were grouped into categories defining the main topics discussed in particular years. The paradigm map was elaborated to analyze the dispersion and interlinkages between the discussed topics.

The analysis based on the primary and secondary data aims to contrast the structural settings and prevailing discourses of the Slovenian national environment in the communist and postcommunist period and also in the contemporary era of globalization and individualization, with the prevailing topics, themes, and discourses provided by the Slovenian sociologists in the selected periods. In that regard, the chapter intends to reveal the role of sociology in constructing a new semiotic order in the dawn of democratization while privileging new variations or leaning on the old constructions based on a specific path dependency with certain ideological orientations.

21.2 Slovenian Structural Trends, Semiosis of National Imaginary, and Sociology

The role sociology has been playing in the construction of the Slovenian national imaginary in the past three decades is inextricably intertwined with the specific historical circumstances from which it emerged as an academic discipline. Whether as a science, profession, or specific expertise, it has developed in the context of cultural, political, and social settings, demarcating the Central and Eastern European region on the one hand and Slovenian national specifics on the other. While sociology was ignited with major social upheavals in Western Europe, specifically industrialization, urbanization and secularization, bureaucratization, and rationalization, it protruded into other European regions with a delayed echo. It has been argued (Forrest Keen & Mucha, 2003; Mucha, n.d., p. 190) that at the end of the nineteenth century, the intelligentsia in the Central and Eastern European region scarcely addressed issues of modernity and industrialization in an analytical way and was more concerned with the emergence of national identities and region's largest social group: the peasants. As a semi-periphery (Adam et al., 2005), it lagged behind the European core, and when industrialization could have developed, World War II broke out, leading to the establishment of the communist regime, which significantly influenced the development and institutionalization of sociology. Slovenia is hardly seen as an exception in that regard. As Adam and Makarovič pointed out (2002, p. 536), the first sociological publications appeared at the beginning of the twentieth century, but sociological knowledge was far from its institutionalization, and it presented merely a supplement to philosophy and pedagogy and with only rudimentary empirical endeavors. The sociological discussions, prevailing discourses, and topics in that period were initiated primarily by Catholic priests and politicians. Their intentions using sociological knowledge to contribute to the development of the Slovenian nation in economic, social, and political terms were quite in vain, as their work almost completely disappeared from the national semantic horizon with the introduction of the communist regime after World War II. It is important to note that even in the transition period, only a few remnants of the first sociological thinking were revived (Adam & Makarovič, 2002).

Sociology as 'a bourgeois science' had been expelled from the academic imaginary until the mid-1950s (Jogan, 1995 in Adam & Makarovič, 2002, p. 536). Since then, its role in constructing a national imaginary has been reinforced. While sociology was controlled or even exploited by the communist regime, it also became institutionalized. In the years 1965–1969, the Association of Sociologists (later renamed into the Slovenian Sociological Association) was established. The infrastructure for empirical research was grounded, and sociologists started to collaborate with the international environment (Adam & Makarovič, 2002, p. 536; Mlinar, 2016, p. 39). Although the prevailing orientation of sociology complied with Marxist ideology, there were also certain inconsistencies with the regime often leading to the conflict between sociologists and the political apparatus. It has been remembered that sociology was knitted with Marxist ideology, and the communist party treated the then Faculty of Social Science as its dependent; nevertheless, it was also receptive to new ways and open to the research sphere in Yugoslavia and worldwide (Hribar, 2016, p. 102). The secession from Stalinism and the introduction of so-called worker's self-management within the communist political system represented an important structural trend inducing certain period of crisis. It enabled new variations of discourses and also their proliferation and retention (cf. Jessop, 2004). The Slovenian Sociological Association regularly organized discussions and consultations regarding wider social issues, such as social conflict, public opinion, and civil society, among others, and it even demonstrated against the Soviet occupation of Czechoslovakia and political oppression toward the scientific endeavors (Mlinar, 2016, p. 23). Sociology contributed to the variation and selection of certain discourses, enabling the reinforcement of civil society, which played an important part in the democratization processes in the 1980s when the communist regime started losing its power. Sociologists often played an active role in that regard, although they could face sanctions, sometimes also imposed through higher education institutions (Podmenik, 2016, p. 278). On the one hand, sociologists contributed to the retention and reinforcement of certain ideological discourses through their work and pedagogical activities, enabling the legitimization of the communist party, while on the other, directly or indirectly, they influenced the new variations opposing the regime. "Sociologists were often praising the idea of self-management offered by the communist party, but it soon turned out that under the concept, we actually understood as social *participation* [...] so the word participation appeared in our studies" (Makarovič, 2016, p. 83). Or, as Andolšek (2016) recalled:

> [...] while its research endeavours and theoretical discussions were knitted with the ideological field of the former socialist system, it was in many cases simultaneously its most important critic, which led to preparing grounds for the transformation and independence of Slovenian society. (p. 93)

With the collapse of the communist regime, a theoretical turning point occurred, leading from a dominance of Marxism to a prevalence of multi-paradigmatic situation (Bernik & Rončević, 2001 in Adam & Makarovič, 2002, p. 537). Slovenian sociology followed certain trends caused by the transformations of the structural order, and it was transformed into a modern science discipline. After Slovenian independence, changes in research topics and interests can be observed. The curriculum went through certain changes, sociologists became much more internationalized, and private higher education institutions dealing with sociology were also established. However, it has been observed that in the transition period, the Faculty of Social Science at the University of Ljubljana, as the leading institution for teaching and researching in the field, did not undergo major structural changes (Adam &

Makarovič, 2002, p. 237). Those who were marginalized in the communist regime gained opportunities to expand their professional career, while those who were advocating communist ideology opted for topics such as feminism, ecology, or social democracy "or portrayed themselves simply as 'neutral' observers of society" (Adam & Makarovič, 2002, p. 538). The decline of the communist system, therefore, did not lead to substantial changes in the employment structure of researchers and professors, and the adaptation to new circumstances was very successful. However, new research interests and topics emerged, embracing the political, cultural, and economic aspects of transition society (Adam & Makarovič, 2001, pp. 392–383). So, the question is, to what extent has sociology followed semantic changes brought by democratization and modernization, how has it adapted to them, and how has it reproduced them?

The period of transition in newly established political systems in Europe was characterized by different economic and political strategies, which caused distinct dynamics of transformation. The fall of the former political system intertwined Slovenia, just as in other countries of East and Southeast Europe, with rapid global transformations on the economic, political, social, and cultural scales. The transition period in European countries took many different forms. Slovenia adopted the path of gradualism (Aghion & Blanchard, 1994; Roland, 2000; Stiglitz, 2002; Mencinger, 2004) along with Hungary, while others, such as the Czech Republic, Slovakia, and Estonia, opted for shock therapy (Lipton & Sachs, 1990; Balcerowitz, 1995). Those transformations occurred at different paces, leading to quite diverse structural outcomes, often explored as varieties of capitalism (Feldmann, 2006; Izyumov & Claxon, 2009; Myant & Drahokoupil, 2012). In addition to structural transformations, major changes also occurred in national semantics. Transitional societies from all over Europe were facing a high level of complexity of variation, pluralization of meanings, and differentiation (Golob, 2013). Contemporary national mythologies were built from various, mutually consistent and coherent, upgrading or concurrent old myths and new ideologies (Velikonja, 1996). The consolidation of the new post-socialist states draws legitimacy from distinct post-socialist mythic constellations, and the past has become reinterpreted in order to suit future needs. Specific national imaginaries were built, articulating particular semiotic orders, which represent specific configurations of genres, discourses, and styles and constitute the meanings of social practices in particular social formations (Jessop & Oosterlynck, 2008). As "each period mentally fabricates its representation of the historical past" (Le Goff, 1992, p. 109), there was a battle between different variants of discourses, which took the form of national collective memories. Slovenian national imaginary has been strongly affected by structural trends occurring after 1991 when multiparty representative democracy was consolidated and a market economy was introduced. Semiotic order followed those changes and was established on new identification codes.

It has been observed that Slovenian sociology put some effort into constructing a new national imaginary. As Adam and Makarovič (2002) pointed out, there was a major shift in theoretical framework. Marxist theoretical background was replaced by a reinterpretation of the sociological classics, such as Schutz's and Weber's concept of rationality and legitimacy and modernization with Parsons and Luhmann and Habermas's public sphere (p. 539). The transition process, democratization, and developmental issues were addressed through their specific impacts on society; however, sociologists rarely cooperated in those endeavors. Studies using opinion polls were prevailing. The attention was also placed on the privatization of social services and industrial relations (Stanojević, 2001); neo-corporatist arrangements and self-regulation; the relationship between the economy, the state, and scientific institutions (Mali, 2000); and elite reproduction (complete overview in Adam & Makarovič, 2001, 2002).

Sociologists also took part in discussions referring to identity issues and collective formations. Ethnic and national symbolic constellations were from the very beginning of independence intertwined with exploring European integration. While analyzing certain issues and narratives legitimating the semiosis on a national imaginary, sociologists contributed to their selection and retention. The formation of Slovenia was accompanied by a series of new political symbols and myths, representing a necessary condition for a country to establish a legitimate and convincing foundation of its history, mythology, and ideology. Those ideas also complied with the idea of a united Europe, referring to Western ideals of freedom and prosperity. A narrative of joining the common European family in terms of the European Union represented the Promised Land in economic, political, and cultural terms (Mastnak, 1996). Europe became a cradle of values, while the Balkans gained the status of the "Other," forming a contrast on which Slovenian national identity was built. Slovenia was also forming itself in relationship to the globalization processes. In that regard, sociologists explored various aspects of identity. They addressed different aspects of ethnic identity and minorities (Komac, Jesih, and Žagar), spatially based identities (Mlinar), studies of nationalism and globalization (Rizman), and Europeanisation, although initially only to a lesser extent (overview in Adam & Makarovič, 2002, p. 541).

With the process of democratization and modernization, Slovenia went through significant structural changes, which tremendously transformed semiotic order, undermining old discourses and consolidating new semantic versions. As represented above, sociologists did play a certain role in the retention, proliferation, and reinforcement of such semiotic order. However, structural changes also enabled the retention and reinforcement of certain old dominant discourses, and the role of sociologists in that regard might be less straightforward.

When analyzing Slovenian national imaginary, one can observe that some discursive mechanisms remained salient, and the nostalgic discourse of the "good old" (communist) times, emphasizing equality and security, has remained significant. One of the discursive sediments of the communist period can be found in the structural formation within the communist political system referring to the form of the so-called worker's self-management, which was characterized by some "liberal" ideas inspired more by Gramscian ideology, which enabled new variation of discourses (Makarovič, 2001). The political system was hindering the selection and retention of those semantic meanings until its end in the early 1990s. Nevertheless, this trend significantly influenced discursive practices in the years when the state was gaining independence and also when negotiating to join the European Union. It integrated into the image, emphasizing Slovenia's leading role among new members of the EU in 2004, as the state was the first postcommunist country to adopt the euro and preside over the Council of the EU.

Another remnant of the communist regime can be found in ideas of state protectionism and the ideology of national interests, which have continued to exist in the new systemic conditions (Bandelj, 2004; Adam & Tomšič, 2012). The old communist structural order was characterized by the explicit patronage of the state ensuing from the dominance of the political subsystem over the other. The state, as a structural and semantic reflection of the system, took responsibility for most aspects of citizens' lives. The latter is still partly present nowadays in terms of memories and discourses transmitting those expectations to the present political order. The nostalgia for secure and favorable living conditions is strongly related to dissatisfaction with political leaders and distrust in political institutions, which has been reactualized with the economic crisis in 2008 when Slovenia experienced severe difficulties in public finances and negative economic trends. As Makarovič (2001) argues, paternalistic understandings of a state and criticism toward politics are strongly interrelated and also firmly maintained through mass media. The higher the expectations from the state in terms of taking care of its citizens, the stronger disappointments with the actual political situation and politicians are. What seems to be even more important is that mild critical stances toward politicians existed even in the communist times due to a softer version of the regime and have been reinterpreted and reaffirmed through new discourses. Semantic versions referring to strong expectations from the state, blaming its leaders for not fulfilling them and believing that nothing can be done anyway, pertain to a certain lack of civic culture, quite typical for postcommunist societies (Sztompka, 1991 in Makarovič, 1996).

Slovenian national imaginary is also signified by an ideological division of two political camps. The discourse of the political "left" draws more on the positive image of the communist past and encourages nostalgia in this regard, while the political "right" tends to see the source of the key Slovenian problems in the insufficient break with the former communist regime. This bipolar division into two political blocs refers to the positions of the two camps in the past, claiming different historical memories. As Adam et al. (2009) argue, their ideological cleavage has heavily marked the political space and also divided Slovenians on the "left" or "right" side of the national story. The latter reveals competing myths, which, in diametrically opposed relationships, deal with the interpretation of communism, the role of the Roman Catholic Church in society, the national liberation struggle, and other events that happened after World War II. Historical memories have thus not yet become consensual, and different interpretations of the national past are still part of political and media discourses. The retention of certain semantics has occurred on the basis of the construction and reinterpretation of the past.

When attempting to elucidate the role of sociology in preserving certain discourses and semantic variations from the past, one cannot avoid the fact that sociology has often been plagued by ideologization. It has been argued (Adam &

Makarovič, 2001, p. 383) that topics such as the reproduction and circulations of elites, the level of democratic development of Slovenian society, and the public role of the Roman Catholic Church often led to different or even opposing sociological interpretations. Similarly, sociologists also represented political stances, such as skepticism toward or opposition to Euro-Atlantic integration, in a way that gave the impression that personal opinions are sociological facts (Adam & Makarovič, 2002, p. 542). "The reasons for this could at least partly be sought in (sometimes latent) world views of researchers, as well as in the lack of an open and tolerant debate through an exchange of views within the social science community" (Adam & Makarovič, 2001, p. 383). Due to the lack of public discussion in the academic sphere, sociologists were often participating in the ideological bind over the cultural struggle. Moreover, as Adam and Makarovič (2002) stated:

> The vast majority of sociologists who take part in such public disputes hold worldviews that reflect a single political faction (which considers itself leftist-liberal) and mostly overlaps with the ruling political parties), so actions by politicians of this faction may be legitimized by being implicitly perceived as based on scientific arguments. (p. 542)

On the one hand, sociology as a social science discipline is on the edge of public interest, but on the other, many sociologists opt for political careers. According to Adam (2015):

> The politicization of social science has reached to an enormous scale […] At the juncture of science and institutions, we are dealing with ideology, based on the impetuous introduction of valuation, and the advocacy of simplified solutions to social problems. […] From quite a lot of debates it follows that capitalism and neoliberalism can be blamed for everything. (p. 89)

Sociology has often been far from value-neutral, scientifically based judgement. While choosing or privileging certain research topics, sociologists have thus been playing a certain role in constructing national imaginary, thus contributing to the selection and retention of discourses.

21.3 Methodology

21.3.1 Search Strategy and Inclusion Criteria

The Cobiss online database was searched for articles published in both selected Slovenian social science scientific journals. In the Slovenian national library system, Cobiss includes all published materials, including scientific journals. Therefore, it includes all published entries in both journals since they started to go public. *Teorija and Praksa* started publishing in 1956, and *Družboslovne razprave* started in 1984. Since the search was initiated by searching all published entries, no initial search keywords were used. We were able to detect a total of 6772 entries published in *Teorija in Praksa* (including editorials, original science articles, reviews, articles, and book reviews) and 1157 published entries (including editorials, original science articles, reviews, articles, and book reviews) in *Družboslovne razprave*.

The following criteria for scanning were further elaborated as follows. First, we selected specific years to be subjected to analysis in the time span between 1987 and 2007. The former was carefully selected as it is known as the year when Issue 57 of *Nova Revija* was published; this issue is considered the cornerstone of the Slovenian demand for democracy. Second, we scanned the articles by specific keywords, assigned to each of the articles by the Cobiss library system (those keywords are "social sciences," "social processes and social dynamics," "sociology," "social groups and social organizations," "society as social structure," and "sociology of culture and sociology of communication"). The two tables below demonstrate the number of articles in individual years as included in the research. The keywords above are attached to articles and preselected by the author when the articles were included in the Cobiss system.

The number of articles containing the outlined keywords was selected for further analysis. At this stage, the sample of articles ready for further analysis is comprised of 287 articles from *Teorija in Praksa* and 79 articles from *Družboslovne razprave*.

After narrowing down the number of analyzed articles, we proceeded with qualitative coding of articles according to predefined additional codes obtained from the Cobiss system. We have checked the specific codes assigned to each of the articles and, where possible, counterchecked with available abstracts from the articles. No limitations to codes were applied this time in order to enable us to obtain more profound insight into the more detailed content of each article.

The coding was prepared in two stages, with the first codes assigned, and in the second stage, broader codes as "categories" were assigned. Categories were analyzed and are presented in the model below. The model offers a tentative solution to the categories Slovenian sociologists were dealing with between the years 1987 and 2017.

21.4 Results

In the time span from 1987 to 2017, several clusters of topics covered by Slovenian sociologists were recognized. These topics vary from the topics of *civil society*, *democracy*, and *state*, predominating in 1987, to topics of *modernization, family*, and *social mobility*, predominating in 1989. The topic of modernization continued to be discussed in 1990, as did the topic of *family* and *in-/equality* (connected to the topic of *social mobility* from the previous year (Fig. 21.1).

Within the new topics, in 1990, *nationalism, socialist society*, and *individualization* emerged in connection with *modernization*). Among new topics in the same year, *welfare state* in connection to *gerontology* appeared along with the topic of *free time*. The year 1992 is again very rich, with the majority connected to topics discussed in previous years (*post-socialism, welfare state, free time*, connected to *lifestyle* and *in-/equality*). As a new topic, *sociological theory* (with the subtopic of

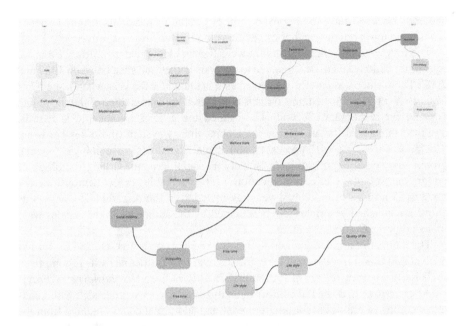

Fig. 21.1 Topics by publication date from two main Slovenian social science journals

postmodernism) emerges. In 1997, the topic of *sociological theory* discussed *postmodernism* and *feminism*; the topic *welfare state* connected *social exclusion* and *in-/equality*. We observe the return of the topic of *gerontology*. The topic of *lifestyle* remains and connects to the previous period. The topic of *quality of life*, as evolved from the topic of *lifestyle* in 1997, continues to be present in 2007, only that it mentions the subtopic of *family*.[1] Additionally, the topic of *in-/equality* connected to the topic of *social exclusion* from 1997 is discussing topics of *social capital* and *civil society*. In this way, we can see the revival of the topic of *civil society* from 1987. In 2007, the topic of *feminism* remains and continues to 2017. In 2017, the topic is upgraded with the subtopic *film theory*. The topic of post-socialism surfaces in 2017 loosely to its emergence in 1992.

In the 7 years surrounding Slovene independence, we are presenting the trends in published topics of two Slovenian social science peer-reviewed journals. We are able to observe the dynamic with fewer sociological topics discussed in the years 1987–1989. In the years marking the most turbulent times of Slovenian history (i.e., the years around independence claims[2]), we can also observe the most vivid scope of discussed topics in both journals. The topics vary, and yet they crystallize in specific threads that also continue to be present in publication activities of sociologies

---

[1] The topic of family was present in publications already in periods 1988 and 1989.
[2] From 1987 with 57th issue of *Nova revija* through 1989 of "May declaration," through the 1990s independence referendum to 1991 proclamation of independence.

in the years to come. The most persistent topics are *social in-/equality*, *lifestyles*, and *feminism* and topics surrounding the questions of *welfare state*.

21.5 Discussion and Conclusion

The main goal of the presented paper was to elaborate and elucidate the role of Slovenian sociology and sociologists in the post-socialist transformations through the prism of cultural political economy. Being able to target the role of sociologists in a period of post-socialist transitions, we focused on the period of second half of the 1980s, more specifically the years following 1987. We considered 1987 to be the cutoff year since this was when the 57th issue of *Nova revija* was published, in which the first claims for Slovenian independence were clearly elaborated. It was in the early 1990s, after the declared independence in 1991, that major structural and semantic changes occurred. However, regardless of the transformations occurring and new narratives emerging along with new discourses and styles, some path dependency with the former structural setting pertained. According to Jessop (2004), such a course is inevitable since, even if new discourses can become privileged in the new era of major transformations, some discourses remain ingrained in individuals and collective routines and identities.

To be able to comprehend the dynamics and transitions of Slovenian sociology, we obtained two paths: the first one is in reviewing the data and information on the role of Slovenian sociology and sociologists in social transformations previously collected by researchers. The review started with the first years of the twentieth century when Slovenian sociology started to develop. The second interesting point was the period of communism and then the period we are most interested in: that of post-socialist transformations. While reviewing secondary data, we also paid attention to the collected interviews and personal opinions by the Slovenian sociologists (in Mlinar, 2016). The empirical part of the chapter evolves around the qualitative analysis of journal articles published in two Slovenian social science journals. The span of 30 years was taken in for analysis with slightly more emphasis on the period between 1987 and 1992. Using the Slovenian online library system Cobiss and applying a method of two-stage coding, we were able to secure 445 scientific journal articles for further analysis. A paradigm map was elaborated, visualizing the dispersion and interlinkages between discussed topics. The dynamics visual from the paradigm map outlines a rich set of topics discussed, with the period being the richest in a number of topics debated in the period 1990–1992. After that, the number of discussed topics decreased, and a question emerged regarding how much both journals are even relevant source to publish by Slovenian sociologists. Namely, both journals were published in the Slovenian language, and with increasing demands for international publications, both *Teorija in praksa* and *Družboslovne razprave* are decreasing the numbers of articles per issue (see Tables 21.1 and 21.2), demonstrating the situation in which the lower number of articles published automatically decreases the number of topics discussed. Nevertheless, the most persistent topics

Table 21.1 *Teorija in Praksa* (Theory and Practice) review of issues covered by topics

Year	Total number of entries	Topics covered						Row Total
		Social sciences	Social processes and social dynamics	Sociology	Social groups, social organizations	Society as a social structure	Sociology of culture and sociology of communication	
1987	247	48	10	–	–	–	–	58
1989	250	18	–	17	13	–	–	48
1990	270	77	7	12	–	7	–	103
1992	205	30	–	11	–	–	4	45
1997	100	6	–	9	4	–	–	19
2007	71	–	5	2	7	–	–	14
2017	52	–	–	–	–	–	–	0
Column Total	1195	179	22	51	24	7	4	287

Table 21.2 *Družboslovne razprave* (Sociological discussions) review of issues covered by topics

Year	Total number of entries	Topics covered						Row Total
		Subsystem and institutions	Social processes and social dynamics	Sociology and directions in sociology	Sociology of culture, sociology of communication	Social structure, society as a social system	Political science	
1987	25	–	–	7	–	6	15	21
1989	43	5	3	5	–	6	–	13
1990	41	–	1	7	–	5	–	18
1992	30	–	2	1	1	–	2	10
1997	13	–	1	–	6	–	–	4
2007	18	–	–	–	3	2	1	10
2017	11	–	–	–	–	–	–	4
Column Total	181	5	8	20	10	19	18	79

in published articles demonstrate that the main topics are *social in-/equality, lifestyles*, and *feminism* and topics surrounding the questions of *welfare state*.

Based on this and turning back to Borut Rončević (Chap. 1), we noted a peculiar dynamic of Slovenian sociology. It was in the transition period with strong institutional support and numerous interventions by Slovenian sociologists. The topics they were researching and publishing about prove their active role in setting the shape of transformation. A strong Slovenian sociological community served as activists with good connections to other professional communities (especially political). However, as noted from the research work, in 2006, another group of sociologists emerged and started gaining prominence in public discourse, but their role remains somewhere between the marginals and voyeurs due to modest funding and weaker institutional support.

Sociology in Slovenia is a fruit of a specific synthesis of scholarly influences from the West corresponding to specific structural and semantic settings of Central and Eastern Europe emerging since the Middle Ages (Keen & Mucha, 2003) and also of the peculiarities of the local situation, which became apparent especially after the social and political cleavages in the early 1990s. In order to comprehend the complex contribution of the sociologist in shaping predominant discourses, further research is needed.

Competing Interests The authors have no conflicts of interest to declare that are relevant to the content of this chapter.

References

Adam, F. (2015). Sociologija med ideologijo in kvantofrenijo. In Z. Mlinar (Ed.), *Kakšna sociologija? Za kakšno družbo?* (pp. 86–90). Fakulteta za družbene vede in SAZU.

Adam, F., & Makarovič, M. (2001). Society in transition as reflected by social sciences: The case of Slovenia. In N. Genov & U. Becker (Eds.), *Social sciences in Southeastern Europe* (pp. 192–222). ISSC and IZ.

Adam, F., & Makarovič, M. (2002). Sociology—Slovenia. In M. Kaase, V. Sparschuh, & A. Wenninger (Eds.), *Three social science disciplines in Central and Eastern Europe* (pp. 536–547). GESIS Social Science Information Centre.

Adam, F., & Rončević, B. (2001). Dialogue of social scientists and public administration in Slovenia. In N. Genov & U. Becker (Eds.), *Social sciences in Southeastern Europe* (pp. 124–133). ISSC and IZ.

Adam, F., & Tomšič, M. (2012). The dynamics of elites and the type of capitalism: Slovenian exceptionalism? *Historical Social Research, 37*, 2.

Adam, F., Makarovič, M., Rončević, B., & Tomšič, M. (2005). *The challenges of sustained development: The role of socio-cultural factors in East-Central Europe*. Central European University Press.

Adam, F., Kristan, P., & Tomšič, M. (2009). Varieties of capitalism in Eastern Europe (with a special emphasis on Estonia and Slovenia). *Communist and Post-Communist Studies, 42*, 1.

Aghion, P., & Blanchard, O. J. (1994). On the speed of transition in Central Europe. In S. Fischer & J. Rotemberg (Eds.), *NBER macroeconomics annual* (pp. 283–320). MIT Press.

Andolšek, S. (2016). Naoge sociologije in družbene spremembe v Sloveniji. In Z. Mlinar (Ed.), *V: Prispevki in izzivi sociologije na slovenskem1. Kakšna sociologija? Za kakšno družbo* (pp. 91–95). Fakulteta za družbene vede in SAZU.

Balcerowitz, L. (1995). *Socialism, capitalism, transformation.* Central European University.

Bandelj, N. (2004). Negotiating global, regional, and national forces: Foreign investment in Slovenia. *European Politics & Societies, 18*(3), 455–480.

Bernik, I., & Rončević, B. (2001). Slowenien: Eine differenzierte Rezeption der differenzierten Theorie. *Družboslovne razprave, 17*(37–38), 15–27.

Čas, B. (1996). Prispevek k zgodovini sociologije na Slovenskem [A contribution to the history of sociology in Slovenia]. In A. Leönik et al. (Eds.), *Kriza socialnih idej* (pp. 459–474). Filozofska fakulteta.

Feldmann, M. (2006). Emerging varieties of capitalism in transition countries: Industrial relations and wage bargaining in Estonia and Slovenia. *Comparative Political Studies, 39*, 7.

Golob, T. (2013). Political rituals and nation building: Exploring the Slovenian statehood day. *Raziskave in razprave, 6*(1), 42–63.

Hribar, S. (2016). Rdeči lemenat? In Z. Mlinar (Ed.), *V: Prispevki in izzivi sociologije na slovenskem1. Kakšna sociologija? Za kakšno družbo?* (pp. 102–105). Fakulteta za družbene vede and SAZU.

Izyumov, A., & Claxon, T. (2009). Models of capitalism and income distribution in transition economies: A comparative perspective. *Journal of Economic Issues, 43*(3), 733–758.

Jessop, B. (2004). Critical semiotic analysis and cultural political economy. *Critical Discourse Studies, 1*(2), 159–174.

Jessop, B., & Oosterlynck, S. (2008). Cultural political economy: On making the cultural turn without falling into soft economic sociology. *Geoforum, 39*(3), 1155–1170.

Jogan, M. (1994). Modern Slovenian sociology. In M. Keen & J. Mucha (Eds.), *Eastern Europe in transformation* (pp. 125–130). Greenwood.

Jogan, M. (1995). Sociologija na Slovenskem: Od konca 19. Do konca 20. Stoletja [Sociology in Slovenia: From the end of the 19th till the end of the 20th century]. In A. Kramberger & Z. Kolarič (Eds.), *V: Zbornik ob 30 letnici slovenskega socioloökega druötva* (pp. 51–58). Slovensko sociološko društvo.

Keen, F., & Mucha, J. (Eds.). (2003). *Sociology in central and Eastern Europe: Transformation at the dawn of a new millennium (Contributions in sociology).* Praeger.

Kerševan, M. (1995). Slovenska sociologija med socialnim okoljem in znanstveno skupnostjo [Slovene sociology between the social environment and the scientific community]. In A. Kramberger & Z. Kolarič (Eds.), *V: Zbornik ob 30 letnici slovenskega sociološkega društva* (pp. 41–50). Slovensko sociološko druötvo.

Le Goff, J. (1992). *History and memory.* Columbia University Press.

Lipton, D., & Sachs, J. (1990). Creating a market economy in Eastern Europe: The case of Poland. *Brookings Papers on Economic Activity, 1990*(1), 75–147.

Makarovič, M. (1996). Neokorporativizem v sistemski perspektivi in njegova vloga v postsocialistični modernizaciji. *Družboslovne razprave, 21*(12), 125–138.

Makarovič, J. (2016). Za angažiranost, globalnost in slovenstvo. Osebni pogled na dozdajšnje uveljavljanje sociologije v Sloveniji. In Z. Mlinar (Ed.), *V: Prispevki in izzivi sociologije na slovenskem1. Kakšna sociologija? Za kakšno družbo?* (pp. 81–85). Fakulteta za družbene vede in SAZU.

Mali, F. (2000). Obstacles in developing university, government and industry links: The case of Slovenia. *Science Studies, 13*(1), 31–49.

Makarovič, M. (2001). Some problems in Luhmann's social systems theory: Differentiation, integration, and planning. *Družboslovne razprave, 17*(37–38), 59–70.

Mastnak, T. (1996). Mit Evrope in religija demokracije (The Myth of Europe and Religion of Democracy). *Družboslovne razprave, 12*(21), 11–19.

Mencinger, J. (2004). Transition to a national and a market economy: A gradualist approach. In M. Mrak, M. Rojec, & C. Silva-Jáuregui (Eds.), *Slovenia from Yugoslavia to the European Union*. The World Bank.

Mlinar, Z. (2016). *Prispevki in izzivi sociologije na slovenskem1. Kakšna sociologija? Za kakšno družbo?* Fakulteta za družbene vede in SAZU.

Mucha, J. (n.d.). *Undated Sociology in Eastern Europe or East European Sociology: Historical and Present*. Retrieved from http://www.ios.sinica.edu.tw/cna/download/proceedings/45.Mucha.Poland.pdf

Myant, M., & Drahokoupil, J. (2012). International integration, varieties of capitalism and resilience to crisis in transition economies. *Europe-Asia Studies, 64*, 1.

Podmenik, D. (2016). Samostojna raziskovalka o uporabnem sociološkem raziskovanju. In Z. Mlinar (Ed.), *V: Prispevki in izzivi sociologije na slovenskem1. Kakšna sociologija? Za kakšno družbo?* (pp. 277–279). Fakulteta za družbene vede in SAZU.

Roland, G. (2000). *Transition and economics: Politics, markets and firms*. MIT Press.

Stanojević, M. (Ed.) (2001). *Uspešna nedozorelost* [Successful immaturity]. Fakulteta za družbene vede.

Stiglitz, J. E. (2002). *Globalization and its discontents*. W.W. Norton.

Velikonja, M. (1996). *Masade duha: Razpotja sodobnih mitologij*. Znanstveno in publicistično središče.

Vičič, V. (Ed.). (1989). *Stanje, vloga in razvojne perspektive družbenih znanosti na Slovenskem* [The condition, role, and developmental perspectives of social sciences in Slovenia]. Marksistični center.

Dr. Tea Golob is Associate Professor in Sociology and the Head of the Institute for Social Morphogenesis at the Faculty of Information Studies, Slovenia. She is a member of the Slovenian National MOST Committee/UNESCO. She has been a leader of various national and European projects, such as the Jean Monnet Module and the scientific project funded by the Slovenian Research Agency. Her research work is related to the issues of digitalization, communities, sustainability, responsibility, transnational challenges, and globalization.

Dr. Tamara Besednjak Valič is a Senior Scientific Associate at the Rudolfovo Science and Technology Centre Novo Mesto and Assistant Professor of Sociology at the Faculty of Information Studies. She is Vice-Dean of Research at the School of Advanced Social Studies (Slovenia). She is particularly interested in topics of steering social systems, including but not limited to innovation ecosystems. She additionally focuses on the role of the entrepreneurial and creative spirit within such ecosystems. Apart from that, research interests include social narratives and their role in social systems' steering.

Chapter 22
The Power of Ukrainian Sociology in Post-USSR Transformations and Russia's War in Ukraine

Olga Kutsenko and Svitlana Babenko

22.1 Introduction

Ukrainian sociology has traveled a long road in its institutionalization, self-identification, formation of ethics, development of research programs, and methodological culture, as well as its recognition by society from the second half of the nineteenth to the twenty-first century. Many features, reasons, and effects of this pathway are rooted in and have arisen from the changing political and economic historical contexts as well as the intellectual and social legacy of sociology, which defined its development essentially as a science and profession, including its impact on post-USSR societal transformations and resistance to Russia's war against Ukraine.

What is the power of Ukrainian sociology in post-USSR societal transformations and Russia's war in Ukraine? How does sociology contribute in response to the challenges which pose threats to national independence, democracy in society, and the development of sociology?

In our theoretical approach to analyzing the role of sociology as a science and profession with an active social position, we primarily rely on the ideas of Michel

---

O. Kutsenko (✉)
Berlin Technical University, Berlin, Germany

Taras Shevchenko National University of Kyiv, Kyiv, Ukraine

S. Babenko
Department of Global Political Studies (GPS), Malmö Institute for Studies of Migration, Diversity and Welfare (MIM), Malmö University, Malmö, Sweden

© The Author(s), under exclusive license to Springer Nature Switzerland AG 2024
B. Roncevic, T. Besednjak Valič (eds.), *Sociology and Post-Socialist Transformations in Eastern Europe*,
https://doi.org/10.1007/978-3-031-65556-2_22

Foucault (1972, 1982) about the relationship between power and knowledge[1] as well as Pierre Bourdieu's later works (1984, 1994, 2003) raising the issue of whether the sociologist has political responsibilities extending to the public domain.[2] We also rely on the positivist-constructivist understanding of the role of sociology, embodied in the professional activities, publications, and research practices of Elena Yakuba (1996), Irina Popova (1996), and Tatiana Zaslavskaya (2007). They share a recognition of the social responsibility of sociology in producing empirically grounded knowledge that reveals the profound structural-cultural-activity mechanisms of society's functioning and transformation, as well as shaping discourses that enhance individual agency and the effectiveness of power functioning in society (Kutsenko, 2008).

We use the concept of the *power of sociology as a science and profession* in a threefold sense, revealing the fundamental dimensions of sociology's interaction with society, namely,

1. *The power of science* as an institutional design and the capacity of sociology to produce comprehensive scientific knowledge. Knowledge production is about what and how to research to identify society's development under historical conditions and to disenchant the strength and weakness of society's response to challenges of multiple conflicts, colonization, and authoritarianism threatening individual and national freedom and civilizational development. These are also the questions about the research focus, conceptual lens, methodology validity, data reliability, professional ethics, and the efficacy of organizational structure of the knowledge production.
2. *The power of discourse* related to discourse formation around core ideas, knowledge transfer, and dissemination, developing sociological discourses via sociological vocabulary, narratives, and imaginaries, which describe, conceptualize, and interpret social phenomena, as well as criticize, construct, and legitimize people's experience of the world. It creates discursive social networks in modes of knowledge dissemination and publicity, including interaction with the media.
3. *The power of doing* reflects the practical utility and social responsibility of sociology in informing and empowering public policy and authorities, businesses, civil society, and communities in their efforts to resolve problems in response to

---

[1] Foucault's ideas allow revealing the power of science through its deep mechanisms. According to M. Foucault, epistemic and discursive frameworks govern its formation in a given historical period. Scientific knowledge produces and is shaped by the epistemic frameworks which contribute to the formation of discourses. These discourses reinforce power relations, enabling institutions and authorities to observe and regulate individuals and public more effectively. At the same time, this knowledge also contributes to the formation of subjectivities via internalizing scientific discourses, adopting certain norms and practices as part of individual's self-identity, which further reinforces society's resilience (Foucault, 1972, 1982; Fader, 2011).

[2] According to Bourdieu (1984, 1994, 2003), the sociologist must engage in a "sociology of sociology" so as not to unwittingly attribute to the object of observation the characteristics of the subject. They ought to conduct their research with one eye continually reflecting back upon their own habitus, their dispositions learned through long social and institutional training.

existential challenges. This is about the independence and responsibility of sociology about public authority and civil society.

The given theoretical lens is used in our research. To substantiate our main research thesis on the active role of Ukrainian sociology, we will first provide a brief characteristic of the long-term discursive structures that emerged during the development of Ukrainian sociology in the nineteenth and twentieth centuries, enabling power of discourse rooted in the national history of sociology and serving as the intellectual pillars for the proactive position of contemporary Ukrainian sociology. We will then outline the current institutional state of sociology as a science and profession. Drawing on data analysis, we will present arguments for the discussion on sociology's power of doing or the influence of Ukrainian sociology on post-USSR transformations, as well as on democracy development, the national-civil identity, the debunking of political-ideological myths, and the resilience of the state and society in resisting Russia's war in Ukraine in recent years.

22.2 Ukrainian Sociology: Building the Power of Science

The studies on intellectual roots and institutionalization trends of Ukrainian sociology attract intense scholarly attention; many studies have already been done recently (Bakirov & Sokurianska, 2020; Bataeva et al., 2018; Stepanenko & Rybschun, 2009; Tancher & Stepanenko, 2004; Reznik & Reznik, 2006), which is a significant aspect of the process of institutionalization of modern Ukrainian sociology and its empowerment within societal transformations. This process involves the theoretical self-reflexivity of Ukrainian sociology in search of its historical roots and identity.

Ukrainian sociology developed its own foundations as a science and academic discipline within the context of emerging European sociology framed with intellectual debates of that time. Ukrainian sociology has its roots in the social philosophical discourses of the nineteenth century, inspired by the ideas of the Enlightenment mainstream concerning natural human rights, the formation of social order, the development of a nation-state, and methods for improving individuals, society, and government. From that time onward, Ukrainian social scientists engaged in critiquing the imperfect social order, political dependence on the Russian as well as Austro-Hungarian Empires against Polish influence, and the system's restrictions on the development of Ukrainian ethnic culture and self-consciousness. Ukrainian sociological discourses and practices have been historically closely connected with the national liberation movement, civil and political activism, nation-building efforts, self-governing community, national identity, and human rights. The sociological contributions of Drahomanov (1868), Kistiakowski (1899), Hrushevsky (1921), and Shapoval (1934) are especially iconic in this concern. The historical engagement with these themes has defined the leitmotif of modern development in Ukrainian sociology.

Having passed through a long and wavelike path of institutionalization, starting from significant achievements in the threshold of the nineteenth and twentieth centuries, setbacks during the Stalinist period, and a revival within the USSR style since the early 1960s, Ukrainian sociology entered a new stage of its institutional development utilizing advantages and responding to the challenges of the new post-USSR reality. The historical analysis of the institutional development of Ukrainian sociology is well represented in the following publications: Bakirov and Sokurianska (2020), Stepanenko and Rybschun (2009), Tancher and Stepanenko (2005), and Reznik and Reznik (2006). With the declaration of the state independence of Ukraine in 1991 and the following post-USSR transformation, sociology in Ukraine has successfully developed a comprehensive professional community, multilevel institutional structure, as well as the principles and rules of doing research, sociological education, and interaction with the public authority, society, and media.

The institutional structure of Ukrainian sociology has actively formed both in academic and applied public and private sectors. The status of Ukrainian sociology today is defined by the professional activity of the powerful, well-developed institutional network that has evolved over the last 30 years under an "umbrella" of the Sociological Association of Ukraine and revolved around two main pillars. The first pillar is the academic sociology which is predominantly represented by the activities both of institutions within the National Academy of Sciences of Ukraine[3] and sociological departments in 27 Ukrainian universities (faculties, chairs, laboratories, research centers, and project groups). The second one is the applied sociology operating mostly both business and in a sector of nongovernmental organizations (numerous sociological, polling and marketing companies, analytical foundations, project groups, etc.). These two pillars form the foundation for the current state of Ukrainian sociology, fostering a dynamic and diverse field that spans both academic and practical applications.

The institutional design of Ukrainian sociology as a science and professional field defines its agency in the societal transformation from 1990 onward. Several outcomes of its professional development significantly shaped the modern scope of Ukrainian sociology and its institutional power, among which are the following:

1. *Establishment of the Sociological Association of Ukraine (SAU) and empowerment of the professional community.* The SAU was founded in 1990 based on the Ukrainian branch of the Soviet Sociological Association, which was quite autonomous, multicomponent, and actively functioned from 1968 to 1990. Currently, SAU unites 21 regional branches, more than 1300 individuals, and 25 collective members (Sociological Association of Ukraine, 2023). Aimed at approving the professional standards in sociologists' community and institutional mechanisms

---

[3] There are three institutes within the Ukraine's National Academy of Sciences: the specialized Institute of Sociology (currently directed by Eugen Golovakha replacing the long-term directorship by V. Vorona); Institute of Demography and Social Policy (directed by Ella Libanova); and Department of Monitoring Based Research on Socio-Economic Transformations at the Institute for Economics and Forecasting (until recently headed by Olga Balakireva).

for their social control, the Code of Professional Ethics of a Sociologist was developed by Natalia Panina with the Commission on Professional Ethics of SAU and adopted in 2004 (Panina, 2004). Since then, compliance with the Charter's and the Code's norms has been mandatory for membership in the Sociological Association of Ukraine. As a vital component of professional sociological culture, a study of these norms is included in all Ukrainian university's sociology curricula.

In order to defend sociology against reputational losses and information-psychological aggression from unprofessional "ratings salesmen" and pseudo-sociologists falsifying sociological information,[4] SAU provides accreditation for polling and research sociological organizations that meet professional standards and have a high professional reputation. The list of professional, trustworthy sociological survey organizations is published on the SAU website and, to date, includes 14 accredited organizations.

SAU publishes two leading academic journals: *Sociology: Theory, Methods, Marketing* (published by the Institute of Sociology at the National Academy of Sciences of Ukraine since 1998[5]) and *Ukrainian Sociological Journal* (published by the V. Karazin Kharkiv National University since 2008[6]). They serve as open-access platforms for presenting and discussing theoretical and empirical research and pressing issues in academic life. The most theoretically and empirically interesting findings from recent research conducted by Ukrainian sociologists, mapping the trends in post-USSR societal transformations in their political, economic, social, and cultural manifestations in contemporary Ukraine, are published in English in the SAU's collective monograph (Bakirov & Golovakha, 2018).

With the onset of Russia's full-scale war against Ukraine in 2022, mass forced migration within and outside the country, constant Russian missile and artillery attacks, direct threats to life with the destruction of university buildings (e.g., in Kharkiv, Mykolaiv, Mariupol, Zaporizhzhia, Sumy), and other essential infrastructure for work and life, the role of SAU in uniting and morally supporting the Ukrainian sociologists has become substantially more significant. The SAU has played a notable role in the collective adaptation of sociologists to the extreme living and working conditions, organizing aid and different support to sociologists, their families, and students who had fled from the war (in particular, the SAU's regional branches in Uzhhorod, Chernivtsi, Lviv, Ternopil). Despite wartime, SAU managed to organize several online conferences and roundtable discussions to explore the societal impacts of the war and prospects for postwar development. Being accompanied by sounds of air raid sirens and explosions, these forums

---

[4] The initiative company of sociologists "TEXTY.ORG.UA" founded in 2015 for fighting against organizations that have been identified in the publication of dubious surveys or engaged in covert political PR counted more than 300 organizations in Ukraine, which over the past 25 years published dubious research results under sociological "umbrella" (Texty.org.ua., 2021).

[5] http://en.stmm.in.ua/

[6] https://periodicals.karazin.ua/usocjour/about

became significant unifying events for the Ukrainian sociologists regardless of their location, which empowered their morale and solidarity.

2. *Establishment of the Institute of Sociology at the National Academy of Sciences of Ukraine* (IS NASU) and *empowerment of methodological culture.* IS NASU was established in 1990, but it was not the first in the history of Ukrainian sociology. Its forerunner was the Ukrainian Sociological Institute formed by Mykhailo Hrushevsky in Vienna in 1919, in emigration. Later, another Ukrainian scientist, Mykyta Shapoval, founded the Ukrainian Institute of Citizenship in Prague in 1924. During the Stalin Soviet regime, Hrushevsky's efforts to relocate Ukrainian sociological institutes from abroad to Kyiv were unsuccessful. However, despite the gap in time, these academic institutions are permeated by a common genetic interest in Ukrainian society; its structural, cultural, and agency grounds; and the production of the corresponding empirically and theoretically well-grounded knowledge.

The IS NASU has become a scientific, intellectual, and methodological center for current sociology in Ukraine, developing high-quality research and methodological culture, producing well-grounded sociological knowledge, and providing a platform for discussions and exchanging sociological expertise. In order to empirically ground the understanding, description, and explanation of Ukrainian society's undergoing transformations, the large-scale annual project of sociological monitoring "Ukrainian Society" was launched in 1992 on the theoretical and methodological basis developed by Panina, Golovakha, and Churylov (Panina, 2005). It has provided a systemic sociological assessment of the reform's policy efficacy and its social impact on Ukrainian society. The monitoring data analysis has resulted in weighty scientific advances in the study of transformation trends; social structure and inequalities; public opinion performance; values and attitudes; social well-being; cultural, ethnic, economic, and political processes; and similar.

Meanwhile, the most significant outcome of the monitoring is the development of a comprehensive methodological and methodical approach to the study of a society undergoing transformation. This approach is based on using a quasi-experimental method within the systemic long-scale monitoring survey on national and regional large samples and applying a cross-cultural analysis of different social groups of Ukrainian society. The institute's scientists have developed unique scales and composite indices to effectively capture social phenomena and the transformative dynamics of Ukrainian society using mass surveys. A collective monograph (Golovakha & Dembitskyi, 2022) summarizes original sociological measurement tools refined and adapted over three decades of monitoring post-USSR transformations. Among these complex tools, there are the Integral Index of Social Well-being (Golovakha, Panina), the Index of Social Tension (Golovakha, Panina, Gorbachyk), the Index of State Subjectivity (Golovakha, Dembitsky), etc.

The annual publication of a collective monograph on the sociological monitoring data since the mid-1990s provides a register for expert analytics on post-USSR transformation. The 2021 issue provides an analytical reflection on changes in Ukrainian society during the 30 years of the state's independence (Vorona & Shulga,

2021). By the end of 2022, the Institute's team presented a collective monograph (Golovakha & Makeev, 2022) analyzing the impact of Russia's war against Ukraine on cohesion, identity, social attitudes, social structure, and activism in Ukrainian society.

3. *Development of private and NGO sectors of sociological research, expertise, and polling* as the market of sociological knowledge production and dissemination. With the attainment of Ukraine's state independence and the strengthening of democratization and marketization processes, the public demand for political, social, and marketing research has increased. The rapid spreading of the nongovernmental sector in polling, research, and expertise has been a response to the growing needs primarily from politicians, businesses, international organizations (such as the World Bank, UNDP, embassies of some countries, etc.), as well as local authorities of some Ukrainian regions and cities. Many nongovernmental sociological and polling institutions have become primary recipients of grants from international and business donors to conduct monitoring, longitudinal, or one-time research. As researchers (Shulga, 2000; Reznik & Reznik, 2006) note, the professional activities of these institutions, their social responsibility, and civic engagement influenced essentially the further post-USSR transformation of Ukraine, its democratization and nation-building, as well as the development of Ukrainian sociology.

Unlike other former Soviet republics, by the time Ukraine gained state independence, there were already several professional sociological institutions with their own national networks conducting large-scale representative sociological surveys and presenting data in mass media. These are the Central Ukrainian Branch of VCIOM (Churylov, Panina), the Sociological Service Center at Verkhovna Rada (the Parliament) of Ukraine (Khmelko, Ossovskyi), and Kyiv Republic Research Sociological Centre affiliated at the SAU (Khmelko, Paniotto). The last one was transformed in 1992 into the first private sociological enterprise, Kyiv International Institute of Sociology (KIIS), cofounded by Ukrainian sociologists Khmelko and Paniotto and American sociologist Swafford. For more than 30 years, the KIIS has occupied a leading position in the market of sociological services in Ukraine (Kyiv International Institute of Sociology, 2023a).

Being a private enterprise, KIIS donates a considerable part of its income to finance academic social research projects, including academic research works of sociology professors and students at the National University "Kyiv-Mohila Academy." For many years, KIIS has been conducting four omnibus surveys per year as regular multipurpose polling of the population by request of a few clients with different goals who finance the poll together. It supports open research data banks, provides financial support to academic journals on sociology, and publishes academic books at its own expense. Since 1992, the Kyiv International Institute of Sociology has pioneered establishing sociological research standards in Ukraine. Moreover, Volodymyr Paniotto, the KIIS's Director General, was the first national representative of the European Society for Opinion and Marketing Research (ESOMAR) in Ukraine. In the early 1990s, on the KIIS's and IS NANU's basis and request, Andrii Gorbachyk[7] developed the first national software, "OSA," for statistical data analysis and sample design (Gorbachyk, 2004). These innovations ensured mass accessibility for Ukrainian sociologists to computer-based statistical tools for sampling and data analysis that remarkably pushed the development of empirical sociology in Ukraine.

Besides KIIS, the impressive contribution to the development of sociology as well as democracy and civil society in Ukraine, enhancing Ukraine's integration into European and Euro-Atlantic structures also has been made by several other nongovernmental professional sociological institutions established mostly in the 1990s, passed the SAU's accreditation, membership of the European Society for Opinion and Marketing Research (ESOMAR) and/or the World Association for Public Opinion Research (WAPOR), and doing sociological research at national and regional levels in compliance with high international standards. Among them, there are the following:

- Ilko Kucheriv Democratic Initiatives Foundation (DIF) under the long-term leadership of Iryna Bekeshkina (Democratic Initiatives Foundation, 2023a). It is one of the oldest and most influential Ukrainian independent think tanks. Founded in 1992, DIF is acclaimed for the combination of classic sociological studies with SMART policy analysis of key events and the development of policy recommendations for decision-making bodies and civil society. It studies the trends of the democratic transformation of Ukraine, the ever-evolving public opinion on key national, regional, and local issues, and tracks specific target groups.
- SOCIS—Centre for Social and Marketing Research headed by Mykola Churilov and Oleksandr Stegniy; later, it forked into the Kantar TNS Ukraine and became a part of the Taylor Nelson Sofres market research group.[8] Since 1994, it has been a member of the Gallup Organization. It also became the first company in Ukraine to be certified by Bureau Veritas according to the international standard for "market opinion and social research."
- The Ukrainian Institute for Social Research, named after Oleksandr Yaremenko, with long-term leadership of Olga Balakireva.[9] The Institute became a pioneer in systemic investigation and monitoring of acute social issues and vulnerability as well as providing social impact analysis of public policy, social and economic reforms in Ukraine focused research on social problems concerning youth, children, family, HIV-infected and tobacco-, drug- and alcohol-addicted groups, unemployment and migration, gender issues, forced displaced people during Russia's war against Ukraine, among other issues. In some respects, the corre-

---

[7] Later, Andrii Gorbachyk was elected as a Dean of Sociology Faculty at T. Shevchenko National University of Kyiv, and during 2004–2012, he was the national representative of Ukrainian team in the European Social Survey.

[8] https://web.archive.org/web/20150915015025/http://www.tns-ua.com/en/

[9] https://www.uisr.org.ua

sponding policymaking in Ukraine was driven particularly by these research findings.
- The Razumkov Centre was the first nongovernmental think tank with the sociological service leadership of Andriy Bychenko and Mykhailo Mischenko.[10] For many years, the Razumkov Centre Sociological Service has been surveying national and civil identity, political attitudes, civic activism, national and local security, and the social impact of public policy.
- The East-Ukrainian Foundation for Social Research directed by Vil Bakirov and Oleksandr Kizilov[11] was founded in Kharkiv at V.N. Karazin Kharkiv National University's Sociological Faculty as a nongovernmental research institution doing sociological regional and nation-based surveys for policymaking. It became a pioneer for Ukraine in a comparative urban study of social issues of city management in the perception of city-dwellers at the request of the Association of Cities of Ukraine (Bakirov & Kushnariev, 1996).
- The Sociological Group "Rating" (Rating Group) is one of the most influential nongovernmental research institutions, established in Lviv in 2008 under the directorship of Alexey Antipovich.[12] Despite the challenges of wartime, they were able to complete more than 20 monitoring surveys in Ukraine within the first year of the full-scale war. Some of the surveys were commissioned by the National Platform for Resilience and Social Cohesion, as well as the International Republic Institute. As a result, a unique database about society during the war was formed, encompassing issues, hopes, experiences, value orientations, activity, adaptation, and resistance in extreme crisis conditions of life. The results of one of the latest studies provide a comprehensive picture of factors contributing to society's resilience during the war and postwar (Sociological Group 'Rating,' 2023b).

The results of these studies published and cited in media enable society to understand better its strength in resisting the extreme challenges of war, making it easier to endure the hardships of war and see a perspective beyond it. For policymakers, this is invaluable for making difficult decisions during wartime and developing a strategy for postwar development in Ukraine.

Since 2014, several Ukrainian sociological nongovernment research and analytical institutions (e.g., DIF, Centre for Social and Economic Research/CASE, Razumkov Centre) became members of the Association of Ukrainian Think Tanks, which consolidates their efforts in promoting reforms and European integration in Ukraine through the Ukrainian Think Tanks Liaison Office in Brussels (Reforms in Ukraine: Public Opinion, n.d.). According to the results of the Global Go To Think Tank Index, which is compiled within the framework of the Think Tanks and Civil Societies Program (TTCSP) at the University of Pennsylvania (USA), the Democratic Initiatives Foundation is rated among the most influential think tanks in

---

[10] https://razumkov.org.ua/en/sociology/press-releases
[11] http://fond.sociology.kharkov.ua/index.php/en/about-en-top
[12] https://ratinggroup.ua/en/about.html

Eastern Europe that is great evidence of growing recognition and prestige of Ukrainian sociology and its public efficacy.

4. *Creation of the Ukraine National Bank of Sociological Data.* In 2015, the Ukraine national sociological databank "Kyiv Archive"[13] was launched. It was initiated by the KIIS and the Centre for "Social Indicators," together with the National University of Kyiv-Mohyla Academy sponsored by the International Renaissance Foundation. The Kyiv Archive has become a partner of the Consortium of European Social Science Data Archives (CESSDA), which comprises 21 member countries and 1 observer.

The Kyiv Archive preserves data from social surveys conducted in Ukraine and makes such data easily and freely accessible to all interested persons or entities both in Ukraine and abroad. It was designed to contain both quantitative and qualitative data archives from 1989 to 1991 until now. However, for the time being, the archive only has quantitative data.

Furthermore, IS NASU has also developed its own Data Bank,[14] which includes a vast dataset of sociological monitoring project "Ukrainian Society," covering the period from 1992 to the present, as well as data from numerous other thematic studies conducted by the research teams of the Institute over the years.

There is no need to emphasize the importance of open data and access to them for conducting research, education, and decision-making. Over the years of post-USSR transformations, Ukrainian sociologists have accumulated an enormous capital of sociological data, enabling them to "see" society in its dynamics and various dimensions. If in the 1990s sociologists experienced a data shortage, today there is a situation of relative data surplus, accompanied by a lack of personnel and time necessary for a systemic and deeper analysis of the data, including conducting fundamental research on the regularities and underlying mechanisms of social processes. Ukrainian sociologists have achieved high proficiency in producing sociological data. However, the richness of data is often used only for relatively superficial descriptions of complex phenomena in public life. In the race for data, sociologists often deprive themselves of the pleasure of pausing to delve into structural and causal analyses of phenomena, thus limiting their ability to reach deeper levels of understanding and forecasting complex processes.

Critical self-reflection, the pursuit of improving professionalism and methodological culture, sensitivity to societal and public policy issues, and the drive to identify and overcome weaknesses in sociology's functioning have been and remain essential pillars of strength for Ukrainian sociology. Critical self-reflection has been a leitmotif at all four congresses of the SAU, as well as at many annual conferences and roundtables of Ukrainian sociologists.[15] The credibility of sociological

---

[13] https://datacatalogue.cessda.eu/?studyAreaCountries.searchField[0]=Ukraine&p=1

[14] https://i-soc.com.ua

[15] Notably illustrative are the proceeding materials of the annual Kharkiv Sociological Readings named after Elena Yakuba and the Sociological Readings in Memory of Natalia Panina (Shulga, 2000; Sociology…, 2009; Golovakha & Stegniy, 2008, 2009; Kutsenko, 2009; Bakirov, 2021).

institutions has a positive but unstable trend. The Kyiv International Institute of Sociology (KIIS) monitored the dynamic of the attitude of the Ukrainian population toward the results of opinion polls and sociological surveys, conducting nationwide opinion polls in 2002, 2004, 2009, and then annually from 2012 (the last one was in December 2021[16]). The level of trust among the Ukrainians in the data of sociological organizations that have long been working and publishing their research results remained high from 2002 to 2021: at 36% in 2002, with the rising rate up to 50–51% in 2012–2016, and the following gradually decreasing to 37% in 2021. Volodymyr Paniotto, Director General of KIIS, comments on the reasons for the decline of trust in sociological research in recent years (Kyiv International Institute of Sociology, 2022, p. 2):

> This [the decline of the trust since 2017] may be due in part to the methodological problems of sociologists themselves (due to COVID and the lack of the Census (the last one was in 2001), the quality of research is declining), but this is not the main reason. In 2019, sociological companies that published the poll results a week before the [presidential] election had a striking coincidence with the election results—and confidence in them still declined. I think the main reasons for the decline in trust are as follows:
>
> - Activities of pseudo-sociological companies that publish fake data.
> - Low level of sociological culture of politicians and journalists (they confuse different types of ratings, electoral ratings, and trust, compare surveys with smartphones with regular telephone surveys, etc., and therefore, they think that there is a big difference between different data);
> - Finally, (and perhaps worst of all) cynical political forces are increasingly using dirty political technologies: political scientists working for them, media owned by them, and bloggers on social networks deliberately destroy trust in professional companies if they consider the results of the poll unfavourable for their political power (even when they consider these results credible). (Kyiv International Institute of Sociology, 2022, n.p.)

This trend aligns with the current development of technologies and the world trend of the so-called "post-truth" society (Malcolm, 2021). In Ukraine, it is also accompanied by Russia's hybrid informational war (Rushchenko, 2015) and a decline in trust in expertise, partly due to the production and mass spread of fakes through social networks and Internet media. Ukrainian sociologists and journalists have launched projects to stop fake news[17] and discover disinformation[18] that collects and analyzes cases from 2014 until now. Currently, they have presented a report on monitoring Russian propaganda and core disinformation issues on Russia's war in Ukraine (Texty.org.ua., 2023).

---

[16] https://www.kiis.com.ua/?lang=eng&cat=reports&t=11

[17] https://www.stopfake.org/uk/golovna/

[18] https://texty.org.ua/tag/dezinformatsija/

22.3 Societal Transformations: The Power of Discourse

Along with the institutionalization of Ukrainian sociology as a science, education, and professional community since the 1990s, sociology also played a significant role in developing the discourse of a good society and nation-state-building. This discourse served as an alternative to the ideological foundations of the "real-socialist society" during the final stage of the USSR. The power of discourses in the post-USSR transformation was grounded in knowledge production through public opinion polls, empirically and theoretically rooted sociological surveys, and the dissemination of research findings through media, public discussions, and academic publications. Additionally, analytical papers and reports were provided to national and local public authorities and civic organizations, leading to public discussions that encouraged self-reflection and social maturation within society. These produced discourses revolved around issues of democratization, historical and cultural legacy, identity and public policy, social inequality and justice, trust and values, political culture, and civic activism. They played a crucial role in searching for key ideas to guide Ukraine's national state-building process.

Sociological projects at the national and regional levels in various dimensions formed an empirical base for a complex of middle-range theories of transforming society developed by modern Ukrainian sociologists. Various concepts were elaborated on the sociological data basis, which better explained the specific features of the Ukrainian post-USSR transformation. Such concepts as "social anomie," "subjective poverty," "double institutionalization" (Golovakha and Panina), "social maturity" (Yakuba), "everyday ideologies," "social cost of the delayed modernization" (Popova), "subjective social well-being" measured through deprivation (Golovakha, Panina, and Zlobina), "society of unequals" (Kutsenko), "value metamorphosis" (Ruchka), "institutionally reproduced inequalities", "extreme-time sociology" (Makeyev), "social subjectivity" (Sokuryanska), "state-that-promotes-development" (Kutuyev), "social mimicry" (Lobanova), "information-cultural styles" (Kostenko), "criminal society" and "hybrid war" (Rushchenko), and others have enriched the theoretical interpretation of the postcommunist transformation of Ukrainian society.

From 1989, the discourse of "back to Europe" was the intellectual and political framework for Eastern European postcommunist transformation, including post-USSR Baltic states, defining the strategy for the reforms and mass-elites agreement about the right way of transformation. However, this discourse was quite marginal both in Ukraine and Ukrainian sociology of that period, remaining in the focus of intellectual debates mostly within the enclaves of the Ukrainian Soviet dissidents and Ukrainian diaspora. Alongside this, institutions founded by Ukrainian diaspora abroad, like the Ukrainian World Congress (uniting the Ukrainian member organizations in 62 countries around the world), Ukrainian Free University (established in 1921-1922 in Vienna-Prague-Munich, and also in New York after the WWII), Harvard Ukrainian Research Institute (founded in 1973 and affiliated with Harvard University, USA), Canadian Institute of Ukrainian Studies (founded in 1976 as an integral part of the Faculty of Arts at the University of Alberta, Canada), as well as The International Renaissance Foundation (IRF, founded in Ukraine in 1990 by George Soros), encouraged and pushed essentially the Ukrainian national sociological renaissance within the frame of European and American intellectual traditions. Besides that, it was in simultaneous balancing with the dominant 'multi-vector' orientations in politics and the wide presence of Russia-centered discourse in Ukrainian sociology of transformation of that time, based on the legacy of the post-Stalinist wave of Soviet sociology institutionalization as well as the intensive communication and intellectual exchanges within the post-Soviet sociological field. The rather popular viewpoint at the time concerning a vision of the post-USSR transformation of Ukraine in the 1990s was argued similarities of the transformational paths for Ukraine, Russia and Belarus due to their common historical legacy and cultural proximity. However, the distinct differences in the transformation paths in Ukraine, Russia, and Belarus were identified in publications from the early 2000s (Churilov et al., 2002). Researchers highlighted Ukraine's specific quality as a "divided society," characterized by party-political and geopolitical polarization, interregional inconsistencies in historical memory, language, and cultural identity deeply rooted in history (Ryabchuk, 2003). They also argued for the divergence of transformation paths and social costs in these countries (Babenko, 2012). Empirical evidence supported the finding that Russian elites and the masses coalesced around imperialistic nationalism, leading away from democracy, while Ukrainian society was mobilized in support of civic nationalism and democracy (Kutsenko, 2006, pp. 56–59; Golovakha & Makeev, 2007).

In the 2000s, the mainstream of Ukrainian sociology gradually shifted its focus toward the necessity of positioning Ukrainian society on the map of Europe as an exemplar of a "better society" and an achievable transformation goal. As a result, sociological debates moved from searching for distinctive features in the mid-2000s to adjusting the discursive agenda. The idea of postcommunist transformation in Eastern Europe as a collective process within the framework of globalization (Genov, 2000) gained more significance as a reference point for discussing the post-USSR transformation in Ukraine. This was evident through various projects initiated by the Open Society Institute/Higher Education Support Program, such as *Changing Diversity: Vectors of Post-Communist Transformation* (Kutsenko & Babenko, 2004), and *European Visions and Divisions: Comparative Studies for Advances in Teaching Sociology* (2009–2011), chaired by Olga Kutsenko and Clair Wallace. These projects contributed to developing the concept of "New Europe," portraying a broadly inclusive European society.

As part of a turn to the discursive agenda, Ukrainian sociology has actively participated in empirical inclusion into the European discourse through its involvement in international comparative research projects such as the European Social Survey (2004–2012), World and European Values Surveys (1995–2021), and the International Social Survey Programme (2008, 2009, and 2019). While Ukrainian sociologists were predominantly fieldwork teams and not the initiators or core coordinators of these projects,[19] their involvement provided an opportunity to place Ukraine in international comparative databases. This, in turn, put Ukrainian sociology on the world sociological map and allowed for analyzing processes in Ukraine from a data-based comparative perspective. Moreover, this participation enhanced the empirical proficiency of the research teams, resulting in the development of a database on Ukrainian society available for comparative analyses in English through international sources. In particular, the data from the World Values Survey and European Values Survey facilitated an assessment of postimperial path dependence in Ukraine, considering the legacies of European empires (Austro-Hungarian, Ottoman, and Russian empires) rooted in the political culture of society, as studied by Kutsenko and Gorbachyk (2015). Furthermore, data from the International Social Survey Programme in 2008, 2009, and 2019 enabled analysis of religiosity and social inequality in Ukraine in comparative temporal and spatial perspectives (Oksamytna & Simonchuk, 2020).

The events of Euromaidan 2013–2014, Russian aggression in Crimea 2014, and Russia's subsequent hybrid war against Ukraine, accompanied by the military conflict in the part of Eastern Ukraine from 2014, stimulated the empowerment of civil society, civic initiatives, and volunteer movement in Ukraine. Civic activism has pushed and controlled the public authorities as well as filled the institutional failures of the state. Not surprisingly, this phenomenon has become a part of sociological reflections and explanations of the ways of post-USSR Ukrainian transformations within the European context (Stepanenko, 2015; CEP, 2022).

The social outcomes of the 30-year post-USSR transformations of Ukrainian society are reflected by sociologists in the collective monograph (Vorona & Shulga, 2021) published shortly before the great new challenge for Ukraine with Russia's full-scale military invasion in February 2022.

Even though Ukrainian society shares many common traits with both Western and Eastern European societies, as Viktoria Sereda (TRAFO, 2022) argued:

> Ukrainian society has faced unique challenges over the last few years; it is not easy to select a comparable case. No other European country is currently under the direct military attack of a global superpower, and nowhere else in Europe are ordinary citizens mobilized and deployed to the front line of the armed conflict. Therefore, a comparison with any of the immediate European neighbors of Ukraine might be misleading. (p. 6)

However, the full-scale war initiated by the Russian Federation consolidated Ukrainian society in its civilizational choice for EU integration and defense of state independence and sovereignty, as numerous sociological data have shown (Golovakha & Makeev, 2022; Paniotto, 2023; Sociological Group 'Rating,' 2023a, 2023b; Hrushetskyi, 2022a, b, c).

---

[19] Such programs and grants were provided from the middle of the 1990s by the International Renaissance Foundation, IREX/USIA, Fulbright Program, Civic Education Program, OSI/HESP, etc.

22.4 Big Challenges: Comprehensive Sociological Responses—*Power of Doing*

Looking back at the past, we can summarize that Ukrainian sociology actively participated in all phases of post-USSR societal transformations. Not only did it establish Ukrainian sociology's national identity within the European sociological space, but it also significantly impacted on the overcoming the consequences of the Chernobyl nuclear disaster of 1986 (Churilov et al., 1994), then democratization, nation-building, state-building, civic development, and consensus-building in Ukraine over more than three decades of post-USSR transformations.

Over the previous three decades, Ukrainian society has encountered rapid and crucial challenges from the fall of the USSR and the renewal of Ukrainian state sovereignty in 1991. The period from 1991 to 2000 witnessed a rapid and multidimensional post-USSR transformation, encompassing democratization, marketization, and nation-building through cultural, social, political, and economic development. This transformative phase was followed by the Orange Revolution in 2004–2005 and the Revolution of Dignity (also known as "Euromaidan") in 2013–2014. Subsequently, on February 20, 2014, Russia invaded and annexed Crimea, and in April 2014, it invaded the eastern parts of the Donetsk and Lugansk regions, marking the beginning of Russia's hybrid war against Ukraine, which persisted in this hybrid form until the end of February 2022. As a result, approximately 20% of Ukraine's territory and population were affected by the war during the period from 2014 to 2021.

Furthermore, Ukraine had to confront the COVID-19 pandemic from 2019 to 2022, which added another layer of complexity to the existing challenges. Finally, on February 24, 2022, Russia initiated a full-scale war.

Throughout these tumultuous times, Ukrainian sociology has demonstrated its power in responding to these challenges through institutional initiatives, self-reflection, and research aimed at addressing the various issues faced by Ukrainian society. It has provided valuable data and disseminated research findings to aid in understanding and tackling the diverse challenges arising during this period.

In this section, we will delve into specific arguments to illustrate the agency of Ukrainian sociology as a part of the driving forces of societal changes.

Sociology played an important historical role in the declaration of the state independence of Ukraine in 1991. Via institutionally established sociological centers, sociological surveys on public opinion about state independence before the referendum in September to October 1991 were conducted. The findings revealed the wish of the vast majority of citizens to live in Ukraine as a sovereign country. These results, presented to the politicians, gave them an additional powerful argument for the political decision regarding the referendum. Moreover, its successful official results in favor of state independence were also confirmed by previous sociological data. Eugen Golovakha (1996), currently Director of IS NASU, commented on this event in his book:

> When people knew from a public opinion survey presented in the media that many wanted independence, they joined the majority. So, sociology played an important role in the development of the civic consensus. And Ukraine managed the first stage of transformation without any military and civic conflicts, unlike most of the post-USSR states. (p. 3)

During the events of the Orange Revolution, sociology was at the center of public focus, dealing with the legitimacy of the elections through the publication of exit poll data from the 2004 presidential elections.

At the beginning of the presidential elections in 2004, the leading national sociological survey and polling centers (KIIS and Razumkov Centre) teamed up in the Consortium of the National Exit Poll 2004. The Consortium has done three national exit polls during the elections, which went three rounds and gave different electoral results to the Central Election Committee. During the second round of the presidential election, especially significant discrepancies were found between the exit poll and the official results. Due to the public trust in the core sociological institutions involved in the exit polls, and whereas the trust in official government organizations and institutions was extremely low at that time, it was the scientific argument for the election falsification which led to mass protests in almost all regions of Ukraine. Subsequently, the case was considered by the Supreme Court of Ukraine and proved the facts of election results falsifications.

The popularity and diversity of multiple data published on behalf of sociologists in the mass media, in particular, have led to many people, including politicians and journalists, misinterpreting the sociological ratings of politicians and parties. Partly, it is the fault of sociologists, as it takes time to agree on the standards for the publication of ratings. That is why leading sociologists from IS NASU, KIIS, and other institutions have held numerous training master classes, tables for journalists, and political and civic activists; they published special comments and even guidelines explaining both the principles of sociological data presentation and interpretation. In particular, drawing on the calculations of Valeriy Khmelko (KIIS's president), the commentary published on the KIIS's website (Kharchenko & Paniotto, 2010; Kyiv Institute of Sociology, 2016) shows that a simpler approach in the sociological research held just before the elections gives better matches with the election results than other models. For this reason, KIIS adopted the following standard for press releases providing two types of ratings: (1) percentages with respect to all and (2) to those who will come and have already decided on the choice at the time of the survey. The second rating gives a better idea of the possible outcome of the election but has a bigger stochastic error owing to the smaller sample. It is a certain estimated rating at the time of the survey (those who were undecided did not give their assessment) rather than the prognosis of the results of future elections. Moreover, this methodology, applied at least in the national exit polls during the presidential and parliamentary elections in 2019, secured a very accurate sociological assessment of the election results.

Ukrainian sociology turns to its public role of classical feedback presentation in the form of public opinion screens, annual presentation of the sociological monitoring's findings in mass media, analytical papers and interviews in newspapers and journals, core national news media channels, as well as expert comments in local mass media of Ukraine, arguing the growing pro-European orientations throughout of Ukraine, debating image of the "divided society," "failure state," and increasing attempts to analyze the processes in Ukraine within the discursive frame of the European trends, European values, or European context. Public intellectuals promoted the explanation of the Euromaidan as a "Revolution of Dignity" in terms of European values and the European future for Ukraine that people of different social classes, ages, ethnic groups, native languages, and all the regions of Ukraine fight for in the face of the threat of the dictatorship of Yanukovich (under his presidency) and Russian scenario of further development. From 2014, this discourse became a part of the mainstream discussions at academic conferences and public lectures based on sociological data and expertise (Golovakha, Bekeshkina, Paniotto, Balakireva, Shulga, Reznik, Chernysh, Brik, and others).

New topics of sociological research have emerged in response to the challenges posed by the COVID-19 pandemic. Different research institutions and projects have been at the forefront of studying these challenges in Ukraine. In particular, in late 2020, KIIS, in collaboration with the DIF, conducted a study of attitudes to the coronavirus crisis and an assessment of government action in the fight against the COVID-19 pandemic (Kyiv International Institute of Sociology, 2022). It was a national part of the Gallup International Association's project, covering 47 countries, including Ukraine. They have monitored by the CATI method (computer-assisted telephone interviews) the development of public attitudes to the pandemic, behavior changes, and the socioeconomic impact of the pandemic on Ukrainian society.

The Razumkov Centre carried out studies on the political and social consequences of COVID-19 in Ukraine. According to the center's multiple surveys (Mischenko, 2021), the citizen's assessments of government actions during the pandemic were relatively low. However, assessments of government efforts in ensuring democracy, interethnic harmony in society, and citizen rights and freedoms, as well as improving Ukraine's international image and foreign policy, were comparatively high. Instead, the government scored the fewest points in addressing socioeconomic issues (remuneration of labor, healthcare, social protection, and pensions, improving the country's economic situation, reducing the influence of oligarchs, combating corruption, and dealing with prices and tariffs). The level of paternalistic expectations among Ukrainians has decreased in recent decades. Increasingly, more citizens assign the state regulation of primary social conditions, providing all citizens with equal opportunities to exercise their fundamental rights through legislation and social programs.

However, the public role of political science experts was much more visible in the course of mass media, and just a few leaders of the sociological professional community played the public sociology role in mass media. The topic of the poor visibility of sociology in public discussions and policy-maling, the public interest in sociology mostly only in connection with electoral campaigns and political ratings was one of the burdens in discussions throughout of the each of professional conferences and congresses of SAU.

Numerous sociological research teams have contributed valuable insights into the effects of the COVID-19 pandemic on various aspects of Ukrainian society (Stepanenko, 2021), helping to shape policy responses and provide guidance for the future.

Since the beginning of Russia's invasion in 2014, Ukrainian sociologists have started researching wartime society, including issues of violence and war crimes, mental health, militarization, de-occupation, forced migration, soldiers returning home, etc. which were accompanied by discussions about the role of sociology and sociologists in wartime and postwar development. The integral task of Ukrainian sociology today is to understand the situation in which Ukrainian society found itself during and after the war (Bakirov, 2021). In the heat of Russia's full-scale war in Ukraine, on July 5, 2022, SAU conducted the first online roundtable with the symbolic title "Ukrainian Society after the Victory," gathering sociologists from all Ukrainian regions.

Despite the war, sociologists study, discuss, and develop an empirically grounded understanding of the social challenges to Ukrainian society caused by the war, the mechanisms of both social resistance to the militant aggressor and social resilience of the nation, the changing social structure and social quality of Ukrainian society in wartime, manifestations of "new" and reinforced "old" social inequalities, civic activism and volunteering, dynamics of social and political attitudes and values, trust and solidarity, social effectiveness of public policy, etc. Regular KIIS surveys register the dynamics of population attitudes toward Russia, Europe, NATO, and other countries (Foreign…, 2023) and trust in Ukrainian social institutions, social attitudes, and readiness for territorial defense (Hrushetskyi, 2022a, 2022b, 2023; Social…, 2022). Makeiev (2022) described the institutional landscape as challenged by wartime, with strong and weak parts to be focused on sustainable development; the issue of social resistance was also a cornerstone of the DIF and KIIS research (Democratic Initiatives Foundation, 2023b; Kyiv Institute of Sociology, 2023b; Razumkov Centre, 2023). Monitoring of social emotions and feelings during the war, as well as volunteering and support of business, is the focus of several research (Dembitskyi, 2023; Bobrova et al., 2023; Gradus, 2023a, 2023b), and knowledge-based scenarios for postwar Ukraine are in the focus of sociological research and thinking.

Russia's war started in 2014 and has pushed new topics and projects aimed at the study of forced internally displaced person (IDP) from the occupied territories since 2014 and refugees since February 2022. The corresponding policymaking in Ukraine, in some respect, has been driven mainly by these research findings, that is, research on IDP adaptation and integration into hosting communities (Balakireva, 2016). Numerous studies on the challenges faced by over 1.5 million internally displaced persons (IDPs) from war-torn regions in Ukraine during the initial years of the conflict were conducted. These studies were followed by a campaign aimed at promoting accessibility to medical support and election rights without requiring registration based on one's place of residence, which ultimately led to a reform in medical accessibility (Kuznetsova & Mikheieva, 2020).

After the full-scale invasion in 2022, there are about five million registered IDPs in Ukraine, and over eight million people have fled to Europe and other countries; over 6.2 million were registered under the European Temporary Protection Declaration and other programs in June 2023 by data[20] of the UNCHR. Through the "Scholars at Risk" programs, hundreds of scholars from Ukraine received temporary positions and research grants that allowed them to support the war-related research agenda. Sociological studies of Ukrainian forced migrants and war refugees, civic activism and societal resilience in wartime have united scholars from Ukraine and hosting universities in Europe, doing research on war refugees' needs assessment; labor market participation; coping and volunteering strategies; support and cooperation in host societies; states' response to the new wave of the migration crisis in the EU; women, children, and divided families; new forms of violence and social inequality, etc.

Gender issues also continued to be the focus of sociological attention during the war. Ukrainian sociologists are implementing projects aimed at studying war-separated families, motherhood under forced migration living conditions, women's activism, volunteering, and special women problems in military forces. Some Ukrainian sociologists also combine their research with holding initiative civic projects. Thus, special attention can be paid to the project "Invisible Battalion" initiated in Ukraine by Tamara Martsenuk in 2015 as a global advocacy project researching and documenting the participation of Ukrainian women in the war against the Russian military invasion. In 2019, the project team filmed documentaries about women at war: "Invisible Battalion" and "No Obvious Signs." The films premiered on national television channels, followed by more than a hundred screenings across the country; the project work continues on the new part of the film during the full-scale phase of the war.[21]

Researching new phenomena and acute societal issues during the war, collecting and regularly publishing empirical data as a kind of societal mirror, empirically debunking Russian propagandistic myths, improving research methodology and explanatory tools as a response to the challenges of wartime, continuing work with students, informing authorities and the public about the state of society, and finally, supporting the cohesion of the professional community all have become vital contributions of Ukrainian sociology in supporting the resilience of the Ukrainian nation and its resistance to external military aggression and the extraordinary problems brought about by the war. These all make the Ukrainian experience unique for European as well as global sociology.

---

[20] https://data2.unhcr.org/en/situations/ukraine
[21] https://invisiblebattalion.org/en/invisbat-2/#invisbat3-0

22.5 Conclusion

The analysis of the path taken by sociology during the years of Ukraine's state independence, which is directly intertwined with multiple societal transformations, nation-building, prodemocratic revolutions, and crises caused by the pandemic and the war, allows us to draw the following key conclusions.

The distinguishing feature of Ukrainian sociology throughout the decades of its institutional development that started at the end of the nineteenth century (with the break in the Stalinist period of forced deinstitutionalization from the late 1920s to the late 1950s) has been its proactive intellectual and social position as a science and profession. Despite institutional ruptures in history, this feature has become deeply rooted in the national tradition of Ukrainian sociology, defining its role as an *activator* of the national liberation movement, democratization, and the processes of nation-state and civil society development. This role is evident in the practices of producing and disseminating sociological knowledge, functioning of sociological discourse, functioning of the sociological community and its institutions, and the subject interaction of sociology with public authority, business, and civil society. The multilevel and diverse impact of Ukrainian sociology on society's self-awareness, decision-making process, and social control over public authority testifies to the power of sociology as a science and profession.

In the difficult times of post-USSR societal transformations, crises, and war, sociology's proactive position ensures the resilience of society. The power of Ukrainian sociology is in producing well-grounded scientific knowledge, shaping socially relevant discourses, and influencing both the self-awareness of civil society and decision-making processes at national and local political and social levels in Ukraine.

The crucial manifestations of the institutional power of Ukrainian sociology include:

- The functioning active, communicative, and well-organized professional community oriented toward the best world and national standards of professional activity;
- A well-developed network of research, educational, and think-tank institutions actively operating in the public, private, and civil sectors, at the national, international, and local levels; and
- Well-established and diverse research and educational infrastructure (curriculum and research programs, databanks, academic journals, communicative platforms, etc.).

Over the previous decades, Ukrainian sociology has played the role of a sounding board, producing discourses for comparing the state of public consciousness and practices, public policies with ideas of a good society, human values and rights, democracy, European integration, and modern civilizational development. This is what defines Ukrainian sociology's power of discourse.

The power of sociology as a science and profession has also been demonstrated through active self-reflection, the development of a national culture of "sociology of sociology," and a systematic effort to critically examine itself, comparing own activities with the best world and national standards, identifying and openly discussing own strengths and weaknesses, and seeking ways to self-improving. Ukrainian sociology is characterized by heightened self-criticism, which, on one hand, stimulates its self-development but, on the other, lowers self-esteem and somewhat reduces competitiveness in the market of knowledge production and dissemination.

Competing Interests The authors have no conflicts of interest to declare that are relevant to the content of this chapter.

References

Babenko, S. (2012). Comparing social cost of post-soviet transformation of Eastern Europe borderland (Ukraine, Belarus, Moldova). *Crossroads Digest, 2012*, 164–191.

Bakirov, V. (2021). Transformation of sociology: Necessity and perspectives. *Ukrainian Sociological Journal, 2021*(26), 9–15. https://doi.org/10.26565/2077-5105-2021-26-01

Bakirov, V., & Golovakha, Y. (2018). *Ukrainian sociology in the 21st century: Theory, methods, research results*. V. N. Karazin Kharkiv National University.

Bakirov, V., & Kushnariev Y. (1996). *City and the state: Problems, concerns and hopes of city-dwellers in Eastern Ukraine*. Fort.

Bakirov, V., & Sokurianska, L. (2020). Sociology in Ukraine: Institutional status and research agenda. *Ukrainian Sociological Journal, 2020*(22), 7–15. https://doi.org/10.26565/2077-5105-2019-22-01

Balakireva, O. (2016). *Forced migrants and host communities: Lessons for effective adaptation and integration*. Institute of Economics and Forecasting, National Academy of Sciences of Ukraine.

Bataeva, K., Burlachuk, V., & Stepanenko, V. (2018). *History of Ukrainian sociology: Study guide*. Kondor Publisher.

Bobrova, A., Nazarenko, Y., Lomonosova, N., Syrbu, E., & Khassai, Y. (2023). *Nine months of full-scale war in Ukraine: Thoughts, feelings, actions*. CEDOS. Retrieved June 25, 2023 from https://cedos.org.ua/en/researches/nine-months-of-full-scale-war-in-ukraine-thoughts-feelings-actions/

Bourdieu, P. (1984). *Homo Academicus*. Polity.

Bourdieu, P. (2003). *Science of science and reflexivity*. Polity.

Bourdieu, P., De Saint Martin, M., & Passeron, J. C. (1994). *Academic discourse: Linguistic misunderstanding and professorial power*. Polity.

CEP. (2022). *Surge in civic activism, overwhelming support to resisting the enemy and fundamental shift in perceiving corruption*. Retrieved June 16, 2023 from https://engage.org.ua/eng/cep-2022-surge-in-civic-activism-overwhelming-support-to-resisting-the-enemy-and-fundamental-shift-in-perceiving-corruption/

Churilov, N., Golovakha, E., Panina, N., & Stegnij, A. (1994). *Tcernobyl*. Einsichten und Erfahrungen einer Schweizer Hilfsaktion.

Churilov, N., Stegniy, O., & Meier-Dallach, H. P. (2002). The regions in Ukraine: Perceptions, fears and hopes of population. In H. P. Meier-Dallach & J. Juchler (Eds.), *Postsocialist transformations and civil society in a globalizing world* (pp. 159–187). Nova Science Pub Inc.

Dembitskyi, S. (2023). *Public opinion in Ukraine after 10 months of war*. Kyiv International Institute of Sociology. Retrieved May 17, 2023 from https://kiis.com.ua/?lang=eng&cat=reports&id=1175&page=1

Democratic Initiatives Foundation. (2023a). *About Ilko Kucheriv Democratic Initiatives Foundation*. Retrieved July 30, 2023 from https://dif.org.ua/en/about

Democratic Initiatives Foundation. (2023b). *Resistance to the aggressor, volunteering, shelling of infrastructure: how the full-scale war affected the lives of Ukrainians*. Retrieved May 26, 2023 from https://dif.org.ua/article/opir-agresoru-volonterstvo-obstrili-infrastrukturi-yak-povnomasshtabna-viyna-vplinula-na-zhittya-ukraintsiv?fbclid=IwAR3mvi67372b0uyFptkB9FnEjH0Zh9ccAHAf5JrJP_JKsZNWm02V6ncqLnM#_Toc128066176

Drahomanov, M. (1868). *Basic of sociology: Introductory words to the study of Ukrainian National History*.

Fader, E. K. (2011). Power/knowledge. In D. Taylor (Ed.), *Michel Foucault: Key concepts* (pp. 55–68). Acumen Publishing.

Foucault, M. (1972). *Archaeology of knowledge*. Pantheon Books.

Foucault, M. (1982). The subject and power. *Critical Inquiry, 8*(4), 777–795.

Genov, N. (Ed.) (2000). Continuing Transformation in Eastern Europe. *Social Studies on eastern Europe*, Vol. 2, Berlin: Trafo Publisher

Golovakha, Y. I. (1996). *Transforming society: Sociological monitoring experience in Ukraine*. Institute of Sociology of the National Academy of Sciences of Ukraine.

Golovakha, Y., & Dembitskyi, S. (Eds.). (2022). *Complex measuring tools in sociological research: Elaborations, adaptations, reliability justifications*. Institute of Sociology of the National Academy of Sciences of Ukraine.

Golovakha, Y., & Makeev, S. (Eds.). (2007). *Ukrainian society through European perspective*. Institute of Sociology of the National Academy of Sciences of Ukraine.

Golovakha, Y., & Makeev, S. (Eds.). (2022). *Ukrainian society in wartime*. Institute of Sociology of the National Academy of Sciences of Ukraine.

Golovakha, Y., & Stegniy, O. (2008). Modern state and development prospects for sociology in Ukraine and Europe. In Y. Golovakha & O. Stegniy (Eds.), *Proceedings of the 1st International Sociological Readings in memory of N. V. Panina*. Institute of Sociology of the National Academy of Sciences of Ukraine.

Golovakha, Y., & Stegniy, O. (2009). Sociology and society today. In Y. Golovakha & O. Stegniy (Eds.), *Proceedings of the 2nd international sociological readings in memory of N.V. Panina*. Institute of Sociology of the National Academy of Sciences of Ukraine.

Gorbachyk, A. (2004). *Guide for user of OCA system (Proceedings with of Sociological Questionnaires) Version 3.01. for Windows 95/98*. Statistical Analysis Bureau.

Gradus. (2023a). *How much do businesses donate and how else do they help solve social issues*. Retrieved July 10, 2023 from https://gradus.app/en/open-reports/how-much-do-businesses-donate-and-how-else-do-they-help-solve-social-issues-ukraine-during-war/

Gradus. (2023b). *Wartime survey of Ukrainian society / Eighth wave*. Retrieved June 15, 2023 from https://gradus.app/en/open-reports/wartime-survey-ukrainian-society-eighth-wave/

Hrushetskyi, A. (2022a). *Dynamics of the population's attitude to Russia and the emotional background due to the war*. Kyiv International Institute of Sociology. Retrieved December 16, 2022 from https://www.kiis.com.ua/?lang=eng&cat=reports&id=1112&page=1

Hrushetskyi, A. (2022b). *Dynamics of trust in social institutions in 2021-2022*. Kyiv International Institute of Sociology. Retrieved December 16, 2022 from https://kiis.com.ua/?lang=eng&cat=reports&id=1174&page=6

Hrushetskyi, A. (2022c). *Sense of personal belonging to the national resistance*. Kyiv International Institute of Sociology. Retrieved July 23, 2023 from https://kiis.com.ua/?lang=eng&cat=reports&id=1158&page=1

Hrushetskyi, A. (2023). *Dynamics of readiness for territorial concessions for the earliest possible end to the war*. Retrieved May 16, 2023 from https://kiis.com.ua/?lang=eng&cat=reports&id=1192&page=1

Hrushevsky, M. (1921). *The beginning of citizenship: Genetic sociology*. Foreign Bureau in Prague.

Kharchenko, N., & Paniotto, V. (2010). Exit polls in an emerging democracy: The complex case of Ukraine. *Survey Research Methods, 4*(1), 31–42.

Kistiakowski, T. (1899). *Gesellschaft und Einzelwesen : eine methodologische Studie / von Th. Kistiakowski STRASSBURG 11*. O. Liebmann.

Kutsenko, O. (2006). Diverging societies: Specificity of system transformations in Russia and Ukraine. *Universe of Russia, 15*(3), 43–61.

Kutsenko, O. (2008). Diagnosis of time through I. M. Popova's eyes. *Sociology: Theory, Methods, Marketing, 2008*(3), 217–219.

Kutsenko, O. (2009). Society and sociological intervention: From functional roles to inversion of subject and object. *Sociological Journal, 2009*(2), 97–103.

Kutsenko, O., & Babenko, S. (Eds.) (2004). Changing Diversities: Vectors, Dimensions and Context of Post-Communist Transformation. Kharkiv, CEP/CEU: Kharkiv University Publisher, 340 p.

Kutsenko, O., & Gorbachyk, A. (2015). *Post-imperial regions: Associated dependence in Eastern Europe development*. In O. Shkaratan, V. Leksin, & G. Yastrebov (Eds.), *Russia as civilization: Food for thought. Part 11* (pp. 441–464). "Mir Rossii" editorial board.

Kuznetsova, I., & Mikheieva, O. (2020). Forced displacement from Ukraine's war-torn territories: Intersectionality and power geometry. *Nationalities Papers, 48*(4), 690–706.

Kyiv International Institute of Sociology. (2016). *Commentary about the Standards for the Publication of the Sociological Ratings*. Retrieved June 20, 2023 from https://www.kiis.com.ua/?lang=eng&cat=background

Kyiv International Institute of Sociology. (2022). *Dynamics of the attitude of the population of Ukraine to sociological surveys, December 2021*. Retrieved January 18, 2022 from https://www.kiis.com.ua/?lang=eng&cat=reports&id=1087&page=1&t=11

Kyiv International Institute of Sociology. (2021) Almost a year with the pandemic: the results of an international Gallup research / KIIS Press Release and Reports. Retrieved from: https://www.kiis.com.ua/?lang=eng&cat=reports&id=1011&page=21

Kyiv International Institute of Sociology. (2023a). *General information*. Retrieved July 30, 2023 from https://www.kiis.com.ua/?lang=eng&cat=background

Kyiv International Institute of Sociology. (2023b). *Opportunities and challenges facing Ukraine's democratic transition*. https://kiis.com.ua/materials/pr/20230223_6/January_2023_Ukraine_wartime_survey_ENG.pdf

Makeiev, S. (2022). Institutional landscape of military order. In Y. Golovakha & S. Makeiev (Eds.), *Ukrainian society in wartime*. Institute of Sociology of the National Academy of Sciences of Ukraine.

Malcolm, D. (2021). Post-truth society? An Eliasian sociological analysis of knowledge in the 21st century. *Sociology, 55*(6), 1063–1079. https://doi.org/10.1177/0038038521994039

Mischenko, M. (2021). Public opinion on socio-economic processes and transformations in the pandemic. In V. Yurchishin (Ed.), *Perspectives for post-coronavirus economic transformations and their impact on the development of countries. The place of Ukraine in the post-crisis world* (pp. 323–358). Zapovit, Razumkov Centre and Friedrich Naumann Foundation.

Oksamytna, S., & Simonchuk, O. (2020). *Dynamics of social inequality perception in Ukraine: On the ISSP data of 2009 and 2019*. Institute of Sociology of the National Academy of Sciences of Ukraine, NU KMA.

Panina, N. (2004). Professional ethics and sociology in Ukraine (towards code of professional ethics of a sociologist SAU). *Sociology: Theory, Methods, Marketing, 2004*(3), 5–8.

Panina, N. (2005). *Ukrainian society 1994–2004: Sociological monitoring*. Institute of Sociology of the National Academy of Sciences of Ukraine.

Paniotto, V. (2023). *What polling says about trends in Modern Ukrainian Society?* Retrieved May 20, 2023 from https://ukraineworld.org/articles/analysis/modern-ukr-society

Popova, I. M. (1996). *Sociology. Propaedeutic course: A textbook for students*. Tandem.

Razumkov Centre. (2023). *Foreign policy orientations of Ukrainian citizens, assessment of the government's foreign policy, attitudes toward foreign countries and politicians* (February-March 2023). https://razumkov.org.ua/napriamky/sotsiologichni-doslidzhennia/zovnishnopolitychni-oriientatsii-gromadian-ukrainy-otsinka-zovnishnoi-polityky-vlady-stavlennia-do-inozemnykh-derzhav-ta-politykiv-liutyi-berezen-2023r

Reforms in Ukraine: public opinion. (n.d.). https://ukraine-office.eu/en/reforms-in-ukraine-public-opinion-3

Reznik, V., & Reznik, O. (2006). Ukrainian sociology after 1991. *Ukrainian Sociological Review, 2004–2005*, 28–58.

Rushchenko, I. P. (2015). *Russian-Ukrainian hybrid war: A sociologist's view*. Pavlenko O.G. Publisher.

Ryabchuk, M. (2003). *Two Ukraines: Real boundaries, virtual games*. Kritika.

Shapoval, M. (1934). *General sociology*. Vilna Spilka.

Shulga, N. (2000). Ukrainian sociology in search for identity. *Sociology: Theory, Methods, Marketing, 2000*(2), 170–177.

Sociological Association of Ukraine. (2023). *About SAU*. Retrieved July 28, 2023 from https://sau.in.ua/pro-sau/

Sociological Group "Rating". (2023a). *Comprehensive research: How the war changed me and the country. Summary of the year*. Retrieved July 20, 2023 from https://ratinggroup.ua/en/research/ukraine/kompleksne_dosl_dzhennyay_yak_v_yna_zm_nila_mene_ta_kra_nu_p_dsumki_roku.html

Sociological Group "Rating". (2023b). *Ukraine's resilience formula: the essential components during war and post-war*. Retrieved July 20, 2023 from https://ratinggroup.ua/en/research/ukraine/ukraine_s_resilience_formula_the_essential_components_during_war_and_post-war_6_11_june_2023.html

Stepanenko, V. P. (2015). *Civil society: Discourses and practices*. Institute of Sociology of the National Academy of Sciences of Ukraine.

Stepanenko, V. P. (2021). *Pandemic COVID-19 in Ukraine: Social consequences*. ТОВ NVP Interservice.

Stepanenko, V., & Rybschun, O. (2009). Ukrainian sociology: Social-historical and ideological context of development. *Sociology: Theory, Methods, Marketing, 2009*(2), 23–46.

Tancher, V., & Stepanenko, V. (2004). *Social transformation: Conceptualization, tendencies, Ukrainian experience*. Institute of Sociology of the National Academy of Sciences of Ukraine.

Tancher, V., & Stepanenko, V. (2005). *Sociological knowledge and power: Contradictory relations of sociological research and political practices*. Stylos.

Texty.org.ua. (2021). *Seller ratings: Database of pseudo-sociologists and hidden pr specialists*. Retrieved July 30, 2023 from https://texty.org.ua/d/socio/

Texty.org.ua. (2023). *The fuhrer stomps his foot. Russian media monitoring report*. Retrieved May 15, 2023 from https://texty.org.ua/articles/109110/the-fuhrer-stomps-his-foot-russian-media-monitoring-report-20-26-february-2023/

TRAFO. (2022). *"Rethinking Ukrainian studies: Interview with Viktoria*. Retrieved May 21, 2023 from https://trafo.hypotheses.org/19157

Vorona, V. M., & Shulga, M. O. (2021). *Ukrainian society: Monitoring of social changes. 30 years of Independence*. Institute of Sociology of the National Academy of Sciences of Ukraine.

Yakuba, E. A. (1996). *Sociology: Textbook for students*. Constanta.

Zaslavskaya, T. I. (2007). *Selected works in 3 volumes*. Economics.

Dr. Olga Kutsenko is Professor of Sociology at Taras Shevchenko National University of Kyiv (Ukraine) and an Einstein Research Professor at the Technical University of Berlin (Germany); Head of PhD Program on Sociology at Taras Shevchenko National University of Kyiv. Since 2007, she has served as Vice President of the Sociological Association of Ukraine. She researches the social-structural and cultural transformations in Ukraine in a comparative European prospect, as well as the dynamics of inequality, democracy support, and civic activism. She is the author of Society of Unequals: Class Analysis in Modern Sociology (2000), the coeditor and author of Changing Diversities: Vectors, Dimensions, and Context of Post-Communist Transformation (2004), and the author of book chapters in Inter-ethnic Integration in Five European Societies (2008), New Europe: Growth to Limits? (2010), Tendencies of Structural Transformation of

Ukrainian Society under Globalization and European Integration (2017), and *Ukrainian Sociology in the 21st Century: Theory, Methods, and Research Results* (2018).

Svitlana Babenko is a Project Researcher at the Department of Global Politic Studies (GPS), Malmö Institute for Studies of Migration, Diversity, and Welfare (MIM), at Malmö University (Sweden). In 2021, she was elected as a Head of Kyiv branch of the Sociological Association of Ukraine. Her current research project is "European Solidarity, Institutional Changes in Migration Policy, and Adaptation Strategies: De-othering and Social Integration of Refugees in the Context of the Russian War in Ukraine." She was Associate Professor at the Department of Social Structures and Social Relations (2009–2023) and Head of MA Program "Gender Studies with Double Degree with Lund University, Sweden" at Faculty of Sociology, Taras Shevchenko National University of Kyiv, Ukraine (2017–2023).

Index

A
Abbott, A., 42
Adam, F., 422, 423, 425, 427
Albania, 67, 68, 72, 73, 77, 83
    post-communist transition, 75–76
Albanian Sociological Association
    (ALBSA), 80
ALBSA, *see* Albanian Sociological
    Association (ALBSA)

B
Babosov, E., 90, 91
Bauman, Z., 54
    intellectuals as interpreters, 36
    intellectuals as legislators, 35
Belarus, 87, 89, 91, 94, 95, 97, 99, 101,
    103, 105
Belarusian Institute of Strategic Studies
    (BISS), 104
Bell, D., 58
Benda, J.
    La Trahison Des Clercs (*The Treason of
    the Intellectuals*), 55
BISS, *see* Belarusian Institute of Strategic
    Studies (BISS)
Bosnia and Herzegovina, 113, 114, 116, 118,
    119, 121–123, 125, 127, 129, 130
Bourdieu, P., 38, 54, 120, 438
Božović, R.R., 296
Bulgaria, 135, 136, 138, 139, 142, 144–146
Burawoy, M., 3, 15, 216, 228, 229, 358
    professional sociology, 33, 42, 151, 215
Búzik, B., 406, 408

C
Calhoun, C., 250
Central and Eastern Europe, 2, 8, 9, 20, 52, 55,
    62, 63, 67, 133, 134, 278
Central Eastern Europe (CEE), *see* Central and
    Eastern Europe
Civil society, 13, 32, 74, 100, 240, 332, 338,
    340, 359, 416, 418, 430
Cold War, 69, 70, 297, 329, 347
Communism, 56, 59, 60, 69, 73, 76, 83, 116,
    122, 327, 330, 332, 342, 347, 348,
    417, 427, 431
Constantinescu, M., 326, 327, 330
Coser, L.A.
    intellectuals as knowledge producers, 40
Croatia, 152, 153, 161–163
Cultural political economy (CPE), 4, 87, 151,
    227, 274, 280, 281, 372, 431
Czechoslovakia, 170–172, 176, 402, 409, 413
Czechoslovak Republic, *see* Czechoslovakia
Czech Republic, 171, 174, 182, 185

D
Dahrendorf, R., 38
Davidjuk, G., 90
    applied sociology, 91
Democracy, 34, 60, 64, 70, 74, 87, 96, 97, 101,
    104, 116, 122, 147, 157, 180, 185,
    194, 227, 251, 258, 264, 265, 276,
    299, 310, 337, 358, 365, 409, 418,
    422, 429, 439, 444, 449, 453, 456
    liberal, 152, 174, 189, 196, 198,
    202, 416

parliamentary, 58, 196, 197
political, 309
Discourse, 5, 6, 18, 30, 99, 102, 117, 157, 175, 180, 192, 216, 227, 230, 233, 235, 239, 251, 275, 278, 280, 283, 299, 315, 326, 352, 357, 359, 363, 365, 372, 373, 382, 385, 387, 391, 421, 422, 426, 431, 448, 449, 453, 456
   academic, 316
   critical, 53, 58, 155, 158, 388, 393
   dominant, 6, 14, 17, 20, 128, 152, 159, 165, 166, 171, 179, 183, 186, 284
   economic, 282
   feminist, 383, 391
   hegemonic, 21, 165, 392
   ideological, 424
   intellectual, 100–103, 316, 346
   internationalist, 383
   liberal, 92, 97, 311
   media, 427
   nationalist, 236, 384
   official, 104, 358
   oppositional, 159
   political, 117, 154, 282, 298, 410, 427
   post-Soviet, 350
   pro-Western, 96
   public, 99, 208, 212, 218, 219, 222, 274, 313, 318, 319, 341, 342, 402, 405, 410, 415, 434
   reformist, 347
   social, 152, 281, 418
   societal, 410
   sociological, 88, 119, 203, 282, 289, 296, 311, 316, 317, 346, 375, 383, 388, 391, 418, 438, 439
Dissident, 57
Dugin, A., 298

E
ECTS, *see* European Credit Transfer System (ECTS)
Elite, 61, 143, 159, 234, 264, 302, 318, 382, 408, 426
   academic, 282, 293
   cultural, 59
   intellectual, 51, 56, 118, 307, 310, 316, 319, 411
   knowledge, 36
   national, 277
   nonstate, 29
   party, 56
   political, 52, 59, 117, 118, 152, 156, 182, 186, 198, 202, 212, 218, 241, 276, 277, 279, 282, 284, 296, 300, 310, 334, 375, 380, 385
   power, 153, 166
   proto-capitalist, 155
   sociological, 358
Emigh, R.J.
   information intellectuals, 29
ESS, *see* European Social Survey (ESS)
Estonia, 189, 192, 195, 198, 201
Etzioni-Halevy, E., 54
EU, *see* European Union (EU)
European Credit Transfer System (ECTS), 259
European Social Survey (ESS), 94, 163, 355, 449
European Union (EU), 2, 18, 102, 162, 189, 210, 232, 260, 285, 298, 307, 314, 318, 325, 333, 342, 385, 409, 418
European Values Study (EVS), 355, 413
EVS, *see* European Values Study (EVS)
Eyal, G., 39

F
Filipescu, I., 325, 335
Filipovic, M., 122
Firsov, B., 349, 350, 364
Foucault, M., 438
   universal intellectuals, 30
Fusaro, D., 302

G
Gál, F., 175, 177, 404, 415
Gender studies, 353, 360
Georgievski, P., 253, 256–258
Giddens, A., 113
Globalisation, 21, 158, 185, 265, 314, 402, 414, 422, 426, 449
Golovakha, Y.I., 442
Gramsci, A., 30
   bourgeois intellectuals, 27
   organic intellectuals, 28, 54
   traditional intellectuals, 27
Greenfeld, L., 328, 330
Grigas, R., 235
Gusti, D., 327
   Gustian school of sociology, 327, 342

H
Havelka, M., 179, 183

I

Ibrulj, N., 122
Ideology, 11, 28, 32, 54, 59, 102, 115, 122, 155, 292, 329, 346, 349, 356, 359, 360, 365, 378, 427
Information society, 175, 185
Intellectuals, 21, 26, 28, 35, 37, 39, 42–44, 52, 54–56, 60, 83, 98, 102, 118, 122, 139, 142, 156, 157, 160, 190–192, 194, 202, 219, 230, 236, 310, 334, 371, 390, 403, 410
  academic, 52, 61, 64
  Belgrade Circle, 379
  Marxist, 164
  non-conformist, 57, 59
  public, 40, 63, 64, 81, 104, 130, 208, 222, 235, 319, 339, 350, 360, 362, 365, 453
Intelligentsia, 27, 53, 56, 58, 138, 140, 179, 190, 316, 383, 423
International Social Survey Programme (ISSP), 94, 239, 355, 413, 449
International Sociological Association (ISA), 3
  Abraham, M., 4
  Hanafi, S., 4
  Pleyers, J., 4
ISA, see International Sociological Association (ISA)
ISSP, see International Social Survey Programme (ISSP)

J

Jessop, B., 273, 281, 431

K

Kabele, J., 175, 177, 180
Katić, N., 295
KIIS, see Kyiv Internation Institute of Sociology (KIIS)
King, L.P., 35, 36
Koludrović, I.T., 156
Komsic, I., 123, 124
Konrád, G., 57, 58
Korosteleva, E.A., 104
Kuljić, T., 383, 388, 390
Kyiv International Institute of Sociology (KIIS), 443
Kyuranov, C., 137, 139, 141

L

LAS, see Lithuanian Academy of Sciences (LAS)
Latvia, 189, 208, 209, 212, 213, 215, 216, 218, 222, 223
Lauristin, M., 196, 198, 199
Lazić, M., 378, 382, 387, 392
Lenin, V.I.
  socialist intellectuals, 27
Levada, Y., 349, 350
Lithuania, 97, 100, 189, 227, 231, 236, 238, 241
Lithuanian Academy of Sciences (LAS), 229

M

Macedonia, 253, 254, 256, 258–260, 266, 267, 269
Machonin, P., 172, 175, 179, 181, 183
  Czech economic sociology, 180
Makarovič, M., 422, 423, 425, 427, 428
Manayev, O.
  Independent Institute of Social-Economic and Political Studies (IISEPS), 97
Mannheim, K., 54
Marxism, 35, 89, 116, 135, 153, 173, 255, 256, 376, 404, 406, 424
Marx, K., 292
Masaryk, T.G.
  Czech sociology, 169
Matějů, P., 179, 180, 183, 185
Merxhani, B.
  Albanian sociology, 79
Migration, 68
Miljovska, D., 255, 258
Milosavlevski, S., 254
Misirkov, P.K., 252
Mladenovski, G., 261, 268
Mlinar, Z., 422
Moldova, 276–278, 281–283, 285
Montenegro, 291, 294, 295, 297, 298, 300–302, 385
Možný, I., 175, 176, 180
Musil, J., 172–174, 177, 181, 403

N

National identity, 96, 114, 173, 212, 356, 423, 426, 439, 451
NATO, see North Atlantic Treaty Organization (NATO)

NGOs, *see* Nongovernmental
  organisations (NGOs)
Nongovernmental organisations (NGOs), 96,
  158, 200, 338, 352
North Atlantic Treaty Organization
  (NATO), 189

O
Oosterlynck, S., 281
Oshavkov, Z., 136

P
Panina, N., 441–443
Paniotto, V., 443, 447
Parsons, T., 38
Path dependence, 152, 165, 314
Path dependency, *see* Path dependence
Perestroika, 87, 93, 139, 195, 350–352, 365
Petkov, K., 141, 146
Petroska, B., 254, 255, 258, 261
Petrusek, M., 180
Poland, 308, 313, 314, 316, 318, 329
Post-communism, 72, 307, 312, 317, 318
Post-communist transformation, 63, 69, 233,
  236, 239, 243, 309, 314
Post-democracy, 296
Post-socialism, 289, 293, 295, 297, 300,
  382, 429
Post-socialist transformation, 2, 6, 10, 21, 114,
  144, 147, 184, 192, 273, 278–280,
  284, 289, 300, 372, 373, 377, 384,
  421, 431
Post-socialist transition, 1, 10, 20, 130, 152,
  275, 332, 378
  See also Post-socialist transformation
Potůček, M., 174, 175, 177, 181,
  182, 185
  Centre for Social and Economic Strategies
    (CESES), 181
Prague Spring, 171, 402

R
Republic of Belarus, *see* Belarus
Republic of Bulgaria, *see* Bulgaria
Republic of Lithuania, *see* Lithuania
Republic of Moldova, *see* Moldova
Republic of North Macedonia, *see* Macedonia
Republic of Srpska, 119
Romania, 276, 325, 329, 332–334, 337,
  339, 341
Rončević, B., 105, 127, 166, 228, 232, 242,
  342, 349, 364, 393, 418, 422, 434

Russia, 92, 102, 296, 345, 357, 360, 361, 363
Russian Federation, *see* Russia

S
Sapiro, G.
  French intellectual field, 39
Schumpeter, J.A., 38
Second World War, *see* World War II
Selectivity
  agential, 8
  discursive, 7
  structural, 7
  technological, 8
Serbia, 373, 374, 376, 377, 381–383, 385, 386,
  388, 390, 393
SFR Yugoslavia, *see* Yugoslavia
SHARE, *see* Survey of Health, Ageing and
  Retirement in Europe (SHARE)
Slovakia, 402, 405, 407, 409, 411, 413,
  414, 416–418
Slovak Republic, *see* Slovakia
Slovenia, 423, 425, 426, 434
Social changes, 31–33, 35, 36, 51, 57, 91, 133,
  135, 137–139, 145, 153, 249, 259,
  264, 267, 269, 290, 291, 293, 297,
  303, 311, 317, 342, 372, 373,
  402, 408
Socialism, 10, 115, 116, 136, 137, 139, 157,
  254, 262, 264, 265, 294, 297, 310,
  311, 313, 329, 347, 372, 374, 376,
  381, 393
  democratic, 154, 164
Social problem, 76, 77, 80
Societal transformation, 3, 7, 11, 13, 14, 16,
  52, 114, 116, 117, 119, 120, 122,
  129, 133, 139, 145, 170, 208, 223,
  381, 437, 439, 440, 451, 456
Sociological development, 80, 87, 89
  in Post-Soviet Belarus, 92–94
Sociological interventions, 26, 36–37
Sociologists, 3, 16, 80, 83, 127, 128, 145, 202,
  220, 237, 270, 302, 331, 333, 336,
  340, 348, 354, 357, 441, 452, 454
  academic, 12
  in Belarus, 103–105
  as critical academics, 215
  East European, 9
  as experts, 12, 198–201
Sociology, 3, 63, 82, 105, 111, 112, 117, 118,
  125, 130, 134–136, 139–142, 147,
  154, 161, 163, 170, 176, 178, 183,
  185, 190, 192, 194, 203, 211, 221,
  223, 241, 249, 250, 253, 258, 260,
  262, 270, 274, 279, 283, 291, 303,

Index 467

    330, 338, 341, 354, 364, 371, 380,
      381, 385, 389–391, 402, 404, 406,
      410, 412, 414, 417, 439, 446, 449,
      451, 455
  academic, 11, 62, 123, 139, 145, 146, 158,
      213, 215, 217, 308, 388, 393
  analytical, 175
  civic, 27, 42–44
  clinical, 4
  as a collaborative activity, 126–129
  as a crisis science, 18–19
  critical, 14, 172, 215, 218, 230,
      238, 315–318
  digital, 243
  empirical, 174, 444
  Marxist, 328
  nationally oriented, 165
  policy, 215, 216, 230, 232
  political, 311, 408
  post-Soviet, 94
  post-transitional, 156
  practical, 156
  pre-communist, 326–328
  public, 3, 26, 31–34, 36, 41, 42, 44, 151,
      218, 230, 234, 355, 362, 453
  as a service science, 19
  socialist, 328
  Soviet, 91
Soviet Union, 87, 105, 135, 189, 196, 208,
      210, 229, 276, 278, 328, 402
Stalin, J., 251, 254
Sum, N.-L., 273
Survey of Health, Ageing and Retirement in
      Europe (SHARE), 239
Szelényi, I., 35, 36, 58

T
Tabuns, A., 208, 209, 211, 218, 219, 222
Tasheva, M., 252, 267

Tisenkopfs, T., 209, 210, 213, 216,
      220, 223
Tito, B., 254
Touraine, A., 36
Turner, J.H., 3

U
Ukraine, 439, 441, 443, 444, 447, 450,
      451, 453
United States, *see* USA
USA, 297, 415
USSR, *see* Soviet Union

V
Vardomatskiy, A.
  NOVAK, 97
Vukićević, S., 292, 294

W
Weber, M., 13, 29, 81
World War II, 68, 76, 180, 254, 328, 335,
      423, 427
WWII, *see* World War II

Y
Yadov, V., 348–350
Yugoslavia, 154, 156, 164, 251, 256, 260, 264,
      268, 291, 297, 299, 303, 337, 375,
      376, 383, 424

Z
Zamfir, C., 325, 332, 335, 337
Zeman, M., 174, 176, 181
Županov, J., 155

Printed in the USA
CPSIA information can be obtained
at www.ICGtesting.com
CBHW071511081224
18663CB00001B/14